P9-DCL-360

UNDERSTANDING
THE CONTEMPORARY
CARIBBEAN

Uɴᴅᴇʀsᴛᴀɴᴅɪɴɢ

Introductions to the States and Regions of the Contemporary World
Donald L. Gordon, series editor

Understanding Contemporary Africa, 4th edition
edited by April A. Gordon and Donald L. Gordon

Understanding Contemporary Asia Pacific
edited by Katherine Palmer Kaup

Understanding the Contemporary Caribbean, 2nd edition
edited by Richard S. Hillman and Thomas J. D'Agostino

Understanding Contemporary China, 3rd edition
edited by Robert E. Gamer

Understanding Contemporary India
edited by Sumit Ganguly and Neil DeVotta

Understanding Contemporary Latin America, 3rd edition
edited by Richard S. Hillman

Understanding the Contemporary Middle East, 3rd edition
edited by Jillian Schwedler and Deborah J. Gerner

Understanding Contemporary Russia
edited by Michael L. Bressler

SECOND EDITION

UNDERSTANDING THE CONTEMPORARY CARIBBEAN

edited by
Richard S. Hillman
Thomas J. D'Agostino

LYNNE RIENNER PUBLISHERS
BOULDER · LONDON

Ian Randle Publishers
Kingston

Published in the United States of America in 2009 by
Lynne Rienner Publishers, Inc.
1800 30th Street, Boulder, Colorado 80301
www.rienner.com

and in the United Kingdom by
Lynne Rienner Publishers, Inc.
3 Henrietta Street, Covent Garden, London WC2E 8LU

Published in Jamaica in 2009 by
Ian Randle Publishers
11 Cunningham Avenue
Kingston 6

© 2009 by Lynne Rienner Publishers, Inc. All rights reserved

Library of Congress Cataloging-in-Publication Data
Understanding the contemporary Caribbean / Richard S. Hillman and
    Thomas J. D'Agostino. — 2nd ed.
        p.   cm.
    Includes bibliographical references and index.
    ISBN 978-1-58826-663-7 (pbk.)
    1. Caribbean Area. I. Hillman, Richard S., 1943–   II. D'Agostino,
Thomas J.
    F2161.U53   2009
    972.9—dc22

                                                        2009002532

British Cataloguing in Publication Data
A Cataloguing in Publication record for this book
is available from the British Library.

Jamaican Cataloguing in Publication Data
A Cataloguing in Publication record for this book
is available from the National Library of Jamaica.
ISBN 978-976-637-399-3

Printed and bound in the United States of America

        The paper used in this publication meets the requirements
 ∞   of the American National Standard for Permanence of
        Paper for Printed Library Materials Z39.48-1992.

     5   4   3

Contents

Illustrations

▓ Figures

Photographs

Preface

The first edition of *Understanding the Contemporary Caribbean* was designed to elucidate essential facts about an often neglected and misunderstood region that has nevertheless made important contributions to global affairs. Our primary goal was to introduce the complex Caribbean region to a wide range of readers. The success of the first edition has encouraged us to provide this updated second edition with the same goal in mind.

We appreciate the participation of each of the contributors to both the first and second editions of *Understanding the Contemporary Caribbean* as well as two new authors who have joined the project for the second edition: Marlene Attzs and Jacqueline Braveboy-Wagner. John Bogdal's creative maps and excellent graphics continue to enhance this updated volume. The chapter authors, who represent a variety of disciplines, have contributed to a book that has proven to be useful in stimulating interest in and enhanced comprehension of the Caribbean. The dedication of each of these experts is a tribute to the highest academic ideals of collegiality, collaboration, and the search for truth.

We remain indebted to Lynne Rienner Publishers for having initially inspired us to launch this project, encouraging us to complete it, and providing critical editorial assistance throughout the lengthy production process. In this context, we acknowledge the helpful critique and useful suggestions put forth by anonymous reviewers. We, of course, take full responsibility for the book's contents.

Richard S. Hillman thanks the US Department of State for having supported the Institute for the Study of Democracy and Human Rights (ISDHR), which he directed until his retirement in 2005. One of the ongoing functions of the ISDHR, an outgrowth of a partnership between the Central University of Venezuela and St. John Fisher College, was to foster research on political institutions in regions in the throes of socioeconomic transition. This book, in exploring these issues in the Caribbean, is a case in point.

Professor Hillman also is grateful to the Semester at Sea and the People to People Ambassador Programs for providing unique opportunities to visit Cuba and speak with university academics, political leaders (including Fidel Castro), and a variety of Cubans from all walks of life. These experiences were particularly illuminating and integral to a more complete comprehension of the Caribbean.

Thomas J. D'Agostino wishes to thank the provost and dean of faculty at Hobart and William Smith Colleges for supporting his involvement in this project, as well as the Andrew W. Mellon Foundation for its support of the Hobart and William Smith Colleges and Union College Partnership for Global Education. A special thanks to Clarence Haydel III and Maureen Smith for their kind assistance.

This project stems from nearly twenty-five years of collaboration between the editors. We are deeply grateful to students and colleagues who have provided feedback and insights in our classes and at conferences over the years. They, along with the many people from the region we have been fortunate enough to encounter, have contributed much to our understanding and appreciation of the Caribbean. Of course, we are thankful for the moral support of our families, who offered constant encouragement and displayed remarkable patience as we were immersed in this project. Their love and understanding sustained us throughout.

—Richard S. Hillman,
Thomas J. D'Agostino

UNDERSTANDING
THE CONTEMPORARY
CARIBBEAN

1

Introduction

Richard S. Hillman

The first edition of *Understanding the Contemporary Caribbean* offered cautious optimism regarding the potential for political, economic, and social progress within the region. Even as this second edition explores many reasons for continued hope that such progress will occur, the global setting and internal dynamics of the Caribbean have presented unpredictable challenges that have exacerbated previous complications.

The post–September 11 world has shifted attention to the Middle East and shaped trade, economic assistance, travel, migration, and human rights in the Caribbean and elsewhere. A full-blown global economic and financial crisis has affected developing countries perhaps even more profoundly than the developed nations. Yet, despite these dramatic and unprecedented events, there are certain constants that were identified in the first edition and continue to characterize the region. For example, the Caribbean is still considerably more important and certainly more complex than is commonly thought.[1] That has not changed.

The popular image of this region suggests an attractive string of underdeveloped island nations in close proximity to the United States, with a pleasant climate and natural attributes that attract large numbers of tourists. Short visits to beautiful beaches and resorts, however, have contributed to a superficial vision of the Caribbean region. It is an interesting, significant, and exciting place for much more profound reasons.

Although there is some truth to the stereotype of the Caribbean as a tropical paradise, the region's historical, cultural, socioeconomic, and political influences far exceed its small size and low status in global affairs. Indeed, political and ideological movements and developments in the Caribbean have provoked international reactions. Moreover, throughout history the people of the Caribbean have been engaged in heroic struggles to liberate themselves from the strictures and exploitation of colonialism, slavery, imperialism, neocolonialism, and dependency.

Historically, the perception of the region has varied, ranging from interest in an extremely valuable asset to one that has elicited benign neglect. Its role as provider of sun, sand, and surf to Americans and Europeans, for example, has obscured the fact that great power rivalries repeatedly have been played out in the Caribbean. In fact, the United States has intervened in the Caribbean more than in any other geographical area of the world. The impacts of migration patterns, investment, and commerce, as well as illicit narcotics trafficking, have been significant not only in the Western Hemisphere but also in Europe and throughout the world. Similarly, Caribbean literature, art, and popular culture have influenced countries around the world.

The Caribbean peoples have made outstanding contributions in many fields, both in their home countries and in those countries to which they have migrated. Their presence is apparent in professions such as health care and education, as

A beach along undeveloped shoreline, Runaway Bay, Jamaica.

United Nations

well as in commerce, construction, music, cuisine, sports, and government. Former US secretary of state Colin Powell, who first rose to the position of chairman of the US Joint Chiefs of Staff, is a first-generation US citizen of Jamaican origin. Baseball legend Roberto Clemente was born in Puerto Rico, and many of the players currently on Major League Baseball rosters come from the Caribbean. Actors like Harry Belafonte and Sidney Poitier, singers like Bob Marley, Wyclef Jean, and the Mighty Sparrow, academics like Orlando Patterson, and writers like Derek Walcott, V. S. Naipaul, John Hearne, Jamaica Kincaid, Aimé Césaire, and Gabriel García Márquez represent the wealth of talent emanating from the Caribbean.

Ironically, as North Americans and Europeans flock to the Caribbean vacationland, the people of the region seek to leave their homelands. Their quest for upward socioeconomic mobility has resulted in large population concentrations abroad. New York City, for example, contains the largest urban concentration of Dominicans outside Santo Domingo. Similarly, New York is the second largest Puerto Rican city next to San Juan. And Miami has become so influenced by Cubans, Jamaicans, and Haitians, among others, it is commonly referred to as "the capital of the Caribbean."

The Caribbean has always been considered a geopolitical and strategic crossroads (see Maps 1.1, 1.2, and 1.3). From the fifteenth century to the end of the twentieth century—from Christopher Columbus to Fidel Castro—the Caribbean has been the focus of external influences (Williams 1979). First, European colonial powers imposed their systems and control. Later the Monroe Doctrine of 1823 conceived of the region as falling within the sphere of influence of the United States. As a consequence, the Caribbean was thought of as the backyard of the United States—a "US lake," so to speak.

The Cold War impinged upon emergent pressures within the Caribbean to define itself autonomously, creating confusion as to the origins and intent of national movements. In the post–Cold War era the potential for continued democratization, expanded free trade, and pragmatic regional integration loomed large on the horizon. The Caribbean was increasingly perceived as a vital link in the realization of the now severely weakened Free Trade Area of the Americas.

In the advent of the twenty-first century, countries across the region are feeling the effects of the global financial crisis as credit contracts, demand for exports declines, and commodity prices fall, resulting in a deterioration of terms of trade. Impending global recession has raised questions about the most effective economic strategies, not only for the industrialized countries but especially for small states such as those in the Caribbean.

Thus, Caribbean leaders are divided in their perspectives on the future. Some see the transfer of power from Fidel to Raúl Castro in Cuba as an opportunity for normalizing relations. Others are hopeful that an emerging coalition of the left led by Venezuela's Hugo Chávez offers a viable alternative to dependence on the United States.

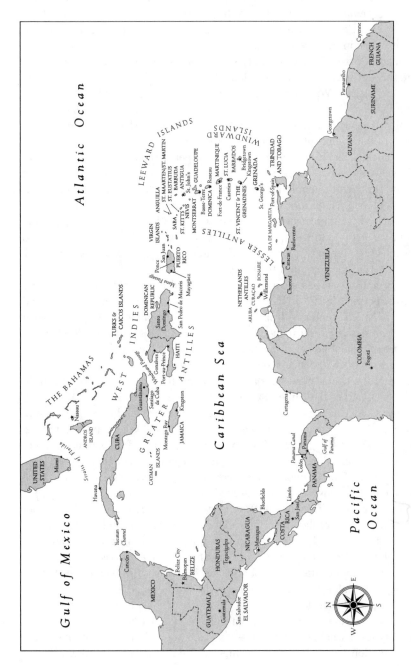

Map 1.1 The Caribbean Region

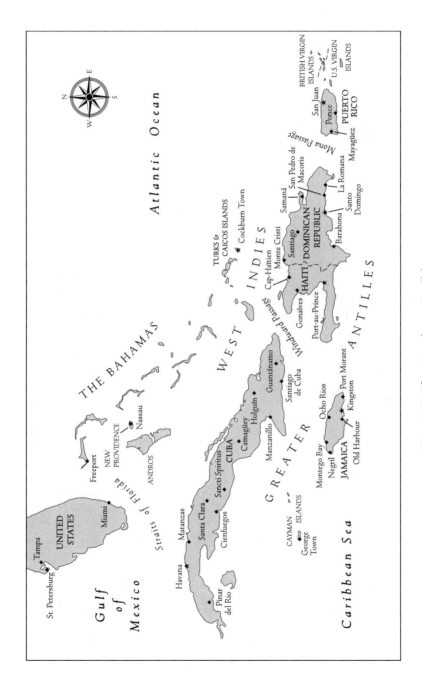

Map 1.2 The Northern Caribbean

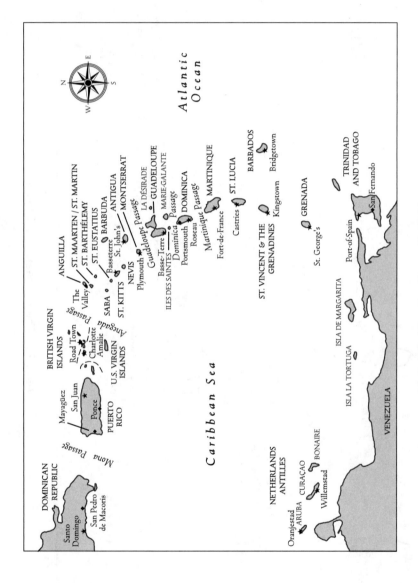

Map 1.3 The Southern Caribbean

Similarly, when asked who would be a better president of the United States for developing countries, Barack Obama or John McCain, former Jamaican prime minister Edward Seaga replied that "there is not much commitment to this region anymore from Washington by either party. The Cold War is over" (*Sunday Gleaner,* October 26, 2008). However, Richard Crawford, lecturer in political science at the University of the West Indies, stated that if Barack Obama were elected, "We would be seeing the end of an era of hostile military-type politics from the United States" (*Sunday Gleaner,* October 26, 2008).

The global crisis, of course, has posed many serious challenges to the region as a whole, as well as individual countries. The Caribbean comprises ministates endowed with widely dispersed and, in some cases, sparse resources. Thus, economic development has been problematic. Political evolution has also been complicated. In countries that have experienced long periods of colonialism, with the attendant institutions of the plantation and slavery, it is difficult to overcome deeply ingrained authoritarian legacies in order to promote the consolidation of democracy. This does not mean, however, that historical legacies will determine the future. Moreover, disparate developments such as the Cuban revolution, the transition toward democracy in the Dominican Republic, and the invasion of Grenada further complicate the absence of a singular paradigm or model that would fit the entire region. Thus, generalizations about Caribbean political and economic development must of necessity be multifaceted and intricate if they are to be meaningful.

Yet the different countries of the Caribbean have much in common. Among the most problematic common features are financial weakness and lack of investment capital. The latter is exacerbated by the global crisis in credit markets.

Most production in the Caribbean has involved food processing, the making of clothing, and the manufacturing of sugar and rum. Efforts to expand these activities to earn additional income and provide new jobs through programs of import substitution and industrialization by invitation have been relatively unsuccessful.[2] Also, West Indian governments have sought to protect local industries by imposing tariffs on the importation of foreign goods, but that drove up the prices of domestically manufactured products, which were often inferior in quality to imported goods.

Among the incentives used to attract investment capital are low-cost labor, factories constructed by governments, reduction in taxes or complete tax abatements for a number of years (free trade zones), government-sponsored training programs, political stability, and proximity to the large North American market.

Companies assembling goods for export to the United States benefit from special US tariffs that either reduce or waive import duties for these products. When duties are imposed, they usually are assessed only on the value added to the products by the Caribbean operations. US firms, seeking to escape high-cost unionized labor, have established assembly maquiladoras (factories) in the Dominican Republic, Haiti, Jamaica, and Barbados. Predominantly female workers typically earn between US$50 and $100 per week in as many as 1,000 maquiladoras throughout the Caribbean employing more than 25,000 workers. A significant portion of the moderately priced clothing sold in the United States is now made in these factories.

Neoliberal economic philosophy purports that it is more beneficial for producers to export their products. Accordingly, the World Bank and the International Monetary Fund (IMF) have required local governments seeking loans to devalue their currencies to reduce the costs of their products overseas, to lower their import tariffs to increase local competition and efficiency, and to reduce domestic spending so that larger financial reserves will be available to pay off the loans. The main problem with this philosophy is that it creates austerity in the home country. Currency devaluation raises local prices; competition from imported goods can drive local firms out of business, exacerbating already high levels of unemployment; and decreased government spending reduces the amount of money circulating within the island's economy, causing political pressures. Recently, the World Bank and the IMF have begun to rethink their overall approach and ease requirements for development loans.

One of the more successful economic mechanisms used by Caribbean nations to fortify their economies has been offshore banking.[3] Some nations provide advantages such as reduction or elimination of taxes on income, profits, dividends, and capital gains in secret accounts.[4] Moreover, legal fees and licenses are charged by the banks, adding valuable foreign currency to the region's economy. Recently, the Netherlands Antilles, especially Curaçao, and then the Bahamas, the Cayman Islands, Antigua, the Turks and Caicos Islands, Montserrat, and St. Vincent became the leading centers in the Caribbean for offshore banking. In the Bahamas and the Cayman Islands, offshore banking is the second leading industry behind tourism, providing 15–20 percent of each country's gross national product.

In sum, although the Caribbean continues to struggle with political and economic challenges, the global scope of the region's impact is inconsistent with its image and size: the Caribbean contains approximately 41 million people—a small percentage of the Western Hemisphere and only a tiny fraction of the world's population. But their impact has been disproportionate to their numbers, and there are many enclaves of Caribbean peoples living in other areas of the world. London, Toronto, Miami, and New York, for example, have a large West Indian presence.

The world continues to become more interdependent, and the Caribbean must be integrated into this emerging global society. Therefore, it is very important to increase our understanding of the contemporary Caribbean. Unfortunately, segregated analyses of the region according to superficial criteria have caused confusion. It has been convenient to refer to linguistic divisions, geographic distributions, and chronological dates of independence, for example. These approaches have reaffirmed obvious differences while obscuring common factors that could help to produce salutary solutions to pervasive problems.

Our earlier research has shown that the Hispanic countries within the Caribbean have been considered an integral part of Latin America, and the English-speaking countries have been excluded based on the assumption that different cultural heritages require a fundamentally different analytical framework. Thus, scholars of Latin America focus on the Latin Caribbean "often to the almost total exclusion of other areas," whereas scholars of the Commonwealth Caribbean "have usually neglected the Latin Caribbean" (Millet and Will 1979:xxi). We have shown that the Caribbean region provides a microcosm of a fragmented third world in which divisions "tenaciously obscure similarities and impede the evolution of common interests and aspirations" and that the absence of a "single, holistic community" has resulted (Hillman and D'Agostino 1992:1–17).

Some authors have argued that there is a "clear dividing line" separating the English-speaking Caribbean countries from their Hispanic, French, and Dutch neighbors (Serbin 1989:146). Some conclude that conflicts in relations between Caribbean countries are due to "misconceptions, misunderstanding, and lack of communication . . . deriving from historical, cultural, racial, and linguistic differences" (Bryan 1988:41). Others have attributed the absence of a single community to the divisiveness of separate Caribbean societies "often fatally hostile to each other" (Moya Pons 1974:33).

Our approach reveals that beneath obvious differences lie similarities in common historical themes, geopolitical and sociocultural contexts, economic experiences, and accommodation patterns that reflect the pressures of congruent sociopolitical environments. Moreover, we believe that there has been significant convergence of mutual economic and political interests to warrant the promotion of improved relations between the diverse Caribbean states. Nicolás Guillén summarizes this idea succinctly when he characterizes the Caribbean archipelago as one "communal yard" due to its common heritage of slavery, imperial domination, and struggle (Guillén 1976:26). And Pére Labat observed in the eighteenth century that the Caribbean peoples are "all together, in the same boat, sailing the same uncertain sea" (Knight 1990:307). We believe that academic and political navigation in this sea can be enhanced through understanding and appreciating the forces that have shaped the contemporary Caribbean.

Therefore, there is a need for an interdisciplinary introduction to the Caribbean region. Academic, business, and policy interests require understanding this complex and significant area, especially in the twenty-first century. But the growing numbers of people who wish to learn about the Caribbean are not able to use narrowly focused studies. Comprehending existing theoretical analyses of the region's socioeconomic and political conditions presupposes expertise and experience.

Further, there is much misunderstanding about Caribbean attitudes, values, and beliefs regarding the conduct of politics, business, and life. Sensationalized media coverage of political instability, external debt, immigration, and narcotics trafficking has overshadowed valiant Caribbean efforts to define uniquely

Caribbean identities and create autonomous institutions, as well as consolidate democracy and promote trade, development, tourism, and regional coopera-tion. Relative to other "developing" areas of the world, the Caribbean's long experience with democracy has been highly valued by citizens—a condition that underlies the legitimacy of any political system. According to Americas Barometer 2006, for example, the Dominican Republic, Guyana, and Jamaica have relatively high ratings for "satisfaction with the way democracy works" (Seligson 2008:268).

Moreover, although the strategic geopolitical relevance of the region has been recognized throughout history, the Caribbean has become critically im-portant in the emerging global economy, within which the volume of trade will significantly affect the entire Western Hemisphere. The Caribbean Basin Ini-tiative of the early 1980s is testimony to this idea. Unfortunately, the persis-tence of flawed policies such as the US embargo against Cuba has impeded, rather than enhanced, regional integration. My visits throughout the region over a number of years have convinced me that there is a great need to promote mutual understanding throughout the hemisphere.[5] The tendency to demonize political leaders with whom there is disagreement has constituted a major ob-stacle to progress in this area. The election of Barack Obama in the US presi-dential election of 2008, however, may result in a reevaluation of the US position regarding Cuba and other Caribbean neighbors. Precedents exist for policies of engagement with Cuba, such as (1) improved relations with China and Vietnam; (2) former president Jimmy Carter's visit to Cuba in May 2002; (3) an increasing number of US members of Congress interested in trade with Cuba; and (4) repeated votes (seventeen years in a row) in the United Nations to end the economic, commercial, and financial embargo imposed by the United States against Cuba. The October 29, 2008, vote was 185 in favor of the amend-ment to end the embargo to 3 against (United States, Israel, Palau), with 2 na-tions abstaining (Marshall Islands, Micronesia).

Attention has been drawn to the region by media accounts of current events, Free Trade Area of the Americas discussions, and tourism, as well as in-creasing business, commerce, and migration from the Caribbean, all of which underscore the need for basic information. In this context, this book provides a basis for comprehension by providing background information about countries within the Caribbean region and introducing major issues, themes, and trends. It is designed as a basic resource that will be useful to those studying the area. The writing style is straightforward, with maps and graphics intended to enhance clarity, comprehension, and appreciation of the traditions, influences, and com-mon themes underlying differences within the Caribbean. *Understanding the Contemporary Caribbean* is intended to contribute to the promotion of inter-est and basic understanding in college and university classrooms, foreign serv-ice seminars, corporate training programs, and the general public.

Because definitions of the Caribbean region vary widely, we provide an integrated text by defining the Caribbean to include the circum-Caribbean, with a focus on the insular Caribbean. In other words, each chapter is primarily concerned with the Greater and the Lesser Antilles. Secondary reference is made to typically Caribbean enclaves in the Atlantic Ocean and on the South American and Central American coasts.

Specifically, the Greater Antilles consists of Cuba, Jamaica, Hispaniola (Haiti and the Dominican Republic), and Puerto Rico. The Lesser Antilles consists of the Leeward Islands and the Windward Islands. The Leewards include Montserrat, Antigua and Barbuda, St. Kitts and Nevis, Saba, St. Eustatius, St. Martin, and Anguilla. (Notice that the French and Dutch halves of St. Martin are spelled differently, St. Maarten [or Sint Maarten] for the Dutch part, and St. Martin for the French part.) The Windwards include Guadeloupe, Dominica, Martinique, St. Lucia, St. Vincent and the Grenadines, and Grenada. The US and British Virgin Islands, Barbados, Trinidad and Tobago, and Aruba, Bonaire, and Curaçao complete the insular Caribbean. The Bahamas, Bermuda, and the Turks and Caicos Islands, although not within the Caribbean Sea, have much in common with the region. Similarly, Belize, Guyana, French Guiana, and Suriname have more in common with the Caribbean than their neighboring Central and South American countries. The same can be said for coastal enclaves in Venezuela and Colombia on the Caribbean coast of South America, as well as the Panamanian, Costa Rican, Nicaraguan, and Honduran coasts of Central America. Finally, for reasons previously stated, it is not inappropriate to include mention of Miami and South Florida in the context of our expanded definition of the Caribbean.

The theme of unity in diversity, drawn from our previous work, provides an organizing concept for this book. There have been many attempts to describe the Caribbean that reflect our basic thesis. The fused, or blended, cultures are "distant neighbors" (Hillman and D'Agostino 1992), a diverse village, a disparate community characterized by "fragmented nationalism" (Knight 1990). The whole is certainly greater than the sum of its parts in a "continent of islands" (Kurlansky 1992), a tropical paradise that exists "in the shadow of the sun" (Deere 1990). Transcending the obvious differences, we explore similarities in the legacies of the colonial experiences, slave trade, plantation life, the imposition of Eurocentric institutions, the difficulties of transition to independence, obstacles to socioeconomic and political development, and ethnographic patterns.

The Caribbean is a unique and complex concatenation of virtually every ethnic group in the world. There are those of African, European, American, and Asian origins. Africans came to the Caribbean as slaves from tribes of the Ibo, Coromantee, Hausa, Mandingo, Fulani, Minas, Yoruba, Congo, Mohammedan, Calabar, Alampo, Whydah, and Dahomean. Europeans—tracing their

ancestries to the Spanish, English, Irish, Scots, French, German, and Dutch—
came as conquerors. Indigenous to the region by virtue of early migrations
from Asia were North American tribes of Taínos, Arawaks, Caribs, Ciboney,
and Guanahuatebey. After the abolition of slavery, indentured servants (from
China, India, and Java) were brought to the Caribbean. Later, small waves of
immigrants arrived from Spain, Portugal, France, England, Germany, China,
the Jewish diaspora (Ashkenazi and Sephardic Jews), Italy, the Middle East
(Syrians and Lebanese), Latin America, and North America (the United States
and Canada).

Each group brought particular traits to the Caribbean. The Africans brought
popular tales and legends, folklore, music, arts, and religious beliefs, as well
as qualities of perseverance and leadership (Herring 1967:109–113). The Europeans brought their religions and culture, military technology, political and
social institutions, scientific discovery, and diseases unknown in the region.
The indigenous contributions are debated due to scant archaeological evidence
(Knight 1990:4–22). However, the Arawaks are reputed to have lived in a pacific
communal society, whereas the Caribs migrated and were more belligerent.
The aesthetic achievements and social structures of the indigenous peoples
were almost completely destroyed by conquest, despite the lasting imprint of
linguistic adaptations—such as words like *bohío* (shack or hut), *guagua* (bus),
cacique (Indian chief or political leader), and *guajiro* (peasant).

Far more interesting and significant than the individual contributions of
the various groups constituting the contemporary Caribbean is the process
whereby their sociopolitical traits have been amalgamated and Eurocentric
dominance has been mitigated. The region has truly been a crucible of various
cultures. This blending, not only of institutions but also of ethnicity, has produced the uniquely Caribbean Creoles.[6] Thus, racial variation can be understood in the context of a fluid continuum. As Gordon Lewis observed, "Columbus
and his followers came to the New World with a baggage of religious intoler-
ance rather than racial phobia" (Lewis 1987:10).

The most popular religious expressions resulted from a syncretizing process
that brought together the elaborate African belief systems with those of the European religious traditions. Thus, elitist practice of Catholicism or mainstream
Protestantism is nominal compared to the dynamic integration into daily life
of Vodou, spiritualism, Obeah, Santería, or other fusions of European and African or indigenous religions. Because the Caribbean was "a society founded on
the gross exploitation, in the name of Christianity, of both Antillean Indian and
African black" people (Lewis 1987:89), these combinations were crucial to a
vast majority of non-Europeans attempting to preserve their beliefs and themselves. Although many perceived that "Catholic proselytization was a lost cause
. . . the Catholic religion saw [its role] as a war against paganism and superstition" (Lewis 1987:195). Lately, evangelical religions have been making inroads
in the Caribbean. As one observer asks, "Who with the slightest missionary

spirit could resist a region of poor countries whose populations are always look-ing for new religions?" (Kurlansky 1992:72).

Occasionally, when it had been impossible to integrate their cultures into the dominant society, certain groups rejected that society and alienated them-selves. The first of these groups were the maroons. The name "maroon" is de-rived from *cimarrón,* which literally refers to a domesticated animal that reverts to a wild state. The name was applied to runaway slaves who escaped from plantations and formed their own enclave societies in the rugged terrain of the Jamaican hinterland. Later on, the Rastafarians rejected Anglo values, creating an Africanist belief system loosely based on allegiance to Haile Se-lassie, the former emperor of Ethiopia.

Understanding the forces that tie Caribbean societies together, as well as those that have challenged and transformed their institutions, requires exploration of the impact of the plantation system, slavery, and the processes through which independence (or pseudo-independence) was gained. Moreover, religion, gov-ernment, society, and current challenges derive in large part from these origins. Simply stated, the relationships between masters and slaves, the rebellions, the heroic struggles, and the tortuous evolution from colonies to independent states reveal inescapable realities that cannot be ignored in our study of the contem-porary Caribbean. The resultant attitudes, values, and beliefs inform our under-standing of this complex region.

Caribbean attitudes toward the United States are ambivalent, ranging from disdain to infatuation. A version of dependency theory in which problems en-demic to the region are attributed to Europe and the United States has become popular in some academic circles. Virulent anti-US sentiment developed early in Cuban history, was cultivated by independence leaders, and given ideological ex-pression through *fidelismo* and Castro's revolution. It was given expression by US as well as Cuban manipulation of the Elián González dispute, in which the question of a father's legal custody over his son became an international incident.

On the one hand, Michael Manley, Maurice Bishop, and other West Indian leaders have flirted with alternative ideologies such as democratic socialism and Marxism as an antidote to dependence on the United States. On the other hand, some Puerto Rican politicians have championed statehood for the island, whereas others fiercely resist it. Some leaders have consistently supported US international initiatives and have always voted accordingly in world forums such as the United Nations. Also, there has been much envy and idolatry of US culture and economic superiority, which has led to massive immigration—both legal and illegal—into the United States. It has also led to "brain drain," whereby Caribbean professionals and the intelligentsia abandon their own countries for US residency and citizenship. This loss of human resources has been extremely problematic for Caribbean societies.

Also, there has been substantial movement within the Caribbean: Domini-cans to Miami and St. Martin; Haitians and Cubans to Puerto Rico, Venezuela,

Poster of Elián González, Havana, Cuba. The poster reads, "Return our Child."

and Miami; Jamaicans to Central America and Miami; Trinidadians to Jamaica and Venezuela; and so on. Movement out of the Caribbean has been a safety valve for overpopulation, political oppression, and especially economic depression. Recently, the European Union began financing border projects on Hispaniola, such that the centuries of animosity between the Dominican Republic and Haiti might be overcome in order to achieve a modicum of economic integration.[7]

Caribbeans nevertheless are proud of their countries, perceiving themselves as holding no candle to the United States or Europe. Michael Manley once remarked to me that "Jamaica is no little dive, it is a sophisticated country" (Hillman 1979:55). Similarly, Edward Seaga told me that "Americans have a dim view" of the third world (Hillman 1979:53). I have known West Indians who have worked their entire lives abroad in order to be able to retire in their homelands. These perspectives ought to be appreciated if we are to develop mutual understanding.

Therefore, *Understanding the Contemporary Caribbean* introduces readers to the region by providing basic definitions, outlining major issues, discussing relevant background, and illustrating the manifestation of these considerations in representative countries. The text employs both thematic and case-study approaches. Each chapter contains a general discussion, key concepts, ongoing questions, and reference to bibliographic resources (see Table 1.1).

Among the major issues discussed in the text, the most prominent are those related to Caribbean identity, socioeconomic and political evolution, debt, immigration, integration, and international relations. Those are understood in the context of a background strongly influenced by the legacies of colonialism and the predominant impact of the United States.

In 2008, the region continues to suffer the consequences of a post-9/11 atmosphere. As one would expect, the scant attention paid to the Caribbean in the past has shifted even further to international terrorism, wars waged in the Middle East, and homeland security. Issues such as human rights, civil rights, travel, economic assistance, trade, the global crisis in credit markets, and the economic recession, have affected Caribbean nationals as much as, perhaps even more, than US citizens.

The text is part of the series entitled Understanding: Introductions to the States and Regions of the Contemporary World. It is designed to generate knowledge and stimulate interest rather than bring these issues to closure. Each chapter is written as if to teach a class on the subject. In "The Caribbean: A Geographic Preface" (Chapter 2), Thomas Boswell discusses the impact of location, population trends, resource availability, and the environment on economic development and the people in the Caribbean. In "The Historical Context" (Chapter 3), Stephen Randall shows how major themes such as colonialism, plantation life, and slavery have created legacies that persist in influencing contemporary realities. In "Caribbean Politics" (Chapter 4), Thomas D'Agostino analyzes the impact of historical legacies on political development. He shows how different institutions converge in similar patterns of patron-clientelism, elite dominance, and Creole fusion.

In "The Economies of the Caribbean" (Chapter 5), Dennis Pantin and Marlene Attzs discuss various attempted solutions to the region's endemic problems and economic programs, the informal economies, tourism, and the emergent trend toward integration. Jacqueline Braveboy-Wagner, in "International Relations" (Chapter 6), employs a conceptual framework that includes cultural identity in her discussion of strategic geopolitical issues, economic regional integration, and external intervention in the region. "The Environment and Ecology" (Chapter 7) by Duncan McGregor contains his treatment of crucial issues such as the ecology of the region—the natural assets and liabilities inherent in essentially tourist economies challenged by hurricanes, depletion of coral reefs, and pollution.

In "Ethnicity, Race, Class, and Nationality" (Chapter 8), David Baronov and Kevin Yelvington elaborate on the significance of large arrays of peoples

16

Table 1.1 Socioeconomic Indicators for Caribbean States

	Population	Population Growth (%)	Urban Population (%)	Life Expectancy (years)	Infant Mortality (per 1,000)	GDP per Capita (PPP $US)[a]	Literacy (%)
Anguilla	14,108	2.33	100	80.53	3.54	8,800	95
Antigua and Barbuda	84,522	1.3	31	74.25	17.49	18,300	85.8
Aruba	101,541	1.5	46.9	75.06	14.26	21,800	97.3
Bahamas	307,451	0.57	91.5	65.72	23.67	28,000	95.6
Barbados	281,968	0.36	55.7	73.21	11.05	18,900	99.7
Belize	301,270	2.2	49.4	68.19	23.65	7,900	76.9
British Virgin Islands	24,041	1.88	63.6	77.07	15.2	38,500	97.8
Cayman Islands	47,862	2.45	100	80.32	7.1	43,800	98
Colombia	46,000,000	1.4	78.5	72.54	19.51	7,400	92.8
Costa Rica	4,000,000	1.38	66	77.4	9.01	11,100	94.9
Cuba	11,000,000	0.25	77.4	77.27	5.93	11,000	99.8
Dominica	72,514	0.2	74.6	75.33	14.12	9,000	94
Dominican Republic	9,500,000	1.5	68.6	73.39	26.93	6,600	87
French Guiana	209,000	0.75	76	75	10.40	17,380	83
Grenada	90,343	0.4	31	65.6	13.58	10,500	96
Guadeloupe	452,776	0.88	100	79	8.41	21,780	90
Guatemala	12,902,500	2.5	50	70.29	27.84	5,200	69.1
Guyana	770,794	0.21	28.5	66.43	30.43	3,700	98.8
Haiti	9,000,000	2.49	45.3	57.56	62.33	1,300	52.9
Honduras	7,000,000	2.02	50.5	69.37	24.61	4,300	80
Jamaica	3,000,000	0.78	54.7	73.59	15.57	7,400	87.9
Martinique	381,427	0.30	98	80.5	6.0	23,931	
Montserrat	5,079	0.31	14.3	72.6	16.46	3,400	97
Netherlands Antilles	225,369	0.75	71.8	76.45	9.36	16,000	96.7
Nicaragua	6,000,000	1.82	58.3	71.21	25.91	2,800	67.5
Panama	3,000,000	1.54	68.7	76.88	13.4	10,700	91.9
Puerto Rico	4,000,000	0.37	98.8	78.58	8.65	18,400	94.1
St. Kitts and Nevis	39,817	0.72	32.4	72.94	14.34	13,900	97.8
St. Lucia	159,585	0.44	28	76.25	13.8	10,700	90.1
St. Vincent and the Grenadines	118,432	0.23	47.8	74.34	13.62	9,800	96
Suriname	475,996	1.09	75.5	73.48	19.45	8,700	89.6
Trinidad and Tobago	1,000,000	-0.8	13.9	67	23.59	25,400	98.6

(continues)

Table 1.1 continued

	Population	Population Growth (%)	Urban Population (%)	Life Expectancy (years)	Infant Mortality (per 1,000)	GDP per Capita (PPP $US)[a]	Literacy (%)
Turks and Caicos	22,352	2.64	45.2	75.19	14.35	11,500	98
US Virgin Islands	109,840	0.002	95.3	78.92	7.72	14,500	95
Venezuela	26,000,000	1.5	93.6	73.45	22.02	12,800	93

Sources: Central Intelligence Agency, *World Factbook 2008,* https://www.cia.gov/library/publications/ The-World-Factbook/ (accessed March 2009); Economic Commission for Latin America and the Caribbean (ECLAC), *Statistical Yearbook for Latin America and the Caribbean 2008,* http://websie.eclac.cl/ anuario_estadistico/anuario_2008/ (accessed March 2009); World Bank, *2008 World Development Indicators* (Washington, DC: World Bank Publications, 2008); United Nations Statistics Division, UNDATA, http://data.un.org/Default.aspx.
Note: a. Gross domestic product per capita purchasing power capacity in US$.

and groups living in the same small area. They also touch on the impact of Eurocentricity and the contribution of the different ethnic groups, as well as the creolization pattern. The contribution of women is the focus of "Women and Development" (Chapter 9), by A. Lynn Bolles. In "Religion in the Caribbean" (Chapter 10), Leslie Desmangles, Stephen Glazier, and Joseph Murphy show how imposed European religions have been embellished by syncretic belief systems such as Rastafarianism, Obeah, Vodou, and Santería.

"Literature and Popular Culture" (Chapter 11), by Kevin Meehan and Paul Miller, discusses the most notable writers and the politicized nature of their work. It also mentions the widespread impact of folklore and music—like reggae, salsa, merengue, rumba, *son, cumbia, tambores,* and calypso. In "The Caribbean Diaspora" (Chapter 12), Dennis Conway shows the geographical diversity and impact of the various groups who leave the region and contribute to brain drain, the safety-valve effect, capital flight, and financial remissions. Finally, in "Trends and Prospects" (Chapter 13), Richard Hillman and Andrés Serbin analyze where the region has been as well as the direction in which it appears to be headed.

Notes

1. The terms *Caribbean* and *West Indies* are used interchangeably throughout this book.

2. The phrase *import substitution* refers to a policy of trying to produce goods locally that were formerly imported. *Industrialization by invitation* is a strategy aimed at attracting foreign capital for investment in local industry.

3. Offshore banking includes financial operations conducted by foreign banks that have branches in countries like those in the Caribbean.

4. This has caused speculation that such operations have become money-laundering facilities for illegal activities such as drug trafficking.

5. Among my travels, I visited Cuba as a professor on the faculty of the University of Pittsburgh Semester at Sea Program and presented a copy of my book, Richard S. Hillman, ed., *Understanding Contemporary Latin America* (Boulder: Lynne Rienner Publishers, 2001), to Fidel Castro during his four-and-a-half hour meeting with Semester at Sea students and faculty in Havana, January 25, 2002.

6. *Creole* is a term used in the Caribbean in reference to the unique admixtures of peoples and cultures.

7. Mireya Navarro, "At Last on Hispaniola: Hands Across the Border," *New York Times,* July 11, 1999, p. 3.

■ Bibliography

Bryan, Anthony T. "The Commonwealth Caribbean/Latin American Relationship: New Wine in Old Bottles?" *Caribbean Affairs* 1 (January–March 1988): 29–44.

Deere, Carmen Diana (coordinator). *In the Shadows of the Sun: Caribbean Development Alternatives and US Policy.* Boulder: Westview, 1990.

Guillén, Nicolás. *Jamaica Journal* 9 (1976): 26.

Herring, Hubert. *A History of Latin America.* New York: Alfred A. Knopf, 1967.

Hillman, Richard S. "Interviewing Jamaica's Political Leaders: Michael Manley and Edward Seaga." *Caribbean Review* 8 (Summer 1979): 28–31, 53–55.

Hillman, Richard S., and Thomas J. D'Agostino. *Distant Neighbors in the Caribbean: The Dominican Republic and Jamaica in Comparative Perspective.* New York: Praeger, 1992.

Knight, Franklin W. *The Caribbean: The Genesis of a Fragmented Nationalism.* 2nd ed. New York: Oxford University Press, 1990.

Kurlansky, Mark. *A Continent of Islands: Searching for the Caribbean Destiny.* New York: Addison-Wesley, 1992.

Lewis, Gordon K. *Main Currents in Caribbean Thought: The Historical Evolution of Caribbean Society in Its Ideological Aspects, 1492–1900.* Baltimore: Johns Hopkins University Press, 1987.

Luton, Daraine. "Jamaica Not High on Obama or McCain's Agenda." *Sunday Gleaner,* October 26, 2008, www.JamaicaGleaner.com.

Millet, Richard, and W. Marvin Will, eds. *The Restless Caribbean: Changing Patterns of International Relations.* New York: Praeger, 1979.

Moya Pons, Frank. *Historia colonial de Santo Domingo.* Santiago, Dominican Republic: Universidad Católica Madre y Maestra, 1974.

Seligson, Mitchel A., ed. *Challenges to Democracy in Latin America and the Caribbean: Evidence from the Americas Barometer 2006-07.* Nashville: Vanderbilt University and USAID, 2008.

Serbin, Andrés. "Race and Politics: Relations Between the English-Speaking Caribbean and Latin America." *Caribbean Affairs* 2 (October–December 1989): 146–171.

Williams, Eric. *From Columbus to Castro: The History of the Caribbean, 1492–1969.* New York: Harper and Row, 1979.

2

The Caribbean: A Geographic Preface

Thomas D. Boswell

Defining regions is not an exact science because not everyone agrees about their boundaries. In a sense, regions are like beauty—they are in the eyes of the beholder. Thus, there is little general agreement on what area is included within the Caribbean region.[1] To some, it includes only the countries and islands within the Caribbean Sea. To most US geographers, it includes those islands in the Caribbean Sea plus the islands of the Bahamas and the Turks and Caicos in the Atlantic Ocean but excludes the Caribbean littoral of Central America and Mexico's Yucatán Peninsula. For many European geographers, as well as residents of the non-Hispanic islands of the Caribbean, it includes all the islands between North America and South America and located east of Central America and Mexico, plus Belize and the northern South American territories of Guyana, Suriname, and French Guiana.

Gary Elbow (1996:115) has suggested that the best way around the problem is to consider the Caribbean to comprise a set of three concentric zones of Caribbean identity (see Map 2.1). The innermost zone is the *core* and includes the islands that everyone considers to be part of the Caribbean. The middle zone is the *fringe,* which includes islands farther away from the core such as the Bahamas and the Turks and Caicos, as well as some of the islands located off the Caribbean coast of Central America. In addition, Belize, Guyana, Suriname, and French Guiana are considered part of the fringe. The outermost zone is the *periphery* and covers southern Mexico, including the Yucatán, and all the Central American countries not included within the fringe. The periphery also includes the northern coasts of Colombia and Venezuela in South America. In this chapter, I concentrate on describing the geographical characteristics of the core of the Caribbean region.

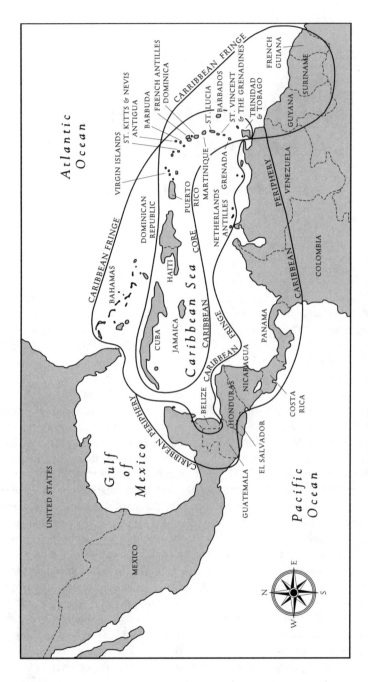

Map 2.1 Subregions of the Caribbean

Considering its size, the Caribbean is certainly one of the more diverse areas in the world (Elbow 1996). This diversity is manifested in virtually every aspect of the islands in the region, including landforms, climates, vegetation, human history, political systems and degree of independence, levels of economic development, religious preferences, and even the languages spoken by residents. Yet as Richard Hillman suggests in Chapter 1, there are unifying themes as well.

The thousands of islands, islets, and keys that comprise the archipelago of the Caribbean stretch approximately 2,200 miles from Cape San Antonio on the western tip of Cuba eastward through the islands of Hispaniola, Puerto Rico, and the Virgin Islands, then southward through the small islands of the eastern Caribbean to the northern coast of Venezuela. However, the aggregate land area of the islands in this region is only about 91,000 square miles, less than the area of the state of Oregon or the island of Great Britain.

It is logical to divide the Caribbean islands into five subregions. The largest is the *Greater Antilles,* encompassing the four islands of Cuba, Hispaniola, Jamaica, and Puerto Rico. Together these islands include 88 percent of the land area in the Caribbean (Table 2.1). The second subregion is the *Lesser Antilles,* including the smaller islands extending from the Virgin Islands east of Puerto Rico and southward to Trinidad. It contains an additional 4 percent of the area of the Caribbean islands. The *Bahamas and the Turks and Caicos Islands* are the third subregion and account for almost 6 percent of the land area of the Caribbean. The remaining two subregions collectively contain less than 1 percent of the area of the Caribbean. These are the *Cayman Islands,* located south of Cuba and west of Jamaica, and the *ABC Islands* (Aruba, Bonaire, and Curaçao) off the coast of Venezuela. Hundreds of other islands are technically located in the Caribbean but are possessions of Central and South American countries; most geographers consider them part of Latin America instead of the Caribbean.

Other terms that require definition are used widely throughout the Caribbean. Perhaps the most important of these is *West Indies,* which is often used interchangeably with *Caribbean.* When Columbus reached the Caribbean during his first voyage in 1492, he thought he had discovered a shorter route to the Orient; he called these islands *Las Indias,* and the natives who lived on them became known as Indians. Later, it was realized that these islands were not the same as those in Southeast Asia; thus they came to be known as the West Indies to distinguish them from the East Indies.

The West Indies were conquered mainly by Spanish, French, Dutch, and British colonialists between the fifteenth and nineteenth centuries, and often they are subdivided according to their respective colonial histories. Thus, the *British West Indies* include the many islands with a British colonial history, including Jamaica, the Cayman Islands, the Bahamas, the Turks and Caicos, the British Virgin Islands, Anguilla, Antigua and Barbuda, St. Kitts and Nevis, Montserrat,

22

Table 2.1 Land Areas and Population Densities in the Caribbean

Countries and Islands	Total Land Area (sq. kilometers)	Population Density (per sq. kilometer), 2005
Anguilla	102	150
Antigua and Barbuda	442	189
Aruba	193	561
Bahamas	10,070	23
Barbados	431	589
Belize	22,806	12
British Virgin Islands	153	146
Cayman Islands	262	199
Colombia	1,038,700	38
Costa Rica	50,660	85
Cuba	110,860	101
Dominica	754	90
Dominican Republic	48,380	197
French Guiana	89,150	2
Grenada	344	298
Guadeloupe	1706	267
Guyana	196,850	4
Haiti	27,560	339
Honduras	111,890	61
Jamaica	10,831	243
Martinique	1060	361
Montserrat	102	55
Netherlands Antilles (excluding Aruba)	960	233
Nicaragua	120,254	42
Panama	75,990	43
Puerto Rico	8870	441
St. Kitts and Nevis	261	188
St. Lucia	606	306
St. Vincent and the Grenadines	389	280
Suriname	161,470	3
Trinidad and Tobago	5128	257
Turks and Caicos Islands	430	71
US Virgin Islands	346	316
Venezuela	882,050	29

Sources: United Nations Population Division, http://esa.un.org/unpp/; Central Intelligence Agency, *World Factbook 2008,* https://www.cia.gov/library/publications/The-World-Factbook/.

Dominica, St. Lucia, St. Vincent and the Grenadines, Barbados, Grenada, and Trinidad and Tobago. The *French West Indies* refer to the French-owned islands of Martinique, Guadeloupe, the northern half of St. Martin, St. Barthélemy, and Haiti (which became independent in 1804). The *Dutch West Indies* (also called the Netherlands Antilles) include the six islands of Aruba, Bonaire, Curaçao, St. Eustatius, Saba, and the southern half of St. Maarten.[2] Finally, Puerto Rico and the US Virgin Islands are in the *US Caribbean*, whereas Cuba and the Dominican Republic—former colonial possessions of Spain—are widely considered part of *Latin America*.[3]

The Lesser Antilles are frequently subdivided by their English- and French-speaking residents in the Leeward Islands and the Windward Islands. The Dominica Passage between Guadeloupe and Dominica is usually regarded as the dividing line, with those to the north called the Leewards and those to the south the Windwards. Interestingly, there is no climate-based logic for such a designation because the islands have similar exposures to the prevailing northeasterly trade winds. One explanation is that Columbus, during his second voyage in 1493, sailed westward between Guadeloupe and Dominica to be on the leeward side of the northern group of Lesser Antilles, thereby gaining some protection from hurricanes that blew in from the east. To complicate matters, the Dutch call their northern islands of St. Maarten, Saba, and St. Eustatius the Windwards, and those to the south the Leewards—the reverse of the British and French uses of these terms. The reason for the Dutch terminology is that Aruba, Bonaire, and Curaçao are much drier than their three northern cousins in the Caribbean.

◼ Climate and Weather Patterns

Taxi drivers in the Caribbean are often amused when newly arriving tourists invariably ask, "How has the weather been?" The truth is that the day-to-day weather is almost always the same at any given location, a characteristic of most tropical locations. Of course, there are variations as well as some marked differences, especially in annual rainfall. For example, drier areas include relatively flat islands (like the Netherlands Antilles), valleys shielded by mountains from moderating sea breezes (like the Enriquillo Depression in the Dominican Republic), and the leeward sides of the Greater Antilles (e.g., the southeastern coast of Jamaica). These drier areas typically have a somewhat greater daily range in temperature than other parts of the region (Boswell and Conway 1992: 10–15).

With the exception of the northern two-thirds of the Bahamas, all the Caribbean lies in the tropics. This factor largely controls the uniform temperatures that typify the area. In tropical latitudes the angle of the sun's rays and the length of the daylight period do not vary as much as they do in the middle and higher latitudes. The variations in average temperatures for the hottest and coolest months here are almost always less than 10 degrees Fahrenheit, a range that decreases closer to the equator. For example, the annual range of temperatures between the coldest and warmest monthly averages for San Juan, Puerto Rico, is 6 degrees Fahrenheit; for Fort-de-France, Martinique, it is 5 degrees; and for Bridgetown, Barbados, and Port of Spain, Trinidad, it is 4 degrees. Even for Nassau, in the Bahamas just north of the Tropic of Cancer, the temperature range is only about 12 degrees. In fact, the winter and summer seasons in the Caribbean differ mainly in the amount of rainfall, not temperature. Summer is the wet season, and winter is the dry season. Daily highs year-round normally range between 82 and 92 degrees Fahrenheit, and the lows range between 70 and 80 degrees. Exceptions occur on the rare occasions when a cold north wind (called *El Norte* in Spanish) blows southward into the Caribbean from the interior of North America, but these incursions affect temperatures only in the Greater Antilles and occasionally the Bahamas.

The West Indies lie in the belt of the northeasterly trade winds, so called because they blow from the northeast to the southwest and because of the role they played in early European settlement and trading patterns in this region. From a climatological perspective, they are significant because their direction determines the leeward and windward sides of the islands, which in turn affects the amount of precipitation and modifies temperature conditions to some extent. Generally, windward coasts are wetter and have somewhat less extreme temperatures. Usually, daily highs on windward coasts range between 2 and 4 degrees Fahrenheit lower than on leeward coasts.

Being surrounded by water has two important climatological consequences for the West Indies. First, the large body of water provides a virtually limitless source of evaporation for the warm tropical northeasterly trade winds that blow over the region, increasing the humidity of Caribbean air masses. Second, because water heats and cools more slowly than land, it helps moderate temperatures on the islands, especially along the coasts. Except for a few sheltered locations, like the Cul-de-Sac Depression of Haiti and the Valle Central of Cuba, temperatures as high as 100 degrees and as low as 60 degrees Fahrenheit are rare in the West Indies.

Air masses in the Caribbean are normally warm and moisture-laden. For rainfall to occur, a mechanism must force this warm, moist air to rise, cooling it enough to create condensation that may result in precipitation. A common geographic feature, island mountain ranges, is one such mechanism. Air is forced to rise on the windward slopes, but it subsides on the leeward sides. As a consequence, the windward sides of the mountains normally experience heavy rainfall (locally known as relief rainfall), whereas the leeward sides are relatively dry, lying in the rain-shadow of the mountains. These windward and leeward effects are most fully developed in the Greater Antilles, where the mountains are higher and the distance traveled by air masses is greater. For example, the city of Port Antonio on Jamaica's northeastern coast receives an average of 125 inches of annual precipitation. Higher up in the adjacent Blue Mountains, about 20 miles inland, rainfall averages nearly 200 inches per year. In Kingston, on the island's southeastern coast, rainfall averages only about 30 inches annually. On the smaller mountainous islands in the Lesser Antilles, rainfall tends to be more symmetrical, without major differences between the windward eastern and leeward western coasts. For example, the coastal lowlands of both the eastern and western sides of St. Vincent average about 70 inches of rainfall, whereas the interior mountains receive more than 125 inches. The flatter island complexes, like the Bahamas and the Cayman Islands, receive much less rainfall than the mountainous ones. Most of the Bahamas receives 40–50 inches of rain, whereas the Netherlands Antilles receives only 20–30 inches per year. In fact, the availability of water for drinking, agriculture, and industry is of major concern in the West Indies. Before the rain that does fall can be used, much of it rapidly runs off to surrounding seas. Some of the islands now strictly ration water. Houses are often built with rain-catching roofs and cisterns, and many of the drier islands, including St. Thomas and St. Martin, have desalination plants. Signs in hotel rooms often urge patrons not to waste water.

A typical summer day on an island in the West Indies will begin with a cool, clear morning with temperatures around 75 to 80 degrees Fahrenheit. By late afternoon, the days warm to between 87 and 92 degrees, and a gentle breeze develops as convectional heating creates a slight low-pressure system over the land relative to the somewhat higher pressures over the cooler sea. Late afternoon convectional showers are intense but of short duration (lasting less than half an hour). The early evenings are warm and muggy because of the high relative humidity. Later at night (around 10 p.m.), the earlier daytime onshore breeze reverses itself to a gentle offshore wind because a weak high-pressure cell develops over the land as temperatures drop. Frequently, spectacular lightning flashes can be seen over the warmer sea as rain falls there. During the winter, temperatures are only slightly lower, but significantly less rain falls. Although there are variations from place to place, normally about 65–75 percent of the precipitation occurs between May and October.

Tropical cyclonic storms develop most often between the tenth and twenty-fifth parallels in the Northern Hemisphere. Although a tropical storm did occur there in 1933, Trinidad is the only island in the Caribbean that is nearly immune to them because it is the southernmost island of the West Indies and therefore the closest to the equator, where the effect of the coriolis force is minimized. This force, caused by the earth's rotation on its axis, causes the winds in hurricanes to spiral around the center of the storm. Low-pressure systems often develop east of the Lesser Antilles in the middle of the Atlantic Ocean. Current wisdom suggests that some of the more fully developed lows originate as thermal bubbles over the western part of Africa's Sahara Desert. As the thermals travel westward off the continent and through the Atlantic Ocean, they can mature into large and destructive storms, officially becoming hurricanes when sustained winds reach 74 miles per hour.

During a typical hurricane season in the West Indies, which officially lasts from June 1 to November 30, perhaps fifty to sixty tropical depressions will develop, but only between ten and fifteen will evolve into named tropical storms, and fewer still (typically between three and seven) will mature into hurricanes. The depressions and storms are notable because of the rain they generate, but hurricanes are the most destructive and dangerous of weather phenomena in the Caribbean. A hurricane's sustained winds can reach more than 150 miles per hour, with gusts exceeding 200 miles per hour. Such powerful winds destroy crops, trees, and physical structures, posing danger to human life. But wind is not the only destructive element of a hurricane. The associated heavy rainfall causes massive flooding and pollutes drinking water supplies by overflowing sewage systems. In addition, virtually all hurricanes are accompanied by a storm surge (typically 5–20 feet in height), which causes massive destruction in coastal areas. Small tornadoes, or vortexes, accompany many hurricanes and add to their destructive effects. Typically, hurricanes follow an east-to-west track through the Caribbean and then curve northward toward the US mainland or the coasts of Mexico and Central America.

Although the use of satellites and reconnaissance aircraft has improved early detection, hurricane paths remain unpredictable, and each year many deaths and millions of dollars in property damage occur. In 1988 Hurricane Gilbert caused massive destruction in the Caribbean. With sustained winds of 185 miles per hour, Gilbert entered the Caribbean, passing over St. Lucia, and then headed for the Dominican Republic and Haiti. Afterward it continued westward to Jamaica, where it traveled the entire length of the island, leaving 500,000 people homeless and destroying much of the island's coffee and banana crops. Finally it headed for Mexico's Yucatán Peninsula, where it did major damage to the resort areas of Cancún and Cozumel. In the end, the damage was estimated to be $5.5 billion, and 341 lives were lost. In 2004, Hurricane Ivan hit the Windward Islands in the eastern Caribbean and then battered Jamaica, the Cayman Islands, and Cuba before it curved northward to come ashore in the southeastern United States. Its sustained winds reached 165 miles per hour, resulting in $19 billion in damage and 124 deaths. In August 2008, Hurricane Gustav's winds reached 150 miles per hour as it stuck the Dominican Republic and wrecked havoc in Haiti. By the time it reached Jamaica, the Cayman Islands, Cuba, and the southeastern United States, estimated damage had risen to $18 billion, and 138 lives had been lost.

▪ A Diversity of Landforms

Some islands in the Caribbean are mountainous, whereas others are virtually flat. A few are volcanically active, and many experience frequent and devastating earthquakes. Elevations range from a high of 10,417 feet at Pico Duarte in the Dominican Republic to about 150 feet below sea level in the Enriquillo Depression in the same country. But the true range in elevations is much greater than suggested by these figures if the depth of the Puerto Rico Trench is considered, about 35 miles off the northern coast of Puerto Rico. It plunges more than 30,000 feet below sea level, deeper than Mount Everest is high.

For the most part, the Caribbean is an extraordinarily active geologic region. There are at least seventeen active volcanoes in the Lesser Antilles, and ten of them have erupted since the days of Columbus. On May 8, 1902, the Caribbean's most famous volcanic eruption occurred at Mount Pelée on Martinique. It buried the town of St. Pierre, killing an estimated 30,000 people. One day earlier, on the island of St. Vincent, the La Soufrière volcano erupted, sending a deadly pyroclastic flow of lava and gases down the mountainside, killing 1,500 people.[4] Another volcano named La Soufrière erupted on the island of Guadeloupe in 1976. Most recently, the Soufrière Hills volcano erupted from 1995 to 1997, burying most of Montserrat's capital city of Plymouth and causing the evacuation of almost two-thirds of the island's population.[5]

The volcanic activity and earthquakes that typify this area reflect its location at the zone of contact of six large, colliding tectonic plates (see Map 2.2). At the center of it all is the Caribbean Plate: its northern and eastern edges contain most of the islands of the West Indies. The most violent collision in the West Indies is occurring along the eastern edge of the Caribbean Plate, where the westward-moving Atlantic Plate is plunging under it at a rate of 1–2 inches

Puerto Rico's South Shore, from the mountains of Jayuya.

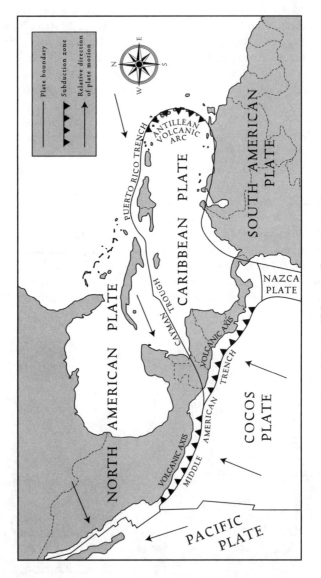

Map 2.2 Caribbean Plate Tectonics

per year. As the more dense Atlantic Plate dives under the lighter Caribbean Plate, the leading edge of the latter deforms, creating a crumpled mountainous landscape with consequent volcanic activity (Boswell and Conway 1992:6–10).

The geologic details of the Lesser Antilles reflect two roughly parallel arcs of islands. The innermost is volcanic in origin and more mountainous and includes most of the larger islands in the Lesser Antilles (St. Kitts, Nevis, Montserrat, Dominica, Martinique, St. Lucia, St. Vincent, and Grenada). The outer arc is more low-lying, of limestone origin or deriving from much older volcanic phenomena that are no longer active. Examples include the Virgin Islands, Anguilla, St. Martin, Barbuda, Antigua, and Barbados (West and Augelli 1989:34–35).

The two halves of the island of Guadeloupe contain examples of both inner- and outer-arc characteristics. The southwestern half, known as Basse-Terre, is a volcanic island whose highest peak (La Soufrière) reaches an elevation of 4,812 feet. Conversely, its northeastern half, Grande-Terre, is a low-lying, undulating island of limestone composition. In addition to Guadeloupe's Basse-Terre and Montserrat, evidence of current volcanic activity is found on Martini-que and St. Vincent. A number of other islands, such as Nevis, St. Lucia, Redonda, Dominica, and Grenada, contain hot sulfur springs that also reflect recent volcanism.

The Greater Antilles are products of much older and probably stronger tectonic forces, dating mainly to between 60 million and 90 million years ago. They are not typified by the recent volcanic activity that characterizes the Lesser Antilles, but when they were exposed to uplifting and volcanism they experienced mountain building that was even greater than that in the eastern Caribbean. As a consequence, the highest mountains on Cuba, Jamaica, and Hispaniola are taller than those on the Lesser Antilles. Even on Puerto Rico, the smallest of the Greater Antilles, the highest elevation of 4,389 feet at Cerro de Punta is comparable to the highest peak in the eastern Caribbean, Guadeloupe's La Soufriére. The main difference in the tectonics of the Greater and Lesser Antilles is that volcanism has ceased on the four largest islands, even though they still occasionally experience devastating earthquakes. For example, Port Royal, the old capital of Jamaica, was completely destroyed by an earthquake in 1692. The current capital, Kingston, was destroyed in 1907 and badly damaged again as recently as 1957. Cap Haitien in Haiti was destroyed in 1842; Port-au-Prince, the capital, was devastated twice during the nineteenth century.

The reasons for the occurrence of earthquakes but not volcanic activity in the Greater Antilles is also explained by the principles of plate tectonics. In the eastern islands, the Caribbean and Atlantic Plates collide head-on, whereas the Caribbean and North American Plates slide past each other. Thus, the force of contact is less intense along the northern coasts of the four larger islands. The friction generated causes pressure to build, and when it is released, it causes the infrequent earthquakes that affect all the northern islands from Cuba to Antigua.

In fact, both the Puerto Rican and Cayman trenches were created by this movement, as well as by earlier subduction forces when the Caribbean and North American Plates confronted each other more directly than today.

The ancient volcanism that created the Greater Antilles was followed by a period of submersion beneath the sea. During this period of several million years, coral formations and dying calcareous marine organisms deposited thick layers of limestone. As a result, many of these islands have limestone soils and rocks that cover the lower elevations of their outer edges. The limestone deposits on the higher elevations of these islands were stripped away when another uplift occurred, raising them once again above sea level. The greater steepness of the slopes at higher elevations intensified the erosive effects of the tropical rainfall on the limestone covering, but the inner volcanic cores of the uplands were more resistant to this degradation. The alluvium washed from the mountains was deposited in the valleys and the narrow coastal plains, where limestone accumulations are most evident today. The older mountainous cores are composed of igneous rocks, evidence of their volcanic origins. However, the mountains on these islands no longer exhibit the symmetrical shape typical of youthful cinder cones because they have been eroded for millions of years.

Several of the low-lying islands (e.g., those in the Bahamas, the Turks and Caicos Islands, Anegada in the British Virgin Islands, and the Cayman Islands) are products primarily of coral reefs that grew on top of submerged sea platforms called banks. They were either lifted above sea level or covered by blowing sand and dying marine organisms that accumulated on top of them. These islands tend to be nearly level, with maximum elevations rarely exceeding 200 feet.

In some places the thick coastal layers of limestone have weathered in geologic formations known as karst topography. Here water has dissolved the underlying calcareous materials into caves with spectacular underground features such as stalactites and stalagmites (spines hanging from the ceiling and columns built up from the ground, respectively). In some places, rivers disappear underground, sinkholes abound, and the surface takes on a jumbled appearance of depressions and low rounded hills known as haystacks. These features are particularly prevalent in parts of the Greater Antilles, especially on their wetter northern coasts, and on Grande-Terre in Guadeloupe. Limestone caves, such as those in the Jamaican cockpit country, are present in less spectacular fashion on many of the other smaller islands. There are also formations called blue holes in the British Caribbean caused by deep seawater intrusions into the limestone bases of these islands.

■ The Caribbean Amerindian Population

The available evidence suggests that the Caribbean islands were occupied by at least three different Amerindian cultural waves prior to the arrival of

Christopher Columbus in 1492. The earliest of these was the Ciboney people, who may have migrated southward from Florida into the Bahamas and then throughout the Greater Antilles as early as 2000 BC. Because they had almost disappeared by the time the Spanish arrived, very little is known about them. There may have been a few thousand still living on the far western end of Cuba and in the southwestern corner of Haiti. They lived adjacent to the coasts and hunted, gathered, and fished but did not practice agriculture (West and Augelli 1989:61–63).

The arrival of the Arawaks from the northern coast of South America, around 300 BC, represented the second wave of Amerindians in the Caribbean. Evidence suggests that these people traveled northward through the Lesser Antilles and into the Greater Antilles. By AD 1500, they occupied mainly the Greater Antilles. As they swept westward through these larger islands, they either absorbed or annihilated most of the earlier-arriving Ciboneys.

The Arawaks had a higher level of technology than the Ciboneys, developing a type of agriculture that is still practiced by many peasant farmers on the mountain slopes of the Lesser Antilles and throughout the Greater Antilles, especially in Haiti and the Dominican Republic. It was a farming strategy known as *conuco*, a variation of shifting cultivation systems practiced throughout humid tropical areas in other parts of the world. The Arawaks first burned the plot of land to remove weeds and leaves on the trees so more sunlight could reach the ground. Then they piled the topsoil in round mounds that were sometimes knee-high and several feet in diameter. Ashes from the burning of the forest cover enriched these concentrations of more fertile soil. On these relatively fertile mounds—humid tropical areas are known for their heavily leached poor soils—the Arawaks planted a variety of native crops, including yucca (also known as cassava), yams (sweet potatoes), arrowroot, peanuts, maize, beans, squash, cacao, various spices, cotton, tobacco, and numerous indigenous fruits such as the mamey and guava. Fish, fowl, and other foods obtained from the nearby water and forests supplemented their diet. When soil fertility declined, the fields were abandoned, new land was cut over, and the process was restarted.

Although the *conucos* looked primitive and unorganized to Europeans because of the way several varieties of crops were intergrown, in fact they represented a logical adjustment to the ecological conditions of the tropical West Indies. Heaping the soil into mounds provided a loose, well-aerated soil; the earthen piles reduced sheet erosion by rainwater; the intercropping of different plants that grew to different heights provided ground cover as further protection against erosion; and the production of a variety of crops offered nutritious variety to the Arawak diet. Additionally, modern research has shown that this kind of companion planting effectively maximizes output of land.

The Caribs, from whom the name Caribbean derived, were the last Indian cultural group to arrive in the region. Like the Arawaks, they also migrated from northern South America. However, they did not begin arriving until about AD 1000, and as a consequence they were found mainly in the eastern Lesser Antilles. Evidence suggests that they were just beginning to encroach on Arawak turf in eastern Puerto Rico when the Spanish arrived.

The Caribs were more warlike, fewer in number, and less technologically advanced than the Arawaks, but they did practice some agriculture, and like the Arawaks and Ciboneys, they also hunted, gathered, and fished. They replaced the Arawaks throughout most of the Lesser Antilles except Trinidad, Tobago, and Barbados. The word *Carib* came to mean cannibal because of their fierceness and reputed practice of eating the flesh of captured male enemies, whether for ritual purposes or merely for food.

Estimates of the number of Amerindians that occupied the Caribbean at the time Columbus arrived vary greatly, usually from 750,000 to as many as 10 million. What happened to these people is a tragedy with few precedents in human history, often referred to as a demographic collapse. The Ciboneys had all but disappeared before AD 1500, and the Arawaks were to virtually vanish from the Caribbean by 1550. The demise of the Arawaks resulted from a number of factors, such as the importation of European diseases to which they had no immunity, the wars of European conquest, destruction of their food supplies, and overwork in mines and as laborers on European-owned farms and ranches. In addition, thousands committed suicide, testimony to the cruel treatment they endured.

The Caribs took longer to defeat because of their more combative nature and because many retreated to the remote forested mountains of the Lesser Antilles. The Spanish did not consider the Lesser Antilles worth the effort it would take to conquer the Caribs; they had become more interested in the riches available on the Latin American mainland. Ultimately, it was the French who defeated the Caribs in Grenada in 1651; the British subdued them on St. Vincent, but not until 1773. Today, there are probably no more than 3,000–4,000 people of recognizable Amerindian descent living in the Caribbean. The few remaining Caribs are found mainly on St. Vincent and Dominica; people with mixed Arawak ancestry are found on Aruba and very infrequently in the Greater Antilles.

▪ Patterns of European Settlement After Conquest

As Stephen Randall details in Chapter 3, Columbus's four voyages throughout the West Indies from 1492 to 1502 paved the way for others to conquer and then settle the new lands in the name of the Spanish crown. With the consolidation of its authority, Spain focused on the exploitation of the region's natural resources. However, Spanish interest in Caribbean possessions quickly diminished except for a few settlements established in the Greater Antilles, especially in Cuba and what is now the Dominican Republic. Still, the Spanish would leave an indelible imprint in the West Indies: forts and cities, architectural styles, and place-names, even on the islands later lost to other European powers. As Thomas D'Agostino points out in Chapter 4, this imprint is also evident within the political systems throughout the region.

Spanish construction of settlements in the Caribbean was determined by the Laws of the Indies, a codified body of laws promulgated by the crown to guide the colonization process. Unless topography demanded otherwise, colonial towns were laid out in a well-defined grid, where streets intersected at right angles. In the center was a town plaza. The settlement's main church (usually the largest building) was located on or close to the plaza. Also, the most important government offices, such as those of the mayor and town council, were located there. Houses were usually built of stone or brick and covered with white stucco and barrel-tile roofs. Their walls were often made of thick masonry to keep out the tropical heat and to protect against hurricanes. Usually, poor people lived on the periphery of these settlements, whereas the middle class and wealthy lived near the town center. Later, a few of the colonial towns grew into large modern metropolitan cities and began to acquire some of the characteristics of North American and European cities; traces of the original structures are still apparent in some cities. The historically reconstructed center of San Juan, Puerto Rico, known as Old San Juan, and parts of Santo Domingo in the Dominican Republic are outstanding examples of colonial Spanish towns (West and Augelli 1989:63–67).

At least ten different powers would eventually play a role in settling the Caribbean: Spain, the United Kingdom, the Netherlands, France, Denmark, Sweden, the Knights of Malta, the United States, and the two German states of Brandenburg and Courland, in addition to independent privateers—but it was the British, Dutch, and French who competed most notably with the Spanish. The Dutch differed from the British and French in their goals in the West Indies because they were interested primarily in trading rather than settlement. The few small islands they settled were primarily trading centers, and none played a major role in the sugar industry that emerged during the 1700s. In addition, the Dutch period of influence was shorter, from 1570 until 1678. Spanning little more than a century, their activities nevertheless had a profound and enduring influence on the Spanish. Dutch privateering damaged Spanish prestige and created enough of a diversion that the British and French were able to settle most of the Lesser Antilles. The Dutch introduced the British and French to the plantation system of sugar production, gained from their earlier experiences in Brazil. They also provided, through loans, much of the capital for these early ventures. In addition, the Dutch shipping industry became the main provider of supplies and slaves for the other Caribbean colonies. In fact, they were so successful in trading that the British and French finally passed laws (called exclusives) that required their respective colonies to trade only with the mother country, much as the Spanish had done earlier. However, by 1678 the

Dutch were eliminated from a significant role in Caribbean trade. As a consequence, they channeled their energies away from the Americas and into their East Indies empire. The only reminders of Dutch activities in the Caribbean are Suriname and six small island possessions in the Lesser Antilles.

Unlike the Dutch, the British and French engaged vigorously in colonization. At first they chose to concentrate their efforts in areas not given much attention by the Spanish, namely, the Lesser Antilles. During the early seventeenth century, they occupied most of the Leeward and Windward Islands, with the exception of Dutch settlements and Carib strongholds like St. Vincent and Dominica. The British occupied St. Kitts in 1623, Barbados in 1625, Nevis in 1628, and Antigua in 1632. The French acquired Guadeloupe and Martinique in 1635. During the latter half of the 1600s, the British and French competed with the Spanish for possessions in the Greater Antilles and stepped up piracy against the Spanish colonies as well as convoys traveling to Spain. In 1655 the British captured Jamaica from the Spanish, and in 1697 the French gained control of what is today Haiti.

The eighteenth century saw frequent wars among the British, French, and Spanish. The greatest concern for each was to maintain the territorial integrity of the home country, so overseas colonies, especially those in the West Indies, often became pawns in diplomacy. The result was sovereignty chaos in the Caribbean during the late 1600s and throughout the 1700s, as individual islands were swapped back and forth many times. For example, St. Lucia changed hands seventeen times, having been held by France nine times and by Great Britain six times and twice being declared neutral. Similarly, St. Eustatius changed hands nine times, both Guadeloupe and Martinique seven times, Tobago six times, and St. Vincent and Grenada four times each (Richardson 1992: 56). Evidence of this confusion is still found in the islands today in their place-names and vernacular speech patterns. For example, although St. Lucia, Dominica, St. Vincent, and Grenada became British possessions during the period 1783–1803 and remained so until their independence during the 1960s, many of their place-names are French, and the local patois spoken informally is a mixture of French and English words.

■ The Rise and Fall of Sugarcane in the West Indies

The first 150 years of settlement in the Caribbean were spent searching for a crop that could be profitably produced and sold in Europe. In addition to food crops grown for subsistence, colonists experimented with cash crops such as indigo, ginger, cotton, and tobacco. But they did not grow enough food to feed even themselves, so from the outset they depended on imports of flour, rice, dried meat, and salted fish. Furthermore, by the mid-1600s, they began to experience serious competition from the colonies of North America in the production of tobacco and, later, cotton.

Sugarcane is ideally suited to the alternating wet and dry periods characteristic of the tropical climate of the West Indies. It requires a year-round growing season of warm temperatures, and the omnipresence of high-intensity sunlight speeds its maturation. Furthermore, sugarcane withstands droughts better than most crops; it benefits from a dry season that makes it easier to harvest; and harvesting can usually be finished before the heart of hurricane season (August and September). The rapidly increasing market for sugar in both Europe and the colonies ensured its early success. Because of the strict temperature requirements and the fact that most of the sugar was exported, plantations were usually located on level or gently rolling land along the coasts and in easily accessible valleys.

Around 1640 the Dutch introduced British and French colonialists to the production of sugarcane. Within fifty years the agricultural foundation of the non-Spanish islands had changed radically. Sugar did not catch on as early in the Spanish colonies because of greater interests in exploiting the Latin American mainland. The Hispanic islands were often used mainly as way stations for supplying and protecting Spanish fleets and for raising cattle to supply dried meat and leather to both Spain and the mainland. Although Spanish and Portuguese entrepreneurs from the Canary Islands and Madeira, respectively, introduced sugar production in Hispaniola and Cuba by the late 1500s, it did not become of major importance on those islands until 250 years later.

At first, labor was provided by indentured immigrants from the British Isles and France because there was no longer an Amerindian population left to exploit. But soon it was clear that another source of workers was needed, which encouraged the black slave trade from West Africa. The infamous triangular trade developed, whereby cloth and manufactured goods were brought from Europe to Africa, Africans were captured and transported against their will to the Caribbean, and sugar, molasses, and rum were shipped back to Europe.

Although estimates vary, some 4–5 million slaves were brought to the Caribbean. This is roughly the same number as were imported to Brazil and approximately ten times as many as were taken to North American colonies. Most arrived in the eighteenth century during the peak of sugar production in the Caribbean. The massive influx of slaves drastically changed the racial and demographic composition of the populations in the British, France, and Dutch colonies. Within a few years blacks were in the majority, a condition that accounts for the prevalence of an African Caribbean majority today in all but the former Spanish territories of Cuba, Puerto Rico, and the Dominican Republic. As noted above, the Hispanic islands did not enter the sugar plantation phase until the middle to late 1700s. Thus, they did not import slaves for as long as the other islands, which explains the smaller proportions of blacks in the populations of Cuba, Puerto Rico, and the Dominican Republic.

The slave trade persisted into the nineteenth century, the British being the first to abolish it in 1807, followed by the Dutch in 1814, the French in 1818, and the Spanish in 1820. The British emancipated their slaves in 1834 but required them to serve an apprenticeship of four years, until 1838, during which time former slaves were required to remain on the plantations as wage laborers. The French freed their slaves in 1848; Puerto Rico and Cuba released theirs in 1873 and 1886, respectively.

Emancipation created a severe labor shortage in the Caribbean because many freed slaves left their plantations, mostly to work on their own small farms. As plantations became desperate to find another labor source, indentured workers were once again enticed to move to the West Indies. Although there were many sources, the largest proportion came from British India (which included present-day India, Pakistan, Bangladesh, and Sri Lanka) and from China. Between 1835 and 1917, almost 700,000 indentured workers were brought in to work in West Indian sugarcane fields (West and Augelli 1989:108). The usual term of indenture was five years, after which most workers left the estates to work on their own small farms or to set up small businesses in the nearby settlements. As a result, indentured workers did not provide a long-term solution to the labor problem. But they did arrive in large enough numbers to significantly affect the ethnic composition of the populations of Trinidad, Guyana, Jamaica, Guadeloupe, Grenada, and St. Martin. In fact, in Trinidad and Guyana persons of South Asian descent roughly equal the number of those of African descent. In both countries they are still associated with the sugar industry, although many now have also opened successful businesses and become skilled professionals in the local towns and cities. The South Asians have had a significant effect on local politics and the landscape, especially through construction of Hindu temples and Muslim mosques. However, on the rest of the islands in the Caribbean they represent a much smaller (but visible) minority and live primarily in cities, where many are merchants and professionals.

By the mid-nineteenth century the Caribbean sugar industry was in decline, although the later date of slave emancipation in the Spanish colonies delayed the decline there until the late 1800s. Several factors account for this deterioration. With emancipation, the cost of labor increased. Soils in some areas eroded and lost their fertility. The price supports that the British and French provided to the West Indies were discontinued, and the protected markets with the homelands were opened to outside competition by the mid-1800s. Because their markets used to be protected, there was little incentive for West Indian producers to modernize their operations. When this protection was removed, the inefficiency of the British and French operations made it difficult for them to compete with new competitors such as Cuba, Mauritius, and Brazil. In addition, sugar beet production in Europe, which was usually heavily protected and subsidized by local governments, provided another source of competition. More recent developments, including the use of corn syrup in sugar production and the use of sugar substitutes such as saccharin and aspartame, further eroded the industry.

Today the sugar industry has all but disappeared from most of the Caribbean and is significant only on a few islands such as Cuba, St. Kitts, Barbados, Trinidad, Guadeloupe, the Dominican Republic, and Jamaica. In fact, on all these islands except Cuba there also has been a significant decline in land used for growing sugar. By the mid-1980s, Jamaica was producing only about half as much sugar as in the 1960s. During the early 1970s, sugar accounted for almost a third of Barbados's exports by value; by the mid-1980s, this figure had declined to about 2 percent. In 1982, for the first time in more than 100 years, Puerto Rico had to import sugar from the US mainland to meet its own needs, and today almost all its sugar comes from somewhere other than the island itself. To survive at all in the Caribbean, the industry had to renew favorable trade agreements with other countries, especially with the European Union and North America. Similarly, the former Soviet Union and allied Eastern European countries used to buy most of Cuba's sugar production at above-market prices. However, the dissolution of the Soviet Union in December 1991 put a stop to that practice. Nevertheless, Cuban sugar is still exported disproportionately to the Eastern European countries and some of the countries of the former Soviet Union, albeit in smaller amounts.

▓ Population Problems

In the West Indies, island size and population numbers are typically directly related: the larger the island, the larger the population. The Greater Antilles collectively contains about 90 percent of the region's population, a figure almost identical to its share of total land area. About 61 percent live in the former Spanish territories of Cuba, the Dominican Republic, and Puerto Rico. Another 24 percent live in the former French colonies of Guadeloupe, Haiti, and Martinique.

Population growth in the Caribbean over the past five centuries has generated extremely high population densities (Table 2.1). In fact, population pressure is nothing new in the West Indies. The population density of the islands has long been much higher than that of the United States, where it is 83 people per square mile (32 people per square kilometer). It has been estimated that the West Indies (not including the Greater Antilles) had population densities that exceeded 100 people per square mile even before the mid-1800s, due largely to the labor demands of sugar production, especially on the British, French, and Dutch islands.

With a population of 41 million in 2008 and an area of approximately 91,000 square miles, the Caribbean has a population density of about 174 people per square kilometer (450 people per square mile), almost 5.5 times that of the United States. There is tremendous variation within the region, however: The Bahamas has the lowest density with 23 people per square kilometer, whereas

Barbados has a density of 589 people per square kilometer—the highest in the West Indies. However, several of the mainland countries of Latin America that are sometimes included within the Caribbean region have much lower densities. For example, French Guiana has a density of 2 people per square kilometer, followed by Suriname (3 people per square kilometer) and Guyana (4 people per square kilometer). Thus, in this context the distinction between the core and the fringe countries shows significant variation.

Such figures do not truly reflect the implications of population pressures. Due to steep slopes, soil erosion, poor drainage conditions, insufficient rainfall, and competition from urban, residential, and industrial uses, only about one-fourth of the land is used for domestic food production. A better indication of population pressure is to consider only land used for agriculture (not including animal grazing), a measure called *physiological density*. The average for all the West Indies is about 696 people per square kilometer of agricultural land, a figure that few regions in the world can match. Coupled with the growing emphasis on cash crop production for export, it is easy to see why Caribbean countries are forced to import food for domestic consumption. Moreover, with 64 percent (and rising) of the region's population living in urban areas, even the concept of physiological density does not fully capture the severity of population pressure. The rapid rate of urbanization has outstripped the ability of national governments to create jobs, build infrastructure, and provide services.

In 1950, the islands of the West Indies had approximately 17 million inhabitants. By the end of the twentieth century, this figure had more than doubled to 36 million and in 2008 it had increased to 41 million, for an annual average (geometric) growth rate of about 1.5 percent for 1950–2008. This rate of growth is about 50 percent higher than that of the United States for the same period. Since the 1960s, West Indian birth rates have steadily declined, but death rates also decreased. As a consequence, by the year 2000 the rate of natural increase (the birthrate minus the death rate) had declined to 1.1 percent, a rate at which a population will double in just over 63 years. For the United States the rate of natural increase is about 0.6 percent, but this is added to by an immigration rate of about 0.3 percent, for a total growth rate of almost 1 percent per year, only slightly lower than that of the Caribbean (see Table 1.1).

▓ Emigration

From its very beginning, the Caribbean population has been migratory. Even the aboriginal Indians who occupied the area before the arrival of Europeans came from elsewhere, most likely what is today Florida and South America. Despite this long history, I focus on emigration patterns since World War II.

Emigration from the Caribbean intensified following World War II. Most of the emigrants went to either the European home country—the United Kingdom, France, or the Netherlands—or to the United States or Canada. During the 1950s, the movement from the British West Indies to the United Kingdom became so great that in 1962 the British government passed the Commonwealth Immigration Act, which greatly restricted the inflow beginning in 1965, when the law became effective. Since then, most of those leaving the former British Islands have gone to the United States or Canada. By the mid-1980s, close to 6 million emigrants from the Caribbean lived either in Europe or in North America, representing about one-fifth of the population still residing in the islands at that time. Approximately three-fourths of the island emigrants lived in the United States, with another 20 percent in Europe and 5 percent in Canada. Of those who migrated to Europe, more than half went to Great Britain, a fourth to France, and a fifth to the Netherlands.

Despite the significant movement to Europe, the United States received by far the greatest number of emigrants from the Caribbean. In 2007 there were 4.9 million people living in the United States who had been born in the Caribbean. That number included 1.5 million born in Puerto Rico and 3.4 million born in the other areas of the West Indies. Although it represented only about 2 percent of the total US population, their presence is more noticeable because they tend to concentrate in a few metropolitan areas. For example, Puerto Ricans, Haitians, Jamaicans, Dominicans, and Trinidadians tend to concentrate in the Northeast, especially in New York City. Cuban immigrants congregate mainly in Miami, with a secondary cluster in New Jersey's Union City in the New York metropolitan area. In addition, there was notable migration to the US Virgin Islands from Puerto Rico, the British Virgin Islands, and the nearby less prosperous Leeward Islands between World War II and the late 1970s, but this pattern has diminished considerably.

Because Caribbean immigrants tend to concentrate in a few cities in the United States, the city with the second-largest number of an island's natives is often located outside the Caribbean. For example, the Miami–Fort Lauderdale metropolitan area has more Cubans (908,000) than does Santiago, Cuba's second-largest city. Similarly, the New York metropolitan area has 1.2 million Puerto Ricans living in it, which is second only to San Juan, Puerto Rico. New York City also is the second leading city of residence for Dominicans, Haitians, Jamaicans, Barbadians, and Trinidadians. Montreal is the third-largest city for Haitians; Paris is the second leading city for both Martinique and Guadeloupe. London is the second for several of the islands in the former British Lesser Antilles, and Amsterdam is the second city for all of the Netherlands Antilles.

Although emigrants from the Caribbean represent only small fractions of the populations of the European and North American countries they moved to, they represent a significant percentage of the islands they moved from. Today, probably more than one-fifth of the West Indian population has moved to countries outside the Caribbean. If these people were to suddenly return to their islands of origin, the result would be catastrophic. For example, in 2007 there were a total of 4.1 million Puerto Ricans living in the United States (including Puerto Ricans born on the US mainland, plus those born in Puerto Rico), which was larger than the population (3.9 million) living in Puerto Rico at that time. Similarly, Barbadian Americans and Jamaican Americans represent one-fourth and one-fifth of the populations living in Barbados and Jamaica, respectively.

As important as emigration has been to the West Indies in serving as an escape valve for population growth, it should not be viewed as a solution to mounting population pressures. Rather, it should be seen as one factor that temporarily slowed what would otherwise have been ruinous population growth on the islands. Some countries that once received significant numbers of immigrants from the Caribbean are now tightening their immigration requirements. In addition to Great Britain's aforementioned Commonwealth Immigration Act of 1962, Canada tightened its immigration policy in 1972, as did the United States in 1986, 1990, and 1996 (Martin and Midgley 1999:17–22).

Even within the Caribbean, serious efforts have been made to reduce interisland movement. For example, Haitian and Jamaican migrations to Cuba have been stopped by Cuban authorities. The Netherlands Antilles has halted the influx from the British and French islands. Jamaica and Barbados have forbidden the immigration of unskilled laborers. Trinidad, much of whose black population initially came from the Windward and Leeward Islands, now has legal barriers against further unrestricted entry. The only islanders not discouraged from immigrating are the skilled and professional groups, and this kind of brain drain is precisely what the islands do not need.

Emigration has served an important function, providing more time for the islands to solve their problem of increasing population pressure caused by continued population growth. Although it is true that fertility rates are currently falling in the Caribbean, emigration continues to serve as an important escape valve for excessive population increase.

Transnational migration, meaning the continued connections between immigrants living abroad and their home islands, has also proven to be an economic and social benefit for the West Indies. Remittances are sent home to support family left behind. Often these remitted funds are essential infusions of foreign currency into the local economies. Not only do they help families subsist in the West Indies, but they provide money for the development of economic infrastructure on the islands. For example, remittances now provide the largest source of foreign capital in Haiti. Some Dominican neighborhood associations in New York City and Boston have built schools, playgrounds, and parks in the Dominican Republic. Similar development programs have been established for other islands in the West Indies by their expatriate communities living in North America and Europe.

▥ Urbanization

People have been migrating from rural to urban areas in the Caribbean since the early 1900s, but this movement has become especially significant since 1945. Today it is one of the most important migration patterns affecting the region, as island populations have been rapidly changing from a predominantly rural and agricultural orientation to an urban focus. In 1960, fewer than 40 percent of the Caribbean population lived in cities. By 1999 this figure had increased to 59 percent, and by 2008 it was 64 percent (Population Reference Bureau 2008). By 2015 about two-thirds of all people living in the West Indies will be residing in urban areas. As Table 1.1 indicates, although there is significant variation, some countries have levels of urbanization comparable to that of the United States (79 percent in 2008). The highest levels of urbanization occur on such islands as Anguilla, the Bahamas, Cuba, the French islands of Guadeloupe and Martinique, Puerto Rico, and the US Virgin Islands. Some of the smaller islands, such as Antigua and Barbuda, Grenada, St. Lucia, St. Kitts, and Trinidad and Tobago have the lowest levels (below one-third) of urbanization.

View of Mahaut, Dominica.

Two related reasons explain Caribbean urbanization: the decline of economic opportunities in rural areas and the perceived increase of such opportunities in the cities. As a result, rural populations are growing at average rates of less than 1 percent throughout most of the Caribbean and are in some cases actually declining. Yet the average annual growth rates in the cities generally exceed 2 percent. To put this in perspective, a city whose growth rate remains 2 percent will see its population double in thirty-five years. In a period of about seventy years, its population will double twice, and thus become four times larger than it started out because growth follows a geometric growth pattern. Such high growth rates make it difficult to provide adequate housing, jobs, and social services for new inhabitants. About one-quarter of this growth is caused by in-migration either from rural areas or from foreign countries, and three-quarters is caused by natural increase (an excess of births versus deaths).

Much of the growth in the Caribbean is taking place in each island's largest city and its surrounding metropolitan area. In 1950 only seven cities in the Caribbean had populations exceeding 100,000, and only Havana had more than 1 million residents. By 2008 there were at least thirty cities with populations exceeding 100,000, and five had metropolitan populations in excess of 1 million: Havana, Santo Domingo, San Juan, Port-au-Prince, and Kingston (United Nations, 2006 Demographic Yearbook, table 8). Almost always, one metropolitan area dominates the urban structure of each island. When the largest city has a population that is more than two or three times as large as its nearest competitor, it is called a *primate city*. Primate cities are primary in almost every respect, dominating the island's economy, culture, politics, and social scene. With the exception of Guadeloupe, whose capital is the small city of Basse-Terre, each island's primate city is also its political capital.

The housing problem has become acute in the primate cities of the West Indies. Many residents live in substandard housing in areas called shantytowns. Houses in shantytowns are often built from scraps of wood, metal, cardboard, or whatever else the owner can find. They usually have one to three rooms, sometimes with a detached kitchen, and an outhouse or pit latrine. Sometimes standpipes are available as a water source, but many residents on the poorer islands still have to buy their water from trucks that travel through the neighborhoods.

If the government does not tear down shantytowns constructed on illegally occupied land, many eventually mature into more substantial housing. As shantytown dwellers find jobs, they begin to make improvements, such as building rooms with cinder blocks and opening a small store in the home. Some suggest that shantytowns help solve the housing problems of the largest Caribbean cities through their self-help nature. In fact, some governments are helping shantytown inhabitants provide for themselves by supplying electricity and water pipes to their neighborhoods. They also have built multistory public apartment units in cities like San Juan, Fort-de-France, Pointe-à-Pitre (on Guadeloupe), and Charlotte Amalie (on St. Thomas), but they have rarely provided long-term solutions to the urban housing problem.

The largest Caribbean cities, with populations over 100,000, have evolved considerably in appearance. Originally, even the British, French, and Dutch cities appeared similar to the typical Spanish colonial town. All the primate cities originated as colonial ports with gridiron street patterns focused around a central square. Usually, the wealthy lived as near as possible to the square, which provided the greatest accessibility to public buildings, businesses, and contact with important people. Today automobile use has become widespread, and the largest cities are beginning to resemble cities in North America and Europe. The central business districts of the West Indian primate cities now have high-rise buildings, but surrounding areas have often deteriorated and become home to the poor instead of the rich. The presence of large shantytowns has become one of the characteristics that distinguishes them from cities of the more developed countries. Often they are located in zones of disamenities, such as areas of poor drainage, unstable hillside slopes, or areas next to noxious land uses such as garbage dumps and unsightly manufacturing areas. Meanwhile, the wealthy and middle classes have moved to the suburbs, as they have in large US cities, and shopping centers have developed on the periphery of metropolitan areas like San Juan and Kingston.

Barrio La Perla, San Juan, Puerto Rico.

▧ Economic Geography

Material well-being varies greatly in the Caribbean. The Bahamas, Barbados, Antigua, the US and British Virgin Islands, Trinidad and Tobago, Cayman Islands, Netherlands Antilles, and French West Indies are more prosperous; Jamaica, the Dominican Republic, Dominica, Grenada, and St. Lucia have middle-range incomes; and the lowest-income country is Haiti. These differences can be traced to a number of factors, such as the country of colonial domination, the country's history of either poor or good leadership, the availability of natural resources, continued or distant ties with more developed countries, and the types of products that dominate the island economies.

Caribbean Agriculture Beyond Sugarcane
The decline of the sugar industry has been so far-reaching that it is only a significant agricultural pursuit on a few Caribbean islands. Still, agriculture has not disappeared from the islands where sugar is no longer important because other crops have also played a significant role in the agricultural economy of the Caribbean.

Spanish missionaries introduced bananas during the early 1500s, but they did not become a major crop until the 1880s. By the beginning of the twentieth century, bananas had become popular in Europe and the United States, and Jamaica was the world's leading producer. There are two general types of bananas that are important in the Caribbean, the sweet dessert variety (familiar to most American and Europeans) and the cooking variety, called plantains. The latter type is used domestically in the West Indies and is not exported in nearly as large quantities as the dessert type. Sweet bananas are most easily grown on fertile alluvial or volcanic soils and on the wetter windward sides of the islands where annual rainfall exceeds 90 inches. Most often they are cultivated on large plantations, where they are grown under carefully supervised conditions. Plantains tolerate less rainfall and are more frequently grown on smaller farms on poorer soils, both on coastal lowlands and in the foothills of the mountains. On several of the Windward Islands of the Lesser Antilles, such as St. Lucia, St. Vincent, Grenada, Martinique, the Basse-Terre side of Guadeloupe, and Dominica, sweet bananas have replaced sugarcane as the main agricultural crop (Grossman 1998:208–222). They are also an important secondary product in the Dominican Republic and Jamaica. But the Caribbean is no longer a leading producer of bananas. Far more are grown in Central America, South America, India, and several countries in Southeast Asia.

Tobacco was one of the earliest cash crops grown in the West Indies. In fact, it was used by the pre-Columbian Indians and may have originated in the Caribbean or possibly in nearby South America. Today, however, it is of greatest significance in Cuba and the Dominican Republic. A little is also grown, mainly for domestic consumption, in Jamaica and Puerto Rico.

Coffee was at one time important as a mountain-grown cash crop on all the islands of the Greater Antilles, and its cultivation eventually extended as far south as Trinidad. But production in the Caribbean could not compete with that in some of the Central American and South American countries, particularly Colombia, Brazil, and Venezuela. Some coffee is still grown for export on mountain slopes in the Dominican Republic, Jamaica, and Haiti. A small amount, mainly for domestic use, is also grown in Puerto Rico.

Cacao, used to make chocolate, originated on the adjacent Central American mainland or perhaps in southern Mexico. It is another crop that used to be widely grown throughout the Caribbean but is no longer as widespread (it is particularly vulnerable to high winds from hurricanes). It is still mildly important today only in the Dominican Republic, Trinidad, and several of the Windward Islands. The world's leading region of production has now shifted from the Caribbean to West Africa, especially to the Ivory Coast and Ghana.

East Indians introduced marijuana (locally called *ganja* in the English-speaking islands) to the Caribbean during the mid-1800s. They brought it with them as a holy plant when they arrived as indentured laborers in the British islands. Marijuana production increased significantly during the 1970s and 1980s, to the point at which it became a billion-dollar industry. It is associated with the region's Rastafarians, a cultural sect, and is cultivated in Jamaica as well as in remote mountainous areas throughout the Caribbean despite the fact that is universally illegal. The locations of the islands, some of which are isolated and uninhabited, make them ideal transshipment points for narcotraffickers.

Other significant commercial crops grown both for export and domestic use in the Caribbean today are pineapples, coconuts, and citrus fruits. Pineapples and coconuts are grown almost exclusively on the coastal lowlands, and citrus trees are raised sometimes on the lowlands (as in Cuba) and sometimes in the low mountains (as in Jamaica and Puerto Rico). But these three crops are grown on almost all the islands in small quantities. The Caribbean is not a major producer of any of these on a world scale, although Cuba did provide much of the citrus consumed in Eastern Europe and the former Soviet Union.

Despite the fact that farming is still widely practiced in the Caribbean, it is also true that not nearly enough food is produced to meet domestic needs. At least 50 percent of the food consumed in the region is imported from other countries, usually located outside the region. In some cases, such as Antigua, Puerto Rico, Barbados, Trinidad, and the Bahamas, the amount imported approaches 80 percent of the food locally consumed. At least five factors account for the region's inability to feed itself. First, population densities are so high on many islands that they could feed themselves only by developing an intensive form of farming similar to that practiced in some parts of eastern and southeastern Asia. Second, much of the best agricultural land is used for cash crops. Food crops are usually grown on peasant farms and in marginal areas that have steeper slopes, less fertile soils, and generally poorer growing conditions. Third, tastes in the Caribbean have changed, and many people prefer to consume products imported from abroad rather than the locally produced cassava, breadfruit, and rum. Fourth, tourists consume some of the food that might otherwise be eaten by locals. Fifth, the food farming operations in the West Indies are generally small-scale operations that are more difficult to mechanize and operate less efficiently than large-scale operations in the United States and elsewhere that can benefit from economies of scale. As a consequence of these five factors, locally produced food is priced 50–100 percent higher in the Caribbean than in the United States, well beyond the means of many local residents.

Mineral Resources

The Caribbean is not blessed with much mineral wealth, with three exceptions: Cuba, Jamaica, and Trinidad. Cuba has the greatest variety of metallic minerals, most of which are located in its mountainous eastern end. It exports some manganese, cobalt, nickel, chrome, and iron from this area, and it has small copper reserves west of Havana near Pinar del Río. Proportionately, minerals are not as important in Cuba as they are in Jamaica and Trinidad.

Jamaica has large reserves of bauxite, the ore from which aluminum is made. It is the world's third-largest producer of this ore, most of which is found in the valleys among the limestone mountains in the center of the island, especially in the area around Mandeville. No aluminum is manufactured in Jamaica because of the high energy requirements of the final processing stage, and as a result most of the alumina is shipped to either the United States or Canada, where it is refined into aluminum. The exportation of both bauxite and alumina provides for almost 60 percent of Jamaica's exports by value, representing the most important element in the island's economy.

Trinidad is the only island in the Caribbean to have significant reserves of oil and natural gas. Its oil and gas industry provides for almost 80 percent of the value of its exports and supplies jobs for approximately 20,000 people. The production of oil and gas, and their refinement into various petroleum products, is by far the island's most important industry.

Other islands have refineries, but none produces its own oil, with the partial exception of Barbados, which has small reserves but not nearly enough to satisfy even its own needs. In fact, the Caribbean is badly deficient in traditional energy sources, a dilemma that complicates economic development as petroleum prices remain volatile. Still, the refining of imported oil is big business on some of the islands, including Aruba, Curaçao, and the Bahamas. About one-sixth of the oil consumed in the United States is refined in the Caribbean.

The Caribbean has a number of oil transshipment terminals in addition to refineries. Approximately 50 percent of the oil imported into the United States passes through Caribbean shipping lanes. The reason is that the largest oil tankers that transport oil from places like Venezuela, Nigeria, and the Middle

East are not allowed access to some ports in the eastern United States because of their size and because of environmental concerns. The supertankers unload their crude oil at Caribbean ports, where it can be transferred to smaller ships to gain access to the lucrative markets on the US eastern seaboard. Most West Indian ports that serve as transshipment terminals take advantage of this situation to refine some oil, earning some profits from this processing stage.

Tourism

The tropical island environment, with some of the world's most beautiful beaches, is an idyllic setting for a vacation, and so tourism has become a significant industry in the Caribbean. The varied history has created a diverse cultural setting in which it is easy to visit English-, Dutch-, French-, and Spanish-speaking islands during a single vacation. Furthermore, the proximity of the Caribbean to the affluent North American market has given it an important advantage.

There was a small but significant Caribbean tourist industry prior to World War II, with a primary concentration in Cuba and a much smaller secondary core in Jamaica. But not until the 1950s, when regular and inexpensive air service became available, did the industry become truly significant. The Puerto Rican government developed tourism during the late 1940s and early 1950s, but the demise of tourism in Cuba that resulted from the revolution in 1959 was the major reason for the success of Puerto Rico's tourism during the early 1960s. This success spurred similar government promotion and development in the US Virgin Islands and the Bahamas during the 1960s and 1970s. Their success, in turn, motivated other islands to promote tourism. Today, tourism accounts for at least 10 percent of the gross national product (GNP) of the Caribbean. This sector of the economy also generates about 20 percent of the region's export earnings, making tourism the number-one earner of foreign currency.

Of course, the importance of tourism differs throughout the West Indies. For example, tourism generates 70–80 percent of the legal GNP of the Bahamas and the Cayman Islands.[6] It accounts for 35–50 percent of GNP in the US Virgin Islands, Antigua, and Barbados. But it provides less than 10 percent of GNP in some of the Lesser Antilles countries like Dominica, St. Vincent, St. Lucia, Martinique, Guadeloupe, and Trinidad and Tobago and in the Greater Antilles countries of Haiti and the Dominican Republic.

Although tourism is the leading earner of foreign currency for the West Indies, the industry there is not big by world standards. The region receives only about 3 percent of the world's tourists (an estimated 22.5 million in 2005) and about 5 percent of its earnings. The number of tourists and the dollars they generate are smaller than in Europe and North America, yet compared to other developing areas, tourism is well established in the Caribbean.

Almost two-thirds of the tourists who visit the Caribbean live in the United States, 8 percent live in Canada, and 10 percent come from Europe. Although the number of interisland tourists traveling within the Caribbean has increased, as a proportion of the total they have decreased since 1970. With the rise of a substantial middle class in the region, more local people are traveling to areas outside the region for vacations, rather than traveling within it from one island to another.

Some people argue that there is a downside to tourism, and they question the logic of depending on this sector as a development strategy. They assert that because tourism is a seasonal venture, it does not provide the type of year-round income and employment that the West Indies need. Also, they note that much of the profits earned by tourism leave the islands for investors living in the more developed countries whence most of the tourists come. For example, many of the tourist facilities are foreign-owned, and much of the revenue they generate is repatriated rather than reinvested in local economies. In addition, overdependence on tourism promotes a monocultural economy that is vulnerable to outside influence beyond the control of local governments and entrepreneurs. Tourism is especially vulnerable to economic fluctuations, and when recessions occur, the number of people taking vacations decreases. They also point out that Caribbean government budgets are a zero-sum game in the sense that money invested in tourism results in less money being spent elsewhere in other economic sectors. Thus, even though tourism generates some revenue and creates some jobs, its contribution to the region's long-term development is questionable. Finally, the tourism critics argue that the local culture is degraded by the large influx of pleasure-seeking tourists. The problem is that there are few other large scale money-making opportunities for which the Caribbean has as much of a comparative advantage as it does for tourism because of its cultural and natural beauty. Therefore, we can expect tourism to continue being a very important industry in the Caribbean.

■ Conclusion

Although the Caribbean's geographic diversity is apparent, there are at least five unifying characteristics that enable us to view it as a single region. First, except for the northern Bahamas, all the Caribbean is located within the tropics, which affects the climates, soils, vegetation patterns, clothing worn, food eaten, and many other characteristics. Second, the Caribbean Sea and the Atlantic Ocean serve as homogenizing factors. Both bodies of water are routes for interisland trade as well as for trade with countries outside the region. Many islanders derive sustenance from the surrounding ocean, which also functions as a source for food and a place of adventure and recreation. Third, the developing countries in the Caribbean are at a disadvantage in their trading relations with the more developed countries in Europe and North America. What the islands do have to export (mainly food products, some minerals, and tourism) usually costs less than what they need to import (e.g., technology, managerial and advertising skills, and manufactured products) from the more industrialized countries of the world. Fourth, each island had a long history of colonial domination, and many only became independent within the past three or four decades. After independence, a new type of economic dependency upon North American and European countries replaced the old-style political colonialism. Despite proximity to one another, the island countries still trade primarily with North America and Europe, more so than with each other. Fifth, the Caribbean's geographic location (sandwiched between the United States to the north, South America to the south, and Mexico and Central America to the west) has been of great importance. It has affected the trading patterns that the West Indian islands have with one another as well as with the nearby United States, Canada, and Latin America. Finally, the fact that all these islands are located close to each other (with much interisland migration and interaction) has created a sense of kinship and neighborhood despite their diversity.

▒ Notes

1. Several years ago I was asked to provide expert testimony in a legal case involving a yacht that had run aground on the Colorado Archipelago, a string of small islands located off the northwestern coast of Cuba. The boat was maneuvered off the reef it had hit and began to limp northward toward Miami. However, the boat never made it. It sank in the Straits of Florida, about a third of the way between Havana and Key West. The yacht had been insured and the policy covered the boat while it was in the Caribbean (not the Caribbean Sea, just the Caribbean). The insurance company involved argued that it was not liable because the boat had not sunk in the Caribbean Sea and, therefore, it had not sunk in the Caribbean. The question I was asked was whether where the boat had sunk was in the Caribbean region. I explained that although there was no unanimity regarding the exact boundaries of this region, it was generally accepted by most scholars that it extended beyond the limits of the Caribbean Sea to include the Straits of Florida, outside the limit of the territorial waters of the United States. The court accepted my explanation, and the insurance company agreed to settle with the yacht's owner.

2. The island of St. Martin is split between the French and the Dutch. The northern half is French St. Martin and the southern half is Dutch St. Maarten (note the difference in spelling). Aruba withdrew from the Netherlands (Dutch) Antilles in 1986 and has since become an autonomous member of the Kingdom of the Netherlands, the same political status as the whole of the rest of the Netherlands Antilles. Independent Suriname (on the northern coast of South America) is also often included within the Dutch West Indies.

3. Puerto Rico is also often considered part of Latin America because of its Spanish colonial roots. We include it in the US Caribbean because it still has a Commonwealth affiliation with the United States, as does the US Virgin Islands.

4. A pyroclastic flow occurs when magma, rocks, mud, and gases mix together and roll down the side of a volcano at speeds up to 60–70 miles per hour. This utterly destructive and often deadly avalanche resembles a mass of boiling boulders.

5. In French the word Soufrière means "sulfur," a chemical that is always present during volcanic eruptions and produces an egglike smell. This word appears repeatedly throughout the mountainous islands of the eastern Caribbean.

6. The illegal drug industry has become well developed in the Bahamas. Because it is a clandestine industry, nobody knows what its precise contribution to the Bahamian economy is, but there is no doubt that it does add very significantly to the country's economy. The 70–80 percent figure just stated for tourism's contribution does not take into consideration profits from the drug industry.

▨ Bibliography

Ashdown, Peter. *Caribbean History in Maps*. London: Longman Caribbean, 1979.

Boswell, Thomas D., and Dennis Conway. *The Caribbean Islands: Endless Geographical Diversity*. New Brunswick, NJ: Rutgers University Press, 1992.

Cameron, Sarah, and Ben Box, eds. *Caribbean Islands Handbook, 2000*. New York: Prentice Hall, 1999.

Caribbean Tourism Organization. "Latest Statistics 2007." Bridgetown, Barbados, http://www.onecaribbean.org/aboutus/ (accessed September 10, 2008).

Elbow, Gary S. "Regional Cooperation in the Caribbean: The Association of Caribbean States." *Journal of Geography* 96, no. 11 (1996): 13–22.

Fukuda-Parr, Sakiko, and Richard Jolly, eds. *Human Development Report 1999*. New York: Oxford University Press, United Nations Development Programme, 1999.

Grossman, Lawrence S. *The Political Ecology of Bananas: Contract Farming, Peasants, and Agrarian Change in the Eastern Caribbean*. Chapel Hill: University of North Carolina Press, 1998.

Klak, Thomas D., ed. *Globalization and Neoliberalism: The Caribbean Context*. Lanham, MD: Rowman and Littlefield, 1998.

Martin, Philip, and Elizabeth Midgley. "Immigration to the United States." *Population Bulletin* 54, no. 2 (June 1999).

Michener, James A. *Caribbean*. New York: Random House, 1989.

Population Reference Bureau. *World Population Data Sheet 2008*. Washington, DC, http://www.prb.org/Publications/Datasheets/2008/2008wpds.aspx.

Potter, Robert, David Barker, Dennis Conway, and Thomas Klak. *The Contemporary Caribbean*. London: Pearson/Prentice Hall, 2004.

Potter, Robert, Dennis Conway, and Joan Phillips. *The Experience of Return Migration: Caribbean Perspectives*. Burlington, VT: Ashgate, 2005.

Richardson, Bonham C. *The Caribbean in the Wider World, 1492–1992: A Regional Geography*. Cambridge, UK: Cambridge University Press, 1992.

United Nations Statistics Division. "Population of Capital Cities and Cities of 100,000 and More Inhabitants." In *Demographic Yearbook 2006*, http://unstats.un.org/unsd/demographic/products/dyb/dyb2006.htm (accessed March 2009).

US Bureau of the Census. *American Community Survey, 2007*. Washington, DC, 2008, http://census.gov.

———. *International Data Base, 1999*. Washington, DC: International Programs Center, http://www.censugov/ipc/www/idbnew.html.

———. *Statistical Abstract of the United States, 2008*. Washington, DC: US Government Printing Office, 2008.

Veregin, Howard, ed. *Goode's World Atlas*. Upper Saddle River, NJ: Prentice Hall, 2005.

West, Robert C., and John P. Augelli, eds. *Middle America: Its Lands and Peoples*. Englewood Cliffs, NJ: Prentice Hall, 1989.

3

The Historical Context

Stephen J. Randall

The complicated historical legacy of the Caribbean, like the colonial legacy throughout Latin America, has largely determined the challenges that the region has faced over the past centuries and those it faces in the twenty-first century. Christopher Columbus, searching for a passage to China, first landed in the area at the end of the fifteenth century. From then on the region has played an important role in international relations, as detailed by Jacqueline Braveboy-Wagner in Chapter 6. The Caribbean was often at the center of European colonial rivalries. Even when the region was of peripheral concern to competing European and North American imperialisms, the competition invariably affected domestic politics, society, and economics.

As Richard S. Hillman indicates in Chapter 1, both unity and diversity characterize the Caribbean. There is a striking cultural and linguistic diversity within the region, as well as significant differences in terms of socioeconomic development and political traditions. For example, some of the islands of the West Indies have traditions of British parliamentary government, whereas Cuba and the Dominican Republic, former Spanish colonies, have experienced authoritarianism and strong presidential regimes. There are contrasts between larger nations such as the Dominican Republic, Haiti, and Cuba, which have played a major role in hemispheric politics in the past century, and the smaller islands of the eastern Antilles. There are also critical differences between the island nations of the Caribbean that remained within the imperial system into the twentieth century and the larger, more powerful mainland nations. Haiti, of course, was the first of the colonies to achieve independence as the result of the 1790s revolt, but burdened with a massive debt by France, it continued to struggle over the next two centuries. African slavery had a substantially lesser impact on Colombia, Venezuela, and Mexico, each of which attained independence from Europe in the early nineteenth century.

Notwithstanding such diverse currents, the countries of the Caribbean have endured common experiences. Settled primarily by English, Spanish, French, and Dutch colonists with imperial interests who rapidly destroyed all but a small remnant of the indigenous populations, the Caribbean took on a different appearance with the massive forced migration of African slaves from the seventeenth century through the middle of the nineteenth century. This forced migration, combined with the institution of slavery and the postemancipation importation of indentured workers from India and China, essentially created the human contours of the region.

Moreover, slavery, economic exploitation, and political domination have profoundly influenced the converging cultural, socioeconomic, and political patterns within the region. Thus, as Thomas J. D'Agostino discusses in Chapter 4, contemporary Caribbean governments and their leaders face similar socioeconomic and political challenges. These governments, despite their disparate structures and traditions, have developed common ways of addressing these challenges.

In this chapter I introduce the major historical developments in the Caribbean region since the end of the fifteenth century and provide background and context for the more specialized chapters that follow. The approach is necessarily synthetic and interpretative, touching on the main historical currents and highlights of the region with a focus on the insular Caribbean.

Conquest and Colonization, 1492–1800

Although debate continues in regard to Christopher Columbus's arrival representing a true "discovery" of the Americas, there can be little disagreement about the historical importance of the colonization of the Caribbean by European imperial powers after 1492. As Thomas Boswell details in Chapter 2, that first voyage ultimately led to the large-scale movement of European, African, and Asian peoples to the Americas, completely altering the demographic composition of the region. It also led to the formation of European colonies throughout the Western Hemisphere, many of which would become independent states during the course of the nineteenth and twentieth centuries.

Columbus conducted four voyages to the Caribbean from 1492 to 1502. The primary interest of Queen Isabella of Spain was not in the settlement of a new world but rather in mineral wealth—particularly gold—believed under the economic theories of the age to be the source of all national wealth. It was only on Columbus's third voyage in 1498 that gold was discovered in Santo Domingo and not until 1508 that Juan Ponce de León would locate deposits in Puerto Rico. Columbus's initial forays into the area, therefore, were of less economic significance than the major developments that followed in Mexico, Peru, and Bolivia, which became the main sources of gold and silver.

Between Columbus's first voyage in 1492 and 1519, when Hernán Cortés invaded Mexico, the Spanish held unchallenged supremacy in the Caribbean. By the time of Cortes's onslaught on the Aztec and Mayan peoples of Mexico, the Spanish had established varying degrees of authority and settlement in Cuba, Santo Domingo (the island of Hispaniola, which became Haiti and the Dominican Republic), Puerto Rico, Jamaica, Trinidad, and Martinique. What was especially important about this period was the rapidity with which the Spanish sought to turn the region into one that could be successfully exploited in the interest of the metropolis, and that interest soon went beyond the quest for gold. For example, Juan de Esquivel set up sugarcane cultivation and processing shortly after establishing a colony in Santo Domingo in 1509, within a few years sending the first shipments of sugar back to Spain.

The Spanish quickly sought to institutionalize the relationship between the metropolis and the new colonies and their peoples (including the indigenous population) and to regulate trade. Prior to the advent of the African slave trade, the indigenous population was the most pressing social concern. At the time of the Spanish arrival in the Caribbean, the indigenous population is estimated to have between 750,000 and 10 million composed primarily of Ciboneys, Arawaks, and Caribs, with the main concentration of the population on the island of Hispaniola (Knight 1978:6) There, the population of perhaps

The Cathedral of Santa María,
Santo Domingo, Dominican Republic.

200,000 was reduced to only a few thousand in less than two decades as the result of warfare, enslavement, and disease. Although there was some outrage in Spanish circles about this devastation, by the time any effort was made to address the problem, the population was already hovering on the brink of extinction. In the Laws of Burgos (1512), the first of the European colonial charters, King Ferdinand sought to address the persistent problems over the treatment of indigenous peoples, recognizing the need for some degree of regulation. The Laws of Burgos, which permitted colonial officials to free native people from the *encomienda* system (in which they were enslaved) when they were Christianized and capable of self-government, in practice simply continued the policy of *repartimiento* (distribution of lands and forced labor) granted to the conquistadors by the Spanish crown. More significant, although perhaps equally ineffectual, was the appointment of friar Bartolomé de las Casas as protector of the Indians. De las Casas, who arrived in Hispaniola in 1502, himself utilized forced Indian labor on his allotted lands until 1515, when he renounced his *repartimiento* of Indians and returned to Spain in an effort to alter Spanish policy. In his efforts to improve the condition of indigenous peoples throughout the region, de las Casas underlined the deficiencies and tragedy of Spanish policies. His historical legacy became one of the major inspirations of modern liberal attitudes toward indigenous peoples and produced an account of Spanish atrocities toward the first inhabitants of the Americas.

Spanish mistreatment of native peoples, the unwillingness of Spanish colonists to engage in agricultural labor, and the singularly exploitative nature of Spanish colonial policy had other, farther-reaching consequences. The rapid decimation of the potential labor force left Spain with few options except to seek alternative sources of manual labor. In 1518 the Spanish crown authorized the importation of African slaves. That initiative would ultimately bring several million African slaves across the Atlantic Ocean to the Americas and create new societies that were an amalgam of European, African, and Asian cultures and peoples.

By the early sixteenth century, Spain began to face increasing challenges to its exclusive presence in the Caribbean, although it was almost another century before it was forced by other European powers to relinquish its monopoly. For much of the sixteenth century, the other major European countries were distracted by other ventures or too weak to confront Spain. Spain controlled the Netherlands until 1568, and though France had the financial capacity to challenge Spain in the Americas, its exploration of North America inspired little initial interest. For much of the century, French raiders were little more than an irritant to Spanish authority in the Caribbean, resulting in intensified security, improved fortifications, and the use of convoys to move shipments of gold to Spain. France made a brief foray into present-day Florida in the 1560s and an equally unsuccessful attempt to colonize in the area of Port Royal in what is now South Carolina. The more serious challenge came from England during the reign of Queen Elizabeth I (1558–1603). English merchants initially sought to legitimately challenge the closed Spanish trading system in the Caribbean. However, the officially sanctioned voyages in the 1560s of John Hawkins, which met a favorable response from Spanish colonists anxious to obtain goods Spain could not provide, provoked a hostile military response from Spain. In 1569 the majority of Hawkins's ships were captured at Veracruz by a Spanish fleet.

Spain's refusal to allow other countries to trade with its West Indian colonies gave other European nations little option but privateering and warfare if they wished to crack the Spanish monopoly. English privateers were the most successful during the balance of the sixteenth century, with Francis Drake the most notable. Having narrowly escaped capture at Veracruz with his cousin John Hawkins, Drake became a major threat to Spanish interests. Operating from a base in Central America and employing native allies and escaped slaves, Drake captured Nombre de Diós on the isthmus in 1572, as well as Spanish ships carrying South American silver to Europe. The following year he captured Panama City, in the process looting its shipments of silver as well. Drake returned from subsequent privateering ventures on the Pacific coast of South America to raid major Spanish ports in the Caribbean region, including Cartagena and Santo Domingo, as well as St. Augustine in Florida.

England and Spain moved to open warfare in 1588, although the Caribbean colonies were almost irrelevant to the conflict. The startling defeat of the Spanish armada by seemingly inferior English naval forces in the English Channel was a minor setback to Spanish power, yet it heralded a more aggressive European challenge to Spanish authority. In 1604 in the Treaty of London and five years later in the Truce of Antwerp, Spain conceded that it could not maintain a monopoly in the Americas. The seventeenth century thus became a period of dramatic change in the Caribbean and of radically increased colonization and mercantile efforts by other European nations, led by the English, the Dutch, and, to a lesser extent, the French.

As much as these nations challenged Spain for hegemony in the Caribbean, they did not seriously threaten the major Spanish colonies or Spain's economic status. The focus of England was on British North America and, like the Dutch, on the smaller islands in the eastern Antilles and on the northern coast of South America in the area that would eventually become the countries of Guyana, Suriname, and French Guiana. Their colonial strategy also differed radically from that of the Spanish, with a stronger emphasis on colonization, the development of agriculture, and imperial trade and less emphasis on the quest for mineral wealth. The Dutch moved expeditiously, for instance, to establish a salt industry on the Caribbean coast of Venezuela. By 1616 they had a foothold in the area that would become Dutch Guiana and later Suriname, and in 1621, to exploit trading opportunities in the region, they established the Dutch West India Company. A few years later they joined the English in settling

St. Croix (part of the present-day US Virgin Islands), and the English in turn gained control over Barbados and St. Kitts in the 1620s. During the seventeenth century, the Dutch moved into Tobago, Curaçao, St. Maarten (the French portion is St. Martin), St. Eustatius, and Saba, all of which, with the exception of Tobago, became part of the Netherlands Antilles. The English gained control of Antigua, Montserrat, and St. Lucia; took Jamaica by force from the Spanish in 1655; and established a firm foothold on the Central American coast in British Honduras (present-day Belize), which proved to be a useful military base and source of tropical timbers and dyes. All of this came at the expense of the Spanish monopoly, although with the exception of Jamaica, given its strategic importance, such gains were made only on the periphery of Spain's Caribbean empire. French acquisitions were even more modest: Martinique and Guadeloupe in the 1630s and a claim to a portion of Guiana. The major French inroad into Spanish territory was the acquisition of the western portion of Santo Domingo in 1697 through the Treaty of Ryswyck, ending the Nine Years' War in Europe. Under French control, St. Domingue (as the colony that would ultimately become Haiti was called) became the wealthiest non-Spanish possession during the eighteenth century.

These inroads by the other European powers may not have threatened Spanish hegemony, but they proved profitable to the other nations and became the source of imperial wars in the seventeenth and eighteenth centuries. Once the other nations had established a presence in the Caribbean, conflict ensued among the other European powers as well as between them and Spain. Between 1652 and 1678 the English and the Dutch fought three wars; in 1669 the Dutch monarch William of Orange ascended to the throne with his English wife, Queen Mary, cementing a military-economic alliance that resolved half a century of conflict. The English, Dutch, and French were also more successful in establishing the economic basis for longer-term prosperity in their colonies, moving quickly to nurture a profitable sugar industry that Spain brought to Cuba only in the nineteenth century. England exported its first shipments of sugar from Barbados in the late 1640s. In St. Domingue, French settlers mixed agriculture and ranching with their share of piracy, and their very occupation of the western half of the island was made possible by the Spanish decision to move Spanish settlers out of that area to reduce support for pirates and smugglers. The Dutch from early in the seventeenth century held a virtual monopoly over salt production and trade. Yet none of these gains did more than nibble at the edges of Spanish authority and hegemony in the area. Spain lost only one major possession—Jamaica—and even what would become St. Domingue had a long road toward economic prosperity after 1697.

For much of the seventeenth century, officially condoned buccaneering by English, Dutch, and French privateers challenged Spain's power in the region. The privateers, often provisioned by colonial officials and given safe haven in colonial ports, cut a swath of terror through the Spanish Caribbean until the end of the seventeenth century, attacking and looting Spanish treasure ships as well as territory. The Englishman Henry Morgan, perhaps the most notorious of the buccaneers, dealt a serious blow to Spanish prestige in 1670 when he and his men captured Panama City and burned it to the ground. Such activities also provided social, political, and economic mobility for a privileged few. In spite of his notorious past, Morgan was later appointed governor of Jamaica. By that time, the other major powers found piracy as disturbing to their own interests in the Caribbean as they had hoped it would be to Spanish authority, with the result that the English and Dutch began to turn their own military might against the buccaneers, bringing to an end a colorful—if violent—period in Caribbean history.

European imperial rivalries, a series of major wars, and continued expansion of and debate over slavery dominated developments in the eighteenth century. The century began with the demise of the Spanish Hapsburg dynasty and the ascendancy of the more reformist Spanish Bourbons, triggering war with Great Britain, which feared a French-Spanish alliance. The War of the Spanish Succession (1701–1714) involved naval actions in the Caribbean as well as land conflicts in North America and Europe. However, the treaties at the end of the war had only limited significance for Spain and other imperial powers in the Caribbean. England's main gain in the Caribbean area was the Spanish concession of the *asiento* (license) to enable England to trade in slaves and other goods in the Spanish colonies. French gains from these conflicts were far more peripheral to Spain's main Caribbean possessions, focusing on the coastal areas of Florida and Texas.

Between 1739 and the mid-1780s, war was constant. One source of conflict between England and Spain was disagreement over the application of the *asiento* at the conclusion of the War of the Spanish Succession. Rather than liberalizing its colonial trade, Spain sought to tighten controls at a time when Spanish demand for European goods continued to increase. With Spain lagging behind both France and England in industrial production, it was unable to meet that demand, and its effort to curtail imports from England only served to exacerbate tensions. War between Spain and England erupted in 1739 over claims by English captain Robert Jenkins that his ear had been severed by zealous Spanish authorities mandated to curtail English trade. The English fleets failed to take the heavily fortified Cartagena and were equally unsuccessful in their attack on Santiago de Cuba, but they seized Portobello in Panama, which had considerable strategic value. The War of Jenkins's Ear involved only England and Spain, but it was evident that in subsequent conflicts England could expect to be confronted by a Bourbon alliance between Spain and France.

By 1740 hostilities had widened into the War of the Austrian Succession, an eight-year conflict. Although the war ended inconclusively, the Spanish decision to cancel the British *asiento* guaranteed future conflict over trade access to the Caribbean. Furthermore, the increased competition between England

and Spain's ally, France, foreshadowed a future Anglo-French war. When conflict (the Seven Years' War/French and Indian War) erupted in 1756, most combat took place in French and British North America, but inevitably the conflict spilled into the West Indies. With France as an ally of Spain, Spanish possessions in the region were fair targets for England's men-of-war, and England—in a crushing blow to Spain's strategic interests as well as its pride—captured the major port of Havana.

Unlike the conclusion of the War of the Spanish Succession, the War of the Austrian Succession, and the War of Jenkins's Ear, the Seven Years' War led to dramatic transfers of power in the Caribbean and the North American mainland. England returned Havana to a humbled Spain, which also retained control over the Floridas. The war had significant implications as well for the evolution of the European presence in North America. France transferred to Spain possession of the lands west of the Mississippi River and its Louisiana Territory at the same time that military losses to the English ended French control over New France as well as disputed territories east of the Mississippi River and south of the Great Lakes. England had emerged as the undisputed hegemon in North America; ironically, when that hegemony was challenged, it came not only from its European rivals but also from North American colonists attempting to sever imperial ties. In diverting its naval and military power to confront the rebellious American colonies after 1775, Britain's capacity to fend off imperial challenges elsewhere in the region was weakened, as evidenced by Spain's regaining control over much of the Floridas as well as temporary possession of British Honduras and the Bahamas.

The French Revolution, hastened not only by an incompetent and arrogant French government but also by the financial disaster occasioned by the unsuccessful Seven Years' War, changed the face of Europe as well as the power structure in the Caribbean. The most significant impact in the Caribbean was France's loss of St. Domingue (Haiti), its most profitable colony and the site of a massive investment in sugar cultivation, processing, and export. When France erupted into revolution in 1789, St. Domingue had an overwhelming majority population of enslaved and free Africans. There were only slightly more than 40,000 whites on the French part of the island, in contrast to more than 440,000 black slaves and some 26,000 free blacks and mulattos (Knight 1978:149–152). In liberating one of the largest slave populations in the Western Hemisphere, the revolt in what would become Haiti also had significance throughout the slaveholding areas of the Americas, including the southern United States.

The slave revolt with the longest-term impact began in St. Domingue in 1791, two years after the outbreak of the French Revolution. The French government not only increasingly lacked the capacity to control its colonies, but the ideology of the French revolutionary governments in the early 1790s, with their emphasis on liberty, fraternity, and equality, tended to favor the end of slavery. In 1791 the French assembly granted full political rights to the free colored population in St. Domingue, and when the white elite refused to accept this act of political enfranchisement, the free colored leaders, perhaps unwittingly, unleashed the mass of black slaves. The French also ended the legal slave trade in 1793 and abolished slavery the following year, but by then the revolt could not be contained. By the end of the decade, the Haitian revolution was led by free blacks and former slaves, the most important of whom were the educated, propertied freedman Toussaint L'Ouverture and his main military commander, Jean-Jacques Dessalines, an African-born former slave. L'Ouverture himself did not survive the rebellion; he was captured and imprisoned in France, where he died. By 1804, however, with France shifting back to empire under Napoleon and departing from its revolutionary ideology, Dessalines had firm control not only of Haiti but also briefly of the rest of the island. Although slavery remained a viable institution in the Spanish Caribbean for another eight decades, the Haitian revolution was a vivid reminder of the potential for change.

Even where major slave revolts did not occur, the resistance to slavery remained a constant fact of life in the slave communities. In most of the slave colonies, the existence of communities of escaped slaves, or maroons, vividly reminded colonial authorities of the resistance to slavery that was always just below the surface, even in times of relative stability. There were large and well-established colonies of escaped slaves in the interior mountainous regions of

Monument commemorating the slave revolt, with the
National Palace in the background, Port-au-Prince, Haiti.

Jamaica, as there were in the less accessible interiors of St. Domingue and eastern Cuba. Such maroon communities were a constant threat not only to the white slaveholding populations of the Caribbean but also to the institution of slavery itself, although the maroons were not in themselves above trading and holding slaves. Although most of the slave opposition to forced labor came in the form of day-to-day resistance, there were also large-scale revolts. White slaveholders, especially on the larger, more isolated plantations, where the ratio of black slaves to white slaveholders overwhelmingly favored the former, lived in constant fear of slave rebellion. There was a serious maroon war in 1734 in Jamaica and another in 1795.

The diversion of French attention from its colonies in the 1790s and its alliance with Spain provided an opportunity for other imperial powers to make gains in the region. England captured Trinidad in 1797 and seized the Dutch islands when France defeated the Netherlands as well as Spain. England also gained temporary control over Martinique, St. Lucia, and Guadeloupe. The Treaty of Amiens in 1802 confirmed English control over the harbors of Trinidad, which occupied a key strategic location near the South American coast.

The Napoleonic Wars and political instability in Spain had a more significant impact on the mainland areas than on the insular Caribbean. Napoleon's conquest of Spain in 1808 disrupted Spain's already tottering capacity to control its American colonies. Spanish energies initially were devoted to resisting the French occupation. In the colonies, loyalties were divided between those who favored a restoration of the Spanish monarchy and liberals who sought political reforms, which they achieved to some degree in the 1812 constitution. By the time Ferdinand II restored the Spanish monarchy in 1814, the level of resistance to Spanish colonialism in the Americas was intense. This resistance served to thwart recolonization efforts over the next decade, as did opposition from the United States and other European powers, especially the English, whose efforts to promote trade would be undermined by the reassertion of Spanish authority. By the early 1820s, Mexico and the rest of Central America, Venezuela, and Colombia had achieved independence from Spain, although Great Britain retained control over British Honduras and Nicaragua's Mosquito Coast. On the northern coast of South America, Britain, the Netherlands, and France still had firm possession of the Guianas. Spain's loss on the mainland was only marginally compensated by its retention of Puerto Rico and Cuba, which remained a powerful foothold in the region for another century.

■ Nation Building and Socioeconomic Transition in the Nineteenth Century

Nothing was of such profound importance in the nineteenth-century Caribbean as the debate over slavery. In the eighteenth century, the Caribbean was the destination for approximately 60 percent of the African slaves forcibly removed to the Americas, with some 5 million people brought to the Caribbean during the course of the slave trade. Eighteenth-century Enlightenment ideas on the equality of man provided an intellectual context for the debate, although more practical considerations led to the termination of the trade and then slavery itself during the nineteenth century. The socioeconomic and demographic impacts of slavery in the Caribbean were profound, as was the impact of emancipation, which opened the door for tens of thousands of immigrant laborers from various parts of the world.

The English and French Caribbean colonies dominated the trade in the eighteenth century, with Dutch vessels providing most of the shipping. In that period the Spanish Caribbean absorbed only some 10 percent of the traffic, in contrast to the nineteenth century, when the Cuban sugar industry took flight, creating a huge demand for labor (Randall and Mount 1998:20). Despite any opposition to slavery and the trade that existed in the Caribbean colonies in the nineteenth century, the critical decisions affecting the institution were made in the metropolitan capitals, which were more insulated from local considerations of racial balance.

Great Britain and the United States declared the international slave trade illegal in 1807–1808, and it was the effort of the British Admiralty to enforce its own decree that significantly curtailed traffic from Africa. Parliamentary action to end the slave trade followed more than a decade of rising opposition within Britain. Antislavery forces established the Society for the Abolition of the Slave Trade in 1787, under the leadership of William Wilberforce, Thomas Clarkson, and others. Wilberforce was clearly the most powerful voice for reform, and his close association with William Pitt added credibility to his cause. Antislavery forces secured passage of the Foreign Slave Bill in 1806, prohibiting the importation of slaves into Britain's territories that had been acquired as a result of the Napoleonic Wars. The following year the British Parliament went farther by banning the slave trade in all British territory.

The Dutch agreed in 1814, at the end of the Napoleonic Wars, to comply with British policy. Britain concluded a treaty with Sweden shortly after, ending a rather marginal Swedish involvement in the traffic. France followed the Dutch example, agreeing by treaty with Britain to end its involvement in the African slave trade by 1818. Responding to critics who found the British expenditure on the initiative excessive, Wilberforce asked: "How can money be so well employed as in thus effecting the deliverance of so great a portion of our fellow creatures from the most cruel scourge that ever afflicted the human race?" (Wilberforce and Wilberforce 1840). However, like officials in the other major slaveholding imperial powers, French authorities turned their backs as another 80,000 slaves entered Guadeloupe and Martinique before the 1830s. Spain paid lip service to the policy by 1820, although there was widespread violation by Spanish colonial officials, with the result that in the decade after official Spanish adherence to that policy, approximately 500,000 African slaves were forcibly removed to Cuba alone, and another 50,000 to Puerto Rico, to toil in the sugarcane fields and processing factories.

Reformers were increasingly disillusioned by the difficulties of enforcement, as even Britain was not vigilant in its enforcement efforts until it declared slavery illegal in its colonies after 1833. Reformers realized that the institution was unlikely to crumble solely through the restriction of international slave traffic. Thus, Wilberforce and his compatriots turned their attention to the abolition of slavery itself in the British Empire, and the legislation finally succeeded in 1833, the year after his death. This was more complicated economically and sociologically than simply ending the traffic, for the end of slavery would result in the loss of a massive investment in forced labor and create an unpredictable racial situation in a number of the colonies. The British government was also sensitive to the fact that its ill-conceived imperial policies had contributed only a few decades earlier to the successful rebellion of the thirteen American colonies. The British approach to emancipation was consequently cautious, but it was still well in advance of thinking in Spain, France, and the southern United States. In 1815 the Parliament passed legislation requiring the registration of all slaves in its colonies. This measure was partially designed to control trafficking, but it was seen as necessary preparation for emancipation. Britain followed its registration policies with legislation in the 1820s to improve the conditions under which slaves lived and worked, although local slaveholders largely ignored and resented such interference. Nonetheless, Britain persisted and appointed an abolitionist, Sir James Stephen, as the administrator of Caribbean affairs within the Colonial Office.

Colonial officials continued to impede application of such legislation, however. In Jamaica, it was not until 1831, two years before actual emancipation, that the colonial legislature passed legislation adhering to the spirit and letter of the Amelioration Acts of the 1820s; even then it did so largely as a response to the massive rebellion that swept through the northwestern section of the island. There, some 40,000 slaves, in part inspired by Baptist lay preacher Sam Sharpe, destroyed several hundred plantations, although the loss of life among white planters was minimal. The rebellion struck fear into planters throughout the Caribbean, but it also inspired the optimism of British abolitionists.

In the aftermath of Sharpe's rebellion, the British Parliament passed the Abolition Act in 1833, ending slavery in British territory. The act provided £25 sterling per capita for compensation to slaveholders, as well as a period of indenture for newly emancipated slaves to ensure the continuity of the labor force. That indenture requirement did not apply to all the colonies. Antigua and Barbados, for example, were exempted. In areas where the policy applied, the indenture was six years for field hands and four years for domestic slaves. There seemed to be no recognition of the irony of compensating slaveholders for their loss of property but not the slaves for their years of free labor and lost freedom.

Although in Cuba and Puerto Rico both the slave trade and slavery itself continued into the late nineteenth century, the passing of the Abolition Act raised serious challenges relating to the labor supply in the British colonies. At the time of emancipation, the overwhelming majority of the slaves—some 300,000—were in Jamaica, with 80,000 in Barbados, 22,000 in Trinidad, 15,000 in British Guiana, and a scattered population in British Honduras. Although there is some evidence that the majority of emancipated slaves remained on the plantations, largely for want of real economic alternatives, there was a near universal belief that slaves would not work the plantations with any enthusiasm after gaining their freedom. Many former slaves in the British colonies also seized the opportunity to become freeholders themselves, even if the landholdings they were able to acquire were often too small to be economically viable. In Jamaica it is estimated that the number of black freeholders in the twenty years after 1838 increased from 2,000 to more than 20,000. In Antigua, freedmen and freedwomen brought thousands of new acres into cultivation after emancipation. In British Guiana, freed slaves between the 1830s and 1848 purchased more than 400 estates with an estimated value of US$100,000 (Randall and Mount 1998:23).

Consequently, there was great interest in attracting immigrant labor in the British Caribbean, particularly in those colonies where the shortage of unskilled labor was most acute. Despite the pressing need for labor, European immigration to the Caribbean in the nineteenth century never approached levels found in North America, Argentina, and Brazil. This may be attributed to several factors, including the climate, the lack of economic diversification in the largely monocultural economies, and the racial composition of the islands. Interestingly, Cuba, despite the continuation of slavery, was, along with Costa Rica, the most attractive to European (almost exclusively Spanish) immigrants, primarily because of the economic boom that accompanied the expansion of the sugar industry.

In the non-Spanish Caribbean, the main immigration was of indentured East Indian workers into Trinidad and British Guiana, along with some Chinese to various colonies. More than 140,000 East Indians arrived in Trinidad between the end of slavery there and World War I. British Guiana was even more active in recruiting East Indian labor, with approximately 238,000 arriving prior to World War I. More than 30,000 East Indians and Chinese came to Jamaica in the nineteenth century, and smaller numbers were brought to St. Kitts, St. Vincent, and Grenada. The indenture system in Trinidad remained in place until 1917, when the British government ended the practice. By that time East Indians and their descendants constituted one-third of the island's population, and the existence of that substantial population was further incentive for continued movement from South Asia (Laurence 1971; Lai 1993). East Asian and South Asian migration into the Caribbean created one of the other enduring features of modern Caribbean history: tension between the Indo-Caribbean and Afro-Caribbean populations. This tension has been especially pronounced in British Guiana and Trinidad.

The pattern of development in Cuba throughout the nineteenth century stood in marked contrast to that of the British Caribbean. With the thriving Cuban economy generating great demand for slave labor, the slave trade (and slavery itself) persisted long after Spain had agreed to end its involvement in 1820. The proportion of Cuban slaves relative to the population increased markedly between the late eighteenth and the mid-nineteenth centuries with the expansion of the sugar industry. Between 1774 and 1827, while the Cuban population increased from approximately 170,000 to more than 700,000, slaves increased from 25 percent to more than 40 percent of the total population (Knight 1978:96–97, 101). That dramatic increase had significant implications for the independence movement as well as for the social and political history of modern Cuba. By 1860, the free colored population in Cuba was only 16 percent of the total population, compared to more than 40 percent in Puerto Rico. Not surprisingly, there was less racial tension in Puerto Rico than in Cuba and less resistance to emancipation (Knight 1978:105). Although the distribution of Cuba's free colored population tended to parallel the urban concentration in the other colonies, Cuba was distinct in the high percentage of the free black population in the largely rural areas of eastern Cuba that a century later provided Fidel Castro with his strongest base of support.

The wealth of the Cuban sugar plantations and slaveholders in the nineteenth century paralleled that of the plantation aristocracy in the United States. They also held a similar degree of political power, although in Cuba it was not muted by the tensions of sectionalism. In terms of their size relative to the black and slave populations, the white populations in Cuba and Puerto Rico also bore greater similarity to that of the southern United States than to the rest of the Caribbean, where slave societies were characterized by the dominance of a small white elite over a massive black majority. As late as 1870, approximately 60 percent of the Cuban population and some 50 percent of the Puerto Rican population were classified as white (Knight 1997:130; Engerman and Genovese 1975).

Between the late 1840s and 1868, small groups of US privateers known as "filibusters"—mainly southerners anxious to extend the area of slavery by annexing Cuba—attempted invasions of Cuba. Unsuccessful as their efforts were, the filibusters were one important manifestation of a long-standing US interest in Cuba, underlined as well by several equally unsuccessful efforts to purchase Cuba from Spain. With the end of the US Civil War in 1865 and the emancipation of US slaves, combined with the extensive trade ties that had emerged between Cuba and the United States, Cuba's colonial status as well as the institution of slavery became increasingly anachronistic. In 1868 Cuban Creole nationalists, frustrated by Spain's refusal to permit a greater degree of political autonomy or to implement meaningful economic reforms, launched their first struggle for independence in what came to be known as the Ten Years' War.

The revolt had little support from the large slaveholding planters in wealthier western Cuba, who had too much at stake to support such an initiative. Neither was there a slave revolt to bolster the ranks of nationalists, led by Carlos Manuel de Céspedes, in large part because the rebels had no clear policy on the abolition of slavery. Although the rebels failed to gain the independence they sought from Spain, the lengthy rebellion had major consequences. The most important was the emancipation of Cuba's slaves over the next few years, providing an additional base of support for later rebellions and reducing some of the power of the slaveholding planter class.

A second important consequence was that the conflict clearly demonstrated that Spain lacked the military power, and perhaps the political will, to suppress a large-scale war for independence. Yet it was also apparent that the rebels did not possess the means to defeat Spain militarily. Without external assistance, Cuban nationalists would likely be condemned in the future to another drawn-out stalemate.

A third significant consequence was the massive destruction of property and the high level of indebtedness that sugar planters and producers suffered. US investors moved in quickly to acquire sugar properties, helping to establish a strong US presence by the time another war for independence broke out in Cuba in the 1890s. By that time, US private direct investment in Cuba exceeded $50 million; bilateral trade, primarily in sugar, industrial goods, and consumer goods, was worth $100 million. Spain had already lost the economic war for its wealthy colony.

Finally, the war spawned nationalist heroes as well as the poet laureate of Cuban nationalism—José Martí. After exile in Spain and Mexico and a brief return to Cuba, Martí settled in New York, where he and other Cuban nationalists established a government-in-exile. Martí wrote extensively on the United States as well as Cuba during his lengthy exile, and his writings on the United States reflected a complex mixture of admiration for US political and economic successes with a fear of the threat the Colossus of the North posed for the Americas' future. By the late 1880s, Martí had become a passionate, idealistic, revolutionary nationalist prepared to lay down his life for his *patria* (country or fatherland). He had also by that time moved away from his earlier disinterest in labor and the peasants to adopt a broader stance of egalitarian, democratic, and racial equality that gave him legendary status with Fidel Castro's revolutionary movement more than half a century later (Ruiz 1968: 62–71).

Support for the nationalist cause from Cubans was strong in the United States, where Martí and other exiles raised funds and recruited forces for the independence struggle. Powerful Cuban exiled nationalists also worked from bases in other countries, including Antonio Maceo in Costa Rica and Máximo Gómez in the Dominican Republic. Ultimately, Cuban discontent with continued

Spanish imperial control and unfulfilled promises of political and economic reforms spilled over into open revolt in February 1895.

Although insurgent forces were stronger and domestic Cuban public opinion more supportive of the independence movement than during the Ten Years' War, this conflict rapidly moved toward a bloody stalemate. Pro-independence sentiments were inflamed by the Spanish anti–guerrilla warfare tactic of reconcentration of the civilian population in the countryside, designed to cut off insurgent forces from food and other supplies. Although the tactic of moving civilians into what were little more than concentration camps was brutal indeed, Spanish forces had little choice if they were to regain control of the insurgent-dominated countryside. For their part, insurgents burned sugarcane fields and destroyed processing plants, plantations, and infrastructure, a good deal of which was US-owned by that time. The widespread violence directed against property and the brutality of Spanish policy under Governor-General Valeriano Weyler—which included the destruction of crops and livestock in an effort to starve out the insurgents—served further to provide a cause célèbre for the yellow press in the United States, primarily Joseph Pulitzer's *New York World* and William Randolph Hearst's *New York Journal,* which vied for circulation with lurid stories of Spanish atrocities.

By 1898 war still raged. Although under US pressure the Spanish government promised to end the policy of reconcentration and move toward political reform, neither the US public, Congress, nor William McKinley's administration were confident that anything short of Cuban independence would end the persistent conflicts on the island. Not only were Cuban-US trade and US investment constantly disrupted by Spain's inability to control its colony, but also the instability in such a strategic area of the Caribbean threatened US security. President McKinley called Cuba's instability a "constant menace" and reluctantly moved toward war (Smith 1965:284–286). A combination of domestic politics, genuine humanitarian concerns, pressure from US commercial interests, and US security concerns, especially following the February 1898 sinking in Havana Harbor of the battleship USS *Maine,* thus led to the US declaration of war against Spain in April of that year.

 The rapid destruction of the Spanish fleet in the Philippines and Cuban waters ended Spain's claim to great power status and marked a significant movement of the United States into world affairs. More than 200,000 Cubans and Spaniards had already perished prior to the US declaration of war, and more than 3,000 US personnel died in the conflict, all but a few hundred from yellow fever and malaria. The war also brought the United States into a new role as colonial administrator in the Caribbean, setting the stage for the next century of US hegemony in the region. The United States established protectorate status over Cuba, formally occupied the island from 1898 through 1902, and returned troops again to restore domestic order in 1906. Under the terms of the Platt Amendment, a rider appended to the Army Appropriations Act of

1901, the United States exercised a high degree of control over Cuba until the amendment was abrogated in 1934.

Cuba was only a protectorate, but Puerto Rico, the Philippines, and Guam became US possessions. As such, the United States wielded considerable influence over the evolution of the Puerto Rican political system. Initially, the US president appointed the governor, cabinet, and all judges sitting on Puerto Rico's supreme court. In contrast to the later occupations of Haiti and the Dominican Republic, where officials appointed to such positions were not nationals of those two countries, at least these appointees were Puerto Rican. In addition, Puerto Ricans were able to elect an assembly on the basis of a franchise that was much wider than in the English and French Caribbean. In 1910, Puerto Ricans elected their first resident commissioner to the US Congress, Luis Muñoz Rivera; seven years later, with the passage of the Jones-Shafroth Act, Puerto Ricans gained US citizenship.

■ The Non-Spanish Caribbean in the Early Twentieth Century

In the late nineteenth century, the British Caribbean enjoyed a greater degree of stability than the Spanish colonies, even before the final collapse in the Spanish-American War. The earlier end of slavery in the British colonies and the arrival of East Indian immigrants in many of those colonies set them on a path toward political maturity and economic development more rapidly than in the colonies of the Spanish Caribbean, although none of them approximated the wealth of Cuba. However, while Cuba was plagued by turmoil and suffered widespread destruction during the war, the British were able to maintain order and stimulate development in their colonies.

Politically, Trinidad and Tobago (united in 1888) and Jamaica remained rigidly under the control of small, mostly white elites. Even the gradual introduction of British parliamentary institutions did not obscure the fact that these societies were neither democratic nor free of imperial dominance at the turn of the century. Jamaica's black population did not gain a legislative majority until the 1920s, although women gained the right to vote just before that, paralleling that development in the United Kingdom and preceding it in the United States. Property and literacy requirements for the franchise remained in effect until 1938, and full racial and gender equality before the law did not come to Jamaica until the adoption of a new constitution in 1944.

In both Jamaica and in Trinidad and Tobago, the effort to improve agriculture and trade involved crop diversification, pest control, and low-interest loans to facilitate the improvement of infrastructure, including the expansion of rail and road links to ease the movement of goods. The attempt to diversify the Jamaican economy met with some success. Although large sugar estates retained their importance, the number of plantation workers declined from 30,000 in 1860 to 20,000 in 1910; the relative importance of sugar to the Jamaican economy also declined, by 1896 representing only 18 percent of the value of Jamaican exports (Randall and Mount 1998:47). Conversely, the number of smaller freeholders operating banana plantations increased, and the country began to export bananas. There was a significant level of Canadian and US investment in the bauxite industry in Jamaica over the next few decades, increasing economic diversification. Yet the demand for labor and the opportunities for economic advancement in Jamaica remained limited, and the lure of either seasonal migratory work or permanent migration from the island became constant. Thousands of Jamaican workers and their families migrated to Panama in the mid-nineteenth century to assist in the construction of the Panama Railroad linking the Caribbean and the Pacific. After the United States gained control of Panama from Colombia in 1903, thousands more sought employment in the construction of the Panama Canal.

Like Jamaica, Trinidad and Tobago experienced some degree of economic diversification in the first half of the twentieth century, in particular with the development of an oil industry after World War I. However, such economic development did not guarantee democratization. Given the high percentage of East Indian immigrants, many of them indentured workers, Trinidad enjoyed less self-government than most of the other British colonies until the end of the indenture system in 1917. Most residents were people of color, and most Europeans were Roman Catholics. What minimal representative government there was disappeared in 1898 as part of the so-called reforms organized by Colonial Secretary Joseph Chamberlain. Chamberlain, who assumed office in 1895 as part of Lord Robert Arthur Salisbury's Conservative cabinet, envisioned a centralized British Empire—a Greater Britain—that would compete with the United States, Russia, and Germany. Before 1898, Trinidad's Legislative Council, which advised the governor, was hardly representative, dominated by wealthy planters, businessmen, and professionals. Even that was too much for Chamberlain. As of 1898, appointees of the Colonial Office would outnumber Trinidadians. Chamberlain also abolished the elective local council in Port of Spain, which had existed since 1853. Despite a high property requirement for the franchise, blacks as well as mulattos had served as councilors, with the result that the abolition of the local council eliminated one of the few avenues for the colored population to participate actively in colonial politics. As late as 1934, only 25,000 Trinidadians out of a total population of more than 400,000 had the right to vote, and in Barbados the franchise was even more restricted, with only 2.5 percent of the population entitled to cast a ballot as late as 1937 (Knight 1978:161).

In terms of its degree of democratization, British Honduras fared little better than Trinidad in the nineteenth and early twentieth centuries. One factor accounting for the limited local self-government in British Honduras was the ongoing threat posed by Guatemala, which maintained a long-standing claim to the territory. From 1814 until 1851, authority rested with the superintendent, a British military officer, and the Public Meeting. At first all free citizens could attend the Public Meeting, but as the society grew, property qualifications—higher for people of color than for whites—became mandatory. A civilian superintendent was appointed in 1851, and in 1854 British Honduras abandoned the Public Meeting, establishing a legislative assembly of eighteen elected members plus three members appointed by the superintendent. Voters had to meet the property requirements; assembly members had to meet even higher ones. In 1862, while the United States was embroiled in the Civil War, Great Britain constituted British Honduras as a formal colony. In 1871 the legislative assembly voted itself out of existence and transferred authority to the governor and his appointees. The threat from Guatemala was not the only factor; the tiny European minority did not want to be governed by the large nonwhite majority. A legislative assembly did not return until 1954, when all literate adults gained the right to vote. In 1964, British Honduras gained full internal self-government, a significant advance but a far cry from the independence enjoyed by Jamaica and Trinidad.

There were similar pressures for more representative government in British Guiana in the late nineteenth century. The emerging Afro-Guyanese middle class was pressing for constitutional reforms, in particular the conversion of the governor-appointed Court of Policy into an elected assembly, as well as less onerous qualifications for the franchise. Yet as in most of the colonies, wealthy planters, who had little difficulty exercising their political influence in London with the West India committee, vigorously resisted such reforms. Nevertheless, by the early 1890s the pressures began to work; voter qualifications were gradually relaxed, the College of Electors was abolished, and eight elected members were added to the Court of Policy to balance the eight appointed members. Still, the governor and planters retained the real power, as the executive duties of the Court of Policy were transferred to an Executive Council that the court controlled. It was not until 1909 that electoral reform made Afro-Guyanese the majority of the voting population. Those reforms were sparked in part by the massive 1905 Ruimveldt riots, which began with a strike by Georgetown stevedores and turned into the country's first general strike uniting urban and rural workers. The strikes and the rioting were quelled by British troops, but the uprising underlined the depth of the discontent that the masses felt with their economic and political condition.

French colonial policies underwent considerable evolution from the early nineteenth through the early twentieth centuries. St. Domingue, prior to its successful revolt against France, had representation in the French National Assembly, as did Martinique and Guadeloupe by 1815. This status went far beyond what England and the United States accorded their possessions by the early twentieth century. The surviving colonies lost that status until after the 1848 revolution in France, although in the intervening years there were some advances in the development of elected councils in both Guadeloupe and Martinique, restricted as the franchise was to men of property. After the failure of the Paris Commune in 1871 and the establishment of the French Republic, French colonial representation in the National Assembly was restored, paving the way for recognition as actual overseas departments of France after World War II (Knight 1978:161).

The legal end of slavery in 1863 in the Dutch West Indies (Aruba, Bonaire, Curaçao, St. Eustatius, St. Maarten, Saba, and Suriname) brought, as elsewhere in the region, economic decline and the search for alternative sources of labor and alternative economic activities. In Bonaire, abolition was followed by a serious and prolonged decline in the production of salt, long the mainstay of the economy. In Aruba, gold mining remained an important economic factor until World War I. Later, as the Venezuelan oil industry experienced rapid growth during the 1920s, Aruba became an important locale for oil refining, by 1929 boasting the largest refinery in the world. Curaçao followed a similar pattern. There the major investments by Dutch Shell in oil refining in the 1920s revived a stagnant economy, and World War II stimulated the development of an offshore oil industry as well. Shell's refinery remained operational until the 1980s, and in the interim the island had also developed, along with Bonaire and Aruba, a vibrant tourist industry.

The experience of Suriname deviated somewhat from that of the other Dutch colonies in this period. As in the others, the abolition of slavery in 1863 was followed by a ten-year transitional period of indentured labor for former slaves, but indentured workers from South Asia significantly supplemented the labor force. Between 1873 and 1916, when the indenture system ended, some 34,000 East Indian contract workers reached Suriname. Most of them were Hindu, but some were Muslim. As with most immigrant labor experiences in the West, the return rate of the Indian indentured workers was high, with an estimated one-third returning to India before the system was discontinued. They left an indelible imprint on the politics, language, culture, and economics in Suriname, and in 1927 their importance was recognized by the grant of eligibility for Dutch citizenship (Hoefte 1998). In the twentieth century, the Surinamese economy came to be dominated by foreign-owned bauxite production and export, most of which was destined for the United States. Rice remained the main agricultural product, supplemented by citrus fruits, bananas, and other tropical crops. In Suriname, as in Curaçao, a complex racial and ethnic mixture of Dutch Europeans, Afro-Caribbeans, Spanish, and Indians has engendered societal divisions and at times spilled over into conflict.

■ The Emergence of US Hegemony, 1898–1930s

After 1898 the United States emerged as the unchallenged power in the Caribbean region. French interest in the construction of a canal across the isthmus of Panama collapsed late in the nineteenth century. With the 1903 separation of Panama from Colombia and the conclusion of the Panama Canal Treaties with Panama, the United States moved rapidly ahead with its plans for a canal linking the Atlantic and Pacific Oceans to facilitate commercial and military naval operations. Distracted with its own colonial problems, mainly in South Africa during the Boer War, and confronted by an increasingly powerful Germany, Great Britain ceded dominance in the Caribbean to the United States. Prime Minister Arthur Balfour renounced any intention of acquiring additional territory in the Americas and explicitly accepted the principles set forth in the 1823 Monroe Doctrine.

No other European power had either the capacity or the political will to challenge the United States in what became a special sphere of influence. Germany, however, briefly presented a challenge early in the century when its warships were active in the Caribbean, protecting and expanding commercial and strategic interests. Without formal colonies in the Caribbean, Germany nonetheless had extensive commercial interests in Venezuela at the time. Confronted with the failure of Venezuelan officials to meet their international financial obligations, Germany blockaded Venezuelan harbors in 1901. During the next few years, German, Italian, and French naval vessels all made shows of force in Caribbean waters. This spurred President Theodore Roosevelt to take a stronger stand against European encroachment, as well as what he considered to be the irresponsible economic practices of Caribbean countries that led them into increased indebtedness abroad.

In the Roosevelt Corollary to the Monroe Doctrine, the president declared that the United States had a responsibility to exercise police power in the Caribbean.[1] His successor, William Howard Taft, pursued a policy called "dollar diplomacy" that substituted financial controls to promote greater political stability and reduce the threat of further European involvement in the region, a concern made more acute with the outbreak of World War I. In fact, the greater willingness of Woodrow Wilson's administration to dispatch US troops, as occurred in Mexico in 1914 and 1917 and in Haiti in 1915, may be attributed as much to the war in Europe as to instability in the Americas.

Much like the specter of communist expansion in the 1920s and the rise of fascism and Nazism in Italy and Germany in the 1930s, the possibility of European encroachment in the Caribbean was perceived as threatening to US security. In response, the United States assumed substantial responsibility for security in the region, as evidenced by the protectorate status of Cuba; the level of control exerted in Puerto Rico; and the establishment of military occupations and/or customs house controls in Nicaragua, Haiti, and the Dominican Republic. This degree of involvement was basically limited to the Caribbean region; with the exception of Mexico during World War I, the more powerful and independent mainland countries remained relatively untouched by direct US action.

Haiti was especially vulnerable and of strategic importance because of its deep-water harbor at Môle St. Nicolas. Although the United States had no

Harper's Weekly, November 21, 1903

"Held Up the Wrong Man"
President Theodore Roosevelt strong-arms Colombia to secure
control of territory for the construction of the Panama Canal.

pressing need for another naval base beyond those it possessed at Guantánamo in Cuba, in Puerto Rico, and in Panama, US officials did not want the port to fall under German control. Seeking stability following the collapse of the government of Guillaume Sam in 1915, President Wilson ordered US forces to occupy Haiti, where they remained until 1934 as the effective power behind a series of governments. Brenda Plummer (1992:110) concludes:

> The Haitian protectorate was unprecedented in its duration, the racism that characterized US behavior in the black republic, and the brutality associated with pacification efforts. . . . The devaluation of Haitian culture by Protestant,

positivist and dogmatic North Americans recalled an age of imperialism that was rapidly becoming obsolete in other parts of the world.

The governance structure imposed by the United States provided for financial oversight of Haitian affairs by US officials, including the power to deal unilaterally with Haiti's creditors, and a national police force commanded by US Marines. There were improvements in health, education, and infrastructure development, as occurred in Cuba and elsewhere in the Caribbean where the United States exercised direct or indirect controls. But US policy measures were universally unpopular in Haiti, and the attitudes as well as the practices of US officials during the lengthy occupation provoked violent resistance.

The political impact of the US occupations was, on the whole, even less positive. In contrast to the British, Dutch, and French colonies, where a variety of civic organizations and political institutions were emerging, the lessons in democracy meted out by US officials seemed to breed more authoritarian than democratic impulses. In the Dominican Republic, for example, where the United States began an eight-year military occupation in 1916, the congress was dissolved and all senior Dominican officials were replaced with US military officers, many of whom did not even speak Spanish. Here, as elsewhere, there were improvements in education, sanitation, and infrastructure. But for all the rhetorical commitments US officials made to equality and democracy, there was little, if any, change in the distribution of wealth and power. Culturally, the US occupation produced a Dominican passion for baseball, which over the coming decades provided a small window of opportunity for economic mobility. But even in that game, the racism that characterized the US presence tended to prevail.

Decades of interventionism and intimidation under the guise of the Roosevelt Corollary, dollar diplomacy, and Wilson's "democratic crusade" engendered considerable ill-will within the region (Smith 1996:64). In recognition of the implications of mounting anti-US sentiment, the United States changed its policy approach toward Latin America and the Caribbean. In his inaugural address on March 4, 1933, Franklin Delano Roosevelt made reference to this new approach: "I would dedicate this nation to the policy of the good neighbor— the neighbor who resolutely respects himself and, because he does so, respects the rights of others." Roosevelt's Good Neighbor Policy sought to enhance the image of the United States and to develop a spirit of cooperation within the hemisphere. Following Herbert Hoover's withdrawal of US forces from Nicaragua in 1933, Roosevelt brought home the remaining troops from Haiti and the Dominican Republic and abrogated the infamous Platt Amendment in 1934. Such measures aside, the United States clearly did not abandon the Monroe Doctrine as the basis of its hemispheric policy. Rather, it was able to pursue its objectives through less confrontational means, including economic leverage and diplomatic pressure (Smith 1994). Although the Good Neighbor Policy appeared to portend improved US-Caribbean relations, the previous era of intervention and occupation left an inauspicious legacy. This legacy set the stage for the eventual rise of brutal dictators such as Rafael Trujillo in the Dominican Republic, Anastasio Somoza in Nicaragua, Fulgencio Batista in Cuba, and François Duvalier in Haiti.

■ The Emergence of Labor Organizations

In the first few decades of the twentieth century, Caribbean colonies and independent states continued to experience political and economic change. As foreign (especially US) investment increased, economic growth, continued imperial control over many colonies, and the growing strength of foreign-owned enterprises stimulated an emergent nationalism. In those nations still under US or European control, this meant an increasingly strong desire for independence. Despite periods of economic growth, high levels of poverty among the majority of previously indentured and enslaved peoples persisted, while political systems throughout the region remained dominated by small, typically white, elite groups. However, the growth of the working class and the slow emergence of a middle class contributed to the formation of labor movements and political parties as much of the Caribbean achieved a greater degree of political institutionalization.

A major development that occurred throughout the Caribbean during the interwar period was the emergence and growing political power of labor organizations. During World War I, the rising cost of living and frequent shortages of basic commodities, including foodstuffs and housing, provoked popular discontent. There were strikes by oil and asphalt workers in Trinidad in 1917, and from 1918 to 1924, strikes and labor violence became more common throughout the region. There were labor disturbances and strikes in Jamaica in 1918 and 1924, in Trinidad in 1919 and 1920, in St. Lucia in 1920, in the Bahamas in 1922, and in British Honduras in 1919 and 1920.

On the mainland, banana workers in the Santa Marta area of Colombia began to organize in the 1920s, with the assistance of European socialist and anarchist groups, which targeted the subsidiaries of the United Fruit Company (UFCO), the main foreign interest in the banana industry throughout the region. Workers tended to have the sympathy as well of local Colombian planters who were seeking with limited success to break UFCO's monopoly over crop transportation and export. Tensions between labor and UFCO climaxed in 1928 in a bloody strike that ended with Colombian troops firing on unarmed civilians, a scene that inspired Gabriel Gárcia Márquez in his brilliant novel *One Hundred Years of Solitude* and that also brought to prominence the young socialist politician Jorge Eliécer Gaitán.

Trade union activity gained momentum in British Guiana, Jamaica, and Trinidad. Led by the popular cricketer Herbert Critchlow, the British Guiana

Labour Union, beginning with black dockworkers and then expanding to encompass East Indian agricultural workers, claimed a membership of 10,000 by the early 1920s. Restricted as trade unions were in Jamaica, the labor movement met with limited success in the 1920s, with only the longshoremen organized briefly by the mid-1920s. Workers realized more success in Trinidad in the interwar years, where Arthur Andrew Cipriani played a crucial role as a labor organizer, encouraging returned veterans and workers to join the Trinidad Workingmen's Association (TWA) in a major dockworkers strike in 1919. Their success emboldened workers who later struck across the island, reflecting a broadened base of participation by sugar workers and tradespeople. Alarmed by the rising level of militancy and violence on the part of labor, British authorities made strike action illegal while simultaneously paying lip service to the need to investigate workers' concerns about wages. Cipriani then shifted his focus to political action, converting the TWA into the Trinidad Labour Party in 1934. In addition to Cipriani, a number of other trade union leaders emerged in Trinidad during the 1930s, including Uriah Butler, who formed the British Empire Workers and Citizens Home Rule Party in 1938. Butler and Adrian Rienzi, a young East Indian lawyer and Leninist activist, contributed to the general strike among oil workers in 1937, the most important labor action in the country to that date.

Jamaica also experienced major labor actions in the late 1930s as workers, whose standard of living continued to decline as economic conditions deteriorated, voiced their growing discontent. The 1938 disturbances began with a major strike on a sugar estate, where striking workers clashed with police. Conflict quickly reached the docks of Kingston and then spread to include public works employees, former soldiers, and cane and banana workers in the rural areas. Suppressed though they were, these strikes led to the establishment of the West India Royal Commission (the Moyne Commission) to study social and economic conditions in the British West Indies, and then to the formation of the Bustamante Industrial Trade Union, which by the end of World War II was the largest labor organization in the Caribbean (Randall and Mount 1998:66–69).

■ War and Cold War, 1939–1959

The period from the end of the Great Depression to the Cuban revolution was turbulent in the Caribbean, although the attention of the great powers was diverted largely to European and Asian affairs. World War II brought tensions to the region, especially with the German defeat of the Netherlands and France, which threatened the future of their Caribbean colonies. Britain's weakness, the defeat of the Dutch and French, and the threat that German submarine activity posed to shipping all contributed to a strengthening of US power in the Caribbean. The war also created unprecedented demand for Caribbean products, from petroleum and bauxite to sugar and other foodstuffs. The unsettled nature of the imperial connections during the war served as a further stimulus to sentiments favoring a greater degree of self-government and liberalization of laws governing political participation.

Events in Europe during World War II sparked concern over the transfer of colonial territories in the Caribbean. When Germany defeated the Netherlands and France by June 1940, US and British officials feared that those countries' Caribbean possessions would fall into German hands. There was also concern that Great Britain, given the threat of German invasion, would be unable to defend its West Indian colonies. In response, the United States and other countries signed the Act of Havana on July 30, 1940, committing to the principle that no territory in the Americas could be transferred from one power to another. They agreed that in the event of an imminent German takeover of colonial territory, one or more countries in the Americas could establish a trusteeship for the duration of the war. In addition, with British consent, Canadian troops moved into Jamaica, the Bahamas, Bermuda, and British Guiana to replace British forces needed in Europe from 1940 to 1946 (Randall and Mount 1998:71). In return for transferring US destroyers to Britain in 1941, the United States also acquired control of a number of British air bases in the region. In the end, although Vichy control over the French colonies posed some problems, there was no transfer of any Caribbean colonies to a hostile power, and no serious security threat emerged during the war.

With European powers debilitated by war, increased political mobilization in their colonies stimulated a growing sense of nationalism and demands for reform. In British Guiana, for example, the Moyne Commission's inquiry underlined the rift between the Afro-Guyanese and the larger Indo-Guyanese population, the latter of which had played little role to that date in the colony's politics. The commission recommended increased democratization of government as well as socioeconomic reforms, including extending the franchise to women and those who did not own land. In contrast to prewar British policy, the commission also encouraged the emerging labor movement. The reforms introduced by Governor Sir Gordon Lethem included reducing property qualifications for holding office and voting and making elected members a majority of the Legislative Council in 1943. By 1952 there was universal adult suffrage, prefacing the movement toward independence.

This political liberalization, albeit limited and with little impact on the distribution of wealth and power, occurred elsewhere, particularly in the British Caribbean. In 1944 suffrage was extended to women in British Guiana, Barbados, and Bermuda. In that same year Jamaica and Trinidad achieved universal adult suffrage, and Jamaica also gained limited self-government. Martinique and Guadeloupe were made overseas departments of France in 1946. Universal adult suffrage came to Barbados in 1950 and to the Leeward and Windward Islands in 1951. After years of debate over its political status, Puerto Rico obtained its first taste of local self-government since the US occupation in

1898, ultimately gaining commonwealth status in 1952. In 1954 the Netherlands Antilles and Suriname were granted the right of internal self-government and universal suffrage and became autonomous parts of the kingdom of the Netherlands.

Along with decolonization, economic development and Cold War tensions dominated the regional agenda in the postwar decades. Puerto Rico experimented with aggressive economic change under the program Operation Bootstrap. Intended to promote industrialization and to diversify the economy, Operation Bootstrap sought to attract large corporations from the mainland with tax incentives and comparatively inexpensive labor. In the short term, at least, the island boomed with manufacturers anxious to take advantage of their ability to export into the US market duty-free. Throughout the region, state planning became increasingly popular in the postwar era, led to a large extent by the United Nations Economic Commission for Latin America and the influential ideas of the Argentine economist Raul Prebisch. The model of industrial development behind protectionist tariff walls was widely adopted in the area during these years, contributing to increased rural-urban migration and the decline of the rural labor force. Economic changes notwithstanding, the traditional polarity between an impoverished rural peasantry and urban proletariat, and a small, largely white urban and landed elite, remained the norm. With inflation rampant by the 1960s, there were few signs that poverty and disparities of wealth were on the wane.

Politically, the non-British Caribbean had slipped decidedly into an authoritarian mold beginning in the 1930s, with the Somozas in Nicaragua, Trujillo in the Dominican Republic, and later with Batista in Cuba and Duvalier in Haiti. Even Colombia came briefly under the control of the military under Gustavo Rojas Pinilla until 1958. Throughout the 1950s, democracy reeled under the onslaught of right-wing dictators considered by the United States to be safe bets in the Cold War struggle. That trend was particularly evident in Guatemala, which emerged with more progressive elements under the leadership of Juan José Arévalo and Jacobo Arbenz. Their efforts to bring sorely needed reforms to landholding and agriculture and to support the rights of labor ran up against US Cold War paranoia as well as the vested economic interests of private capital, in particular the United Fruit Company (UFCO). Confronted with what US officials considered to be a wedge for communism, Dwight Eisenhower's administration in 1954 gave support (through the Central Intelligence Agency) to the reactionary forces of the Guatemalan military, led by US-trained colonel Carlos Castillo Armas, in overthrowing the democratically elected government of Arbenz. In addition to rolling back a decade of socioeconomic and political reform, this coup ushered in three decades of repressive military rule.

In the postwar years the British Caribbean experimented less with revolution than with political evolution, including a failed attempt at federation between

1958 and 1962 (the West Indies Federation) involving Jamaica, Barbados, Trinidad, and the Windward and Leeward Islands. The federation was less a colonial initiative than one inspired by British officials anxious to curtail the costs of empire for a weakened postwar Britain while seeking to minimize the impact of decolonization on the smaller island economies unable to survive on their own. The federation was doomed to fail as an artificial creation that accurately represented neither the political will of the majority nor the historical reality of the ties among the British West Indies. Ultimately, Jamaica's physical separation from and weak economic links to the other islands led to its withdrawal. When Trinidad followed suit, the British House of Commons was left with little choice but to end the short-lived federation in 1962. The failure of the West Indies Federation presented an early indication of the obstacles to political changes that might address historical inequities in the Caribbean.

The onset of severe East-West tensions heightened concerns in the United States and other imperial powers over the threat of communism specifically and political radicalism generally. However, it was Fidel Castro's seizure of power in 1959 and the Cuban revolution's turn to socialism that brought home the realities of the Cold War in the Western Hemisphere.

▪ The Cuban Revolution

No event in the postwar years had a more significant impact on the Caribbean than the 1959 Cuban revolution. In toppling the regime of dictator Fulgencio Batista, Fidel Castro initiated a true revolution that resulted in a massive redistribution of political, social, and economic power in the insular Caribbean's largest and most powerful nation. This revolt, and Castro's subsequent embrace of Soviet-style socialism, dramatically affected the East-West balance of power and made Castro and Cuba a symbol of defiance against the United States, one that has endured for some fifty years.

Cuba's alliance with the Soviet Union appeared to provide communism a beachhead in the Western Hemisphere. It conditioned the US response to any political change in the area that seemed to portend radical socioeconomic transformation or provide more leverage for Soviet- and Cuban-supported insurgencies. The first and only direct US effort to overthrow Castro, with the use of a surrogate force of Cuban exiles, ended in disaster at the Bay of Pigs in April 1961. The Cuban Missile Crisis in October 1962 resulted in a more cautious, if still determined, effort to undermine the Castro regime. The rupture of diplomatic relations and the US-imposed economic embargo by the Organization of American States in 1962 heightened Cuba's isolation within the region, ultimately leading to a greater level of dependence on Soviet aid and trade with Eastern bloc countries. Although the embargo did take a toll on the average Cuban, for whom basic necessities would become scarce, as well as

A portrait of Fidel Castro in a cigar shop in Cuba.

on the infrastructure of the island, it failed to bring about Castro's demise. In fact, he and the revolution have endured, and Cuba has wielded considerable influence both within the Caribbean as well as on the world stage.

Among other things, the Cuban revolution served to increase the paranoia and sensitivity of Western powers and Cuba's neighbors to political change in the region. Thus, after civil war broke out in the Dominican Republic in 1965 when supporters of ousted president Juan Bosch tried to return him to power, Lyndon Johnson's administration sent 23,000 troops to forestall what was perceived as a threat of revolutionary change. Ultimately, US forces helped to defeat the pro-Bosch movement, preventing the restoration of the democratically elected government and facilitating the establishment of an authoritarian regime headed by longtime Trujillo associate Joaquín Balaguer.

The Cuban revolution and the Cold War also brought tension to the British Caribbean, in particular to British Guiana (independent Guyana after 1966) and Jamaica. In the former, US and British authorities were concerned with the political dominance in the early 1960s of the left-leaning Cheddi Jagan and his People's Progressive Party (PPP). Canada also had extensive economic investments in the country, primarily in the financial sector, and generally shared the US desire to avoid a political crisis. Under US pressure, the British government in 1964 introduced a new electoral system employing proportional representation, a significant departure from traditional British electoral politics, in order to provide an opportunity for the People's National Congress (PNC) under Forbes Burnham and other opposition parties to break the stranglehold of the PPP. The tactic worked, with the PNC winning the election and establishing a minority government in alliance with the United Force Party in 1964. Ironically, Burnham himself drifted to the left and adopted a more radical stance in the early 1970s, nationalizing a number of foreign-owned enterprises, including the extremely important bauxite holdings of the Canadian-owned company Alcan, and establishing closer links with Cuba, Libya, North Korea, and East Germany.

Further evidence of the Cuban influence can be found throughout the 1970s. With the nationalization of bauxite production in Guyana, greater attention was focused on production in Jamaica, where Alcan's holdings had more potential and where there were also extensive investments by Anaconda, Kaiser, Revere, and Reynolds. The political situation in Jamaica in the early 1970s was viewed with alarm in the United States, as the electoral victory by the People's National Party (PNP) in 1972 led to the formation of a government committed to a program of democratic socialism under the leadership of Michael Manley. Manley and the PNP won reelection in 1976 and proceeded to establish diplomatic relations with the Soviet Union and to host an official visit by Fidel Castro in late 1977, provoking an ever-more hostile response from the United States.

By the end of the decade, the worst fears of the United States—the potential expansion of Cuban and Soviet influence—seemed to have been confirmed. Cuba's military activism in Africa, particularly its remarkable success intervening in conflicts in Angola (beginning in 1975) and Ethiopia (1977), did much to enhance the country's global stature, as did Havana's hosting of the Sixth Nonaligned Summit in 1979. The success of the Sandinista National Liberation Front (Frente Sandinista de Liberación Nacional, or FSLN) in overthrowing the regime of Anastasio Somoza in Nicaragua in 1979 provoked a crisis within the region and raised US fears of a second Cuba in what had become known as the Caribbean Basin. That same year, Maurice Bishop's New Jewel Movement came to power in Grenada after overthrowing the regime of Sir Eric Gairy and made immediate overtures to Castro. With Cuba attempting to expand its economic and political ties throughout the region, this period marks the high point of Cuban power and prestige in the Caribbean. However, as Jacqueline Braveboy-Wagner examines more fully in Chapter 6, such revolutionary change precipitated ongoing hostilities with the United States and varying degrees of military intervention that contributed to a diminishing of Cuban influence as time went on.

▇ The Post–Cold War Years

The dismantling of the Berlin Wall at the end of 1989 and the collapse of the Soviet Union in 1991 marked the end of a half century of Cold War. To a significant extent those changes also wrought a different dynamic in the Caribbean. Castro's Cuba remained an irritant in domestic and foreign policy for the United States even with the departure from power of Fidel Castro, initially in 2006 and more formally in 2008, when titular power passed to his brother Raúl. Yet it was an irritant that had lost its Cold War symbolism. Nor did Cuba cast a long shadow over the politics of the region in the way it had during the height of the Cold War. Hugo Chávez's Bolivarian revolution in Venezuela had a far more important impact on politics and foreign policy in the Caribbean Basin as he sought to deepen relations with Cuba and influence political events in Colombia, Nicaragua, and elsewhere in Latin America. In 2005 Chávez took the lead in hosting the first Caribbean Energy Summit in Puerto La Cruz. Thirteen countries participated in the summit, which Chávez touted as part of Venezuela's commitment to exporting cheaper oil to Caribbean countries faced with high-cost imports and to enhance technological development. In 2006 Chávez was also a vocal presence in the months leading up to the Nicaraguan election that returned an aging Daniel Ortega and the Sandinista National Liberation Front to power. In early 2008 he engaged in saber rattling over the brief entry into Ecuador by Colombian forces attacking a base belonging to the Revolutionary Armed Forces of Colombia (Fuerzas Armadas Revolucionarias de Colombia, or FARC).

Chávez's posturing, even with the leverage provided by the nation's oil wealth during years of high oil prices in the early twenty-first century, appeared to matter little to the region as a whole. In the post–Cold War period, Caribbean political leaders have focused more on expanding trade relations within the region; coping with the same pressures of globalization that face the major powers; and dealing with the continuing challenges of poverty, organized crime, and out-migration that have long characterized the region. The early promise of the potential benefits of a Free Trade Area of the Americas rapidly faded as the initiative lost momentum in the first decade of the twenty-first century, and the conclusion in 2005 of the Central American Free Trade Agreement by the United States heightened anxieties among Caribbean nations that they would be left further behind in the increasingly competitive global marketplace. The Association of Caribbean States (ACS), established at Cartagena in 1994, has been particularly focused on addressing issues of regional economic integration and protecting the interests of the smaller economies in the context of the World Trade Organization (WTO). Remittances to families in the region from family members who have migrated to North America or Europe have had some positive impact, especially in Jamaica, but remittances are hardly a substitute for real economic development and a reduction of the region's continued dependency.

Even as Chávez's Venezuela has been the economic powerhouse in the Caribbean basin, Haiti has continued to struggle with political instability and economic weakness. There were raised hopes for Haiti when Jean-Bertrand Aristide was elected president by a large popular majority in 1990, but those hopes were dashed when he was overthrown by military coup in September 1991. After a period of exile in Venezuela and the United States, he was returned to power with US military support during the Clinton administration in Operation Restore Democracy. During rule by the military junta, the international community, including the OAS and UN, imposed economic sanctions on Haiti, which had little impact on the junta but intensified the suffering of the Haitian populace. Aristide was succeeded ultimately by René Préval in 1996, who served his full presidential term (1996–2001). In 2000, Aristide's Lavalas Family Party won control of the Senate, and later that year Aristide himself was returned to the presidency in an election that was boycotted by most of the opposition parties. Faced with mounting violence, military opposition, and international pressures, Aristide once again left office in 2004, fleeing into exile first in Jamaica and then the Central African Republic.

The internationally supervised presidential and parliamentary elections in 2006 that returned Préval to the presidency were viewed as relatively free of problems and a promising indication of increasing stability in Haiti. Préval appealed to the international community for the kind of substantial and long-term development aid that is essential if the country is to move beyond its endemic economic problems. However, socioeconomic and political stability have continued to elude what is by all accounts the poorest country in the Western Hemisphere.

Jamaica, governed after 2002 by the fourth successive government led by the People's National Party (PNP), also experienced times of turbulence, driven in large part by inflation in the cost of such basic commodities as gasoline. Troubled by perceived high levels of illegal immigration from Jamaica, the British government in 2003 for the first time imposed visa requirements on Jamaicans wishing to enter the United Kingdom. The Dominican Republic also witnessed violent public protests in 2003 in response to the high cost of consumer goods and energy shortages. The previous year, Patrick Manning, the prime minister of Trinidad and Tobago, had felt compelled to suspend parliament in the face of an ongoing political crisis but was returned to power in the third election in only three years. Dominica also faced serious economic problems in the first years of the new century confronted as it was by a decline in both exports and tourism.

◼ Conclusion

Some historical patterns have emerged from this discussion. First, the insular countries of the Caribbean have had divergent colonial experiences, yet they share to varying degrees common problems of underdevelopment, out-migration, and political instability. A second important feature is the continuing interaction between the insular Caribbean and the larger Caribbean Basin, in particular with such major countries as Venezuela. A third characteristic of the region has been the range of political experiences as the former colonies achieved independence, from the earliest experience of Haiti and its slave revolt against both planter and French authority to the more gradual and constitutional transitions experienced by the British Caribbean.[2] Aside from those remaining vestiges of colonial power, governance in the region ranges from authoritarian to constitutional democracy. Although the colonial heritage imparted different traditions, values, and institutions to the region, the movement toward political independence has done little to foster economic autonomy. As Dennis Pantin and Marlene Attzs demonstrate in Chapter 5, the economic dependency of the region may have lessened somewhat with the greater diversification of national economies, but dependency rather than self-sustaining economic growth is more the norm than the exception. In Chapter 4, Thomas J. D'Agostino explores the political implications of this condition. The countries of the Caribbean have endured a common historical experience of slavery, economic exploitation, and political domination. Confronting the implications of this historical legacy remains the main challenge for the Caribbean nations in the twenty-first century.

Notes

1. On December 6, 1904, in a message to Congress, Roosevelt stated:

Any country whose people conduct themselves well can count upon our hearty friendship. If a nation shows that it knows how to act with reasonable efficiency and decency in social and political matters, if it keeps order and pays its obligations, it need fear no interference from the United States. Chronic wrong-doing, or an impotence which results in a general loosening of the ties of society, may in America, as elsewhere, ultimately require intervention by some civilized nation, and in the western hemisphere the adherence of the United States to the Monroe Doctrine may force the United States, however reluctantly, in flagrant cases of such wrong-doing or impotence, to the exercise of an international police power. (P. Smith 1996:38)

2. The current and former British West Indies had the most complicated road to independence of the Caribbean territories. Some, like Anguilla, the British Virgin Islands, the Cayman Islands, Montserrat, and the Turks and Caicos Islands, remain possessions of the United Kingdom with internal self-governments. Others, like most of the former British Lesser Antilles and the Bahamas, have become independent. The first to become independent were Jamaica and Trinidad and Tobago in 1962. Barbados became independent in 1966, and the rest achieved independence during the 1970s and early 1980s, with St. Kitts and Nevis being the most recent to become independent in 1983.

Bibliography

Andie, F. M., and T. G. Mathews, eds. *The Caribbean in Transition: Papers on Social, Political, and Economic Development.* San Juan: University of Puerto Rico Press, 1965.
Ardila, Martha, compiler. *El Gran Caribe: Historia, cultura, y política.* Bogotá: Universidad Externado de Colombia, 2005.

Beckles, Hilary. *Freedom Won: Caribbean Emancipation, Ethnicities and Nationhood.* Cambridge: Cambridge University Press, 2006.

Black, Clinton. *A History of Jamaica.* London: Longman, 2003.

Bryan, Anthony. *Trading Places: The Caribbean Faces Europe and the Americas in the Twenty-first Century.* Occasional Paper 27. Miami: University of Miami North-South Center, 1997.

Buhle, Paul. *C. L. R. James: The Artist as Revolutionary.* New York: Verso, 1988.

Bush, Barbara. *Slave Women in Caribbean Society, 1650–1838.* Bloomington: Indiana University Press, 1990.

Craton, Michael. *Founded Upon the Seas: A History of the Cayman Islands and Their People.* Kingston: Ian Randle, 2003.

Curtin, Philip D. *The Atlantic Slave Trade: A Census.* Madison: University of Wisconsin Press, 1969.

Domínguez, Jorge. *International Security and Democracy: Latin America and the Caribbean in the Post–Cold War Era.* Pittsburgh: University of Pittsburgh Press, 1998.

Domínguez, Jorge I., Robert A. Pastor, and R. DeLisle Worrell, eds. *Democracy in the Caribbean: Political, Economic, and Social Perspectives.* Baltimore: Johns Hopkins University Press, 1993.

Dupuy, Alex. "From Jean-Bertrand Aristide to Gerard Latortue: The Unending Crisis of Democratization in Haiti." *Journal of Latin American Anthropology* 10, no. 1 (April 2005): 186–205.

Engerman, Stanley, and Eugene Genovese, eds. *Race and Slavery in the Western Hemisphere.* Princeton, NJ: Princeton University Press, 1975.

Geggus, David, ed. *The Impact of the Haitian Revolution in the Atlantic World.* Columbia: University of South Carolina Press, 2001.

Gordinga, Cornelius. *A Short History of the Netherlands Antilles and Suriname.* The Hague: M. Nijhoff, 1979.

Green, W. *British Slave Emancipation: The Sugar Colonies and the Great Experiment, 1830–1865.* Oxford: Clarendon Press, 1965.

Hart, Richard. *Slaves Who Abolished Slavery: Blacks in Rebellion.* Kingston: University of the West Indies, 2002.

Hartog, Johannes. *Curaçao: From Colonial Dependence to Autonomy.* Aruba: De Wit, 1968.

Henry, Paget, and Paul Buhle, eds. *C. L. R. James's Caribbean.* Durham, NC: Duke University Press, 1991.

Hoefte, Rosemarijn. *In Place of Slavery: A Social History of British Indian and Javanese Laborers in Suriname.* Gainesville: University of Florida Press, 1998.

Ince, B., ed. *Contemporary International Relations of the Caribbean.* Trinidad: University of the West Indies Press, 1978.

James, C. L. R. *The Black Jacobins: Toussaint L'Ouverture and the San Domingue Revolution.* 2nd ed. New York: Vintage, 1963.

Johnson, Howard. *The Bahamas from Slavery to Servitude, 1783–1933.* Gainesville: University of Florida Press, 1996.

Knight, Franklin W. *The Caribbean: The Genesis of a Fragmented Nationalism.* New York: Oxford University Press, 1978.

———, ed. *General History of the Caribbean,* Vol. 3: *Slave Societies of the Caribbean.* London: UNESCO and Macmillan, 1997.

Knight, W. Andy, and Randolph B. Persaud. "Subsidiarity, Regional Governance, and Caribbean Security." *Latin American Politics and Society* 43, no. 1 (Spring 2001): 29–56.

Lai, Walton Look. *Chinese and Indian Migrants to the British West Indies, 1838–1918.* Baltimore: Johns Hopkins University Press, 1993.

Lane, Kris E. *Blood and Silver: A History of Piracy in the Caribbean and Central America.* Oxford: Signal Books, 1999.

Langley, Lester D. *Struggle for the American Mediterranean: United States–European Rivalry in the Gulf-Caribbean, 1776–1914.* Athens: University of Georgia Press, 1976.

———. *The United States and the Caribbean, 1900–1970.* Athens: University of Georgia Press, 1980.

Latin American Crisis Group. *Haiti After the Elections: Challenges for Préval's First 100 Days.* Latin America/Caribbean Briefing no. 10, May 11, 2006.

Laurence, K. O. *Immigration into the West Indies in the Nineteenth Century.* Barbados: Caribbean Universities Press, 1971.

Lewis, Rupert, and Patrick Bryan, eds. *Garvey: His Work and Impact.* Jamaica: Institute of Social and Economic Research, 1988.

Matthews, Gelien. *Caribbean Slave Revolts and the British Abolitionist Movement.* Baton Rouge: Louisiana State University Press, 2006.

McLean Petras, Elizabeth. *Jamaican Labor Migration: White Capital and Black Labor, 1850–1930.* London: Westview, 1988.

Moya Pons, Frank. *History of the Caribbean: Plantations, Trade and War in the Atlantic World.* Princeton: Markus Wiener, 2007.

de Onís, Juan. *The America of José Martí.* New York: Funk and Wagnalls, 1953.

Pantojas-García, Emilio. "Trade Liberalization and Peripheral Postindustrialization in the Caribbean." *Latin American Politics and Society* 43, no. 1 (Spring 2001): 57–77.

Parry, J. H., and P. M. Sherlock. *A Short History of the West Indies.* London: Macmillan, 1965.

Pastor, Robert A. *Whirlpool: US Foreign Policy Toward Latin America and the Caribbean.* Princeton, NJ: Princeton University Press, 1992.

Plummer, Brenda Gayle. *Haiti and the United States: The Psychological Moment.* Athens: University of Georgia Press, 1992.

Randall, Stephen J., and Graeme S. Mount. *The Caribbean Basin: An International History.* London: Routledge, 1998.

Raup, Henry. *The Life and Writings of Bartolomé de las Casas.* Albuquerque: University of New Mexico Press, 1967.

Ruiz, Ramón Eduardo. *Cuba: The Making of a Revolution.* New York: Norton, 1968.

Schoonover, Thomas. *Uncle Sam's War of 1898 and the Origins of Globalization.* Lexington: University of Kentucky Press, 2003.

Smith, Daniel, ed. *Major Problems in American Diplomatic History.* Boston: D.C. Heath, 1965.

Smith, Gaddis. *The Last Years of the Monroe Doctrine, 1945–1993.* New York: Hill and Wang, 1994.

Smith, Peter H. *Talons of the Eagle: Dynamics of US–Latin American Relations.* New York: Oxford University Press, 1996.

Solnick, B. B. *The West Indies and Central America to 1898.* New York: Knopf, 1970.

Stinchcombe, Arthur L. *Sugar Island: Slavery in the Age of Enlightenment.* Princeton, NJ: Princeton University Press, 1995.

Thomas, Hugh, *The Slave Trade: The Story of the Atlantic Slave Trade, 1440–1870.* New York: Simon and Schuster, 1997.

Tulchin, J. S., and R. H. Espach, eds. *Security in the Caribbean Basin: The Challenge of Regional Cooperation.* Boulder, CO: Lynne Rienner, 2000.

Turton, Peter. *José Martí: Architect of Cuba's Freedom.* London: Zed Books, 1986.

Wilberforce, Robert Isaac, and Samuel Wilberforce, eds. *The Correspondence of William Wilberforce.* London: John Murray, 1840.

Wilgus, A. C., ed. *The Caribbean: Its Hemispheric Role.* Gainesville: University of Florida Press, 1967.

4

Caribbean Politics

Thomas J. D'Agostino

Much that is deeply embedded in Caribbean political culture has continued to influence the outcome of political events in the twenty-first century. Yet there have been several important changes: Raúl Castro replaced his brother Fidel as Cuba's leader in 2008, Hugo Chávez has sought to generate a coalition of Caribbean nations that would challenge US hegemony in the region, and the post–September 11 political climate has focused US attention on areas other than the Caribbean. Perhaps most momentous, however, has been the devastating impact of the deepening global economic crisis. Interestingly, Barack Obama's leadership in the United States commencing in 2009 could offer a new approach to each of these changes and the issues associated with them. But to understand contemporary politics in the Caribbean region, we need not only to recognize significant events that shape the driving forces and issues affecting people's lives but also to appreciate the uniquely Caribbean attitudes, values, and beliefs that have formed over time.

▓ The Past as Prelude

The protracted and disparate colonial experiences that Stephen Randall discusses in Chapter 3 have profoundly influenced contemporary Caribbean political systems. The Caribbean contains remarkably diverse institutional structures and constitutional traditions, ranging from Cuba's revolutionary communist system to Westminster-style parliamentary democracies in the Commonwealth Caribbean to emerging democracies elsewhere, from independent states to colonial dependencies to states with varying relationships with metropolitan powers (see Basic Political Data at the back of this book). Thus, on the surface at least, generalizing about Caribbean politics is a challenging task.

The perception that Caribbean political systems are too different from one another to merit serious comparison has led to the tendency to segregate analyses by subregions, defined primarily by linguistic and cultural criteria. The result has been a dearth of pan-Caribbean political studies that are truly comparative.

Superficial differences between Caribbean societies, however, have tended to obscure underlying commonalities in their political systems. Some scholars observe that Caribbean societies, despite their unique features, have all been shaped by a host of common experiences (Lewis 1985; Knight 1990). The legacies of conquest, European colonialism, the plantation system, African slavery, and the persistent influence of external powers have produced similar patterns of political change and are evident in the values, practices, and institutions prevailing throughout the region. Contemporary Caribbean political systems reflect the blending of traditional and modern patterns, yielding hybrid systems that exhibit significant structural variations and divergent constitutional traditions yet ultimately appear to function in similar ways (Wiarda and Kryzanek 1992). In other words, though they may diverge in theory, the political systems across the Caribbean converge in practice.

This becomes apparent when evaluating the performance of Caribbean governments over time. Conventional wisdom has maintained that by virtue of their British colonial heritage, the states of the Commonwealth Caribbean are more likely to sustain stable democratic governance than other countries in the region. To be sure, many of the difficulties experienced by Haiti and some of the Spanish-speaking countries of the circum-Caribbean may be attributed to highly centralized authoritarian rule derived from the colonial and postcolonial eras and the concomitant paucity of viable political institutions. In contrast, the democratic structures and values Britain imparted to its Caribbean possessions, coupled with its policy of gradual decolonization in the region, facilitated the transition to independence and contributed to the relative success of democratic governments among the Commonwealth states. However, British rule also included long periods of semiauthoritarian "crown colony" administration and the imposition of a plantation economic system sustained by African slavery and indentured labor. The legacies of this colonial experience are reflected in contemporary political systems that manifest, like many throughout the region, the trappings of formal democracy yet remain elite-dominated and exclusionary, operating on the basis of personalism and patron-clientelism. Political crises in Grenada, Guyana, Jamaica, and Trinidad and Tobago since the early 1980s have tarnished the popular image of Anglo-Caribbean democracy, revealing these countries to be vulnerable to the same socioeconomic and political pressures as elsewhere in the region.

Though many scholars point to the record of democratic stability as the feature that has most distinguished the Caribbean from other developing areas, recent trends are unsettling (Griffin 1993; Ryan 1994; Huber 1993; Domín-guez, Pastor, and Worrell 1993; Edie 1994). With the onset of a devastating economic crisis in the 1970s and 1980s, governments across the Caribbean struggled to meet the basic needs of their populations. The struggle intensified in 2008 as the global economic crisis impacted the region. As frustration and cynicism have mounted, the exodus of West Indian peoples has continued to accelerate, and many of those who remain increasingly question the efficacy of political systems that they believe have failed to sufficiently provide for or represent them. At present, then, the challenges confronting regional governments and leaders—regardless of cultural, linguistic, and political traditions—as well as the internal and external constraints under which they operate are daunting.

What are the primary factors that have contributed to the development and maintenance of democratic political systems in the Caribbean? What has hindered the ability of governments to meet popular demands? What, if anything, can be done to make governments more responsive and to enhance their capacity to provide for citizens? Is the future of democracy in the Caribbean imperiled, and, if so, where might that lead? Will the emergence of a new administration in the United States have significant implications for the Caribbean? In this chapter I explore the political repercussions of historical processes and current trends in order to address these questions and assess the future of Caribbean politics.

External Influences, Internal Dynamics, and New Forms

For more than five centuries, the Caribbean has been affected by events and processes originating outside the region. The islands of the West Indies and the mainland areas bordering the Caribbean Sea were irrevocably transformed as a result of European conquest and colonization. Following the consolidation of Spanish control, other European powers sought to challenge Spain and intensified efforts to make inroads in the region. By the early 1600s Spanish hegemony was beginning to erode, precipitating major changes throughout the Caribbean.

Nearly constant warfare among the British, Dutch, French, and Spanish resulted in many colonies changing hands throughout the sixteenth and seventeenth centuries (e.g., Jamaica was ceded to Britain from Spain in 1655). Of even greater importance was the introduction of the plantation system by Dutch colonizers expelled from Brazil around 1640.

This innovation sparked the "sugar revolution" that transformed the agricultural, demographic, and socioeconomic character of the Caribbean and greatly enhanced its economic and strategic value. For example, land tenure patterns were altered dramatically as vast tracts were concentrated in the hands of the wealthy planter class, with production geared for export to metropoles.

More significantly, the demand for labor far exceeded the available pool, stimulating the growth of the African slave trade. As David Baronov and Kevin Yelvington discuss in Chapter 8, the importation of millions of African slaves as laborers forever changed the demographic composition of the region and led to the formation of a rigid three-tier social hierarchy (white minority elite on top, black slaves on the bottom, and a mixed colored population in the middle), the legacies of which remain evident today (Knight and Palmer 1989:7). Although the nonwhite population dwarfed the white European population throughout virtually the entire region, whites retained their economic and political dominance, reflecting the pervasive elitism within Caribbean societies.

The French colony of St. Domingue (later to become Haiti) provides another example of how external events have impacted the Caribbean. After France gained control over the western third of Hispaniola in 1697, the introduction of a slave-based sugar plantation economy enabled St. Domingue to become one of the most lucrative colonies in the world. However, the onset of the French Revolution in 1789, with its ideals of liberty, equality, and fraternity, contributed to the outbreak of a slave revolt in 1791 and the first challenge to colonial rule in the region. Even the abolition of the slave trade in 1793 and of slavery itself in 1794 in St. Domingue could not stop the revolt that culminated in the formation of the first independent black republic in the Americas: Haiti.

Stephen Randall notes in Chapter 3 that efforts to abolish slavery in the Caribbean were subject to fits and starts. Once again, external forces proved to have a major impact, as the debate over slavery in Britain during the early 1800s set into motion events that slowly curtailed the practice of slavery in the region. The actual implementation of policies to end the slave trade and then slavery itself occurred at different intervals by the respective colonial powers (Williams 1970). Regardless of when abolition occurred, the implications for Caribbean political systems and societies were extraordinary.

One of the most significant implications in the Anglo-Caribbean, where emancipation occurred earliest, was the need for an alternative source of labor. Attention turned to Asia, resulting in the influx of tens of thousands of indentured laborers primarily from India but also from China and elsewhere (CIA World Factbook 2009).

Although abolition technically gave freedom to millions of slaves, it did not alter the inequitable distribution of economic resources or political power.[1] The rigid stratification of Caribbean societies by race and class persisted, with the white minority planter class still in control. Nevertheless, it began a long process of enfranchisement that ultimately challenged the political dominance of elites, who opposed any measures that would open political systems to the nonwhite majority. Literacy and property requirements were imposed to delay the extension of the franchise and thereby preserve elite control over local representative institutions (i.e., legislative assemblies). As pressure to open systems escalated, several assemblies, including those in British Honduras and Jamaica, voted themselves out of existence rather than allow the nonwhite majority to gain control. This paved the way (along with the 1865 Morant Bay rebellion in Jamaica) for the end of the "old representative system" that had been established in 1661 and the implementation of "crown colony" administration throughout the British Caribbean. Designed to perpetuate British control over increasingly vocal colonial societies, this inhibited political development and bestowed a legacy of semi-authoritarian centralized executive power that contrasts with the democratic structures inherent in Anglo-Caribbean systems.

While Britain retained tight control over its colonies well into the twentieth century, Spain's power in the Americas deteriorated dramatically by the early 1800s following the loss of its mainland possessions and the Dominican Republic, leaving only Cuba and Puerto Rico under its control by 1825. This decline was paralleled by the gradual emergence of the United States as a significant presence in the region. The 1823 Monroe Doctrine underscored US interest in Latin America and the Caribbean, particularly the countries in closest geographic proximity to its borders. Initially, it did little to curtail European interventionism, because the United States had no means to enforce the doctrine. However, following the end of the Civil War, the United States began to assert itself, and the flow of US investment into the region greatly increased. Thus, concerns about regional stability precipitated a more aggressive approach that enabled the United States to exert enormous influence across the region.

A variety of actions underscored the centrality of the circum-Caribbean to US economic and national security interests, as well as US determination to consolidate its hegemony within the region. US involvement in the 1895 border dispute between Venezuela and British Guiana reflected a heightened assertiveness and European recognition of the growing stature of the United States. The construction of the Panama Canal facilitated US commercial and strategic dominance. But it was the defeat of Spain in the Spanish-American War that brought the Caribbean within the US sphere of influence and marked the advent of US preeminence in the region.

US intervention in Cuba's struggle for independence had major regional implications. Spain's defeat and its loss of colonial possessions (Cuba, Puerto Rico, Guam, and the Philippines) effectively ended its reign as a colonial power. Although Britain, France, and the Netherlands each retained a number of Caribbean possessions, the mantle of power had been passed to the United States (Richardson 1992). This marked the beginning of the "American Century" in the Caribbean, during which US preeminence would be established, challenged, and later confirmed with the end of the Cold War.

By intervening in the military conflict between Spain and those forces seeking Cuban independence, the United States denied Cuba its opportunity to gain independence on its own. Instead, after defeating Spain the United States established a protectorate over Cuba, motivated in part by the magnitude of US investments there. The insertion of the infamous Platt Amendment as part of Cuba's 1902 constitution—which forbade Cuba from incurring foreign debt, provided for the establishment of a US naval coaling station at Guantánamo Bay (still in operation), and gave the United States the right to intervene in Cuban affairs—provoked strong anti-US sentiment that later fueled the fight for Cuban "independence" in the 1950s.

Elsewhere in the Caribbean, the early part of the twentieth century witnessed varying forms of US intervention and heightened anti-US sentiment. The US preoccupation with regional stability was exemplified by President Theodore Roosevelt's 1904 Roosevelt Corollary to the Monroe Doctrine. In asserting the right of the United States to exercise an "international police power" in the hemisphere, Roosevelt was "extending the Monroe Doctrine to justify US intervention to prevent European intervention" (Molineau 1990: 41). Over the next three decades, US policymakers acted to protect commercial and strategic geopolitical interests from the threat of European encroachment. For example, fears that mounting Caribbean debts might provoke a response from European creditors led to the establishment of customs receiverships in the Dominican Republic, Haiti, and Nicaragua. At the same time, concerns that instability would threaten US interests and invite European incursions in the region (particularly given the escalation of tensions prior to World War I and during the interwar period) led to direct military interventions and occupations in a number of countries.

Notwithstanding the fiscal benefits derived from the receiverships, as well as the infrastructure improvements carried out by US occupation forces, the political repercussions of US interventionism were more problematic. Despite efforts to tout the US democratic mission in the circum-Caribbean, these interventions not only stultified the development of democratic institutions and values but actually paved the way for the emergence of a number of repressive authoritarian regimes. Ironically, even though President Franklin Delano Roosevelt's Good Neighbor Policy was intended to improve relations with Latin American and Caribbean countries by putting an end to direct US intervention, the withdrawal of US forces in favor of local institutions ("national guards") designed to maintain stability actually facilitated the rise of notorious dictators such as Rafael Trujillo, Fulgencio Batista, Anastasio Somoza, and François Duvalier. In each case, domestic political development was sacrificed in the interest of preserving the status quo and safeguarding US national security, sowing the seeds of future conflict that would involve further US intervention, albeit in different forms (see Table 4.1).

▓ The Case of Puerto Rico

Puerto Rico represents something of an anomaly in the study of US involvement in the Caribbean. Acquired by the United States from Spain concurrently

**Table 4.1 US Military Involvement in the Caribbean
During the Era of Intervention, 1898–1934**

Country	Years
Cuba	1898–1902, 1906–1909, 1912, 1917–1922
Dominican Republic	1912, 1916–1924
Haiti	1915–1934
Mexico	1914, 1916–1917
Nicaragua	1909–1910, 1912–1925, 1926–1933
Panama	1903
Puerto Rico	1898–1900

Source: Harold Molineau, *US Policy Toward Latin America* (Boulder, CO: Westview, 1990), p. 51.

with Cuba, Puerto Rico was subject to military intervention and occupation like the cases discussed above. By contrast, however, the US occupation of Puerto Rico was comparatively brief and gave way not to brutal dictatorship but to stable civilian rule closely tied to the United States. Puerto Rico is further distinguished from the other cases in that it never gained independence, remaining a US possession to this day.

Puerto Rico's central location in the Caribbean, its special relationship with the United States, and the relatively advanced level of development on the island have brought attention to it as a unique case. Yet despite its distinctiveness, Puerto Rico has much in common with its Caribbean neighbors, especially in terms of social problems, economic challenges, and external domination.

A brief overview of past developments helps to clarify the similarities and differences between Puerto Rico and the rest of the Caribbean. After Spain ceded Puerto Rico to the United States in 1898, the US military occupied the island until President William McKinley signed the Foraker Act in 1900, providing for a civilian government. Under that act—whereby Puerto Rico became an unincorporated territory of the United States—the US president appointed the Puerto Rican governor, the members of an executive council, and the justices of the Supreme Court. And though the House of Delegates and resident commissioner were popularly elected, the United States continued to exercise substantial governmental control.

The Foraker Act also facilitated US control over the Puerto Rican economy. In providing "the legal framework for economic dependency," the act extended the US tariff structure, currency, and commercial regulations to the island (Silvestrini 1989:148). Among other things, this prevented Puerto Rico from entering into commercial treaties with other nations and required that US vessels transport all products shipped between the island and the mainland. Coupled with its administration of the education, health care, and criminal justice systems, deemed "pivotal in the Americanization process," it is evident that US control was pervasive (Silvestrini 1989:153).

In response to demands from Puerto Rican political leaders for increased autonomy and self-rule for the island, the 1917 Jones-Shafroth Act provided for the popular election of the nineteen-member Senate as well as US citizenship for the island's residents. Although that did enhance local authority to a degree, continued US control was ensured by virtue of the US president's appointment power.

The Puerto Rican economy underwent significant change during the early part of the twentieth century, growing more closely integrated with the US economy in the process. This sparked changes in the social structure as well as land tenure and employment patterns. The pace of rural-urban migration increased and, after the onset of economic problems in the 1930s, so did the exodus to the United States. Debate continued on the political status question, however, with political parties emerging to represent the three options: autonomy, independence, and statehood.

More far-reaching changes occurred in the 1940s. Following its creation in 1938, the Popular Democratic Party (Partido Popular Democrático) swept the 1940 legislative elections under the leadership of Luis Muñoz Marín. Its decision to shift from agriculture to industrialization as the development focus led to the implementation of Operation Bootstrap in 1947. This program of "industrialization by invitation"—designed to attract foreign investment with tax breaks and other incentives—triggered substantial economic growth, with profound implications for Puerto Rican society and politics in the coming decades.

After World War II, the United States was under increasing pressure from the United Nations to modify its colonial relationship with Puerto Rico. President Harry Truman signed the Elective Governor Act in 1947, paving the way for the election of Muñoz as the island's first elected governor the following year. In 1950 the US Congress approved Public Law 600, which set into motion the process of establishing a constitution for Puerto Rico. Following its approval by referendum in Puerto Rico, where it was opposed by the independence movement, the process culminated on July 25, 1952, with the creation of the Estado Libre Asociado de Puerto Rico—the Free Associated State (or Commonwealth).

The new constitution modified the structure of government in Puerto Rico, allocating more power to the elected government and legislature. Even still, the United States retained considerable powers that had been provided in the Foraker and Jones-Shafroth Acts. It has been suggested that the 1952 constitution bestowed "a new veneer of respectability to the home rule provided for Puerto Rico," an important international consideration for the United States at the time, but "did not in fact bring any fundamental change in the powers of government" (Gautier-Mayoral 1994:167). This situation is characterized as one of "limited democracy," whereby the elected government has control of local matters, while a host of key areas and issues (including, in addition to defense and foreign relations, customs, citizenship, immigration, the post office, and minimum wages) that affect the daily lives of people on the island remain under US control. As a result, the debate over the status question did not end with the promulgation of the Commonwealth constitution. On the contrary, it has continued over the past half-century with no definitive resolution in sight.

Despite impressive rates of economic growth during the 1950s and 1960s, producing a level of prosperity exceeding that of most regional neighbors, it became apparent that the Puerto Rican developmental model was beset by problems (Silvestrini 1989; Gautier-Mayoral 1994). First, the development of capital-intensive industry created far fewer new jobs than the number needed to reduce already high levels of unemployment. That was exacerbated by the collapse of the rural agricultural economy and displacement of peasant farmers, a trend that sparked large-scale urban and out-migration (mainly to the United States) and necessitated costly food imports as production declined.

Second, the influx of US companies and investment capital, though stimulating growth, also had a downside. The government undertook a massive infrastructure development program in order to accommodate the emerging industrial economy, causing public debt to skyrocket. At the same time, much of the profit generated by the companies, most of which received substantial tax breaks to locate on the island, was repatriated rather than reinvested locally. Thus, aside from the jobs that were created, the presence of these companies in Puerto Rico was not nearly as beneficial to the local population as statistical growth rates would seem to suggest.

Finally, over time Puerto Rico grew increasingly dependent on the United States as a source of capital, markets, technology, and expertise as the island economy became more closely integrated with the US economy. In addition, the level of US federal assistance increased dramatically as more and more island residents came to rely on public services and social welfare programs. Puerto Rico receives more than US$3 billion annually in federal grants. This heightened dependence has had significant political ramifications, for it represents "a formidable obstacle in the quest for self-determination" (Gamaliel Ramos and Rivera 2001:7). This point is echoed by another scholar, who concludes that the massive transfer of federal funds has produced "a bipartisan political system with alternation and cogovernance of the two major parties and fewer opportunities for a political status change" (Gautier-Mayoral 1994:168). Efforts to promote greater local autonomy or pursue statehood were thus "largely neutralized."

For all its idiosyncrasies, Puerto Rico faces challenges similar to those in other small, dependent, resource-scarce Caribbean states seeking to adapt to a global economy dominated by the world's major industrial powers. It has much in common with other "welfare colonies" in the region, including the Dutch and French possessions, whose decolonization has been "deferred" and who enjoy "prosperous dependence" through heavy subsidies from metropolitan powers (Gautier-Mayoral 1994). This extreme dependence breeds a "politics of immobility" with regard to the status issue. In the case of Puerto Rico, support for those favoring statehood and those favoring the existing commonwealth status had been more or less evenly divided in recent elections and referenda. However, in the gubernatorial election held in November 2008 Luis Fortuno, the leader of the pro-statehood New Progressive Party (Partido Nuevo Progresista, or PNP) and Puerto Rico's representative in the US Congress, soundly defeated the incumbent governor Anibal Acevedo-Vila of the pro-commonwealth Popular Democratic Party (PPD). The incoming government has indicated that its first priority will be to address the island's severe fiscal problems and it is unlikely that a change in status will occur anytime soon. Nevertheless, Puerto Rico's political status continues to be an important issue, which determines the kind of relationship the island can have with its Caribbean neighbors as well as with other countries of the world.

As in most of the Caribbean, tourism—a major capital producer for Puerto Rico—declined from 2005 through 2008 due to the economic downturn in the United States and elsewhere. Concomitant increases in joblessness and social malaise, including an escalation in rates of crime and violence, as well as workers' strikes and cases of political corruption, plagued the island in the first decade of the twenty-first century.

■ Socioeconomic Conditions and Political Consciousness

Outside Central America and the non-English-speaking Greater Antilles, where US interventionism was most pervasive, the late nineteenth and early twentieth centuries saw substantial socioeconomic changes. The political repercussions were particularly profound in the Anglo-Caribbean, where export-driven development contributed to the expansion of the nascent urban working and middle classes, primarily non-Europeans. As the level of popular political consciousness rose, however, political systems throughout the region remained under the firm control of the small, predominantly white elite. Largely excluded from the political process, the working and middle classes recognized that despite divergent objectives, they had a mutual interest in reforming the anachronistic colonial political order (Knight and Palmer 1989:12).

While the middle classes sought more gradual constitutional reform, the working classes demanded immediate change. Despite the proliferation of organizations promoting popular interests, their limited access to legitimate political channels compelled them to employ extralegal methods to express their demands. The depth of popular discontent throughout the Anglo-Caribbean was manifested by a plethora of violent disturbances, including the water riots in Trinidad in 1903 and the 1905 Ruimveldt riots in British Guiana. These events, calling attention to deteriorating socioeconomic conditions and exclusionary political systems, served as a precursor to the turmoil that engulfed the region in the 1930s.

With the onset of the Great Depression, tensions within the working classes were exacerbated by massive return migration on top of already heightened levels of unemployment (Knight and Palmer 1989). Amid intensifying nationalist fervor and demands for self-rule, violent labor disturbances culminated in the 1938 riots in Jamaica and British Guiana. In the aftermath, the Moyne Commission's inquiry into the causes of the unrest focused on the dire poverty afflicting the masses and led to a call for sweeping reform within the British territories.

The impact of external events on Caribbean affairs was again evident with the outbreak of hostilities in Europe in the late 1930s. As noted by Stephen Randall in Chapter 3, World War II led the United States to assume greater responsibility for security in the Caribbean and also bolstered nationalist sentiments within the region. Coupled with the repercussions of the labor disturbances, this brought pressure on the European powers to reassess their colonial policies and set the stage for significant change in the postwar era.

France and the Netherlands pursued a policy of decolonization very different from that of Britain. Confronted with escalating tensions in other colonies following World War II, France and the Netherlands took measures to more fully integrate their respective Caribbean possessions with the metropolitan center. Following a plebiscite in which each approved political union with France, French Guiana, Guadeloupe, and Martinique became *départements d'outre mer* (French overseas departments) in 1946. Among other things, this arrangement entitled the departments to elected representation in the French legislature as well as government subsidies. The Dutch granted internal self-government and universal suffrage to the Netherlands Antilles (comprised at that time of Aruba, Bonaire, Curaçao, Saba, St. Eustatius, and St. Maarten), which in 1954 was granted autonomy in international affairs and attained constitutional equality with the Netherlands and Suriname, joining with them to form the kingdom of the Netherlands. Suriname went on to acquire full independence in 1975. In 1986 Aruba became a separate self-governing unit in anticipation of a ten-year transition to independence. In 1990, however, Aruba rescinded its petition in order to remain within the kingdom. Compared to other areas within the Caribbean, Aruba and the Netherlands Antilles (with only a few incidents of unrest) have been stable while enjoying pacific governance and a relatively high standard of living.

■ Postwar Transitions

In contrast to the French and Dutch approach to colonial reform, Britain responded to demands for reform by initiating a gradual process that differed markedly from its policy in Africa and Asia. A lengthy period of "tutelary democracy" ensued whereby the structural apparatus of Britain's Westminster parliamentary system was introduced to facilitate the transition to local self-government and, ultimately, independent statehood. Such an institutional inheritance, in and of itself, has not necessarily guaranteed democratic stability, for "form seldom defines function" (Knight 1993:32). In the case of the Anglo-Caribbean, ostensibly democratic institutional structures were grafted onto societies that had experienced a protracted period of highly centralized, semi-authoritarian governance under crown colony administration. Through a process of "institutional adaptation" (Stone 1985:15), the Westminster parliamentary system was "Caribbeanized" (Payne 1993:72), or adapted, to the socioeconomic, political, and cultural realities of the Caribbean. This process has yielded hybrid or blended political systems that combine first world theory and institutions with third world conditions (Hillman and D'Agostino 1992; Payne 1993). Such systems boast formal democratic institutions and processes, yet in practice they tend to operate on the basis of personalism, patron-client relationships, and the exclusion of the popular classes.

Compared to other developing areas of the world, the Anglo-Caribbean historically has maintained an impressive record of stable democratic rule. Many scholars attribute this, at least in part, to the institutional and attitudinal legacies imparted by Britain to its Caribbean colonies.[2] These legacies (though perhaps not as democratic as is widely perceived) were a great deal more beneficial than those passed on to Haiti and the former Spanish colonies of the circum-Caribbean. After centuries of colonial rule the latter states, with deep-rooted authoritarian political cultures, were ill-prepared for nation building, much less democratization. With the removal of colonial authority, the newly independent states were confronted by a vacuum of power in societies devoid of any viable political institutions and democratic traditions.

Into this vacuum stepped rival military leaders, such as Henri Christophe and Alexandre Pétion (following the death of Jean-Jacques Dessalines) in Haiti and Pedro Santana and Buenaventura Báez in the Dominican Republic, competing to assert control over the state and its resources. The dominance of powerful caudillos (strong leaders, often military figures who dominate politics through the use of force) had profound repercussions throughout Central America and the Greater Antilles, perpetuating the dearth of institutions by impeding the development of those central to democratic societies. What followed, in the wake of the Great Depression, the Good Neighbor Policy, and the withdrawal of US forces from the region, was the emergence of brutal regimes such as those led by Trujillo, Somoza, Batista, and Duvalier.

The repressive rule and instability experienced in these countries following World War II stood in stark contrast to the gradual process of decolonization that characterized the territories controlled by the British, as well as the processes of reform employed by the Dutch and the French. These divergent experiences may be attributed to a variety of factors. Some scholars point to the disparity in the level of institutionalization in explaining the relative stability of the non-Hispanic Caribbean (excluding Haiti) as compared to other areas (Grugel 1995; Stone 1985). In the Anglo-Caribbean, the emergence of a vibrant civil society, particularly labor unions and political parties, served to channel heightened levels of social mobilization engendered through modernization, while enhanced linkages with the metropolitan centers helped to preserve stability in the Dutch and French territories, as well as in Puerto Rico. The paucity of viable institutions in Haiti and many of the former Spanish colonies, however, left opposition groups little choice but to pursue extraconstitutional means to challenge authoritarian regimes and effect change.

Scholars also focus on the response of elite groups to demands for reform in explaining divergent experiences since World War II (Grugel 1995:10; Stone 1985:47–48). In the Anglo-Caribbean, the rapidly growing and increasingly well-organized popular classes posed a significant threat to the political dominance of elites. Following the disturbances of the late 1930s, elites took measures to provide working classes with improved benefits and limited opportunities to participate in the political process under their tutelage within the existing power structure (Hillman and D'Agostino 1992).

The situations in the Hispanic Caribbean (excluding Puerto Rico) and in Haiti were very different. In those countries the growth of the urban working class was more gradual, and the labor movements were much smaller, less dynamic, and not nearly as well organized. Consequently, those in power (and their elite supporters) did not feel compelled to accommodate pressures for reform and, instead, utilized coercion and repression to marginalize and depoliticize the popular classes.

It is important to consider the influence of the United States in these areas during the early post–World War II era. US activism and intervention were primarily confined to the non-English-speaking Greater Antilles and Central America in what some consider the true US sphere of influence (see, e.g., Molineau 1990). The onset of the Cold War heightened US sensitivity to the potential for instability and communist insurgency within the region. Seeking to forestall revolutionary change that might threaten its interests, the United States supported self-professed anticommunist dictatorships (such as those identified above), effectively "putting the Good Neighbor Policy in mothballs and giving the Monroe Doctrine new life" (Maingot 1994:87). Through the Central Intelligence Agency, the United States also supported forces that ousted the democratically elected government of Jacobo Arbenz in Guatemala in 1954.[3] Arbenz was perceived by conservatives in the US government as being too far to the left because his reformist agenda threatened US business interests, especially the United Fruit Company. With the removal of Arbenz, the Caribbean again took center stage in the struggle between the world's great powers.

■ The Case of Cuba

The 1959 Cuban Revolution, by effecting a complete social transformation in the largest insular Caribbean state, was a regional and global watershed. The revolution produced a unique alternative political and socioeconomic model within the Caribbean.

The 1898 US intervention and subsequent occupation compromised Cuban independence. A pattern of strongman rule and military intervention in politics ensued. The overthrow of Gerardo Machado, who was elected in 1924 but maintained power illegally until 1933, led to a brief revolutionary period under Ramón Grau San Martín. Then Fulgencio Batista led a military revolt, leading to his domination of Cuban politics over the next decade, initially behind the scenes and later through direct rule from 1940 to 1944. During this period the United States strengthened its economic and political ties to Cuba. Any democratic alternative, severely undermined by widespread corruption and endemic political violence, was eliminated in March 1952 when Batista again seized power.

Batista cultivated ties with the United States, which maintained close scrutiny over Cuban affairs, given its proximity and the extensive US business interests on the island. Cuba, compared to other Caribbean nations, was relatively prosperous, yet there were considerable disparities in the distribution of wealth as well as between urban areas and impoverished rural areas. Thus, broad opposition to Batista's increasingly repressive regime emerged. Among the various groups seeking to oust the dictator was the 26th of July Movement, named after the date in 1953 on which its leader, Fidel Castro, launched an ill-fated attack on the Moncada military barracks. After his release from prison, Castro went to Mexico, where he plotted the overthrow of Batista. The struggle began in 1956, when Castro and his forces (numbering fewer than 100) returned to Cuba and waged a remarkably effective guerrilla campaign against Batista's well-equipped (by the United States) army of some 40,000. With his forces unable to quell the rebellion, Batista increased repression against students and other groups who led urban-based opposition to the regime, as well as those suspected of sympathizing with the rebels. Lacking any substantial popular support and having lost US backing, Batista fled into exile on January 1, 1959, and Castro marched triumphantly into Havana.

As the broad revolutionary coalition began to splinter, Castro's faction, including his brother Raúl and the Argentine revolutionary Ernesto "Che" Guevara, became the dominant force. The ultimate direction that the revolution would take was unclear at this time, largely due to uncertainty as to Fidel's ideological orientation. Although Guevara, an avowed Marxist, maintained that Fidel was not a Marxist prior to the revolution, Fidel Castro himself has given conflicting accounts. He was not a member of the prerevolutionary Communist Party, instead focusing his appeal on the middle sectors as a nationalist

A political rally in Bayamo, Cuba, July 1982, to hear
President Fidel Castro's address at a celebration
commemorating the Cuban revolution.

reformer. However, initial uncertainty as to his intentions gave way to the realization that Castro was committed to a radical program intended to transform Cuban society and to assert Cuban sovereignty and independence from US influence.

The Castro regime immediately set about dismantling the country's dependent capitalist economy, nationalizing property of both domestic and foreign owners. This action, coupled with the movement toward an authoritarian single-party state, led to the exodus of thousands of upper- and middle-class Cubans. This exodus (and subsequent ones like the 1980 Mariél boatlift) served as a kind of safety valve for Castro, helping to defuse internal opposition.

His charismatic presence did much to fill the institutional void left in the wake of Batista's collapse, and Committees for the Defense of the Revolution and other organizations were formed to mobilize support for the regime. Support was also generated by an ambitious program to address the glaring inequalities that characterized pre-1959 Cuba. Land redistribution, educational reform, a literacy campaign, and improvements in health care and other services were introduced to raise the standard of living of Cuba's masses and to ensure that their basic daily needs would be met.

Emboldened by Cuba's deepening ties with the Soviet Union, which provided a market for Cuban sugar and a new source of technology (and, later, military assistance), Castro's anti-US rhetoric intensified. The revolution's increasingly radical tone, coupled with the seizure of US holdings, prompted

John Kennedy's administration in 1961 to launch a Guatemala-style invasion by US-backed Cuban exiles at the Bay of Pigs. Instead of fomenting a counterrevolution within Cuba, the poorly organized operation failed miserably. A monumental victory for Castro and for Cuban nationalism, the Bay of Pigs substantiated Castro's contention that the United States was the mortal enemy of revolutionary Cuba; many contend that the failed invasion pushed Cuba further into the embrace of the Soviet bloc.

Castro then formally declared himself, and the revolution, Marxist-Leninist. Within months, Soviet leader Nikita Khrushchev ordered the installation of missile bases on the island, transforming Cuba into a stage for a confrontation that brought the world's superpowers to the brink of nuclear war. The Cuban Missile Crisis of October 1962 was resolved when Khrushchev, under pressure from the Kennedy administration, agreed to withdraw Cuba-based Soviet missiles in exchange for a US pledge not to invade the island.

Mural depicting Ernesto "Che" Guevara, Havana, Cuba.

Cynthia Sutton

Graffiti in Cuba:
"The Committees for the Defense of the Revolution,
will always continue fighting."

Over the next three decades Cuba became a key Soviet ally in the third world. The relationship provided the Soviets with access to a strategic location in the Western Hemisphere, and Soviet efforts to assist communist movements in Africa were bolstered by Castro's desire to export revolution and his willingness to contribute troops and other personnel to missions in Angola and Ethiopia. In return, the Soviet Union provided the military support and economic and technical assistance that helped institutionalize the revolution and enabled Cuba to survive the embargo imposed by the United States in the early 1960s.

Critics of the revolution argue that Castro, despite his rhetoric about asserting Cuba's independence from foreign powers, merely exchanged US dependence for Soviet dependence. Although supporters counter that since 1959 Cuba has belonged to Cubans rather than to foreign investors, Soviet influence was pervasive. Castro maintained a greater degree of autonomy than the leaders of most Soviet satellites, but his longevity in power was due, in part, to Soviet backing. To be sure, Castro depended heavily on Soviet aid to provide the benefits that endeared him to the Cuban masses. But Castro's popularity also derived from his willingness to confront the United States, which greatly enhanced the sense of national pride and dignity among Cubans. His longevity may also be attributed to a centralized authoritarian state in which legitimate opposition was not tolerated and dissent was severely repressed.

The Cuban Revolution has been influenced profoundly by the prevailing international context. The bipolar structure institutionalized during the Cold War enabled Castro to parlay Cuba's strategic geopolitical location into leverage in dealing with the Soviet Union. However, the situation changed dramatically with the emergence of Soviet leader Mikhail Gorbachev in 1985 and the introduction of reforms such as glasnost and perestroika. Soviet rapprochement with the West meant that Cuba soon became a costly burden, both economically and politically. As the Cold War wound down and the Soviet domestic crisis deepened, the Soviet Union's diminished ability and willingness to subsidize Cuba led to a reduction in assistance. Further, as Cuba's trade partners began to demand hard currency payments, Cuba was forced to borrow from abroad, accruing a substantial foreign debt.

The collapse of regimes throughout Eastern Europe and the dissolution of the Soviet Union deprived Cuba of its primary trading partners and its source of economic and technical assistance. Coupled with the long-standing US embargo, the loss of Soviet-bloc assistance has caused serious economic hardship in Cuba. Ironically, in being left to fend for itself, Cuba may be considered truly independent for the first time since formally gaining independence more than a century ago.

Despite rhetorical slogans like "Socialism or Death!" Fidel Castro adopted a more pragmatic approach to maintaining the revolution in the long term. For example, in an effort to attract much-needed hard currency, Castro allowed for the dollarization of the Cuban economy in 1993, enabling people to trade in US dollars. He also sought foreign investment, establishing joint ventures with foreign firms to stimulate the economy. In particular, Cuba has banked on a revitalization of the once-vibrant tourist industry to keep the economy, and possibly the regime itself, afloat. However, the influx of tourists has exacerbated the sense of deprivation felt by many Cubans. This could prove especially troubling among Cuba's youth, who face bleak prospects with few opportunities and who lack the strong emotional attachment to Castro and the revolution felt by the previous generation. Nevertheless, as Richard Hillman points out in Chapter 1 of this book, the Elián González case illustrated that Cuban nationalism is tied inextricably to anti-US sentiment and the desire for Cuba to chart an independent course.

The transition from Fidel Castro to his brother Raúl, formalized in February 2008, has raised many questions about the future of the Cuban Revolution. Although some analysts consider Raúl to be even more doctrinaire than Fidel, restrictions on Internet access recently were eased, and some economic incentives have been implemented—giving rise to speculation that under his regime Cuba could become more openly practical than ideological. Yet Fidel continues to publish articles in *Granma,* the daily communist newspaper—giving the appearance of his continued leadership—at least symbolically. Cuba has also sought to bolster its relations with other countries, including continuing to deepen its ties with Venezuela, as evidenced by Raúl Castro's state visit in December 2008. Interestingly, at the same time Raúl indicated a willingness to negotiate directly with President Barack Obama, Cuba has revitalized relations with Russia. President Dmitry Medvedev visited Havana in November 2008, and the following month Russian naval ships stopped in Cuba for the first time since the dissolution of the Soviet Union in late 1991.

For countries in the Western Hemisphere, the repercussions of the Cuban Revolution were far-reaching. Fidel Castro's consolidation of power and Cuba's alliance with the Soviet Union aroused US fears of the potential for socioeconomic and political change throughout the Americas. After 1959, US policy in the region focused on preventing a "second Cuba." In 1961, the Alliance for Progress was introduced by the Kennedy administration to stimulate development and ameliorate the conditions believed to foster communism. The determination to confront regimes deemed leftist was evident in Guyana, where pressure on Britain to alter electoral laws brought down the government of Marxist Cheddi Jagan in 1964 and, on a grander scale, in the Dominican Republic following its 1962 elections.

The Case of the Dominican Republic

After coming to power in 1930, Rafael Trujillo established a highly centralized authoritarian state whereby he would rule until his assassination in 1961. During this time the Dominican Republic evolved into a police state in which Trujillo came to exercise absolute control and the regime relied upon intimidation, repression, and terror to maintain power. Although the country was transformed from a traditional rural society to a more modern urban one under Trujillo, his unwillingness to accommodate the demands of an increasingly mobilized populace, particularly the emerging urban working and middle classes, contributed to his demise. Political development had been so constrained under his rule that "the country was only slightly more advanced in 1961, when Trujillo was assassinated, than in 1844, when independent life began" (Wiarda 1989:434).

Rapid modernization in the post-Trujillo era continued to alter the composition and structure of Dominican society, as well as the expectations and values of the populace. The Dominican Revolutionary Party (Partido Revolucionario Dominicano, or PRD), led by Juan Bosch, mobilized the newly emergent groups and won the nation's first competitive democratic election in 1962. However, the PRD's democratic experiment faced serious obstacles, including opposition from domestic elites who, along with the United States, feared Bosch's progressive policies and viewed events in the Dominican Republic as a prelude to Cuban-style revolution.

Whereas the PRD's victory appeared to promise an opening of the political system, Bosch's ouster by a coalition of powerful elites and the military after only seven months in office underscored the lack of national consensus as to the future direction of Dominican politics. The suppression of the PRD and its supporters following the coup did not bode well for the maintenance of stability. Mass discontent and violence ultimately erupted in April 1965, when Bosch supporters attempted to restore him to the presidency.

Lyndon Johnson's administration sent some 23,000 troops to assist loyalist forces in quelling the revolt, seen as a threat to stability and US hegemony in the region. After the defeat of the pro-Bosch constitutionalist forces, Dominicans returned to the polls in 1966 to elect Joaquín Balaguer, a former Trujillo associate. Balaguer's conservative agenda endeared him to the Dominican elites, the international business community, and particularly the US government, whose overt support of Balaguer over Bosch was one of several factors that compromised the electoral process. Over the next twelve years Balaguer ruled in a manner reminiscent of the Trujillo era, employing electoral fraud and repression in a process of authoritarian restructuring that stultified democratic development in the Dominican Republic.

▨ The Anglo-Caribbean

While Cuba embarked on a period of revolutionary change and the Dominican Republic reverted to its authoritarian past, the Anglo-Caribbean was on the

Dominican presidential candidate
Juan Bosch during his 1990 campaign.

verge of a new era as well. As Stephen Randall describes in Chapter 3, the West Indies Federation (WIF) was created in 1958 to facilitate the transition to independence for a number of British colonies. However, the WIF faced substantial obstacles from its inception and was "doomed from the start by lukewarm popular support" (Knight and Palmer 1989:15). Many of the obstacles derived from Britain's own colonial policies. For example, Britain fostered a sense of division among its colonies as a way to enhance its control. There was little direct communication and trade among the colonies, as each dealt primarily with London. Significant disparities in the level of economic and political development among the British colonies also undermined efforts to promote a sense of cohesiveness and unity of purpose.

Thus, there was little sense of regional identity or regionwide nationalism within the British Caribbean (Grugel 1995:115–116). On the contrary, one of the commonalities that emerged among the British colonies was a fierce sense of nationalism in the early twentieth century. This nationalism was island-specific and fostered a strong desire for independence rather than a desire to belong to an artificial supranational creation. That regional interests would be subordinated to those of individual states became evident early on: the federation "quickly foundered on the uncompromising insular interests, especially of its principal participants, Trinidad and Jamaica" (Knight and Palmer 1989:15).

The eventual demise of the federation came as a result of Jamaica's decision to withdraw following a referendum held on September 19, 1961. The legacies of fragmentation and uneven development played a significant role: Jamaica's ties to the other members were limited, and there was a widespread perception among Jamaicans that their country, as the federation's largest economy, would be subsidizing its less developed partners. With Trinidad subsequently announcing its decision to withdraw, the WIF was officially dissolved on May 31, 1962. Later that year, on August 6, Jamaica became the first British colony in the region to gain its independence.

■ The Case of Jamaica

Jamaica provides an interesting case in exploring the transition to independence as well as the challenges confronting newly independent states. Such analysis demonstrates the extent to which the legacies of British colonial rule shaped the postindependence political systems in the Anglo-Caribbean (Payne 1993).

Jamaica's independence marked an end to more than 300 years of British colonial rule. During this time, political institutions and values inherent in the British parliamentary tradition were transplanted in Jamaica, along with the crown's other West Indian possessions. These institutions and values were adapted over time to the country's socioeconomic realities, producing a uniquely Jamaican political system—yet one that has been influenced deeply by the country's colonial heritage.

"Free Me from Federation"
Opponents of the West Indies Federation in Jamaica argued
that their country would suffer when smaller member states
drained resources from the federation's largest economy.

Following its seizure from Spain in 1655, Jamaica experienced a brief period of military rule. The "old representative system" was in place from 1661 to 1865, dominated by a governor and a council forming an upper house appointed by the king. The lower house consisted of a representative assembly chosen by an electorate limited by a variety of restrictions. This assembly represented the interests of the landowning plantocracy and, in the nineteenth century, some professional and mercantile interests as well. The system was exclusionary, leaving the vast majority without representation.

In the wake of emancipation in 1838 (slavery itself was abolished in 1834) and the subsequent arrival of indentured workers from Asia, disturbances erupted periodically between landowners and laborers frustrated with the lack of responsiveness to their demands. This turmoil culminated in the 1865 Morant Bay rebellion, which resulted in the dismantling of the old representative system and its constitution and the imposition of a crown colony government in which the governor enjoyed nearly autocratic power and in which political activity was discouraged. It wasn't until 1944, after a series of disturbances in 1937–1938, that crown colony rule was rescinded. A new constitution was proclaimed, restoring representative government and facilitating the transition to self-rule.

The labor unrest and incipient nationalism that emerged in the 1930s gave rise to charismatic leaders and organizations that would lead Jamaica into independence. Frustrated by the dearth of institutions through which their demands could be effectively channeled, workers began to organize. Movement toward the unionization of labor provided a vehicle for the organization of political expression. One of the leaders of this movement was Alexander Bustamante, who formed the Bustamante Industrial Trade Union in 1938 and captured the imagination of the Jamaican masses. At the same time, as sentiment for self-government mounted, Norman Manley established the People's National Party (PNP) as a nation-building organization. Bustamante subsequently founded the Jamaica Labour Party (JLP) while the PNP was initially linked to the Trade Union Council and later established its trade union affiliate, the National Workers' Union. This nexus between political parties and labor unions played a critical role in Jamaica's transition to independence and democratic rule, facilitating the institutionalization of a dominant two-party system in which both major parties relied upon labor organizations for electoral support.

This support was secured through an elaborate system of patron-client relations in which political parties and their leaders distribute employment and other material benefits in exchange for loyalty and support from the masses. In this manner, "the Jamaican ruling groups have been able to anesthetize popular discontent by a politics of clientelism, keeping the masses quiet by a politics of 'jobs for the boys' at every social level" (Lewis 1985:227). Party loyalty was also derived from the dominance of "big personalities" such as Bustamante and Manley, a pattern in Caribbean politics in which "loyalties have traditionally been given to leaders on a highly deferential, almost messianic, basis" (Payne 1993:72).

Beginning with the 1944 election, Jamaica's first with universal adult suffrage, the JLP and PNP went on to alternate as majority and opposition, with Bustamante and the JLP winning in 1944 and 1949 and Norman Manley and the PNP prevailing in 1955 and 1959. These parties were representative of the two main ideological tendencies in the post–World War II Caribbean. However, both the "working-class and peasant-based populism" of Bustamante's JLP and the Fabian-inspired "social democracy" of Manley's PNP had much in common and "represented dual types of centrist ideological tendencies that supported economic and social reform on behalf of the majority classes but rejected either right-wing conservatism or left-wing Marxism/Leninism" (Stone 1985:41). The moderate platforms supported by each party attracted broad support, minimizing ideological conflicts and contributing to an orderly transition to independence.

Jamaica's transition to becoming an independent democratic state was facilitated by several factors deriving from its colonial experience. However, it is important to note that the country's gradual evolution toward self-rule differed markedly not only from the experiences of its non-English-speaking neighbors but also from those of Britain's possessions in other areas. As one scholar has noted:

> Unlike their counterparts in Britain's African and Asian colonies, the nationalist movements that emerged in the Commonwealth Caribbean during this time eschewed armed struggle and stuck to legal methods of bringing about change. Ruled directly by Britain under the Crown Colony system from the mid-Victorian period until decolonization, the Caribbean possessions never knew sustained and crude repression of the sort that Spain visited upon Cuba and Puerto Rico. As a result, violent anti-British sentiment never reached significant proportions in these countries. (Griffin 1993:88)

In addition, the duration and intensity of the colonial experience in the Commonwealth Caribbean set the region apart from other areas controlled by Britain. For example, "unlike in Africa and Asia, British rule in the Caribbean had been uninterrupted for centuries" (Domínguez, Pastor, and Worrell 1993: 16). Consequently, the institutions and values imparted by Britain could become more firmly embedded in Jamaican society.

Most observers agree that Anglophone Caribbean states have benefited from the Westminster parliamentary system, firmly rooted by the time of independence. In contrast to the presidential system found in former Spanish colonies, the parliamentary system, coupled with a stable party system, enables governments to function more efficiently by virtue of their control over both the executive and legislative branches (Huber 1993).

A vibrant civil society developed during the colonial era also contributed to the solid institutional base upon which Jamaican democracy was established. In particular, the emergence of labor organizations, political parties, and other civic associations provided opportunities for political expression and some degree (albeit limited) of political participation. The ties between the major parties and their union affiliates were critical to both the transition to independent statehood and the consolidation of Jamaican democracy. At the time of independence in the Commonwealth Caribbean, the "party-union complex was firmly established in terms of electoral effectiveness and as one pillar of the democratic order" (Domínguez 1993:16–17).

A dynamic democratic political culture also took root in Jamaican society during the colonial era. According to one scholar, "The record suggests that Anglophone Caribbean societies are *structurally* and *culturally* hospitable to democratic attitudes, institutions, and processes. These countries hold traditional values that reflect a distaste for excessive and arbitrary authority and a belief in individual autonomy" (Griffin 1993:89). The broad acceptance of democratic values has bolstered democratic governments in Jamaica and throughout the Anglophone Caribbean. The movement toward self-rule, for example, was aided by the fact that, with few exceptions, "the leading political figures who contested power in the Commonwealth Caribbean at the time of independence possessed values that were more deeply rooted in liberal democratic politics than in any other ideology" (Payne 1993:60). At the same time, democracy was widely embraced by the masses, who demonstrated their support through their active participation in the electoral process.

Yet it is also true that certain aspects of the British colonial legacy inhibited Jamaica's pursuit of independence and democratic stability. Some contend that the decolonization process deprived Jamaicans of a true "revolutionary" experience and that independence amounted to "separation but not transformation." Formal independence created no abrupt alterations in a political culture defined by great continuity with the past, and the basic socioeconomic and political structures and traditions remained intact, with indigenous Jamaican elites replacing British colonial elites.

The legacy of elitism inherent in British colonial rule endured in the postindependence era, and "as a result, Jamaican politics acquired a markedly elitist character" (Grugel 1995:118). This was apparent within the political parties created by elites in order to integrate the masses into the existing framework of power (Edie 1991). In the absence of real ideological differences between them, support for the rival parties derived from emotional images of charismatic leaders (Bustamante and Norman Manley) who consolidated power through personal appeal and promises to provide material benefits in the form of jobs, housing, access to education and health care, and other kinds of social welfare. Thus, with power highly concentrated within a narrow leadership, the parties served (and continue to serve) as vehicles of elite dominance rather than as aggregators of mass interests.[4] In co-opting the masses into a corporatist framework through such patron-client linkages, the party system channeled popular participation and served as a stabilizing agent during Jamaica's transitional period. However, even though this method of mobilizing mass support ensured maintenance of the status quo in the short term, its tenability has been challenged.

Jamaica's parliamentary system enjoyed a high degree of legitimacy from a broad cross-section of society in the immediate postindependence era. To a large extent that was due to a period of substantial economic growth spurred by favorable market conditions for Jamaican exports. Rising export revenues, coupled with increased investment and aid flows, helped to sustain the "statist bargain," enabling the government to provide material benefits and foster the perception that it was "delivering" (Domínguez, Pastor, and Worrell 1993; Huber 1993). As Trevor Munroe observed:

> The period of decolonization saw the consolidation of the system based on a version of party clientelism and state welfarism that improved the standard of living of the people and facilitated upward social mobility of the underclass. On this foundation, the postcolonial state, democracy, and constitutional government retained sufficient legitimacy among the people and performed effectively until the beginning of the 1970s. (Munroe 1996:104)

In fact, the system began to show signs of strain during the late 1960s. A series of disturbances broke out, including the 1968 Rodney riots (sparked by the deportation of a popular university professor). These outbursts reflected rising frustration and discontent among the Jamaican masses and served as the latest in a long tradition of violent uprisings against the deep-seated inequities inherent in Jamaican society. As was the case following the 1865 Morant Bay rebellion and the 1938 labor disturbances, the unrest of the late 1960s ushered in a period of substantial change.

It is ironic that although the postwar economic boom in Jamaica provided the resources to mollify a broad range of society through patronage, it also created conditions that ultimately provoked instability. This economic expansion has been characterized as "growth without development," meaning that expansion was generated externally through foreign investment in tourism, bauxite and other mineral extraction, and light manufacturing (Payne and Sutton 1993: 11). Most of the wealth produced was repatriated, with little reinvested in Jamaica, and the number of jobs created was far below that needed to reduce unemployment. Working-class Jamaicans, relatively speaking, benefited little from their country's economic success.

With the economic boom came rapid social changes: increased urbanization, greater access to media outlets and other forms of communication, heightened levels of social mobilization, and improvements in education and literacy. Over time the public demonstrated a greater degree of political awareness, and popular expectations and demands upon government increased. Unfortunately, this trend coincided with a period of economic decline in the late 1960s and early 1970s that undermined the government's ability to maintain the statist bargain and the extensive clientelistic linkages it relied upon for support. As the quality of life for Jamaica's masses deteriorated, they blamed the JLP government that had been in power since independence.

In 1972 the Jamaican electorate turned to the PNP and its new leader, Michael Manley (Norman's son), whose campaign featured slogans like "Power to the People" and "Better Must Come." Over the next eight years Manley pursued an agenda that asserted Jamaica's economic and political independence, sparking a sharp ideological division within Jamaican society and rancor in relations with the United States. The rift between the PNP, which aligned with the anti-imperialist rhetoric prevailing throughout the third world, and the more conservative JLP was indicative of the ideological polarization that typified the region over the next two decades.[5]

* * *

Franklin Knight asserts that the 1960s was "a major turning point" marking "the beginning of some fundamental restructuring of the politics and society of the Caribbean region. . . . Politically the Caribbean entered a period of intensified restlessness" (Knight 1993:29–30). This restlessness and restructuring were evident in Jamaica in the late 1960s and the 1970s. The disturbances fueled by the black power movement and deep socioeconomic inequalities were a portent of rioting that erupted elsewhere, including in Curaçao in 1969 and Trinidad in 1970. As discontent swelled, Manley and other Caribbean leaders explored common interests and forged links with other developing countries. This effort to diversify relations, coupled with the influx of alternative ideological currents, was viewed by the United States as a threat to regional stability and provoked a strong response.

■ Decades of Challenge and Change: The 1970s and 1980s

Reflecting the restlessness of the 1960s, the 1970s and early 1980s saw numerous instances of political restructuring and a host of regime changes. In the context of these regime changes, some states experienced a transition from colonial status to become independent liberal-democratic states (Antigua, 1982; Belize, 1981; Dominica, 1978; St. Lucia, 1979; and St. Vincent, 1979); in others liberal-democratic systems gave way to "leftist-socialist one-party states" (Grenada, Guyana, and Suriname); and one (the Dominican Republic) evolved from a conservative authoritarian system to establish an embryonic liberal democracy (Stone 1985).[6]

In other cases significant restructuring occurred. In Haiti, François "Papa Doc" Duvalier died in 1971, having ruled the country since 1957. He was succeeded by his then nineteen-year-old son, Jean-Claude "Baby Doc" Duvalier. Although the Duvalier dynasty endured under Jean-Claude's direction until 1986, his style of leadership and the nature of his regime differed from that of his father. His ties to the mulatto business community centered in Port-au-Prince contributed to the erosion of the regime's traditional base of support among the rural black peasantry. Its collapse in 1986 ushered in a period of violence and instability that underscored the dearth of viable political institutions in Haiti.

In Jamaica, Michael Manley's pursuit of "democratic socialism"—an alternative model of development independent of Western capitalism and Soviet communism—was a significant departure from his predecessors' policies. The decided shift to the left during the 1970s, in Jamaica and much of the region, reflected the influx of new ideological currents as well as Cuba's increasing influence. Analysis of these patterns reveals many challenges confronting governments across the Caribbean and provides insight into conditions under which democracies flourished—or foundered.

In contrast to other cases to be examined, Jamaica's shift to the left occurred within the framework of the country's parliamentary system, the result of a peaceful transfer of power. Manley and the PNP were not seeking to fundamentally restructure Jamaican society or its political system but rather to experiment with an alternative developmental model.

Jamaica's experience from 1972 to 1980 illustrates the considerable external constraints under which many Caribbean governments have had to operate. For example, the oil crises and the economic decline that beset the developed world severely hindered the ability of Manley and other leaders to sustain patron-client linkages. In addition, Manley's program of democratic socialism aroused US concerns in light of his aggressive stance toward multinational corporations operating in Jamaica. In particular, a new tax (or levy) imposed on foreign-owned bauxite companies was viewed as a potentially dangerous precedent for other exporters of raw materials.

Manley's cordial relations with Cuba and his close ties to Fidel Castro also earned him the enmity of the United States. The concern was that this relationship served to further legitimize Castro at a time when Cuba's global stature was peaking. Some observers, as well as Manley himself (Hillman and D'Agostino 1992), maintain that US opposition to Jamaica's socioeconomic and political agenda at this time led to a campaign aimed at isolating the PNP government and destabilizing the Jamaican economy. The bauxite levy engendered strong opposition from the companies as well as the US government, including production cutbacks and transfers, lawsuits, and a media campaign designed to undermine the tourist industry (Edie 1991:95). Plagued by significant international and domestic constraints, the Jamaican economy deteriorated in the late 1970s, hindering Manley's ability to deliver for his constituents. In an election marred by unprecedented political violence (some 800 people were killed during the campaign), Edward Seaga and the JLP soundly defeated Manley and the PNP in 1980. This marked the end of democratic socialism in Jamaica and was part of a wave of electoral victories from 1979 to 1982 by conservative candidates in Barbados, Dominica, and St. Lucia.

The situations in British Guiana/Guyana, Grenada, and Suriname differed sharply from that in Jamaica, where the shift to the left occurred within the existing liberal-democratic political framework. In these cases, the emergence of leftist-socialist regimes with close ties to Cuba resulted from the collapse of liberal-democratic systems inherited from the colonial era.

In Suriname, allegations of corruption, unfulfilled promises of political and socioeconomic reform, and widespread discontent within the military undermined support for the government of Henck Arron that had come into power at the time of independence in 1975. Arron was ousted in a coup d'état on February 25, 1980, and by early 1981 Suriname had embarked on a revolutionary socialist course under the leadership of Desi Bouterse.

The erosion of democratic institutions and values in Guyana and Grenada illustrated the fragile nature of liberal democracy in the face of endemic corruption, severe repression, and elite-dominated exclusionary political systems. It also underscored the fact that Westminster-type parliamentary democracy—

a remnant of British rule adapted to the realities of the Caribbean—has not always functioned as envisioned in the region. The electoral victories by Cheddi Jagan, an avowed Marxist, in British Guiana in 1953, 1957, and 1961 sparked concern in both London and Washington of the potential for expanded Soviet influence in the region. In 1953, with Jagan in office only five months, the constitution was suspended, and Jagan and the People's Progressive Party (PPP) were removed from power. Britain's decision in the aftermath of the 1961 contest to introduce a new type of electoral system (proportional representation, replacing the traditional first-past-the-post system used throughout the Anglo-Caribbean) enabled Jagan's former associate, Forbes Burnham, to win the 1964 election and to lead British Guiana into independence.

Burnham unleashed a campaign of repression against Jagan's PPP in advance of the 1968 election, which his People's National Congress (PNC) won amid allegations of massive fraud. Initially viewed as a social-democratic alternative to Jagan, Burnham himself disavowed the capitalist economic model and declared Guyana to be a socialist cooperative republic in 1970. By the mid-1970s, more than three-quarters of the national economy was under state control as Guyana evolved into a militarized single-party state. Racial and ethnic conflicts escalated as the Afro-Guyanese-based PNC, which retained power through blatantly fraudulent elections, dominated at the expense of the PPP, whose strength was centered in the majority East Indian community. Burnham's power was further augmented with a new presidential-style constitution introduced in 1980, although the onset of a severe economic crisis and mounting tensions with Ronald Reagan's administration plagued his regime until Burnham's death in 1985.

As in Guyana, Grenada's Westminster-type system was undermined by rampant corruption, extensive state-sponsored repression, economic decline, and the extreme centralization of power and concomitant exclusion of the masses from the political process. However, Grenada merits special attention given the extraordinary international context in which its revolution occurred. In July 1979 in Nicaragua, just months after the ouster of Grenada's longtime leader Sir Eric Gairy, the Sandinista National Liberation Front (Frente Sandinista de Liberación Nacional, or FSLN) toppled the regime of Anastasio Somoza Debayle. Later that year in December, the Soviet Union invaded Afghanistan. Coupled with the 1980 election of US President Ronald Reagan, these events sparked a resurgence of Cold War tensions with major implications for the nations of the Caribbean. Indeed, the perceived threat posed by the revolutionary turmoil resulted in a new era of US interventionism.

The Case of Grenada

The March 1979 coup that toppled Gairy marked the first time that a leader in the Anglo-Caribbean had been removed from power by force. Gairy first emerged in 1951, establishing a labor union (the Grenada Manual and Mental Workers Union) and later a political party (the Grenada United Labour Party) that enabled him to take power with the support of the newly enfranchised masses. With the exception of 1962–1967, Gairy ruled Grenada for nearly three decades, during which time the political system deviated from the traditional British parliamentary model and increasingly centered on his individual leadership. Often known simply as Gairyism, it was a system of authoritarian rule in which political power was highly personalized, extensive patron-client linkages assured the regime of mass support, and coercion and intimidation were regularly employed to quell opposition. According to one scholar:

> The trajectory of a matter-of-fact, routine liberal parliamentary democracy which brings in the masses as voters, producers of wealth, and consumers of colonial hegemony while leaving real political, social, and cultural power in the hands, pockets, and institutions of a minority elite—the Gairy Revolution and administration derailed that. Gairyism was its replacement—that synthetic, contradictory mix of part popular empowerment and part open dictatorship, with the personal and political figure of Gairy—not English rule—as the icon of ideology and politics. (Williams 1970:100)

By the early 1970s, amid a deepening economic crisis in which unemployment reached a staggering 44.6 percent and underemployment was estimated at nearly 75 percent, opposition to Gairy escalated. Popular disillusionment over the regime's assaults on civil liberties and democratic institutions, rendered all but meaningless, also undermined Gairy's support. After opponents of the regime, including the New Jewel Movement (NJM; formed in 1973), carried out a series of strikes and demonstrations aimed at forcing Gairy from office, they faced even greater levels of repression carried out by the notorious Green Beasts (a paramilitary group) and Mongoose Gang (Gairy's secret police). With the NJM asserting itself as the leading opposition, the regime fell in March 1979, paving the way for the emergence of the People's Revolutionary Government (PRG)—the second successful socialist revolution in the hemisphere.

The PRG inherited leadership of a country beset by a host of socioeconomic and political problems. Long-standing democratic institutions had been seriously debilitated, subordinated to the highly centralized personal power wielded by Gairy. The inequitable distribution of wealth, pervasive unemployment and underemployment, inadequate infrastructure, and foreign domination of key sectors of the economy posed daunting challenges to the new government (Smith 1993). The PRG attributed these conditions to the legacies of Gairyism and British colonial domination, as well as to neocolonialism. In rejecting the Westminster model and Grenada's links to Western capitalism, the PRG pursued an alternative form of political organization and socioeconomic development that sparked tensions with neighbors as well as with the United States.

If Gairy contributed to the degradation of the Westminster-type representative democracy in place in Grenada, the PRG and its leader, Prime Minister Maurice Bishop, were determined to eliminate it altogether. They viewed this system, considered by many to be central to the maintenance of relative stability throughout the Anglo-Caribbean, as elite-dominated and unrepresentative. Their objective was to replace the system they derisively referred to as "two-second democracy" (for the amount of time they claimed a citizen would actually participate in the system every five years, i.e., by voting) with a system of community-based "participatory democracy." This new structure was intended to foster grassroots organization and the integration of the masses into the political process.

Seeking to facilitate the transition to socialism and to address mounting economic problems, the PRG adopted the Soviet Union's model of noncapitalist development. A program of socioeconomic restructuring was initiated in which the state was to play a dominant role in a mixed economy. Seeking to boost productivity and enhance the quality of life among Grenada's masses, a variety of agrarian reform initiatives and physical and social infrastructure projects were undertaken. To reduce the country's external dependence, the government sought to diversify its international relations to include other developing and socialist states. Tourism was the key to the PRG's program of economic restructuring, appearing to offer the best opportunity for short-term growth that would generate the revenue needed to invest in both the agricultural and manufacturing sectors. Ironically, the focal point of the PRG's policy to bolster the tourist sector—the construction of the international airport at Point Salines—was to be cited by the United States as one of the primary factors leading to the US invasion in October 1983.

The economic performance of the PRG was decidedly mixed (Smith 1993). Overall growth rates from 1979 to 1982 were positive, enabling the government to deliver substantial improvements in the so-called social wage—a PRG term referring to benefits in areas like education, health care, housing, and transportation. However, this image was misleading, for it did not reflect the serious sectoral imbalance in the economy. Most of this growth resulted from government-funded construction aimed at infrastructure development, but state and cooperative sectors lagged. Expectations for growth in tourism were dashed as arrivals and receipts declined precipitously, particularly from the United States, given the PRG's pro-Soviet rhetoric. Dwindling private-sector investment weakened the manufacturing sector as well. These trends, exacerbated by the dearth of external funding, hindered the PRG's ability to reduce unemployment and deliver benefits. Thus, even though some socioeconomic gains occurred, they were tempered by the regime's inability to sustain growth. Ultimately, to forestall the deepening economic crisis, the PRG entered into an agreement with the International Monetary Fund (IMF) in August 1983. Such a step was inherently at odds with the PRG's agenda and did much to erode regime support.

Although the deteriorating economic conditions were problematic, the PRG's efforts at political restructuring were even more damaging. Its attempt to establish a more participatory system did stimulate the development of a number of mass-based organizations, albeit under the direction of NJM officials. The extent to which this integrated the masses into the political process in a meaningful way was limited, as "there was little real popular involvement in policy making and implementation" (Thorndike 1993:163). This failure to open the system and broaden participation, coupled with frustration with the lack of elections and limitations on basic civil liberties, further undermined popular perceptions of the PRG. Bitter infighting within the PRG, pitting Bishop against the more militant Bernard Coard, did little to enhance its public image.

Although a variety of factors contributed to the revolution's demise, the principal cause of its collapse was the imposition of Marxism-Leninism in a context ill-suited for it: "The Grenadian revolutionary experiment, in both theoretical and practical terms, was far removed from the values that informed the traditional Eastern Caribbean model" (Thorndike 1993:158). The 1979 coup and formation of a one-party militarized state were an aberration in the eastern Caribbean, an area in which democracy is deeply rooted and a culture of constitutionalism pervades. Given the centrality of competitive elections and peaceful transfers of power, the events of October 1983 proved particularly unsettling for regional observers. More ominously, the coup in which Bishop was arrested and executed—with power shifting to a Revolutionary Military Council led by General Hudson Austin—provided a pretext for the US-led invasion (Operation Urgent Fury) that toppled the regime and marked a renewed era of US intervention.

■ The Resurgence of US Interventionism

US policy in the Caribbean Basin during the 1980s differed markedly from the approach employed by President Jimmy Carter (1977–1981). The Carter administration's role in pressuring the military in the Dominican Republic to respect the results of the country's 1978 election, along with its agreement to transfer control of the Panama Canal to the government of Panama, engendered positive relations with Latin American and Caribbean countries. However, the Soviet invasion of Afghanistan, the revolutions in Grenada and Nicaragua (and turmoil elsewhere in Central America), and the election of Ronald Reagan in 1980 sparked a resurgence in Cold War hostilities that exacerbated tensions within increasingly polarized societies. Coupled with the devastating economic crisis that engulfed the region, this trend ensured that the 1980s would be volatile. Events during this period illustrated the extent to which politics in the Caribbean continued to be shaped by the power of external actors and by changes in international geopolitics.

That was clearly illustrated by the 1983 invasion of Grenada as well as the Reagan administration's actions in Central America, included within its definition of the Caribbean Basin. In Nicaragua, the 1979 revolt brought an end to a US-backed dynasty that dated back to the mid-1930s. Although the United States initially sought amicable ties with the revolutionary coalition led by the FSLN, relations deteriorated, and by 1981 the Reagan administration had initiated a campaign to destabilize what it saw as a Marxist-Leninist ally of Cuba and the Soviet Union. The US policy of economic sanctions and support for anti-Sandinista counterrevolutionary forces (the contras) exacted a considerable toll on the regime. The physical and economic devastation caused by the sanctions and the contra war, which threatened to engulf Honduras and Costa Rica (the longest-standing democracy in Central America), prevented the Sandinista government from delivering on its pledge to improve the standard of living, undermining its popular support. Thus, even though US policy never brought about military victory over the Sandinistas, it did serve to badly discredit them and contributed to their electoral defeat in 1990. The FSLN and its leader, Daniel Ortega, went on to suffer decisive defeats in 1996 and 2001. However, the FSLN returned to power after winning the 2006 election, a victory tempered by the fact that Ortega received only 38 percent of the vote in defeating a fragmented opposition.

In El Salvador, the Reagan administration continued its quest to confront communist aggression. Massive economic and military assistance, totaling nearly US$2 billion from 1981 to 1986, was provided to a succession of military-backed governments threatened by an insurgency led by the Farabundo Martí Front for National Liberation (Frente Farabundo Martí para la Liberación Nacional, or FMLN). US involvement dramatically escalated the conflict and prolonged a civil war that dragged on for more than a decade, with neither side able to gain a decisive victory. Aside from the billions of dollars in damage and lost productivity caused by the conflict, some 75,000 lives were lost, mainly civilians. Among them was Oscar Romero, the popular archbishop of San Salvador who was assassinated while saying mass in March 1980.

In the insular Caribbean, Reagan's first term (1981–1985) coincided with an ideological shift to the right. Electoral victories by conservative parties brought to power Edward Seaga in Jamaica, Tom Adams in Barbados, Eugenia Charles in Dominica, and John Compton in St. Lucia. In addition, the first postinvasion election in Grenada was won by the New National Party, a coalition of parties led by Herbert Blaize. These leaders cultivated close ties with the United States, campaigning on the basis that their ideological affinity with the Reagan administration would bring a foreign aid and investment windfall. This struck a chord of resonance among electorates weary of economic stagnation and seeking amelioration of endemic socioeconomic problems.

Great optimism accompanied the emergence of these leaders and the regional economic development program proposed by the United States, yet the

1980s proved to be a trying period for the Caribbean. The Reagan administration's eagerly awaited Caribbean Basin Initiative (CBI), originally conceived by Adams and Seaga as a mini–Marshall Plan, could not stem the economic crisis that gripped the region. This "lost decade," as the 1980s became known, was characterized by skyrocketing inflation, rising unemployment and external debt, and deteriorating living conditions. With limited resources and heightened demands, the challenges confronting governments across the Caribbean were daunting, and many fell victim to their inability to fulfill expectations. This is perhaps best illustrated by events in Jamaica and the Dominican Republic during the mid-1980s.

It is ironic that Jamaica, which under Seaga was considered by the Reagan administration as the centerpiece of the CBI, would experience the level of economic strife that it did. As a proponent of the neoliberal free market economic policies favored by international lending agencies, Seaga quickly endeared himself to Reagan. However, despite a substantial infusion of assistance from the United States, the economic performance of the Seaga government was disappointing at best. What went wrong?

An analysis of this case reveals the structural constraints under which Caribbean leaders must operate. Seaga worked closely with the IMF, implementing the prescribed structural adjustment measures in return for a series of loan packages. Jamaica's economic recovery, however, was derailed by a confluence of factors. The global economic slowdown of the 1980s proved especially problematic, limiting foreign investment and shrinking markets for traditional exports such as bauxite. Domestic political reaction to the imposition of austerity measures, including currency devaluations, tax increases, and public sector layoffs, was oftentimes swift and furious, as illustrated by rioting that broke out in January 1985. Seaga, therefore, had to contend with the conflicting demands of dual constituencies, one external and one internal, neither of which he was able to satisfy. His government repeatedly failed to meet benchmarks set forth in its agreements with the IMF, and the leverage he enjoyed through his once cordial ties with the United States diminished over time. So, too, did his and his party's stature with the Jamaican electorate, culminating in the JLP's defeat in 1989 and the return to power of Michael Manley.

The experience in the Dominican Republic during this period closely parallels that of Jamaica. In the historic 1978 election, the opposition PRD and its candidate, Antonio Guzmán, defeated three-term incumbent Joaquín Balaguer. Guzmán's death shortly before the end of his term led the party to nominate Salvador Jorge Blanco to be its candidate in 1982. Widely viewed as a reformist, Jorge Blanco's pledge to raise the standard of living and respect human rights and civil liberties helped him to defeat Balaguer. Soon after taking office, however, Jorge Blanco negotiated with the IMF for an emergency loan that was conditioned on the imposition of an austerity program. The announcement of a currency devaluation in April 1984 dramatically increased the cost of many basic items and sparked rioting that was brutally suppressed. By 1986 the PRD was deeply divided and badly discredited in the eyes of its traditional popular constituency, which had expected reform but was rewarded with austerity.

Both cases reveal the lack of real autonomy for Caribbean political leaders who, despite domestic political considerations, are compelled to follow strict policy guidelines in order to qualify for desperately needed funds. With little choice but to accept the loan conditions, Seaga and Jorge Blanco carried out austerity programs and suffered the political consequences. This also points to the extent to which the leaders of Caribbean countries located within the US sphere of influence are subjected to external pressures. With respect to Jamaica,

> this gives substantial power over the Jamaican political directorate to a range of external forces, from US political leadership in the White House and various US departments of state, to the officials of the IMF, the World Bank, and other US-dominated international financial agencies, to the managers of major multinational corporations with investments and interests in Jamaica. (Payne 1993:51)

The fact that Seaga's JLP and Jorge Blanco's PRD were defeated at the polls following IMF-related riots reveals the depth of popular outrage with these programs as well as with governments that impose them. However, in both cases power was transferred peacefully to the opposition through competitive elections (Manley and the PNP in Jamaica, and Balaguer and his Social Christian Reformist Party in the Dominican Republic), a testament to the level of democratic institutionalization attained in each society. The stability that characterized these transitions, however, stands in stark contrast to the experience of Haiti during the late 1980s and 1990s. A lack of viable institutions, extreme inequalities, a deeply entrenched elite, and a praetorian military have frustrated efforts to introduce democratic reforms following the collapse of the Duvalier regime in 1986.

The Case of Haiti

Under French rule, Haiti became one of the most valuable colonial possessions in the world. Nearly two centuries after acquiring independence, it is now widely regarded as the most impoverished country in the Western Hemisphere.

The massive importation of slave labor required for Haiti's sugar plantation economy engendered profound social and racial divisions that persist to the present day. The slave uprising that culminated in independence in 1804 left the country in economic ruin. In addition, the removal of colonial authority left the country without viable political institutions, a void filled by a succession of personalistic authoritarian military leaders.

As a result of postindependence economic decline, Haiti fell deeply into debt. Coupled with escalating political strife, this prompted the US intervention and occupation from 1915 to 1934. The US failure to foster the development of democratic institutions paved the way for the election of François Duvalier in 1957. Papa Doc employed Vodou, *noirisme* (a political ideology aimed at empowering the black majority), and the repressive Tonton Macoutes (a private security force) to consolidate power, appealing primarily to the rural masses. He declared himself president for life in 1964, transferring power prior to his death in 1971 to his son, Jean-Claude.

Baby Doc's policies, particularly his close ties with the mulatto elite in Port-au-Prince, alienated many traditional supporters of Duvalierism. Economic decline in the rural areas and the mobilization of church opposition, particularly following the 1983 visit of Pope John Paul II, further undermined the regime. The withdrawal of long-standing US support hastened the collapse of the dictatorship, and Baby Doc Duvalier fled into exile after pilfering the national treasury in February 1986.

Several aborted attempts at democratic transitions preceded the 1990 election of Jean-Bertrand Aristide. Enormously popular among Haiti's poor majority and perceived as threatening by elites and the military, Aristide was overthrown less than a year into his term. Following the coup, security forces and paramilitary groups killed an estimated 3,000 supporters of Aristide's Lavalas movement, and thousands more fled to the United States. Protracted negotiations, an international embargo against the Haitian military government led by Raoul Cédras, and the threat of US military action succeeded in returning Aristide to power in October 1994. This marked the first time that the United States had intervened in order to restore a democratically elected Caribbean leader (Stotzky 1997).

Aristide's return and the subsequent peaceful transfer of power to his ally and successor, René Préval—the first such transfer between democratically elected leaders in Haiti's history—were positive steps in the promotion of democracy. However, significant obstacles remained. Although Préval's victory in the 1995 election (he officially took office in 1996), coupled with Lavalas's sweep of legislative contests, seemed to bode well, a dispute erupted within the movement that led Aristide and his supporters to break and establish a rival organization, Fanmi Lavalas (FL). Senate and local elections held in 1997, marred by allegations of fraud and extremely low voter turnout, were followed by a period of gridlock; the split had fueled partisan rancor and brought the legislative and executive branches into conflict and the government to a standstill.

This gridlock prevented the organization of local and legislative elections scheduled for late 1998. With members' terms having technically expired in the absence of these elections, virtually the entire legislature—all members of the Chamber of Deputies and two-thirds of the Senate—were dismissed, enabling

Jean-Bertrand Aristide

the president and prime minister to rule by decree. After further delays, elections were finally held on May 21, 2000. Despite a strong turnout (more than 60 percent) and a broad range of candidates, the electoral process was seriously compromised by the manipulation of results to benefit the governing coalition and the poor performance of the Provisional Electoral Council charged with overseeing the contest. Opposition groups coalesced to protest and to pressure the government to call for new elections. International efforts to resolve the crisis, led by the Organization of American States and the Caribbean Common Market and Community (CARICOM), were unsuccessful, prompting all major opposition groups to boycott the subsequent presidential and Senate elections held on November 26, 2000. Aristide returned to power, winning nearly 92 percent of the vote, and his FL party swept the Senate contests.

Nevertheless, Aristide remained a deeply polarizing figure, and as political violence and economic strife intensified, a rebellion broke out that culminated in Aristide fleeing into exile on February 29, 2004. As Jacqueline Braveboy-Wagner explains in Chapter 6, a UN force was brought in to help stabilize the country, and nearly two years passed before an election was held. René Préval defeated nearly three dozen candidates to return to office but was faced with seemingly intractable fiscal problems. In April 2008 Préval's prime minister, Jacques-Edouard Alexis, was ousted by opponents who blamed him for failing to manage the economic crisis. It was not until September that agreement was reached on a successor, Michele Pierre-Louis, who became the second female prime minister in Haiti's history.

Haiti's turbulent past, lack of experience with participatory institutions, debilitated economy, and polarized citizenry have combined to produce a political culture that provides very little foundation for democracy. Although many aspects of these problems are specific to Haiti, the country also faces a host of challenges typical of other countries within the region.

■ An Era of Uncertainty: The 1990s and 2000s

Given its past, Haiti's struggles with its first real experience with democratic governance might have been anticipated. However, the problems afflicting some of the region's well-established democracies in the late 1980s and 1990s came as a surprise to many and served as a portent of the adversities that have come to confront governments across the region. In Trinidad and Tobago, a coup attempt was launched by a Muslim extremist group, the Jamaat al-Muslimeen, in July 1990. Although the group surrendered after holding the prime minister and most of the cabinet hostage for almost a week, their demand that the government address the economic burden stemming from IMF austerity measures reflected popular frustration with inequities and deteriorating living standards.

In Venezuela—one of the most advanced democracies in the Americas—the imposition of an IMF austerity program sparked massive riots in 1989. Despite the country's relative prosperity, the lower classes were largely excluded from the rapid economic growth of the 1970s. Deepening inequalities, an elite-dominated exclusionary political system, and allegations of massive corruption heightened opposition to the government of Carlos Andrés Pérez and prompted two coup attempts in 1992. These attempts dealt a serious blow to Venezuela's democratic system, as did the eventual removal and impeachment of Pérez. Ironically, the leader of the first coup attempt, Hugo Chávez, a former military officer who was imprisoned after the attempt, went on to win the presidency in 1998. His success and the subsequent dismantling of the institutional structures that had been in place since 1958 underscored the depth of the discontent with a system that was viewed as serving only the interests of the privileged (Hillman 1994). However, Chávez's attempts to promote a "social revolution" alienated the middle and upper classes, who supported protests and work-stoppages designed to leverage an early election. Consequently, Venezuela was paralyzed from December 2002 through February 2003. César Gaviria, secretary general of the Organization of American States, and former US president Jimmy Carter were unsuccessful in their attempts to mediate. However, a nonbinding referendum on Chávez's presidency held on February 2, 2003, revealed levels of support sufficient not only to allow Chávez to continue in office but also to embolden his efforts to implement radical reforms.

After defeating a referendum in December 2007 that would have allowed the president of Venezuela to be reelected continuously, the opposition was optimistic that Chávez's popularity was diminishing. However, the state and municipal elections of November 23, 2008, dashed expectations that the opposition candidates would gain significant victories. In fact, Chávez's United Socialist Party (Partido Socialista Unido de Venezuela, or PSUV) took seventeen of the nation's twenty-two governorships, 80 percent of the mayoral posts, and all but three state legislatures. *Chavistas* gained an absolute majority of the popular vote after ten years in office—an impressive outcome.

In addressing the issues of poverty, illiteracy, and health with missionary zeal, Chávez has delivered substantial improvements to marginalized Venezuelans, and he continues to count on their ardent support. Hence, it has been within democratic structures that Chávez is able to continue radical reforms that are unfortunately linked to virulent anti-American rhetoric. One program with regional significance has been Venezuela's supply of cut-rate oil to Caribbean countries—including Cuba. Of course, his programs were bolstered by high oil prices (Venezuela continues to supply around 14 percent of petroleum imported into the United States). The precipitous drop in the global price of a barrel of oil in late 2008 commenced a period of reevaluation of Venezuela's economic status. Increased inflation, joblessness, and the societal consequences of the pressures associated with these problems, along with extreme polarization between a growing minority opposition and a dwindling majority of *Chavistas,* have thrust Venezuela into difficult times. Sadly, most Venezuelans consider personal security to be the number-one issue facing their country.

To some the Chávez presidency represents a truly popular democratic example of a regime that has begun to attack endemic issues affecting the lives of the impoverished majority. To others it is a corrupt administration devolving into the typical authoritarianism that suppresses opposition as well as legitimate conflict resolution. It remains to be seen if in 2009 the Obama administration will be able to engage in constructive interaction with Chávez and Venezuela— an extremely important influence within the Caribbean region.

As the Venezuelan and the other examples clearly illustrate, the health of democratic political systems across the Caribbean increasingly has been called into question. The defeat of numerous incumbent governments, including in the Bahamas (May 2007), Barbados (January 2008), Belize (February 2008), and Grenada (July 2008), points to the seemingly insurmountable challenges confronting Caribbean leaders.[7] A particularly noteworthy case is that of Jamaica, where the PNP had been in power from 1989, when Michael Manley regained the prime ministership, past the turn of the century. When Manley resigned due to poor health in 1992, he was succeeded by P. J. Patterson of the PNP, who became the longest-serving prime minister in Jamaican history. Portia Simpson-Miller, also of the PNP, became the first female prime minister in Jamaica when she replaced Patterson in 2006. After eighteen years of PNP control, the opposition JLP narrowly defeated the incumbent government, and Bruce Golding assumed power in September 2007.

Voter participation rates traditionally have been extremely high throughout the Caribbean, particularly in the Anglophone countries. However, participation has diminished since the early 1990s (Venezuela is an anomaly), reflecting mounting alienation and frustration, especially among Caribbean youth (Munroe 1996). Potentially more devastating are declining rates of political party identification and loyalty. The demise of some of the region's most noteworthy political parties, especially in Venezuela, raises serious questions, given the critical role that parties play in the consolidation of democratic regimes (Huber 1993; Mainwaring and Scully 1995).[8]

The Caribbean, especially the Anglo-Caribbean, has been widely recognized as the most democratic and stable of all the developing areas. Given that Caribbean political systems are subjected to many of the same adversities confronting these other areas, what accounts for the region's distinctive record in promoting democracy? Most important, what do the trends outlined above mean for the democratic systems prevailing throughout the Caribbean today?

With respect to the former British colonies, many observers point to the nature and duration of colonial rule as key to the region's success. The introduction of the Westminster-type parliamentary system provided the necessary framework within which Caribbean democracies could flourish, and the liberal political culture that would sustain this system became deeply rooted in West Indian societies. The long, gradual process of decolonization in the Anglo-Caribbean differed markedly from the experiences of British colonies in Africa and Asia, providing the opportunity for institutional development, nation building, and "tutelage" in the ways of democratic governance.

Among the other pillars upon which Caribbean democracy has rested is a well-established institutional infrastructure. The emergence of strong political party systems, regular competitive elections, and vibrant civil societies (including labor unions, professional associations, and the like) has done much to bolster the cause of democracy in the Caribbean. Although the level of institutionalization in the Anglo-Caribbean has been greater than that in some other parts of the region, particularly the former Spanish colonies in Central America (excluding Costa Rica) and on Hispaniola, significant progress has been achieved in a number of countries.

To a large extent, the legitimacy of democratic institutions and governments in the Caribbean has derived from their ability to deliver material benefits to the people. Thus, perhaps the most important pillar on which Caribbean democracy has been based has been the statist bargain:

> Caribbean states invested the income derived from favorable international circumstances (high prices for commodities, new investments in tourism and other sectors, and foreign aid) to improve the standard of living for many

Caribbean citizens. The Caribbean state was the midwife; economic growth gave birth to social welfare. Because this practice continued in the 1960s even after independence in the larger countries of the Anglophone Caribbean and in the 1970s in the Dominican Republic . . . as it democratized gradually, the allegiance of citizens to democratic states was enhanced: Democracies delivered material gain. (Domínguez 1993:12)

State-sponsored patron-clientelism, then, contributed significantly to the legitimization of emerging democracies across the region. As Caribbean citizens gained access to an array of social services, including improved education and health care, they increasingly viewed political parties (as the primary dispensers of patronage) and democratic governments as worthy of their loyalty and electoral support.

More recently, however, economic decline has undermined the statist bargain. As the fiscal resources needed to sustain patron-client linkages have diminished, the foundation of Caribbean democracy has eroded.

Ironically, the Caribbean has suffered from a *lack* of US interest in recent years. With the end of the Cold War, US security and economic interests have been focused on other areas, including the former Soviet Union and Eastern Europe, China, and the Middle East. The terrorist attacks of September 11, 2001, also caused the United States to direct huge amounts of political and financial resources toward the war on terrorism. As a result, there has been a significant reduction in US aid to and investment in the Caribbean. At the same time, commodity prices for many traditional Caribbean exports have stagnated or, in some cases, declined. Although the tourist sector has remained strong, foreign exchange revenues have struggled to keep pace with spending in many countries.

The adoption of neoliberal economic policies has limited the ability of Caribbean governments to fund social welfare programs and thereby maintain the statist bargain. This has had a deleterious impact on the quality of life for millions across the region, a problematic trend given the heightened expectations held by increasingly mobilized populations. The failure to fulfill such expectations, drastically exacerbated by the global economic crisis in the first decade of the twenty-first century, has undermined the public's faith in political parties, popularly elected leaders, and democratic politics in general.

This loss of confidence has been exacerbated by popular perceptions that the institutions of democracy have failed to represent the interests of the masses, as evidenced by the tendency for the burden of structural adjustment to fall squarely on their shoulders. The traditional pattern of elite domination of parties, with mass participation effectively limited to providing electoral support, is no longer tenable. The prospects for long-term stability within the Caribbean will remain tenuous at best until democracy is deepened and the masses are integrated into the democratic process in meaningful ways.

Despite their divergent origins and structures, political systems through-out the Caribbean have much in common. All have been influenced by the legacies of colonialism—slavery, economic exploitation and dependence, ex-ternal domination, and elite-dominated exclusionary rule. The evolution of these systems has been conditioned by external forces, in many cases the United States being the most obvious. Caribbean leaders are confronted by a host of common problems, including deteriorating living standards; pervasive frustra-tion and alienation; corruption and violence stemming, in large part, from the illicit narcotics traffic; and the inherent constraints imposed upon small, re-source-scarce states in the global economy. Caribbean political systems func-tion in similar ways in seeking to address these issues. Unfortunately, they have demonstrated a common inability to find long-term solutions to the endemic problems within the region.

▣ Notes

1. "It is almost a truism that emancipation did not transform the nature of Carib-bean societies, nor the fundamental pattern of race relations, nor the way power was held and exercised, nor even the values and attitudes that had most prestige" (Brereton 1989:85).

2. "Similar institutional inheritances collapsed quickly enough in other ex-British colonies, notably in Africa" (Payne 1993:59); this underscores the point that a variety of other factors also contributed to the region's record of democratic success.

3. For the best account of this event, see Stephen Schlesinger and Stephen Kinzer, *Bitter Fruit: The Untold Story of the American Coup in Guatemala* (Garden City, NY: Doubleday, 1982).

4. According to one scholar:

There is a deep gulf which separates the political elite, composed of impor-tant members of both parties and their allies in the trade unions, business and the administration, and the mass of Jamaican citizens. Politics "at the top" has very little relevance to the needs and concerns of the ordinary Jamaican citizen, with the parties functioning to ensure votes and to promote party identification but without creating channels for the incorporation into the po-litical agenda of demands from the party bases. The parties operate from the top downwards. (Grugel 1995:118)

And here is a comment on the role of political parties throughout the Common-wealth Caribbean: They "have generally been conceived . . . as tools for mobilizing the vote and winning elections. They have not been built up as mass organizations in the sense of constituting vehicles by which ordinary members can enter the policymaking process" (Payne 1993:71).

5. According to one scholar:

Between the Black Power revolt in Trinidad in 1970 and the implosion of the Grenada revolution in 1983, significant social sectors in the region turned to-ward radical Left alternatives within and outside the framework of liberal democracy and market-driven economies. The successive administrations headed by Michael Manley in Jamaica (1972–80), the People's Revolutionary government in Grenada (1979–83), and the Forbes Burnham government in Guyana represented the highest development (and also the deformation) of these tendencies in the Commonwealth Caribbean. This turn to the Left was influenced by the reality as well as the perception that the democratic governance and state interventionist market economies of the 1960s in the region had deepened, rather than reduced, economic and social inequalities. (Munroe 1996:104)

6. According to the broad definition of *circum-Caribbean* employed in this book, Nicaragua should be recognized as having experienced a regime change. In 1979 the FSLN ousted the dictator Anastasio Somoza Debayle, marking a shift from a conservative authoritarian regime to a leftist-socialist one-party state.

7. There have been some notable exceptions to this trend, however. In Trinidad and Tobago, the People's National Movement (PNM) and its leader, Patrick Manning, took power in late 2001 and subsequently won elections in 2002 and 2007 to retain power. In St. Vincent and the Grenadines, Prime Minister Ralph Gonsalves and the United Labour Party won election in 2001 and again in 2005. Venezuelan president Hugo Chávez was first elected in 1998 and was reelected decisively in 2000 and 2006. Leonel Fernández served as president of the Dominican Republic from 1996 to 2000 but was constitutionally prohibited from running for reelection. This provision was later rescinded, however, allowing Fernández's successor, Hipólito Mejía, to seek reelection in 2004. Fernández soundly defeated Mejía in 2004 and was reelected in 2008.

8. In his introduction to *Democracy in the Caribbean: Political, Economic, and Social Perspectives,* Jorge Domínguez (1993) writes: "Can democratic regimes survive if the partisan institutions that have been at the heart of politics can no longer provide organized political support and opposition?"

▓ Bibliography

Barrow-Giles, Cynthia, and Tennyson S.D. Joseph. *General Elections and Voting in the English-Speaking Caribbean, 1992–2005.* Kingston, Jamaica: Ian Randle, 2006.

Brereton, Bridget. "Society and Culture in the Caribbean: The British and French West Indies, 1870–1980." In *The Modern Caribbean,* edited by Franklin Knight and Colin Palmer, pp. 85–110. Chapel Hill: University of North Carolina Press, 1989.

CIA (Central Intelligence Agency). *World Factbook.* http://www.cia.gov/library/publications/the-world-factbook/ (accessed January 2009).

Crandall, Russell. *Gunboat Democracy: US Interventions in the Dominican Republic, Grenada, and Panama.* Lanham, MD: Rowman and Littlefield, 2006.

Domínguez, Jorge I. "The Caribbean Question: Why Has Liberal Democracy (Surprisingly) Flourished?" In *Democracy in the Caribbean: Political, Economic, and Social Perspectives,* edited by Jorge I. Domínguez, Robert A. Pastor, and R. DeLisle Worrell, pp. 1–25. Baltimore: Johns Hopkins University Press, 1993.

Domínguez, Jorge I., and Abraham Lowenthal. *Constructing Democratic Governance: Latin America and the Caribbean in the 1990s—Themes and Issues.* Baltimore: Johns Hopkins University Press, 1996.

Domínguez, Jorge I., Robert A. Pastor, and R. DeLisle Worrell, eds. *Democracy in the Caribbean: Political, Economic, and Social Perspectives.* Baltimore: Johns Hopkins University Press, 1993.

Edie, Carlene. *Democracy by Default: Dependency and Clientelism in Jamaica.* Boulder, CO: Lynne Rienner, 1991.

———. *Democracy in the Caribbean: Myths and Realities.* Westport, CT: Praeger, 1994.

Ellner, Steve. *Rethinking Venezuelan Politics: Class, Conflict, and the Chávez Phenomenon.* Boulder, CO: Lynne Rienner, 2008.

Fatton, Robert, Jr. *The Roots of Haitian Despotism.* Boulder, CO: Lynne Rienner, 2007.

Gamaliel Ramos, Aarón, and Angel Israel Rivera. *Islands at the Crossroads: Politics in the Non-Independent Caribbean.* Boulder, CO: Lynne Rienner, 2001.

Gautier-Mayoral, Carmen. "Puerto Rico: Problems of Democracy and Decolonization in the Late Twentieth Century." In *Democracy in the Caribbean: Myths and Realities,* edited by Carlene Edie, pp. 163–179. Westport, CT: Praeger, 1994.

Griffin, Clifford E. "Democracy in the Commonwealth Caribbean." *Journal of Democracy* 4, no. 2 (April 1993); 84–94.

Grugel, Jean. *Politics and Development in the Caribbean Basin.* Bloomington: Indiana University Press, 1995.

Hartlyn, Jonathan. *The Struggle for Democratic Politics in the Dominican Republic.* Chapel Hill: University of North Carolina Press, 1998.

Henke, Holger, and Fred Reno, eds. *Modern Political Culture in the Caribbean.* Kingston, Jamaica: University of West Indies Press, 2003.

Hillman, Richard S. *Democracy for the Privileged: Crisis and Transition in Venezuela.* Boulder, CO: Lynne Rienner, 1994.

Hillman, Richard, and Thomas J. D'Agostino. *Distant Neighbors in the Caribbean: The Dominican Republic and Jamaica in Comparative Perspective.* New York: Praeger, 1992.

Huber, Evelyne. "The Future of Democracy in the Caribbean." In *Democracy in the Caribbean: Political, Economic, and Social Perspectives,* edited by Jorge I. Domínguez, Robert A. Pastor, and R. DeLisle Worrell, pp. 74–95. Baltimore: Johns Hopkins University Press, 1993.

Knight, Franklin. *The Caribbean: The Genesis of a Fragmented Nationalism.* 2nd ed. New York: Oxford University Press, 1990.

———. "The Societies of the Caribbean Since Independence." In *Democracy in the Caribbean: Political, Economic, and Social Perspectives,* edited by Jorge I. Domínguez, Robert A. Pastor, and R. DeLisle Worrell, pp. 29–41. Baltimore: Johns Hopkins University Press, 1993.

Knight, Franklin, and Colin Palmer. *The Modern Caribbean.* Chapel Hill: University of North Carolina Press, 1989.

Lewis, Gordon. "The Contemporary Caribbean: A General Overview." In *Caribbean Contours,* edited by Sidney W. Mintz and Sally Price, pp. 219–250. Baltimore: Johns Hopkins University Press, 1985.

Maingot, Anthony. *The United States and the Caribbean.* Boulder, CO: Westview, 1994.

Mainwaring, Scott, and Timothy R. Scully. *Building Democratic Institutions: Party Systems in Latin America.* Stanford: Stanford University Press, 1995.

Mintz, Sidney W., and Sally Price. *Caribbean Contours.* Baltimore: Johns Hopkins University Press, 1985.

Molineau, Harold. *US Policy Toward Latin America.* Boulder, CO: Westview, 1990.

Munroe, Trevor. "Caribbean Democracy: Decay or Renewal?" In *Constructing Democratic Governance: Latin America and the Caribbean in the 1990s—Themes and Issues,* edited by Jorge I. Domínguez and Abraham Lowenthal, pp. 104–117. Baltimore: Johns Hopkins University Press, 1996.

Oostindie, Gert, and Inge Klinkers. *Decolonising the Caribbean: Dutch Policies in a Comparative Perspective.* Amsterdam: Amsterdam University Press, 2004.

Payne, Anthony. "Westminster Adapted: The Political Order of the Commonwealth Caribbean." In *Democracy in the Caribbean: Political, Economic, and Social Perspectives,* edited by Jorge I. Domínguez, Robert A. Pastor, and R. DeLisle Worrell, pp. 57–73. Baltimore: Johns Hopkins University Press, 1993.

Payne, Anthony, and Paul Sutton. *Modern Caribbean Politics.* Baltimore: Johns Hopkins University Press, 1993.

Peeler, John. *Building Democracy in Latin America.* Boulder, CO: Lynne Rienner, 1998.

Richardson, Bonham C. *The Caribbean in the Wider World, 1492–1992: A Regional Geography.* Cambridge, UK: Cambridge University Press, 1992.

Ryan, Selwyn. "Problems and Prospects for the Survival of Liberal Democracy in the Anglophone Caribbean." In *Democracy in the Caribbean: Myths and Realities,* edited by Carlene Edie, pp. 233–250. Westport, CT: Praeger, 1994.

Silvestrini, Blanca G. "Contemporary Puerto Rico: A Society of Contrasts." In *The Modern Caribbean,* edited by Franklin Knight and Colin Palmer, pp. 147–167. Chapel Hill: University of North Carolina Press, 1989.

Smith, Courtney. "The Grenadian Revolution in Retrospect." In *Modern Caribbean Politics,* edited by Anthony Payne and Paul Sutton, pp. 176–197. Baltimore: Johns Hopkins University Press, 1993.

Stone, Carl. "A Political Profile of the Caribbean." In *Caribbean Contours,* edited by Sidney W. Mintz and Sally Price, pp. 13–54. Baltimore: Johns Hopkins University Press, 1985.

Stotzky, Irwin. *Silencing the Guns in Haiti: The Promise of Deliberative Democracy.* Chicago: University of Chicago Press, 1997.

Thorndike, Tony. "Revolution, Democracy, and Regional Integration in the Eastern Caribbean." In *Modern Caribbean Politics,* edited by Anthony Payne and Paul Sutton, pp. 176–197. Baltimore: Johns Hopkins University Press, 1993.

Von Mettenheim, Kurt, and James Malloy. *Deepening Democracy in Latin America.* Pittsburgh: University of Pittsburgh Press, 1998.

Wiarda, Howard. "The Dominican Republic: Mirror Legacies of Democracy and Authoritarianism." In *Democracy in Developing Countries,* vol. 4, edited by Larry Diamond, Juan J. Linz, and Seymour Martin Lipset, pp. 423–458. Boulder, CO: Lynne Rienner, 1989.

Wiarda, Howard, and Michael J. Kryzanek. *The Dominican Republic: A Caribbean Crucible.* Rev. ed. Boulder, CO: Westview, 1992.

Will, W. Marvin. "A Nation Divided: The Quest for Caribbean Integration." *Latin American Research Review* 26, no. 2 (1991): 3–37.

Williams, Eric. *From Columbus to Castro: The History of the Caribbean.* London: Andre Deutsch, 1970.

5

The Economies of the Caribbean

Dennis A. Pantin and Marlene Attzs

Contemporary Caribbean economies evolved as a consequence of the post-Columbian history of colonization by European powers whose primary purpose was to grow sugarcane for export. As Stephen Randall shows in Chapter 3, the impact of this history on each of the region's countries has been profound and lasting. Therefore, understanding the historical evolution of Caribbean economies is essential for an informed analysis of current and projected economic problems challenging the countries and the region.

The idea of a singular Caribbean is a recent development.[1] In keeping with the theme set forth by Richard S. Hillman in Chapter 1, we focus in this chapter on the insular Caribbean and refer to the island economies within the Caribbean Sea together with the bordering mainland states of Belize, Guyana, French Guiana, and Suriname; some mention also will be made of other countries on the northern coast of South America and eastern coast of Central America.

The insular Caribbean is comprised of twenty-eight distinct political entities: Most are islands and twelve are dependent territories. In a region with a total estimated population of 41 million, there are many areas of commonality among the individual political entities. In this chapter, therefore, we begin with a historical overview of the Caribbean and then turn to a review of current economic structures, their economic performance, and future economic challenges.

■ Common Economic History

The region shares a prehistory, that is, the period prior to the European colonization initiated by Christopher Columbus' voyage in 1492. Today, little remains—

other than historical artifacts and a few isolated communities throughout the Caribbean—of the indigenous peoples who inhabited the region. It is in this sense that the term *prehistory* is used relative to the indigenous peoples, who still make up a significant share of the population in some South American countries. All Caribbean economies are also linked by a common economic history and, in particular, two specific economic characteristics.

The first common point of economic history is that of plantation slavery together with the indentureship that followed the end of the slave trade and the subsequent abolition of slavery itself. This occurred by 1838 in the English-speaking Caribbean, following which indentured laborers were introduced from India and elsewhere, particularly in Trinidad, Guyana, and Surinamc. The result has been the creation of multiracial and plural religious societies, the legacies of which are evident today in the social, political, and economic systems in these countries.

There is a particular school of Caribbean economics—the plantation economy school—that has sought to explain the functioning of the Caribbean economy on the basis of this historical origin.[2] The plantation economy literature was influenced by the notion of "plantation America," which encompassed the southern US states, northeastern Brazil, and other pockets of slavery throughout North, South, and Central America, in addition to the Caribbean (Wagley 1960).[3] What is specific and special about the Caribbean, according to the plantation economy school, is that plantation economic systems have continued to persist. But some of the other countries in plantation America, by contrast,

UN photo 154282, Nicole Toutounji

An outdoor market in Port-au-Prince, Haiti.

have become integrated into more complex economic systems, including settler agriculture, manufacturing, and scientific and technological development. The United States is the best example of this.

The plantation economy school hypothesizes that the original (slave) plantation economies of the Caribbean have been bequeathed a legacy of non-dynamic responses to changes in the external world economic environment (see Best and Levitt 1968:32). The plantation economy theorists suggest that this legacy not only persists in the traditional agricultural sectors that still exist (especially sugarcane production) but is also evident in other sectors, notably minerals, manufacturing, and services.

A second common legacy among Caribbean economies is dependence on natural resources for the generation of export earnings. These small, open, export-led economies began as totally dependent on the generation of sugarcane exports for their internal production, employment, income, and consumption. Therefore, soil fertility determined fortunes as cane producers shifted to newer territories and hence virgin soils. Following the emancipation of slaves and the collapse of the sugar industry in the nineteenth century, diversification was marked by a shift to other agricultural exports such as cocoa, coffee, citrus, and, later, bananas.[4] In the twentieth century, there was also the growth of mineral export dependence, whether bauxite (Jamaica, Guyana, Suriname), oil or, more recently, natural gas (Trinidad and Tobago) and tourism (all Caribbean economies). We provide more detail on the significance of the tourism industry to Caribbean economies later in this chapter. Regional economies therefore remain largely dependent on natural resources for their economic survival.

■ Some Differences

There are several points of difference among Caribbean economies. First, the dominant languagååe in the insular Caribbean, in terms of the sheer number of speakers, is Spanish. The primary language in Cuba, the Dominican Republic, and Puerto Rico, Spanish is spoken by 60 percent of the region's population. The second most common language is French, particularly the Creole variant, as spoken in Haiti, Martinique, and Guadeloupe (combined, roughly 22 percent of the regional population), but also alongside English in St. Lucia and Dominica. English is the third language (17 percent) and Dutch the fourth (1 percent).

These language differences, of course, result from the most dominant or long-lasting metropolitan colonization.[5] Most language groups have tended to retain a closer linkage—in both economics and communications—with the country of original metropolitan colonization than with each other, although the United States became a more significant and, in some senses, unifying metropolitan country of influence throughout the twentieth century. Language differences have contributed to both limited economic relations within the Caribbean and limited cooperation among these economies in interacting with the rest of the world. Intraregional trading and investment opportunities are therefore sometimes constrained by these language barriers.

A second point of difference can be found in the nature of their political systems. All Caribbean countries have effectively embraced the legal, juridical, and political systems of the original colonial power, although as Thomas J. D'Agostino notes in Chapter 4, some local adaptation has been added. Cuba is, of course, a significant exception to this generality. Such differences can also serve as an impediment to trade and investment within the Caribbean, given the lack of familiarity about other subsystems, a tendency exacerbated by language differences.

The third significant difference derives from Caribbean states' political status. Most are, at least formally, politically independent, but a minority still retain a formal political linkage with a metropolitan power. Puerto Rico, Martinique and Guadeloupe, Montserrat, and the Netherlands Antilles are in this category.[6] On the one hand, those that have acquired their political independence enjoy a degree of self-determination unknown among those that have maintained metropolitan ties. On the other hand, Caribbean economies in which formal quasi-colonial relations have been retained benefit in several ways, including free movement of labor and access to metropolitan institutions for education, health care, and sometimes other social services.

A fourth distinction among Caribbean economies involves the ideological underpinnings of the various economic system types found throughout the region. One may contrast, for example, Cuba's socialist economic system with variants of the market economy that prevail throughout the remainder of the region.

A fifth point of difference flows from size as defined in population and area terms. In terms of population, Caribbean economies range from Cuba with some 11.4 million people and the Dominican Republic with 9.5 million to, at the other extreme, Montserrat with fewer than 6,000.

The most populous and largest Caribbean economies (in terms of area) exist in the northern Caribbean—Cuba, Hispaniola (the Dominican Republic and Haiti), Puerto Rico, and Jamaica—and the southern Caribbean, particularly Guyana (roughly 83,000 square miles, with a population of 766,000) and Trinidad and Tobago. The size of Caribbean economies (in population and area size) decreases as one moves south of Hispaniola or north of Guyana and Trinidad and Tobago. As will be discussed below, there appears to be no particular advantage of size in terms of economic performance in the Caribbean. In fact, at times the larger economies have experienced greater difficulties.

The sixth area of difference has to do with linkages among Caribbean economies. As Jacqueline Braveboy-Wagner details in Chapter 6, the English-speaking countries of the Caribbean share a relatively higher degree of intercountry linkages. In 1967, the English-speaking Caribbean economies formed the Caribbean Free Trade Association (CARIFTA), which was transformed in

1973 into the Caribbean Common Market and Community (CARICOM). Within this grouping, there are even closer linkages between the subgroup of the Organization of Eastern Caribbean States that share a common currency and central bank (the Eastern Caribbean Central Bank, or ECCB).

More recently, there have been several efforts to broaden the base of intraregional cooperation. These initiatives include the Caribbean Forum (known as CARIFORUM), which links CARICOM with Haiti (now a member of CARICOM) and the Dominican Republic. Another development has been the formation of the Association of Caribbean States (ACS), linking Caribbean and Central American countries with Mexico, Colombia, and Venezuela. The ACS has identified trade, transportation, sustainable tourism, and natural disasters as its four areas of policy focus.

A seventh and final area of difference among Caribbean economies is the extent of diversification away from the original dependence on sugarcane or a substitute traditional agricultural export. In the twentieth century, there was an increasing divergence away from traditional agricultural exports. The main form of diversification was seen in the growth of tourism.[7] However, there also was a shift to mineral exports (bauxite in the case of Jamaica, Guyana, and Suriname and petroleum in the case of Trinidad and Tobago) and, more recently, a smaller shift to information processing (Barbados, the Dominican Republic, and Jamaica), offshore financial services (Antigua and Barbuda, the Bahamas, Barbados, the Cayman Islands, the Netherlands Antilles, St. Vincent and the Grenadines), and some specialty agroindustrial and medical/pharmaceutical exports (particularly Cuba).

■ An Overview of the Economic Structure of Caribbean Economies

Caribbean economies continue to be dominated by their export sectors, which in turn tend to be concentrated on one to three products based on the region's natural resource endowment. Caribbean economies vary in the significance of non-export-producing sectors. Domestic food production is the most common area of nonexport production. However, in some islands (particularly the more arid or limestone islands such as Aruba, Curaçao, and Barbados), there is little domestic agricultural production. Manufacturing also exists in some Caribbean economies, although there tends to be a dependence on imported products. There are also four other sectors of significant growth, although all began from a low initial base, in some Caribbean economies.

1. Offshore financial services: This sector is of particular importance in Antigua and Barbuda, the Bahamas, Barbados, the Cayman Islands, the Netherlands Antilles, and St. Vincent and the Grenadines.

2. Export-processing zones:[8] These have become important in the Dominican Republic and, to some extent, Jamaica.

3. Information processing: In 1993, the level of employment in this sector in the region was estimated at some 5,000 persons. By the mid-1990s, there were some seventy-four export-oriented information processing firms in the Caribbean, employing 7,500 persons, an increase of 50 percent within two to three years (Pantin 1999).

4. Exported labor, as indicated by remittances by the Caribbean population living abroad: The significant economic role of this Caribbean diaspora, examined in greater detail by Dennis Conway in Chapter 12, is reflected in the impact of remittances on home country economies. The percentage of native-born Jamaicans living abroad in the late 1980s relative to the resident population on the island was 40 percent, similar to Guyana. Of the English-speaking Caribbean countries, Jamaica has been the largest recipient of transfers, with remittances to that country increasing from US$184 million in 1990 to US$1.466 billion in 2004, an increase of 697 percent over the fifteen-year period, or 46 percent per year. The main sources of remittances to Jamaica are the United States (60 percent), the UK (25 percent), Canada, and the Cayman Islands (5 percent each). As Figure 5.1 shows, between 1996 and 2001 remittances accounted for an estimated 11–13 percent of GDP in Jamaica. Remittances also comprised a significant percentage of gross domestic product (GDP) in Guyana, Belize, Barbados, and to a lesser extent in the Bahamas and Trinidad and Tobago.

◼ Tourism as a Major Economic Activity

As noted earlier, in addition to the sectors identified above, it is widely acknowledged that perhaps the most dynamic economic activity in many of the Caribbean countries is tourism. The tourism sector, which covers activities such as sports and culture, cruise ship tourism and yachting, and all-inclusive stopover visits, is the most economically significant sector for many of the Caribbean islands. The Economic Commission for Latin America and the Caribbean (ECLAC) in 2006 noted, for example, that for most of the Caribbean economies, tourism had a catalytic effect on manufacturing, transportation, communications, and especially on the construction sector. That report suggests that not only do direct benefits accrue to economies from tourism activity—reflected in the share of government revenue earned from the sector—but so do many indirect benefits, including employment. To more accurately gauge the multiplier impact of tourism on Caribbean economies, some of the islands have begun to develop Tourism Satellite Accounts (TSA).

Tables 5.1, 5.2, and 5.3 provide selected indicators of the economic significance of the tourism sector. From 1995 to 2004, visitor arrivals to the region

Figure 5.1 Remittances as a Percentage of GDP in Selected CARICOM Countries, 1996–2001

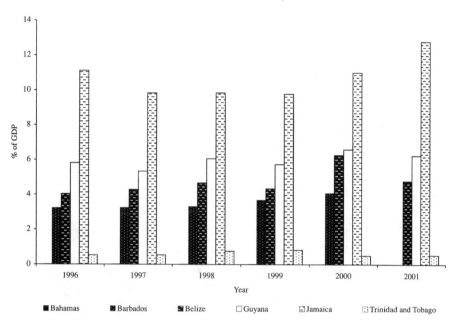

Source: Adapted from Claremont Kirton, "Remittances: The Experiences of the English-Speaking Caribbean," in *Beyond Small Change: Making Migrant Remittances Count*, edited by Donald F. Terry and Steven R. Wilson (Washington, DC: Inter-American Development Bank, 2005).

increased from 16 million to 21.8 million—a 36 percent increase over the period. Employment in the sector, particularly in accommodation establishments (hotels, guesthouses, and the like) experienced a drastic increase over the period—from an estimated 122,000 in 1995 to 900,000 in 2000. Table 5.3 illustrates another important dimension of the contribution of tourism to Caribbean economies. The table shows that in some of the countries visitor expenditures accounted for a significant share of national GDP. For some of the smaller island states in the Caribbean, such as Anguilla, Antigua and Barbuda, Grenada, St. Lucia, and the Virgin Islands (British and US), the contribution of visitor expenditures to GDP has consistently been around 50 percent, ranging even higher in some cases. For some of the larger island states, including Puerto Rico and Trinidad and Tobago, visitor expenditures account for less than 5 percent of GDP. In the case of Trinidad and Tobago, the fairly insignificant contribution of tourism is in part due to that country's reliance on the oil and gas sectors. Jamaica and the Bahamas stand out as exceptions since though they are large island states, their dependence on tourism is not insignificant.

Table 5.1 Selected Indicators of Tourism in the Caribbean

Indicator	1995	2000	2004	% Change 1995–2000	% Change 2000–2004	% Change 1995–2004
Estimates of visitor expenditure (US$ millions)	14,022	19,847	21,636	41.54	9.01	54.3
International visitor arrivals (millions)	16	20	21.8	25	9	36.25
Employment in accommodation establishments	122,237	900,000	NA	636	NA	NA

Source: Caribbean Tourism Organization, *Caribbean Tourism Statistical Report, 2003–2004* (St. Michael, Barbados: Caribbean Tourism Organization, 2005).

Los Patos beach, Barahona, Dominican Republic.

Visitor Expenditure and Employment

Figure 5.2 illustrates foreign exchange that enters the region through the tourism industry. In 1989, visitor expenditure amounted to $US6.82 billion. By 1995, visitor expenditure increased to US$14.02 billion. The expenditure generated by visitors to the region increased during the five-year period 1995–2000 by an average of 7.3 percent (Caribbean Tourism Organization 2000–2001).

Table 5.2 Hotel Room Capacity and Related Employment

Destination	Number of Rooms			Persons Employed	Employee/ Room Ratio
	1995	2000	2003	2003	2003
Anguilla	951	1,067	1.48	1.48	1.48
Antigua and Barbuda	3,317	3,185	1.15	1.15	1.15
Aruba	6,881	7,500	1.15	1.15	1.15
Bahamas	13,421	14,701	1.09	1.09	1.09
Barbados	5,084	6,456	0.99	0.99	0.99
Belize	3,708	4,106	0.68	0.68	0.68
Bermuda	4,141	3,339	0.99	0.99	0.99
Bonaire	1,125	1,050			
British Virgin Islands	1,459	1,666	1.33	1.33	1.33
Cancun	19,411	25,434			
Cayman Islands	3,585	5,364			
Cozumel	3,367	4,101			
Cuba	27,928	38,072			
Curaçao	1,950	2,941			
Dominica	588	890	1.22	1.22	1.22
Dominican Republic	32,746	51,916	0.83	0.83	0.83
Grenada	1,652	1,822	1.07	1.07	1.07
Guadeloupe	7,917	8,136			
Guyana	639	730			
Haiti	1,758	1,758			
Jamaica	20,896	23,630	1.24	1.24	1.24
Martinique	7,210	8,733			
Montserrat	710	264			
Puerto Rico	10,312	12,353	1.13	1.13	1.13
Saba	186	80			
St. Eustatius	139	62	0.30	0.30	0.30
St. Kitts and Nevis	1,563	1,754	1.00	1.00	1.00
St. Lucia	3,974	4,525	1.38	1.38	1.38
St. Maarten	3,707	3,545			
St. Vincent and Grenadines	1,176	1,747			
Suriname	1,024	1,276			
Trinidad and Tobago	3,107	4,532	1.05	1.05	1.05
Turks and Caicos	1,068	2,023			
US Virgin Islands	5,154	5,008	0.77	0.77	0.77

Source: Caribbean Tourism Organization, *Caribbean Tourism Statistical Report, 2003–2004* (St. Michael, Barbados: Caribbean Tourism Organization, 2005).

Table 5.3 Estimates of Visitor Expenditure as a Percentage of GDP, 1997–2004

Destination	1997	1998	1999	2000	2001	2002	2003	2004
Anguilla	84	79.6	66.8	65.1	69.5	63.5	64.2	63.7
Antigua and Barbuda	59.5	57.1	56.9	50.4	45.3	44.8	46.8	49.5
Aruba	41.9	37.3	38.4	39.7	38.9	34.2	32.2	38.1
Bahamas	35.9	32.3	34.6	35.6	33.3	34.9	33.4	
Barbados	36.4	36	32.7	33.7	32.5	31.9	34.5	33.1
Belize	16.9	18.4	17.4	16.5	16.1	16.7	18.2	22.4
Bermuda	16.3	15.6	15.3	12	9.6	9.6	8.1	
British Virgin Islands	65.5	47.7	46.3	50.1	48.9	41	41.4	44.7
Cayman Islands	41.3	33.5	30.4	31	31.6	31.4	25.9	
Cuba	9.1	10.7	6.9	7.4	6.8	6.4	7	
Curaçao			12.9	10.7	11.5	12.4	12.6	
Dominica	23.5	21.5	22.5	20.9	20.8	21.6	25.9	37.2
Dominican Republic	13.9	13.5	14.5	14.5	12.9	12.6	18.6	
Grenada	56.3	53.5	54.5	53.1	50	52.6	50.2	
Guyana	9.8	10.1	10.5	14.8	14.7			
Haiti	21.4		7.7	11.2	11.2			
Jamaica	16.7	16.7	17.9	18.2	16.3	15.5	18.2	
Montserrat	15.5	17.1	27.2	30.5	27.8	26.6	21.6	28.1
Puerto Rico	4.3	4.1	3.6	3.9	3.9	3.5	3.6	
St. Kitts and Nevis	29.1	31.5	26.3	20.6	21.1	19.2	24.8	
St. Lucia	57.7	52.1	49.8	51.5	41.6	37.1	47.7	
St. Vincent and Grenadines	28.6	27.3	27.6	29.2	30.9	30.5	29.4	
Suriname	9.4	5.7	9.7	7.6				
Trinidad and Tobago	3.3	3.2	3.1	2.6	2.3	2.6	2.3	
US Virgin Islands	49.6	48.9	49.3	51.6	49.8	50	49.8	

Source: Compiled by the authors from Sean Smith (statistical specialist) and Adrian McAllister (research assistant) of the Caribbean Tourism Organization, 2005.

The dip in expenditure in 2001 mirrors the decrease in the number of visitors in the same year. Expenditure peaked in 2004 at US$20.9 billion with a significant decrease the following year to US$15.0 billion (Caribbean Tourism Organization, Caribbean Tourism Performance Reviews, various years).

Pantin et al. (2002) reported that for some small islands, including St. Lucia and Barbados, tourism accounts for 30–50 percent of total employment and generates upward of 50 percent of GDP. In its annual statistical report published in 2000, the Caribbean Tourism Organization noted that the tourism sector in the region employed approximately 900,000 persons, directly and indirectly.

Figure 5.2 Visitor Expenditure in Caribbean Destinations, 1997–2005

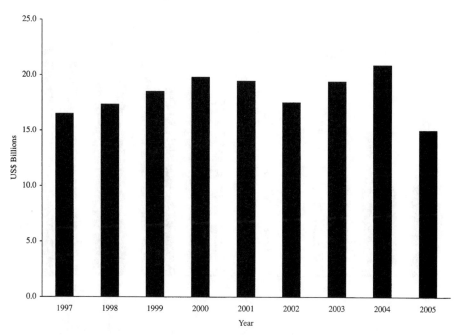

Source: Compiled by authors from Caribbean Tourism Organization, http://onecaribbean.org/.

Tourist Arrivals

The constant increases in tourist arrivals over the decade 1990–2000 are an indication of the region's ability to attract visitors, as shown in Figure 5.3. In 1991, 12.8 million people visited the Caribbean. By the end of 2000, this number had increased to 20.3 million—a 63 percent increase. The years 2001 and 2002 saw small decreases in arrivals to 20 and 19 million, respectively, perhaps due in part to global events that put a damper on the buoyancy of the Caribbean tourism industry. However, there was a recovery in 2003 with the number of tourist arrivals rising to 20.4 million, and by 2005 the number of visitors had reached 22.2 million. This upward trend suggests that while CARICOM tourist destinations have faced increased competition from other destinations in the region—including Mexico's Caribbean coast, Belize, Honduras, and Cuba—CARICOM destinations have succeeded in retaining their market share and, in some specific cases, have increased their share of tourist arrivals.

Government Revenue

Overall government revenue from tourism for the year 2002 for some islands is shown in Figure 5.4. The intake for Jamaica and for Trinidad and Tobago far

Figure 5.3 Tourist Arrivals to Caribbean Destinations, 1989–2005

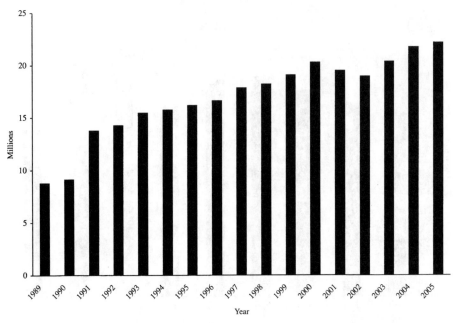

Source: Compiled by authors from Caribbean Tourism Organization, http://onecaribbean.org/.

Figure 5.4 Government Revenue from Tourism, 2002

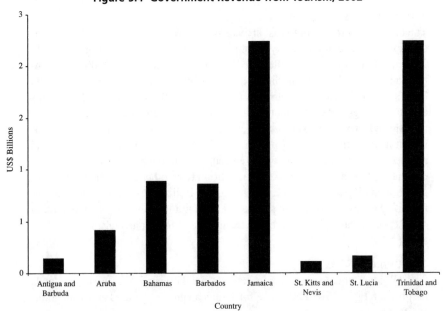

Source: Compiled by authors from Caribbean Tourism Organization, http://onecaribbean.org/.

exceeded the rest. The former had revenue of US$2.244 billion, whereas Trinidad and Tobago's revenue from tourism totalled US$2.224 billion. Hotel occupancy taxes are a source of revenue for Caribbean economies. Chandana Jayawardena (2005) acknowledges the scarcity of data that measures revenue of this type but provides data for the US Virgin Islands, Aruba, Antigua and Barbuda, St. Lucia, and the British Virgin Islands, each of which may be considered mature Caribbean destinations. Revenue from hotel occupancy taxes in these locations totalled US$11.2 million, US$10.1 million, US$8.3 million, US$6.6 million, and US$4.4 million, respectively.

Cruise Ship Arrivals

According to the Florida–Caribbean Cruise Association (F-CCA), the global cruise industry's growth has been spearheaded by the Caribbean region. The cruise industry has grown at an average of 8.5 percent per year since 1980. The Caribbean region had a market share of 46.4 percent of all global itineraries in 2006, making it the industry's number-one destination in the world (F-CCA, "Cruise Industry Overview—2006").

Figure 5.5 depicts the increasing significance of cruise tourism to the region. In 1990, cruise arrivals accounted for 60.5 percent of total tourist arrivals to the region. This tourism subsector, unlike land tourism, did not show signs of decline in 2001. By 2001, cruise arrivals had increased to 71.6 percent, and by 2003, 85.2 percent of the tourists visiting the Caribbean arrived by cruise ship.

The F-CCA suggested that the direct economic benefits from the cruise industry to host destinations come from three sources (F-CCA, "Economic Impact of Cruise Tourism on the Caribbean Economy," October 2006). First, passengers spend money onshore mainly on jewellery and clothing. Second, the crew spends on food and beverages, transportation, clothing, and electronic equipment. Finally, the cruise lines spend on food and beverages, services at the ports, and port fees and taxes.

In 2005–2006, the F-CCA conducted a survey of nineteen cruise destinations, revealing that passengers on average spent approximately US$100 onshore. In that time period, cruise lines spent US$236.8 million for port fees and taxes and navigation services. The amounts spent on port fees and local supplies vary by destination, as a result of differences in the number of calls to ports and the needs of ships. Total expenditure by passengers, crew, and cruise lines amounted to US$1.8 billion. Approximately 25,000 jobs were created across these nineteen destinations with annual wages of US$344 million.

The Caribbean is a desirable place to visit in large part due to the region's extraordinary natural endowments—sun, sea, and sand. However, along with the benefits that accrue to the region from the tourism sector, there are several challenges facing the regional tourism industry. One major challenge, as discussed by Thomas Boswell in Chapter 2 and Duncan McGregor in Chapter 7, is the frequency and intensity of windstorm-related events, particularly hurricanes that affect the region and are predicted to be exacerbated by climate

Kathy Gillman

A cruise ship on its way to the Bahamas.

change. The impact of hurricanes and the potential impact of climate change on Caribbean economies are explored in further detail later in this chapter. Another challenge is to keep tourism within the eco-cultural carrying capacity of the region (see Pantin et al. 2001).

■ Current Economic Performance

In terms of economic performance, the Caribbean can be grouped into four categories: independent larger island states (Cuba, the Dominican Republic, Haiti, and Jamaica), smaller island states (Antigua and Barbuda, the Bahamas, Barbados, Dominica, Grenada, St. Lucia, St. Kitts and Nevis, St. Vincent, and Trinidad and Tobago), mainland states (Belize, Guyana, Suriname), and the twelve dependent territories (Girvan 2001). Table 5.4 provides a summary comparison of these groupings in terms of size (population and territory) and GDP; further details on the individual countries within each group are shown in Table 5.5.

Table 5.5 also illuminates the performance of Caribbean countries based on the Human Development Reports published by the United Nations Development Programme (UNDP). The UNDP produced its first worldwide Human Development Report in 1990, introducing a new Human Development Index (HDI) based on combined indicators of life expectancy, educational attainment, and income. The HDI captures more qualitative indicators of development

**Figure 5.5 Cruise Passengers vs. Total Tourist Arrivals
to Caribbean Destinations, 1989–2005**

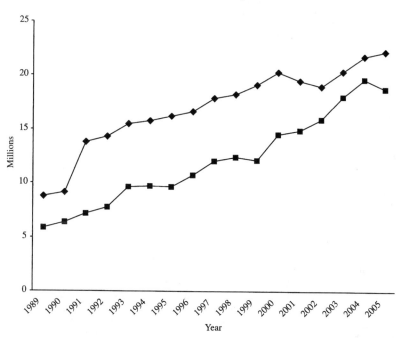

Source: Compiled by authors from Caribbean Tourism Organization, http://onecaribbean.org/.

than the GDP and therefore allows for a better, albeit general, comparison of development trends across countries. The most significant declines in HDI in the Caribbean during the period 2000 to 2008 were recorded in Jamaica, Belize, and Suriname, with changes of –15, –22 and –11, respectively. Some of the smaller island states of the Organization of Eastern Caribbean States (OECS) subregion also recorded negative trends in the HDI over the period, including Dominica (–10), St. Kitts and Nevis (–10), and St. Lucia (–6).

A number of factors explain varying economic performances among Caribbean countries. The first, of course, is size of economy. The smaller the economy, the easier it is for any positive microtrends to express themselves in macroeconomic significance. The data in Table 5.5 also illuminate the challenges posed to these island states by poverty. Perhaps one of the main indicators of development is the level of poverty, which is especially stark in Caribbean countries when one considers the relatively small populations of the islands (Cuba, Haiti, and the Dominican Republic excluded).

A second and related factor is the role of tourism. The Caribbean economies with more positive macroeconomic trends, namely GDP, are largely those with growing, or already dominant, tourism sectors.

Table 5.4 Gross Domestic Product, Population, and Land Area in the Caribbean

	Per Capita GDP at Constant Prices (100=2000)	GDP at Constant Prices (100=2000) (millions of $)	Per Capita GDP at Constant Prices (100=2000)	GDP at Constant Prices (100=2000) (millions of $)	Per Capita GDP at Constant Prices (100=2000)	GDP at Constant Prices (100=2000) (millions of $)
	1995		2000		2003	
Larger island states						
Cuba	2,062	22,538	2,535	28,206	2,708	30,358
Dominican Republic	2,114	16,944	2,707	23,655	2,769	25,413
Haiti	413	3,236	427	3,665	403	3,630
Jamaica	2,979	7,403	2,848	7,374	2,924	7,721
Smaller island states						
Trinidad and Tobago	4,461	5,666	6,270	8,154	7,981	10,492
Barbados	5,233	1,465	6,025	1,726	5,830	1,690
Bahamas	14,409	4,040	16,506	5,004	16,594	5,233
OECS						
Antigua and Barbuda	7,926	539	8,665	665	9,078	734
Dominica	3,584	246	3,962	271	3,757	256
Grenada	3,182	313	4,278	430	4,345	450
St. Kitts and Nevis	6,108	263	7,149	329	7,121	341
St. Lucia	4,150	606	4,627	707	4,566	720
St. Vincent and the Grenadines	2,544	287	2,889	335	3,073	362
Mainland						
Belize	2,904	7,091	3,400	8,398	3,810	8,989
Guyana	701	518	807	593	825	609
Suriname	1,772	716	1,775	775	1,986	887
Dependent territories[a]						
Aruba						
Netherlands Antilles						
Anguilla						
Montserrat						
British Virgin Islands						
Cayman Islands						
Turks and Caicos						
French Guiana						
Guadeloupe						
Martinique						
Puerto Rico						
US Virgin Islands						
CARICOM	60,366	32,390	69,628	38,424	72,294	42,114

Sources: Economic Commission for Latin America and the Caribbean, Statistics and Economic Projections Division, *Statistical Yearbook for Latin America and the Caribbean 2007,* March 2008, http://websie.eclac./anuario_estadistico/anuario_2007; Caribbean Tourism Organization, http://onecaribbean.org/.

Note: a. Some data not available for dependent territories.

Per Capita GDP at Constant Prices (100=2000)	GDP at Constant Prices (100=2000) (millions of $)	Per Capita GDP at Constant Prices (100=2000)	GDP at Constant Prices (100=2000) (millions of $)	Per Capita GDP at Constant Prices (100=2000)	GDP at Constant Prices (100=2000) (millions of $)	Population (1000's mid-year)	Land Area (square kilometers)
2004		2005		2006		2007	
2,824	31,721					110,860.0	11,251.0
2,762	25,746	2,972	28,140	3,240	31,133	48,442.0	87,716.5
383	3,502	384	3,566	386	3,648	27,750.0	8,131.5
2,933	7,817	2,956	7,928	3,101	8,124	11,424.0	2,635.4
8,654	11,416	9,310	12,323	10,389	13,801	5,128.0	1,282.4
6,088	1,771	6,313	1,843	6,534	1,914	432.0	271.6
16,594	5,328	16,930	5,474	17,293	5,660	13,864.0	316.0
9,600	787	9,917	824	11,014	926	440.0	78.6
4,001	272	4,147	281	4,381	296	750.0	71.2
3,996	418	4,526	476	4,545	480	344.0	104.8
7,568	367	7,827	385	8,219	409	269.0	47.3
4,757	758	4,985	804	5,129	836	616.0	160.6
3,246	385	3,345	399	3,618	433	389.0	106.7
3,895	9,364	3,942	9,743	4,073	10,194	22,966.0	273.7
837	619	820	606	859	635	215,000.0	767,500.0
2,125	955	2,229	1,009	2,344	1,067	164.0	441.4
						180.0	94.2
						220.0	960.0
						91.0	12.2
						102.0	4.5
						150.0	21.3
						260.0	42.5
						417.0	22.0
						1,373.0	438.8
						1,060.0	381.4
						8,875.0	3,878.5
						342.0	110.7
74,675	43,758	77,631	45,659	81,884	48,423		

Table 5.5 Human Development in the Caribbean: Growth and Poverty

Caribbean States	GDP per Capita ($US), 2005	GDP per Capita (PPP), 2005	Human Development Category, 2007–2008	HDI Change, 2000–2008	GDP per Capita Annual Growth Rate, 1980–1990 (%)	GDP per Capita Annual Growth Rate, 1990–2005 (%)	Poverty (%)
Larger island states							
Cuba	n.a.	6,000	High	+4	n.a.	3.5	42.2
Dominican Republic	3,317	8,217	Medium	+15	-0.1	3.9	80
Haiti	500	1,663	Medium	0	-0.7	-2.0	14.8
Jamaica	3,607	4,291	Medium	-15	-1.7	0.7	
Smaller island states							
Antigua and Barbuda	10,578	12,500	High	-5	6.4	1.5 (shorter period)	n.a.
Bahamas	17,497 (2003)	18,380	High	-8	2.3	0.4 (shorter period)	9.3
Barbados	11,465	17,297	High	0	1.5	1.5 (shorter period)	n.a.
Dominica	3,938	6,393	Medium	-10	3.1	1.3 (shorter period)	30
Grenada	4,451	7,843	Medium	1	5.6	2.5 (shorter period)	32
St. Kitts and Nevis	9,438	13,307	High	-10	6.6	2.9 (shorter period)	31
St. Lucia	5,007	6,707	Medium	-6	4.5	0.9 (shorter period)	19
St. Vincent and the Grenadines	3,612	6,568	Medium	-2	4.8	1.6	33
Trinidad and Tobago	11,000	14,603	High	-9	-7.3	4.3	17
Mainland							
Belize	3,786	7,109	Medium	-22	0.4	2.3	33.5
Guyana	1,048	4,508	Medium	+6	-6.6	3.2	35
Suriname	2,986	7,722	Medium	-11	-5.7	1.1	70

Sources: UN Development Programme, *Human Development Report 1992* (New York: Oxford University Press); UN Development Programme, *Human Development Report 2002* (New York: Oxford University Press); and UN Development Programme, *Human Development Report 2007/2008* (New York: Palgrave Macmilan); World Bank, *World Development Indicators 2004* (Washington, DC: World Bank, 2004).

Notes: Data unavailable for dependent territories.
n.a. indicates data not available.

Port in Oranjestad, Aruba.

   A third factor that explains the variation in economic performance is macro-economic management, government use of fiscal, monetary, and other economic policies to influence the level of overall economic activity. One particularly significant component of this is the exchange rate policy between a national currency and foreign currencies. The exchange rate is extremely important to small Caribbean economies that are highly dependent on imports for both consumption and production. Significant volatility in the exchange rate can have deleterious impacts on the standard of living and, by inference, on social stability.

   There are four exchange rate options open to small economies. The first is to have no national currency, as occurs in Panama, which relies on the US dollar. A second option is to fix, or peg, the exchange rate to a hard currency such as the US dollar. A third strategy would be to permit one's national currency to float and hence be determined by the forces of supply and demand. A final option is to link the supply of national currency to reserves in hard currency, or foreign exchange. This final option, a currency board, was long practiced in the British colonies. According to currency board arrangements that include a fixed exchange rate system, the national currency is backed—completely or partially—by reserves of hard currencies.

   Most Caribbean economies currently operate pegged or floating single-currency systems. The members of the Eastern Caribbean Central Bank, who share a common currency that is based on a modified currency board system, are exceptions. ECCB member countries have recorded a more stable economic performance than their larger cousins in the English-speaking CARICOM. The latter set of countries (Jamaica, Guyana, Trinidad and Tobago, and Barbados) have operated with fixed exchange rates, subject to devaluation, and more recently (with the exception of Barbados) with floating exchange rates, subject to depreciation. Puerto Rico, of course, uses the common US currency, and the French departments draw on the French franc. The Netherlands Antilles use the guilder as their currency.

▪ Current and Projected Economic Challenges

There are perhaps six main economic problems that Caribbean economies will face, in common, in the near-term: (1) the collapse of preferential arrangements for traditional exports; (2) liberalization in the context of globalization, such as agreements made under World Trade Organization (WTO) rules and new trading agreements with the European Union Economic Partnership Agreement (EU-EPA); (3) stubborn unemployment, particularly among youth, and concomitant growing social deviance, including violence, crime, and drugs; (4) foreign debt burdens; (5) market risks faced by the more dynamic sectors of recent years—tourism, offshore finance, and information processing; and (6) vulnerability to natural disasters, exacerbated by climate change (also a longer-term concern).

The Collapse of Preferential Arrangements
Although there has been substantial economic diversification in the Caribbean, traditional agricultural exports still loom large. Cuba, Jamaica, and Guyana continue to operate significant sugarcane industries, particularly in terms of employment. Some other Caribbean economies, like those in the Windward Islands, share a similar dependence on banana exports. Long-established preferential agreements with the European Union (EU) under the Lomé Convention were challenged by recent WTO rulings, giving way to less favorable arrangements.[9] This has led to a decline in the Caribbean banana industry, triggering increased unemployment, mounting social tensions, and a concomitant domino effect on other economic sectors.

Adjusting to Liberalization and Globalization
The near-term collapse of preferential arrangements for small Caribbean economies is complicated by globalization and its institutional expression in economic liberalization. Globalization may be defined, generally, as the increasing integration of the world economy. Liberalization involves negotiation of binding contracts by nations to remove barriers to the opening of their economies. The WTO is the forum for such negotiations, which are reinforced in many instances by loan agreements signed by countries with the World Bank or International Monetary Fund.

One of the key issues in negotiations is the time allowed individual countries to adjust to the demands of liberalization. In the case of the WTO, for example, countries such as the United States have been able to negotiate a decade-long transitional period to liberalize markets for textiles and garments. The Caribbean, to date, has not had the negotiating clout to achieve similar results for some traditional export industries such as bananas.

The implications of globalization and liberalization include the end of differential treatment for nationally owned firms in the tourism, financial, agricultural, and manufacturing sectors. According to some interpretations of WTO rules, for example, Caribbean economies may no longer be able to require significant or total local ownership of small hotels, tour operators, and the like. If this proves to be the case, then the share of national ownership in many Caribbean industries may come under threat from transnational corporations. Although some increased competition is not without benefits, a sudden and large-scale denationalization of industry is likely to have negative impacts, including resentment toward foreign ownership of major industries, particularly those that were previously nationally owned. The commitment of foreign firms to national development objectives also is likely to be weaker.

Unemployment, Underemployment, Poverty, Crime, and Drugs

Another constraint is the existence of unemployment, underemployment, and poverty throughout the region, particularly in the more populous Caribbean economies. The data reveal a concentration of unemployment among the youth of the region. Therefore, it is not difficult to suggest a link between the frustration of unemployed youths and growing levels of crime, particularly drug-related offenses. In Chapter 4, Thomas J. D'Agostino also notes that mounting frustration and cynicism among Caribbean youths has undermined support for political parties and elections, critical components of the democratic systems within the region. Trade and investment patterns are sensitive to national stability that can be disrupted, particularly in small economies, by factors such as deviant behavior and crime. As explained by Dennis Conway in Chapter 12, the general paucity of economic opportunities in many Caribbean states is a primary factor contributing to outmigration. This, in turn, has produced a brain-drain that undermines future economic development as the region continues to lose vital human resources.

The Foreign Debt Burden

One of the constraints that some Caribbean economies face, particularly those with significant socioeconomic problems, stems from substantial foreign debt burdens that consume a large share of fiscal revenue. This is true of Jamaica and Guyana and, to a lesser extent, the Dominican Republic. Facing the challenges noted above is likely to require substantial fiscal expenditures to fund programs, including retraining workers displaced in the process of globalization and liberalization and upgrading infrastructure for new investments (e.g., telecommunications). However, countries with significant debt burdens are constrained to service such prior liabilities before addressing future needs.

Risks Facing Nonpreferential Export Sectors

Even the nonpreferential and globally competitive export industries of the Caribbean will not remain unaffected by global trends. Tourism, for example, is the most dynamic sector in the Caribbean. However, the prospects are not always bright. The larger question is the sustainability of the regional tourism industry. The Caribbean faces the danger, for example, of killing the proverbial goose that lays the golden egg by expanding tourism beyond its eco-cultural carrying capacity. The challenge is to develop sustainable tourism, which simultaneously stays within carrying capacity limits (whether sociocultural, economic, or ecological), while maximizing the retention of the majority of the economic rents accruing from the sector.[10]

The prospects are not as bright for other sectors, with the partial exception of natural gas in Trinidad and Tobago. However, the distribution of rents from that sector is still problematic, given substantial tax holidays and dominant foreign ownership.

The offshore financial sector faces a decline in light of changing metropolitan tax laws targeting centers of money laundering and tax evasion. A 2002 report by the Organization for Economic Cooperation and Development (OECD) on harmful tax competition listed forty-seven countries, including fifteen from the Caribbean with offshore financial services and nominal corporation taxes, claimed to be causing injury to tax regimes in OECD countries (OECD 2002). Offshore investment trusts, foreign sales corporations, and offshore insurance companies have been identified as instruments of OECD tax losses. The Caribbean has been attempting to seek support from individual OECD countries, particularly in the European Union, to stave off punitive changes in the relevant tax laws.[11]

The information-processing sector, as noted earlier, is dominated by low-end data-entry activities. Competitive erosion by the increasing automation of such functions, among other things, is facilitating the use of non-English-speaking data entry services in regions of the world with lower labor costs, particularly Asia.

Vulnerability to Natural Disasters and Climate Change

One of the major challenges to sustainable development in the Caribbean, and particularly to the tourism sector, is the annual passage of hydro-meteorological events (hurricanes and tropical storms as well as other windstorm-related events). These types of natural hazards are the most common in the region. They account for more than half of all natural hazards and disasters. There is also significant flooding in the region, related to the aftereffects of hurricanes and windstorms. Larger economies in the region, including Haiti, Cuba, the

Dominican Republic and Jamaica, have clearly been most affected in terms of the frequency of natural disasters (see Table 5.6).

Hurricane Damage to the Tourism Sector

In 1995 Hurricanes Luis and Marilyn caused severe damage to hotels and other properties in Antigua and Barbuda's tourism industry. The effects of hurricanes also led to a 17 percent decrease in the number of tourist arrivals and adversely affected employment and foreign exchange. The country had similar experiences in 1998 and 1999 with the passage of Hurricanes José, Georges, and Lenny. In 1998 Hurricanes Georges and Mitch affected Jamaica's tourism sector. Hurricane Lenny caused approximately a quarter million dollars worth of damage in 1999 to the tourism infrastructure in Dominica, mainly along the western coast. Tourism arrivals in St. Kitts were negatively affected by the passage of hurricanes Luis and Marilyn (1995), Georges (1998), and José (1999), significantly reducing the inflow of capital (Attzs 2002).

Table 5.6 Number of Disasters by Country and by Disaster Type, 1980–2007

Country	Drought	Earthquake (seismic activity)	Extreme Temperature	Flood	Storm	Total
Anguilla	0	0	0	1	3	4
Antigua and Barbuda	1	0	0	0	6	7
Bahamas	0	0	0	1	10	11
Barbados	0	1	0	1	5	7
Belize	0	0	1	2	8	11
Cayman Islands	0	0	0	0	5	5
Cuba	6	1	0	19	22	48
Dominica	0	1	0	0	8	9
Dominican Republic	0	1	0	14	17	32
Grenada	0	0	0	0	5	5
Guyana	2	0	0	4	0	6
Haiti	4	0	0	34	21	59
Jamaica	2	0	0	7	15	24
St. Kitts and Nevis	0	0	0	1	6	7
St. Lucia	0	1	0	0	10	11
St. Vincent and the Grenadines	0	0	0	3	6	9
Suriname	0	0	0	2	0	2
Trinidad and Tobago	0	1	0	2	4	7

Source: EM-DAT: Office of US Foreign Disaster Assistance/Centre for Research on the Epidemiology of Disasters (OFDA/CRED) International Disaster Database, Université Catholique de Louvain, Brussels, Belgium, www.em-dat.net (accessed March 2009).

More recently, in 2004 Hurricane Ivan severely affected the tourism sector in Grenada and other countries. According to the Organization of Eastern Caribbean States, an estimated 90 percent of the guest rooms in the tourism sector in Grenada were damaged or destroyed, equivalent to approximately 29 percent of that country's GDP. Table 5.7 shows the economic impact of disasters in selected Caribbean countries. For most of the countries identified, tourism is their economic base. However, as an industry where sustainability is dependent upon providing a pleasing environment to vistors, the vulnerability of tourism to hurricanes and other natural disasters poses significant challenges to government policymakers and the general citizenry alike.

In 2005, the Caribbean suffered through the most active hurricane season ever recorded. There were a total of twenty-eight tropical and subtropical storms, fifteen of which became hurricanes. Several storms toward the end of the season were named after letters in the Greek alphabet once the list of hurricane names was exhausted.[12] The data from the 2005 season, along with data about Dean (2007) and Gustav, Hanna, and Ike (2008), suggest that the frequency and intensity of hurricanes have increased in recent years. Clearly, hurricanes and other natural disasters pose a significant challenge to the development of a sustainable tourism industry in the Caribbean. Climate change will exacerbate the impact of hurricanes in the future, as noted in the Third Assessment Report of the Intergovernmental Panel on Climate Change (IPCC 2001:854): "while there is no consensus related to the behaviour of tropical cyclones in a warmer world, individual studies have reported the likelihood of a possible increase of approximately 10–20% in intensity of tropical cyclones under enhanced CO_2

**Table 5.7 Economic Impact of Natural Disasters in
            Selected Caribbean Countries**

Hurricane Name (Year)	Affected Country	Disaster Damage as % of GDP
Gilbert (1988)	Jamaica	65
Hugo (1989)	Montserrat	200
Debbie (1994)	St. Lucia	18
Luis/Marilyn (1995)	Antigua	65
Michelle (2001)	Jamaica	1
Keith (2000)	Belize	46
Ivan (2004)	Jamaica	8
	Bahamas	7
	Cayman Islands	183
	Dominican Republic	2
	Grenada	212

Source: Economic Commission for Latin America and the Caribbean (ECLAC), http://www.eclac.org (accessed March 2009).

conditions." The Fourth Assessment Report (2007) of the IPCC reinforces this point. The report also notes that the likely impacts of climate change on small and island developing states (SIDS) include sea-level rise and increased seawater temperature, which will cause beach erosion and coral bleaching, negatively affecting the tourist sector's heavy dependence on coastal resources. It is not difficult to imagine that the sustainability of the tourist sector could be directly vulnerable to climate change. Indirectly, climate change could reduce the number of visitors traveling from temperate countries to the warmer island states. Also, changes in climate could result in water shortages and increases in vector-borne diseases—all of which could reduce tourist arrivals in the Caribbean.

▓ Conclusion

The major challenge facing Caribbean economies is to find mechanisms for regional collaboration and cooperation in addressing seven key issue areas: (1) loss of preferences; (2) liberalization and globalization; (3) unemployment, poverty, crime, and violence; (4) foreign debt; (5) risks to the dynamic sectors of tourism and offshore finance; (6) information processing; and (7) vulnerability to natural disasters. In each of these challenges, the advantages of cooperation should be obvious, but it will require surmounting a deep-seated legacy of limited interaction.

Three of these challenges—the collapse of preferential agreements, liberalization and globalization, and foreign debt burdens—require individual Caribbean economies to enter into negotiations with the same global players, whether multilateral or national. Cooperation among them can facilitate their leverage in such negotiations. The same holds true for the threats facing the offshore financial sector. The commonality of concerns as to the other challenges—such as unemployment, drugs and crime, and vulnerability to natural disasters—also suggests benefits from the sharing of experiences, expertise, and resources. In terms of tourism, the Caribbean Tourism Organization already joins regional governments with the mission of promoting the regional industry. The quest for sustainable tourism reinforces this need for cooperation and collaboration, including the sharing of experiences.[13]

As noted by Jacqueline Braveboy-Wagner in Chapter 6, some forms of cooperation and collaboration already exist. However, these cooperative ventures need to encompass new issues and concerns as they are both deepened and expanded.

▓ Notes

1. See Girvan (2001) for a helpful review of differing definitions of the Caribbean and of the view of Gaztambide-Geigel (1996), as cited in Girvan, that the very concept of the Caribbean originated only toward the end of the nineteenth century.

2. See Best (1967), Best and Levitt (1968), and Beckford (1972), for elaboration on the plantation economy school. For a review of critiques and update on this school, see Pantin (1980) and Pantin and Mahabir (1999).

3. For more general reviews of Caribbean economic thought, see Brown and Brewster (1974), St. Cyr (1984), and Lalta and Freckleton (1992). See Lewis (1950) for a pioneering effort to analyze Caribbean economic reality from the perspective of the majority peoples of the region.

4. See Eric Williams's seminal articulation (1944) of the linkage between the economic fortunes of the sugar industry and slavery and then emancipation.

5. Some Caribbean countries have run the gamut of European colonizers—French, Spanish, English, or Dutch.

6. The relationship between Caribbean countries and more urban countries cannot be simply described as colonial because the majority of the population of the former continues to support these links.

7. For a discussion of the cultural, economic, environmental, and social repercussions of the growth of tourism in the Caribbean, see Polly Pattullo (1996).

8. The export-processing zone (EPZ) is a demarcated physical area within a country in which a range of host-country domestic laws—particularly trade-related laws—do not apply and in which the entire output of resident firms is normally exported. The first EPZ in the Dominican Republic was established in 1969. By 1980 some 16,440 jobs had been created, and by 1992 an estimated 101,300 people were employed in nearly twenty EPZs. The vast majority—an estimated 70 percent—are involved in the production of apparel and textiles. Companies have been attracted to the Dominican EPZs because of low wages, relative political stability, and access to the North American market. For further analysis of EPZs in the Dominican Republic, see Jonathan Hartlyn (1998) and Emelio Betances (1995).

9. For details on WTO rulings on the European Union's banana regime and the implications for the Caribbean, see Pantin, Sandiford, and Henry (1999).

10. For a review of the literature on sustainable tourism and its application to the Caribbean, see Pantin (1999). Also see Pattullo (1996) for a critical review of the contribution of the tourist industry to Caribbean development.

11. A report in the *Trinidad Guardian* of March 11, 2000, on a meeting between French president Jacques Chirac and sixteen CARIFORUM countries in Guadeloupe was captioned, "Region Wants French to Halt [OECD] Offshore [Financial Sector] Assault."

12. Alpha, Beta, Gamma, Delta, Epsilon, and Zeta were the names given to the last six storms in 2006.

13. The Association of Caribbean States has set a target of 2020 for the achievement of a sustainable tourism zone in the Caribbean.

Bibliography

Attzs, Marlene. *Preliminary Review of the Economic Impact of Climate Change on Caribbean Tourism: What Is at Risk and Adapting for Sustainable Tourism Development.* OAS Meeting on Adaptation to Climate Change, Caribbean Tourism Sector Workshop, Grenada, May 27–28, 2002.

Beckford, George. *Persistent Poverty: Underdevelopment in the Plantation Economies of the Third World.* New York: Oxford University Press, 1972.

Best, Lloyd. "A Model of Pure Plantation Economy." *Social and Economies Studies* 17, no. 3 (September 1967).

Best, L., and Kari Levitt. "Externally Propelled Industrialisation and Growth in the Caribbean." 4 vols. Montreal: McGill Centre for Developing Area Studies (mimeo), 1968.

Betances, Emelio. *State and Society in the Dominican Republic.* Boulder, CO: Westview, 1995.

Brown, Adlith, and H. Brewster. "A Review of the Study of Economics in the English-Speaking Caribbean." *Social and Economies Studies* 23, no. 1 (March 1974).

Byron, Jessica. "The Association of Caribbean States: Growing Pains of a New Regionalism?" *Pensamiento Propio* 3, no. 7 (May–August 1998): 33–57.

Caribbean Tourism Organization (CTO). Caribbean Tourism Statistical Report, 1999–2000. Bridgetown, Barbados: Caribbean Tourism Organization, 2003.

Centre for Research in the Epidemiology of Disasters (CRED). EM-DAT: The OFDA/CRED International Disaster Database. Université Catholique de Louvain, Brussels, www.em-dat.net.

Florida-Caribbean Cruise Association. "Cruise Industry Overview—2006." Pembroke Pines, Florida, www.f-caa.com/downloads/overview2006.pdf.

———. "Economic Impact of Cruise Tourism on the Caribbean Economy." Pembroke Pines, October 2006, www.f-caa.com/research.html.

Gaztambide-Geigel, Antonio. "La invención del Caribe en el Siglo XX: Las definiciones del Caribe como problema histórico e metodológico" (The invention of the Caribbean in the twentieth century: Definitions of the Caribbean as a historical and methodological problem). *Revista Mexicana del Caribe* 1, no. 1 (1996): 75–96.

Girvan, Norman. "Reinterpreting the Caribbean." In *New Caribbean Thought,* edited by Folke Lindahl and Brian Meeks. Kingston, Jamaica: University of the West Indies Press, 2001.

Hartlyn, Jonathan. *The Struggle for Democratic Politics in the Dominican Republic.* Chapel Hill: University of North Carolina Press, 1998.

Intergovernmental Panel on Climate Change. *Climate Change 2001: IPCC Third Assessment Report.* Arendal, Norway: GRID-Arendal (a UNEP-collaborating center), 2003, http://www.grida.no/publications/other/ipcc_tar/.

Jayawardena, Chandana, ed. *Caribbean Tourism: People, Service, and Hospitality.* Kingston, Jamaica: Ian Randle, 2005.

Lalta, Stanley, and Marie Freckleton. *Caribbean Economic Development: The Second Generation.* Kingston, Jamaica: Ian Randle, 1992.

Lewis, W. Arthur. "The Industrialisation of the British West Indies." *Caribbean Economic Review* 12 (May 1950).

OECD (Organization for Economic Cooperation and Development). "Harmful Tax Practices." *Annual Report 2002.* Paris: OECD Public Affairs Division, 2002, p. 41.

Pantin, Dennis A. "The Plantation Economy Model and the Caribbean." *IDS Bulletin* 12, no. 1 (December 1980): 17–23.

———. "The Challenge of Sustainable Development in Small Island Developing States: Case Study on Tourism in the Caribbean." *Natural Resources Forum* 23, no. 3 (August 1999): 221–234.

Pantin, Dennis, Jennifer Edwards, Suzanne Shillingford, Maria Bellot, Marlene Attzs, and Michelle Mycoo. *The Greening of Tourism in the Caribbean and Its Adaptation to Climate Change.* UWI-SEDU Report to the UWI Ford Foundation Project, 2001.

———. "Environmental Management Insertion in Tourism Sector Policies of the Caribbean." Final Report, submitted by the Sustainable Economic Development Unit (SEDU), Department of Economics, University of the West Indies, to the Inter-American Development Bank (IADB/UWI-SEDU), 2002.

Pantin, Dennis A., and Dhanyshar Mahabir, eds. "The Plantation Economy Revisited." *Maroonage* 1, no. 1 (March 1999).

Pantin, Dennis A., W. Sandiford, and M. Henry. *Cake, Mama Coka or? Alternatives Facing the Caribbean Banana Industry Following the April 1999 WTO Ruling.* Study for the West Indian Farmer's Association, the Caribbean Development Policy Center, and OXFAM, September 1999.

Pattullo, Polly. *Last Resorts: The Cost of Tourism in the Caribbean.* New York: Monthly Review Press, 1996.

Riley, Liz. "Sustainable Tourism: Repositioning the Sector to Manage Disaster Risk, a Context for Discussion." Paper presented at the Association of Caribbean States (ACS) Workshop on Disasters and Sustainable Tourism, Port-au-Prince, Haiti, November 14, 2007. Bridgetown, Barbados: Caribbean Disaster Emergency Response Agency.

Schwartz, Anna J. *Do Currency Boards Have a Future?* Twenty-Second Wincott Memorial Lecture. Occasional Paper 88. Mona, Kingston, Jamaica: Institute of Economic Affairs, University of the West Indies, 1992.

St. Cyr, Eric. *Caribbean Economic Thought.* Occasional paper. St. Augustine, Trinidad: Institute of International Relations, University of the West Indies, 1984.

Steinmetz, Thomas. "Caribbean Tourism: Unplanned and in Crisis." *Global Travel Industry News,* June 29, 2008. http://www.eturbonews.com/3397/caribbean-tourism-unplanned-and-crisis (accessed August 7, 2008).

Thomas, Petal. *Evaluation of Activities of All Inclusives and Cruise Ship Operations in the Caribbean.* Master's Thesis, University of the West Indies, St. Augustine, Trinidad, 2007.

United Nations Development Programme (UNDP). *Human Development Report 2007/ 2008 Fighting Climate Change: Human Solidarity in a Divided World.* http://hdrstats .undp.org/countries/ (accessed September 9, 2008).

Wagley, Charles. "Plantation America: A Culture Sphere." In *Caribbean Studies: A Symposium,* edited by Vera Rubin. Seattle: University of Washington Press, 1960.

Williams, Eric. *Capitalism and Slavery.* Chapel Hill: University of North Carolina Press, 1944.

6

International Relations

Jacqueline Anne Braveboy-Wagner

The Caribbean appears to the casual observer as a region comprising numerous small states that may be attractive tourist destinations and tax havens, but with little global significance. There are two exceptions: (1) Cuba has played an intriguing role as an anti-American communist anomaly in the US "sphere of influence"; and (2) Haiti, because of successive crises, has attracted primarily negative global attention over the years.

In the twenty-first century, the region risks marginalization in both the global economy and the global polity. Yet the Caribbean also offers many lessons in survival to the small independent states that now form the bulk of nations in the world.[1] Moreover, it is important to recognize that the Caribbean is a culturally diverse region that was once important enough to have been a major arena of colonial competition.

In this chapter, I address several of the major aspects of the Caribbean's international relations under three rubrics: (1) the impact of culture and identity, (2) the role of geopolitical framing in the region's security, and (3) issues affecting the region's foreign economic relations.

* * *

Clearly, as Richard Hillman outlines in Chapter 1, all the island states of the Caribbean Sea, as well as the countries located in the circum-Caribbean, may be included in an inclusive definition of the region. Since this chapter deals with international relations, however, the focus is on the *independent* states because they have the capacity to conduct formal foreign policies.

Within the broader Caribbean, the subgroup that comprises the Caribbean Community (CARICOM), the central economic integration arrangement in the region, includes not only island states such as Haiti[2] but also the continental states of Belize, Guyana, and Suriname. I view these continental states as having a Caribbean identity.

The countries *not* included in this chapter, however, also have some claim to a Caribbean identity by virtue of their location in the circum-Caribbean. Central American nations are not normally recognized as part of the central Caribbean core. The Caribbean Basin concept has been employed to incorporate these countries and has been used in formulating US policy in the Caribbean and Central America. In addition, although Mexico, Venezuela, and Colombia sustain varying degrees of Caribbean interests, their main identities lie elsewhere. Thus, the Central American nations as well as Mexico, Venezuela, and Colombia are treated in this chapter as an outer circle of countries with which the core Caribbean countries share special but not primary interests.

■ The External Effects of Caribbean Culture and Identity

The study of international relations and foreign policy has generally focused on realist (power) and liberal (cooperative) explanations. However, the field has benefited much in recent years from the rise of constructivism, an approach that focuses on the effect of nonmaterial structures (that is, shared ideas, beliefs, and values about external behavior). Constructivists believe that the social identities of political actors are shaped by such normative and ideational structures, and that those identities inform the actors' interests and actions.[3] Indeed, to understand the Caribbean, it is important to address the culture and identities that have shaped it. The region has amalgamated different cultures brought to the region by different colonial powers—Spanish, English, French, and Dutch. This Creole amalgamation of indigenous and colonial cultures in different countries resulted in separate and distinct patterns of interaction that have inhibited mutual understanding and cooperation.

Haiti was the first country in the region to declare its independence, beginning the struggle in 1791 and separating from France in 1804. But the ensuing period of isolation, during which Haiti had conflicted relations with France, Germany, and the United States, was attributable in no small measure to international disdain as well as concern generated by the republic's violent birth through slave uprisings and postrevolutionary chaos. The still-expanding United States feared the potential influence of African nationalism in Haiti on its own slave-holding states, particularly Louisiana. Haiti's négritude also differentiated the republic substantially from the new criollo nations of the hemisphere that were fighting for their independence from Spain during much of the nineteenth century, so much so that Haiti was not invited to attend the Bolivarian-inspired Spanish American congresses, the precursors to the creation of the pan-American system. Although Haiti went on to become a founding member of the League of Nations and a consistent participant in regional and global affairs, this initial period of ostracism and conflict deepened Haitian nationalism and limited its external partnerships.

Next door to Haiti, the Dominican Republic was subject to Haitian control from 1822 to 1844, and Haiti continued to be a military threat until 1895. Thus Haitian dominance strengthened Dominican nationalism and the desire to develop an identity separate from the country with which it shares the island of Hispaniola. Anti-Haitianism became compounded by color distinctions between the predominantly mixed-race *dominicanos* and the predominantly black Haitians, and it has continued to adversely affect relations between the neighbors. Anti-Haitianism helped to sustain border violence, with the worst occurring in 1937 when some 20,000 Haitians were massacred, as well as a history of arbitrary removals of Haitian migrants in the Dominican Republic.[4]

Cuban identity, known widely as *cubanidad*,[5] evolved from its difficult independence from Spain (it was acquired by the United States after the 1898 Spanish-American War), the rise of nationalism that preceded independence, and the particular blend of African, Spanish, and indigenous culture that has over time infused Cuban literature, music, and life. However, after almost fifty years of the Cuban Revolution, *cubanidad* also reflects the socialist norms with which Cubans have been imbued, resulting in strong stances against imperialism and racism and in favor of global equity and social justice.

Comprised of numerous island states and the mainland enclaves of Belize and Guyana, the English-speaking Caribbean inherited an Anglophone identity along with English institutions and values. Perhaps most notably, this subregion holds a deep commitment to representative democracy that distinguishes it from many other parts of the world. A common cultural bond among these states has been strengthened by complex social linkages resulting from intramigration, travel, and intermarriage. Even if these bonds have not provided

This mural in Havana, Cuba, reads, "Imperialists, we have absolutely no fear of you."

Bernhard Streitwieser

a sufficient foundation for political integration, they have propelled the economic integration and functional cooperation that have been the basis for CARICOM.

Suriname has been a member of CARICOM since 1984. Its Dutch heritage and language have contributed to a pattern of external interaction more with Europe than with others in the hemisphere. However, its Creole culture— a mix of African, Javanese, and East Indian—shares some influences with other countries in CARICOM, allowing for deepening links with its neighbors in recent years. In particular, Trinidad and Tobago and Guyana share with Suriname a particular ethnic mix of African and East Indian elements—in each case about 40 percent of the national population is East Indian, a legacy of the system of indentured labor from the eighteenth and early nineteenth centuries (detailed by Stephen Randall in Chapter 3). The bulk of the remaining population in each country is classified as African or "mixed."

Cultural distinctions have made for a divided and sometimes divisive Caribbean. Although some observers have recognized significant commonalities among Caribbean states, historically a pan-Caribbean identity has been lacking, and interaction among subregions (the Anglo-Caribbean, the Hispanic Caribbean, the Dutch Caribbean, and the French Caribbean) has been defined primarily by colonial heritage (Hillman and D'Agostino 1992). However, recognition of mutual economic and political interests that transcend linguistic and cultural barriers has gradually evolved. Distances between Caribbean states have diminished as business elites across the region develop closer ties and policymakers collaborate on transnational issues such as migration, security, and the environment.

CARICOM, originally comprised of Anglophone Caribbean states, reflects this trend. Suriname and Haiti have become full members, and several others enjoy observer status, including Colombia, Mexico, Venezuela, and the Dominican Republic, which has become more active in CARICOM affairs. Although Haiti historically had little contact with its Anglophone neighbors, CARICOM states moved closer to Haiti during the exile of President Jean-Bertrand Aristide, and troops from CARICOM states participated in peacekeeping efforts in Haiti after the US-led multinational intervention of 1994. Haiti's acceptance into CARICOM, effective in 2002, has further reduced the intergovernmental distance, if not yet the distance between Haitians and the peoples of other member nations.

Historically, Cuba attracted many English-speaking Caribbean migrants who worked in the sugar plantations and stayed to add a West Indian flavor to Cuba's cultural diversity, especially in Cuba's Oriente province.[6] Although in the early 1960s the English-speaking countries were wary of Fidel Castro's socialism and regional ambitions, a sense of camaraderie with Cuba developed after 1972 when the four original members of CARICOM (Barbados, Guyana, Jamaica, and Trinidad and Tobago) established diplomatic relations with Cuba. Since then Cuba has sought to deepen relations, as evidenced by its joining the African-Caribbean-Pacific (ACP) group and the Caribbean Forum (CARIFORUM) in the early 2000s.

CARICOM nations have accelerated their interaction with Central and South America over the past few decades by increasing economic ties and joining institutions such as the Organization of American States (OAS), beginning with Trinidad and Tobago's membership in 1967; the Economic Commission for Latin America and the Caribbean (ECLAC), the second "C" having been added in 1984; the Sistema Latinoamericano Económico (SELA), formed in 1975; the Rio Group, created in 1986; and the Association of Caribbean States (ACS), formed in 1994. These increased connections have led some English-speaking states, such as Trinidad and Tobago, to more closely identify with their Latin American counterparts.

In the cases of Belize, Guyana, and Suriname, their location on the mainland suggests that they would seek stronger relationships with their Latin American neighbors. However, in the case of the first two, tensions stemming from territorial disputes after independence were the norm. Guatemala claimed Belize, based on Britain's violation of treaty promises, and Venezuela claimed the Essequibo region of Guyana, a significant portion of that country's present territory.[7] Over the years, the attention focused on these (unresolved) disputes has diminished, allowing Belize and Guyana to deepen ties with their neighbors. Belize, in particular, saw an influx of Spanish-speaking refugees as a result of the civil wars that ravaged Central America in the 1970s and 1980s; this, along with strong economic links created by membership in the Central American Integration System (SICA) has certainly heightened Belize's Latin identity.

Notwithstanding their cultural distinctions, the normative stances and postures assumed by the Caribbean nations in world affairs can be traced to some overarching identities. As former colonies as well as multiracial societies, they have all adopted anticolonialism and antiracialism as norms that they consistently articulate in the United Nations. Living in the shadow of a superpower, these nation-states have defended the need for respect for political and economic sovereignty. Cuba and Guyana have played major roles in the non-aligned movement (NAM), a forum in which these norms are predominant and which most Caribbean states joined in the 1970s and 1980s. Haiti, St. Vincent and the Grenadines, Antigua and Barbuda, Dominica, the Dominican Republic, and St. Kitts and Nevis were cautious about holding more than observer status in the NAM during the Cold War, but in the post–Cold War "unipolar" environment, they have all joined their Caribbean neighbors as full members.

It was noted earlier that the English-speaking Caribbean inherited from Britain an attachment to democratic norms and institutions. As a result, externally they have been perceived as generally stable nations. Indeed, the persistence of these values is underscored by their continued membership in the British Commonwealth. However, there have been a few exceptions to that history of stability: two coup attempts in Trinidad and Tobago in 1970 and 1991, a political takeover in Grenada in 1979 and the subsequent breakdown of order that provoked an invasion by the United States in 1983, and creeping and then consolidated authoritarianism in Guyana under Forbes Burnham from the 1970s to the mid-1980s. The other Caribbean states have struggled in varying degrees to maintain democracy: Suriname began to consolidate its democracy only after a period of military and military-civilian rule from 1980 to 1987; in the Dominican Republic democracy was strengthened only after 1996; Haiti has seen near-constant instability; and Cuba still claims popular but not recognizably representative democracy. Despite all Caribbean nations' public support for human rights norms (reflected in their adherence to the UN and Inter-American Conventions on Human Rights), there have been significant violations of human rights under authoritarian governments in a number of countries.

The countries of the Caribbean identify themselves, and are widely recognized as "small states," a reality that has profoundly affected their external relations. Even though there is no definitive upper population limit for a small state, Cuba, the largest Caribbean state, has only about 11.4 million people. The smallest state, St. Kitts and Nevis, has fewer than 50,000 people. Caribbean states are unmistakably small by any global standard. And small state status has dramatically affected their global affairs in multiple ways.[8]

A small state may be able to wield some influence internationally by virtue of strategic or economic advantages. Strategically, Cuba has played a far more prominent role than its relative size would suggest, particularly during the post-1959 period. Economically, Trinidad and Tobago's oil endowments give it some limited influence beyond the region. But small states are also highly vulnerable to a variety of threats, including intervention and pressures from larger neighbors, resource and infrastructure limitations, difficulties in achieving economies of scale, and excessive trade dependence. In their external behavior, small states are generally thought to have limited options as they confront these vulnerabilities.

Like other small states, therefore, Caribbean states have (with some exceptions) attempted to carefully balance their interests with the interests of their large North American neighbor. They have also joined coalitions to increase their bargaining strength and sought admission to a relatively large number of international organizations as a way to lower their "transaction costs," that is to say, to achieve their goals efficiently and at a low (economic and political) cost for the individual state.[9] In this regard, joining and participating in the UN and its agencies have clearly been a priority. A number of other organizational memberships of Caribbean states have already been mentioned, including the OAS, SELA, the ACS, the NAM, CARIFORUM, and, of course, CARICOM itself. The English-speaking Caribbean states have maintained their membership in the Commonwealth, an association of former colonies of

Britain—the cost of membership is low, and the cultural, economic, and diplomatic benefits are relatively rewarding. The Alliance for Small Island Developing States, formed in 1990 to bring attention to the particular environmental vulnerabilities of members, demonstrates the advantages of forming coalitions. Caribbean states were instrumental in its formation, and the organization has been very effective at the UN as well as in networking with relevant global communities.[10]

▉ The Geopolitical Framing of Security

From Colonialism to the Cold War

Despite the small size of the Caribbean states, they have at times played important roles in global and, particularly, hemispheric relations. Students of classical realism know well the advantages ascribed by great powers to strategic location. Classical geopolitical doctrine, particularly as put forward by Alfred Thayer Mahan, emphasizes great power rivalry for control and dominance over contiguous islands and coastal continental areas.[11] More modern geopolitical thinking, however, has also included strategic economic considerations, particularly the importance of securing sources of raw materials such as bauxite and petroleum.

The great powers of the seventeenth and eighteenth centuries—the Dutch, Spanish, French, and English—fought over the Caribbean islands for access to raw materials. Many of the frequent transfers of power from one colonial regime to another in the islands and littoral, however, were only incidental to wars fought on the European continent. As colonial powers vied for dominance over ocean routes between the New World and the Old, the Caribbean islands formed a natural bridge between the Atlantic and the Caribbean Sea. Thus, they provided important bases, ports, and fortified garrisons. As H. Michael Erisman (2003) notes, the most significant territories were those adjacent to several narrow choke points that the maritime traffic had to traverse, the most prominent being the Yucatán Channel; the Straits of Florida; and the Windward, Mona, and Anegada passages (see Maps 1.1, 1.2, and 1.3).

In addition to their strategic military value, the Caribbean territories were also prized colonial possessions because of their economic role as suppliers of sugarcane, which was produced cheaply through slave labor on large plantations and exported wholesale to the metropolitan powers. The importance of sugar was such that at one point England considered acquiring Guadeloupe and Martinique by trading all of Canada for them (Erisman 2003). Sugar was the main attraction in Sir Walter Raleigh's search for El Dorado, which, although not bearing fruit in his time, was a preview of the gold rush that brought so many Englishmen to British Guiana in the mid-1850s.[12]

Decolonization did not bring an end to the geopolitical maneuverings of the major powers. However, the Monroe Doctrine (1823) warned against European encroachment in the Western Hemisphere. Henceforth, the United States found itself embroiled in the affairs of the Latin American and Caribbean nations. The United States ostensibly sought to champion Latin American independence, and soon came to view Haiti, Cuba, and the Dominican Republic as countries with essential geopolitical significance.

By the late nineteenth century, the United States was competing vigorously with European economic interests in Haiti. Concerned about the consequences of chronic political instability in the country, the United States took over customs operations and eventually intervened in 1915. These US actions occurred in the wake of European threats of intervention to collect debts and fears of German aggression. They were followed by an arrangement under which the United States controlled Haiti, installing pliable local leaders to run the country's institutions. This arrangement lasted until 1934.

Similar concerns led to US intervention in the Dominican Republic between 1916 and 1924. The Dominican Republic became independent in 1844 after having seen its declared independence in 1821 superseded by Haitian control. Meanwhile, the United States grew in global and hemispheric stature after the Spanish-American War of 1898, during which it supported an insurgency challenging Spanish control in Cuba. After Spain withdrew, a US military government ruled Cuba until 1902. However, the Platt Amendment of 1901 became part of Cuba's 1902 constitution, giving the United States the unilateral right to intervene in the island's affairs. The United States repeatedly intervened in Cuba until the amendment was abrogated as a result of President Franklin Roosevelt's Good Neighbor Policy in 1934. The Platt Amendment also gave Guantánamo Bay to the United States as a naval base, a cession that has continued to vex Cuba to the present day.

During World War II, the United States established military bases throughout the Caribbean. The Netherlands agreed to a US base in Suriname to protect the bauxite mines, and the United States leased bases from Britain in several locations, including Bermuda, the Bahamas, Jamaica, Antigua, Saint Lucia, and British Guiana.[13] Chief among these was the Chaguaramas naval base in Trinidad, leased in 1941 for ninety-nine years in exchange for fifty destroyers. Trinidad and Tobago's fight for sovereignty over the base between 1956 and 1967 was protracted, helping to engender a postcolonial foreign policy that has included a pointed wariness of the United States. These bases were later deactivated or minimized, some immediately after the war, others in the 1960s and 1970s. However, the United States continues to maintain facilities in the Bahamas, Panama, and Puerto Rico, along with Guantánamo Bay in Cuba; in some cases this has served to perpetuate a wariness of the US but also underscores the ongoing US concern with events in the region.

"Next"
In the early twentieth century, the United States perceived itself as responsible for the states of the circum-Caribbean.

The Cold War

The United States has always considered the Caribbean to be a vital strategic area due to its geographic proximity. The level of interaction between the Americas and the Caribbean has remained high, including interventions and the installation of military bases, tourism, migrations of people, and international commerce. Such proximity and interaction have both benefited and challenged countries within the region and, as Thomas J. D'Agostino describes in Chapter 4, the significance of the Caribbean was magnified even further after World War II. With the onset of the Cold War, the countries in the Caribbean soon found themselves embroiled in global and regional ideological rivalries, while the United States sought to maintain ideologically friendly governments in the Caribbean, its immediate sphere of influence.

Events in Cuba illustrated the virulent anticommunist sentiment pervading Washington as well as the depth of US concern regarding possible Soviet influence in the circum-Caribbean. Following World War II, democratically elected governments in Guatemala under the leadership of Juan José Arévalo and Jacobo Arbenz implemented a series of socioeconomic and political reforms that brought them into conflict with conservative elements in Guatemala as well as with the United States. Arbenz in particular was viewed as a threat to US hegemony in the region because of a sweeping agrarian reform measure that targeted US business interests. Efforts to destabilize the government culminated in US support for a coup led by Colonel Carlos Castillo Armas that toppled Arbenz in 1954 and ushered in a period of authoritarian rule and closer ties to the United States.

Until 1959, Cuba was a haven for US investments and tourism as well as a political ally whose authoritarian government under Fulgencio Batista was strongly supported by Washington as an anticommunist bulwark in the region. Fidel Castro's revolution and transformation of Cuba into a socialist state with close ties to Moscow posed a unique geopolitical challenge for the United States, given Cuba's proximity to the US mainland. In response, the United States sought to overthrow Castro by supporting Cuban exiles who unsuccessfully invaded the island at the Bay of Pigs in 1961.

In the wake of the invasion, Cuba allied itself with the Soviet Union in order to defend against potential attacks in the future. The US discovery in 1962 of Soviet missiles in Cuba caused a major confrontation that brought the world's superpowers to the brink of nuclear war. Although John F. Kennedy and Nikita Khrushchev were the principal actors in the Cuban Missile Crisis, the role of Fidel Castro was catalytic. This incident brought the Caribbean once again to the forefront of international relations, reminiscent of the era when tensions among European colonial powers sparked conflicts throughout the region.

The tenuous peace that followed the Soviet removal of the missiles was backed by a US promise not to invade Cuba, but the superpowers' global ideological rivalry continued to have implications for the region. The Caribbean became a center of Cold War competition as Cuba enthusiastically supported leftist insurgencies and regimes in a number of countries, while the United States sought to isolate Cuba through a strict economic embargo. In response to the Soviet and Cuban challenges in its sphere of influence, the United States provided substantial economic, technical, and military assistance to bolster ties with "friendly" Caribbean states. For example, the Alliance for Progress was designed to provide development aid in order to ameliorate the conditions that US policymakers viewed as conducive to leftist insurgency. One of the conditions for aid was the initiation of land reform programs, based on the belief that such "pacific revolutions" would make violent revolutions avoidable. "Reform, not revolution" became the mantra of those seeking alternatives to the Cuban model.

The revolutionary Cuban regime embarked on an activist foreign policy throughout the Americas as well as in Africa. Castro was committed to exporting his revolution to the rest of Latin America and the Caribbean, providing arms and assistance to various guerrilla groups and using Cuba as a training ground for insurgents from other countries. Support for revolutionary movements in Angola, Ethiopia, and Mozambique, among other African states, demonstrated Cuba's burgeoning international influence.

In 1963 Cuba's involvement in Venezuelan antigovernment guerrilla activity led to the imposition of sanctions by the OAS, which had already excluded Cuba from participation in 1962. In the Dominican Republic, concerns that Cuba was supporting an effort to restore democratically elected Juan Bosch to power led to the deployment of some 23,000 US troops in 1965. The deployment of such a large number of troops attracted substantial regional as well as extraregional criticism that was only placated by the conversion of the US force into a broader inter-American peace force.

Despite turning toward domestic consolidation, by the 1970s Cuba was again involved in supporting militant and nationalist regimes, independence fighters, and guerrilla groups in Africa as well as Latin America, particularly in Central America where civil wars erupted, and in the Caribbean. These activities were viewed by the West as proxy wars for the Soviet Union. Most significantly for the region, Cuba developed close relations and gave technical assistance to what the United States perceived as leftist-leaning regimes. For example, Cuba assisted Guyana, which had become a socialist "cooperative" republic in 1970. Similarly, in the early 1970s Cuba made inroads in Jamaica, which under Prime Minister Michael Manley had pursued a program of "democratic socialism." The Castro regime also provided material and technical assistance, along with a variety of personnel, to Grenada when the New Jewel Movement (NJM) seized power, leading to the emergence of the People's Revolutionary Government (PRG) in 1979.

In the case of Jamaica, the perception of Manley's increasing radicalism led to capital flight, a decline in tourism and foreign investment, and US economic pressure that ended when the conservative government of Edward Seaga was elected in 1980. The United States continued to tolerate the authoritarian government of Forbes Burnham in Guyana because the Guyanese opposition was led by Cheddi Jagan, an avowed Marxist. The death of Burnham in 1985 and the influence of a new global era of liberalism led to greater democracy in the 1990s. Grenada's PRG, however, had embraced more extensive military and economic contacts with and assistance from Cuba and other socialist allies. In 1983, factionalization and breakdown within the regime gave the United States an opening to intervene militarily. With the support of several Eastern Caribbean states and Jamaica, the PRG was removed from power and the Reagan administration proclaimed that it had restored democracy in Grenada.

Under Ronald Reagan, the United States grew increasingly unyielding about maintaining its geopolitical advantages in the circum-Caribbean, a region that was a major supplier of bauxite and petroleum to the United States. The region had also become a transportation channel for half of US exports and two-thirds of its imports (US State Department 1982). To that end, the United States as well as Britain and Canada provided substantial economic as well as military assistance to countries throughout the region, with the notable exception of Cuba. In addition to increased military aid to individual states, including the Dominican Republic, Jamaica, and other members of CARICOM, a new regional security system was established. Centered in the Eastern Caribbean, the security system was designed to police the region after the Grenada invasion. As a complement to military aid, a number of economic support programs were implemented in an effort to promote socioeconomic development and ameliorate conditions that were viewed by the Reagan administration as conducive to leftist insurgencies. Most notable among these programs was the Caribbean Basin Initiative (CBI), initiated in 1982 to provide preferential terms of trade for Caribbean products in the US market.

Of course, none of these aid programs was targeted to Cuba, which continued to deepen its role as a supporter of the Soviet Union throughout the Cold War. A rapprochement between Cuba and the United States did occur in the late 1970s when President Jimmy Carter introduced a policy of dialogue that included negotiations on immigration and territorial issues and the opening of an "interests section" as a proxy for an embassy in Havana.[14] However, this experiment was halted by the end of the 1970s, when the United States grew increasingly alarmed at Cuban intervention in Africa. When hostility between the United States and the Soviet Union peaked after the Soviet invasion of Afghanistan, Carter's "softer" policy was replaced by a hard-line approach centered on the stiffening of the embargo and support for human rights groups trying to maintain a toehold in Cuba.

In sum, although the region was always considered important, US policy had not always been as centered on the Caribbean as it was during the Cold War. The ideological rivalry between the superpowers enhanced the Caribbean's significance as a vital strategic area. Thus, most Caribbean countries desiring development assistance and support were able to capitalize on the interests of the United States and the West—or in the case of Cuba and a few other nations from time to time, on the Soviet Union and the Eastern bloc. The disproportionate international role of the Caribbean countries relative to their size and wealth, especially during the Cold War era, exemplified the complexities of interaction between small states and superpowers, in which the lines of influence and control were not always clearly drawn.

After the Cold War

After 1991, when the Soviet Union ceased to exist, socialist Cuba found itself largely abandoned by Russia and yet unwilling to democratize as demanded by the United States. Under the Helms-Burton Act of 1996, not only was the economic embargo extended to foreign companies, but no Cuban government that included the Castro brothers, Fidel and Raúl, was deemed acceptable to the United States. In view of the changed global and domestic circumstances, Cuba embarked on a program to partially liberalize its economy, opening up some areas (tourism in particular) to controlled foreign investment. Cuba also expanded its ties with European countries that considered the Helms-Burton Act to be inapplicable and offensive and with Latin American and Caribbean countries that had long opposed the US embargo.

Meanwhile, the end of Cold War rivalries reduced external interest, and hence intervention, in the Caribbean. Yet the United States designated the region as its "third border" and formally launched its Third Border Initiative in 2001. Through this program, grant funding has been provided for, among other things, HIV/AIDS prevention, disaster preparedness and mitigation, law enforcement cooperation, and education programs (White House 2001). The Caribbean is clearly vulnerable to multidimensional security challenges, including drug trafficking, financial crime, natural disasters, HIV/AIDS, migrant and refugee movements, trafficking in arms and persons, smuggling, and possible terrorist activities, a heightened global concern after the events of September 11, 2001. The region's foreign security policy has involved substantial cooperation with the United States, as well as Canada and Europe, on drug trafficking, terrorism, and financial crime in particular, as well as cooperation with international agencies on environmental and social development issues.

Supporters of Jean-Bertrand Aristide celebrate
his presidential election victory, Haiti.

For Haiti, basic political stability remains an elusive goal. The country endured a coup that deposed popularly elected President Aristide in 1991, followed by a period of military rule characterized by severe human rights violations and violence directed at Aristide supporters. In 1994, Aristide was restored to his elected position with US support. This US intervention on behalf of a democratically elected president marked a departure from the historical norm of US support for right-wing authoritarian leaders and appeared to offer hope for Haiti's future. However, as Thomas J. D'Agostino notes in Chapter 4, bitter political infighting and gridlock plagued the government of René Préval, who succeeded Aristide in 1996, and Aristide's reelection in 2000 was marred by a boycott by the main opposition parties and allegations of fraud that led to the suspension of aid from the United States and Europe. Amid mounting political violence and economic turmoil, a rebellion broke out in 2004, culminating in Aristide being forced from power on February 29. After repeated delays due to security and logistical issues, an interim government backed by a UN force (United Nations Stabilization Mission in Haiti, or MINUSTAH) oversaw elections in 2006 that brought René Préval back into office. The removal of Préval's Prime Minister, Jacques-Edouard Alexis, in April 2008 and a protracted impasse in the appointment of his successor underscored the depth of Haiti's political problems.

Such profound political instability has severely undermined efforts to promote economic and political development in Haiti. Combined external efforts by bilateral and multilateral donors and nongovernmental organizations have centered on supporting democracy and human rights, relieving Haiti's debt, and attracting financial inflows of aid as well as long-term investment.

The Role of Venezuela

Scholars of geopolitics tend to focus on the great powers, but there are also regional powers that have geopolitical ambitions on a smaller scale. In the case of the Caribbean, Venezuela has sought to play a more active role in the region over the past few decades. By the early 1970s, Venezuela had openly redefined its foreign policy to focus on its Caribbean "front yard," where it sought to counteract Cuban influence. To promote its influence in 1973, Venezuela embarked on a period of intense economic diplomacy, fueled by the influx of petrodollars. Venezuela's program of assistance to the region included the financing of joint ventures, the creation of a trust fund within the Caribbean Development Bank (CDB), and in particular, an initiative undertaken with Mexico in 1980 called the San José Accord. Under this agreement, Central America and the Caribbean would receive oil at subsidized prices, part of Mexico's effort to gain regional and third world influence under the populist government of Luis Echeverría.

Venezuela's growing interest in the Caribbean brought it into conflict with Trinidad and Tobago, which had undertaken its own petro-diplomacy and saw

Hugo Chávez in
front of a portrait
of Simón Bolívar.

Sheila Steele, from Flickr.com

its own arrangements—including an ambitious aluminum smelter plant involving Guyana, Jamaica, and Mexico—downgraded in favor of alternative
arrangements with Venezuela. A tense period ensued as Trinidad and Tobago
cautioned its neighbors about Venezuelan imperialism, stressing Venezuela's
continuing territorial claims in Guyana as well as Bird Island, which is close
to Dominica and under Venezuelan control. Trinidad's efforts, however, were
less than successful as Venezuela improved its relations with other countries
in the region, including Cuba. Moreover, in the 1980s and into the 1990s,
Venezuela positioned itself as a mediator and peacemaker in the conflicts in
Central America and Haiti, enhancing its stature as a leader in the region.[15]

The post–Cold War period brought a new phase in Caribbean relations
with Venezuela. Under President Hugo Chávez, who came to power in 1998,
Venezuela adopted a new radicalized foreign policy in keeping with its plans
for domestic social transformation. Along with bringing Venezuela closer to
Iran, a reinvigorated Russia, China, and other independent-minded countries

outside the hemisphere, Chávez joined Cuba in vigorously opposing neoliberalism and, in particular, US-supported plans for hemispheric free trade. Instead, he offered his own Bolivarian Alternative for the Americas (Alternativa Bolivariana para las Américas, or ALBA), which emphasizes regional integration as well as support for development and antipoverty programs in Latin America and the global South. Since the launch of ALBA in 2004, Cuba and Dominica have joined Nicaragua, Bolivia, and Honduras as members, while Haiti and St. Vincent and the Grenadines have been attending the meetings of the group.

Boosted by increased oil revenues, Chávez has also offered new economic incentives to Caribbean countries. For example, a program of concessionary financing and bartering oil for agricultural products called Petrocaribe was launched in 2005. All but two Caribbean countries have been eager participants in this agreement. Trinidad and Tobago, whose own energy arrangements have been disrupted, would not participate. Nor would Barbados, preferring to continue its existing energy relationship with Trinidad and Tobago. In addition to Petrocaribe, the San José Accord has been renewed every year since its inception in 1980. Moreover, Guyana and Suriname have been drawn more tightly into Venezuela's orbit. They participate in the new Union of South American Nations (UNASUR), an initiative for continental integration launched in 2004–2005 with considerable input and financing from Venezuela as well as Brazil.

▓ Economic Relations

Vulnerabilities

The Caribbean territories were once prized colonial possessions because of their large-scale sugarcane production.[16] Although some countries continue to generate significant revenue from such production, the value of sugar as an export commodity today is far less than it once was. By the twentieth century, national enterprises had replaced the foreign corporations that took over from colonial planters, perpetuating dependence on a precarious economic system.

In Jamaica and the Windward Islands, large-scale banana production began in the 1920s and 1930s.[17] Some Caribbean countries are also mineral producers. Trinidad and Tobago began to produce oil commercially in the early twentieth century. Similarly, Suriname began producing bauxite in 1920, and Jamaica and Haiti followed in the 1940s. In the nineteenth century, gold was discovered in Guyana and is still exploited commercially, as is ferronickel in the Dominican Republic. But after independence, the Caribbean's role as a primary producer of a few key agricultural or mineral products continued to deepen the dependence of the region on trade with a few metropolitan markets.

Over time, geographical proximity and the sheer size of the US market helped shift almost all Caribbean countries toward greater dependence on the

United States. As a result, Haiti, the Dominican Republic, Belize, St. Kitts and Nevis (which today is no longer a sugar producer), and Trinidad and Tobago now send considerably more than half their exports to the United States. Moreover, most Caribbean countries receive more than a quarter of their imports from the United States (see Tables 6.1 and 6.2). However, the main banana-producing countries of the eastern Caribbean (Dominica, St. Lucia, and St. Vincent) have remained focused on the European market. Suriname, which has continued to focus on the Netherlands and other European partners while gradually increasing its trade with the United States, is also an exception to the trend.

Caribbean policymakers recognized the need to diversify products for exportation to expanded markets. In their effort to reduce their dependence on agricultural production, most Caribbean countries industrialized to whatever extent possible, but only Cuba, the Dominican Republic, Trinidad and Tobago, and Jamaica are large enough to be classified as significant exporters of manufactured products.

As Dennis Pantin and Marlene Attzs detail in Chapter 5, most Caribbean countries have relied on tourism to generate capital. However, revenues from the tourist industry are highly variable, depending on the quality of offerings from competitors (including intra-Caribbean competitors), the vagaries of demand in relatively concentrated markets, and often unpredictable environmental, social (especially crime), and political factors. Some Caribbean countries have opted for the more lucrative area of providing financial services and tax shelters. Those exercising that option early on, in particular the Bahamas and the Cayman Islands (an overseas territory of the United Kingdom), have been very successful. Among those countries starting later, Antigua and Barbuda and Barbados have also been relatively successful. However, this later group has relied quite heavily on offshore services, drawing special scrutiny from the developed countries adversely affected by corporate and individual tax evasion, as well as the consequences of money laundering. As a result, they have had to deal with increasingly strict and more onerous regulations passed by the Organization for Economic Cooperation and Development.[18]

Some of the issues generated by the Caribbean's trade dependence are similar to the problems caused by the region's reliance on foreign aid. Caribbean countries are listed as middle- to upper-income countries by the international financial institutions, such as the World Bank and the Inter-American Development Bank. But this designation has not eliminated heavy reliance on external assistance. As with trade, the bulk of this assistance comes from a few aid donors, primarily the United States, the United Kingdom, Canada, France, Germany, Japan, and the Netherlands. The less wealthy Caribbean countries have also received official development assistance from UN agencies, particularly the UN Development Programme, the region's own CDB, the World Bank, and the International Monetary Fund (IMF). Aid dependence brings with it varying levels of vulnerability to the demands of bilateral and multilateral

Table 6.1 CARICOM Trade with Selected Partners, 2006 (US$ millions)

Country	Flow	Total	United States	Canada	UK	EU[a]	CARICOM[b]	ALADI[c]	CACM[d]	Japan	Asia[e]
Antigua and Barbuda	Imports	670.8	248.2	8.1	23.2	58.2	84.5	14.0	1.1	18.5	39.6
	Exports	n.a.	n.a.	0.01[f]	n.a.	n.a.	2.3[f]	0.00[f]	n.a.	0.02[f]	0.02[f]
Barbados	Imports	1,629.0	602.3	60.1	94.9	220.1	428.9	65.7	14.7	59.9	153.1
	Exports	299.4	43.3	7.4	28.3	38.7	126.3	0.8	0.4	0.1	4.5
Belize	Imports	660.3	256.0	7.2	9.1	42.5	13.4	72.1	72.1	9.8	54.1
	Exports	268.2	112.2	0.3	44.3	84.4	22.2	8.6	26.3	2.7	2.7
Dominica	Imports	166.9	58.2	4.5	9.6	19.3	53.6	6.3	1.4	6.6	14.8
	Exports	40.5	1.3	0.0	7.6	7.6	25.7	n.t.	n.t.	n.t.	0.0[g]
Grenada	Imports	298.9	116.4	7.1	16.7	37.6	73.4	15.0	5.2	11.8	32.8
	Exports	18.2	3.5	0.6	0.1	1.9	11.4	0.0[g]	n.t.	n.t.	0.0[g]
Guyana	Imports	882.3	234.7	18.9	42.4	88.7	309.4	69.8	4.6	31.4	112.8
	Exports	647.8	121.0	137.7	98.7	182.2	123.6	6.9	0.1	1.0	30.0
Jamaica	Imports	5,043.0	1,806.0	123.5	133.0	466.5	670.8	885.6	97.9	211.5	550.8
	Exports	1,952.3	584.0	308.3	204.3	476.3	46.5	6.9	1.0	28.7	337.4
St. Kitts and Nevis	Imports	249.5	138.1	6.5	13.2	17.9	45.4	5.8	0.4	10.7	15.4
	Exports	35.2	29.9	0.02	n.t.	0.1	1.8	n.t.	0.0[g]	0.01[h]	0.00
St. Lucia	Imports	592.2	204.7	16.1	40.8	77.4	150.1	21.6	4.7	37.4	61.9
	Exports	52.0	5.5	0.05	0.1	19.3	24.9	n.t.	0.00	0.01	0.04
St. Vincent	Imports	271.5	87.4	9.9	19.5	36.5	88.5	13.3	1.8	10.5	24.7
	Exports	33.8	0.6	0.07	9.3	9.4	22.9	n.a.	n.t.	n.t.	0.0[g]
Suriname	Imports	1,008.9	303.2	8.1	5.3	240.3	245.2	51.7	3.4	43.2	106.7
	Exports	n.a.	n.a.	n.a.	n.a.	n.a.	n.a.	n.a.	n.a.	n.a.	337.4
Trinidad and Tobago	Imports	6,579.3	1,790.7	146.3	180.7	689.4	97.9	1,732.1	28.6	227.8	730.3
	Exports	14,118.9	8,010.2	170.1	116.8	1,222.3	2,397.7	531.0	86.0	72.6	83.7

(continues)

Table 6.1 continued

Country	Flow	Total	United States	Canada	UK	EU[a]	CARICOM[b]	ALADI[c]	CACM[d]	Japan	Asia[e]
Groupings and percentages											
CARICOM	Imports	18,082.9	5,858.3	417.1	589.8	1,996.9	2,272.7	2,953.3	236.0	674.0	1,899.1
	Percent[i]	100.0	32.4	2.3	3.3	11.0	12.6	16.3	1.3	3.7	10.5
	Exports	17,466.8	8,911.6	624.4	528.4	2,042.2	2,803.5	554.7	113.7	105.2	458.3
	Percent[i]	100.0	51.0	3.6	3.0	11.7	16.1	3.2	0.7	0.6	2.6
OECS	Imports	2,280.0	865.2	53.0	124.3	249.3	507.2	76.3	14.6	97.0	191.3
	Percent[i]	100.0	37.9	2.3	5.5	10.9	22.2	3.3	0.6	4.3	8.4
	Exports	180.4	40.9	0.8	36.1	38.3	87.1	0.5	0.00	0.01	0.04
	Percent[i]	100.0	22.7	0.4	20.0	21.2	48.3	0.3	0.0	0.0	0.0

Source: Caribbean Community Secretariat, Statistics Sub-Program database, http://www.caricomstats.org/.

Notes: n.a. indicates data not available.

n.t. indicates no trade.

a. The European Union includes the United Kingdom.

b. Does not include the Bahamas or Haiti, which are not members of the common market. Some export data for Antigua and Barbuda and Suriname are not available.

c. *Asociación latinoamericana de integración* (Latin American Integration Association); members include Argentina, Bolivia, Brazil, Chile, Colombia, Cuba, Ecuador, Mexico, Paraguay, Peru, Uruguay, and Venezuela.

d. Central American Common Market.

e. Selected countries: China, Hong Kong, India, Japan, Singapore, South Korea, Taiwan, and Thailand.

f. Figures are from 2005.

g. Total trade amounts to less than US$500.

h. Preliminary data for 2007.

i. Rows do not add to 100 percent because data are not included for all trading partners.

Table 6.2 Direction of Trade, Non–Common Market Countries, 2006

Country	Flow (US$ millions)	Total	Developed Countries, Americas[a]	EU	CARICOM	ALADI[b]	CACM[c]	Developed Countries, Asia[d]	Other Countries, Asia[e]
Bahamas	Imports[f]	10,179.1	2,573.5	1,436.7	67.6	1,910.4	10.8	1,339.3	1,538.0
	Percent[f]	100.0	25.3	14.1	0.7	18.8	0.1	13.2	15.1
	Exports[f]	2,135.7	452.6	1,249.9	8.5	17.2	108.1	77.8	79.3
	Percent[f]	100.0	21.2	58.5	0.4	0.8	5.1	3.6	3.7
Cuba	Imports[f]	8,917.1	880.2	2,345.4	59.2	3,257.3	38.1	140.6	1,668.7
	Percent[f]	100.0	9.9	26.3	0.7	36.5	0.4	2.2	18.7
	Exports[f]	2,569.0	555.7	843.7	120.2	116.1	18.2	555.7	603.1
	Percent[f]	100.0	21.6	32.8	4.7	4.5	0.7	0.9	23.5
Dominican Republic	Imports[f]	12,541.6	6,042.9	1,222.4	273.1	3,313.1	275.1	309.8	839.5
	Percent[f]	100.0	48.2	9.7	2.2	26.4	2.2	2.6	6.7
	Exports[f]	5,817.1	4,327.3	814.1	79.8	174.1	54.1	47.4	245.5
	Percent[f]	100.0	74.4	14.0	1.4	3.0	0.9	1.1	4.2
Haiti	Imports[f]	1,911.2	920.3	220.8	17.3	244.3	29.7	43.2	173.8
	Percent[f]	100.00	48.2	11.6	0.9	12.8	1.6	2.3	9.1
	Exports[f]	579.1	479.7	21.6	0.6	12.9	0.7	1.3	8.5
	Percent[f]	100.0	82.8	3.7	0.1	2.2	0.1	0.4	1.5

Source: United Nations Conference on Trade and Development (UNCTAD), *Handbook of Statistics 2008* (New York and Geneva: United Nations, 2008), http://www.unctad.org/.

Notes: a. Defined by UNCTAD as the United States, Canada, Bermuda, Greenland, St. Pierre, and Miquelon.
b. ALADI refers to members of the Asociación latinoamericana de integración (Latin American Integration Association). Its members are Argentina, Bolivia, Brazil, Chile, Colombia, Cuba, Ecuador, Mexico, Paraguay, Peru, Uruguay, and Venezuela.
c. CACM stands for Central American Common Market.
d. Defined as Japan and Israel.
e. Eastern, southern, and southeastern Asia.
f. Percentages do not add to 100 percent because data are not included for all trading partners.

donors. Caribbean countries have been subject to a number of pressures, ranging from IMF "conditionality" to demands for political change. In Jamaica and Guyana, for example, the United States attempted to "destabilize" regimes it thought moved too far left. Other pressures included threats of decertification in the case of countries not deemed to be cooperating in drug interdiction, and the demand for environmental safeguards and greater transparency in governance in the current era of liberalization.

Since the 1990s, various indices of economic vulnerability have been developed by the United Nations and the Commonwealth Secretariat. One such index includes measures of openness to trade, export diversification, access to and reliance on external financial flows, export dependence, international transportation costs, and vulnerability to natural disasters. According to this index, the degree of a country's dependence and its ecological vulnerability are mitigated by gross domestic product as a measure of resilience. Of the CARICOM countries in the late 1990s, Antigua and Barbuda ranked as the most vulnerable nation (indeed, the second most vulnerable of the 111 developing nations surveyed), the Bahamas ranked fourth, Guyana and the eastern Caribbean countries were above average, all ranking below thirty, Trinidad and Tobago was about average, and Haiti and Suriname ranked as the least vulnerable, perhaps because of lower market exposure and, in Suriname's case, because there was a lower exposure to environmental shocks.[19]

Caribbean economic vulnerability has been deepened by energy dependence. With the exception of Venezuela and Mexico, Trinidad and Tobago has been the only major energy exporter in the region and therefore the most resilient in this regard. High energy prices in both the 1970s and 2000s undermined development plans and slowed the pace of regional integration, forcing countries to expand their revenues through nonregional trade. The dramatic increase in the cost of oil, particularly from 2005 to 2008, has severely curtailed expenditures in countries that were already struggling to be competitive in a climate of economic liberalization and globalization.

Major Programs

Since the 1970s, most Caribbean countries have relied on favorable terms of trade for their exported goods to Europe and North America. The Lomé Convention, a trade program negotiated by the African-Caribbean-Pacific (ACP) countries in 1975, 1980, 1985, 1990, and renewed in 1995, extended preferences for bananas and rum production by the European Community/European Union. Additional protocols to these accords covered sugar and rice preferences. With the expiration of the Lomé Convention in 2000, a new arrangement between Europe and the ACP countries was established. The Cotonou Agreement is broader in scope than its predecessor, allowing for the participation of non-state actors and local governments and mandating enhanced political dialogue on issues including human rights, immigration, and security. Although it has been a member of the ACP group since 2000, Cuba has not joined the Cotonou Agreement, despite having applied for membership in 2000 and 2003.

In addition, the Caribbean Basin Initiative, enacted through the Caribbean Basin Economic Recovery Act, was converted into a permanent program in 1990. The CBI was then expanded by the Caribbean Basin Trade Partnership Act of 2000 and later extended through 2010. The 2000 extension allowed the region to resist some of the adverse effects of the North American Free Trade Agreement (NAFTA), which came into effect in 1994. Another system of preferences, the Caribbean Canada Trade Agreement (CARIBCAN), provided benefits similar to those offered by the CBI.

Although Cuban-European relations have historically been good, Cuba relied heavily on the Soviet Union following the imposition of the US embargo in 1962, trading its sugar for much-needed oil and joining the Committee for Mutual Economic Assistance in 1972. In the post–Cold War era, Cuba has expanded trade with Europe and with the Caribbean and Latin America.

In the changed environment of the 1990s and 2000s, the most significant challenge facing the Caribbean has been the need to adjust to the anticipated loss of preferential arrangements with Europe. Central American banana-producing countries, backed by US multinational corporations, challenged these arrangements, and the World Trade Organization (WTO) ruled in their favor. The sugar regime was also declared to be incompatible with WTO rules and was renegotiated several times. Finally, the rum regime was phased out in the 1990s. In place of preferences, in 2007 the CARIFORUM countries (except Cuba) negotiated an Economic Partnership Agreement with the European Union, under which 87 percent of trade would be liberalized in fifteen years (with a three-year grace period on most products and a seven-year grace period on others), and all trade would be liberalized within twenty-five years.[20] A new temporary sugar quota was negotiated, adding a moderate 160,000 tons to the existing regional quota but with the provision that the Dominican Republic could export an additional 30,000 tons.

While negotiations with Europe have attracted the most attention, similar negotiations on freeing trade with Canada were initiated by CARICOM countries in 2007 and 2008. During the period of temporary continuation of the CBI, CARICOM is expected to move toward a free trade agreement with the United States as well. The Dominican Republic, already a strong trading partner with Central America as well as a participant in many of that region's integration activities, entered CAFTA in 2004.

CARICOM Integration
Beyond North America and Europe, the most important set of relations in this region has been those *within* the CARICOM. It originated as the Caribbean Free Trade Association (CARIFTA) in 1967, an attempt by the English-speaking

Caribbean nations to counteract deficiencies of size and scale by removing internal barriers to trade. Such regional integration was highly favored at the time by the United Nations Economic Commission for Latin America (ECLA) and by the global South as a whole in the context of the strategy of collective self-reliance. Then, despite some reluctance by those members of CARIFTA dissatisfied with the distribution of benefits up to that point, it was upgraded to a common market in 1973. The Bahamas chose not to join.

Unfortunately, CARICOM's progress toward a common market was sluggish, disrupted by Cold War ideological differences, dislocations caused by high energy prices in the 1970s, and nationalist as well as technical disagreements. After the US intervention in Grenada in 1983, CARICOM leaders moved to revive the integration movement, which was later made more urgent by the anticipated unification of Europe in 1992. Since then, CARICOM states have moved (albeit very slowly) toward a genuine community, completing arrangements for a common external tariff, launching a single market and economy in 2006, introducing some labor mobility (for university graduates, artists, media, and sports personnel), easing intraregional travel, and forming a regional stock exchange among some of the larger countries. The institutional structure was streamlined in 2001, a Court of Justice launched in 2005, a charter on civil society passed in 1992, a (very weak) parliamentary assembly established in 1994, and a new regional security framework put in place in 2006.

At the center of the regional market is Trinidad and Tobago, which is the main trading partner for the other countries and is particularly important to the smaller Eastern Caribbean states (see Table 6.1). It is also the main beneficiary of integration, exporting about $2.4 billion within the region in 2006, well above second-level exporters like Barbados ($126 million) and Guyana ($123.6 million), respectively.

Although I focus in this chapter on CARICOM, it should be noted that within the larger organization, the eastern Caribbean islands—Antigua and Barbuda, Dominica, Grenada, Montserrat (an overseas territory in the United Kingdom), St. Lucia, St. Vincent, and St. Kitts and Nevis—are members of a tightly knit subgroup called the Organization of Eastern Caribbean States (OECS). The OECS was formed in 1981 among states with a strong history of functional cooperation, a common currency, and success in forming their own common market. However, given their small size, the OECS states have had limited capacity to act.

CARICOM also maintains relationships with the Hispanic Caribbean and circum-Caribbean. The Dominican Republic has been an observer in CARICOM since 1982, and Venezuela, Colombia, and Mexico (along with Puerto Rico) were accepted as observers in 1990. Venezuela and Colombia deepened their ties by signing one-way free trade agreements with CARICOM in 1993 and 1994, respectively; the Dominican Republic did so in 1998, and Costa Rica in 2003. In 1993, an exploratory Cuba-CARICOM commission was established, followed by negotiation of a free trade agreement in 2000 and an investment agreement the following year. CARICOM also committed to negotiating similar arrangements with the Andean Community and with the Common Market of the South (Mercosur).[21]

In addition to these arrangements, CARICOM nations have paid particular attention to formalizing linkages with the Central American Integration System (SICA), and it was their initiative that led to the creation of the Association of Caribbean States (ACS) in 1994. The ACS includes Central American and Caribbean states and territories, as well as Colombia, Mexico, and Venezuela. The ACS's mandate is to serve as a forum for consultation and cooperation on trade promotion and related issues, and eventually contribute to the integration process. However, some members have given priority to CARICOM and SICA, and few countries have been willing to lend the ACS the support that it needs to flourish.

Some Caribbean states, most notably the Dominican Republic, Trinidad and Tobago, and Jamaica, for example, have taken a proactive stance toward the US-supported Free Trade Area of the Americas. However, negotiations begun in 1994 stalled in the late 1990s as some Latin American countries, in particular the members of Mercosur, turned instead to strengthening their own integration processes. Moreover, the small states of the eastern Caribbean were already skeptical of hemispheric free trade and called (with limited success) for special measures to allow small states to integrate gradually.

The strengthening of CARICOM relations with Latin America has come in the context of the urgent need for diversification of trade in light of the high priority given to global free trade (though it should be noted that global free trade talks stalled in 2003 and the global recession of 2008 has raised questions about the dynamics of a free market system). Caribbean nations have therefore tried to strengthen trade ties outside the Americas. A number of countries, particularly Cuba, the Dominican Republic, Jamaica, and the Bahamas, have turned to Japan as a major source of imports, a growing export market, and a source of investment and tourism revenue. Some countries have developed links with Southeast Asian countries such as Singapore, Malaysia, and Indonesia. Perhaps most important, over the past several years China has become a major player in the region, ranking just behind Japan in exports to CARICOM states. Moreover, China has been providing generous aid to some countries, as it searches for raw materials and seeks to offset Taiwan's influence in the region. Some smaller eastern Caribbean countries, as well as Haiti and the Dominican Republic, have maintained relations with Taiwan, but China's efforts have been so successful that most have switched their allegiance to the mainland in the 2000s.[22]

■ Challenges for the Future

The Caribbean states face a number of notable challenges in their international relations in the coming decades. The major challenge is how to survive and grow in a global economic environment that is relatively inhospitable to small, dependent economies that must compete with larger, more self-sustaining (though interdependent) economies.

CARICOM countries took a long time to embrace liberalization and have continued to rely, perhaps excessively, on the promise of regional and "global South" bargaining. But by 2008, they had recognized the urgent need to diversify their economies, find additional trade partners, and develop new sources of assistance. As Dennis Conway shows in Chapter 12, the large Caribbean diasporas located in North America and Western Europe are increasingly seen as sources of economic assistance. For many countries, remittances from abroad are very significant and are rising in importance. For example, in 2006 remittances accounted for 31.2 percent of Grenada's gross domestic product, 26.4 of St. Vincent's, 21.1 percent of Haiti's, 18.5 percent of St. Kitts and Nevis's, and 18.3 percent of Jamaica's.[23]

Also, securing stable energy supplies through various regional and extraregional arrangements, as well as the development and sourcing of alternative energy, are crucial needs for the region in an era of high energy prices. Currently, ethanol and solar power appear to be the favored targets for Caribbean development.

The economic challenges are even more complex for Cuba. When leadership passed from the ailing Fidel Castro to his brother Raúl in 2006, there appeared to be a shift in focus. Economic reforms have moved forward, including the passage of new rules allowing market pricing for agricultural production and permitting Cubans to purchase previously prohibited high-tech products. In addition, Cuba has maintained a productive energy partnership with Venezuela that dates back to the 1980s but has been strengthened considerably in the 2000s. However, given the lack of competitiveness of its economy and limited prospects for expanded trade, Cuba faces particular challenges. Specifically, without substantive political and human rights reform, Cuba has not been able to enjoy competitive access to the United States and many northern markets. However, the election of Barack Obama as US president could have an impact on US-Cuban economic relations.

Another major contemporary challenge for the region is how best to meet the diverse transnational threats facing small states. There is broad recognition of the need for sustainable environmental development, which includes the enactment of measures to preserve biodiversity, prevent deforestation, deal with land and marine pollution, and prevent flooding and other man-made disasters. Another important consideration is the institution of more responsible tourism development (including responsible eco-tourism), better management systems and regulations to reduce the impact of natural disasters, and international collaboration to anticipate and address future environmental problems such as the rise in sea levels and the depletion of the ozone layer. These issues are discussed in greater detail by Dennis Pantin and Marlene Attzs in Chapter 5 and by Duncan McGregor in Chapter 7.

Caribbean nations have been in the forefront of the effort to bring global attention to the special environmental needs of small island developing nations. They are founding members of the Alliance for Small Island Developing States, an advocacy group that has participated actively in relevant UN-sponsored talks on environmental issues.

Given their small size and limited resources, Caribbean states have to strengthen regional collaboration as well as harness international support to help meet transnational security challenges such as narcotrafficking, piracy, and environmental degradation, among others. They must at the same time deal effectively with the anxieties of their bilateral and multilateral partners. CARICOM has a particular responsibility to assist Haiti in achieving its basic goals of political and economic stability by helping the country to prepare for participation in the regional democratic community and single market.

Finally, CARICOM itself faces the challenge of consolidating its integration arrangements. Progress toward an integrated Caribbean economy has been notably slow, with the date of adoption now pushed to 2015. Even functional cooperation is lagging, especially in the area of regional transportation. Adherence to the Court of Justice is still partial, and leaders do not agree on institutional measures to give the body more supranational powers. Not surprisingly, various proposals for political union, both within the OECS and parts of CARICOM, have failed to garner widespread support.

Throughout its history, the Caribbean has been profoundly influenced by the world's major powers. During the protracted colonial period and through the independence and Cold War eras to the present day, the region has been buffeted by powerful economic and political forces beyond its control. However, the region's historical strategic and economic significance has given way to potential marginalization in world affairs. At the same time, it has grown increasingly vulnerable to ecological, economic, and other transnational threats. Ultimately, proactive leadership and skilled diplomacy will be needed in order to develop an appropriate mix of bilateral, expanded regional, and global collaborative strategies to effectively address these challenges.

▓ Notes

1. In terms of population, the traditional measure of a state's size, China and India are outliers with more than 1 billion people, and some 147 nations and territories of the 201 listed by the World Bank have populations at or below 15 million. See World Bank 2008, Tables 1 and 6. Available at http://go.worldbank.org/2IL9T6CGO0.

2. The members of CARICOM are Antigua and Barbuda, the Bahamas, Barbados, Belize, Dominica, Grenada, Guyana, Haiti, Jamaica, Montserrat (not independent), St. Lucia, St. Kitts and Nevis, St. Vincent and the Grenadines, Suriname, and Trinidad and Tobago. Haiti was suspended from CARICOM in 2004 but readmitted in 2006.

3. For a succinct overview of constructivism, see Reus-Smit (2005:188–212).

4. For a good discussion of Haitian treatment in Dominican *bateyes* (sugar compounds), see Martínez (1995).

5. On *cubanidad* see, for example, two books by Antoni Kapcia (2000, 2005).

6. According to Richardson (1989: 210–212), some 50,000 Jamaicans migrated to Cuba in 1919–1920 to work in the sugar fields, Smaller numbers came from Barbados and the Leeward Islands.

7. See Braveboy-Wagner (1984) for details regarding Venezuela's claim.

8. For an excellent discussion of the implications of "smallness" for Caribbean states, see Dennis Conway (1998).

9. This is an argument made by neoliberal institutionalists in support of international organizations and regimes. See, for example, Keohane (1984).

10. One example of the effectiveness of the Alliance for Small Island Developing States has been in addressing issues of sustainable development, such as global climate change. Details of CARICOM's international organizational behavior can be found in Braveboy-Wagner (2007:140–166).

11. Mahan had a strong influence on US strategy. See Mahan (1918).

12. The occupation of the Essequibo by gold prospectors provides one of the bases for Guyana's claim to ownership. See Braveboy-Wagner (1984).

13. For details on the region's strategic linkages in the military arena, see Braveboy-Wagner (2007:89–106).

14. For more on Carter's policies, see Erisman (1985:91–94) and Pastor (1992: 42–64).

15. Venezuela was a member of the Contadora Group, which mediated the Central American conflicts in the 1980s. The other members were Colombia, Panama, and Mexico. Venezuela has also been a member of the group of friends (with the United States, Canada, and France) that have mediated conflict in Haiti in the 1990s.

16. For more detailed information on foreign economic relations, see Braveboy-Wagner (2007:55–87, 106–125).

17. For a history of the banana industry in the Caribbean, see Clegg (2002).

18. For information on OECD operations in this regard, see http://www.fatf-gafi .org, the website of the Financial Action Task Force.

19. For more on this composite vulnerability index, see Atkins, Mazzi, and Easter (2000).

20. The Economic Partnership Agreement has been criticized by some scholars as well as policymakers on various grounds, including the harm the most-favored nation provision can do to third-party negotiations, the lack of adequate protection for uncompetitive sectors, and the possible adverse impact on CARICOM cooperation. Guyana and Haiti had not yet agreed to sign it as of September 2008.

21. Mercosur was established in 1991 by Argentina, Brazil, Paraguay, and Uruguay. Venezuela was later admitted as a full member. Associate member status has been granted to Bolivia, Chile, Colombia, Ecuador, and Peru.

22. Countries switching to China in the 1990s and 2000s were the Bahamas, Dominica, Grenada, and St. Kitts and Nevis. St. Lucia switched from Beijing to Taiwan.

23. In volume, the Dominican Republic had the highest total ($2.7 billion), with Jamaica at $1.9 billion and Haiti $1 billion. See International Fund for Agricultural Development (2008), http://www.ifad.org/events/remittances/maps/latin.htm.

▓ Bibliography

Atkins, G. Pope. *Latin America and the Caribbean in the International System.* Boulder, CO: Westview, 1999.

Atkins, Jonathan R., Sonia Mazzi, and Christopher D. Easter. *A Commonwealth Vulnerability Index for Developing Countries: The Position of Small States.* London: Commonwealth Secretariat, 2000.

Blight, James G., and Philip Brenner. *Sad and Luminous Days: Cuba's Struggle with the Superpowers After the Missile Crisis.* Lanham, MD: Rowman and Littlefield, 2002.

Braveboy-Wagner, Jacqueline Anne. *The Venezuela-Guyana Border Dispute: Britain's Colonial Legacy in the Caribbean.* Boulder, CO: Westview, 1984.

————. *Small States in Global Affairs: The Foreign Policies of the Caribbean Community (CARICOM).* New York: Palgrave Macmillan, 2007.

————. "The Diplomacy of Caribbean Community States: Searching for Resilience." Paper presented at Workshop on the Diplomacy of Small States, sponsored by the Center for International Global Governance, Waterloo, Canada, and the Institute of International Relations, University of the West Indies, February 19–22, 2008.

Clegg, Peter. *The Caribbean Banana Trade: From Colonialism to Globalization.* New York: Palgrave Macmillan, 2002.

Conway, Dennis. "Microstates in a Macroworld." In *Globalization and Neoliberalism: The Caribbean Context,* edited by Thomas Klak, pp. 51–63. Lanham, MD: Rowman and Littlefield, 1998.

de la Garza, Rodolfo O., and Harry Pachon, eds. *Latinos and US Foreign Policy: Representing the "Homeland"?* Lanham, MD: Rowman and Littlefield, 2000.

Desch, Michael C., Jorge I. Domínguez, and Andrés Serbín. eds. *From Pirates to Drug Lords.* Albany: State University of New York Press, 1998.

Dupuy, Alex. *Haiti in the New World Order: The Limits of the Democratic Revolution.* Boulder, CO: Westview, 1997.

Erisman, H. Michael. *Cuba's International Relations: The Anatomy of a Nationalistic Foreign Policy.* Boulder, CO: Westview, 1985.

————. "International Relations." In *Understanding the Contemporary Caribbean,* edited by Richard S. Hillman and Thomas J. D'Agostino, pp. 149–177. Boulder, CO: Lynne Rienner, 2003.

Erisman, H. Michael, and J. M. Kirk. eds. *Redefining Cuban Foreign Policy: The Impact of the "Special Period."* Gainesville: University Press of Florida, 2006.

Gregory, Steven. *The Devil Behind the Mirror: Globalization and Politics in the Dominican Republic.* Berkeley: University of California Press, 2006.

Griffith, Ivelaw L., ed. *Caribbean Security in the Age of Terror.* Kingston, Jamaica: Ian Randle, 2004.

Hall, Kenneth O., and Denis Benn, eds. *Caribbean Imperatives: Regional Governance and Integrated Development.* Kingston, Jamaica: Ian Randle, 2005.

Hillman, Richard S., and Thomas J. D'Agostino. *Distant Neighbors in the Caribbean: The Dominican Republic and Jamaica in Comparative Perspective.* New York: Praeger, 1992.

International Fund for Agricultural Development. Rural Poverty Portal, World Remittances Forum, April 1, 2008. http://www.ifad.org/events/remittances/maps/latin.htm.

Kapcia, Antoni. *Cuba: Island of Dreams.* Oxford: Berg, 2000.

————. *Havana: The Making of Cuban Culture.* Oxford: Berg, 2005.

Keohane, Robert O. *After Hegemony: Cooperation and Discord in the World Political Economy.* Princeton, NJ: Princeton University Press, 1984.

Mahan, Alfred Thayer. *The Interest of America in Sea Power, Present and Future.* Boston: Little, Brown, 1918.

Martínez, Samuel. *Peripheral Migrants: Haitians and Dominican Republic Sugar Plantations.* Knoxville: University of Tennessee Press, 1995.

Pastor, Robert A. *Whirlpool: US Foreign Policy Toward Latin America and the Caribbean.* Princeton, NJ: Princeton University Press, 1992.

Plummer, Brenda Gayle. *Haiti and the Great Powers, 1902–1915.* Baton Rouge: Louisiana State University Press, 1988.

Reus-Smit, Christian. "Constructivism." In *Theories of International Relations,* edited by Scott Burchill, Andrew Linklater, Richard Devetak, Jack Donnelly, Mattthew Paterson, Christian Reus-Smit, and Jacquie True, pp. 188–212. 3rd ed. New York: Palgrave Macmillan, 2005.

Richardson, C. Bonham. "Caribbean Migrations, 1838–1985." In *The Modern Caribbean,* edited by Franklin Knight and Colin Palmer, pp. 203–228. Chapel Hill: University of North Carolina Press, 1989.

Serbin, Andrés. *Sunset over the Islands: The Caribbean in an Age of Global and Regional Challenges.* London: Macmillan, 1998.

Sutton, Paul. *Europe and the Caribbean.* London: Macmillan, 1990.

Tulchin, Joseph S., and Ralph H. Espach, eds. *Security in the Caribbean Basin: The Challenge of Regional Cooperation.* Boulder, CO: Lynne Rienner, 2000.

Tulchin, Joseph S., Andrés Serbín, and Rafael Hernández, eds. *Cuba and the Caribbean: Regional Issues and Trends in the Post–Cold War Era.* Latin American Program at the Woodrow Wilson International Center for Scholars. Wilmington, DE: Scholarly Resources, 1997.

US Department of State. "Caribbean Basin Initiative Speech: President Reagan's Address to the Organization of American States." *Department of State Bulletin,* Washington, DC, March 1982.

White House, Office of the Press Secretary. *Fact Sheet Caribbean: Third Border Initiative.* Washington, DC, April 21, 2001.

Williams, Gary. *US-Grenada Relations: Revolution and Intervention in the Backyard.* London: Palgrave Macmillan, 2007.

World Bank. *World Development Report: Agriculture for Development.* Washington, DC: World Bank, 2008.

7

The Environment and Ecology

Duncan McGregor

M any have argued that the Caribbean environment has been, and is being, altered at a pace that is resulting in significant environmental degradation (Watts 1987; Paskett and Philoctete 1990; McElroy, Potter, and Towle 1990; Richardson 1992; McGregor 1995; Eyre 1998, GEO-LAC 2003; Potter et al. 2004; Baver and Lynch 2006). This degradation occurs in three major areas. Widespread *ecological degradation* has occurred through the depletion of both flora and fauna. *Soil degradation* is exemplified by the removal of topsoil by erosion as well as pollution of the land by agrochemicals and a range of human and industrial wastes. *Marine degradation* is most clearly seen in reef degradation, though a general depletion of marine life through overfishing and pollution has been a fact of Caribbean life for decades.

As Dennis Pantin and Marlene Attzs show in Chapter 5, economic development in most, if not all, of the Caribbean has been achieved in three ways: agriculture, extractive industry, and tourism (with industry and tourism leading to ever-increasing urbanization, particularly in the coastal zone). Each of these has had, and continues to have, a significant effect on the environment. The longest acting driver is agriculture, and in this respect environmental degradation has been a fact of Caribbean life for centuries. Regionwide increases in soil erosion associated with the conversion of natural forest to plantation agriculture have been documented (Watts 1987; Richardson 1992). It has also been argued that historically entrenched land use patterns virtually ensured that soil erosion and land degradation would continue to be a problem after emancipation, once rural population pressures built up in agriculturally marginal hillside farming regions (Barker 1989).

Today, environmental degradation and loss of topsoil is ubiquitous through-out the Caribbean and is at critical levels in Haiti in particular (Watts 1995; McClintock 2003). It has continued apace despite numerous attempts at water-shed rehabilitation (see, e.g., Paskett and Philoctete 1990; McGregor and Barker 1991; McGregor 1995; Edwards 1998; McClintock 2003). Watershed defor-estation leads to increased levels of soil erosion as well as to deteriorating water supplies; negative impacts on stream, estuarine, and marine plant and animal life; and the reduction of reservoir capacity. Again, the interdependence of nat-ural and human systems is apparent, and a holistic perspective is critical to in-forming the discussion of environmental degradation.

The roots of environmental degradation can be found in the history of the plantation economies and the colonial legacy (Watts 1987; Richardson 1992; Potter 2000; Potter et al. 2004). However, the colonial legacy is more than en-vironmental degradation and economic dependency on the exploitation of nat-ural resources; it is also about the greater ability of national governments to control interactions between humans and their environment (Bryant and Bai-ley 1997). A common manifestation is exploitation at the expense of the envi-ronment (e.g., Jamaica's bauxite industry and the effects of tourism; see France and Wheeller 1995; Pattullo 1996). Such exploitation is most often driven by global economic forces, which are largely controlled by national governments or by individuals and groups who have the opportunity to influence government thinking. The outcome for local people and their environment is frequently dis-advantageous. The agriculture industry will serve as an example.

Much of Caribbean agriculture suffers from entrenched *structural dualism,* defined in this context as a situation whereby a large-scale commercial sector uses the best land for produce destined for the export market and a small-scale traditional sector produces mainly for the local market, often relying on mar-ginal land such as steeply sloping hillsides (Barker 1993).

A second major constraint on agriculture is the periodic disruption caused by natural hazards, such as hurricanes, floods, storm surges, and landslides, as well as hazards exacerbated by human activity, such as accelerated soil ero-sion. Additionally, the economic vulnerability characteristic of small states is linked to this hazardous nature and arises from a number of underlying causes, principally the limited supply of quality agricultural land, the high population densities of many Caribbean islands, limited aquifer (groundwater) storage of water, and small catchments with rapid transfer of the effects of environmen-tal damage (Brookfield 1990; McElroy, Potter, and Towle 1990; Barker 1993; Potter 2000). For example, soil eroded from cultivated upland slopes in small islands such as Dominica and St. Lucia is rapidly incorporated into the hillside streams, with their relatively steep gradients and rapid flows, and is rapidly trans-ported by these streams through the catchments and out into the near-shore sea zone.

◼ The Physical Setting

Although Thomas Boswell discusses the geographic setting of the Caribbean in Chapter 2, I begin with a brief explanation of the nature of the environment and of recent environmental change in order to understand fully the pressures that shape human behavior in the contemporary Caribbean.

Geologically, the islands of the Caribbean may be divided into four main groups. The Bahamas consists of more than 700 islands, most of which are composed of limestone and many of which are uninhabited. The four largest islands in the Caribbean—Cuba, Hispaniola, Puerto Rico, and Jamaica—form the Greater Antilles and owe their origins to tectonic activity at the interface between the North American Plate and the northward- and eastward-moving Caribbean Plate, most notably during the late Miocene and Pliocene geological periods, between about 10 million and 4 million years ago (Draper et al. 1994; Potter et al. 2004:6–14).

The Lesser Antilles comprise two parallel chains of islands: an inner arc built around volcanic cones or cone groups (such as Montserrat, Dominica, St. Lucia, and St. Vincent), and a discontinuous outer arc of islands of coral limestone (Anguilla, Barbuda, Antigua, Grande Terre, and Barbados). These islands have been constructed from mid-Eocene times (about 45 million years ago) along the arc-shaped eastern edge of the Caribbean Plate. A number of the volcanic cones are still intermittently active, as witnessed most dramatically by the eruptions of the Soufrière Hills volcano (1995 to as recent as 2003) in Montserrat; many islands experience intermittent earthquake activity.

A fourth group of islands close to the South American mainland, including Trinidad and Tobago, although geologically varied, owe their current form and position to Andean folding and faulting, predominantly of Miocene age.

The region is characterized by northeasterly trade winds and relatively high temperature regimes with little seasonal variation. Rainfall is generally highest in the summer months, and a drier period is commonly present between December and April. Orographic rainfall is important, in which rain-bearing clouds are forced to rise upon encountering mountain ranges, causing the air to cool and precipitate its moisture as rain on the northeasterly-facing mountain slopes. "Rain-shadow" effects are common on the larger islands or those such as Dominica, which are dominated by mountain terrain, where relatively little rain remains to fall in the southwest-facing side of the mountains. For example, the eastern slopes of the Jamaican Blue Mountains have up to 197 inches of rainfall in the average year, but that drops to 31.52 inches in Kingston, only a short distance to the leeward side of the Blue Mountains peaks.

Tropical storms and hurricanes are regular features of Caribbean life, with most heavy storms being experienced during August and September. They are born in the warm waters of the western Atlantic or the Caribbean Sea, in areas

where sea temperatures exceed the critical threshold of 26 degrees Celsius required to provide the heat energy for their development. Although varied and
unpredictable, most hurricanes track from east to west across the Caribbean
before frequently moving to a more northerly track as they approach the
Lesser Antilles or the North American or Central American mainlands.

In this area of relatively abundant rainfall and equable tropical temperatures, natural vegetation consists mainly of tropical and seasonal rainforest, except in rain-shadow areas, where drier forms of seasonal rainforest are found
(Table 7.1). Cactus-thorn forest-scrub communities are found on the dry coastal
fringes of many islands, more extensively in the Bahamas and other well-drained
limestone areas. Significant vegetation community types include lowland savanna grasslands, freshwater and saltwater swamp vegetation, mountain forest
formations, and coastal fringe formations such as mangrove communities.
Lowland savanna grasslands (which formerly covered about one-third of Cuba),
have long been exploited for agriculture, including extensive conversion to plantation monoculture. Also, mangrove communities were formerly much more
widespread, forming an important buffer to coastal erosion by waves and storm

Table 7.1 Lowland Vegetation Formations in the Caribbean

Vegetation Type	Tropical Rainforest	Seasonal Rainforest	Seasonal Rainforest (dry)	Cactus-thorn Forest-scrub
Annual precipitation (inches)	78.74	49.21–78.74	29.53–49.21	19.69–29.53
Number of dry months	0–2	3–5	6–7	8–10
Predominant soils	Ferralitic[a] latosols and podsols	Relatively rich organic; some concretions near surface	Relatively rich organic; some concretions near surface	Young, often closely related to bedrock
Nutrient cycling	Rapid; storage in vegetation	Slower; litter accumulation, some storage in soil as well as vegetation	Slower; litter accumulation, some storage in soil as well as vegetation	Slow

Source: Adapted from D. Watts, *The West Indies: Patterns of Development, Culture, and Environmental Change Since 1492* (Cambridge, UK: Cambridge University Press, 1987), p. 28.
   Note: a. These are iron-rich soils, formed by the relative accumulation of iron through the gradual loss by leaching of other minerals.

surges and acting as a trap of material eroded from cleared land and natural erosion.

High natural rates of chemical weathering are another result of the combination of high temperatures and rainfall. The soils that are produced are deeply weathered, heavily leached, and highly susceptible to erosion. On steeper slopes in particular, attempts at permanent forms of agriculture inevitably lead to accelerated soil erosion and thin soils of relatively low chemical fertility (see, e.g., Paskett and Philoctete 1990; McGregor 1988, 1995). Younger volcanic soils and soils developed on low-lying coral limestone may, in contrast, be very fertile, and these soils have formed a long-term basis of successful agriculture where carefully husbanded (Watts 1987). Examples of fertile volcanic soils included those of Montserrat before its recent volcanic eruptions; sugarcane plantations have thrived for centuries on limestone soils such as those of Barbados.

The Caribbean islands have in the past supported a rich range of flora and fauna, with the distribution of plant species varying according to rainfall regime and altitude. Seasonal rainforest is the natural vegetation cover of most lowland areas of the West Indies below 660 feet in elevation, and it has been the principal focus of clearance. Precipitation increases with altitude in many locations, and with human clearance of natural vegetation for plantations, as well as other forms of agriculture, seasonal rainforest is frequently succeeded upslope by tropical rainforest.

Most remnants of Caribbean rainforest fall into the precipitation regime envelope depicted in Figure 7.1. Significant variation can be seen within this envelope, which affects the ability of the rainforest to recover from disturbance. Whereas most Caribbean island areas are small in size and many subareas exhibit a high degree of specialized plant habitat adaptation (e.g., Cockpit Country, Jamaica), the potential for species extinction is high.

The same may be said of Caribbean fauna. The island situation limits the number of land-mammal fauna compared with adjacent South America. Reptile fauna and native birds are relatively diverse, reflecting easier migration from island to island, but endemism is relatively high. Only Trinidad, closest to the continental area, has a large range of species. For example, as Robert Potter and his colleagues note, "400 species of birds have been recorded in Trinidad compared with 250 in Jamaica, even though Trinidad is a smaller island. Yet Jamaica has 30 endemic bird species compared with only one endemic bird in Trinidad" (2004: 30).

Near-shore sea margins have in the past supported an immensely varied wildlife system, with large populations of fish, shellfish, and amphibians. A notable consequence of the relatively warm seas that have characterized the Caribbean over at least the last 10,000 years has been the growth and nourishment of coral reef communities. Reef coral is still actively forming in some areas, but in many more the vitality of the coral has been progressively reduced

Figure 7.1 Caribbean Tropical Rainforest Regime

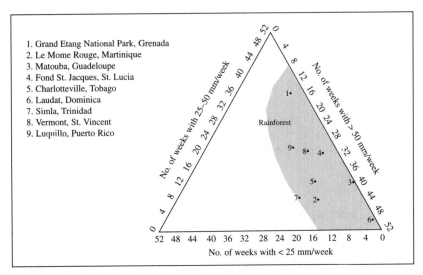

1. Grand Etang National Park, Grenada
2. Le Mome Rouge, Martinique
3. Matouba, Guadeloupe
4. Fond St. Jacques, St. Lucia
5. Charlotteville, Tobago
6. Laudat, Dominica
7. Simla, Trinidad
8. Vermont, St. Vincent
9. Luquillo, Puerto Rico

Source: Adapted from L. A. Eyre, "The Tropical Rainforest of the Eastern Caribbean: Present Status and Conservation," *Caribbean Geography* 9, no. 20 (1998): 101–120.

by damaging effects. Dead or severely damaged reefs are unfortunately no longer remarkable in the region, as a tourist submarine excursion around Montego Bay on Jamaica's northern coast will readily testify. As a result, the coastal zone suffers more from the effects of storm surges associated with hurricanes and tropical storms.

The most radical terrestrial influence on environmental change in the Caribbean over the past three and a half centuries has been the progressive destruction of natural vegetation (Watts 1987; Richardson 1992; Potter et al. 2004). Haiti is the worst example, now reported as being less than 1 percent forested (Wilson, Brothers, and Marcano 2000). Progressive deforestation, although primarily affecting the terrestrial environment, has led directly to the increased discharge of eroded soil particles into the coastal and near-shore zones, with an attendant reduction in the vitality of coastal vegetation and reef communities.

More recently, human activities relating to increasing urbanization and tourism have focused primarily on the coastal zone (Potter et al. 2004). Throughout the insular Caribbean, significant degradation of this zone has been the result (see discussion below).

For the foreseeable future for the Caribbean region, the Intergovernmental Panel on Climate Change Fourth Assessment Report forecasts, on the basis of improved global climate models, regional precipitation decreases and increased seasonality, with regional rises in temperatures (Christensen et al. 2007; Mimura et al. 2007). Those changes will affect terrestrial and marine ecosystems that have already been weakened by human action. In many ways, the resulting loss of soil and/or marine productivity will directly affect the livelihoods of farmers and fishermen alike, which in turn will lead to greater pressure, through rural-urban migration, on the social systems of regional towns and cities in the coming decades.

These negative influences on the Caribbean island environment will be discussed in detail in this chapter.

▓ Historical and Recent Land Use Change

The introduction of sugarcane to Barbados in about 1640 triggered the large-scale clearance of native vegetation, and by 1665 only isolated pockets of forest remained in Barbados (Watts 1987). A similar process was under way on lowlands throughout the islands, fueled progressively by imported slave labor. Reports of accelerated soil erosion followed almost immediately (Richardson 1992). Native plant species were replaced to some extent by imported species such as breadfruit. Emancipation of the slaves in the 1830s and 1840s exacerbated environmental deterioration in many cases. In Jamaica, for example, the freed slaves were forced to more marginal ground, often steeply sloping hillsides, where they persisted with the deleterious practices of fire clearance and clean weeding that caused erosion (Barker and McGregor 1988). The combination of preoccupation with cash crops on the best land, the intensification of domestic food production on more marginal land, and increasing population pressures brought many small-farmer systems throughout the Caribbean to the point of collapse. Inevitably, a drift away from agriculture has led to increasing urbanization, particularly in the western Caribbean. Enlightened colonial land management practices and land reform structures have helped promote environmental conservation to an extent in the eastern Caribbean (Mills 2006).

Hillside agriculture and urban growth are linked by the increasing pressures on land as well as by increasing throughputs of mass and energy. In the case of hillside agriculture, this is seen in the growing transfer of sediment through terrestrial runoff from the slope to the near-shore zone, something that is likely to continue for some time. In the urban zone, pressures on space and amenities are increasing urban hazards, such as flooding, slope failure, traffic congestion, and health risks such as local outbreaks of cholera and typhoid caused by the contamination of domestic water supplies.

Clearly, the ability to tackle these problems has to do partly with economics—the cost-benefit equation of whether it is more expeditious to attempt to solve the problem or to live with it. In this context, it is becoming increasingly apparent that attitudes toward land and the environment determine whether

The sign announces this area as a Green Area Restoration Project,
Santo Domingo, Dominican Republic.

environmental problems are perceived as such. In turn, such perceptions will influence whether problems are addressed and, if so, how they will be addressed.

As for agricultural land, some general points can be made as to how Caribbean peoples perceive the land. First, there is a fundamental paradox, which is perhaps Caribbean-wide, in people's perceptions of "family land" (Besson 1987). On the one hand, family land is seen as scarce in relation to the dominant plantation sector, partly because slaves did not receive enough land to support themselves and their families during the transition from slavery (Besson 1987). The effect on an individual piece of land is often overuse. On the other hand, land is seen as an unlimited resource in light of the long-term role of land held by the family for absent kinsfolk. That attitude often manifests in voluntary nonuse of parcels in recognition of the rights of absent family members. Such idle land, widespread in some areas of Jamaica, leads to underproduction. This perception of land, partly a protection for kinsfolk, may well maintain some land in a relatively undegraded condition in more traditional rural areas. The net effect, however, is more pressure on the land that is in regular use.

According to Bonham Richardson (1992:188), "The control of land signifies freedom and provides a partial buffer against external economic oscillation." This suggests that within the region, land is primarily seen as an economic asset. However, there seems now to be a clear disjunction between agricultural land use (seen as traditional and unattractive) and the urban-centered tourist industry (seen as a more attractive economic proposition). The social implications include a drift toward an aging agricultural labor force as younger people migrate to the cities, as well as increased crime and prostitution in the cities as young people seek urban employment and housing.

Although these perceptions focus only on one aspect of a complex social process, such views of the value of land, if extrapolated to the wider Caribbean, imply the continuation of rural-urban drift. They suggest the aging agricultural labor force will have to cope with an increasingly hostile environment, and pressures on the already stretched urban areas will increase. In addition, the continuing development of tourist-based activities will likely lead to the further diminution of indigenous and agricultural activities.

The Human Impact: Deforestation and the Environment

Demand for land has led to historically high rates of deforestation throughout the Caribbean (Lugo and Brown 1981; Watts 1987). Ongoing and allegedly unsustainable rates of deforestation (e.g., an estimated rate of 3.3 percent per annum for Jamaica) were subsequently revised upward to 5.3 percent per annum (Eyre 1987, 1996).

Estimates of deforestation rates on thirteen islands in the eastern Caribbean from Puerto Rico to Trinidad, though varying enormously, indicate an annual deforestation rate of around 1.5 percent (Eyre 1998). Although it may not seem high compared to Jamaican deforestation, at present only 30 percent of the area capable of supporting rainforest is not under cultivation or some other form of development (Eyre 1998; see Table 7.2). This represents deforestation of some 70 percent (compared to the 1996 calculation of 67 percent of Jamaica's former forest cover lost).

It should be noted, however, that much of the speculation on rates of Caribbean deforestation has been based on partial analysis and on data of varying

Land degradation
due to hillside farming
in Jamaica.

Table 7.2 Status of Rainforests of the Eastern Caribbean

	Area with Humid Climate (sq. kilometers)	Area in Rainforest (sq. kilometers)	Area in Rainforest (%)	Rainforest in National Parks and Adequately Protected Reserves (%)
Puerto Rico	2,896	700	24	83
Saba	15	3	20	0
St. Eustatius	5	1	20	0
St. Kitts	28	20	71	0
Nevis	55	8	15	0
Guadeloupe	1,050	196	19	98
Dominica	751	342	46	30
Martinique	898	150	17	31
St. Lucia	579	189	33	0
St. Vincent	389	67	16	0
Grenada	180	39	22	49
Tobago	145	69	48	92
Trinidad	2,986	1,194	40	68[a]
Eastern Caribbean	9,977	2,978	30	34

Source: Adapted from L. A. Eyre, "The Tropical Rainforests of the Eastern Caribbean: Present Status and Conservation," *Caribbean Geography* 9, no. 2 (1998): 101–120.
   Note: a. Categorization of "adequate" is dubious.

quality. Although large-scale deforestation has undoubtedly taken place in the past and is continuing (albeit probably at lower rates), accurate rates of contemporary Caribbean-wide deforestation have yet to be convincingly established. More recent analyses using remote-sensing imagery and more rigorous definition of land and land use categories have led in some cases to much lower estimates of ongoing deforestation. Some scholars (e.g., Evelyn and Camerand 2003) not only postulate a low deforestation rate for Jamaica between 1989 and 1998 of 0.1 percent per annum but point to Food and Agriculture Organization data that suggest a positive change in forested areas in some Caribbean islands such as Cuba and Guadeloupe (FAO 2001a, 2001b).

The Implications for Hillside Agriculture

Whatever its rate, deforestation induces accelerated erosion due to a combination of steep slopes and high-intensity rainfall events, and although crops as they grow impart a progressively better protection against raindrop impact, fields are at their barest and most vulnerable when newly planted at the start of the rainy season. Hillside farming systems throughout the Caribbean are therefore characterized by high rates of soil erosion and widespread land degradation (Watts 1987; Barker and McGregor 1988; Paskett and Philoctete 1990; McGregor and Barker 1991; McGregor 1995). For example, one study demonstrated experimentally that soil losses from an intensely cultivated St. Lucian agricultural watershed were twenty times higher than those from an adjacent forested watershed (Cox, Sarangi, and Madramootoo 2006).

Many Caribbean agricultural plots consist of small and fragmented holdings, caused by landholdings being split among the heirs when a farmer retires from the land or dies. In addition, family land may be subdivided between family members so that each can work a separate parcel. When allied with common practices such as fire clearance and clean weeding, and coupled with population pressure on resources, those practices make a recipe for land degradation. Fire clearance and clean weeding are a legacy from plantation management methods and have persisted despite many governments' efforts to ban the use of fire to clear land.

Systematic soil erosion control schemes, such as those established in Jamaica through the Land Authority projects in the period 1950–1969, and through subsequent projects, have proved to be ineffective (Edwards 1995). The principal reasons for these failures include a lack of funding; the breakdown of integrated systems of structures and waterways; the application of inappropriate control measures in inappropriate topographic locations; and the basic physical limitations of slope, soil, and climate.

Local factors also contribute to progressive deforestation, such as the cutting of poles to support yam vines. In Jamaica alone, the annual requirement is estimated to be up to 40 million new poles each year (Barker and Beckford 2003). This particular requirement is driven by farmers' perception that yams are one of the crops most suited to cultivation on steeply sloping land; perceptions undoubtedly play a part in the overall failure to manage land appropriately. To cite one example from the Blue Mountains area of Jamaica, few farmers surveyed perceived soil erosion as a problem, despite having a good understanding of the process and despite almost universal employment of soil conservation structures (McGregor and Barker 1991). Further, few perceived a direct link between soil erosion and declining yields, blaming a variety of factors from climate to the Jamaican government. Given rural poverty and the short-term planning horizons that it creates, farmers have neither the time nor the financial ability nor the perception of the problem to plan on their own for a sustainable future.

It should be noted here that in recent years there has been significant expansion of housing onto both forested and agricultural land. Trinidad provides examples of both trends, first where land in the Northern Ranges is being developed for housing, and second where land formerly under sugarcane is converted to housing (allegedly in an attempt by the ruling People's National Movement [PNM] party to curry favor among voters).

Government housing built on former
sugarcane land near San Fernando, Trinidad.

The Human Impact: Urbanization and
Ecology in the Coastal Zone

Contemporary Caribbean societies are strongly urban in character. Recent data
indicate that the Caribbean is considerably more highly urbanized than the developing world and exhibits a higher urban proportion than the world as a
whole (Potter 1995, 2000). More than 60 percent of the total population of the
Caribbean resides in urban settlements, compared to a global urbanization figure of about 50 percent (McGregor and Potter 1997). The urban population of
the Caribbean grew at around 2.4 percent per annum during the 1990s. Notice-
ably, levels of urban primacy—the phenomenon whereby more and more people are attracted to the national or regional capital city—are high, with 40–60
percent of national populations living in the capital. Further, the ongoing extension, due to the dictates of tourism and manufacturing activities, of a highly
concentrated coastal-based "plantopolis" settlement pattern is a feature that
presents a series of environmental challenges in Caribbean territories (Potter
1995, 2000). This plantopolis settlement pattern has its roots in the colonial
era, whereby present-day patterns of settlement and transportation links are inherited from the original plantation distributions of location, transportation,
and trade. Such high levels of urbanization and marked urban primacy are associated with urban housing and urban infrastructure problems. For example,
in Jamaica more than 50 percent of the total population is now classed as

urban, approximately half of which live in the Kingston metropolitan area alone. Growth rates in the decade 1982–1991 peaked at 2.3 percent per annum for Portmore, a commuter settlement near Kingston, and 1.9 percent per annum for the tourist-oriented Montego Bay (Thomas-Hope 1996). Portmore has continued to grow, almost doubling in size between the 1991 and 2001 censuses (from 90,138 to 156,467 people) (see Brinkhoff 2007). Substandard housing is a critical problem throughout the region, with inadequate sanitation and water supply, urban transportation, and waste disposal among the associated effects.

The Environmental Impact of Urban Development

The effects of urban development on the Caribbean environment are wide-ranging and widespread. They range from the effects of building in the coastal zone to the destruction of wetlands and the degradation of marine environments (see Table 7.3). In particular, the expansion of tourism throughout the region has exacerbated many of the problems of water supply, traffic congestion, and building blight, as well as increasing the impact of social problems such as prostitution and petty crime.

Table 7.3 Some Environmental Problems Facing the Caribbean Region

Problem	Possible Cause
Declining ratios of arable land per capita	Urban growth
Unequal balance between agricultural production and consumption	Decline in domestic crops
Soil erosion, infertile land, cleared forests	Past and present land use
Forest usage for energy and manufacturing	Tourism; informal industry; foreign-owned industry
Limited water availability	Tourism; industrial development
Wetland degradation	Housing; industrial development; tourist developments; pollution
Overfishing and overhunting of rare species	Export industry; informal sector
Removal of sand from beaches	Urban construction; tourist developments
Pollution (lack of control and limited infrastructure)	Overpopulation; tourist industry; irregular housing; industrial development; informal sector
Degradation of marine environments	Tourism; industrial development
Degraded urban environments	Uncontrolled urbanization; inefficient resources; lack of basic services; poverty

Source: D. F. M. McGregor and R. B. Potter, "Environmental Change and Sustainability in the Caribbean: Terrestrial Perspectives," in *Land, Sea, and Human Effort in the Caribbean,* edited by B. M. W. Ratter and W-D. Sahr, Beiträge zur Geographischen Regionalforschung in Latinamerika, no. 10 (Hamburg: Institut für Geographie der Universtat Hamburg, 1997), pp. 1–15.

Increasingly, urban systems in the Caribbean cannot cope with the effects of runoff, sediment, and waste. The urban area presents a more or less sealed surface, particularly because sediment and urban waste choke parts of the urban drainage system. Already, significant areas of Kingston, Jamaica, flood during storms, and the roads often become a temporary stream network with concomitant disruption of traffic. This problem is often at its most acute in squatter settlements, where drainage infrastructure is lacking. For example, the Four-a-Chaud area of Castries, St. Lucia, a squatter area constructed on reclaimed land adjacent to the waterfront, regularly floods during peak rainfall events.

In Jamaica, the Kingston metropolitan area and Montego Bay both illustrate the pressures of urbanization on environmentally fragile areas, including reclaimed coastal lands liable to an increasing risk of flooding under conditions of rising sea levels. Portmore, a rapidly growing coastal-zone suburb of Kingston, is particularly at risk, as some areas of urban expansion, built behind artificial barriers, are already below sea level; Portmore is situated in a tectonically active area with the associated risk of earthquake and tsunami damage. In light of the potentially increased storm-surge levels associated with the combination of more intense hurricane conditions and a progressively drowned protective coral reef, Portmore may be seen as a disaster waiting to happen.

Open sewage canal, Cité-Soleil, Haiti.

The Marine Environment: Reefs and Near-Shore Fisheries

The southerly parts of coastal East Asia and the Caribbean are the two areas of the tropics where reefs are most at risk (Bryant et al. 1998), due to a combination of circumstances, including coastal development, marine-based pollution, overexploitation, and land-based pollution and erosion. More than 60 percent of the Caribbean's reef area is at medium to high risk, with the risk being higher where onshore population concentrations are greatest (Jamaica, Haiti, much of the Lesser Antilles, and Tobago). Jamaica exhibits some of the worst degradation, with storm damage from hurricanes, reef bleaching, and unchecked algal overgrowth all adding to the range of human-related sources of pollution. The reef in Montego Bay, despite its designation as a marine park in 1966, is the most seriously degraded, a reflection of the small size and unmanaged nature of the park. The Montego Bay Marine Park was reestablished in 1990, but the reef continues to be affected by poaching, pollution from the city and airport, and runoff and sediment from inland agricultural and building activities. As a result, some economic activities (e.g., fishing and tourism) become less possible or attractive, and the potential for onshore storm damage grows.

Out of the total of 367 reef areas worldwide, the Caribbean region has 139 areas with protected-area status (totaling slightly more than 15,000 square miles), a greater regional coverage than anywhere except Australia's Great Barrier Reef (Bryant et al. 1998). There has, however, been criticism in the region of the degree to which parks (both marine and terrestrial) are in fact protected. Some critics use the phrase "paper parks," that is, areas protected by legislation but lacking enforcement.

Caribbean peoples have relied on the sea for food for centuries, but today stocks of all edible species are severely depleted. Some species, such as sea turtles, have been afforded conservation status, yet turtles are still widely available for consumption. Some ascribe reports of widespread fish kills in the region in 1998 to the effects of raised sea surface temperatures on shallow reef fish. But there are also hypotheses of waste contamination by cruise ships, pathogens transported by the Orinoco River, and even Montserrat's volcanic activity (Caribbean Environment Programme 1999). Negative media coverage of the fish kills reduced consumption and tourism, adversely affecting local fishermen.

Wetlands are a vital linkage between land and sea activities. They have often formed an integral part of local indigenous (artisanal) fisheries (e.g., see Johnson 1998's discussion of the Black River Morass in Jamaica) and are now under threat from a variety of exploitative and destructive practices. Moreover, much of the eastern Caribbean's coastal wetland areas are degraded, and in particular mangrove destruction has been significant. Of 195 sites investigated, 47 percent were seriously degraded, with the principal culprits being landfill and solid waste dumping, vegetation clearance (particularly unregulated cutting of mangrove and other species for timber or charcoal production), reclamation for agriculture, alteration of natural drainage patterns, and pollution

Fishermen from Dominica returning with a day's catch.

by factory and domestic effluents (Bacon 1995). In addition, the delicate water and sediment balances of many eastern Caribbean wetland areas have been adversely affected by changes in land use, both agricultural and urban, within their catchments. The highest percentage of degradation was shown by wetlands in Barbados (100 percent), St. Vincent (75 percent), and St. Kitts (63 percent). However, rehabilitation of wetland areas may be inexpensive and effective, usually involving replanting mangroves, strictly managing exploitation, cleaning up dumped wastes, and reestablishing natural flushing systems (Bacon 1995). Clearly, where these areas have been built upon, to fulfill the demand for housing or tourist accommodation and facilities, such solutions are more problematic.

Pollution of coastal waters is thus a significant environmental problem throughout the Caribbean. Coastal resource management has become a key focus of institutional concern, and many programs have emphasized environmental education. Involving communities in policing and managing coastal resource use offers a way forward. For example, this is illustrated in a study of three polluted coastal ecosystems in Cuba and Venezuela that shows how community perceptions of problems can provide a basis to improve better resource management structures (Gómez et al. 2006).

Tourism: Destroyer or Savior?
As for tourism, the official views of governments and tourist bodies frequently contrast with the views of environmentalists, researchers, and the media. There

is no doubt that island governments see tourism as the savior of faltering economies or that the economic benefits of tourism have been offset by environmental degradation (see Table 7.3). The sustainability of tourism has frequently been called into question (e.g., France and Wheeller 1995; Pattullo 1996; France 1998, Potter et al. 2004). The prospect of introducing forms of ecotourism, whereby sustainable environmental considerations and strict conservation requirements are central themes of development, has received similarly mixed reviews (e.g., Weaver 1994; Woodfield 1998). The "hawking of heritage," ranging from museums of colonial artifacts and accounts of the slave trade and early plantation life to displays of traditional forms of livelihoods, is seen as a commercial expediency, often of a contrived nature (Potter 2000).

The case study of the Jalousie Plantation Resort in St. Lucia, where development was permitted in an area of outstanding natural beauty and within a sacred Arawak site, is perhaps one of the more prominent of a number of controversial developments (Pattullo 1996; France 1998). This development was situated within an area (the Pitons Management Area) subsequently designated (2004) as a World Heritage Site by the United Nations Educational, Scientific, and Cultural Organization. With no local sand source, sand was imported from Guyana to form a tourist beach. Local politicians often play a role in such developments, with the implication that environmental interests are taking a back seat to personal profit (Pattullo 1996).

The problems arising from coastal tourist development are many and include beach erosion, marine and coastal pollution, reef degradation, dumping of untreated sewage and other wastes, sand mining, and the destruction of wetlands and salt ponds. The market response to a degraded environment is often swift. For example, the southern coast of Barbados, where coastal erosion and sewage pollution have been significant, has suffered declining tourist numbers in recent years, despite measures to stem erosion and the construction of a new sewage plant. Yet the environmental lessons do not seem to have been fully taken on board. In Barbados, for example, the mid-1990s development of the Royal Westmoreland estate, an up-market tourist resort, has led to increased flooding risk along its coastal fringe, partly due to the use of scarce water resources to maintain a championship golf course. Proposals for a hotel and tourist complex at Graeme Hall Swamp, the island's largest inland body of water, have been on the table for some time. The swamp forms part of a wetland RAMSAR site (a designation referring to the 1971 international Ramsar Convention on Wetlands) and includes a nature sanctuary. The debate has raged for nearly a decade now and still rouses local passions (see, for example, the *Barbados Free Press* website). A recent twist was a proposal by developers to construct a water park within the swamp.

Although the attraction of tourism is understandable, the situation in which Caribbean nations have found themselves since the early 1990s—of increasing debt, declining prices for their goods and raw materials, and the negative impact of liberalization policies on traditional markets (driven in part by the

US government)—means that the environmental price of tourism has been substantial and requires addressing.

◼ Climate Change and Caribbean Environments

The most likely future climate scenario for the Caribbean Basin projected by global climate models is one of regional precipitation decreasing by about 12 percent by the 2080s (Christensen et al. 2007:912), accompanied by a likelihood of increased seasonality and a tendency toward fewer, but more intense, rainfall events.

An increase in air temperatures, currently estimated for the Caribbean Basin to be about 2.0 degrees Celsius by the 2080s (Christensen et al. 2007: 912), would potentially lead to significant and wide-ranging changes in environmental conditions (Wigley and Santer 1993). For example, increases in sea surface and shallow water temperatures above a critical threshold of 30 degrees Celsius lead to significant increases in coral bleaching (Milliman 1993).

Coral Bleaching

Coral bleaching occurs when corals, under stress from rising sea surface temperatures, lose much of their symbiotic algae, which supply nutrients and color. The immediate environmental effect of coral bleaching is a reduction in the vitality of the coral. Severe or prolonged bleaching can lead to coral mortality. An add-on effect is the reduction of the protective effect of fringing coral reefs on Caribbean coastlines.

A significant number of incidences of coral bleaching in the Caribbean have been documented since the late 1980s (Bryant et al. 1998). A major event occurred throughout the tropics in 1998, ascribed by some to the El Niño event of 1997. In the Caribbean, the Belize reefs were the worst affected, though regionwide bleaching was reported. A further major coral bleaching event occurred in September–October 2005 throughout the basin. Scientists in Puerto Rico reported colonies representing over 40 species being totally bleached at many sites, with up to 95 percent bleaching in some areas. Surveys showed that reefs in Grenada suffered up to 70 percent bleaching (Butler 2005). Modeling of historical temperature data in the eastern Caribbean suggests that such conditions will likely become more frequent and will most likely be due to human-induced climate change (Donner, Knutson, and Oppenheimer 2007). In a warmer world, the rate at which bleaching occurs is likely to outstrip the ability of coral to colonize cooler waters.

Coral bleaching damages one of the world's most complex ecosystems, causes the loss of habitats and species, and reduces the ability of the reefs to protect the onshore land from storm surges. The critical link here is the ability of the coral reefs to grow fast enough to keep pace with the rising sea levels projected by global warming. An unhealthy reef unable to grow fast enough to keep pace with rising sea levels will become progressively drowned, and the degree of onshore protection from storm-surge waves will be reduced. It is too early to predict with any accuracy what will happen in the Caribbean Basin in this respect, but the present rate of reef degradation is clearly unsustainable.

The Potential Influence of
Climate Change on Hurricane Activity

It has long been postulated (Shapiro 1982; Emmanuel 1987) that the increases in sea surface temperatures that will follow from increased atmospheric temperatures could increase the intensity and frequency of tropical storms. A simple tabulation seems to bear this out (Table 7.4). It can be seen that the average number of tropical storms, and of those that developed into hurricanes, was much higher in the five-year period from 2000 to 2004 than in the preceding fifty-year period. That period included the relatively stormy 1930s and 1950s, but it may be further evidence of increasing storm activity that the 2005 season (Table 7.4) was the most active since the 1930s, with a modern record of twenty-seven named storms (and another that was unnamed), of which fifteen developed into hurricane strength. It is worthy of note that the 1995 season was the previously most active season since the 1930s, with nineteen tropical storms recorded, eleven of which developed into hurricanes, but this "record-breaker" was significantly exceeded in 2005. In contrast, 2006 was a relatively

Table 7.4 Incidence of Tropical Storms and Hurricanes Since the 1950s

	Tropical Storms	Hurricanes	Intense Hurricanes
Long-term average, 1950–			
1999	9.3	5.9	2.3
2000	14	8	3
2001	15	9	4
2002	12	4	2
2003	17	8	3
2004	14	9	6
Average, 2000–			
2004	14.4	7.6	3.6
2005	28	15	4
2006	9	5	2
2007	15	6	2

Source: Caribbean Weather Site (CARIBWX), http://www.caribwx.com/cyclone.html (accessed March 2009).

quiet season, while still reaching the long-term average, but in 2007 figures again reached those of the early 2000s.

Additionally, hurricane tracks may change due to the changing position of the weather systems associated with the Intertropical Convergence Zone (ITCZ), the zone of atmospheric turbulence where warm, moist tropical air meets cool subtropical air, in particular toward a more northerly penetration of the ITCZ. Areas such as the Leeward Islands and the Greater Antilles, which lie to the north of a major hurricane track across the Caribbean Sea, may in the next few decades become more at risk from hurricane activity (Reading and Walsh 1995).

Although perhaps the most publicized losses through hurricane activity are to life and property, losses to agriculture are significant in most years. For example, Hurricane Ivan effectively destroyed Grenada's agriculture and severely reduced agricultural production in Jamaica in 1994. Jamaica's main banana crop was virtually destroyed by Hurricane Dean (late August 2007) and again by Hurricane Gustav (late August 2008), to the extent that the island's principal banana producer is considering pulling out of banana production.

Water Supply

A continuing regional precipitation decrease will undoubtedly exacerbate existing water-supply problems throughout the region. However, the number of heavy rainfall events is currently increasing in the Caribbean, which implies that the trend is indeed toward a stormier rainy season, contrasting with a more drought-prone dry season (Mimura et al. 2007). Seasonal water deficits already exist, as witnessed by the example of the Mavis Bank area of Jamaica, an area of relatively intense hillside farming (Jamaica, Ministry of Agriculture, n.d.). This area, in common with much of the western Caribbean Basin, experiences two periods of moisture deficit annually (see Figure 7.2). Although they do not present a significant problem in a normal year, farmers' reports of drought conditions affecting the crop cycle have been more frequent in recent years. For example, early season droughts have severely affected Jamaican agriculture in 2004, 2005, and 2008.

A trend of rising temperatures and decreasing rainfall will increase the net moisture deficit, partly through increasing evaporation. In respect to the Mavis Bank example (Figure 7.2), the overall rainfall total may not change dramatically or may decrease. But the annual distribution may show lower dry season rainfalls (the period from December to April) and therefore a more pronounced summer peak, and potential evaporation (the dotted line in Figure 7.2) will rise along with increasing temperature. The net result is likely to be a long dry period of moisture deficit from December to July or even August, as well as a much shorter single growing season.

Progressive loss of vegetative cover will also exacerbate this trend. A further factor in increasing evaporation rates is the projected increase of wind

Figure 7.2 Seasonal Water Deficits in a Jamaican Hillside Context (millimeters of rainfall)

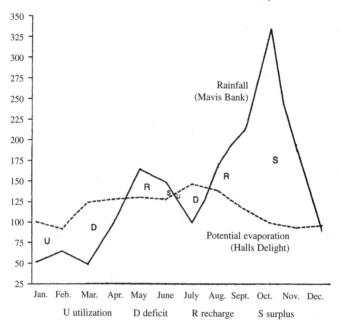

Source: Ministry of Agriculture, Jamaica, *Mavis Bank: Agricultural Development Plan* (Kingston, Jamaica: Ministry of Agriculture, undated).

speeds. In addition to increases in upper-level winds associated with intensified tropical cyclone activity, increases in surface wind speeds are consistent with projections; trends in data from Jamaica and Trinidad and Tobago support this contention (Gray 1993).

Decreasing regional rainfalls will lower average stream flows as well as the amount of water available for recharging groundwater aquifer resources. Water table levels will drop, and water supply problems will be exacerbated in urban and tourist areas. The potential for the intrusion of saline seawater into freshwater aquifers in the coastal zone will increase, particularly where overabstraction of the freshwater aquifer occurs due to urban expansion or increased demands from the tourist industry. If more freshwater is being extracted than can be replaced quickly enough by the natural flow of fresh groundwater from inland, then saltwater will seep in from the sea and contaminate the coastal groundwater supply.

Finally, a drier but stormier climate regime will lead, through increased surface runoff into stream channels, to more flash floods. This has implications not only for water supplies but also for risk scenarios associated with the urbanization of floodplain areas.

Sea-Level Rise

Sea-level rise associated with the expansion of ocean volumes and the melting of polar ice caps is a major potential threat to coastal lowlands in the Caribbean, especially critical for small island states, which have high ratios of coastal lands to interior lands. Much of the urban settlement and economic activities of island states in the Caribbean, including tourism, occur in the coastal zone.

It has been estimated the sea level has risen in the region at an average of 1 mm (0.04 inches) per year over the twentieth century, more rapidly in recent years, though considerable variation is evident throughout the basin (Hendry 1993; Mimura et al. 2007). The causes of this variation are not clear but are likely related to underlying vertical tectonic movements, which affect the land levels on which the tide gauges are located (Mimura et al. 2007). Increases in sea level will inevitably have significant effects in the coastal zone, where large urban populations and the tourist industry are concentrated throughout the Caribbean region. Flooding, especially on reclaimed coastal lands, is a particular risk. Many of the beaches upon which tourism depends are likely to suffer significant erosion as wave and tidal forces react to the increasing depth of water in the near-shore zone.

Particularly at risk of economic losses will be locations with beaches and preexisting infrastructure. Not only are they already relatively well developed, but also they are prime targets for a combination of urban- and tourism-related expansion (e.g., Ocho Rios and Montego Bay in Jamaica, St. Lawrence/Oistins in Barbados, Grand Anse in Grenada, Castries-Gros Islet in St. Lucia, and Condado Beach in San Juan, Puerto Rico).

The Implications for Food Security

A warmer climate may increase seasonality, with reduced precipitation during dry periods and possibly fewer but higher-magnitude rainfall events in wet seasons (Christensen et al. 2007; Mimura et al. 2007). Increased wind speeds are forecast, with attendant increased evaporation rates, which points to a tendency for longer periods of net moisture deficit in parts of the region. There is precedent for this: droughts have been recorded in the Caribbean Basin in the past and have caused significant crop failures leading to food shortages and "occasionally famine" (Watts 1995:6).

In addition to direct effects on crop yields and potential crop failure, the projected climatic conditions would accelerate soil erosion, particularly at the start of the wet season, through reduction of protection afforded to topsoil from the reduced biomass cover present during the intensified dry season. Thus, the climate change projection will inevitably lead to land degradation on heavily used upland farming areas unless proactive steps are taken to protect upland watersheds.

Although climate changes on the scale proposed for the Caribbean region would have relatively little direct influence on crop growth patterns "as long as pests and diseases can be kept under control," new crop pests and diseases may appear, or those already present may become worse (Watts 1995:9). Such problems might be controlled by vigilance and appropriate proactive measures. However, some crops grown successfully in the region could lose viability as the combination of reduced rainfall and increased temperatures affect germination probabilities and growth rates. In the absence of any research data, this urgently requires attention.

For tropical areas in general, temperature increases of around 1.5 degrees Celsius would, in areas already close to marginality, raise the rates of temperature-dependent evapotranspiration (moisture losses from the soil surface layers and from plant tissue) by 5–15 percent (Parry 1990). Unless local rainfall increased, such losses would reduce yields. Regional increases in rainfall are unlikely in the Caribbean region for the foreseeable future, and yield declines seem inevitable without adding extensive irrigation systems, which in turn require much more careful water planning than is generally the case in the Caribbean at present.

Traditional staple crops, particularly those such as yams that mature underground, are likely to survive the projected climate changes for the foreseeable future, though yields may decline. The more significant problem may lie with the dualism in agriculture developing throughout the basin (see Barker 1993 for a discussion of the Jamaican case). Better land is progressively given over to export monocropping, and crops grown for family consumption and the domestic market are becoming marginalized, that is, forced to less fertile or steeper lands. Although that may not in itself necessarily lead to greater risk from pests and diseases, it will almost certainly lead to greater risk in the event of more frequent drought conditions and in the event of more frequent and intense hurricanes.

With more intense use of agricultural land, the economic effects of extreme events will become more pronounced. Coastal low-lying areas are particularly vulnerable to storm surges and groundwater intrusion during hurricane events, causing coastal flooding and the saturation of agricultural land by seawater. Upland agriculture suffers significantly from the excessive landslide activity and accelerated erosion associated with high-magnitude events. Such effects are most notable in Haiti, the poorest state in the Western Hemisphere. Centuries of deforestation and misuse have severely degraded Haiti's uplands, leading to entrenched rural poverty (Paskett and Philoctete 1990; McClintock 2003). Even without the series of hurricanes that have hit Haiti since 2000, the country has long since been unable to produce sufficient food to feed its population. Political instability and a crippling debt burden have contributed to Haiti's problems. One author proposes agroforestry as the only sustainable solution for the rehabilitation of Haiti's hillside agriculture (McClintock 2003).

Yet agroforestry is not immune from the effects of hurricanes, as shown by Hurricane Ivan's destruction of Grenada's nutmeg and other forest tree products in 2004.

■ Sustainability and the Environment: Some Reflections

In examining the application of sustainable development in small Caribbean states, it remains true that there is "an understandable and unavoidable tension everywhere between the demands of employment, improved wages and living conditions today and the environmental sustainability of economic policies implemented to achieve these demands" (Pantin 1994:10). In the Caribbean, even those who are sensitive to environmental issues have not yet found solutions to the inherent problems of economic survival, the difficulty of assessing the environmental impact on natural resources of socioeconomic activities, and the ability to prevent or even mitigate environmental disasters in the region (Pantin 1994). A sustainable approach to development is of paramount importance in island states (Barker and McGregor 1995, Potter et al. 2004). At present, however, there are more questions than answers, among them the following: (1) Are Caribbean ecosystems inherently fragile, or can they resist environmental change? (2) Are the types of damage currently happening in the Caribbean more or less recoverable than the degradation being experienced in developed countries, such as large-scale industrialization and urbanization? The fact that the future of the Caribbean island states, due to their relatively small physical size and small economic turnover, depends on maintaining a balance between resource use and human needs makes an understanding of the relative resilience of Caribbean ecosystems all the more important.

From a historical perspective, current environmental problems in the insular Caribbean result directly from externally focused colonial trade and extraction policies (Richardson 1992). Centuries of change and development in the Caribbean region, including relatively rapid urbanization and economic activity, have altered the natural and human environments. Although most Caribbean islands are now independent, they are still subject, in varying degrees, to external economic dependency that is unlikely to change radically in the future (Thomas 1988; Deere et al. 1990). Yet still, as Dennis Conway and Benjamin Timms (2003) point out, regional and national debates about economic development continue to reveal a distinct lack of concern with population-environment interactions and with environmental conservation, as well as the repeated failure by Caribbean governments to place environmental concerns toward the front of the agenda. It should be said, however, that the specter of climate change has recently focused the attention of regional authorities on the importance of protecting their Caribbean environments.

Despite this equivocation by their governments, it is noteworthy that Caribbean peoples are experienced and adaptable in shaping survival strategies, especially in the face of the plantation hegemony and its legacy regarding access to land resources (Mintz 1985; Hills 1988; Hills and Iton 1983). Imposed upon the traditional means of earning a livelihood, the importation of Western models of development and recent economic restructuring agreements with the International Monetary Fund have presented new challenges to the people of the region in terms of survival, development paths, and sustainability.

Past environmental degradation was inextricably linked to European colonial settlement and associated plantation economies (Watts 1987; Richardson 1992). Yet the environmental crisis today can also be attributed to increasing poverty, economic restructuring, inappropriate industrial policy, rapid urbanization, and social deprivation (Lloyd Evans and Potter 1996). A fundamental issue is whether the environment should take precedence over economic development or vice versa. In a report on sustainable development in the region, the Economic Commission for Latin America and the Caribbean (ECLAC) stated that its prime objectives were development and the sustainable management of natural resources and the environment and that the real challenge involved improving the standard of living for the majority of the population in a time of economic liberalization (ECLAC 1991). Under conditions of economic austerity, the tendency is to transfer natural resources into exports and foreign exchange earnings in order to improve living standards; environmental concerns are relegated to second place. Little, if anything, has changed since ECLAC's pronouncement.

Trying to make development sustainable assumes that it is possible to recognize what is unsustainable (Thomas-Hope 1996). If sustainability is concerned with meeting the needs of the present generation as well as those of future generations, then the Caribbean is replete with examples of unsustainable development. Table 7.3 highlights some human activities that give rise to environmental problems. The environmental impact of coastal-zone development, agricultural practices, urbanization, and tourism are critical aspects of development planning that need immediate attention.

Studies of Caribbean tourism illustrate contradictions surrounding environmental sustainability and provide numerous examples of negative environmental impacts and doubtful sustainable benefits. Coastal resources, including inshore fisheries, are radically affected by tourism in a number of ways, such as overfishing, reef mining, pollution, and reef degradation. However, much of the research on the impact of Caribbean tourism tends to be project-specific (and hence location-specific), and the broader national or regional perspective may be lacking. For example, the legacy of environmental degradation from colonial plantation agriculture in Antigua has continued in the modern period and is being replicated and exacerbated through short-sighted tourism developments that threaten the environmental integrity of the coastal zone (Lorah 1995). Similar issues have been raised by those concerned that ecotourism is becoming a clever marketing ploy rather than a genuine effort to develop a sustainable form of tourism (Cater and Lowman 1995; France and Wheeller

1995; France 1998; Woodfield 1998). The multiple appearances of tourism in Table 7.3 suggests that it is likely to be central to future regional sustainability because it impinges on many aspects of physical, economic, and cultural environments.

Yvan Breton and colleagues (2006) argue that the way forward in reconciling tourism with sustainable coastal zone management is through community participation and the engagement of all levels of stakeholders. Though this may seem uncontroversial, it is more difficult to implement in practice. They show what is possible in a series of case studies of community-based projects throughout the insular and continental Caribbean. Yvan Breton and Brian Davy (2006) emphasize the importance of indigenous environmental knowledge and the resilience to environmental degradation that it can promote if accessed appropriately. Dennis Pantin and Marlene Attzs examine the economic issues associated with tourism in the Caribbean in Chapter 5.

The nature of Caribbean food systems also illustrates the complexities and contradictions of sustainability in geographically small tropical islands (McElroy and de Albuquerque 1990; Spence 1996). The colonial period established outward-focused agricultural economies devoted to export. Little has changed since independence to alter the economic orientation of commercial agriculture, though now the financial benefits may be more likely to remain in the Caribbean, with the gradual increase in locally owned businesses. Concern about dependence on undiversified agriculture has persisted through several decades, resurfacing in the 1990s in relation to the survival of banana producers (Welch 1996; Grossman 1998). Yet efforts to increase yields and modernize agricultural production are fraught with new environmental problems as agricultural pollutants begin to have an impact on water supply and on marine ecosystems. Similarly, the study of decisionmaking by small farmers can highlight the multifaceted dilemmas of sustainability (Meikle 1992; Davis-Morrison 1998; Beckford and Barker 2007). How can the natural capital of land resources be conserved while producing export food crops and a sustainable supply of domestic food for a growing domestic population? How can small farmers provide a decent standard of living for their families in the face of global trade liberalization and a renewed flood of cheap food imports into the region?

Some Caribbean nations are not overly concerned with the preservation of agricultural land for domestic food production, but rather rely on imports for food security (Lynch 2006). Others such as Cuba, with its strongly centralized government, have tried to promote food security by focusing on domestic agriculture. In Cuba's case, "Green Revolution" technology has underpinned a technology-driven rather than farmer-driven approach, with emphasis on biofertilizers, biological crop protection, improved water management techniques, animal traction, and improved pasture management (Lynch 2006). Lynch argues that elements of Cuba's approach, although not uniformly successful, provide pointers to a more sustainable and productive domestic agriculture.

Generally speaking, discussion of sustainability issues connotes a medium-to long-term planning horizon, but high-magnitude natural disasters such as hurricanes, earthquakes, and volcanoes can have immediate disruptive effects on sustainability. Hurricanes such as Gilbert (1988), Hugo (1989), and Ivan (2004) brought entire islands to a state of emergency (see Barker and Miller 1990 for an example), and the effects of recent volcanic activity on Montserrat have been devastating to that island's survival. Though natural hazards have plagued the region for centuries, their impacts are likely to become more significant in the future as populations increase, as infrastructure becomes more developed and sophisticated, and as the environment becomes more degraded. Add to that trends such as global warming, which could have a severe impact in the insular Caribbean, widespread reef degradation, more violent patterns of hurricane activity, and subregional drought. Thus, hazards, whether natural or human-induced, also play a crucial role in the sustainability equation because of their unpredictable impacts on the resource base, land use, and human settlement (Skinner 2006).

Recommendations for policy and research emphasis in the search for sustainable development in the insular Caribbean have been made (see McElroy, Potter and Towle 1990; see also Table 7.5). Realization of objectives will require progress on two basic issues: environmental damage control and habitat restoration, and breakthroughs in our understanding of potentially sustainable resource uses. However, such recommendations underscore the importance of

Table 7.5 Recommendations for Sustainable Development in the Caribbean

1. Agricultural policy should focus on small-scale diverse crop farms.
2. Small-farm orientation should promote agroforestry options.
3. Such small-farm focus would justify legal retention of agricultural resource use on criteria other than commercial viability.
4. Research required to determine ways to enhance local benefits of traditional tourism (applies also to ecotourism).
5. A regional institute is required to promote new technologies and to undertake assessments of their impacts.
6. New planning and user-friendly indices of environmental vulnerability are required.
7. Systems for promoting interisland transfer of resource management skills are needed.
8. Fostering of local specialists to gauge impact of international trends on insular economies is required.
9. External agencies and host governments must devise new ways to facilitate effective resource decisionmaking and policy implementation.

Source: J. L. McElroy, B. Potter, and E. Towle, "Challenges for Sustainable Development in Small Caribbean Islands," in *Sustainable Development and Environmental Management of Small Islands,* edited by W. Beller, P. d'Ayala, and P. Hein (Paris: UNESCO; Carnforth, UK: Parthenon, 1990), pp. 299–316.

social development in achieving these goals. For example, there is a need to channel investment into appropriate environmental education and training as well as the promotion of environmental awareness throughout society.

Environmentalists contend that development strategies should focus on the social needs of the people while respecting the natural environment. In this respect, it is also important that any approach should be gender-sensitive, as women often undertake the primary role in environmental management (Dankelman and Davidson 1988; Braidotti 1994). Environmental conservation is often predicated on social inequality, especially on the basis of class, ethnicity, and gender; those in power drive their own agenda, sometimes to the detriment of others (Thomas-Hope 1996; Peake 1998). This demands the promotion of more sustainable and indigenous development programs, with empowerment as a major goal. Local environmental management will require community collaboration and the promotion of equity between different social groups (Lloyd Evans 1998). Sherrie Baver and Barbara Lynch (2006:6) argue for a political ecology approach, which recognizes the importance of local cultural identities and social groups within the wider globalization context.

Environmental awareness heightened in the 1990s, which were characterized by the proliferation of nongovernmental initiatives in which environmental projects played a key role in mobilizing community development. There was progress on three such projects in St. Lucia, and similar efforts have been documented even in crisis-torn Haiti (Conway and Lorah 1995; Maguire 1994). In many ways, such initiatives reflect a more enlightened and progressive attitude on the part of international, national, and regional power brokers, as well as genuine enthusiasm and involvement on the part of Caribbean peoples.

The most important resource in the Caribbean region is the human resource. In order to harness the true potential of people, Caribbean nations need to channel investment into education and training, the provision of basic needs, and creative employment opportunities (Lloyd Evans 1998). Education of the next generation and the promotion of environmental awareness throughout society must be given a central role in any future agenda. Caribbean peoples will determine the shape of sustainable development, whether it becomes a useful intellectual concept or an attainable human goal. Central to sustainability must be the future protection of the already degraded Caribbean environment.

▣ Bibliography

Bacon, P. E. "Wetland Resource Rehabilitation for Sustainable Development in the Eastern Caribbean." In *Environment and Development in the Caribbean: Geographical Perspectives,* edited by D. Barker and D. F. M. McGregor, pp. 46–56. Kingston, Jamaica: University of the West Indies Press, 1995.

Barker, D. "A Periphery in Genesis and Exodus: Reflections on Rural-Urban Relations in Jamaica." In *The Geography of Urban-Rural Interactions in Developing Countries,* edited by R. B. Potter and T. Unwin, pp. 294–322. London: Routledge, 1989.

———. "Dualism and Disaster on a Tropical Island: Constraints on Agricultural Development in Jamaica." *Tidjschrift voor Economische en Sociale Geographie* (Journal for Economic and Social Geography), no. 84 (1993): 332–340.

———. "Yam Farmers on the Edge of Cockpit Country: Aspects of Resource Use and Sustainability." In *Resource Sustainability and Caribbean Development,* edited by D. F. M. McGregor, D. Barker, and S. Lloyd Evans, pp. 357–372. Kingston, Jamaica: University of the West Indies Press, 1998.

Barker, D., and C. Beckford. "Yam Production and the Yam Stick Trade in Jamaica: Integrated Problems for Resource Management." In *Resources, Planning and Environmental Management in a Changing Caribbean,* edited by D. Barker and D. F. M. McGregor, pp. 57–73. Kingston, Jamaica: University of the West Indies Press, 2003.

Barker, D., and D. F. M. McGregor. "Land Degradation in the Yallahs Basin, Jamaica: Historical Notes and Contemporary Perspectives." *Geography* 783, no. 2 (1988): 116–124.

———. *Environment and Development in the Caribbean: Geographical Perspectives.* Kingston, Jamaica: University of the West Indies Press, 1995.

Barker, D., and D. J. Miller. "Hurricane Gilbert: Anthropomorphising a Natural Disaster." *Area* 22, no. 2 (1990): 107–116.

Baver, S. L., and B. D. Lynch. "The Political Ecology of Paradise." In *Beyond Sun and Sand: Caribbean Environmentalisms,* edited by S. L. Baver and B. D. Lynch, pp. 3–16. Rutgers, New Brunswick: Rutgers University Press, 2006.

Beckford, C., and D. Barker. "The Role and Value of Local Knowledge in Jamaican Agriculture: Adaptation and Change in Small-Scale Farming." *Geographical Journal* 173 (2007): 118–128.

Besson, J. "A Paradox in Caribbean Attitudes to Land." In *Land and Development in the Caribbean,* edited by J. Besson and J. Momsen, pp. 13–45. Warwick University Caribbean Studies series. London: Macmillan, 1987.

Braidotti, R., ed. *Women, the Environment, and Sustainable Development: Towards a Theoretical Synthesis.* London: Zed Books, 1994.

Breton, Y., D. Brown, B. Davy, M. Haughton, and L. Ovares, eds. *Coastal Resource Management in the Wider Caribbean: Resilience, Adaptation, and Community Diversity.* Kingston, Jamaica: Ian Randle, 2006.

Breton, Y., and B. Davy. "Analytical Insights, Lessons Learnt, and Recommendations." In *Coastal Resource Management in the Wider Caribbean: Resilience, Adaptation, and Community Diversity,* edited by Y. Breton, D. Brown, B. Davy, M. Haughton, and L. Ovares, pp. 223–254. Kingston, Jamaica: Ian Randle, 2006.

Brinkhoff, Thomas. City Population. "Jamaica." 2007. http://www.citypopulation.de/Jamaica.html.

Brookfield, H. C. "An Approach to Islands." In *Sustainable Development and Environmental Management of Small Islands,* edited by W. Beller, P. d'Ayala, and P. Hein, pp. 23–23. Paris and Carnforth, UK: UNESCO and Parthenon, 1990.

Bryant, D., L. Burke, J. McManus, and M. Spalding. *Reefs at Risk: A Map-Based Indicator of Threats to the World's Coral Reefs.* Washington, DC: World Resources Institute, 1998.

Bryant, R. L., and S. Bailey. *Third World Political Ecology.* London: Routledge, 1997.

Butler, R. A. "Coral Reefs Suffer Severe Coral Bleaching Event." Mongabay.com, 2005, http://news.mongabay.com/2005/1220-reefs.html.

Caribbean Environment Programme (CEP). "Caribbean Fish Kills." *CEP Newsletter* 14, no. 2 (1999): 9.

Cater, E., and G. Lowman, eds. *Ecotourism: A Sustainable Option?* Chichester, UK: Wiley, 1995.

Christensen, J. H., et al. "Regional Climate Projections." In *Climate Change 2007: The Physical Science Basis. Contribution of Working Group I to the Fourth Assessment Report of the Intergovernmental Panel on Climate Change*, edited by S. Solomon, D. Qin, M. Manning, Z. Chen, M. Marquis, K. B. Averyt, M. Tignor, and H. L. Miller, pp. 847–940. Cambridge, UK: Cambridge University Press, 2007.

Conway, D., and P. Lorah. "Environmental Protection Policies in Caribbean Small Islands: Some St. Lucian Examples." *Caribbean Geography* 6 (1995): 16–27.

Conway, D., and B. Timms. "Where Is the Environment in Caribbean Development Theory and Praxis?" *Global Development Studies* 3 (2003): 91–130.

Cox, C. A., A. Sarangi, and C. A. Madramootoo. "Effect of Land Management on Runoff and Soil Losses from Two Small Watersheds in St. Lucia." *Land Degradation and Development* 17 (2006): 55–72.

Dankelman, Irene, and Joan Davidson, eds. *Women and the Environment in the Third World: Alliance for the Future*. London: Earthscan Publications, 1988.

Davis-Morrison, V. "The Sustainability of Small-Scale Agricultural Systems in the Millbank Area of the Rio Grande Valley, Portland, Jamaica." In *Resource Sustainability and Caribbean Development*, edited by D. F. M., McGregor, D. Barker, and S. Lloyd Evans, pp. 296–316. Kingston, Jamaica: University of the West Indies Press, 1998.

Deere, C., P. Antrobus, E. Melendez, P. Phillips, M. Rivera, and H. Safa, eds. *In the Shadows of the Sun: Caribbean Development Alternatives and US Policy*. Boulder, CO: Westview, 1990.

Donner, S. D., T. R. Knutson, and M. Oppenheimer. "Model-Based Assessment of the Role of Human-Induced Climate Change in the 2005 Caribbean Coral Bleaching Event." *Proceedings of the National Academy of Sciences* 104 (2007): 5483–5488.

Draper, G., T. A. Jackson, and S. K. Donovan. "Geologic Provinces of the Caribbean Region." In *Caribbean Geology: An Introduction*, edited by S. K. Donovan and T. A. Jackson, pp. 3–12. Kingston, Jamaica: University of the West Indies Publishers' Association (UWIPA), 1994.

ECLAC (Economic Commission for Latin America and the Caribbean). *Sustainable Development: Changing Production Patterns, Social Equity, and the Environment*. Santiago: United Nations, 1991.

Edwards, D. *Small Farmers and the Protection of the Watersheds: The Experience of Jamaica Since the 1950s*. Occasional Paper no. 3, University of the West Indies, Centre for Environment and Development. Kingston, Jamaica: Canoe, 1995.

———. "Protection of the Hillsides Occupied by Small Farmers in Jamaica: Lessons of History and Prospects for Public Initiatives." In *Resource Sustainability and Caribbean Development*, edited by D. F. M. McGregor, D. Barker, and S. Lloyd Evans, pp. 341–356. Kingston, Jamaica: University of the West Indies Press, 1998.

Emanuel, K. A. "The Dependence of Hurricane Intensity on Climate." *Nature*, April 2, 1987, 483–485.

Evelyn, O. B., and R. Camirand. "Forest Cover and Deforestation in Jamaica: an Analysis of Forest Cover Estimates over Time." *International Forestry Review* 5 (2003): 354–363.

Eyre, L. A. "Jamaica: Test Case for Tropical Deforestation." *Ambio* 16 (1987): 338–343.

———. "The Cockpit Country: A World Heritage Site?" In *Environment and Development in the Caribbean: Geographical Perspectives*, edited by D. Barker and D. F. M. McGregor, pp. 259–270. Kingston, Jamaica: University of the West Indies Press, 1995.

———. "The Tropical Rainforests of Jamaica." *Jamaica Journal* 26, no. 1 (1996): 26–35.

———. "The Tropical Rainforests of the Eastern Caribbean: Present Status and Conservation." *Caribbean Geography* 9, no. 2 (1998): 101–120.

FAO (Food and Agriculture Organization of the United Nations). *Global Forest Resources Assessment 2000: Main Report.* FAO Forestry Report 12. Rome: FAO, 2001a.

————. *State of the World's Forests 2001.* Rome: FAO, 2001b.

France, L. "Sustainability and Development in Tourism on the Islands of Barbados, St. Lucia, and Dominica." In *Resource Sustainability and Caribbean Development,* edited by D. F. M. McGregor, D. Barker, and S. Lloyd Evans, pp. 109–125. Kingston, Jamaica: University of the West Indies Press, 1998.

France, L., and B. Wheeller. "Sustainability Tourism in the Caribbean." In *Environment and Development in the Caribbean: Geographical Perspectives,* edited by D. Barker and D. F. M. McGregor, pp. 59–69. Kingston, Jamaica: University of the West Indies Press, 1995.

GEO-LAC (Global Environment Outlook–Latin America and the Caribbean). *GEO Latin America and the Caribbean: Environment Outlook 2003.* Mexico D.F.: United Nations Environment Programme, 2003.

Gómez, L. M., L. C. Marcano, Z. Poggy, M. E. C. Gonzalez, and C. E. M. Vera. "Community Mobilization and Education in Contaminated Coastal Ecosystems." In *Coastal Resource Management in the Wider Caribbean: Resilience, Adaptation, and Community Diversity,* edited by Y. Breton, D. Brown, B. Davy, M. Haughton, and L. Ovares, pp. 137–171. Kingston, Jamaica: Ian Randle, 2006.

Gray, C. R. "Regional Meteorology and Hurricanes." In *Climate Change in the Intra-Americas Sea,* edited by G. A. Maul, pp. 87–99. London: Edward Arnold, 1993.

Grossman, Lawrence S. *The Political Ecology of Bananas: Contract Farming, Peasants, and Agrarian Change in the Eastern Caribbean.* Chapel Hill: University of North Carolina Press, 1998.

Hendry, M. "Sea-Level Movements and Shoreline Change." In *Climate Change in the Intra-Americas Sea,* edited by G. A. Maul, pp. 115–161. London: Edward Arnold, 1993.

Hills, T. L. "The Caribbean Peasant Food Forest: Ecological Artistry or Random Chaos?" In *Small Farming and Peasant Resources in the Caribbean,* edited by J. S. Brierley and H. Rubenstein, pp. 1–28. Manitoba Geographical Studies no. 10. Winnipeg: University of Manitoba, 1988.

Hills, T., and S. Iton. "A Reassessment of the 'Traditional' in Caribbean Small-Scale Agriculture." *Caribbean Geography* 1 (1983): 24–35.

Jamaica, Ministry of Agriculture. *Mavis Bank: Agricultural Development Plan.* Kingston, Jamaica: Ministry of Agriculture, n.d.

Johnson, A. M. "The Artisanal Fishery of the Black River Lower Morass, Jamaica: A Traditional System of Resource Management." In *Resource Sustainability and Caribbean Development,* edited by D. F. M. McGregor, D. Barker, and S. Lloyd Evans, pp. 390–404. Kingston, Jamaica: University of the West Indies Press, 1998.

Lloyd Evans, S. "Gender, Ethnicity, and Small Business Development in Trinidad: Prospects for Sustainable Job Creation." In *Resource Sustainability and Caribbean Development,* edited by D. F. M. McGregor, D. Barker, and S. Lloyd Evans, pp. 195–213. Kingston, Jamaica: University of the West Indies Press, 1998.

Lloyd Evans, S., and R. B. Potter. "Environmental Impacts of Urban Development and the Urban Informal Sector in the Caribbean." In *Land Degradation in the Tropics,* edited by M. J. Eden and J. T. Parry, pp. 245–260. London: Pinter, 1996.

Lorah, P. "An Unsustainable Path: Tourism's Vulnerability to Environmental Decline in Antigua." *Caribbean Geography* 6 (1995): 28–29.

Lugo, A. E. "Development, Forestry, and Environmental Quality in the Eastern Caribbean." In *Sustainable Development and Environmental Management of Small Islands,* edited by W. Beller, P. d'Ayala, and P. Hein, pp. 317–342. Paris and Carnforth, UK: UNESCO and Parthenon, 1990.

Lugo, A., R. Schmidt, and S. Brown. "Tropical Forests in the Caribbean." *Ambio* 10 (1981): 318–324.

Lynch, B. D. "Seeking Agricultural Sustainability: Cuban and Dominican Strategies." In *Beyond Sun and Sand: Caribbean Environmentalisms,* edited by S. L. Baver and B. D. Lynch, pp. 86–108. New Brunswick, NJ: Rutgers University Press, 2006.

Maguire, R. E. "Sisyphus Revisited: Grassroots Development and Community Conflict in Haiti." *Caribbean Geography* 5 (1994): 127–135.

McClintock, N. C. "Agroforestry and Sustainable Resource Conservation in Haiti: A Case Study." Working paper, North Carolina State University, Raleigh, 2003, http://www.ncsu.edu/project/cnrint/Agro/resource_home.htm.

McElroy, J. L., and K. de Albuquerque. "Sustainable Small-Scale Agriculture in Small Caribbean Islands." *Society and Natural Resources* 3 (1990): 107–129.

McElroy, J. L., B. Potter, and E. Towle. "Challenges for Sustainable Development in Small Caribbean Islands." In *Sustainable Development and Environmental Management of Small Islands,* edited by W. Beller, P. d'Ayala, and P. Hein, pp. 299–316. Paris and Carnforth, UK: UNESCO and Parthenon, 1990.

McGregor, D. F. M. "An Investigation of Soil Status and Land Use on a Steeply Sloping Hillside, Blue Mountains, Jamaica." *Singapore Journal of Tropical Geography* 9 (1988): 60–71.

———. "Soil Erosion, Environmental Change, and Development in the Caribbean: A Deepening Crisis?" In *Environment and Development in the Caribbean: Geographical Perspectives,* edited by D. Barker and D. F. M. McGregor, pp. 189–208. Kingston, Jamaica: University of the West Indies Press, 1995.

McGregor, D. F. M., and D. Barker. "Land Degradation and Hillside Farming in the Fall River Basin, Jamaica." *Applied Geography* 11 (1991): 143–156.

McGregor, D. F. M., and R. B. Potter. "Environmental Change and Sustainability in the Caribbean: Terrestrial Perspectives." In *Land, Sea, and Human Effort in the Caribbean,* edited by B. M. W. Ratter and W.-D. Sahr, pp. 1–15. Beiträge zur Geographischen Regionalforschung in Latinamerika (Contributions to regional geographic research in Latin America), vol. 10. Hamburg: Institut für Geographie der Universtat Hamburg, 1997.

Meikle, P. "Spatial-Temporal Trends in Root Crop Production and Mobility in Jamaica." *Caribbean Geography* 3 (1992): 223–235.

Milliman, J. D. "Coral Reefs and Their Response to Global Climate Change." In *Climate Change in the Intra-Americas Sea,* edited by G. A. Maul, pp. 306–321. London: Edward Arnold, 1993.

Mills, B. "'The Bad Old Days Look Better': Enlightened Colonial Land Management Practices and Land Reform in the British Windward Islands." In *Environmental Planning in the Caribbean,* edited by J. Pugh and J. Momsen, pp. 21–31. Aldershot, UK: Ashgate, 2006.

Mimura, N., L. Nurse, R. F. McLean, J. Agard, L. Briguglio, P. Lefale, R. Payet, and G. Sem. "Small Islands." In *Climate Change 2007: Impacts, Adaptation, and Vulnerability. Contribution of Working Group II to the Fourth Assessment Report of the Intergovernmental Panel on Climate Change,* edited by M. L. Parry, O. F. Canziani, J. P. Palutikof, P. J. van der Linden, and C. E. Hanson, pp. 687–716. Cambridge, UK: Cambridge University Press, 2007.

Mintz, Sidney W. "From Plantation to Peasantries in the Caribbean." In *Caribbean Contours,* edited by Sidney W. Mintz and Sally Price, pp. 127–154. Baltimore: Johns Hopkins University Press, 1985.

Pantin, Dennis. *The Economics of Sustainable Development in Small Caribbean Islands.* Kingston, Jamaica, and St. Augustine, Trinidad: Centre for Environment and Development, University of the West Indies—Jamaica, and the Department of Economics, University of the West Indies—Trinidad, 1994.

Parry, M. L. *Climate Change and World Agriculture.* London: Earthscan, 1990.

Paskett, C. J., and C.-E. Philoctete. "Soil Conservation in Haiti." *Journal of Soil and Water Conservation* 45 (1990): 457–459.

Pattullo, Polly. *Last Resorts: The Cost of Tourism in the Caribbean.* London: Cassell, 1996.

Peake, L. J. "Living in Poverty in Linden, Guyana, in the 1990s: Bauxite, the Development of Poverty, and Household Coping Mechanisms." In *Resource Sustainability and Caribbean Development,* edited by D. F. M. McGregor, D. Barker, and S. Lloyd Evans, pp. 171–194. Kingston, Jamaica: University of the West Indies Press, 1998.

Potter, R. B. "Urbanisation and Development in the Caribbean." *Geography* 80 (1995): 334–341.

———. *The Urban Caribbean in an Era of Global Change.* Aldershot, UK: Ashgate Publishing, 2000.

Potter, Robert B., David Barker, Dennis Conway, and Thomas Klak. *The Contemporary Caribbean.* Harlow, UK, and New York: Pearson and Prentice Hall, 2004.

Reading, A. J., and R. P. D. Walsh. "Tropical Cyclone Activity Within the Caribbean Basin Since 1500." In *Environment and Development in the Caribbean: Geographical Perspectives,* edited by D. Barker and D. F. M. McGregor, pp. 124–146. Kingston, Jamaica: University of the West Indies Press, 1995.

Richardson, Bonham C. *The Caribbean in the Wider World, 1492–1992: A Regional Geography.* Cambridge, UK: Cambridge University Press, 1992.

Shapiro, L. J. "Hurricane Climatic Fluctuations, Part II: Relation to Large-Scale Circulation." *Monthly Weather Review* 110 (1982): 1014–1023.

Skinner, J. "Disaster Creation in the Caribbean and Planning, Policy, and Participation Reconsidered." In *Environmental Planning in the Caribbean,* edited by J. Pugh and J. Momsen, pp. 53–72. Aldershot, UK: Ashgate, 2006.

Spence, B. "The Influence of Small Farmers' Land Use Decisions on the Status of Food Security in Jamaica." *Caribbean Geography* 6 (1996): 132–142.

Thomas, C. Y. *The Poor and the Powerless: Economic Policy and Change in the Caribbean.* London: Latin American Bureau, 1988.

Thomas-Hope, E. *The Environmental Dilemma in the Caribbean Context.* Grace Kennedy Foundation Lecture 1996. Kingston: Institute of Jamaica and Grace Kennedy Foundation, 1996.

Walsh, R. P. D. "Climatic Changes in the Eastern Caribbean over the Last 150 Years and Some Implications in Planning Sustainable Development." In *Resource Sustainability and Caribbean Development,* edited by D. F. M. McGregor, D. Barker, and S. Lloyd Evans, pp. 26–48. Kingston, Jamaica: University of the West Indies Press, 1998.

Watts, D. *The West Indies: Patterns of Development, Culture, and Environmental Change Since 1492.* Cambridge, UK: Cambridge University Press, 1987.

———. "Environmental Degradation, the Water Resource, and Sustainable Development in the Eastern Caribbean." *Caribbean Geography* 6 (1995): 2–15.

Weaver, D. "Ecotourism in the Caribbean Basin." In *Ecotourism: A Sustainable Option?* edited by E. Cater and G. Lowman, pp. 159–176. Chichester, UK: John Wiley, 1994.

Welch, B. *Survival by Association: Supply Management Landscapes of the Eastern Caribbean.* Kingston, Jamaica, and Montreal: University of the West Indies Press and McGill-Queens University Press, 1996.

Wigley, T. M. L., and B. D. Santer. "Future Climate of the Gulf/Caribbean Basin from the Global Circulation Models." In *Climate Change in the Intra-Americas Sea,* edited by G. A. Maul, pp. 31–54. London: Edward Arnold, 1993.

Wilson, J. S., T. S. Brothers, and E. J. Marcano. "Land Cover Contrasts on the Haitian/Dominican Border." *Caribbean Geography* 11 (2000): 244–249.

Woodfield, N. "The Role of Ecotourism in Grenada: A Marketing Ploy or a Step Towards Sustainable Development?" In *Resource Sustainability and Caribbean Development,* edited by D. F. M. McGregor, D. Barker, and S. Lloyd Evans, pp. 148–168. Kingston, Jamaica: University of the West Indies Press, 1998.

8

Ethnicity, Race, Class, and Nationality

David Baronov and Kevin A. Yelvington

In order to understand cultures other than our own, we must overcome pre-conceived ideas and stereotypes. The concepts used in this chapter, based on modern anthropological and sociological definitions, are designed to provide an objective approach to comprehending intuitive concepts such as ethnicity, race, class, and nationality.

Ethnicity may be best conceived of as a set of ideas concerning a group's real or imagined cultural links with an ancestral past. It suggests identification with a certain group based on cultural and historical traditions, including language and religion, and provides basic insights into the nature and origins of a group of people as well as explanations for their modern beliefs, behaviors, and accomplishments. Inherent in this concept is the notion that the members of a distinct ethnic group share some set of common characteristics that sets them apart from the broader society.[1]

With the conquest and colonization of Africa and the Americas in the fifteenth and sixteenth centuries, Europeans for the first time developed sustained relationships with markedly different peoples and societies. Rationalizing and legitimizing their control required an ideological foundation based in a presumed superiority, prompting the creation of racial categories reflecting the idea that humankind is naturally divided into divergent physical and biological types. An array of characteristics was associated with each type, with an inherent hierarchy that reflected European superiority. The result was the division of the world's population into a fixed number of "pure" *races,* each representing bundles of traits (physical differences in skin color, hair, facial features, and the like) given differing values.

Scientists have demonstrated that humankind, in fact, cannot be neatly or meaningfully categorized into races. To begin with, there is no scientific reason to believe that people would conform to any racial ideal or so-called pureblood model even if there were no miscegenation (mixing) between races. Even without miscegenation, the frequencies of genes responsible for the bundle of traits will change through time due to the forces of evolution. At least half of the world's population today displays bundles of racial traits not anticipated in the supposedly scientific traditional view of "the three races." Rather, they combine a number of physical traits thought to pertain to one race. The distribution of genes responsible for the bundle of traits is dispersed throughout the world. There are no sharp breaks between gene distributions, as one would find if the traditional view were correct. In fact, scientists have shown that there is much more genetic variation within groups regarded as races than exists between members of different races. Race must be viewed, therefore, as socially constructed.[2]

Social class is a complex concept for which there are a variety of competing interpretations.[3] The idea of class reflects social power relations and is a critical determinant of access to social resources, social mobility, social status and acceptance, and social identity.

Importantly, various forms of social stratification can cut across class lines. Ethnicity and race are given further meaning within the context of social class and intersect with class in different ways. Often, a person's ethnic or racial identity may be a stronger determinant of social power than his or her class position. For example, ethnic and racial discrimination—such as that against Dominicans in Puerto Rico—cuts across class lines. At times, a person's ethnic or racial identity may be a determinant of class position, as was the case with those of African descent during the era of slavery and with East Indians and Chinese who came to the Americas as indentured laborers.

The multidimensional nature of social class—along with the influences of ethnicity, race, and nationality—provides avenues for strategic cross-class alliances as well as occasional intraclass conflict. Thus, social class must be understood as part of an ongoing, fluid process of contestation rather than as fixed, static, and unchanging categories. The control and distribution of social resources is the basis for a good deal of social conflict within the Caribbean and elsewhere. Understanding how social class, as well as ethnic-racial and national identity, shape this conflict is essential for an understanding of Caribbean society and culture.

Although nationality shares much with the concepts of ethnicity and race, there remains a crucial distinction. Discussions of ethnicity often center on a group's ultimate origins and how they have supposedly remained unchanged throughout the ages. *Nationality,* in contrast, reflects an ideology suggesting that there is a homogeneous and unifying cultural identity confined to geographically defined territories that is somehow able to overcome ethnic-racial differences within the population. In other words, regardless of the varied origins of different ethnic groups within a given society, there are certain characteristics common to the entire population. These commonalities uniquely define the people as a nation.[4]

In this chapter we provide an overview of the nature of ethnicity, race, class, and nationality across Caribbean societies. In the process, it will shed light on how these concepts are interpreted and understood, as well as on how they have affected the lives of those who reside in the region.

▨ The Mix of Ethnicity, Race, Class, and Nationality Across the Caribbean

US racial categories would be almost unrecognizable to most Caribbeans, and vice versa. In contrast to most of the Caribbean, where gradations of light or dark skin color, rather than pure racial types, tend to define racial identities, the US tradition has been that a person of African or European descent is either African American or white.[5] This is based on the so-called one-drop rule: one drop of African American blood makes one African American. The offspring of an African American and a white person has, by custom, been considered African American. This harkens back to earlier racist ideologies based on the fiction of pure racial bloodlines.

Writing about Puerto Rico, Isar Godreau (2000) suggests that popular notions of ethnicity, race, class, and nationality can be characterized by what she calls *la semántica fugitiva* (slippery semantics). *La semántica fugitiva* refers to the indeterminacy and negotiation involved in everyday notions of ethnic-racial identity. There is often extensive use of indirectness and metaphor in everyday conversation. Rural Puerto Ricans, for example, often use descriptions for various degrees of rainfall as analogies for racial types. Thus, *aguacero* (hard rainfall) designates someone who is very dark-skinned, and *lloviznas* (mild rainfall) refers to those deemed medium in skin color. *Opaco* (cloudy) denotes *trigueños bastante oscuro* (dark, wheat-colored people), that is, those with kinky hair but not completely dark skin (Gordon 1949:298).

La semántica fugitiva is reflected in the idea of *mestizaje* (*métissage* in French), meaning "miscegenation" or "race-mixing" as well as "cultural blending." An equivalent term is *creolization*. The word *Creole* is taken from the Spanish word *criollo,* meaning "of local origin." Creolization in Caribbean popular culture extols a process of ongoing cultural and ethnic-racial blending. *Mestizaje* is coupled with the ideology of *blanqueamiento* (whitening). In the dominant belief system, whiteness is given special value, representing and embodying European-derived culture. Whiteness becomes the aesthetic standard to which people aspire.

The larger point is, therefore, that ethnicity, race, class, and nationality (as manifested in the ideology of nationalism) are mutually constituting. Ethnic-racial identities influence social class by acting as a resource (or a liability) in securing social capital and prestige. Social class affects nationalism insofar as the privileged classes define and principally benefit from the dominant ideology of nationalism. Nationalism affects ethnicity and race in that those who are defined as white, mulatto, and so on—and the value accorded to each—in one nationalist context may not be so defined in another.

◼ Historical Legacies

As Stephen Randall details in Chapter 3, the modern Caribbean rests on the bedrock of three formidable institutions: colonialism, the plantation system, and slavery. The legacy of colonialism for the Caribbean is evident today in the chorus of Dutch, English, French, and Spanish voices echoing across the region. When Europeans first reached the Caribbean, they encountered a small collection of thriving Amerindian societies, which were almost totally eliminated as distinct cultural groups by the 1530s. European powers captured and either enslaved or slaughtered the indigenous Amerindian population and then set out to repopulate the newly claimed area with Europeans and African slaves.

For nearly the first two centuries of colonial rule in the Caribbean, the entire region belonged to the Spanish Empire. The British, Dutch, and French did not arrive until the seventeenth century, but by the 1780s the French colony of St. Domingue (what would become independent Haiti) was the world's leading sugar producer, its plantations generating great wealth.

The defining feature of colonial rule and the plantation system in the Caribbean was slavery (Eltis 2000; Klein 1986, 1999; Shepherd and Beckles 2000). Over the 350-plus years of the Atlantic slave trade, as many as 10–12 million Africans were kidnapped from their homelands and forced to work as slaves in the Americas. Of these, it is estimated that roughly 40 percent reached the Caribbean. Another 40 percent were taken to Brazil; 16 percent landed in Spanish Latin America; and about 4 percent reached British North America (the colonies and later the United States). The category of slave was reserved by Europeans exclusively for persons of African descent. There were other forms of forced labor, however, and each was associated with a distinct ethnic-racial group. The *encomienda* system of forced labor was for Amerindians, whose spiritual salvation was entrusted to Christianizing Europeans. Indentured servitude was only available to Europeans (and later some Asians). Europeans sent their criminals and political prisoners to the Caribbean as unfree labor, although they were never slaves. After serving a definite period of indenture, they were freed from service. Their masters had no claims of ownership over them or any of their offspring, as was the case for slaves.

Africans were kidnapped from across the span of Africa. Branding all slaves as Africans was therefore a convenient excuse for ignoring the significant ethnic-cultural differences among African peoples, who constituted as varied and distinct a population as existed on any continent. Table 8.1 illustrates the diverse regional origins of the Africans taken as slaves, though it cannot account for the full extent of the ethnic and cultural diversity of their societies. Table 8.2 provides additional details regarding the regional origins of Africans sent to major British colonies at the advent of the plantation system. Importantly, a slave's regional origins cannot be completely confounded with a slave's ethnic affiliation (called "nations" by slavers and planters at the time and later by the slaves themselves). Both tables portray a certain homogeneity in the regional origins of these slaves and provide clues about the cultures of the Africans taken to these colonies.

Ethnic differences among Africans were not lost on the slave traders. Europeans made sharp distinctions between African ethnic groups as they related to the population's supposed temperament, tendency to rebel, health, work habits, and native intelligence—all critical factors for plantation productivity. The journals and correspondences of the planters are full of their reflections on these issues as well as their requests for specific types of Africans. An early scientific society centered in the bustling port and commercial center of Cap François, St. Domingue, called the Cercle des Philadelphes carried out detailed investigations into the lives of slaves. This did not, of course, stem from any humanitarian concern but from the interest in maintaining a profitable colonial economy. The Cercle undertook a general survey of agriculture in 1787 and sent out a questionnaire. Among its 250 questions, the survey asked slaveholders to identify which work suited which kinds of Africans and which Africans were the easiest to discipline (McClellan 1992).

A further concern related to African ethnicity was the fear of slave revolts. Planters avoided buying too many members of the same ethnic group for their plantations. It was reasoned that a common language and culture would facilitate planning and conspiracy. Indeed, a number of slave revolts across the Caribbean were led by one ethnic group or another. In the only completely successful slave revolt—the protracted and bloody war beginning in 1791 that brought about Haitian independence in 1804—Kongo soldiers, military tactics, and political ideology all played a role. Other slaves, rather than revolting, often formed maroon communities of runaway slaves. This was especially true in areas where the rugged terrain aided such escapes, as in Jamaica and Suriname.

Colonialism, the Plantation System, Slavery, and the European Notion of Whiteness

The lasting legacy of colonialism, the plantation system, and slavery has been the European fixation on race and the notion of *whiteness*. With colonial rule, multiple European ethnic identities soon began to fuse into a single white racial identity. The Spanish conquest of the Caribbean occurred at the time of

Table 8.1 Estimates of Regional Distribution of Slave Exports to the Americas from Africa, 1662–1867

Years	Senegambia	Sierra Leone	Gold Coast	Bight of Benin	Bight of Biafra	West-Central Africa	Southeast Africa	Total	Annual Exports
1662–1670	3,232		12,174	23,021	34,471	9,695	91	82,684	9,187
1671–1680	5,842		20,597	22,753	24,021	15,794	309	89,316	8,932
1681–1690	10,834		15,333	71,733	21,625	32,760	5,392	157,677	15,768
1691–1700	13,376		17,407	103,313	12,115	30,072	190	176,473	17,647
1700–1709	22,230	34,560	31,650	138,590	23,130	109,780	0	359,940	35,994
1710–1719	36,260	6,380	37,540	138,690	51,410	132,590	0	402,870	40,287
1720–1729	52,530	9,120	65,110	150,280	59,990	179,620	0	516,650	51,665
1730–1739	57,210	29,470	74,460	135,220	62,260	240,890	0	599,510	59,951
1740–1749	35,000	43,350	83,620	97,830	76,790	214,470	0	551,060	55,106
1750–1759	30,100	83,860	52,780	86,620	106,100	222,430	0	581,890	58,189
1760–1769	27,590	178,360	69,650	98,390	142,640	266,570	0	783,200	78,320
1770–1779	24,400	132,220	54,370	111,550	160,400	234,880	0	717,820	71,782
1780–1789	15,240	74,190	57,650	121,080	225,360	300,340	0	793,860	79,386
1790–1799	18,320	70,510	73,960	74,600	181,740	340,110	0	759,240	75,924
1800–1809	18,000	63,970	44,150	75,750	123,000	280,900	0	605,770	60,577
1810–1815	19,300	4,200		34,600	33,100	111,800	8,700	211,700	42,340
1816–1820	48,400	9,000		59,200	60,600	151,100	59,600	387,900	77,580
1821–1825	22,700	4,000		44,200	60,600	128,400	43,200	303,100	60,620
1826–1830	26,700	4,900		70,500	66,700	164,400	58,100	391,300	78,260
1831–1835	27,400	1,100		37,700	71,900	102,800	3,000	243,900	48,780
1836–1840	35,300	5,700		50,400	40,800	193,500	99,400	425,100	85,020
1841–1845	19,100	200		45,300	4,400	112,900	20,300	202,200	40,440
1846–1850	14,700	700		53,400	7,700	197,000	66,700	340,200	68,040
1851–1855	10,300	300		8,900	2,900	22,600	12,800	57,800	11,560
1856–1860	3,100	300		14,000	4,400	88,200	11,300	121,300	24,260
1861–1865	2,700	0		2,600	0	41,200	2,700	49,200	9,840
1866–1867	0	0		400	0	3,000	0	3,400	1,700
Total	599,864	756,390	710,451	1,870,620	1,658,152	3,927,801	391,782	9,915,060	48,131

Source: Herbert S. Klein, The Atlantic Slave Trade (New York: Cambridge University Press, 1999), pp. 208–209.

the *reconquista* (the "reconquering" of Spain from the Moors) and the expulsion of the Jews from Spain. The resulting racial ideology was referred to as *limpieza de sangre* (purity of blood). Once introduced to the Caribbean, *limpieza de sangre* translated into a system of racial privilege in which whiteness stood at the top of an ethnic-racial hierarchy that put African and Amerindian physical features at the lowest end of the continuum. Within this system of racial privilege, race mixtures that occurred between pure races (and later mixed races) could be charted and—through precise mathematical computations—persons could be assigned differential rights and privileges. Table 8.3 indicates the profusion of racial terms (and their meanings) from eighteenth-century New Spain (Mexico).

As one might imagine, the resulting system of supposed racial types produced a confusing pattern of classification across the Spanish, British, French, and Dutch Caribbean territories. Indeed, a comparison of racial terms and categories on Spanish-, French-, and British-ruled islands at the time provides a clear illustration of the social construction of race. In this regard, a comparison of Table 8.4 and Figure 8.1 is instructive. Table 8.4 presents the exacting measures taken by elites in the French Caribbean to ascertain a person's precise degree of whiteness, and Figure 8.1 depicts similar efforts on the part of Jamaican elites.

Table 8.5, meanwhile, examines the 128 racial combinations and the (at least) eleven racial types identified by the Creole observer Médéric Louis Élie Moreau de Saint-Méry (1750–1819) in his three-volume *Description topographique, physique, civile, politique, et historique de la partie Française de l'isle de Saint-Domingue* (Topographical, physical, civil, political, and historical description of the French part of the island of Santo Domingo). The common thread running through all of these systems was the Caribbean elite's

Table 8.2 Distribution of the African Regional Origins of Slaves Arriving in Major British Colonies, 1658–1713 (percentage)

	Chesapeake	Barbados	Jamaica	Antigua	Montserrat	Nevis
Senegambia	34.2	5.3	5.4	2.5	21.8	8.9
Sierra Leone	0	0.8	0.5	3.0	0	5.0
Windward Coast	0	0.2	0.4	0	0	2.9
Gold Coast	16.5	39.6	36.0	44.8	37.8	32.1
Bight of Benin	4.0	25.7	26.0	13.9	8.1	12.0
Bight of Biafra	44.0	13.4	11.5	32.3	12.6	24.7
West-Central Africa	1.2	10.2	20.1	3.6	0	13.1
Southeast Africa	0	4.8	0.2	0	19.7	1.4
Number of slaves	7,795	85,995	72,998	8,926	2,037	14,040

Source: David Eltis, *The Rise of African Slavery in the Americas* (Cambridge, UK: Cambridge University Press, 2000), p. 245.

Table 8.3 Racial Categories in Eighteenth-Century New Spain (Mexico)

1. Spaniard and Indian beget mestizo.
2. Mestizo and Spanish woman beget *castizo*.
3. *Castizo* woman and Spaniard beget Spaniard.
4. Spanish woman and black man beget mulatto.
5. Spaniard and mulatto woman beget *morisco*.
6. *Morisco* woman and Spaniard beget *albino*.
7. Spaniard and albino woman beget *torna atrás* (turn away, as in "from white").
8. Indian man and *torna atrás* woman beget *lobo*.
9. *Lobo* and Indian woman beget *zambaigo*.
10. *Zambaigo* and Indian woman beget *cambujo*.
11. *Cambujo* and mulatto woman beget *albarazado*.
12. *Albarazado* and mulatto woman beget *barcino*.
13. *Barcino* and mulatto woman beget *coyote*.
14. *Coyote* woman and Indian man beget *chamiso*.
15. *Chamiso* woman and mestizo beget *coyote mestizo*.
16. *Coyote mestizo* and mulatto woman beget *ahí te estás* (there you are).

Source: Magnus Mörner, *Race Mixture in the History of Latin America* (Boston: Little, Brown, 1967), p. 58.

Table 8.4 Some Terms Used in the French Caribbean for Race Mixtures and Degrees of Whiteness

Putative Ancestry	Term	English Equivalent	Reputed Degree of Whiteness
Offspring of white and black	*mulâtre*	mulatto	1/2 white
Offspring of white and *mulâtre*	*quarteron*	quadroon	3/4 white
Offspring of white and *quarteron*	*métis* or *octavon*	octoroon	7/8 white
Offspring of white and *octavon*	*mamelouc*	mustee	15/16 white
Offspring of white and *mamelouc*	*sang-mélé*	musteephino	31/32 white
Offspring of black and *mulâtre*	*griffe*	sambo	1/4 white
Offspring of black and *griffe*	*sacatra*	sambo	1/8 white
Offspring of black and *sacatra*	*marabou*	sambo	1/16 white

Source: Adapted from W. Adolphe Roberts, *The French in the West Indies* (New York: Bobbs-Merrill, 1942), p. 134.

grave concern for determining a mixed individual's exact degree of proximity to (or distance from) whiteness.

The classic image of the ethnic, racial, and class structure of colonial Caribbean society during slavery is one of a pyramid. A small section at the apex represented whites. A thin band beneath this represented the mulatto population;

Figure 8.1 Grades of Color in Early Nineteenth-Century Jamaica

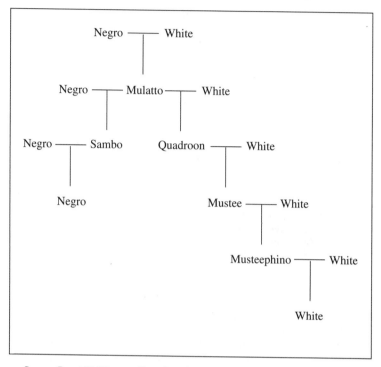

Source: Barry W. Higman, *Slave Population and Economy in Jamaica, 1807–1834* (Cambridge, UK: Cambridge University Press, 1976), p. 139.

the rest of society constituted the vast majority of African slaves. But that can be only a general, impressionistic guide. Ethnicity, race, and social class were never in perfect alignment, and often conflicts broke out within the top echelons of Caribbean society. The Haitian revolution provides a case in point. On the eve of the revolution, the "free people of color"—known as the *affranchis*—represented a small but influential portion of the overall population and in many ways were responsible for precipitating the revolution. Table 8.6 provides a breakdown of ethnicity and status in the colonies of Santo Domingo (the Dominican Republic) and St. Domingue (Haiti) at the end of the eighteenth century.

At the same time, there were profound class and status divisions within and across each segment of the social pyramid in St. Domingue that tended to mitigate the structural simplicity. For example, among whites there were *grands blancs* (high-status landowning whites), as well as *petit blancs* (lesser whites). Many *affranchis* owned slaves. There were also mulatto former slaves

Table 8.5 Racial Categories in St. Domingue, Late Eighteenth Century

Category	Parts White	Parts Black
Noir (black)	0	128
Sacatra	16	112
Griffe	32	96
Marabou	48	80
Mulâtre	64	64
Quarteron	96	32
Métis	112	16
Mamelouc	120	8
Quarteronné	124	4
Sang-mêlé	126	2
Blanc (white)	128	0

Source: Médéric Louis Élie Moreau de Saint-Méry, *Description topographique, physique, civile, politique et historique de la partie Française de l'isle de Saint-Domingue* (Topographical, physical, civil, political, and historical description of the French part of the island of Santo Domingo), 3 vols. New edition edited by Blanche Maurel and Étienne Taillemite (Paris: Société de L'Histoire des Colonies Françaises and Librairie LaRose, 1958 [1797–1798]), vol. 1, p. 100.

and well-to-do Afro-Haitians among the group of free coloreds, as they were called. The Haitian revolution avowedly upheld the power of Afro-Haitians. The resulting constitution of 1805 barred whites from owning property and equated the Haitian identity with "blackness"—a conscious effort to turn the colonial racial system privileging whites on its head. Despite such declarations, postrevolutionary power generally remained in the hands of an organized mulatto elite, and the division between this mulatto elite and the broader Afro-Haitian masses has plagued Haiti ever since. Following the revolution, mulattoes tended to exert significant economic and political control, whereas Afro-Haitians occupied the lower rungs of the social ladder.

The Aftermath of Colonial Rule and Slavery

As critical as slavery was for the development of ethnicity, race, class, and nationality across the modern Caribbean, the period immediately preceding and following the abolition of slavery has left an equally indelible mark (Scott 1985; Fraginals, Pons, and Engerman 1985; Baronov 2000). The process of abolition itself was by no means uniform throughout the Caribbean. The competing colonial powers ended slavery at different times. The dramatic slave uprising and revolution in Haiti was far from the norm. More typical was the case of the British Empire. A combination of free-market forces and humanitarian interests eventually ended the slave trade in 1807, with slavery itself abolished by 1838. Cuba was the final holdout, maintaining slavery until 1886.

Table 8.6 Ethnicity and Status in Santo Domingo and St. Domingue at the End of the Eighteenth Century

	Santo Domingo (1794)	St. Domingue (1789)
Whites	35,000	40,000
Slaves	15,000–30,000	450,000
Free/mixed	38,000	30,000

Source: Anthony P. Maingot, "Race, Color, and Class in the Caribbean," in *The Americas: Interpretive Essays,* edited by Alfred Stepan (New York: Oxford University Press, 1992), p. 230.

The paths following slavery with respect to the plantation system and the treatment of former slaves also differed significantly across the Caribbean. In many cases, slaves were initially forced into systems of apprenticeship (called *patronato* in Cuba). The purpose of apprenticeship—or so it was claimed—was to ease the transition for former slaves into their new lives. In fact, apprenticeship was primarily used to assist planters while they set about to replace slaves with new forms of coerced labor. Following apprenticeship, former slaves faced two basic options. They could continue to work on plantations under new structures of coercion, or, in areas where land was available, they could venture out and try to form independent peasant communities. Others occasionally migrated to other locations.

The immediate concern of planters on the eve of abolition was to maintain ready access to an easily coerced labor force. To resolve this dilemma, a global network of forced labor migration was instituted. This enormous undertaking ferried huge numbers of workers from the distant reaches of the British, Dutch, Portuguese, and Spanish Empires to the Caribbean. Chinese and East Indian laborers represented the majority of workers forced to migrate. More than 125,000 indentured Chinese laborers came to Cuba, Guyana, Jamaica, and Trinidad. From 1838 to 1917, more than 400,000 East Indians were taken to Jamaica, Guyana, and Trinidad. Today East Indians comprise about 40 percent of the Trinidad and Tobago population and 55 percent of the Guyanese population. More than 100,000 East Indians were sent to Martinique, Guadeloupe, and French Guiana. Another 35,000 went to Suriname, where they were joined by about 22,000 laborers from Java. Amerindians from the Yucatán were also sent to the Caribbean, along with a number of West African laborers and indentured workers from Madeira who wound up in Trinidad and Guyana. Thus, the end of slavery in the Caribbean resulted in one of the most ethnically and culturally diverse regional gatherings in the world.

In addition to the forced migration to the Caribbean there was a sizable amount of migration within the Caribbean. Migrants from Haiti as well as the British West Indies traveled to Cuba during the sugar boom. Puerto Ricans crossed the Mona Passage to the Dominican Republic for similar reasons. Laborers from Curaçao moved to Suriname to work on the railway. This massive movement of labor flooded the Caribbean region and greatly reduced the bargaining power of former slaves. If former slaves refused to work, they were easily replaced. If former slaves refused to work under certain harsh conditions, they were threatened with the prospect of losing their job to an imported laborer. In addition, the forced global gathering of varying nationalities, ethnicities, and religions guaranteed a degree of internecine conflict that could effectively keep the powerless masses continuously divided.

Ethnic, Racial, and National Minorities in Caribbean Society

Few regions of the world today can match the Caribbean's cultural diversity. The ongoing migration into the Caribbean both before and since the end of slavery has created an extraordinary blending of peoples, languages, and faiths. As discussed, the long period of the slave trade and plantation system brought a diverse mix of African ethnic groups. The plantation system, of course, also brought European traders and planters from Spain, the Netherlands, England, Denmark, and France. The next wave of forced labor migration in the mid-nineteenth century brought people from China, India, and Portugal as well as additional laborers from West Africa and other parts of Central America and the Caribbean. Later waves of migration brought a still more diverse collection of peoples, including communities of Germans, Italians, Syrians, and Lebanese.

By the end of the twentieth century, the panorama of nationalities, languages, and religions across the Caribbean was staggering. Beyond the languages of the original colonizers (Spanish, English, French, Dutch, and their Creole versions) one should not be surprised to hear Chinese, Hindi, Arabic, German, or Italian spoken throughout the region. Furthermore, as Leslie Desmangles, Stephen Glazier, and Joseph Murphy describe in Chapter 10, the region has communities of worship for every major world religion, including Hinduism, Islam, Buddhism, Judaism, and Christianity, as well as a multitude of uniquely Caribbean syncretic religions.

The Afro-Caribbean population clearly represents the largest ethnic-racial group in the Caribbean. At the same time, though Afro-Caribbean peoples have achieved political power and prominence in many countries, they remain notably lacking among the region's social and economic elites. Thus, despite their declining numbers—as a percentage of the population—and dwindling political clout since the abolition of slavery, Caribbean whites continue to exert disproportional social, political, and economic influence. This is in large measure due to the enormous concentration of wealth and resources in the territories still under their control. In Martinique, for example, as late as eighty-seven years following abolition, in 1935, 3 percent of all landowners continued to own 61 percent of the cultivable soil. By the 1950s, just five large corporations effectively controlled Martinique's agricultural production. The great majority of the island's wealth and strategic resources were controlled by Creole whites, referred to as *békés*. In 1960, it was estimated that the *békés* held as much as two-thirds of the invested capital in the island.

The role of the white elite is complemented by that of the so-called trading minorities, which are ethnic-racial groups across the Caribbean who operate as merchants and traders. They facilitate intraisland trade and commerce as well as trade between the islands and other regions of the globe. Because nearly all Caribbean islands rely heavily on export trade for economic survival, trading minorities occupy a powerful position with great influence over the daily lives of the masses in society. The potential for broad resentment and antiminority sentiment in the face of an economic downturn is a constant concern. The Chinese in Trinidad, Martinique, Guyana, and Jamaica are a case in point. Middle Eastern immigrants in Haiti, Trinidad and Tobago, and the Dominican Republic (such as Syrians and Lebanese) or Jews in Curaçao and Jamaica are additional examples.

In multiethnic societies such as Trinidad and Tobago, where there is social and economic competition among several groups, things can be especially complicated. Historically, Afro-Trinidadians and East Indians have lagged far behind whites, browns, and others. Table 8.7 looks at income distribution by ethnic-racial group in Trinidad and Tobago in the 1970s. Afro-Trinidadians and East Indians today each represent about 40 percent of the population. Following the oil boom of the 1970s and the expansion in state employment and entrepreneurial opportunities, Afro-Trinidadians and East Indians have made notable progress. A 1993 report on ethnic-racial business ownership, however, indicated that Afro-Trinidadians are virtually absent from the senior management of firms owned

Table 8.7 Income Distribution in Trinidad and Tobago by Ethnic Groups, 1971–1972 and 1975–1976 (average monthly income, Trinidad and Tobago dollars)

Ethnic Group	1971–1972	1975–1976
Black	279	412
East Indian	240	454
Others	442	630

Source: Adapted from Jare Harewood and Ralph M. Henry, *Inequality in a Post-Colonial Society: Trinidad and Tobago* (St. Augustine, Trinidad: Institute of Social and Economic Research, University of the West Indies, 1985), pp. 64–65.

by whites, Syrians, Lebanese, Chinese, or East Indians. Thus, despite progress
in closing the gap, the disparities remain sharp. In the early 1990s Afro-Trini-
dadian males earned US$0.75 and East Indian males US$0.64 for every dollar
earned by males from other ethnic-racial categories. Female wages were US$0.77
and US$0.70, respectively, for Afro-Trinidadians and East Indians (Centre for
Ethnic Studies 1993).

Lasting African Influences

As noted, the vast majority of Caribbean people trace their heritage to Africa.
It is interesting to consider what this identification with Africa means to those
in the Caribbean who also identify themselves as Martinicans, Jamaicans, Trinidadians, Cubans, Grenadians, Barbadians, and so forth. To begin, it is helpful
to reiterate the danger of generalizing too greatly about the conditions that African slaves first encountered in the different slave societies of the Caribbean or
about the mix of African ethnicities that were brought over. The only experience common to all was the brutal and barbaric treatment at the hands of Europeans. Based upon their enslavement and the forced mixture of African
cultures, Caribbean slaves forged new folk traditions, belief systems, and sus-
taining ideologies. Sidney Mintz and Richard Price emphasize the significant
ethnic heterogeneity of Caribbean slave populations. They have argued against
any assumptions of historical connections between a single specific culture in
West Africa and Afro-Caribbean cultures. "The Africans who reached the New
World did not compose, at the outset, *groups*. In fact, in most cases, it might
even be more accurate to view them as *crowds,* and very heterogeneous crowds
at that" (Mintz and Price 1992:18).

What seem at first glance to be purely African cultural forms in the
Caribbean are, in fact, better conceived of as broad cultural continuities. The
evolution of Afro-Caribbean culture has entailed the constant making and re-
making of sociocultural practices and beliefs consistent with an ongoing cultural transformation and adaptation to the new Caribbean social reality. Some
of the results of this dynamic process of continuity and change have been religious systems such as Santería (or Lukumí) in Cuba, Vodou in Haiti, the Orisha religion in Trinidad, and Myal and Kumina in Jamaica. Creole languages,
as well as various forms of dance, art, and music, have also flourished within
this unique cultural transformation. Table 8.8 details the mix of language influences shaping the modern Caribbean.

In this context, the image of Africa has become a potent symbol in
Caribbean consciousness. It has been held up as the motherland or homeland
by a variety of social movements at different times. The work of Jamaican
Marcus Garvey (1887–1940) and his Universal Negro Improvement Association is a case in point. At its height in the 1920s, Garvey's association listed
more than 1,000 branches internationally. Rastafarianism—known the world

Table 8.8 Caribbean Language Situations

Multilingual: Trinidad has standard and nonstandard forms of English, a French-based
Creole, nonstandard Spanish, Bhojpuri, Urdu, and Yoruba. Suriname has Dutch, Sranan,
Saramaccan, Ndjuka, Javanese, and Hindi.

Bilingual: St. Lucia, Dominica, and Grenada have standard and nonstandard forms of
English and a French-based Creole. The Netherlands Antilles has Dutch and Papiamentu
(with English and Spanish widely used).

Diglossia: In Haiti and the French West Indies, French and a French-based Creole exist
but are kept relatively separate.

Continuum: Guyana, Antigua, Jamaica, Montserrat, and St. Kitts have different graded
levels of language beginning with a polar variety commonly called "Creole" or "Patois"
and moving through intermediate levels to a standard norm of English at the other pole.

Monolingual: Barbados, Cuba, the Dominican Republic, and Puerto Rico have a standard
and a nonstandard form of European languages (English in the first case, Spanish in
the others).

Source: Mervyn C. Alleyne, "A Linguistic Perspective on the Caribbean," in *Caribbean Contours,* edited by Sidney W. Mintz and Sally Price (Baltimore: Johns Hopkins University Press, 1985), p. 166.

over for its association with reggae music—was born of this African-inspired social movement in Jamaica. In the 1930s, Ethiopian emperor Haile Selassie I was declared God on Earth by Jamaican preachers and their followers, prompting some Rastafari from across the Caribbean to try to enlist for war when Italy invaded Ethiopia in 1935 (Yelvington 1999).

▓ Imagining the Caribbean Nation

In the Caribbean there are several ways of "imagining" the national community (Anderson 1983). It is perhaps best to view these competing versions as variations on a theme rather than as distinct and unrelated. What they have in common is their genesis in eighteenth-century European conceptualizations of the state. In addition, nationalisms in the Caribbean revolve around the notion of a national culture. This is taken to mean a number of things, most especially popular forms of expression such as music (Manuel et al. 1995).

The extent to which dominant ethnic-racial groups are able to cast their vision as the accepted image of nationalism among the masses has far-reaching implications. Indeed, it is argued here that there are four essential frameworks for imagining the nation in the Caribbean: *mestizaje-créolité* (racial mixing/ creolism), racial democracy, national race, and multiculturalism. This is not to suggest that any particular nationalist ideology is wholly subscribed to by all citizens or that it imposes a uniform pattern of social relations. For example, anti-Haitian sentiment is the cornerstone of nationalism in the Dominican Republic, but it is mitigated by ongoing cooperative relationships between Haitians and Dominicans in the border zones. In Trinidad and Tobago, the competition between Afro-Trinidadians and East Indians that typifies competing visions of the nation exists alongside bonds of kinship between members of each group.

Mestizaje-Créolité

Nationalism in many Latin American countries is characterized by the concept of *mestizaje* (Yelvington 1997), which revolves around the image of Amerindians and the offspring of Amerindians and Europeans who represent a unique, new ethnic identity. Two beliefs are fundamental: (1) Due to the lack of pure European ethnicity, the traditional European model of nationhood—built on a supposed European national character—is rejected; and (2) at the same time, notions of backwardness and lack of civilization attach to the claims of local ethnic distinctiveness. Thus, ethnic-racial identities that form the ideological basis for nationhood in the European model are, in this case, treated as handicaps to be overcome. The ruling elites step in to argue that heterogeneous Caribbean ethnic-racial identities stand in the way of creating a harmonious and homogeneous nation. The project of national identity thus becomes inextricably linked to the interests of Caribbean ruling elites and is based largely on the elites' ability to construct a notion of nationhood around their ethnic-racial identity.

Certain contradictions are inevitable in this process. Contemporary Amerindian peoples are actively marginalized, while symbols of a noble pre-Hispanic Amerindian culture are recast as national characteristics in recognition of the mixed ethnic-racial past. This process is exemplified by the case of Martinique, where leading intellectuals—such as Patrick Chamoiseau, Raphaël Confiant, and Jean Bernabé—promote a *créolité* cultural politics. These writers are often responding to the négritude (an ideology extolling manifestations of blackness) of Aimé Césaire, a major Martinican thinker and politician. They promote Creole language, culture, and music as celebrations of a supposedly authentic Martinican culture and history. These *créolistes* attempt to present themselves as products of a historical process that resulted in a new Creole culture. Herein lies the danger and the deception: national history becomes a tool of domination by elites.

The basic argument of the *créolistes* is that harmony rather than conflict characterized early Martinican society. It is claimed, for example, that the plantation—the site of the creolization process—was characterized by a relatively mild form of slavery as compared to elsewhere in the Caribbean. In Puerto Rico, Cuba, and the former French territories, one also hears the argument that slavery was somehow more benign and that relations between slaves and masters were less onerous or objectionable than in other plantation societies such as Jamaica and the United States. It is easy to see how this fits with a nationalist project of *mestizaje-créolité*. Unlike in those countries colonized

Children of African
descent in a barrio
in Santo Domingo,
Dominican Republic.

by the "cold" northern Europeans, there is no basis for modern ethnic-racial conflict because there was so little conflict in the past. We are, after all, one big, happy family united around common core values. Or so the story goes.

For all the claims of a harmonious and equal mix of cultural influences, European origins remain dominant. For example, the Creole language is an integral component of national identity. For the *créolistes,* however, Creole does not reflect the influence of African languages. Rather, modern Creole is thought to have resulted from the dialects spoken by the early French colonists. This selective, creative reconstruction of Martinique's history has allowed elites to popularize a fictional account legitimizing and justifying their rule. Insofar as the *créolistes* have been able to position themselves as both heroic chroniclers of the "true" past and, coincidentally, as the very embodiments of a mythical, mixed ethnic-racial identity and tradition, they have been able to mask the self-serving effects of *francisation* (identification with French culture, or "Frenchification").

Racial Democracy

Cuban nationalist José Martí (1853–1895) recognized the strong potential for ethnic-racial conflict within the revolutionary forces organized to overthrow Spanish colonialism during the Cuban war of independence (more commonly known as the Spanish-American War). As a result, he sought to unite Cubans with an ideology of nonracial nationalism. In his influential 1893 essay "Mi raza" (My race), Martí wrote, "Man is more than white, more than mulatto, more than black. Cuban is more than white, more than mulatto, more than black." There was an effort in the early twentieth century by many nationalist thinkers, of all ethnic-racial identities, to revive the work of Martí and to define the cultural essence of what it meant to be Cuban. As was the case in Martinique, harmony was emphasized over conflict. Both the *negristas* (the middle-class Afro-Cubans, mulattoes, and their white allies who proclaimed the national culture to be uniquely mulatto) and the Hispanicists emphasized the role of a Spanish-based Creole culture where ethnic-racial problems were minimal because Afro-Cubans, mulattos, and whites each shared this culture (Davis 1997).

This notion of ethnic-racial harmony has shaped Cuban nationalism for the past century—notwithstanding recurrent Afro-Cuban mobilizations against racism. Given the impact of twentieth-century US interventions on ethnic-racial relations and nationalism in Cuba, Puerto Rico, Haiti, and the Dominican Republic, the language of racial democracy often also takes the form of anti-imperialism. Racial democracy—with healthy doses of anti-imperialism—became a central tenet of the Cuban national identity that framed the 1959 Cuban revolution. Fidel Castro has often referred to Cuba as a "Latin-African" nation. Because racial democracy emphasizes national cultural integration that idealizes ethnic-racial relations, there has been a tendency to soften the Afro-Cuban identity by presuming a mulatto or Creole national cultural identity. Racial democracy precludes identification with specific ethnic-racial groups as a threat to national unity. Consequently, the postrevolutionary Cuban leadership has often come under criticism for its failure to effectively deal with the race issue.

The complexities inherent in defining national identities in the Caribbean are evident in a curious controversy that emerged in Puerto Rico. In 1997 the Mattel Corporation introduced a new Puerto Rican Barbie as part of its Dolls of the World Collection. Although Mattel had introduced Mexican, Peruvian, Brazilian, and Spanish versions of the doll, as well as the nonspecific Hispanic Barbie in the United States, none generated as much debate in the popular media as the Puerto Rican doll. Many objections centered on the doll's physical appearance and costume.

Puerto Rican Barbie wore a long, white cotton dress trimmed with lace, pink ribbon, and floral adornments, evoking Spanish influence. The doll's long, wavy hair and the pink ribbon around its waist were accented with an amapola flower, which symbolizes the *jíbara* (a female peasant in the mountainous interior region). In Puerto Rico, the *jíbaro* (male peasant) plays a crucial symbolic role

Schoolchildren in Cuba.

shaping national identity. Considered to possess the simple values and indomitable spirit of rural folk everywhere, the *jíbaro* also embodies the process of *mestizaje-creolization*. He is descended from a mixture of the three races and cultures said to constitute Puerto Ricans: the Spanish colonizers, the Amerindians (or Taínos), and the African slaves. Yet the *jíbaro*, intended to represent racial democracy in Puerto Rico, is invariably depicted as white, effectively denying all but the most insignificant Amerindian heritage along with all traces of an African heritage. Similarly, Puerto Rican Barbie's fair skin and long, flowing hair were viewed by some as sending an implicit message regarding social standards of beauty, while the doll's impossibly thin waist but full-bosomed figure was said to promote a distinctly US cultural vision of beauty.[6]

Journalist Juan Manuel García Passlacqua argued that Puerto Rican Barbie was mulatto based on a popular vision of Puerto Rico as a *mestizo-mulatto* society. In a column in the *San Juan Star,* he lauded Puerto Rican Barbie's "mulatto complexion, her almond eyes, her thick nose, her plump lips, her raven hair and her most magnificently simple but gorgeous local folkloric dress."[7] This tendency to treat the mulatto identity as the exclusive national image—at the expense of the Afro-Caribbean presence—is not unusual among nationalist writers (particularly males) in the Spanish-speaking Caribbean. As Arlene Torres has argued, "The crux of the matter is that Puerto Rico is *mulato* as a nation *cuando nos conviene* (when it is convenient to be so)" (Torres 1998:288). The controversy surrounding Puerto Rican Barbie underscores the profound implications of racial and ethnic identity in the region, a topic we will return to later in this chapter.

National Race

In the Dominican Republic, an Afro-Caribbean identity is commonly associated with Haitian lineage. If one is "truly" Dominican, one is not Afro-Caribbean; Dominican and Afro-Caribbean identities are mutually exclusive. National race, as an ideology of nationalism, tends to conflate nationality with ethnicity. In the Dominican Republic, this has its roots in the dictatorship of Rafael Trujillo (1930–1961) and his anti-Haitian paranoia and prejudice. Although considered a mulatto himself—his maternal grandmother was Haitian, and he was consequently denied membership to the white elite's social clubs—Trujillo sought at every turn to valorize white civilization and culture. He instituted a policy of *hispanidad* (Spanishness), by which the national identity and culture of the Dominican Republic were rooted in a glorious European past. Roman Catholicism, Spanish literature, the conquistadors, and even the bullfight were upheld as the true legacy of the nation.

Trujillo's machinations were more than rhetorical. In the depths of the Great Depression, with sugar prices low and unemployment high, he ordered the security forces to massacre Haitian sugarcane workers. An estimated 20,000–30,000 Haitians were killed from October 2 to 4, 1937. Importantly, despite popular ideology suggesting that all Afro-Caribbean people in the Dominican Republic must be Haitian, not all Afro-Caribbeans were simply taken aside and slaughtered; steps were taken to distinguish Afro-Caribbeans who were Dominican from Afro-Caribbeans who were actually Haitian. Haitians were known to have difficulty pronouncing the word *perejil* (parsley). This follows from the fact that, within Haitian Creole, the *r* sound is pronounced like an *l*. Based on this test, Haitians were identified and killed (Yelvington 1997). This method of distinguishing Haitians from Dominicans testifies to the fact that Dominicans, at least at some level, recognize that there is such a person as an Afro-Dominican—a Dominican who is identical to a Haitian in appearance.

Although this episode represented an extreme form of racist nationalism in the Caribbean, virulent anti-Haitian sentiment has remained a staple of Dominican politics. During the 1994 presidential election, Joaquín Balaguer, a multiterm president and Trujillo protégé, based much of his campaign on an appeal to voters based on anti-Haitian bigotry. It was argued that victory for his opponent, José Francisco Peña Gómez—the Afro-Dominican former mayor of Santo Domingo—would risk a tidal wave of Haitian immigration that could threaten the nation. Balaguer's campaign produced a video showing Peña Gómez attending a faith-healing ceremony that they tried to link to Haitian Vodou worship. A pamphlet was circulated characterizing Peña Gómez's election as part of a centuries-old Haitian plot to take over the Dominican Republic. Many

Dominicans rejected Balaguer's racist appeals. Nevertheless, amid charges of fraud, the Central Elections Board eventually declared Balaguer the winner by a slim margin.

A more recent example of the depth of anti-Haitian sentiment in the Dominican Republic occurred in 2005, when the Movement for Dominican Women of Haitian Descent helped galvanize the fight for two ethnic Haitian children who had been born in the Dominican Republic and were later denied Dominican birth certificates. The children's case was taken to the Inter-American Court for Human Rights, which sided with the children and ordered the Dominican government to provide each child a birth certificate and $8,000 restitution. In addition, the court ordered the Dominican Republic to open its schools to all children, regardless of national origin. It was a landmark case: for the first time in the court's history, it upheld human rights laws prohibiting racial discrimination in access to nationality and citizenship. The victory, however, was short-lived.

Taking advantage of an ambiguity within the Dominican constitution, the Dominican Supreme Court ultimately ruled against the children. The constitution grants citizenship to those born in the Dominican Republic, with the exception of those considered to be "in transit" through the country. Those born to Haitian seasonal workers, such as the children in this case, fall into this category and are not extended citizenship. Haiti, by contrast, offers citizenship to the offspring of any Haitian citizen, no matter where they are born.

The court's decision sparked a series of human rights abuses, with government officials openly challenging the citizenship of many Dominicans of Haitian descent. That treatment further deepened the second-class status of darker-skinned Dominicans in general and of Dominicans with Haitian backgrounds in particular. Indeed, in 2007, the US Embassy urged its staff members to avoid a very popular nightclub in Santo Domingo after a number of African American diplomats were refused entry.

At the center of much of this controversy was Sonia Pierre, the director of the Movement for Dominican Women of Haitian Descent, who was born to Haitian parents in the Dominican Republic and has spent most of her life advocating for the equal rights of persons of Haitian descent in the country. Sonia Pierre's activism began in the mid-1970s, when at the age of thirteen, she helped organize Haitian and Dominican sugarcane workers to protest the working conditions and abuses of Dominican bosses. In 2006, she was awarded the Robert F. Kennedy Memorial Center Human Rights Award. Predictably, shortly after receiving this honor, her Dominican opponents attacked her, and the government began questioning her rightful citizenship. The Administrative Chamber of the Dominican Republic's Electoral Board threatened to revoke her and her children's citizenship. Carlos Morales Troncoso, the Dominican foreign minister, formally protested to Ethel Kennedy, the late senator's widow, suggesting that the selection of Sonia Pierre was ill-advised. The Dominican government remained adamant in defense of its policies toward Haitians.

In accepting the RFK Human Rights award, Sonia Pierre remarked:

In my country, my community is a victim of violence and repression expressed in different ways, among which are the massive roundups and expulsions to Haiti, during which families are split and women and children are subject to sexual violence by military personnel in charge of immigration. This year [2006], according to the data from the Migration Office more than 25,000 persons have been illegally and arbitrarily expelled to Haiti. Racism, discrimination and anti-Haitian sentiments developed in such a way that Haitian communities have been attacked by violent groups. Last summer, the national media reported tens of attacks and assassinations, which included five persons who were burnt alive. It is disheartening that government authorities and the police remain indifferent to these acts, and do not conduct the appropriate investigations to find and punish culprits.[8]

Multiculturalism

Things are somewhat different in the former British and Dutch colonies such as Jamaica, Guyana, Trinidad and Tobago, and Suriname. In these nations, nationalism and ethnic-racial identities intertwine in a manner that departs from the previously considered patterns. Nationalism here can be seen as part of a two-pronged process. First, multiculturalism is emphasized. National mottoes often reflect this orientation. Guyana refers to itself as the "Land of Six Peoples." Jamaica's national motto is "Out of Many, One People," and Trinidad and Tobago's is "Together We Aspire, Together We Achieve." In this respect, ethnic-racial differences and complementarity are both highlighted to prove and justify each group's indispensable contribution, authenticity, and citizenship.

Second, debates often emerge regarding which ethnic-racial group has historically contributed the most to the national culture, implying a right to certain social privileges. In this process, the Eurocentric hierarchy is turned on its head. The formerly subordinate become the privileged, while the formerly privileged become the scorned. A social status hierarchy among ethnic-racial groups emerges in these societies along a continuum of so-called givers and takers. Europeans are at the bottom of the hierarchy, viewed as takers who benefited from society more than they contributed. Afro-Caribbeans and East Indians wage a never-ending contest to prove that they are the ultimate givers and that their group contributes the most to the nation. It is only fair—or so it is argued—that the biggest givers have the greatest say in the allocation of social and political resources.

From this upended social hierarchy a homogenizing synthesis emerges that conflates the concepts of nation, state, and ethnic-racial identity. As a result, the notion of *nonethnicity* is created, wherein someone is either an authentic representative of a national culture (a Trinidadian or Jamaican, for example) or is considered an "other" within a larger national setting. These others are portrayed as belonging to ethnic-racial groups that have retained their non-Trinidadian or non-Jamaican identity while continuing to reside in Trinidad or Jamaica. Afro-Caribbean and colored elites have developed a unique tactic, incorporating this inverted social hierarchy to anchor their privileged social position. This strategy—known as Afro-Creole nationalism—identifies national consciousness with images of Africa in a show of anticolonial zeal (Hintzen 1997). These elites celebrate various popular Afro-Caribbean cultural forms to identify with historical oppression and legitimize their views of national culture among the larger masses.

■ Contemporary Realities and Caribbean Identities

Today's Caribbean reality forms an intricate tapestry. In addition to the complex intersection of ethnicity, race, class, and nationality is the growing phenomenon of migration, which is creating a new web of transnational Caribbean communities (Basch, Schiller, and Blanc 1994). Dennis Conway reveals in Chapter 12 that the constant movement between the Caribbean and other lands is continuously reshaping Caribbean identities in new ways. This principle applies to few places more aptly than Puerto Rico. Returning to the earlier Puerto Rican Barbie controversy highlights striking differences in perceptions and values within Caribbean communities, depending upon one's location within the larger diaspora.

Given the extraordinary influence of US popular culture exported to Puerto Rico, the debate regarding the appearance of the Puerto Rican Barbie doll invariably raised questions of identity, along with deeper political concerns. "Puerto Rico has a history of [external] control that makes the people insecure about who they are," observed Roberta Johnson, a professor of political science at the University of San Francisco. "A lot of people don't want to be consumed by the English-speaking country to the north." The Barbie package, for example, describes Puerto Rico as having been "discovered in 1493 by Christopher Columbus, who claimed it for Spain." That ignores Puerto Rico's original Amerindian inhabitants (the Taínos) and their contributions to Puerto Rican cultural identity. "I was insulted," said Gina Rosario, a school art director of Puerto Rican descent who lives in Alexandria, Virginia. "She looks very, very Anglo, and what was written [in the package's brief history of Puerto Rico] was very condescending—'The US government lets us govern ourselves.' If you're going to represent a culture, do it properly—be politically honest," she said.

The Barbie episode underscored significant differences between Puerto Ricans living in Puerto Rico and Puerto Ricans living in the United States regarding cultural and national identity. For many in Puerto Rico, the doll was a welcome, if belated, attempt to valorize Puerto Rican culture. In the United States, Puerto Rican identity has different implications, and the very same symbols can generate alternative meanings. Ethnic-racial discrimination, social class, nationalism, and sexism all affect Puerto Ricans differently, depending on whether they live in the United States or in Puerto Rico. Negative media stereotypes and prejudice tend to hit Puerto Ricans living in the United States especially hard. Sensitivity to how Puerto Ricans are depicted—and by whom—means that US Puerto Ricans feel a need to be in control of these representations and, as a result, have developed a heightened political consciousness.

Puerto Ricans in the United States have actively engaged in efforts to define and shape representations of Puerto Rican culture—to extol its virtues while confronting damaging stereotypes. Puerto Rican Barbie, with her Spanish colonial dress and Anglicized physical features, undermined these efforts. The contrasting receptions of Puerto Rican Barbie also have to do, in part, with disagreements over Puerto Rico's political status. As Thomas J. D'Agostino explains in Chapter 4, Puerto Rico is currently a commonwealth of the United States, subject to US law and jurisdiction, with limited self-governance and no voting representation in the US Congress. Although those in Puerto Rico are closely divided over statehood and the current commonwealth status, a clear majority of Puerto Ricans in the United States favor keeping the commonwealth status, strongly opposing Puerto Rico's annexation. "In Puerto Rico, the issue is recognition for this little island," said Angelo Falcón of the Institute for Puerto Rican Policy in New York City. "Over here, there's a real question of how we're presented." By contrast, writing for a Puerto Rican newspaper, García Passlacqua argued that what is important is that the doll "will help us explain ourselves, as we are, to all Americans."

Race—and particularly the implications of racial identity—has been the focus of much artistic expression in Puerto Rico as well as throughout the wider Caribbean. Tego Calderón is an Afro–Puerto Rican musician who since the late 1990s has developed an original interpretation of reggaeton, a musical style originating in Panama in the 1990s. Calderón's musical influences include an eclectic mix of reggaeton, hip-hop, mambo, salsa, and the blues. Through his music and in his personal life, Calderón identifies deeply with the Afro-Caribbean community of Loíza on the east coast of Puerto Rico. In confronting the loose racial hierarchy that persists in Puerto Rico, favoring those with lighter skin, Calderón's music resonates strongly with Afro-Puerto Ricans and represents an especially radical challenge with its prideful message and unapologetic tone.

This is reflected in the lyrics from his 2002 song, "Loíza," in which Calderón sharply condemns Puerto Rican society for its racist attitudes, blatant discrimination, and a legal system based on racial preferences. In particular, Calderón inveighs against the popular ideological belief that there are no blacks or whites in Puerto Rico because everyone is a mix of Spanish, African, and Taíno. This notion of a benevolent racial trilogy, Calderón argues, is belied by the everyday experiences of darker-skinned Puerto Ricans, especially at the hands of the legal system. In "Loíza," Calderón implores:

> For my community that I love so much!
> From Calderón to all of Loíza!
> Listen!
> I am in no hurry
> But your slow pace angers me
> And those who do not fight for Loíza
> (No, does not fight!)
> Want to make me think
> That I am part of a racial trilogy
> Where everybody's the same, without special treatment
> I know how to forgive
> It is you who does not know how to absolve
> So, you are able to justify so much evil
> because your history is shameful
> Amongst other things
> You changed chains for handcuffs
> We are not all equal in legal terms[9]

■ The Growing Diaspora

Conflicting notions of authenticity and identity between Caribbean communities living in their country of origin and those living abroad are not unique to Puerto Ricans. Everywhere they settle, Caribbean migrant communities maintain transnational linkages with their homelands while forging new communities and identities in their adopted countries. The implications of such linkages are explored in greater detail by Dennis Conway in Chapter 12. Indeed, today London, New York, Amsterdam, Toronto, Miami, and Paris are home to many migrants, including second- and third-generation communities. Table 8.9 traces the path of significant Caribbean communities outside the region; Table 8.10 provides an overview of Caribbean migrants in the United States by country of origin.

This transformative migration experience has been well captured by many Caribbean writers' reflective (and quasi-autobiographical) works of fiction. The growing list of Caribbean migrant literature includes Samuel Selvon's *The Lonely Londoners* (1956), Paule Marshall's *Brown Girl, Brownstones* (1959), V. S. Naipaul's *Mimic Men* (1967), Julia Álvarez's *How the García Girls Lost Their Accents* (1991), Edwidge Danticat's *The Dew Breaker* (2004), and Junot Díaz's *The Brief Wondrous Life of Oscar Wao* (2007). Each of these works attempts to understand the unique pressures and experiences shaping Caribbean migrant communities. For example, "La guagua aérea" (The flying bus), a short story written in 1994 by Puerto Rican writer Luis Rafael Sánchez, chronicles

Table 8.9 Caribbean Migrants in the Metropoles

Country	Year	Home Population	Migrants Living in the Metropolis	Metropolis	Migrants in the Metropolis as a % of Home Population
Puerto Rico	1980	3,196,520	2,014,000	United States	63
	1990	3,522,037	2,651,815		75
Suriname	1975	365,000	150,000	Netherlands	41
	1980	356,000	176,000		49
	1990	422,000	228,722		54
Martinique	1982	326,717	95,704	France	29
	1990	359,572	109,616		30
			175,200 (ancestry)[a]		48.7
Guadeloupe	1982	328,400	87,024	France	26
	1990	386,987	101,934		26
			161,806 (ancestry)[a]		42
Dutch Antilles	1990	248,000	75,722	Netherlands	30.5
Jamaica	1990	2,404,000	435,024 (ancestry)[a]	United States	18
			685,024 (includes extralegal migrants)		28.5
			325,000 (ancestry) [a]	United Kingdom	13.5
			1,010,024	United States and United Kingdom	42
Haiti	1990	6,349,000	289,521 (ancestry)[a]	United States	4.5
			689,521 (includes extralegal migrants)		10.8
Dominican Republic	1990	6,948,000	520,151 (ancestry)[a]	United States	7.4
			745,151 (includes extralegal migrants)		10.7
Cuba	1983	9,771,000	910,867	United States	9.3
	1990	10,500,000	1,053,197		10

Source: Adapted from Ramón Grosfoguel, "Colonial Caribbean Migrations to France, the Netherlands, Great Britain, and the United States," in *Caribe 2000: Definiciones, identidades y culturas regionales y/o nacionales* (Caribbean 2000: Definitions, identities, and regional cultures and/or nationalities), edited by Lowell Fiet and Janette Becerra (San Juan: Facultad de Humanidades Universidad de Puerto Rico, 1997), p. 64.

Note: a. "Ancestry" refers to citizens of the metropolis of Caribbean descent. Other numbers refer to migrants, both legal and extralegal.

**Table 8.10 Caribbean-Origin Populations by US State,
1980 and 1990 (percentage)**

State	Year	Puerto Rican[a]	Cuban[a]	Dominican	Jamaican	Haitian
New York	1980	49	10	79	54	60
	1990	41	7	69	44	39
New Jersey	1980	12	10	8	6	6
	1990	11	8	5	6	7
Florida	1980	5	59	4	13	19
	1990	9	64	7	22	37
Other	1980	34	21	9	27	15
	1990	39	21	19	28	17
Total	1980	2,014	803	169	197	92
population	1990	2,652	1,053	357	343	229
(thousands)						

Source: Alejandro Portes and Ramón Grosfoguel, "Caribbean Diasporas: Migration and Ethnic Communities," in *Trends in US-Caribbean Relations, Annals of the American Academy of Political and Social Science,* vol. 533, edited by Anthony P. Maingot (New York: American Academy
of Political and Social Science, 1994), p. 61.
Note: a. The percentages under "Puerto Rican" and "Cuban" refer to US citizens of Puerto
Rican or Cuban descent; foreign-born persons are included for the other three countries.

the initial period of air travel between San Juan and New York City in the
1960s. The humorous story, which was made into the film *The Flying Bus: A
Flight of Hope* in 1995, shows how such travel transformed the lives of both
those leaving Puerto Rico and of the family members who remained.

The role of nationalism often takes on heightened meaning abroad, where
segregated communities sharpen national identities. The Washington Heights
neighborhood of New York City is home to a large immigrant population from
the Dominican Republic, and Haitians and those from the English-speaking
Caribbean concentrate in Brooklyn. Miami includes neighborhoods such as
Little Haiti and Little Havana.

While drawing distinctions between themselves and other Caribbean communities, Caribbean migrants also emphasize certain differences between themselves and host cultures and ethnicities. British West Indian migrants in Central
America often proclaim the superiority of their British heritage over the local
Hispanic traditions and Spanish language. In North America, Afro-Caribbean
West Indians must learn to deal with everyday forms of racism. This is done, in
part, by forming an insulating politics of blackness while attempting to differentiate themselves from non-Caribbean African Americans. Haitian youths in
the United States, by contrast, often become "cover-ups," denying their Haitian
heritage so as to avoid the strong anti-Haitian social stigma.

The status of Haitians contrasts strongly with that of Cuban immigrants. Haitians seeking to come to the United States typically are categorized as economic refugees. Those attempting to reach the United States by boat are, therefore, intercepted by the US Coast Guard on the high seas and barred from entry. Cubans, by contrast, continue to benefit from Cold War–era policies that privilege Cuban refugees above others. At the same time, in sharp contrast to Haitians, Cubans in the United States overwhelmingly think of themselves as white. When the Cuban-orchestrated Mariél boatlift in 1980 sent thousands of Afro-Cuban and mulatto Cubans to the shores of South Florida, a decidedly hostile reaction awaited, and there was a general call for them to be sent back. In this respect, the so-called Cuban success story conceals significant ethnic-racial and class differences within the Cuban immigrant community. Cubans retain a strong preference for standard spoken Spanish in everyday life. At the same time, young Cuban Americans born in the United States continue to celebrate their cultural hybridism by extolling their command of Spanglish while proudly announcing their Cubanness—in a social context where it is convenient to do so—and emphasizing their linkages to an imagined homeland.

Conclusion

Just as 500 years ago the Caribbean was defined by the massive waves of migration into the region, today the Caribbean is notable for the ebb and flow of its peoples between the Caribbean and other regions of the former colonial empires. As new communities form and flourish within the diaspora, fresh identities and cultural patterns develop. Notions of ethnicity, race, class, and nationality are transported along with personal belongings to new lands, where these fluid and ever-changing concepts are, once again, socially constructed to fit the contours of the new environment. Thus, as soon as we think that we have grasped the essential truths of ethnicity, race, class, and nationality in the Caribbean, we inevitably discover a new metamorphosis leading to a richer, fuller description and meaning.

Although these concepts may be interpreted and understood in different ways across the Caribbean, the fact that ethnicity, race, class, and nationality continue to exert a profound influence on the lifestyles and expectations of peoples throughout the region is a common pattern that transcends political boundaries and cultural traditions.

Notes

1. Ethnic identity is seen by the people involved to draw from three principal spheres of influence: biological (or natural) factors; culture-bound traits; and otherworldly,

sacred, or spiritual forces. Importantly, it is often held that there is a causal relationship between these factors, which combine to provide a real and cohesive basis of group identity. The particular weight given to each factor and the direction of causation vary significantly among different ethnic groups.

2. The characteristics of race differ according to which society we happen to be within. When a phenomenon has no universally agreed upon criteria for describing and defining it, we say it is "socially constructed." This means that race is constructed—it is given meaning—by people within individual societies. Therefore, when applying such concepts across cultures, we do not have the luxury of assuming standard meanings.

3. There are three predominant interpretations of social class to consider. The first—and the most common use in the United States—associates class position with personal income. The principal concern is how much money one has via salary or investments. The second interpretation of class emphasizes social status as a measure of class position. Social status revolves around a host of culturally shaped social values that grant higher or lower status to certain communities, occupations, or activities. The third interpretation of class associates class position with one's social role within a society's economic system. In this formulation, a person's social power is determined by one's relation to the production process.

4. This notion is captured by Benedict Anderson's concept of the "imagined community" (Anderson 1983). This is not to suggest that national identity is somehow dreamed up or fictitious. Rather, it implies that nationhood emerges as a widely accepted ideology among group leaders and members. *Community* is understood not in the sense of a small, face-to-face society. Rather, it flows from the notion of a physically dispersed group of persons who are somehow alike in fundamental ways and who could, therefore, form a community. Nationality is no less contested than ethnicity, race, or class. Indeed, especially in the Americas, ethnic-racial pluralism confronts national ideals of homogeneity. Nationalism, therefore, supports dominant ideologies—promulgated by privileged elites—and tends to legitimate a particular configuration of social power.

5. In this regard, it should be noted that throughout this chapter we have substituted the term *Afro-Caribbean* (or *Afro-Haitian, Afro-Dominican,* etc.) for the racial category generally referred to as *black* in the United States. In this way, we are distinguishing between Afro-Haitians (or blacks in Haiti) and mulatto Haitians.

6. Mattel refused our request to include a photo of the Puerto Rican Barbie doll.

7. The information and quotes on the Puerto Rican Barbie controversy come from the following two newspaper articles: *Charlotte Observer,* December 30, 1997; and *New York Times,* December 27, 1997.

8. The text of Sonia Pierre's remarks in accepting the award can be found on the Robert F. Kennedy Memorial website, http://www.rfkmemorial.org/legacyinaction/2006_soniaspeech/%22.

9. The translation into English was provided by Maria Soledad Baronov.

Bibliography

Alleyne, Mervyn C. "A Linguistic Perspective on the Caribbean." In *Caribbean Contours,* edited by Sidney W. Mintz and Sally Price, pp. 155–179. Baltimore: Johns Hopkins University Press, 1985.

———. *Construction and Representation of Race and Ethnicity in the Caribbean and the World.* Kingston, Jamaica: University of the West Indies Press, 2002.

Álvarez, Julia. *How the García Girls Lost Their Accents*. Chapel Hill, NC: Algonquin Books of Chapel Hill, 1991.

Anderson, Benedict. *Imagined Communities: Reflections on the Origin and Spread of Nationalism*. London: Verso, 1983.

Barnes, Natasha. *Cultural Conundrums: Gender, Race, Nation, and the Making of Caribbean Cultural Politics*. Ann Arbor: University of Michigan Press, 2006.

Baronov, David. *The Abolition of Slavery in Brazil*. Westport, CT: Greenwood, 2000.

Basch, Linda, Nina Glick Schiller, and Cristina Szanton Blanc. *Nations Unbound: Transnational Projects, Postcolonial Predicaments, and Deterritorialized Nation-States*. Langhorne, PA: Gordon and Breach, 1994.

Buscaglia-Salgado, José. *Undoing Empire: Race and Nation in the Mulatto Caribbean*. Minneapolis: University of Minnesota Press, 2003.

Centre for Ethnic Studies. *Employment Practices in the Public and Private Sectors in Trinidad and Tobago,* Vol. 2: *The Private Sector.* St. Augustine, Trinidad: Centre for Ethnic Studies, University of the West Indies, 1993.

Curtin, Philip D. *The Atlantic Slave Trade: A Census*. Madison: University of Wisconsin Press, 1969.

Danticat, Edwidge. *The Dew Breaker.* New York: Alfred A. Knopf, 2004.

Davis, Darién J., ed. *Beyond Slavery: The Multilayered Legacy of Africans in Latin America and the Caribbean*. Lanham, MD: Rowman and Littlefield, 2007.

Davis, Darién J. "¿*Criollo o Mulato?* Cultural Identity in Cuba, 1930–1960." In *Ethnicity, Race, and Nationality in the Caribbean,* edited by Juan Manuel Carrión, pp. 69–95. San Juan: Institute of Caribbean Studies, University of Puerto Rico, 1997.

Díaz, Junot. *The Brief Wondrous Life of Oscar Wao*. New York: Penguin/Riverhead Books, 2007.

Eltis, David. *The Rise of African Slavery in the Americas*. Cambridge, UK: Cambridge University Press, 2000.

Fraginals, M., F. Pons, and S. Engerman. *Between Slavery and Free Labor: The Spanish-Speaking Caribbean in the Nineteenth Century*. Baltimore: Johns Hopkins University Press, 1985.

Godreau, Isar P. "La semántica fugitiva: 'Raza,' color, y vida cotidiana en Puerto Rico" (Slippery semantics: "Race," color and everyday life in Puerto Rico). *Revista de Ciencias Sociales* 9 (2000): 52–71.

Gordon, Maxine W. "Race Patterns and Prejudice in Puerto Rico." *American Sociological Review* 14, no. 2 (1949): 294–301.

Grosfoguel, Ramón. "Colonial Caribbean Migrations to France, the Netherlands, Great Britain, and the United States." In *Caribe 2000: Definiciones, identidades, y culturas regionales y/o nacionales* (Caribbean 2000: Definitions, identities, and regional cultures and/or nationalities), edited by Lowell Fiet and Janette Becerra, pp. 58–80. San Juan: Facultad de Humanidades, Universidad de Puerto Rico, 1997.

Harewood, Jack, and Ralph M. Henry. *Inequality in a Post-Colonial Society: Trinidad and Tobago*. St. Augustine, Trinidad: Institute for Social and Economic Research, University of the West Indies, 1985.

Higman, Barry W. *Slave Population and Economy in Jamaica, 1807–1834*. Cambridge, UK: Cambridge University Press, 1976.

Hintzen, Percy C. "Reproducing Domination Identity and Legitimacy Constructs in the West Indies." *Social Identities* 3, no. 1 (1997): 47–75.

Hoetink, H. "'Race' and Color in the Caribbean." In *Caribbean Contours,* edited by Sidney W. Mintz and Sally Price, pp. 55–84. Baltimore: Johns Hopkins University Press, 1985.

James, C. L. R. *The Black Jacobins: Toussaint L'Ouverture and the San Domingo Revolution*. 2nd ed. New York: Vintage Books, 1963.

Kempadoo, Kamala. *Sexing the Caribbean: Gender, Race, and Sexual Labor.* New York: Routledge Press, 2004.

Klein, Herbert S. *African Slavery in Latin America and the Caribbean.* New York: Oxford University Press, 1986.

———. *The Atlantic Slave Trade.* New York: Cambridge University Press, 1999.

Maingot, Anthony P. "Race, Color, and Class in the Caribbean." In *The Americas: Interpretive Essays,* edited by Alfred Stepan, pp. 220–247. New York: Oxford University Press, 1992.

Manuel, Peter, with Kenneth Bilby and Michael Largey. *Caribbean Currents: Caribbean Music from Rumba to Reggae.* Philadelphia: Temple University Press, 1995.

Marshall, Paule. *Brown Girl, Brownstones.* New York: Random House, 1959.

Martí, José. "Mi raza" (My race). In *La cuestion racial* (The racial question), pp. 25–29. Havana: Editorial Lex, 1959 [1893].

———. "Our America." In *Our America by José Martí: Writings on Latin America and the Struggle for Cuban Independence,* edited by Philip S. Foner and translated by Elinor Randall, Juan de Onís, and Roslyn Held Foner, pp. 84–94. New York: Monthly Review Press, 1977 [1891].

McClellan, James E. III. *Colonialism and Science: Saint Domingue in the Old Regime.* Baltimore: Johns Hopkins University Press, 1992.

Mintz, Sidney. *Caribbean Transformations.* Chicago: Aldine, 1974.

———. *Sweetness and Power: The Place of Sugar in Modern History.* New York: Viking, 1985.

Mintz, Sidney, and Richard Price. *The Birth of African-American Culture: An Anthropological Perspective.* Boston: Beacon Press, 1992.

Misir, Prem. *Ethnic Cleavage and Closure in the Caribbean Diaspora: Essays on Race, Ethnicity, and Class.* Lewiston, NY: Edwin Mellon Press, 2006.

Monge Oviedo, Rodolfo. "Are We or Aren't We?" *Report on the Americas* 25, no. 4 (1992): 19.

Moreau de Saint-Méry, Médéric Louis Élie. *Description topographique, physique, civile, politique et historique de la partie Française de l'isle de Saint-Domingue, avec des observations générales sur sa population, sur le caractère & les mœurs de ses divers habitans; sur son climat, sa culture, ses productions, son administration, &c. &c* (Topographical, physical, civil, political, and historical description of the French part of the island of Santo Domingo, with an overview of the character types and customs of its various inhabitants, as well as a study of its climate, its culture, its production, and its administrative system . . .). Philadelphia: Author, 1797–1798.

———. *Description topographique, physique, civile, politique, et historique de la partie française de l'isle de Saint-Domingue* (Topographical, physical, civil, political, and historical description of the French part of the island of Santo Domingo). 3 vols. New edition edited by Blanche Maurel and Étienne Taillemite. Paris: Société de L'Histoire des Colonies Françaises and Librairie LaRose, 1958 [1797–1798].

———. *A Civilization That Perished: The Last Years of White Colonial Rule in Haiti.* Translated, edited, and abridged by Ivor D. Spencer. Lanham, MD: University Press of America, 1985 [1797–1798].

Mörner, Magnus. *Race Mixture in the History of Latin America.* Boston: Little, Brown, 1967.

Naipaul, V. S. *The Mimic Men.* London: Andre Deutsch, 1967.

Portes, Alejandro, and Ramón Grosfoguel. "Caribbean Diasporas: Migration and Ethnic Communities." In *Trends in US-Caribbean Relations.* Annals of the American Academy of Political and Social Science, vol. 533, edited by Anthony P. Maingot, pp. 48–69. New York: American Academy of Political and Social Science, 1994.

Roberts, W. Adolphe. *The French in the West Indies.* New York: Bobbs-Merrill, 1942.

Sánchez, Luis Rafael. *La guagua aérea* (The flying bus). San Juan: Editorial Cultural, 1994.

Scott, Rebecca. *Slave Emancipation in Cuba.* Princeton, NJ: Princeton University Press, 1985.

Selvon, Samuel. *The Lonely Londoners.* New York: St. Martin's, 1956.

Shepherd, Verene A., and Hilary McD. Beckles, eds. *Caribbean Slavery and the Atlantic World.* Princeton, NJ: Markus Weiner, 2000.

Torres, Arlene. "La gran familia puertorriqueña 'Es prieta de beldá'" (The great Puerto Rican family "is really really black"). In *Blackness in Latin America and the Caribbean: Social Dynamics and Cultural Transformations,* Vol. 2: *Eastern South America and the Caribbean,* edited by Arlene Torres and Norman E. Whitten Jr., pp. 285–306. Bloomington: Indiana University Press, 1998.

Williams, Brackette F. *Stains on My Name, War in My Veins: Guyana and the Politics of Cultural Struggle.* Durham, NC: Duke University Press, 1991.

Yelvington, Kevin A. "Patterns of Ethnicity, Class, and Nationalism." In *Understanding Contemporary Latin America,* edited by Richard S. Hillman, pp. 209–236. Boulder, CO: Lynne Rienner, 1997.

———. "The War in Ethiopia and Trinidad, 1935–1936." In *The Colonial Caribbean in Transition: Essays on Postemancipation Social and Cultural History,* edited by Bridget Brereton and Kevin A. Yelvington, pp. 189–225. Gainesville: University Press of Florida, 1999.

———. "Caribbean Crucible: History, Culture, and Globalization." *Social Education* 64, no. 2 (2000): 70–77.

9

Women and Development

A. Lynn Bolles

U nderstanding Caribbean women's significant contributions to overcoming the legacies of slavery and colonialism, as well as their role in the development of the modern Caribbean, provides a more complete vision than the popular images of sensuality and exoticism that have been attributed to Caribbean women throughout history. In order to enhance our understanding, this chapter analyzes the sociocultural context of Caribbean women; their early struggles during the colonial era; similarities and differences between the Hispanic and Anglophone Caribbean; women's continuing struggles in the twenty-first century; women in organized labor and the workforce; gender, class, and familial organization; the "independent" woman in the contemporary Caribbean; women in national politics; and women in the Organization of American States (OAS) and other international agencies.

■ The Sociocultural Context of Caribbean Women

In Chapter 1 of this book, Richard S. Hillman proposes an inclusive definition of the Caribbean region. Named after one of its indigenous groups, the Caribs, the region includes twenty-seven island and mainland territories, four major European language groups, countless vernaculars and dialects, and a myriad of races and cultures. Despite these differences, the people of the region have a shared identity—West Indian/Antillean/Caribbean—that results from a shared history. There is no denying that the Caribbean region experienced two of the most extreme forms of exploitation known in human societies: slavery and colonialism. Contact between Europeans and the indigenous populations almost eradicated the latter through warfare, forced labor, diseases, and genocide.

As David Baronov and Kevin Yelvington illustrate in Chapter 8, slavery and colonial oppression introduced two additional cultural systems—African and European—which, through the process of creolization (the blending of peoples and traditions), gave rise to particularly complex social formations. Consequently, because of the legacy of slavery that marked free and nonfree on the basis of phenotype (skin color), Caribbean societies are highly stratified by race, color, class, ethnicity, and gender inequality (Barriteau 1998).

Contemporary Caribbean women are descended from the victims of the largest forced migration in modern history (arising from the enslavement of the African peoples) and of the coerced relocation of nineteenth-century indentured laborers, such as the East Indians. They are the survivors of European expansionism and its annihilation of Amerindians (Knight and Crahan 1979). In the Caribbean, however, one finds women with ethnic backgrounds from various regions of the world besides the predominant Africa and Europe. They include the Indian subcontinent, China, Lebanon, Syria, and other areas of the former Ottoman Empire.

For most island Caribbean societies, the Amerindian contribution to culture is reduced to a faint memory inscribed in archaeological sites but is evident in some cultural traits such as language, place-names, home furnishings, and some food customs. However, the recognition of and pride in Taíno heritage is resurfacing in certain quarters in the Dominican Republic and Puerto Rico, where festivals are held in commemoration of the Amerindian heritage (Davila 1997:223–227). There are groups of Amerindians living in tropical forests in southern Guyana and Suriname. For contemporary Carib women from St. Vincent and their relatives, as well as the Garifuna from coastal Guatemala and Belize, their Amerindian culture continues into the twenty-first century (McLaurin 1996). There is no doubt that these indigenous groups paid a high price for their survival. Caribs who survived battles against the French and the English were forcibly removed and relocated. Britain moved Carib peoples beyond the tropics and even resettled a group in a northern colony (Nova Scotia, Canada). However, the Caribs did not go quietly. In 1651, a year after the Caribs of Grenada allowed a French expedition from Martinique to buy extensive landholdings, hostilities resumed between the indigenous people and the French. Seeing that their efforts were futile, the last forty Caribs jumped to their deaths from a precipice on the extreme north coast of Grenada rather than submit to French rule (Ecumenical Program for Inter-Communication and Action 1982).

The East Indian population, constituting the largest ethnic group in both Guyana and Trinidad, brings critical cultural contributions from the subcontinent, both Hindu and Muslim. The vicissitudes of British colonial rule, the political economy, and immigration flows have affected the indentured populations. Many more men than women were conscripted, thereby skewing the demographics and altering cultural expectations for both men and women.

Only when the male-female ratio evened out did the Hindu- and Muslim-prescribed roles of women and men manifest themselves in the Caribbean. Gender constructs of the society of origin weigh heavily on how Indo-Guyanese and Indo-Trinidadian women were viewed historically and how they are understood at present (Mohammed and Shepherd 1999).

Caribbean women of European descent predominate in the Spanish-speaking countries of the Dominican Republic, Puerto Rico, and Cuba, although these societies are primarily mixed-race, reflecting the sociocultural and racial context of creolization—the blending of two or more groups such as African, European, or Amerindian. Here, as in the rest of the region, class and color are fundamental indicators of a woman's social position. There are also Caribbean women of Chinese and Middle Eastern descent, among others, representing distinct ethnic and religious affiliations. Ironically, notwithstanding the Creole nature of these societies, in the official census there are also categories of people designated as mixed (Yelvington 1995:22–23).

The majority of women who live in the Caribbean, however, are of African descent. Furthermore, the sociocultural contributions of different African ethnic groups (e.g., Akan, Yoruba, Ibo, and Twi) were significant. Subsequently, their language, music, religion, and other aspects of social organization contributed to the creolization process in all island and mainland territories (Manuel et al. 1995). In addition, the intensity of particular African ethnic cultural contributions is often the dominant element of Caribbean society. For example, as Leslie Desmangles, Stephen Glazier, and Joseph Murphy show in Chapter 10, there are Trinidadian Yoruba songs, as well as religious practices of Kumina in Jamaica, Vodou in Haiti, and Santería in Puerto Rico and Cuba (Warner-Lewis 1979; Rey 1999). These cultural practices evolved within the context of slavery and the founding economic structures of the region.

During early colonization, white indentured servants could not follow the prescriptive norm, or generally accepted standard of behavior for women, due to their social status. Technically, these white women were not free. English, Irish, Welsh, and Scottish women contracted as indentured laborers to escape incarceration as political prisoners, prostitutes, and convicts; to avoid leading a life of abject poverty; and of their own accord (Shepherd 1999:20–39). However, after their time of servitude ended, those who remained in Barbados, Jamaica, or St. Kitts could become a part of the respectable class if they were lucky enough to find a mate to marry or to profit from their business acumen. Because they were white, they were aided in these endeavors by their color, as it was a major social marker for being free.

During the sixteenth and seventeenth centuries, increasing numbers of African women were enslaved and brought to Caribbean colonies. These women satisfied two significant needs of these expanding sugar empires. First, there was the urgent necessity of replenishing labor due to the high volume of production and high mortality rates among enslaved workers. African women who

were familiar with agricultural work proved to be more than adequate workers in the sugarcane plantations. Subsequently, slave traders began to capture
both men and women in Africa (Higman 1999:116).

By the close of the eighteenth century, women in the slave societies of the
English-speaking Caribbean outnumbered the men. For example, in Barbados
there were consistently more women than men up until emancipation in 1834.
In Jamaica, by 1827 women constituted more than half of the enslaved population (Higman 1999:116). Mature women hoed the soil, dug drains, cut and
bundled canes, planted new canes, carried baskets of manure to the fields, and
performed other physically demanding tasks. Younger women did lighter tasks
such as weeding, tending cattle, and the like (Mathurin Mair 1975).

Fulfillment of the second need benefited slaves as well as those who required a replenished workforce on their estates. The community of slaves
made it possible for human nature to take its course, and love and procreation
brought children into the world. Given the structure of the slave society, however, these children were property and could be sold as a business transaction.
Furthermore, white overseers, masters, and other slaves raped enslaved women.
Power over the slave woman turned her own biology into a sexual commodity.

Children born to enslaved women assumed the social rank of their mothers. Some women who found themselves pregnant due to rape, or just despon-
dent about their life as a slave, resorted to taking herbal remedies that induced
spontaneous abortions. As historians have documented, women distraught
over their lives as slaves could not endure the thought that their own children
would face a similar fate. Taking matters into their own hands, women ended
potential life before it began. Incidences of infanticide were not uncommon.
Guyanese poet Grace Nichols uses this imagery in her 1983 epic poem, "I Is a
Long Memoried Woman," which depicts a slave mother throwing her newborn
overboard during the Middle Passage and then committing suicide herself.

In Jamaica, an anonymously authored popular poem titled "The Sable
Queen: An Ode" appeared in 1765 (Bush 1990:11). The poem offers a positive
image of brown and black women in glowing verse, remarking on their physical beauty and pleasing feminine attributes. While its stanzas exclaim over the
desirability of these beauties, the poem does not mention the circumstances
that brought these women from their distant homelands in Africa to the Caribbean. Furthermore, the poem never mentions that the majority of these pleasing, graceful women were enslaved or descendants of slaves. It also does not
share with the reader that because of their status as slaves, the exotic sable
women were readily available to European men by any means of coercion or
for a price affixed by her master.

The Sable Queen was a most desired sexual commodity, whether free or
enslaved, but she was still a woman of color. By reason of their skin color,
brown-skinned women occupied a social status far below that of European
women. Consequently, the economic activities of the sable queens of the poem

and the sable queens who labored in the sugarcane plantations all came to illustrate the multiple roles women played historically in Caribbean societies. Neither type of sable queen, however, was symbolized by a dusky English rose on a pedestal for all to admire and whose sole purpose was home and hearth. They were women whose lives and experiences were complicated because society denigrated any skin color but white.

Following the revolution that freed the slaves of Haiti, emancipation occurred at different times across the region. As Stephen Randall notes in Chapter 3, the British outlawed the slave trade in 1807 but did not emancipate their enslaved populations until 1838, followed by a five-year amelioration period. The Dutch (1863), Danes (1847), and French (1848) emancipated their populations at different times, leaving the Spanish colonies as the only remaining practitioners of slave labor. Puerto Rico emancipated its people in 1870 and Cuba in 1886, but they were not independent countries. Haiti (1804) and the Dominican Republic (1844) functioned as autonomous nations following their respective emancipations, but as their histories tell us, they continued to be constricted by neocolonial and island strife (Sagás 2000).

In Chapter 5, Dennis Pantin and Marlene Attzs analyze the economic impact of the sugar industry in Caribbean development. Women, men, and children across the Caribbean carved out livelihoods under severe economic conditions resulting from the collapse of the international price of sugar. During this transition from slavery, former slaves' freedom to create new villages and urban settlements in the Caribbean can be understood only within the ongoing neocolonial context. The aftermath of uneven social and economic development propagated by colonial administrations and the landed elite restricted the opportunities and living conditions available to peoples in Caribbean societies (Deere et al. 1990). More specifically, the social divisions of society (based on race and color, class and gender, and access to education and training) assigned black women to the low end of the socioeconomic ladder (Shepherd 1999:90).

Caribbean Women's Early Struggles

The pioneering work of the Jamaican feminist historian Lucille Mathurin Mair brought the previously unrecognized black woman into Caribbean history (Mathurin Mair 1975). The images about women found in conventional historical texts conveyed the idea that either the experiences of slavery and postemancipation life were homogeneous (essentially those of men) or that black women and men had different aspirations, needs, and functions in pan-Caribbean societies. Recent texts document female participation in resistance, in the development of culture and society, and in challenging male-centered, almost misogynistic interpretations of history (Shepherd, Brereton, and Bailey 1995; Shepherd 1999; Matos-Rodríguez 1999).

The new scholarship on Caribbean women analyzes the nature of surviving enslavement and various ways of living under colonial strictures. Since the mid-1970s, Caribbean feminist history has illustrated how an alternative view can bring people, especially women, and events into their proper light while providing a more inclusive vision of society. Women, enslaved or free, across classes, races, and ethnicities, used a range of cultural and social formations to challenge gender barriers. Abiding by prescribed gender norms and behavior, as well as adopting nontraditional roles, Caribbean women were instrumental in changing their societies.

As Mathurin Mair comments, it is essentially awareness of oneself as a human being that makes the individual refuse to be reduced to the level of a non-human in the way that slavery attempted (Mathurin Mair 1975:18). West African traditions of production, kinship, and family also supported the positive valuation of motherhood and the equality fostered by the plantation labor force.

Conventional histories of slavery assert that women in slave society were more readily and firmly attached to white society. This interpretation suggests that black women accommodated more readily to slavery than their male counterparts (Patterson 1982). Presumably, a domestic slave woman's physical proximity to white men placed her in a contradictory position of devotion and betrayal. However, ample accounts of slave revolts in the British and French West Indies leave little doubt that there was an outright rejection of slavery by peoples of African descent in the region. Furthermore, both men and women found many ways in their everyday lives to frustrate their masters. The psychological and physical security of planters rested on believing behavioral stereotypes of blacks in order to retain their own honor and power in slave society. Daily resistance on the part of women slaves was the response to this denigration. In fact, resistance to enslavement began from the moment of capture, through the Middle Passage, and on to emancipation, which began in the Caribbean with the Haitian revolution and continued to 1886, when Cuba finally freed its slaves.

As historian Barbara Bush argues, female insubordination took on various forms, including feigning illness, refusing to go to work, using abusive language (tongue lashings), leaving the estate without permission, losing articles of clothing from the master's laundry, withholding or using sexuality for their own benefit, and using the slave codes in their own favor, especially concerning maternity rights (Bush 1990). Poignantly, one of the most powerful weapons in the hands of women cooks was their skillful use of poisons.

Other forms of resistance arose in the Caribbean as well. Maroons (from the Spanish *cimarrón,* or "runaway") were groups of people who escaped slavery and set up their own communities, usually in inaccessible areas such as swamps, forests, and mountains. Around 1769 in St. Domingue (the French form of Santo Domingo, and the early name for Haiti), a group of maroon women persuaded another group of women, who pounded grain and did other domestic chores, to join them. Although women refrained from running away in large numbers because of their kinship ties and children, it is now clear that they engaged in daily resistance and were often severely punished for these offenses against the planter class.

The work of Barbara Bush shows that on a daily basis, women caused more trouble than the men. According to contemporary histories written by men, few women seem to have taken part in the uprisings that plagued the Caribbean during the days of slavery (Higman 1999). Yet as Bush suggests, the absence of the names of female slaves from official records and contemporary accounts of slave uprisings and conspiracies does not constitute proof that they played no active part. Nanny, the legendary Jamaican windward maroon, provides an example of the role women played in their battle for freedom from slavery in the region.

Nanny was known by her own people and the British as an outstanding political and military leader. A junior British officer described her in the following way: "[She] had a girdle round her waist, with nine or ten different knives hanging in sheaths to it, many of which I doubt not had been plunged into human flesh and blood" (Mathurin Mair 1975:36). Legend also has it that Nanny slew and captured English soldiers with impunity and that she had supernatural powers. Yet in 1739, when the British were finally defeated, they refused to recognize Nanny as the maroon leader during the signing of the treaty. Nonetheless, sociologist Rhoda Reddock signals that Nanny figures prominently in Caribbean women's history because she led her people with courage and religious conviction and inspired them to maintain the spirit of independence that was their rightful inheritance (Reddock 1994).

It was only after the tremendous social, economic, and cultural changes that took place in the nineteenth century (e.g., the Haitian revolution; the independence of the Dominican Republic; emancipation in the English, Danish, Dutch, and French colonies; the rise of the peasantry; indenture; the wars of independence with Spain at the end of the century) that the region would be in a position to look for a female figure who could reclaim the spirit invoked by Nanny. One such figure is Doña Mariana Grajales de Maceo of Santiago de Cuba. Born a free woman of color in the early nineteenth century, Mariana was the mother of thirteen children, nine of whom lost their lives in the Ten Years' War (1868–1878), including the most famous, Antonio Maceo. Antonio Maceo (the Bronze Titan) has military standing that is likened to that of Toussaint L'Ouverture of Haiti's revolution. Caribbean historian Jean Stubbs remarks that Mariana—"the mother of Cuba"—has acquired legendary proportions akin to Nanny, "but the focus is on her status as a self-sacrificing mother, and not as a political or military leader" (Stubbs 1995:297).

Nanny and Mariana Grajales de Maceo each represent an aspect of womanhood that is fostered in the region. Each worked exceptionally hard to reach her own goals. Mariana nursed her sons, as well as other wounded soldiers, in the fight for independence. She lived in exile, and her own life was in jeopardy for decades. Nanny's status as a warrior-mother rekindles the heritage of the Akan peoples, who were prominent in the early enslaved populations. Nanny fought the battles but was denied recognition by the British because of her gender. Both women are now valued by their respective countries. One of the highest accolades bestowed on a Cuban mother is to be compared to Mariana Grajales de Maceo. Nanny is Jamaica's only national heroine, and her visage appears on the Jamaican $500 bill.

▓ Women in the Hispanic Caribbean

For the most part, the domestic arena of home and hearth was the ideal, prescriptive norm for Spanish-speaking women of the Hispanic Caribbean. Therefore, unless they were poor, a member of the peasantry, or in urban domestic service, they had less visibility than their Anglophone counterparts in public life. Women in parts of the Hispanic Caribbean, however, managed to be exceptional while retaining the traditional domestic role designated for them. Thus, the similarity between them and their Anglophone Caribbean counterparts becomes significant (Safa 1995; McLaurin 1996).

The fact that women in Venezuela and the Dominican Republic have become politicians, business executives, and professionals, for example, appears to contradict the typical Latin American *machista* (male-dominated) culture. Yet movement toward sexual equality has occurred, in part, from necessity. High divorce rates, widespread infidelity, rampant promiscuity that produced second families, large numbers of single teenage mothers, and male refusal of paternal responsibility have forced women to fend for themselves.

The double standard is poignant for women across class and color lines. The tradition of *marianismo* (treating women as if they were the Virgin Mary) persists. Ironically, there is political currency in having a mistress. Extramarital affairs, politically problematic in the United States, are a sign of power in the Caribbean, where *machismo* has yet to be completely overcome.

Life in the extended family is considered sacrosanct. The extended family incorporates the system of *compadrazgo* (godparents—*padriños*—and distant relatives) as the norm despite the resultant non-Euro-centered family structure. Women find themselves in positions of discord or incongruity between what they say or do and what is expected of them. In other words, they are caught in a double standard supported by the male-dominated culture and corporate sponsorship. An example is the importance and popularity of beauty contests that promote contestants for Miss Universe on the basis of their European physical features as well as their resemblance to an "authentic" Taíno queen (Davila 1997). A range of "beauty" products are central to a gendered female identity. However, insofar as Caribbean women's preoccupation with glamor gains them professional success and equality, this prescriptive norm is not necessarily incompatible with femininity.

Cuban women were active in their country's revolution. They also contributed to the subsequent literacy and health programs and today play an important role in professional and managerial life. Women occupy 28 percent of the positions in the Cuban government and 16 percent of those in the Dominican Republic, compared to the Latin American average of 15.4 percent. The US and world averages are both 16 percent (Htun 1999:148–152; Center for American Women and Politics 2009).

Also, women's participation in the economy of the Hispanic Caribbean has increased dramatically. Although there is still a wage gap between women and men as well as significant problems in applying new laws recognizing the equal rights of women, illiteracy among women has decreased, and women constitute more than half of the students in primary, secondary, and university education. Women in the Hispanic Caribbean, therefore, have made much progress in overcoming historical obstacles and modern stereotypes.

■ Caribbean Women's Continuing Struggles

Early in the twentieth century, Caribbean women continued their struggles for equality and suffrage. Women played viable and assertive roles in Puerto Rican politics, particularly after the Spanish-American War (1898), whereby Puerto Rico came under the control of the United States. Combining politics and labor movement activism, women waged legal battles for suffrage and improved working conditions for both men and women. A major figure of the early twentieth century was Luisa Capietillo (1880–1922), a socialist labor organizer and writer. Literary scholar Edna Acosta-Belén tells us that Capietillo argued on behalf of equal rights for women and tried to raise the consciousness of workers (Acosta-Belén 1993). Challenging social conventions, Capietillo is remembered as being the first woman in Puerto Rico to wear slacks in public. Her writings placed her well ahead of her time, as she urged women to go forward and not shy away from social change. Likewise, Dominican novelist Julia Álvarez's *In the Time of the Butterflies* (1994) contributes to our historical knowledge of women's political engagement. The novel is based on the historical fact that three sisters participated in dangerous underground activities against Rafael Trujillo, the Dominican dictator. During thirty-one years of terror, Trujillo and his secret police tortured and murdered dissenters. The three sisters, immortalized by Álvarez, illustrate the range and depth of women's political commitment.

During the worldwide Great Depression of the 1930s, Anglo-Caribbean women were poised to reclaim the political spirit invoked by Nanny of the maroons, most obviously through their role in labor unions. The general strikes

A women's group in La Vega, Dominican Republic.

and worker insurrections that blazed across the English-speaking Caribbean in the late 1930s gave rise to two significant outcomes: (1) a more self-confident working class demanding its rights; and (2) trade union workers who called for the right to strike, labor representation, adequate pay, and decent working conditions. Working conditions had not improved since the days of slavery, which had ended 100 years earlier in the British territories. The trade unions, following British organizational structures, considered men to be the primary workers, although they did recognize the fact that women constituted a major segment of the British West Indian labor force. During the strikes, there were women on the picket lines engaged in their own anticolonial struggle and exerting their right to self-determination. There were women who were fiscally responsible for those fledgling labor organizations—the early women trade union leaders (Bolles 1996). Yet these women are absent from much of the Caribbean historical literature.

One unique feature of the English-speaking Caribbean is the historically high incidence of female participation in the labor force. The organized labor activity of women trade union leaders in the Caribbean came about through the circumstances of their own work, their life experiences, and the acknowledged deplorable working conditions of many others around them. Coming from a range of class backgrounds, the women entered the labor movement with the faith that their actions, together with those of others of like mind, would contribute to making their country a better place in which to live and work.

Like men in the labor movement, women trade union leaders continue now to have a sense of collective consciousness: they recognize the benefits of collective action on behalf of the common good of working people. Once they were members of a trade union and their talents became apparent to those in leadership positions, or to their peers, these women took on responsibilities beyond mere membership. To this day, however, only a handful of women trade union leaders are included in the highest levels of decisionmaking in their organizations. Again, it is not a question of women's capabilities, but the nature of the deterrents put in their way.

Women from middle- and working-class backgrounds have become trade union leaders for the last fifty years of the Caribbean labor movement's history (Bolles 1996). From the turn of the twentieth century to contemporary times, Caribbean women activist leaders have been able to carry out public political, social, and economic work on behalf of women, men, and children of their country, the region, and the world. Additional factors in women's success include individual charismatic personalities, organizational skills, political savvy, and specific family histories. However, part of the success of Caribbean women leaders may be attributed to cultural cues that served their ancestors well—the ability to speak their minds, stand their ground, and use the most appropriate adaptive strategy available. For middle-class women, this often meant upending their socialization.

Young middle-class women were not encouraged to move beyond the home by dictates of class position and colonial rule guided by local patriarchy. Across class lines, women's power was located at home. Female power seems to exist at a somewhat subterranean level, especially in regard to kinship and the family (Anderson 1986:320). In the workforce, women's power was severely curtailed, relegated to gender-segregated activities and duties that confer low status (Bolles 1996). With the exception of British expatriate wives' clubs and similar social welfare groups, organizations did not question male domination or female subordination. Leadership and public speaking were male constructs that implied conduct unbecoming of a lady. Although public speaking became a critical asset for all women activists, it is the use of other skills that marked the talents of women leaders for improved quality of life and social change.

The following excerpts are from a collection of life stories of Commonwealth Caribbean women trade union leaders representing three generations. At age seventy-three, a member of the Barbados Workers' Union recalls how she joined the labor movement:

> They used to have meetings and all there in the market square and there'd be something with Toppin, the primer from The Advocate [*sic*] and all like that and I used to go and listen to these things and all like that so I knew about the union. So when the organizer came I was only too glad but then after I got in there then I got another reinforcement behind me, his nickname "Commisah,"

and he explained certain things and I talk with him and when I couldn't talk
with Frank Walcott [CEO of the union]. (Bolles 1996:95)

A leader from the Jamaica Teacher's Association (JTA) states:

Let us put it this way, from 1954 I recognized myself as a trade union person, having started to accept the responsibility to represent the teachers in
council of the JTA. I think that 1966 when we had our first strike, running
around Kingston and making sure that the schools were closed are things that
I will never forget. (Bolles 1996:102)

Continuing the tradition, an Antiguan woman in her twenties remarks: "I
am a person who believes in human rights and I saw I could make a difference" (Bolles 1996:103).

The outpouring of scholarship from the 1970s onward allowed researchers
to critically examine archives and to engage in interdisciplinary study. It is in
this vein that the analysis of women in the workplace has advanced beyond the
basics of employment trends. Critical examination gives insight into the poor
working conditions that continue to characterize the lives of women across the
Caribbean, despite efforts to unionize and high labor force participation rates.
As political scientist Luz del Alba Acevedo argues in "Feminist Inroads in the
Study of Women's Work and Development," scholars must move their analyses beyond women's marginalization in the workforce and study the effects of
"the feminization of the labor force and the economic inequalities inherent in
a gendered hierarchical occupational structure in developing countries" (Acevedo
1995:70). If we examine the evidence published by the United Nations Statistics Division, it demonstrates that women's participation in the labor market is
substantial (see Table 9.1).

However, for a more complete vision we must simultaneously analyze the
data on the gendered differences in part-time employment and unemployment.
For example, the cases listed in Table 9.2 reflect the greater propensity for women
to be engaged in part-time employment. Even more striking is the disparity in unemployment rates between women and men throughout the region, as depicted in
Table 9.3. With few exceptions the unemployment rate among women is higher,
in some cases (Belize, Dominican Republic, French Guiana, Grenada, and Suriname) exceeding male unemployment by more than 10 percent.

Labor-force participation rates for women have always been high within
the English-speaking Caribbean, with some countries showing higher rates than
others. The countries that have experienced severe fiscal problems, difficult
transitions into the global economy, and high unemployment rates in the formal
sector have high percentages of women who are self-employed. Self-employment
can include activities that range from working as a domestic selling goods in
the local market to skilled work as seamstresses and high-tech consultants.

The United Nations Economic Commission for Latin America and the
Caribbean (ECLAC) states that in absolute terms, the number of Latin American

Table 9.1 Percentage Distribution of the Labor Force for Women and Men, by Status in Employment

Country	Year	Employees		Employers		Own-account Workers		Contributing Family Workers	
		W	M	W	M	W	M	W	M
Bahamas	1995	88	83	n.a.	n.a.	n.a.	n.a.	n.a.	n.a.
Barbados	2003	91	80	n.a.	n.a.	8	18	n.a.	n.a.
Belize	1999	71	62	n.a.	n.a.	25	34	4	3
Dominica	1997	71	61	6	15	19	22	3	1
Dominican Republic	2001	68	48	2	4	28	46	n.a.	n.a.
Jamaica	2003	69	58	1	3	27	38	2	1
Netherlands Antilles	2000	92	84	1	5	3	8	1	0
Puerto Rico	2003	92	80	n.a.	n.a.	7	19	n.a.	n.a.
Saint Lucia	2000	71	59	3	7	24	31	1	1
Suriname	1998	87	78	n.a.	n.a.	9	19	n.a.	n.a.
Trinidad and Tobago	2002	82	74	3	6	12	18	2	0

Source: United Nations Statistics Division, "Distribution of Labor Force by Status in Employment," *The World's Women 2005: Progress in Statistics,* http://unstats.un.org/unsd/demographic/products/indwm/ww2005/tab5e.htm (accessed March 2009).

Note: n.a. indicates data not available.

and Caribbean people living in poverty hovers around 210 million. This figure is higher now than ever before. Of every 100 new jobs created between 1990 and 1995, eighty-four were in the informal sector (often self-employment). Young females under the age of twenty-five in Jamaica had the highest rate of unemployment. According to UN statistics for 2003, half of young women between the ages of fifteen and twenty-four in St. Lucia were unemployed. In places like Dominica, the overall female unemployment rate was 27.2 percent; in the Dominican Republic, 28 percent; in Grenada, almost 25 percent; and in St. Lucia and St. Vincent and the Grenadines, around 23 percent each. For those who are employed, inflation is a serious issue. For example, Jamaica raised its minimum wage from $J2,400 (set in 2005) to J3,200 for a forty-hour workweek. At the 2008 exchange rate of J$71.75 to US$1, Jamaican workers earn a little more than US$1 an hour if they work forty hours per week. The Dominican Republic faces a similar situation. According to International Monetary Fund 2007 data on minimum wages, in the Dominican Republic laborers who work outside the free trade zone (FTZ) earn approximately US$1.16 per

Table 9.2 Adult Employment That Is Part-Time and Women's Share of Part-Time Employment (percentage)

Country	Year	Adult Part-Time Employment		Women's Share of Part-Time Employment
		W	M	
Bahamas	2002	12	10	54
Barbados	1999	14	8	60
Belize	1999	26	12	49
Dominica	1997	28	12	65
Dominican Republic	2003	23	12	50
Grenada	1998	36	30	46
Jamaica	2001	16	10	52
Netherlands Antilles	1998	19	7	69
Suriname	1998	32	12	59
Trinidad and Tobago	2002	10	7	45

Sources: United Nations Statistics Division, "Part-time Employment," *Statistics and Indicators on Women and Men,* http://unstats.un.org/unsd/demographic/products/indwm/tab5b.htm (accessed March 2009); United Nations Statistics Division, "Part-time Employment," *The World's Women 2005: Progress in Statistics,* http://unstats.un.org/unsd/demographic/products/indwm/ww2005/tab5b .htm (accessed March 2009).

hour. However, the predominantly female workforce of the FTZ plants earns less than US$.50 per hour.

In 2000, 189 United Nations member states and at least twenty-three international organizations, such as the World Bank, agreed to a plan of action to end poverty and seven other major social and economic problems facing the developing world, including the Caribbean. The plan, the Millennium Development Goals (MDGs), has a target date for ending extreme poverty (an income of less that US$1.25 per day according to the World Bank) and its associated social elements by 2015. Besides ending poverty, the MDGs include reducing child and maternal mortality, fighting diseases and epidemics such as HIV/AIDs, achieving and maintaining environmental sustainability, providing debt relief for the most destitute nations, and developing a global partnership for development. As Caribbean feminist activist Peggy Antrobus (2004) notes, the adoption of the MDGs provides a new focus for women's activism in areas of special concern for them, such as gender equity at work, maternal health, and the needs of youth. In this respect, the MDGs are quite welcome. Nonetheless, Antrobus cautions women's groups about what the MDG partnerships might mean for the structure, operation, control, and implementation of activities, especially as they legitimize neoliberal (globalization) policies that have had a checkered rate of success for women and girls in the wider Caribbean. No matter what it

Table 9.3 Unemployment Rate in the Caribbean for Women and Men 15 Years of Age and Older (percentage)

Country	Year	Women	Men
Anguilla	2002	10	6
Antigua and Barbuda	2001	9	8
Aruba	1997	8	7
Bahamas	2007	9	7
Barbados	2004	11	9
Belize	2005	17	7
Cuba	2006	2	2
Dominica	2001	10	12
Dominican Republic	2005	29	11
French Guiana	2006	35	24
Grenada	1998	22	11
Guadeloupe	2006	31	24
Guyana	2002	15	10
Haiti	1999	8	6
Jamaica	2007	14	5
Martinique	2006	27	23
Netherlands Antilles	2007	14	10
Puerto Rico	2007	10	12
St. Lucia	2004	25	17
St. Vincent and the Grenadines	1991	22	18
Suriname	1999	20	10
Trinidad and Tobago	2007	10	4

Source: United Nations Statistics Division, "Adult Unemployment," *Statistics and Indicators on Women and Men,* http://unstats.un.org/unsd/demographic/products/indwm/tab5f.htm (accessed March 2009).

is called, globalization is the outcome of unconstrained capitalism in the modern period, contributing to social and economic inequality within nations and across the world (Bolles 2007).

From a gendered perspective, because unequal power relations exist between women and men, it is women whose socioeconomic rights are not being advanced by globalization (Steady 1993). Additionally, gender inequality is compounded by other dimensions of differences, such as race, class, ethnicity, sexuality, religion, region, and other distinctions that may vary across cultures.

Gender, Class, and Familial Organization

Much of the social science literature from the 1930s to the early 1970s stresses apparent differences between aspects of culture that are perceived as "European."

Features designated as European (white- or light-skinned, upper or middle class) are considered as the social "norm." Falling outside this so-called norm are the African-based Creole cultural systems of the majority. More than four centuries of European colonization resulted in the sociopolitical hegemony of the upper classes and accompanying derision of the cultures of the masses. Light skin color and middle-class status approximated the socially approved norm, whereas the African cultural patterns and dark skin of the black majority were cause for disparagement. In the case of Trinidad and Guyana, East Indians imported as indentured servants were allotted a rank below that of Afro-Caribbeans; Chinese, Lebanese, Jews, and Portuguese fell below whites.

Family forms were couched in ideal typologies. For example, decades of social science research categorized West Indian family forms and household organizations in three patterns, listed here in descending order: nuclear family (wife, husband, children), common-law family (nuclear without legal sanctions), and visiting unions (woman and children with a nonresident boyfriend or nonresident children's father) (Mohammed and Perkins 1998). Research in the French and Dutch Antilles followed the British model, and studies in Cuba, the Dominican Republic, and Puerto Rico utilized the Spanish class-color specificities of *mestizo* culture.

Often, marriage was neither economically feasible (because of the cost of a wedding or of setting up a household) nor a given in the Caribbean reality of gender relations. Indeed, having a child does not connote or necessitate the forming of a nuclear family. Therefore, the predominant Caribbean family forms stray from the ideal Eurocentric nuclear family. Caribbean domestic organization privileges female-headed households, other variations in household structures, the double standard in mating relations, the normative experience of extramarital mating, and the commonplace acceptance of birth outside of wedlock (Mohammed and Perkins 1998).

As research conducted in the 1950s demonstrates, particularly the work by anthropologists Michael Horowitz (*Morne-Paysan: Peasant Village in Martinique*) and Miriam Slater (*The Caribbean Family: Legitimacy in Martinique*), the very notion of West Indianness refers primarily to peoples of African descent or of mulatto or *mestizo* origins. To a large extent, these terms exclude the East Indian experience. This is particularly true in the discussion of family organization. The East Indian family structure was able to draw on its South Asian foundations when the ratio of men and women was less skewed. When there were twice as many men as women, there were a variety of relationships, none of which even came close to approximating traditional ones. Hindu and Muslim marriages were not legally sanctioned in Trinidad and Guyana until the mid-twentieth century. For those living primarily on sugar plantations, the estate manager usually settled marital disputes and other domestic conflicts according to colonial Eurocentric family norms and values. In contrast to subcontinental practices, couples resided with the husband's parents for only a few years, the father was no longer the sole trustee of family resources, and wives were given more say in family events. The caste system and caste endogamy (marrying within your own group by Hindus) was totally undermined. Arranged marriages within castes became impossible to attain (Mohammed 1995:39).

The domination of European constructs of gender-appropriate role, status, and place in society can be seen in the laws and policies enacted throughout the region in the twentieth century. For example, the mass-marriage campaigns of the post–World War II period attempted to convince Jamaicans to transform common-law relationships into patriarchal legal marriages and enlisted churches, schools, the press, the radio, and welfare agencies in the effort (Smith 1962). This effort was also a remedy for another problem, as marriage would legitimize offspring who were deemed bastards under the law. Despite the media blitz, the mass-marriage campaign was a failure because of the customary economic requirements necessary for legal marriage, as well as the cultural acceptance of all children regardless of the circumstances of their birth. As a matter of fact, since the late 1970s, starting with Jamaica, most Commonwealth Caribbean governments have enacted a status-of-the-child law that finally put an end to questions of bastardy. This law states that a person cannot be held responsible for the consequences of his or her birth. In effect, illegitimacy is now a moot point, and all children are legitimate under the eyes of the law. In her text *Legitimate Acts and Illegal Encounters* (1994), Mindie Lazarus-Black studies how poor women, legally married or not, are taking their baby's father to court and demanding child care payments because they are legal heirs to the man's property.

However, it was not the question of children that was viewed as a problem but the prevalence of female-headed households that concerned first colonial and now duly elected governments. Furthermore, this situation, most prominent for poor and working-class women, dovetailed with increasing levels of social inequality.

Decades of detailed investigations by anthropologists and sociologists documented that Afro-Caribbean families did not represent disorganized or pathological adaptations to the conditions of slavery (Barrow 1996). Such a view resulted from looking at female-headed households in the Caribbean through middle-class European or US eyes or both. For example, the model household of a family as two adults of the same generation but different sexes, who are the biological parents of children with whom they live, rests in part on a gendered division of labor requiring a male breadwinner and a female homemaker, as well as on the belief that conjugal relations are more important than consanguineous ones. Eventually, feminist researchers challenged this notion of gender and family. The Creole Caribbean family differs from it not only in reality but also in beliefs about what a family is and what is appropriate for its members to do. Anthropologists learned that, in attempting to understand both the economic support of households and children and the performance of domestic responsibilities such as laundry, meal preparation, and child care, they could not assume that the boundaries of a dwelling define a family and what it does. Often, eating, sleeping, financial support, and child rearing were shared among a network of male and female relatives and neighbors (Bolles 1996). However, research in the former Spanish colonies of Cuba, the Dominican Republic, and Puerto Rico shows the majority of households following a Eurocentric model, except for poor domestic units, which tended to be female-headed and whose members were of African descent (Brown 1975).

For subcontinental Indians, who were indentured laborers primarily in Trinidad and Tobago and Guyana, the organization of family did not resemble the norm in India at all. More men than women were indentured, and all lived in barracks on sugar estates. Sociologist Patricia Mohammed examined the life of East Indian women who carried on wage labor on the estates and performed the prescribed gender roles of cleaning, cooking, and washing for a spouse— and often barrack mates (Mohammed 1995). Only when the numbers of males and females became more equal did the Indo-Caribbean peoples develop domestic units similar in structure to those in India (albeit nuanced differently for life in the Caribbean). Indo-Caribbean family structure became a catalyst for the revival of Indian culture in the West Indies. Pride over India's independence in 1947, and the arrival of Muslim preachers and artists, made family and religious ceremonies once again the center of Indian life. However, Indo–West Indian culture had evolved its own creolization. Marriage was one of the first traditions to be compromised. Parents' criteria for selection of marriage partners emphasized security, wealth, and family status, but the younger generation looked for new and modern ways. The legally sanctioned nuclear family is still the most popular marital union, although common-law and visiting unions are becoming more prevalent than before. Young Indo–West Indians are also enjoying greater equality between spouses. A 1982 study noted that married women under the age of forty typically experience more autonomy than the generation of women before them.

The complexities of West Indian plantation life distorted the division of labor brought by slaves from Africa while, ironically, reinforcing it. For example, many mothers understood the cruelty of bringing children into slavery and resisted the master's encouragement to do so. The use of women as laborers in the fields beside men also revealed biases of color and gender; the majority of field slaves were black women. Although men and women labored equally in the field gangs, the chances of females doing any other task were slim (Mathurin Mair 1975). Furthermore, there is a sharp division in the organization of household labor. Dorian Powell's 1984 study stresses the point that women perform a disproportionate amount of housework and usually carry the enormous responsibility of ensuring the survival of family members, a set of activities that Victoria Durant-Gonzalez calls "the realm of female responsibility." She states that a large proportion of women in the English-speaking Caribbean are "in charge of [the] economics of producing, providing, controlling, or managing the resources essential to meeting daily needs" (Durant-Gonzalez 1982:3).

In *The Myth of the Male Breadwinner* (1995), anthropologist Helen Safa conducted a comparative study of contemporary women, family, and factory work in Cuba, the Dominican Republic, and Puerto Rico. She notes that by the 1980s, women had assumed more authority in the household than was culturally prescribed in the past because they were employed in jobs outside the home. The additional authority does not necessarily come from their economic contribution but more from the fact that now there was more than one source of family income. Not only is the erosion of the man's role as economic provider at issue; his ability and willingness to share this role with his wife also come into play. It makes for more equitable marital relationships. In Puerto Rico and the Dominican Republic, where male marginalization was most severe due to unemployment, the percentage of female-headed households was on the rise by the 1980s. As a matter of fact, the data show that women headed 25 percent of all households (Safa 1995:180). In contrast to the prevailing cultural patterns of male domination within families in the Hispanic Caribbean, the question is: Will these trends start to approximate marital patterns found in other areas of the Caribbean, or will new forms appear?

Of significance to the welfare of families, regardless of organizational structure, is the incidence of domestic violence. This social issue came to the forefront when in 2000 all Caribbean Community (CARICOM) governments signed and ratified the Convention on the Elimination of All Forms of Discrimination Against Women (CEDAW). CEDAW requires each member government to report every four years on the steps it is taking to assist victims of these crimes and to provide shelter, support, and legal and other services for them. Needless to say, without enforcement capabilities, self-reporting is a flawed process.

In her book *Everyday Harm* (2007), Mindie Lazarus-Black examines Trinidad's Domestic Violence Act and how it is viewed and enacted by citizens, law enforcement, and the family court system. Lazarus-Black discusses what she calls the "cultures of reconciliation." Notions of common sense combined with cultural practices not only keep potential litigants out of court, but they also allow officials charged with implementing the law to use discretion. Police, probation officers, lawyers, and magistrates, like litigants, are influenced by the force of "cultures of reconciliation."

▓ The "Independent" Woman in the Contemporary Caribbean

With the prominence of women heading households, we see the price of the inclusive concept of motherhood that pertains to the Caribbean. Because most Caribbean women are either employed in low-paying, low-skilled, and menial

This sign reading "Zero tolerance toward violence against women" is part of a campaign to combat violence against women, Santo Domingo, Dominican Republic.

jobs or are unemployed, how can they fulfill all that is expected of them? The ideological support mechanisms found in the African-based traditional role of women in Caribbean societies prove to be invaluable cultural assets. Work—no matter how dead-end—has meaning and value for women. It not only meets their family responsibilities but also plays an important role in the development of women's self-image and the conception of "independent" womanhood (Bolles and D'Amico-Samuels 1990).

Independent is a word often used to describe West Indian women and how they carry out their responsibilities. Independence is a quality based on having one's own source of economic support—from employment, other income-generating activities, and, where possible, savings—while at the same time organizing and utilizing support from others (Barrow 1986). *Autonomy,* by contrast, implies exercising options while making decisions for oneself and having control over one's own destiny with no strings attached.

Independence, then, is not coterminous with female autonomy. Economic self-sufficiency is far beyond the grasp of most to whom the term *independent* has been applied in the Caribbean context. Rather than acting on behalf of a single person, autonomy implies interdependence among a number of individuals.

Autonomy is highly valued, and lifetimes are spent fulfilling obligations to others so as to reinforce that reciprocal support in time of need. Christine Barrow (1986) has observed "one is considered foolish to refuse support from those who give, especially if they have a culturally prescribed obligation to do so."

One mechanism used to preserve autonomy in the Caribbean is the maintenance of reciprocal relationships within networks. Borrowing from Christine Barrow, there is an etiquette of network exchanges such that "independence," or at least the public image of it, is maintained. The most critical characteristic of successful network management is avoiding total dependence on one source of support, particularly a male partner. If a relationship endures over the years, the mate support tends to become secure. However, it can never be fully relied upon, because at any stage of marital union—whether visiting (in which the man visits his girlfriend and perhaps their children), common-law (in which a couple lives together), or points in between—the relationship can be temporarily or completely terminated. Therefore, Caribbean women's control over their lives is a function of their degree of economic autonomy, which includes the nature of their earning, spending, saving, and property ownership, and the sexual division of money matters.

According to Barrow, female autonomy in the English-speaking Caribbean is encouraged from an early age, and education is emphasized as the means to get a good job. The major lifelong strategy, then, to "cut and contrive," involves female networks that assist mothers, sisters, daughters, and in-laws (children's

A women's literacy program, Jacmel, Haiti.

father's female relatives) alongside income-generating activities (Barrow 1996). Although the notions of independence and autonomy are essential aspects of women's survival in the region, they should not be romanticized.

One of the developments that further exemplifies notions of interdependence, autonomy, women's employment, and the varied kinds of Caribbean households is the immigration of women of the region to the United States, Britain, and Canada. During the 1970s, the numbers of Caribbean women migrants from all areas of the region rose dramatically, changing the migration pattern from a male-dominated one to a female- and family-centered one. Telephones, accessible international air travel, and email connect extended family to one another and allow for kin ties to be maintained across the miles. Sociologist Dwayne Plaza's (2000) research on "frequent-flyer grannies" describes how successful sons can facilitate travel plans for their mothers between Trinidad and Toronto. In the large enclaves of Miami and the Washington Heights neighborhood of Manhattan, Spanish is the dominant language, and Cuban and Dominican cultural patterns are the norm (Grasmuck and Pessar 1991; Portes and Stepick 1993). Likewise in Little Haiti in Miami and in Brooklyn, New York, Haitian creole and Jamaican patois are the local vernaculars (Stepick 1998; Foner 2001). Carole Boyce Davies (2007) studies Caribbean women as migrating subjects who navigate US interests and their own by moving from one locale to another over time and with different purposes in mind. In her interviews with and narratives of twenty-five Caribbean women, Boyce Davies saw similarities but also differences among two generations of women migrants. The older group migrated to the United States for economic success, whereas the younger set saw relocating as but "one option in a series of possibilities." Nonetheless, the movement and labor of women has made this transnationalism possible.

Women in Regional and International Politics

The importance of gender issues has gained international attention, and Caribbean women are represented on the Inter-American Commission of Women (CIM), headquartered in Washington, D.C. Created by the Sixth International Conference of American States (Havana, 1928), the CIM acts as the Organization of American States's advisory body on matters related to women in the Western Hemisphere and reports to the governments on the progress accomplished and the problems that need to be addressed, suggesting ways those problems can be resolved. Many high-profile women have been involved in CIM, including a variety of government ministers and legislative representatives from the thirty-four member states of the OAS. An executive committee composed of seven members elected by an Assembly of Delegates directs the CIM. The committee for the period 2006–2008 includes members from Antigua and Barbuda, Brazil, Colombia, Guatemala, Haiti, Peru, and Uruguay.

The first meeting of the Caribbean region on Women in Politics, organized by the Network of Nongovernmental Organizations for the Advancement of Women of Trinidad and Tobago, was held in Port of Spain, Trinidad and Tobago, May 11–13, 1998. Other meetings on women's issues, including a conference on sexual abuse, have yielded important data and policy recommendations.

Since the early 1970s, the governments of CARICOM states have supported efforts to improve the status of women in the region. Two leading figures on the international level, the late Dame Nita Barrow of Barbados and Dr. Lucille Mathurin Mair of Jamaica, represent the Caribbean's extraordinary influence in contributing to the advancement of women throughout the world. The careers of these two women truly underscore the cornerstone concepts of justice, social equity, and change promoted by the United Nations Development Fund for Women (UNIFEM). Dame Nita was the ultimate international leader, convening the nongovernmental organizations' meeting, Forum 85, held in Nairobi, Kenya, marking the close of the UN Decade for Women in 2004. She was Barbados's representative to the United Nations from 1986–1990 and ran a hotly contested campaign for the Secretary-General position. Nita began her career as a nurse educator when she migrated to Canada for her training. This was followed by her tenure as a Young Women's Christian Association (YWCA) international organizer. After her role as a diplomat, she ended her career of service as the governor general (Queen Elizabeth's representative) to Barbados.

Mathurin Mair, the pioneering feminist Caribbean historian, has also had a career of service to her country and the world. She began her professional life at the University of the West Indies (UWI) in Jamaica, where she was a staff member for more than two decades. Mathurin Mair moved into foreign affairs, representing Jamaica at the UN as a diplomat and helping to draft the 1975 Declaration of Mexico, which recognized the urgency of improving the status of women. After working with the United Nation's Children's Fund and UNIFEM, she became a founding member of Development Alternatives with Women for a New Era , an influential international group that focused on economic rights and social justice for women. Returning to UWI, Dr. Mair ended her career by helping to establish and guide the Center for Gender and Development at the University of the West Indies on its three campuses in Jamaica, Trinidad and Tobago, and Barbados.

Women in Electoral Politics

The lack of inclusion of women in power and in civil society decisionmaking became apparent in the aftermath of the UN Decade for Women (1975–1985). The engagement of women in the political process of their respective countries as voters created an illusion of women's political power. Real power accompanied the ascension of women to elected political offices throughout the region.

Two trailblazing women who held the highest political office in their respective countries were Dame Eugenia Charles of Dominica and Janet Jagan of Guyana.

Charles was "first" in many areas of public service. She was the first woman lawyer in Dominica when she was called to the bar in 1949. She was appointed to the legislature in 1970, cofounded the conservative Dominica Freedom Party, and became the leader of the opposition in 1975. She became the first woman prime minister in the Caribbean in 1979, following Dominica's independence, and was the first female elected head of government in North America, a position she held for fifteen years (1980 to 1995). Queen Elizabeth knighted her in 1992 for her distinguished career as a lawyer and politician.

Known as the "Iron Lady of the Caribbean," Charles ruled Dominica in a stern manner, focusing more on anticorruption measures and anti-Cuba policies than on social welfare programs. She is best known as a fiscal conservative and for her support for the US invasion of Grenada. She was featured prominently in media accounts of the time standing next to US president Ronald Reagan. Following 1983, "Concrete and Current," which signified building roads and rural electrification, became the cornerstones of her administration. Her policy was sustained by the United States as a reward for Dominica's support of the invasion. Charles was an isolated woman in politics, and her personal life was the object of abuse by her many critics across the political spectrum. She never identified with feminist issues and never gave Caribbean women any particular consideration.

Janet Rosenberg Jagan entered electoral politics after years of activist work with organized labor, women's organizations and journalism. She came to what was then British Guiana in 1943 as the bride of Cheddi Jagan, an Indo-Guyanese dentist whom she met when they were both students in her native Chicago. Trained as a nurse, she worked in her husband's dental clinic for ten years, but at the same time became immersed in the labor struggles and politics of postwar British Guiana. With other women, she founded the Women's Political and Economic Organization, now known as the WPO. In 1950 she cofounded the People's Progressive Party (PPP) and held numerous posts in that organization. A few years later, she was appointed first editor of *Thunder,* the official media outlet of the party. During a period of limited self-government in British Guiana, the PPP won the election and Janet Jagan was one of the three women to enter the legislature, becoming the first woman deputy speaker. However, by 1955 efforts to thwart what was perceived as communist infiltration led the British to suspend the constitution. Janet Jagan, along with her husband and other members of the PPP, were jailed for six months. When released, they were confined to Georgetown and had to report to the police on a weekly basis. Guyana became independent in 1966, but the political atmosphere was still charged with racial and ethnic tensions. Nonetheless, Jagan continued her service in government in various capacities. From 1970 to 1997, she was a newspaper editor as well as an elected member of Parliament. Following the PPP electoral victory in 1992, Janet Jagan was designated First Lady of the Republic and temporarily served as Guyana's representative to the United Nations. Following her husband's death in 1997, she was sworn in as Guyana's first woman prime minister and first female vice president. She was the first US-born and the first Caucasian woman to lead the nation. Later that year, following the PPP victory in the elections, Janet Jagan became prime minister in her own right and served as commander in chief until 1999, when poor health caused her to resign her post. Her accolades include the 1997 Gandhi Gold Medal for Peace, Democracy, and Women's Rights, presented by the United Nations Educational, Scientific, and Cultural Organization.

Other than these two leading figures, the number of women in Caribbean electoral politics remains low, and in some cases the socially prescribed role of women tends to undermine future success. According to political scientist Luz del Alba Acevedo (2008), the number of women elected to office in Puerto Rico rose consistently during the 1990s, reaching its peak in 2000 with the election of the first woman governor, Sila María Calderón of the Popular Democratic Party. She stepped down from the party and electoral politics after one term. Calderon was not new to politics. She had served as secretary of state and chief of staff to Governor Pedro Roselló González and was the mayor of San Juan, the island's largest city and capital. Her objectives for her first term included removing the US Navy from Vieques Island; fighting crime and drug smuggling, and resolving the Puerto Rico's status issues. After four years of dealing with disputes among the three major political parties, her ineffectiveness in implementing programs and policies, the increase in crime, the brutal criticism of her management style, and the attention placed on her personal life, Calderon did not seek reelection. The title of a *New York Times* article from July 25, 2004, "Extra Dose of Drama," expresses the tenor of Calderon's administration. Obviously, the "shattered glass ceiling of women's political representation" and the ongoing challenges associated with gender politics in Puerto Rico require further examination.

Perhaps more than the other women politicians in the Caribbean who came before her, Jamaica's Portia Simpson-Miller worked her way up the political ladder one rung at a time. She had neither higher education nor social position. The February 27, 2006, edition of the BBC Caribbean described her as one of Jamaica's most popular politicians, having served in the People's National Party (PNP) for thirty-four years. She began her career in local government, where she won a hotly contested seat representing one of the tough inner-city constituencies. At the same time, Simpson-Miller worked her way up to leadership positions in the PNP Women's Movement. When the PNP returned to power in 1989, Simpson-Miller was appointed minister of labor, social security, and sport. Thus commenced her service in a variety of ministerial positions in the 1990s. Her reputation as a "road warrior" and a "tough comrade" was exemplified by her ability to effectively deal with the devastating impact of the September 11, 2001, terrorist attacks on Jamaica's tourist sector. Simpson-Miller quickly and efficiently executed measures that revived the industry in 2002 and set up plans for a sustainable development program in tourism for the future. These actions were recognized outside Jamaica, and she was asked to serve in numerous international organizations. Nonetheless, "she has never forgotten her roots, and has for decades committed herself to the mission of uplifting the poor and marginalized" (People's National Party). Her concern for the welfare of the country's overseas farm workers led her to reform the Overseas Farm Workers Program. Unfortunately, her ministerial portfolios were characterized by allegations of mismanagement and corruption. Her supporters argued that "Sista P," as she is known, had a distict style of management. In the meantime, Simpson-Miller earned a bachelor's degree and took courses in management to prove that she was capable of executive decision-making. Beginning in the 1990s, Simpson-Miller waged campaigns within the PNP with an eye toward becoming the president of the PNP, so that she would be eligible for the office of prime minister if the PNP gained a parliamentary majority in national elections. In fact, Simpson-Miller won the presidency of the PNP in 2006 by a very small margin and replaced P. J. Patterson, the outgoing PNP prime minister. Even before she could finish celebrating, her detractors from within the party and naturally from the opposition suggested that she did not have the intellectual capacity to lead Jamaica and to represent the country at the international level. They also took aim at her personal life and targeted her humble class, level of education, and demeanor, couched in the rhetoric of charges of mismanagement. Although supporters called her selection "a proud moment for the women of our region and the women of the world," Portia Simpson-Miller was prime minister for just nineteen months, and the PNP lost the general election in 2007. Since 2008, Simpson-Miller, now the leader of the opposition, has resisted the challenge of party rivals to her presidency of the People's National Party.

In their study of women's political participation in Jamaica from 1944 (the year of universal suffrage) and 2007 (the year of Portia Simpson-Miller's election as prime minister), social scientists Mark Figueroa and Natasha Mortley examine social, cultural and economic barriers facing women in public administration. They conclude that "in the English-speaking Caribbean the taboo against female leadership still has currency and the women represent a second choice for leadership." The authors note further that "in fields where men are inclined to participate and still find it lucrative to do so they are well placed to use a range of conscious and unconscious strategies that give them an advantage and exclude women" (Figueroa and Mortley 2008:13).

In Chapter 4, Thomas D'Agostino refers to a historical legacy of instability in Haiti, the first predominantly black independent nation in the Western Hemisphere. Despite a long history of male-dominated despotism and military rule, however, Haitian women gained suffrage in 1950. Eleven years later, a woman won a seat in Parliament. In 1995, President Jean-Bertrand Aristide named Claudette Werleigh prime minister with responsibility for foreign affairs and religion. Michele Duvivier Pierre-Louis became Haiti's second female prime minister in September 2008. Pierre-Louis was confirmed when former prime minister Jacques-Edouard Alexis was dismissed after a three-month political stalemate and charged with failure to manage Haiti's impoverished economy. Since 1995, Pierre-Louis, an economist who had led Knowledge and Freedom (one of Haiti's most successful nonprofit organizations funded by the Soros Foundation), has worked to foster economic development. Despite being welcomed by those who were "tired of Haitian-style, male-dominated politics as usual" (Brea 2008), Prime Minister Pierre-Louis was faced with the daunting task of ameliorating Haiti's food scarcity crisis, lowering soaring fuel costs, and mending the ravages of violent weather. Hence, the legislature's reluctance to comply with Pierre-Louis's initiatives has raised questions about the impact of gender in politics.

Jamaican feminist activist Linnette Vassell (2003:8) notes "although there has been some visibility of women in some Parliaments because of non-elected positions, such as president or vice-president of the Senate, it does not bring women within the most sensitive centers of decision-making." Little value has been placed on women's leadership and what they were able to achieve, despite the obstacles they had to overcome. From the 1980s onward, women's movements and actions brought attention to issues such as violence, education and training, grinding poverty, and the practical needs in the environment and their communities. Barriers of class, color, education, and misogyny, as well as negative media representations and other impediments, constrict women's civic engagement on the local and national levels. Vassell (2003) calls for transformative leadership-training practices that embed a gender analysis and participatory governance as central ideas. It is the conscious and unconscious strategies of pernicious gender ideologies that are at work in maintaining an unacceptable status quo.

■ Conclusion

Women of the region, whether poor or from the working or the upper classes, have been subject to inequities based on their gender. These gender inequities have historical precedents so pronounced that the resultant socioeconomic structures continue to affect every contemporary Caribbean country. Enslavement and its impact on the majority of women of African descent fostered the development of Creole cultures. The social system constructed hierarchies based on color and class and, after emancipation, the indentured status of immigrant workers. Yet women developed resistance strategies, surviving enslavement and postemancipation challenges. Across the region, women took action on behalf of themselves, their children, and men. Whether it was pursuing political activities, organizing labor, or making a living, Caribbean women worked against the odds. Still, even today, they are denied access to resources (in relation to their class position), and their potential is minimized because they are not full participants in the development of their countries due to gender bias. As we learn more about the past and the contributions women have made to Caribbean life and culture, however, we will be better equipped to resolve contemporary problems, as well as those that may arise in the future.

▣ Bibliography

Acevedo, Luz del Alba. "Feminist Inroads in the Study of Women's Work and Development." In *Women in the Latin American Development Process,* edited by Christine E. Bose and Edna Acosta-Belén. Philadelphia: Temple University Press, 1995.

———. "Rebuilding the 'Glass Ceiling' . . . New Gender Challenges to Political Representation in Puerto Rico." Paper prepared for the thirty-third meeting of the Caribbean Studies Association, San Andres, Colombia, May 2008.

Acosta-Belén, Edna. "Puerto Rican Women in Culture, History, and Society." In *The Puerto Rican Woman,* edited by Edna Acosta-Belén. New York: Praeger, 1986.

———. "Defining a Common Ground: The Theoretical Meeting of Women's, Ethnic, and Area Studies." In *Researching Women in Latin America and the Caribbean,* edited by Edna Acosta-Belén and Christine E. Bose. Boulder, CO: Westview, 1993.

Acosta-Belén, Edna, and Christine E. Bose, eds. *Researching Women in Latin America and the Caribbean.* Boulder, CO: Westview, 1993.

Álvarez, Julia. *In the Time of the Butterflies.* Chapel Hill, NC: Algonquin, 1994.

Anderson, Patricia. "Conclusion: WICP." *Social and Economic Studies* 35, no. 2 (1986): 291–324.

Antrobus, Peggy. *The Global Women's Movement.* Kingston, Jamaica: Ian Randle 2004.

Barriteau, Eudine. "Theorizing Gender Systems and the Project of Modernity in the Twentieth-Century Caribbean." *Feminist Review* 59 (Summer 1998): 186–210.

Barriteau, Eudine, and Alan Cobley. *Stronger, Surer, Bolder: Ruth Nita Barrow.* Kingston, Jamaica: University of the West Indies Press, 2001.

Barrow, Christine. "Finding the Support: A Study of Strategies for Survival." *Social and Economic Studies* 35, no. 2 (1986): 131–176.

———. *Family in the Caribbean: Social and Economic Studies.* Kingston, Jamaica: Ian Randle, 1996.

BBC Caribbean Com. "Portia Simpson: Profile," February 27, 2006, www.bbc.co.uk/caribbean/news/story/2006/02/060227_whoisportia.shtml.

Bolles, A. Lynn. *We Paid Our Dues: Women Trade Union Leaders in the Caribbean.* Washington, DC: Howard University Press, 1996.

———. "Of Land and Sea: Women Entrepreneurs in Negril, Jamaica." In *Women's Labor in the Global Economy,* edited by Sharon Harley. New Brunswick, NJ: Rutgers University Press, 2007.

Bolles, A. Lynn, and Deborah D'Amico-Samuels. "Anthropological Scholarship on Gender in the English-Speaking Caribbean." In *Gender and Anthropology,* edited by S. Morgen. Washington, DC: American Anthropological Association, 1990.

Bose, Christine E., and Edna Acosta-Belén, eds. *Women in the Latin American Development Process.* Philadelphia: Temple University Press, 1995.

Boyce Davies, Carol. "Caribbean Women, Domestic Labor, and the Politics of Transnational Migration." In *Women's Labor in the Global Economy*, edited by Sharon Harley. New Brunswick, NJ: Rutgers University Press, 2007.

Brea, Jennifer. "Michele Pierre-Louis, Haiti's New Prime Minister." Global Voices Online, August 9, 2008, http://globalvoicesonline.org (accessed March 25, 2009).

Brown, Susan. "Love Unites Them and Hunger Separates Them: Poor Women in the Dominican Republic." In *Toward an Anthropology of Women*, edited by Rayna R. Reiter. New York: Monthly Review Press, 1975.

Bush, Barbara. *Slave Women in Caribbean Society, 1650–1838*. Bloomington: Indiana University Press, 1990.

Caribbean Community (CARICOM) Secretariat. "Dame Mary Eugenia Charles." www.caricom.org/jsp/projects/personalities (accessed October 2008).

Center for American Women and Politics. Eagleton Institute, Rutgers University, 2009, www.womenscenter.com (accessed March 2009).

Cole, Johnnetta. *All American Women*. New York: Free Press, 1986.

Davila, Arlene. *Sponsored Identities*. Philadelphia: Temple University Press, 1997.

Deere, Carmen Diana, et al. *In the Shadows of the Sun: Caribbean Development Alternatives and US Policy*. Boulder, CO: Westview, 1990.

Durant-Gonzalez, Victoria. "The Realm of Female Responsibility." In *Women in the Family*. Cave Hill, Barbados: Institute of Social and Economic Research, 1982.

Ecumenical Program for Inter-Communication and Action (EPICA). *Grenada: The Peaceful Revolution*. Washington, DC: EPICA, 1982.

Figueroa, Mark, and Natasha Mortley. "Women and Leadership in Jamaican Government Politics and State Administration." Paper prepared for the thirty-third meeting of the Caribbean Studies Association, San Andres, Colombia May, 2008.

Foner, Nancy, ed. *Islands in the City: West Indian Migration to New York*. Berkeley: University of California Press, 2001.

Grasmuck, Sherri, and Patricia Pessar. *Between Two Islands*. Berkeley: University of California Press, 1991.

Green, Vera M. *Migrants in Aruba*. Assen, Netherlands: Van Gorcum, 1974.

Higman, Barry. *Writing West Indian Histories*. London: Macmillan Education, 1999.

Ho, Christine. *Salt-Water Trinnies*. New York: AMS Press, 1991.

Horowitz, Michael. *Morne-Paysan: Peasant Village in Martinique*. New York: Holt, Rinehart, and Winston, 1967.

Htun, Mala. "Women in Latin America: Unequal Progress Toward Equality." *Current History* (1999). Reprinted in *Global Studies: Latin America*, edited by Paul B. Goodwin, pp. 148–152. 9th ed. Guilford, CT: Dushkin/McGraw-Hill, 2000.

International Monetary Fund. *World Economic Outlook Database*. http://www.imf.org/external/pubs/ft/weo/2008/02/weodata/index.aspx."Jagan, Janet, O.E., Profile of: First Woman President of Guyana." Cheddi Jagan Research Centre, 1999, http://jagan.org/janet_jagan3.htm.

Johnson-Odim, Cheryl, and Margaret Strobel, eds. *Expanding the Boundaries of Women's History: Essays on Women in the Third World*. Bloomington: Indiana University Press, 1992.

Knight, Franklin W., and Margaret E. Crahan. "The African Migration and the Origins of an Afro-American Society and Culture." In *Africa and the Caribbean*, edited by Margaret E. Crahan and Franklin W. Knight. Baltimore: Johns Hopkins University Press, 1979.

Lazarus-Black, Mindie. *Legitimate Acts and Illegal Encounters*. Washington, DC: Smithsonian Institution Press, 1994.

————. *Everyday Harm: Domestic Violence, Court Rites, and Cultures of Reconciliation.* Urbana: University of Illinois Press, 2007.

Lewis, Oscar. *La Vida: A Puerto Rican Family in the Culture of Poverty.* New York: Random House, 1966.

Manuel, Peter, with Kenneth Bilby and Michael Largey. *Caribbean Currents: Caribbean Music from Rumba to Reggae.* Philadelphia: Temple University Press, 1995.

Mathurin Mair, Lucille. *The Rebel Woman in the West Indies During Slavery.* Kingston, Jamaica: Institute of Jamaica, 1975.

Matos-Rodríguez, Félix. *Women and Urban Change in San Juan, Puerto Rico, 1820–1868.* Gainesville: University Press of Florida, 1999.

Matos-Rodríguez, Félix, and Linda C. Delgado. *Puerto Rican Women's History: New Perspectives.* Armonk, NY: M. E. Sharpe, 1998.

McLaurin, Irma. *Women of Belize: Gender and Change in Central America.* New Brunswick, NJ: Rutgers University Press, 1996.

Millennium Development Goals Indicators, 2008, http://mdgs.un.org/unsd/mdg/default.aspx (accessed March 25, 2009).

Mohammed, Patricia. "Writing Gender into History: The Negotiation of Gender Relations Among Indian Men and Women in Post-indenture Trinidad Society, 1917–1947." In *Engendering History,* edited by Verene Shepherd, Bridget Brereton, and Barbara Bailey. Kingston, Jamaica: Ian Randle, 1995.

Mohammed, Patricia, and Althea Perkins. "Freedom and Responsibility: New Challenges to Gender Relations in the Family." In *Gender and the Family in the Caribbean,* edited by Wilma Bailey. Kingston, Jamaica: Institute of Social and Economic Research, University of the West Indies, 1998.

————. *Caribbean Women at the Crossroads: The Paradox of Motherhood Among Women of Barbados, St. Lucia, and Dominica.* Kingston, Jamaica: Canoe Press, University of the West Indies, 1999.

Mohammed, Patricia, and Catherine Shepherd. *Gender in Caribbean Development.* Kingston, Jamaica: Canoe Press, University of the West Indies, 1999.

Moitt, Bernard. "Women, Work, and Resistance in the French Caribbean During Slavery." In *Engendering History,* edited by Verene Shepherd, Bridget Brereton, and Barbara Bailey. Kingston, Jamaica: Ian Randle, 1995.

Momsen, Janet H., ed. *Women and Change in the Caribbean.* Kingston, Jamaica: Ian Randle, 1993.

Ortiz, Altagracia, ed. *Puerto Rican Women and Work: Bridges in Transnational Labor.* Philadelphia: Temple University Press, 1996.

Patterson, Orlando. "Persistence, Continuity, and Change in the Jamaican Working-Class Family." *Journal of Family History* 7 (1982): 135–161.

People's National Party. "Candidate, Portia Simpson-Miller." http://www.pnpjamaica.com.

Plaza, Dwayne. "Frequent Flyer Grannies." Paper presented at the History of the Family Conference, Carlton University, Ottawa, May 15–16, 1997.

————. "Transnational Grannies: The Changing Family Responsibilities of Elderly African Caribbean-Born Women Resident in Britain." *Social Indicators Research* 1, no. 1 (2000): 75–105.

Portes, Alejandro, and Alex Stepick. *City on the Edge: The Transformation of Miami.* Berkeley: University of California Press, 1993.

Powell, Dorian. "The Role of Women in the Caribbean." *Social and Economic Studies* 33, no. 2 (June 1984): 97–122.

Reddock, Rhoda. *Women, Labour, and Politics in Trinidad: A History.* London: Zed Books, 1994.

Rey, Terry. *Our Lady of Class Struggle*. Trenton, NJ: Africa World Press, 1999.

Safa, Helen I. *The Myth of the Male Breadwinner.* Boulder, CO: Westview, 1995.

Sagás, Ernesto. *Race and Politics in the Dominican Republic.* Gainesville: University Press of Florida, 2000.

Shepherd, Verene, ed. *Women in Caribbean History.* Kingston, Jamaica: Ian Randle, 1999.

Shepherd, Verene, Bridget Brereton, and Barbara Bailey, eds. *Engendering History: Caribbean Women in Historical Perspective.* Kingston, Jamaica: Ian Randle, 1995.

Slater, Mariam K. *The Caribbean Family: Legitimacy in Martinique.* New York: St. Martin's Press, 1977.

Smith, M. G. "Introduction: My Mother Who Fathered Me." In *West Indian Family Structure,* by M. G. Smith. Seattle: University of Washington Press, 1962.

Steady, Filomina Chiona. *Women and Children First: Environment, Poverty, and Sustainable Development.* Rochester, VT: Schenkman Books, 1993.

Stepick, Alex. *Pride Against Prejudice.* Boston: Allyn and Bacon, 1998.

Stubbs, Jean. "Social and Political Motherhood of Cuba: Mariana Grajales Cuello." In *Engendering History,* edited by Verene Shepherd, Bridget Brereton, and Barbara Bailey. Kingston, Jamaica: Ian Randle, 1995.

United Nations Statistics Division. "Adult Unemployment," http://unstats.un.org/unsd/demographic/products/indwm/tab5f.htm (accessed 2009).

———. "Distribution of the Labor Force by Status in Employment." In *The World's Women 2005: Progress in Statistics,* http://unstats.un.org/unsd/demographic/products/indwm/ww2005/tab5e.htm (accessed 2009).

———. "Part-time Employment." In *Statistics and Indicators on Women and Men,* http://unstats.un.org/unsd/demographic/products/indwm/tab5b.htm (accessed 2009).

———. "Part-time Employment." In *The World's Women 2005: Progress in Statistics,* http://unstats.un.org/unsd/demographic/products/indwm/ww2005/tab5b.htm (accessed 2009).

Vassell, Linnette. "Women, Power, and Decision-Making in CARICOM Countries." In *Gender Equality in the Caribbean,* edited by Gemma Tang and Barbara Bailey. Kingston, Jamaica: Ian Randle, 2003.

Warner-Lewis, Maureen. "The African Impact on Language and Literature in the English-Speaking Caribbean." In *Africa and the Caribbean,* edited by Margaret E. Crahan and Franklin W. Knight. Baltimore: Johns Hopkins University Press, 1979.

Yelvington, Kevin. *Producing Power: Ethnicity, Gender, and Class in a Caribbean Workplace.* Philadelphia: Temple University Press, 1995.

10

Religion in
the Caribbean

Leslie G. Desmangles, Stephen D. Glazier,
and Joseph M. Murphy

Vodou, Santería, the Spiritual Baptists, and Orisha are religions native to the Caribbean. For their devotees, these terms hold the keys to some of life's most profound concerns, but for many fans of Hollywood, they evoke mysterious religious beliefs and practices related to destructive supernatural forces, zombification, cannibalism, and all sorts of religious wizardry. These popular notions are far from the truth, and an objective examination of these religions reveals that none of their beliefs and rituals confirms such views.

Caribbean religions are practiced by millions of people whose lives are affected profoundly by their teachings. Like other religions of the world, they give meaning to life, uplift the downtrodden, and instill in their devotees a need for solace and self-reflection. They also relate humans to powerful divine beings believed to govern the universe. These demiurges are said to live in sacred abodes whose invisible "portals" can be opened with the proper rituals to provide assistance to their devotees in their daily lives.

Caribbean religions are global religions. They embrace a wide range of cultural elements, personal creeds and practices, including forms of folk medical practices and systems of ethics transmitted across generations through proverbs, stories, songs, dances, and other artistic forms of expressions. In short, if one important aspect of religion is to offer a unique dimension of experience that motivates the believers to interpret their whole lives by such experiences, then the Caribbean religions are more than religious phenomena. They are intrinsic parts of the cultures that they serve.

There are significant numbers of religions indigenous to the Caribbean, and scholars who study them often include those of the Brazilian state of Bahia as well as those of the countries found on the northern coast of South America (Venezuela, Suriname, and Guyana). As Stephen J. Randall shows in Chapter

3, relatively long periods of colonial domination, a history of slavery and resistance to slavery, modes of production deriving from forced labor, and political and socioeconomic developments that resulted from these historical events are common experiences within the region.

■ Categories of Caribbean Religions

For theoretical purposes, Caribbean religions may be classified into five major categories (Simpson 1978:14). First are the African-derived religions, which developed within the context of slavery and preserved a fair amount of African religious traditions alongside Roman Catholic or Protestant beliefs and practices. They include Vodou in Haiti; Santería in Cuba, the Dominican Republic, and Puerto Rico; and Candomblé and Macumba in Brazil. To this category can be added other African-derived and ancestral religions that have preserved fewer African traditions but have been combined with various forms of Protestantism imported to the Caribbean by Christian missionaries during the nineteenth and twentieth centuries: they include the Spiritual Baptists and Orisha groups in Trinidad and Tobago, the Kumina (or Pukumina[1]) and Convince in Jamaica, the Big Drum in Grenada and Carriacou, and the Kele in St. Lucia (Simpson 1978:14).

The second category includes the Revivalist religions, nineteenth- and twentieth-century phenomena that are related to charismatic Protestant movements imported from the United States. They encompass the Pentecostals, Baptists, Seventh-Day Adventists, and Revival movements throughout the Caribbean; Shouters in Trinidad and Tobago, St. Vincent, Grenada, and Guyana; Shakers and Streams of Power in St. Vincent; Tie Heads (members of the Jerusalem Apostolic Spiritual Baptist Church) in Barbados and St. Lucia; Jordanites of Guyana; Spirit Baptists in Jamaica; and the Cohortes and Holiness movements (Pentecostal-derived groups) in Haiti.

The third category emphasizes divination (the intuitive reading of one's future into an object), folk healing,[2] spiritual healing, and divine revelation through mediumship. It encompasses Myalism in Jamaica; revival movements (including, among others, the Native Baptist [formerly the Ethiopian Baptist] Church and the Jamaican Baptist); Espiritismo, Karedicismo, and the various spiritist sects in Puerto Rico and Cuba; Umbanda in Brazil; and María Lionza in Venezuela.

The fourth category includes what we may call *redemptionist* groups or religio-political movements that developed sporadically as early as the eighteenth century and address many issues related to neocolonialism and social and economic injustice. They include the Rastafari (also called Rastafarians) and Dread movements that originated in Jamaica (but have become widespread throughout the Caribbean), as well as the Nation of Islam from the United States.

A fifth category comprises the religious traditions imported to the Caribbean from Europe, the Middle East, Asia, and South Asia: Judaism, Islam, and Hinduism, brought to the region with the arrival of hundreds of thousands of indentured laborers in Brazil, Guyana, Trinidad, Suriname, Curaçao, and other parts of the Caribbean.

The divisions that exist between these categories, however, are merely theoretical, for in reality they are not mutually exclusive but take diverse local forms in which the theology of some in one category may be included in the beliefs and practices of another. This chapter cannot allow for a description of all the religions found within the Caribbean. We have therefore selected Vodou, Santería, the Spiritual Baptists, the Pentecostal-derived movements, the Rastafari, Judaism, Islam, and Hinduism for several reasons: their importance to the historical development and future direction of Caribbean religious thought; the significant number of adherents who practice them; and their important influence on the lives of millions of Caribbean immigrants currently living abroad.

In short, Caribbean religions consist of religious traditions that derived from five continents, namely Europe, Africa, Asia, and the Americas. But most

St. George's Cathedral, Georgetown, Guyana.

Maureen Smith

scholars who study them regard them as *Creole* or New World creations because these traditions were altered with time from their original forms by environmental conditions and unique economic, historical, and cultural factors in the Caribbean. The different admixture of African religious traditions represented in various parts of the Caribbean, as well as the inclusion of Christian theology, transformed African beliefs and practices permanently into something different from those of the motherland.

Most Caribbean religions have taken divergent forms and consist of loosely organized structures with independent local cells that maintain differing beliefs and practices. These cells operate independently of each other rather than through a centralized point of authority. Despite divergences in the cells' theological and ritual details, they exhibit some common elements. First, they are tied informally to each other by a system of *reticulation,* or a weblike character, in which the leaders and members of one cell visit those of other cells and participate together in occasional religious festivals and pilgrimages (Gerlach and Hine 1970). Second, they hold common attitudes about the nature of faith itself. Their members regard religion strictly in practical terms; faith does not consist of a self-surrender to mysticism or to complicated theological debates. Religion is a way of life, and one's faith must satisfy actual needs and answer some of the profound existential questions. As noted in Joseph Murphy's description of Santería in this chapter, the spirits must serve as founts of wisdom that address practical matters of life. Third, except for the Spiritual Baptists and Opa Orisa in Trinidad, Caribbean religions maintain neither theological nor ecumenical centers for the training of their leaders, nor presses, editorial staff, or publications; hence, their leaders receive no formal training but learn their skills from other practitioners through inheritance or through social contacts. New leaders establish their religious authority in their local cells by their knowledge of the theology, their public commitment to their faith, and their religious fervor (as in the case of the Pentecostals in their ability to prophesy). As Stephen Glazier observes in this chapter, recent attempts to create training centers and establish a universal creed among the Spiritual Baptist churches of Trinidad have been hotly contested and largely unsuccessful.

Because these religions lack an established orthodoxy, it is difficult to present a complete documentation of their beliefs and practices. But despite differences between local cells, it is nonetheless possible to discover the internally consistent systems that exist between them. What follows, then, is not intended to portray the universal beliefs and practices of Caribbean people. Rather, it is a description of those beliefs and practices most commonly held by the devotees.

■ The Colonial Setting and Religious Diversity

Caribbean religions are amalgams of various religious traditions that originated in Africa, Asia, Europe, and the Americas. The blending of these traditions began with Christopher Columbus's arrival in the Western Hemisphere and with the establishment of the first European settlement on Hispaniola in December 1492, where the new settlers encountered a native population of Amerindians (Arawaks and Caribs) who derived originally from the Taíno.

In the years following that encounter, the European presence had profound effects on this native population. Consumed by their determination to discover gold reputed to exist on these islands, the Spanish *conquistadors* subjected the Indians to hard labor. The tyranny was so severe that just fifteen years after the Europeans' arrival, nearly four-fifth of the Amerindian population had perished. Various diseases imported from Europe, against which the Amerindians were not immune, decimated their numbers. Estimates are that by the end of the seventeenth century, the number of Amerindians in the region had been reduced from about half a million to 60,000 (Desmangles 1992:18). Amerindian cultures might have disappeared completely due to centuries of oppression, but many religious traditions have survived to the present day. Taíno, Carib, and Ciboney "protector spirits" are included in the traditions of Brazilian Umbanda; Puerto Rican Espiritismo; shamanism in Trinidad, Puerto Rico, and Suriname; and some of the regional practices of Cuban Santería.

The rapid decline in the Amerindian population necessitated a new source of labor, and Bartolomé de las Casas, an influential Spanish Catholic missionary who had become sympathetic to the Indians' mistreatment and had taken their plight before the Spanish Crown, endorsed a plan to replace the Amerindians with African laborers.[3] Although no one is sure of the exact date the slave trade began in the Americas, some historical records indicate that it was as early as 1512, a mere twenty years after Columbus's arrival in the Caribbean, and that the number of Africans brought over totaled more than 12 million (Bastide 1971:5).

The Africans taken to the Caribbean as slaves came from a variety of ethnic nations covering a wide region of West Africa. They brought with them their religious traditions, which permeated the fabric of the region's colonial life. In contacts with each other, they shared religious traditions and succeeded in fashioning religious amalgams that left an indelible mark on the cultures of the region and resulted in the continuity of African cultural traditions in the Caribbean.

If African religious traditions survived in the Caribbean, it was largely due to *maronnage*. The word *maroon* derives from the Spanish *cimarrón,* a term used to designate a domesticated animal that had reverted to a wild state. The term soon came to be applied to the slaves who ran away from the plantations and gathered in the interior of the colonies to form secret societies known as maroon republics (Bastide 1971:51). The Africans who joined these republics probably congregated along ethnic lines, and thus the religious traditions in each republic depended upon the particular ethnic mix in each. The republics' theological diversity helps explain the local divergences in beliefs and practices that exist in Caribbean religions today. Depending on the geographic area, some emphasized particular African ethnic traditions and not others. Despite these ethnic divergences, however, the demographic distribution of Africans who came to each country in the Caribbean derived overwhelmingly from specific regions of Africa, and consequently the religious traditions of the more prominent ethnic groups prevailed over others. Thus, Santería in Cuba derives largely from Nigerian Yoruba beliefs and practices, whereas Haitian Vodou theology derives largely from Dahomey (contemporary Benin) and Congo, the homelands of many Africans.

Despite some similarities, Caribbean religions do not replicate those in West Africa. Environmental conditions, the historical contexts of the region, and the admixture of African religious and ethnic traditions represented in the Caribbean permanently transformed African beliefs into something different. Thus, Caribbean religions cannot be characterized as African religions but rather as African-derived religions whose beliefs and practices originated largely in West Africa.

An important aspect of Caribbean religions is how they incorporated Christian traditions into their theology. The degree to which Christianity was included within the theology of these religions differed from Catholic to Protestant colonies. By and large, the territories under British rule were Protestant and tended to be less syncretic than the Catholic-dominated ones (e.g., the French and the Spanish colonies). Also, the period in which Protestants undertook the systematic evangelization of Africans began much later and consequently was shorter than in the Catholic areas. Unlike the Spanish and French in the Catholic areas, where there were significant missionary efforts to convert slaves to Christianity, the British thought that Christianity was too sophisticated for Africans to understand and therefore considered slaves unfit for its practice. In Jamaica, for example, the Church of England (Anglican) did not make a concerted attempt to evangelize the slaves in any systematic way until the 1820s, shortly after the arrival of Moravian and Methodist missionaries from the United States. By contrast, the French began to convert the slaves to Christianity as early as the sixteenth century. Two reasons account for such a difference. First, the Catholic emphasis on hagiology (the biography of the saints) and sacred iconography made it compatible with the retention of many African religious traditions in the Catholic colonies. As we shall see later, many of the symbols associated with the saints resembled those for African gods, and such similarities facilitated the reinterpretations of Catholic theology in terms of African traditions. Second, the degree to which African religious traditions were preserved in the Protestant areas depended on the peculiar historical circumstances and the length of colonial rule in the region. A prolonged European influence in a country tended to lessen that country's ability to maintain African traditions and thus increased the prevalence of Protestantism. In effect, continuous contact with Europeans over a relatively long period tended gradually to abrade the prevalence of African religious traditions.

Apart from the Anglican Church, which entrenched itself in the lives of colonists as early as the seventeenth century in the British territories, Protestantism was barely represented in the overwhelmingly Catholic Spanish and French Caribbean areas until the early nineteenth century. Protestant missions in the areas where Catholicism was the predominant religion were limited, the number of adherents relatively small. In these areas, Protestantism did not gain importance until the late nineteenth and early twentieth centuries, with the arrival of missionaries from the United States. Among the major Protestant denominations, the religious groups that gained the most adherents were evangelical in nature. They include Pentecostals, Baptists, Seventh-Day Adventists, Jehovah's Witnesses, and, more recently, the Church of the Latter Day Saints (Mormons). The number of Pentecostals and Baptists today exceeds those of the other Protestant groups, perhaps because of their religious zeal and ardent recruitment of new members. In the case of Pentecostals and Holiness groups, the possibilities of engaging oneself directly with the spirit world through spiritual trances and glossolalia (speaking in tongues) have traditionally been kindred to the African ritual styles entrenched in Caribbean society and might have contributed to the conversion of thousands of devotees.

African-Derived Traditions

Vodou

Vodou is the religion indigenous to Haiti. The word *Vodou* derives from *vodu* or *vodun* in the Fon language of Benin on the western coast of Africa and means "deity" or "spirit." Thus, Vodou relates the life of its devotees to thousands of incommensurable spirits called *lwas* (from a Yoruba word for "spirit"), who govern all of life in addition to the entire cosmos. *Lwas* are believed to manifest themselves in nature and through the bodies of their devotees in spirit or trance possession.

The theology of Vodou was born on the sugar plantations of the French colony of St. Domingue (as Haiti was known during the colonial period). Little is known about the slave communities in the colony during that period, but historical sources indicate that the Africans who came to St. Domingue originated (among other places) in Dahomey (presently known as Benin), Congo, Angola, and Nigeria. They were agricultural and pastoral peoples who brought their religious traditions with them, which they wove into the fabric of Vodou's theology as it exists today. But despite Vodou's Africanness, it cannot by any stretch of the imagination be called an African religion. St. Domingue's history of social oppression altered African religious traditions permanently, making Vodou a religion exclusive to the Americas. African beliefs and rituals were adapted to their new milieu in the New World, and many bear no resemblances to their African forebears.

During the eighteenth century, St. Domingue became France's wealthiest colony. Large plantations were established, employing a large slave labor force and exporting, among other yields such as mahogany, cotton, coffee, and rum, 65 percent of the world's sugar.[4] The colony's thriving economy attracted a significant number of French landowners and investors who sought to make their fortune. The majority of them were Roman Catholics who regarded Vodou as an aberration and sought to eliminate it from colonial society. They were quick to enact a number of edicts such as the Code Noir (Black Code) of 1685 that made it illegal for the slaves to practice their African religions openly. The severity of such laws drove African rituals underground. To circumvent interference in their rituals by their masters, slaves learned to overlay African practices with the veneer of Roman Catholic symbols and rituals. They used symbols of the church in their rituals as "white masks over black faces"—veils behind which they could hide their African practices.[5] The presence of these symbols prompted the slaves to use them in their rituals and to use the Catholic feast days to honor the African gods. They established correspondences between the African spirits and Catholic saints consisting of a system of reinterpretations in which particular symbols associated with the gods in African mythology were made to correspond to similar symbols associated with the saints in Catholic hagiology. For example, the Dahomean snake deity Damballah was made to correspond with St. Patrick because of the Catholic legend about St. Patrick and the snakes of Ireland. In effect, the slaves succeeded in creating what is known as a religious *symbiosis* (Desmangles 1992:8). The word *symbiosis* as used here has a different meaning from that of the biological sciences, where it refers to the living together of dissimilar organisms in a mutually beneficial relationship. Etymologically, symbiosis is from the Greek *sun* (with) and *bios* (life, or life together with). In the ethnological sense, symbiosis is the spatial juxtaposition of diverse religious traditions from two continents that coexist without fusing. Like the tiny parts of a stained-glass window juxtaposed to form a whole, parts of the Vodou and Catholic traditions are juxtaposed in space and time to constitute the whole of Vodou.

The encroachment of Vodou practices on Catholic theology was embarrassing for church clerics, who from time to time launched vehement campaigns against fetishism in Haitian society. Haitians have continued to practice two religions simultaneously and maintained their allegiance to both in parallel ways (Desmangles 1992:50–53). An often quoted Haitian proverb is that one must be Catholic to serve the Vodou *lwas*. The truth of that statement illustrates the reality of Haitian culture as a product of African and European cultures. It also illustrates what seems logical to Vodouists: that the world is governed by the Godhead whom they call *Bondye* (from the French *bon Dieu,* meaning "Good Lord") or *Gran Mèt* (Grand Master) and that the *lwas* (or by extension the Catholic saints) are nothing more than the manifestations of Bondye. Vodou is therefore a monotheistic religion in that each *lwa* is a different facet of the complex persona of Bondye.

A Vodou altar showing chromolithographs of Catholic saints, Haiti.

Leslie G. Desmangles

Vodouists also believe that the human body is a manifestation of Bondye. It contains a soul with several compartments, characterized by their psychic functions. In some ways, the Vodou notion of the compartmentalized self is analogous to Sigmund Freud's description of the theoretical divisions of the human psyche. The first compartment of the human soul in Vodou is the *gwo bon anj* (the big good angel), a life force, the source of divine energy that is implanted in the human body and is associated with the act of breathing itself. It is also the source of dynamic energy from which derives physiological movement: the beating of the heart, the flow of blood throughout the body. The second compartment of the human spirit is the *ti bon anj* (the little good angel), the "ego soul" that is identified with the personality, is manifested in one's deportment and facial expressions, and is displaced in trance possession. The third compartment is the *mèt tèt* (the master of the head); it is the part of the soul that is the manifestation of a guardian *lwa* who has protected a person from danger throughout his or her life.

A ritual called *desounen* (the uprooting of life) is performed shortly after death. It extracts these compartments of the spirits from the body and dispatches them to their respective abodes: the *gwo bon anj* and the *mèt tèt* to Ginen, the underworld where the spirits of the dead reside; the *ti bon anj* to heaven (because of the Catholic influence); and the body to the navel of the earth, where it will disintegrate and never rise again. The Vodou cycle of funerary rites constitutes an elaborate set of observances performed by members of the family that can last an entire year after a person's death.

As in Africa, ancestral spirits exercise direct authority over the living. They join the community of the "living dead" ruled by Gede, the master of Ginen. In time, they are thought to acquire a sacred wisdom that allows them to observe the community of the living. They are conceived to exist in other dimensions of time, possessing the ability to see far into the future and the past, and are called upon to guide the living in their daily lives. They are also considered to be demigods whose lives are remembered and preserved as a valuable legacy for the future prosperity of the living's progeny. They impart their wisdom in trance possession or in intuitive ways.

Trance possession can be defined as an altered state of consciousness in which the self is experienced as disembodied and replaced by a supernatural entity. During trance possession, a Vodouist believes that his or her body becomes a vessel that harbors a *lwa.* The self is then disembodied and replaced by the community's envisaged mythological persona of a spirit. The temporary surrender of one's identity to that of a supernatural entity, and the alternate behavior that accompanies such states, is pursued by a person who longs for a transcendent experience whereby they embody a spirit. It also serves as a symbol of direct communication between the sacred and profane worlds. Trance possession is one of the elements that characterizes Vodou as a democratic religion. Indeed, it is a means by which a devotee can experience firsthand a direct engagement with the spirit world, for by being possessed, the Vodouist does not come to know the *lwas* by merely observing or imagining them through the myths but by *becoming* them by being possessed by them. Trance possession is an important part of a Vodou ceremony because it is through the body of a devotee that a spirit can embody the mythology of the community, enact the events that surround the lives of the *lwas,* and share their wisdom with that community. Conversely, it is also through the same medium that the members of the community can share their concerns with the embodied spirit. Thus, trance possession is not only a symbol of the commitment of the community to a *lwa* but also a quintessential spiritual achievement in a believer's religious life because it is a public commitment to the religion that testifies to his or her religious fervor.

In ceremonies, Vodouists use every sensory means at their disposal to invoke the spirits and to petition them to invade the bodies of their devotees. Each *lwa* has its own songs, its own dances and drum rhythms, and its own symbols. These symbols are known as *vèvès*—geometric, Kabbala-like traceries that symbolize the personae and the functions of the *lwas.* When a *lwa* is invoked in a ritual, the priest or priestess (*oungan* or *mambo*) traces the *lwa's* *vèvè* on the floor of the temple by sifting corn flour with the thumb and the forefinger of his right hand. Vodouists believe that these visual and auditory media summon the *lwas* to leave their abode and to possess their devotees. In a sense, Vodou's use of these depictions for the *lwas* is analogous to the literary and artistic vehicles upon which mythologies of other cultures, including those of Christian Europe, often rely for the portrayal of their deities.

In conclusion, Vodou constitutes a set of beliefs and practices related to powerful spirits (or saints) that are implicated in every aspect of life. Vodou, like African traditional religions, is not a religion in the Western sense in which one may or may not choose to identify oneself with a system of thought. Vodou is not a belief system to be affirmed or rejected. Vodouists contend that spiritual reality cannot be the subject of scientific investigation but is based on what is self-evident: that the entire cosmos is filled with the presence of incommensurable spiritual forces whose awesome powers no one can escape.

Santería

Santería is a Cuban religious tradition that originated among the Yoruba peoples of West Africa and has since spread around the world. Santería (meaning "way of the saints" in Spanish) reminds us that African traditions in the Caribbean developed though an oppressive encounter with European colonialism. Nearly 1 million African men, women, and children were enslaved and carried to Cuba to work on sugar plantations, where they earned enormous profits for European landholders and venture capitalists. In the midst of the systematic atrocities of a society built on slave labor, many Africans in Cuba were able to find power and healing in the religious traditions brought from their homelands. The Yoruba in Cuba paralleled their clandestine rites to African spirits with those of the Catholic saints supported by the colonial ethos. And so the tradition came to be called Santería, a way of venerating Yoruba spirits likened to Catholic saints.

At the end of the eighteenth century, Yoruba people were brought over in large numbers to Cuba in response to two events. First, the successful revolution in Haiti ended European control of one of the most lucrative sugar plantation colonies in the world. Liberated Haitians turned to subsistence farming, and European investors were forced to look elsewhere to realize large profits from enslaved labor. Second, the West African empire administered from the Yoruba city of Oyo disintegrated due to a series of challenges from without and within. Fulani from the north, Dahomeans from the west, and rival Yoruba city-states pulled the empire apart, and the Yoruba were plunged into years of war. From the late eighteenth century through the first decades of the nineteenth century, perhaps as many as 1 million Yoruba displaced by these wars were sold along the "Slave Coast" of West Africa and carried to the Americas.

The European demand for sugar, the loss of Haitian slave labor and plantations, and the ready supply of enslaved Yoruba led to the rapid development of the sugar industry in Cuba. Hundreds of thousands of Yoruba cleared, planted, and harvested sugar on hundreds of new plantations. The large and rapid influx of people sharing the Yoruba language and culture established Yoruba ethnicity as a permanent part of Cuba's cultural mosaic. They came to be called *Lucumi* after an old name for *Oyo*. Today those who would emphasize this heritage in their religion will speak of *la religión lucumi* or *la regla lucumi*.

The development of Santería (*la religión lucumi*) was greatly enhanced by the formation of ethnic mutual-aid societies called *cabildos africanos*. In the cities and towns of Cuba, Lucumi—enslaved and free—were able to join together for mutual benefit, protection, and recreation. The *cabildos* assisted the infirm, buried the dead, held accounts for the purchase of members' freedom, and venerated the spirits of their homelands. Several other African peoples formed *cabildos* in colonial Cuba, although of the scores of African ethnicities documented on the island, only a few were able to incorporate themselves into assemblies. Congos from central Africa, Carabali from the Niger Delta, and Arara from Dahomey made lasting impressions on the Cuban ethnic landscape, and their distinctive religious traditions continue to be maintained today. Yet the numerical plurality of the Yoruba gave their traditions a visibility and prestige that have only grown throughout the twentieth century.

Out of the leadership of the Lucumi *cabildos* came the lines of initiation that sanction Santería priesthood today. Lucumi tradition recognizes two categories of interdependent priesthood: those of *Orula*, the patron of divination; and those of individual spirits called *orichas*. The priests of Orula are called *babalaos* (the fathers of the mystery) and are extensively trained to divine for devotees by means of an ancient oracle called *Ifa*. By the random fall of specially prepared palm nuts, the *babalao* can interpret the destiny of individuals and groups and develop their relationship to the multitude of *orichas* who empower life. Devotees will seek out the services of a *babalao* for advice in securing the power of the *orichas* to meet the challenges of life: for health, for security, for love.

The other category of priest is called either *iyalocha* (mother of the *oricha*, if a woman) or *babalocha* (father of the *oricha*, if a man). The often-used Spanish equivalents are *santera* and *santero*, respectively. These people have been consecrated to the service of a particular *oricha*, though they may be authorized to serve as priests to other spirits as well. They have received the power of the *orichas* "in their heads" and so may at times embody the presence of the *orichas* for other devotees. Each *iyalocha* or *babalocha* is free to establish her or his own spiritual house (*ilé*) and thus conduct ceremonies independently as well as cooperatively with other houses. *Iyalochas* and *babalochas* who initiate others into their houses are addressed as *madriña* (godmother) and *padriño* (godfather) and are expected to be treated with great respect by their godchildren.

A contemporary Santería house functions in many of the same ways as the nineteenth-century Lucumi *cabildos*. Godchildren gather for mutual aid and recreation, yet the principal feature of a contemporary house is the organization of the cycle of ceremonies for the *orichas*. Ceremonies may be held for the initiation of new members, anniversaries of initiation, further advanced initiations for priestesses and priests, ceremonies of petition and thanksgiving to the *orichas* for special intentions, and the annual feast days of the spirits. Santería, like Vodou, has inherited its calendar from the colonial authority of the Roman Catholic Church and so celebrates its calendar feasts on the days of the *oricha*'s Catholic equivalent.

The analogy of the *orichas* with Catholic saints is imperfect but useful in understanding Santería theology. The *orichas* proceed from one almighty God who has delegated and divided his power (*aché*) among them. Through the currency of this divine *aché,* the *orichas* may be petitioned for help in securing earthly success and heavenly wisdom. The *orichas* are powerful, invisible entities who act as the source of the energies of the world. Each *oricha* is the "owner" of a particular cluster of energies that can be seen in natural phenomena such as rivers, fire, wind, or iron. These energies also give rise to the personalities of the *orichas,* so that Ochún, for example, who is the *oricha* of the river, is manifested as a life-giving, sensuous, woman; and Changó, *oricha* of thunder and lightning, is a bold warrior king. Each *oricha* has hundreds of stories that detail its exploits and explain its powers and avenues of approach. And each *oricha* is venerated with special stones, herbs, beads, colors, foods, rhythms, and songs appropriate to it.

A life with the *orichas* usually begins with a critical problem in an individual person's life: an illness, an errant lover, a lost job. He or she might consult a *babalao* or *iyalocha* to determine if an *oricha*'s aid might be effective in meeting the crisis. The proper oracles would be consulted and a solution offered that would involve a sacrifice appropriate to the *oricha* whose power is most suited to the resolution of the problem. A sacrifice may be a very simple one of candles lit and prayers said; if the oracles so prescribe, however, there are much more elaborate undertakings involving the preparation of special foods and the cooperation of the entire community. At its most lavish, a Santería sacrifice might require the services of many highly trained priests and priestesses, professional musicians who have mastered the vast musical repertoires of the *orichas,* and the accumulation of costly foods and live animals for ritual slaughter.

As the ceremonial exchanges with the *orichas* and with the community grow, it is likely that a particular *oricha* will begin to assert itself as the individual's patron or patroness. Once divination has determined the identity of this *oricha,* the individual will be called to the Santería priesthood through a lengthy ordination ceremony called *asiento* (seating) in Spanish and *kariocha* (*oricha*-crowning) in Lucumi. Here the individual and the *oricha* form an irrevocable bond in which the *oricha* is enthroned or seated in the "head," or deepest personality, of the individual. The new priest now bears the responsibility to represent his or her *oricha* at the ceremonies of the community. With the *oricha* in his or her head, the priest may act as a medium for the *oricha,* as with trance possessions among Vodouists, losing his or her own personality in the rhythms of the drumming and dancing and manifesting the personality of the *oricha* patron or patroness. Thus Ochún and Changó, for example, are seen to actually appear at ceremonies, manifested through the service of their human priestly mediums. The *orichas* may speak with the community to admonish, prophesy, and heal. The appearances of the *orichas* through the bodies of devotees are greeted with reverence and joy by the congregation and are the dramatic high point of Santería's ceremonial life.

The vibrant idioms of Santería ceremony have crossed over into Cuban popular culture in many ways. The rhythms of the sacred drums have been adapted to recreational dances like the mambo, rumba, and cha-cha. Many of the gestures and steps of these dances originate in the attitudes of the *orichas* when they manifest themselves through their human mediums. Cuba's socialist government has sponsored Afro-Cuban culture as an authentic expression of the island's independent Creole identity, the most notable product being the internationally recognized Conjunto Folklórico Nacíonal, which presents dance performances on *oricha* themes. In the 1990s the government began subsidizing prominent *santeros* and *santeras* and facilitated their meeting with foreign devotees in order to instruct and initiate them.

An official Asociación Cultural Yoruba de Cuba was formed to act on the government's behalf in matters related to Afro-Cuban traditions. The association publishes an annual *Letra del Año* (Sign for the Year), an Ifa divination for the nation that seeks to orient Cubans to the *oricha* energies at work in the coming year. Other Ifa groups on the island and abroad publish their own *Letras del Año,* which they say are untainted by the political concerns of the Cuban government.

Officially or unofficially, foreign seekers come to Cuba to learn about and be initiated into Afro-Cuban traditions. Of course, with them comes much-needed hard currency, and so the governmental interest in this kind of commerce underscores the visibility and influence of Santería in Cuban life. Cuba has become famous for Santería and a point of pilgrimage for seekers and tourists alike. When Pope John-Paul II came to Cuba in 1998, the government made every effort to deemphasize the extent of Catholicism in the nation, and many officially sanctioned publications proclaimed Santería as the religion of the Cuban people. Again the strategic value of such support is apparent, yet the central role of Santería in representations of nation is clear as well.

Santería faces a host of challenges as it expands beyond the Caribbean to the international arena. The very name *Santería* is often seen by many practitioners as both parochial and tied to a colonial ethos that the religion heroically resisted. Now, independent of colonial attitudes and persecution, the religion might stand on its own in the company of other world traditions. Alternative names might be *Yoruba* (recognizing the African ethnic origins of the tradition) or *Lucumi* (demonstrating the importance of the religion's development in Cuba), or perhaps simply *Oricha* (respecting the spirits venerated). Regardless of the label, the tradition is engaged in the difficult process of developing systems of authority and of sanctioning a priesthood and canonizing texts. As the religion continues to grow, particularly among populations only distantly aware of Cuba (or even the struggle for justice among communities abroad), the religion's leaders will have to adapt to new meanings and initiatives. For example, the religion is represented at hundreds of Internet sites that disseminate information far beyond the influence of the most conscientious and dedicated elders.

Afro-Cuban religion is one of dynamic aesthetics, spiritual depth, and heroic resistance to oppression and despair. It is one of the great contributions of the Caribbean to the world and a model for intercultural worlds of the future.

The Spiritual Baptists

The Spiritual Baptists of Trinidad are part of a rapidly expanding international religious movement with congregations in St. Vincent (where many Trinidadian Spiritual Baptists claim their faith originated), Trinidad and Tobago, Grenada, Guyana, Venezuela, London, Toronto, Los Angeles, and New York City. In addition, there are a number of similar religious movements on other Caribbean islands whose rituals parallel those of the Spiritual Baptists (i.e., the Tie Heads of Barbados, the Jordanites of Guyana, and the Spirit Baptists of Jamaica). Spiritual Baptists, however, do not consider members of those other religions to be a part of their religion and seldom participate in joint worship services, pilgrimages, missions, and other activities with them. They do, however, maintain close and active ties with brethren in St. Vincent, Guyana, Grenada, Venezuela, the United States, Europe, and Canada.

Like other religions of Caribbean origin, Spiritual Baptist membership is predominantly black, and—like many other Afro-Caribbean groups—the Spiritual Baptists seem to have started out as a religion of the oppressed. In recent years, however, congregations in Trinidad have attracted membership among middle-class blacks, as well as sizable numbers of wealthier East Indians, Chinese, whites, and individuals of mixed heritage. Although some Spiritual Baptist leaders take great pride in their multiethnic congregations, it is possible to overplay the influence of other ethnic groups. The Spiritual Baptist faith is still overwhelmingly a black religion, with Asians and whites representing less than 5 percent of total adherents. Recent membership in Trinidad and Tobago has fluctuated between 10,000 and 12,500.

Many Trinidadians confuse Spiritual Baptists and followers of the African-derived Orisha movement.[6] They assume that Spiritual Baptist and Orisha rites are identical. Members of these two faiths, however, do not share this confusion. A large percentage of Spiritual Baptists condemn Orisha rites as heathen worship.

Orisha devotees, for their part, assert that the Spiritual Baptists copy their ideas and try to "steal their power." On occasion, Spiritual Baptist leaders have picketed Orisha centers prior to Orisha ceremonies.

Another complicating factor is the growing number of Spiritual Baptist leaders who are also involved in the Kabbala. The influence of Kabbala was noted briefly by George Eaton Simpson, who remarked on Spiritual Baptists' widespread use of the Sixth and Seventh Books of Moses while conducting fieldwork in the 1960s (Simpson 1966). It is in the nature of Kabbala to be secretive, and Simpson's informants (who were mostly from churches along the Eastern Main Road) did not provide him with much information. Beginning in the late 1970s, Stephen Glazier conducted fieldwork with many informants from the same geographical area as Simpson's sources (Glazier 1991). Although at least two of the informants were heavily involved in Kabbala, Glazier encountered similar challenges in obtaining information. Since Kabbala rites are private and not readily shared, ethnographic research in this area did not open up prior to the pioneering work of Kenneth Lum starting in 1986.

Kabbala rituals are similar to those of American and Latin American spiritualism and Puerto Rican Karedicismo. A major difference is that during Kabbalistic séances, spirits from the "other side" communicate exclusively via a series of alternating short and long taps, which are simultaneously transcribed and translated by a medium. Kabbalistic rites are usually performed apart from Spiritual Baptist worship, most often in private homes. Sometimes, however, Kabbala tappings are embedded within regular Spiritual Baptist worship. In 1999 Glazier noted Kabbala being performed in the midst of Sunday morning services in Arima and Maraval, respectively. In both cases, Kabbala spirits communicated as part of a healing ceremony that was conducted by a Spiritual Baptist shepherd and nurse in the right-hand corner of the church. The paramount leader served as medium. Hidden behind a lace veil, the paramount leader transcribed the tappings. His interpretations were given in a private consultation at the conclusion of worship.

It should be emphasized that Kabbala has never been a major part of Spiritual Baptist worship in some Trinidadian churches and may be unknown among Spiritual Baptists on other Caribbean islands. Wallace Zane (1999) has noted that the religion is practiced neither in St. Vincent nor in New York City but is widespread among Spiritual Baptists in Trinidad. Séances are conducted so unobtrusively that only the initiated recognize what is taking place. To the uninitiated, the tapping of a shepherd's crook on an earthen floor (like pounding pews, ringing bells, and clapping hands) is simply taken as another aspect of Spiritual Baptist musical expression. This is exactly the intention of Kabbala operators and one reason Spiritual Baptist services are considered such a good cover for Kabbala rites.

Orisha rites, many of which are conducted outdoors in crowded residential areas, are not as secretive. Drumming and possession, which are the major components of Orisha rites, are public and highly visible. In examining the connections between Spiritual Baptist churches and Orisha centers, four distinct types of relationships may be discerned: Spiritual Baptist churches with Orisha connections; Spiritual Baptist churches without Orisha connections; Orisha centers with Spiritual Baptist connections; and Orisha centers without Spiritual Baptist connections. These distinctions reflect the ways in which members of these religions think of themselves. Are they, for example, Spiritual Baptists who also "do" Orisha work or followers of the Orisha who also "do" Spiritual Baptist work?

Members of all four types of organizations may also sponsor Kabbala rites, but Kabbala is most common among Spiritual Baptists who maintain close connections with Orisha and least common at Orisha centers without Spiritual Baptist ties. Of course, there are also many Kabbalists in Trinidad who do not participate in either Spiritual Baptist or Orisha rites.

Spiritual Baptists as well as devotees of Orisha combine beliefs and practices from a variety of religious traditions. A major difference is that Spiritual Baptist rituals are directed to their version of the Holy Trinity, whereas Orisha rites are directed toward and incorporate African-derived deities. Spiritual Baptists profess that they are Christians. We do not mean to imply that Spiritual Baptists do not acknowledge the power of the Orisha. They believe strongly in the power of African deities but do not believe that those deities should be venerated. A frequent assertion is that Spiritual Baptists do not fear the Orisha because "Christ gives us power over Orisha."

Although they practice separate traditions, Spiritual Baptists and Orisha devotees are interrelated on a number of levels. Their memberships overlap, and perhaps 90 percent of all Orisha devotees in Trinidad and Tobago also participate in Spiritual Baptist services; perhaps 40 percent of all Spiritual Baptists also participate in African-derived religions. Of course, there are degrees of participation. Not all leaders in the former religion are necessarily officials in the latter and vice versa.

Close associations between Spiritual Baptist churches and Orisha are unique within the Caribbean. Participants in other African-derived faiths—like Cuban Santería and Haitian Vodou—maintain ties with the Catholic Church; for example, the first step in serving the Haitian *lwas* is a Catholic baptism. Spiritual Baptists, however, are the only Protestant group in the region that serves as an institutional base for an African-derived religion. The relationship between Orisha devotees and Spiritual Baptist churches could be described as symbiotic. Spiritual Baptists maintain permanent buildings, whereas most Orisha devotees do not. Spiritual Baptists meet twice a week, while Orisha feasts are held only once or twice a year. Thus, Spiritual Baptist churches provide a convenient location for Orisha devotees to organize feasts and plan their activities and are also a setting for opening prayers for Orisha ceremonies.

For the Spiritual Baptists, the most central and controversial rite is the ritual known as mourning. Mourning ceremonies, Spiritual Baptists claim, make their religion distinct from all other religions in the world. The Spiritual Baptist concept of mourning differs greatly from that of many other religious traditions. Among Spiritual Baptists, it does not relate directly to physical death and bereavement but is an elaborate ceremony involving fasting, lying on a dirt floor, and other so-called deprivations, although contemporary rites give greater emphasis to symbolic deprivation than actual physical deprivation.

As in African initiation, death symbolism is apparent in mourning rites, but the ritual's central role has always been to remind mourners of human frailty and imperfection amid life. Spiritual Baptists say that they participate in mourning ceremonies for a variety of reasons—to cure cancer, to see the future, or to communicate with the deceased. On a more mundane level, mourning enables Spiritual Baptists to temporarily escape family obligations, gives them an opportunity for fellowship, and even provides the possibility of weight loss (though fasting is no longer encouraged, some mourners find it easy to diet within the context of the ceremony). For many, it is a vision quest, an attempt to discover the "true" self in relation to God the Father and God the Holy Ghost. The major stated goal of mourners, however, is to discover one's true rank within a twenty-two step church hierarchy. Every Spiritual Baptist is expected to mourn often, and every Spiritual Baptist desires to advance within the church hierarchy.

Many Spiritual Baptists complain that the mourning ceremony has been radically misinterpreted by outsiders. Rather than emphasize deprivations (visual, sleep-related, dietary), these Spiritual Baptists see the rite as a time of meditation—like a Catholic retreat. As noted above, Spiritual Baptist leaders frequently take it upon themselves to make mourning rites less demanding. Over the past twenty years, most ceremonies in the majority of churches have been abbreviated from three weeks to one week to three days. Mourning rites are no longer uniform for all participants, and most vary from one local community or cell to another. Older mourners may be assigned a full-time nurse (this is a spiritual rank, but very often nurses have had some medical training) for the entire duration of the rite. Leaders are expected to assess the health of each potential participant and adjust the rite accordingly. Greater care is taken in terms of diet (only the prohibition on salt remains; all other food restrictions are left to the discretion of the individual leader). Those who want to observe a strict "fast" are encouraged to do so at home.

Lastly, mourners are no longer anonymous. In the past, mourners in the chamber were given numbers and referred to as "Mourner number 1," "Mourner number 2," and so on throughout the rite. This underscored the loss of individuality associated with death. Now, senior mourners, especially those of higher ranks, are referred to by name during the ceremony. This represents an abrupt departure from prior practices.

As noted, mourning is believed to have curative powers, and because so many individuals enter the rite in an unhealthy condition, occasionally participants die during the ceremony. It has happened several times since the mid-1970s.

Deaths may prompt a routine government inquiry and perhaps a lawsuit. In government inquiries, the government attempts to determine whether poor diet and damp conditions in the mourning room could have been contributing factors in the mourners' deaths. Government officials assert that Spiritual Baptist leaders should refuse participation to mourners believed to be too weak to withstand the rigors of the ceremony.

Leaders defend themselves by claiming that they take every possible precaution to ensure the mourner's physical survival but point out that their primary responsibility is for the spiritual survival of the mourner. According to Spiritual Baptist ideology, mourning rituals are believed to have been spiritually effective even if the mourner dies. Religious interpretations seem to have prevailed. No Spiritual Baptist leader has been indicted as a result of a government inquiry.

Without exception, Spiritual Baptist leaders interpret attempts to scrutinize the mourning ceremonies as an assault on religious freedom. Those leaders who claim religious persecution make much of a 1917 ordinance (the Shouters Prohibition Ordinance) introduced in the Trinidad and Tobago Legislative Council banning "shouting," bell ringing, and other components of Spiritual Baptist worship. The ban on shouting remained in effect from 1917 to 1953. Similar ordinances were introduced and passed on other islands of the British West Indies, most notably on Jamaica, Grenada, St. Kitts, and St. Vincent.

A number of sources stressed that the Trinidad ban lasted longer and was more rigorously enforced than on other islands. But leaders who do not believe that the Spiritual Baptist faith has been subjected to persecution point out that the ban was sporadically enforced and that it did little to slow the spread of the Spiritual Baptist religion. For example, the Belmont church, alleged to have been the target of the original ordinance, continued to conduct weekly services throughout the period of the ban. It has been alleged that in five instances Spiritual Baptist leaders were fined (in 1940, 1941, and 1945; see Thomas 1987). Although that has not been verified, it is possible to discern evidence of governmental interference and censorship of Spiritual Baptist practices in calypsos composed during the 1930s and 1940s. One source cites Growling Tiger's 1939 calypso tune, "What Is a Shouter?" (Rohlehr 1990). The lyrics reflect the attitudes of the time:

> The Shango, of course, is quite disagreeable
> For the drum is miserable
> But the Kookoo and goat and nice white rice
> I mean the rum and the coffee is nice
> But the Shouters is a husband, children, and wife
> And they livin' miserable, a corrupted life
> If is that they call civilization
> It's a disgrace to my native land.

A persistent theme in Spiritual Baptist sermons is that the faith has made great progress in the face of adversity, and the period of the ban is likened to the ancient Israelites' forty years in the wilderness.

A number of dramatic changes have taken place among the Spiritual Baptists since the mid-1970s. The most dramatic changes relate to the roles of women within the faith. When Glazier began fieldwork, Spiritual Baptist women were not permitted to occupy the same ritual space as men. In 1976, about 26 percent of the churches Glazier attended observed separate seating for males and females (males on the right, females on the left). Today, this practice has largely been abandoned.

In the past, Spiritual Baptist women were expected to direct their attention toward a raised platform at the center of the church (known as the center pole), while men conducted church services from a raised platform (the altar) near the front of the church. Women never spoke from the altar platform but addressed their concerns to the congregation in the form of a prayer kneeling at the center pole. Only uninitiated men, women, and children gravitated toward the center pole. All men—even men who were not Spiritual Baptists—were encouraged to speak from the front. When asked if a woman was ever allowed to stand on the altar, one respondent told Glazier that women were allowed up there only to "dust and mop" (Glazier 1991).

Although many churches still do not allow women to preach from the front altar, some larger suburban churches encourage low-ranking males to make their comments from the center pole and higher-ranking females to preach from the front of the church. Women have become much more prominent in denominational affairs. There are now two female bishops. In addition, two women serve as faculty members at the Herman Parris Spiritual Baptist Southland School of Theology in La Brea, Trinidad, founded in 1981.

The status of women has also changed dramatically among followers of Orisha. Tracey Hucks (2006; see Glazier, 2008) indicates two main Orisha groups in Trinidad: the Orisha Movement and Opa Orisa. Of the two groups, Opa Orisa is the most prominent by virtue of highly publicized lectures and media presentations; attendance at Orisha conferences in Africa, New York, and the Caribbean; and its strong Internet presence (Castor 1999). Opa Orisa represents itself as "a return to orthodoxy." Many of its leaders—including its founder, Patricia McLeod—were first initiated in Africa, have studied the Yoruba language, and have been formally trained in traditional (Ife) divination techniques. McLeod is a devotee of Shango, an Orisa warrior god. That created something of a controversy since prior to McLeod, Shango's most prominent followers in Trinidad have always been male, and Shango's compounds have been dominated by males (see Bascom 1972; Glazier 2008). Orisha, of course, are neither male nor female, and on other Caribbean islands, Shango's devotees are predominantly female and Shango is identified with Santa Barbara, a Christian patron saint and martyr.

The 1990s ushered in a period of increasing respectability and visibility for both Orisha followers and members of the Spiritual Baptist faith. In 1996, a general conference of Spiritual Baptist bishops and leaders was held at the Central Bank Auditorium in Port of Spain, Trinidad, one of the nicest, best-equipped conference facilities in the Caribbean. Not coincidentally, the Central Bank Auditorium was selected by the bishops because it was seen as a center of political and economic power. Several speakers (Spiritual Baptist and non-Baptists) began their talks by remarking, "Who would think that the Baptists be here?" Senator Michael Ramsharam and other dignitaries were invited to address the conference. Future prime minister Basdeo Panday was also said to have been in the audience. Panday was instrumental in establishing a national holiday in honor of the Spiritual Baptists.

The proceedings of this conference have been published under the title "Call Him by His Name, Jesus: Spiritual Baptists—Christians Moving into the 21st Century."[7] They have been widely distributed in local bookstores and throughout the Caribbean by the World Council of Churches. The proceedings contain the full texts of all bishops' remarks as well as questions and comments from the floor. It is a remarkable document. Most notable is Archbishop Alexander Murrain's address calling for a new cathedral with a library for researchers who want to "make a history" of the Spiritual Baptist faith, establishment of a trade school to help Spiritual Baptists get better jobs, and development of a "Spiritual Baptist Park" that will serve as a pilgrimage site for Spiritual Baptists in the Caribbean and throughout the world.

The day of the repeal of the Shouters Prohibition Ordinance in 1953 has been designated as a national holiday in Trinidad and Tobago, and Spiritual Baptists have been granted land to establish an open space—a national memorial park—and to build a Spiritual Baptist cathedral and a trade school. The church has also established a governing body, the Council of Elders, with headquarters on Saddle Road in the town of Maraval. They are located in the midst of an expensive residential area on the main road to Moka golf course and the beach. The headquarters themselves are in a modest house that is in disrepair, but its highly visible sign on a high traffic road underscores Spiritual Baptist obsessions with location.

A number of Spiritual Baptist bishops have openly stated that they would like to see the Spiritual Baptists become more like other churches. They pursue their goal with a zeal that would have surprised even chroniclers of rationality in religious organizations like Max Weber (1960) and Ernst Troeltsch (1960). To become more like the other churches, a seminary (Southland School of Theology) was established for training ministers. It is hoped that these ministers will qualify for ordination and be legally entitled to marry and bury parishioners, unlike prior generations of Spiritual Baptist leaders. Many Spiritual Baptist leaders dislike the fact that members of their congregations must look elsewhere for weddings and funerals because Spiritual Baptist ministers are seldom licensed. Ordination, however, may not have the anticipated impact. Funerals for Spiritual Baptists are usually held in Catholic, Anglican, or Pentecostal churches. A complicating factor is that families arrange for funerals to take place in the family's home church, and unless other family members are Spiritual Baptists, they will be unlikely to hold their funerals in Spiritual Baptist churches.

A comprehensive Spiritual Baptist minister's manual was published in 1993. Its 238 pages include detailed instructions for conducting dedication of infants, baptisms, and mournings, as well as a suggested Order of Worship and a list of appropriate hymns and scriptural passages for each juncture of the service. For a religion that prides itself in following the spirit, it seems ironic that such a manual should exist at all. But it should be added that the manual does accurately reflect Spiritual Baptist practices—even if in a somewhat stifled way.

It is extremely difficult to gauge the impact of these proposed changes on rank-and-file believers. Thus far the impact has been minuscule. The Southland School of Theology has no full-time students; the Spiritual Baptist ministers' manual is rarely consulted; and construction has yet to begin on the park, the trade school, and the cathedral. The majority of Spiritual Baptist churches are small, and they lack a solid financial base. For the average church member, things continue pretty much as before.

▓ The Revivalists: Pentecostals

Pentecostalism is a sect of Christianity that originated in the United States in 1906 with Charles Parham (1872–1929), a zealous evangelist who inspired the Asuza Street Revival in Los Angeles, California. Pentecostalism's teachings are based on the story reported in the New Testament's book of Acts, in which it is said that after Christ's death and resurrection, Christ's disciples gathered in a room, and "tongues, as of fire, appeared to rest on each of them, and they were then filled with the Holy Spirit," endowing them with the gift of grace to preach, to prophesy, to witness of their faith in many languages, and to heal the sick (Acts 2:1–21). Pentecostals believe that the miracle at Pentecost can be reenacted in their lives today and that they can achieve a state of "holiness" by exercising spiritual self-discipline and by resisting the devil's temptations. Glossolalia (speaking in tongues) occurs during brief instances of trance in which Pentecostals believe that they are sanctified by the Holy Spirit, who is said to "fill" their minds and bodies. During these trances in the religious services, glossolalists believe that they receive revelations from the Holy Spirit that they reveal to the community on the spot, and that they are empowered to heal the sick. They are also endowed with the gift to interpret dreams, which are conceived as divine revelatory media. Glossolalia and trance, therefore, are states of profound spiritual achievement that not only intensify the devotees' commitment to the faith but also heighten their exercise of religious authority in the community. For these reasons, devotees wish to experience trances many times in their lives.

Pentecostals view the present world as abysmally evil and corrupt. Therefore, they must remain pure in their thoughts and in their conduct. Such purity is achieved by rejecting the world and adopting a religious discipline that makes the scriptures and the affairs of the religious community the center of one's life. Moral conduct such as abstinence from premarital and extramarital sex, from dancing outside of the worship services, and from the use of tobacco, alcohol or drugs are central to an authentic Christian life.

Pentecostals are millenarian to the core, for they believe that the Second Coming of Christ and the Last Judgment are imminent. They conceive of time as linear, beginning with the creation and ending with the destruction of the world by cataclysm and fire. Jesus will appear at the end of days to punish the unworthy and gather the righteous, who will be caught up with him and all the angels in a rapture in which they will be lifted up to the sky. As the Good Shepherd, Jesus will lead them into the "New Jerusalem," believed to be a city where everyone will be liberated from pain and from the fallibility of sin. Pentecostals hold two views about the New Jerusalem. Some say that it is "otherworldly" and that those who are "born again" will rise from the earth and enter into this holy city in the sky; others believe that the New Jerusalem is "thisworldly" and that it will be on earth, which will be destroyed but redeemed and purified by God and the angels. Because the end of the world is imminent, it is essential that one remains pure and sinless to prepare oneself for the final event. Pentecostals also hold a collective concept of salvation, in that they regard themselves as the elect of God and the bearers of good tiding to the world; they see themselves as the new Israel whose mission is to save the world before the end of time.

The Pentecostal's most important spiritual attainment is to reach a state of inner perfection. Salvation can be achieved by believing in the literal interpretation of the scriptures and by "breaking the Bible" (reading the Bible) daily. Accepting Christ and recognizing that he is the "Savior and the Lord" of one's life is the first step in one's spiritual journey. Devotees must also make a public confession of their sins in which they declare openly to the community that they take a vow to conduct themselves according to the teachings of the New Testament. This public affirmation must be symbolized by the ritual of baptism. Pentecostals and Baptists in the Caribbean believe in the efficacy of adult baptism, a ritual by which a believer's body is immersed in water. Baptism not only actualizes a person's participation in the death and resurrection of Christ, but can be seen as a liminal rite which symbolizes a person's ontological transformation from a state of sinfulness and imperfection to one of saintliness and perfection. By being raised from the water, one passes from death to life and from sin to sainthood; one is therefore born anew into a new being.

Pentecostals believe in the immanence of evil as a negative force in one's life. They reject the beliefs and practices of the devotees of the African-derived religions and segregate themselves from these practices. But they recognize the power of the spirits revered in these religions as real and regard them as demonic (Glazier 1980:71–75). They are demiurges that must be exorcised from a person or wherever they are said to reside. Illness is caused by the devil, and spiritual healing returns a person to wholeness by uprooting the demons from his or her body. Moreover, evil manifests itself in the secular and economic pursuits of society's members and detracts from the central questions of spirituality. Because evil is ubiquitous in the world, Pentecostal devotees pit themselves against the secularism of society and seek to change the world by converting those who have gone astray. They are therefore *conversionists* in that they believe that the inherent power of the "Word" (the Bible) can engender a complete transformation of the world into a state of spiritual perfection.

The Pentecostals and Baptists have left their mark on the religious lives of Caribbean peoples. The theology of these groups has inspired the formation of religious sects throughout the Caribbean, many of which have combined traditional African ritualistic styles of worship with evangelical Protestant theology. The Africanness of these sects can be seen in the belief in ancestral reverence, in the importance of the revelatory nature of dreams, in the styles of worship that include antiphonal calls and answers between the leaders and congregants, in the hymns sung in rhythmical patterns accompanied by drums, and in the cadenced sways of the congregants' bodies. In short, much like African traditional religions, the Caribbean's Pentecostal and Baptist styles of worship use every possible visible and auditory vehicle to engage the congregants actively in their rituals. These rituals are "danced out" rather than conceived intellectually; they do not separate the mind from the body by merely leading a participant to high-flown intellectual exercises, but they claim the entire person.

Because these religious groups comprise local cells that are independent of each other, it is difficult to determine their number, but there may well be no less than 100 different types of such movements in the Caribbean, each existing as a variation on a theme. The most well-known are the Tie Heads of the Jerusalem Apostolic Spiritual Baptist Church in Barbados, the various Cohortes and Holiness movements (Pentecostal-derived sects, for the most part) in Haiti and the Dominican Republic, the Shakers and the Streams of Power in St. Vincent, the Spirit Baptists and Kumina sects in Jamaica, and the Shouters and Spiritual Baptists in Trinidad.[8]

■ The Religio-Political Movements: The Redemptionists, the Rastafari, and the Dread

The Rastafari and the Dread are religio-political movements and twentieth-century phenomena. They address issues of social and economic injustice among blacks in Jamaica and elsewhere in the world and oppose the social ills as well as the institutions that perpetuate such ills. The Rastafari express their resistance to the established order in theological terms, in that they have a millenarian orientation. Their members believe that they are destined to return to Ethiopia, which they envision as the promised land.

Historically, the Rastafari movement began in Jamaica in the early part of the twentieth century. Its theology follows from a long tradition of redemptive religious movements in Jamaica. As early as 1784, an American slave named George Liele (also known as George Sharp, the surname of his owner in Savannah, Georgia) founded one of the first Baptist churches in Jamaica. After his owner's death, he was placed in the service of one Colonel Kirkland, who manumitted him in 1783. In the same year, Kirkland emigrated from the United States to Jamaica and took the young George Sharp with him. It was there that he changed his name to George Liele and began to evangelize and convert the slaves who worked on the plantations in and around Kingston and Spanish Town.

The significance of Liele's church to the Rastafari is its name. He called it the Ethiopian Baptist Church, and it was later renamed the Jamaican Baptist Church. The reference to Ethiopia doubtless had symbolic value and derived meaning from various biblical passages in which the word *Ethiopian* is used interchangeably with *Nubian* and *Cushite.* In the Bible, the word *Cushite,* from the Hebrew *cush,* means "black skin" or "burned skin." In the Bible, *cush* was translated by the Greek term *ethiop;* thus, in modern times *Ethiopia* became *Africa* ("the land of the burnt-skinned people"), and most Rastafari today equate these terms and use them interchangeably.[9]

The virtues of Ethiopia or Africa as holy places continued to be extolled in Jamaican religious thought during the period of the Great Revival (1860–1920). This period saw the meteoric rise of scores of religious movements such as the Convince and the Kumina (Pukumina or Pocomania) mentioned earlier in this chapter, the Revival bands, and different forms of spiritual healing sects called Myalism, which stressed ancestor reverence and trance possession and had a millenarian or utopian vision of the world. An important feature of such movements is their message of redemption, in which they prophesy the end of the world followed by the establishment of a new kingdom in which the meek and the oppressed poor will be redeemed. One of these movements during the Great Revival was the Native Baptist (or Bedwardite) church, which became significant during the early part of the twentieth century.

The Native Baptist Church was founded by Alexander Bedward around 1891. Born of slave ancestry in 1859, Bedward was reared in the spirit of the Great Revival and lived on the Mona Estate, the current site of the main campus of the prestigious University of the West Indies. As a young man, he is said to have had a vision in which a spirit gave him the gift of healing and he was later anointed as the incarnate Christ on Earth. He claimed that the end of the world was near and that he would ascend to heaven, taking his followers in the sky with him. Shortly after their ascension, cataclysmic disasters would destroy the world, after which a New Jerusalem would be established on the earth, and the mighty would be brought down and serve the poor and the meek.

Some parallels exist between Native Baptist teachings and those of the Rastafari. First, the Native Baptists believed in the spiritual efficacy of fasting. The Rastafari say that fasting cleanses, sanctifies, and prepares one to face the spiritual struggles in the maintenance of one's faith in an alienating environment. Second, the Native Baptists, like the Rastafari today, believed in the regenerative power of the sun; they often formed bands of devotees who went on sacred excursions through the night to greet the rising sun. Third, the Native Baptists called upon the powers of God to crush the whites, whom they saw as the incarnations of the Pharisees and Saducees in the New Testament, and believed that Bedward's prophecy would come to pass: that white civilization would eventually be destroyed.

The Native Baptists' millennial visions survived well into the 1920s and were instrumental to the emergence of Garveyism and the subsequent rise of the Rastafari movement in Jamaica. Marcus Garvey was born into a Roman Catholic family in the Parish of St. Ann in Jamaica on August 17, 1887. His father was a proud man who traced his ancestry to the early maroon freedom fighters such as Quaco and Cudjoe, who battled the British army in Jamaica for nearly a century.

Very early in his life, Garvey had become aware of the problems of inequality, poverty, and social injustice in Jamaican society. After the emancipation of the slaves in the early 1830s, three social classes emerged in Jamaica: the wealthy white elite, who were usually descendents of British slave owners; a relatively small middle class of black Jamaican professionals; and at the bottom, a large number of blacks who were so poor that they lived below a minimum standard of subsistence. The majority blacks were uneducated, with little hope of ever improving their lot. Many of them were unemployed, and those few who did work received low wages. Between 1910 and 1914, Garvey tried relentlessly to acquaint Jamaican authorities with the plight of poor blacks. He visited Panama and England to evaluate the social and economic conditions of the large numbers of Jamaicans in these countries and discovered that they were equally poor there as well. He returned to Kingston and founded the Universal Negro Improvement Association (UNIA) in 1914. The goal of this organization was to lobby for the cause and improve the lot of poor Jamaicans. In 1916, he moved the headquarters of the UNIA to New York City, where he thought his work would be more effective, far from the intimidation of Jamaica's British colonial government. He struggled with the rank and file in the British colonial government over issues related to higher wages, civil liberties, the granting of political rights (including universal suffrage), and the ownership of land among the disenfranchised.

The UNIA's focus might have been secular, but Garvey's speeches echoed many of the religious themes found in the earlier revivalist movements in

Jamaica. He declared that blacks were the chosen people of God and that they had been forced to live in the diaspora against their will when their ancestors were brought to the New World as slaves. For more than 300 years they had been subjected to white racism, social oppression, abject poverty, and economic exploitation. Black people's devils were therefore whites, who had created corrupt civilizations that would eventually meet their own demise. Blacks in the Americas should therefore look to Africa, from where a king would rise: he would be a long-awaited messiah who would liberate them from oppression. Just as blacks here looked with hope to Africa, so, too, "princes would come out of Egypt," and Ethiopia would be the first of all African nations to "soon stretch out her hands unto God" (Psalms 68:31). To Garvey, the kingdom of heaven was to occur on earth and would entail the repatriation of all blacks to Africa. Although Garvey did not actively undertake blacks' return to Africa, his writings and speeches (published in the *Negro World,* the official newspaper of the UNIA) inspired significant numbers of them to return there. Garvey was a persuasive and eloquent orator, and his articulation of these issues and his personal struggles over these questions undoubtedly set the stage for the millenarian theology of the Rastafari.

It is important to distinguish between the Rastafari and Garveyism, on the one hand, and the Native Baptists on the other with regard to their beliefs about whites. Bedward taught that white civilization would be destroyed, but he regarded whites as superior to blacks. He suggested however, that like the redeeming quality of Jesus' suffering, blacks' oppression would serve as a means to their eventual redemption. In the end, blacks would become superior by replacing whites in the new kingdom to come. In contrast, the Rastafari (as well as Garveyism), believed in the superiority of blackness and affirmed that God, Jesus, and all the prophets were black, not white (Chevannes 1994:109).

The Rastafari emerged in Jamaica shortly after 1930, the year that Haile Selassie, son of Ras Makonen, became emperor of Ethiopia. His enthronement was covered widely by the international press, not only because of the opulence that surrounded it but also because of the new monarch's flamboyant titles.[10] He was to be known as Ras Tafari, that is, the "King of Kings and Lord of Lords, the Conquering Lion of the Tribe of Judah." He also claimed to be the 225th descendent in an unbroken succession that originated with King David and the Queen of Sheba.

The emperor's celebrated enthronement caused many poor Jamaicans to remember both Garvey's prophecy about Africa as well as the use of the term *Ethiopia* by the Ethiopian Baptists. For the Rastafari, Ethiopia became the "land of the blacks," the long-awaited promised land, and the emperor himself the messiah. According to the Rastafari, all blacks in the Americas were the reincarnation of ancient Israelites and could also be likened to the dispersed Jews in the diaspora. As Jah's (God's) chosen people, the Rastafari believe that they should make a vow to separate themselves from whites.[11] The Rastafari believe that Jah is black, as were Adam and Eve, Christ, all the prophets, and all the great religious figures of the Bible. Blacks are therefore superior to whites because they were the chosen people of God.

During the period of slavery, Europeans transported blacks to the Americas and forced them to live in a society created by whites. The Rastafari regard white civilization as Babylon, that is, an abysmally corrupt and evil world, one that is therefore not worthy of their participation. They believe that God allowed blacks to be exiled in the Americas as slaves because of their past transgressions and those of their ancestors, but that the advent of the invincible emperor was a sign that their sins had been expiated and that the end of their suffering was near. Like the ancient city of Babylon, the world of whites was a hopeless hell and would be destroyed. That destruction would then open the way for God to enact His covenant with His people and ensure their safe and final passage to Ethiopia—the promised land. They believed that the emperor who was God became manifest in the flesh to ensure their safe repatriation to Ethiopia and that he was working out the details with the leaders of the nations of the world. Following their repatriation, a new order would be established that would reverse the present social order, for whites would become subservient to blacks.

As in other Caribbean religions, not all the Rastafari sects hold to these tenets, nor do they give the same interpretations to them. Indeed, since the death of Haile Selassie in 1974, many Rastafari have placed less emphasis on the movement's otherworldly millennial dream and have insisted that deliverance would not come from the outside, but internally within Jamaican society.[12] For them, Ethiopia is a symbol of religious unity and racial identity. It is also an international symbol of black unity and hope in the face of white oppression.

Since the 1950s, the Rastafari have tended to live in close-knit religious communities that simulate the organizational structures of traditional African compounds. This communal setting prompted clearer formulations of Rastafari theology: the elaboration of symbols and ritual forms, the popularization of ritual music and drumming, and the designation and observances of religious festival days. The long sessions of theological debates among the men (known as "reasonings") are occasions to identify key biblical passages that underlie their theology and substantiate the relations between their beliefs and the world's current state of affairs.

During this period the Rastafari developed peculiar notions of what they consider "natural" and thus in keeping with biblical tradition (Chevannes 1994). These notions have affected the Rastafari lifestyle in profound ways. The wearing of beards and dreadlocks, something that already existed in the movement, did not gain importance until the 1950s. The Rastafari allude to several sources for leaving their hair untouched and natural and ascribe many symbolic meanings to their dreadlocks. Some cite the biblical passage in which one who takes a holy "vow of separation [referring to their separation from the whites], no razor shall come upon his head," but he should "let his locks of hair hang by the side of his head" (Numbers 6:9). Others, like the Dreads, emphasize the long suffering of the "people of God" in a "strange land." Dreads wear natural locks that symbolize tears resulting from the sorrow that they experienced during centuries of oppression, injustice, and deprivation. The locks of hair and their seemingly unkempt appearance symbolize their categorical rejection of Babylon. Still others believe that, historically, blacks are the descendants of kings and queens and are therefore of royal pedigree, and their "manes" recall the emperor's honorific title as the Conquering Lion of Judah. Moreover, Rastafari thought emphasizes that all things natural and untouched (and many would claim that growing out their locks and beards manifests that belief) are a manifestation of a natural physiognomy that was given to humankind at creation—one that is neither changed by cosmetics nor sculptured by human hands. Such emphasis on the natural also underlies Rastafari's strict dietary rules.[13]

The Rastafari believe that the killing of an animal for human consumption does nothing more than promote death, for killing the animal removes from it the life-giving power of Jah that resides within it. Hence, the meat that is cut off from a dead animal is unfit for human consumption because it does not hold Jah's life force, a divine essence that is equivalent to the *gwo bon anj* in Vodou and *aché* in Santería. In contrast, a flower may continue to bloom even after it has been severed from its stem, a fruit will continue to ripen even after it has been cut from the tree, and a grain removed from the plant continues to hold within it the power of regeneration when it is planted into a fertile ground. The Rastafari follow a vegetarian diet that incorporates dairy products. They believe that a vegetarian diet is sacred, for it allows one to derive from nature Jah's life-sustaining force.

The use of ganja, or marijuana, which is so important to the *reasonings,* became important in the 1950s as well. Ganja was introduced into the Caribbean by East Indian immigrants in the nineteenth century, and was later adopted strictly for ritual use by the Rastafari devotees. The most common reason for using the sacred plant comes from a biblical passage in which, during the sixth day of the creation, God declared that he made the grasses and all vegetation for mankind's enjoyment (Genesis 1:29). The Rastafari also believe that ganja is a holy weed that can promote clearer visions of Jah. In effect, the use of ganja is a highly sacramental act that infuses within the body the sacred power of the spirit as it derives from nature. It also opens the mind to the will of Jah and allows for the miraculous and unexpected revelations from the Almighty.

Throughout the 1950s and 1960s, many Rastafari communities established themselves in the urban centers of Jamaica, and their members overtly criticized whites, entrepreneurs, and Jamaican black police officers, whom they regarded as traitors to their race. They criticized the established clergy for its lack of moral integrity and its service to two masters: God and Satan. During this period, militant Rastafari sought to create rapid changes in Jamaican society and incited violent civil disturbances in Kingston that threatened socioeconomic and political stability. These disturbances might not have been as threatening as they were perceived by Jamaican authorities, but the aura of mystery that surrounded their communal lifestyle, their conscious decision not to participate in Jamaica's national life, and the dreadlocks (which many perceived as bordering on the grotesque and the savage), engendered a profound fear of them among many Jamaicans. The Jamaican government undertook a detailed study of the Rastafari, undoubtedly to allay the fears of its citizens. After a relatively long inquisition into their beliefs and lifestyle, the government published a favorable report (and the first of its kind) about the movement (Augier et al. 1960).

Today the militancy of the Rastafari can be seen in their opposition to many aspects of contemporary society that they perceive as Babylon. It includes the hegemony of the West and the mighty arm of its multinational corporations. For this reason, many do not participate in Jamaica's national life. But their withdrawal from society has ironically rendered a service to Jamaican culture, for their emphasis on blackness has stimulated a new sense of identity among Jamaicans (Barrett 1977). The terms of endearment and the forms of address (such as "Brother," "Sister," and "Rastaman"), as well as the customary greeting ("peace and love") that the Rastafari use among themselves have awakened among black Jamaicans a communal attachment to a common culture that transcends social class. Another mode of address that the Rastafari use is the phrase "I and I" when referring to themselves, meaning that they and their neighbors share the living spirit of Jah.

The Rastafaris' rejection of Jamaican society has created a need for artistic venues that have been embraced by the very culture that has rejected them in the past. These art forms have made significant contributions to the development of Jamaican popular culture. In the domain of music, the use of the *akete* drum and its music has contributed to the development of reggae. The Rastafari have also written scores of poems and essays and have produced sculptures and paintings that symbolize various aspects of their theology. Their depictions of contemporary society have influenced Caribbean music and literature in general. Indeed, the Rastafari have called for an awareness of the region's pan-African heritage well before it became fashionable in the late 1960s.

It is art—and especially the reggae music popularized by Bob Marley and others—that has contributed to the international reputation that the Rastafari currently enjoy. Since the late 1960s, Rastafari culture has spread to many parts of the world, and many communities have been formed in urban centers throughout the world. Not all of them are religious communities, however, for many have adopted the hairstyle, the diet, the secular use of ganja, and the sense of communal identity without the religious dimension central to the movement.

Three sects, each with its corresponding cells, have emerged in Rastafari thought and practice in the past sixty years or so. They all teach the divinity of Haile Selassie and the dignity of blacks, but the difference between them lies largely in their understanding of blacks' African origins and in some nuances in the ways in which certain theological assumptions affect the Rastafari's religious lives. The first of these is the Nyabinghi Order, or the Theocratic Priesthood and Livity of the Order of Nyabinghi, which derives its name from Queen Nyabinghi of Uganda, who is believed to have resisted British colonialism in the nineteenth century. The Nyabinghi is the oldest sect that focuses on the divinity of Haile Selassie and the eventual return of blacks to Africa. The Bobo Shanti (or Bobo Dreads) was founded in the 1950s in Jamaica by Prince Emmanuel Charles, who is revered, like the emperor, as the reincarnation of Jesus Christ in the New World. *Bobo* means "black" and *Shanti* derives from the name of the Ashanti tribe in Ghana. Hence, the Bobo Shanti derive their ancestry and give emphasis to aspects of Ashanti beliefs such as the importance of ancestral reverence. Bobo Shanti members wear long flowing robes and turbans around their dreads resembling those of Ashanti chiefs. They follow the Jewish dietary laws, particularly those concerning hygiene noted in Leviticus in the Bible, and some ritually carry brooms with them to symbolize their cleanliness.[14] They live separately in closed communities, apart from other Rastafari groups and from society in general. They emphasize the repatriation of blacks to Africa and demand monetary reparation for slavery. Finally, the Twelve Tribes of Israel was founded by Vernon "Prophet Gad" Carrington in 1968 and is the most liberal of the Rastafari groups because it allows its members to worship in churches of their own choosing. It also emphasizes the belief that their members belong to one of the twelve tribes (or houses) of Israel, as determined by the month in which they were born.

In short, Rastafarianism is probably the most culturally diverse and internationally diffused of all the Caribbean religions. The movement's appeal is not merely its music or various art forms but its universal message that befits the current conditions of the contemporary world. Despite sectarian differences, the Rastafari propound a common theme that echoes the conditions of many people across the world: they decry neocolonialism, social oppression, and the economic exploitation of the poor by the wealthy.

■ Other Imports from Europe, the Middle East, and Asia

Judaism

The story of Judaism in the Caribbean has received little attention in historians' accounts of slavery and plantocracy, piracy and military skirmishes by European colonial powers competing for new territories in the New World. Indeed, relatively little has been written about the Jewish religious communities in the Caribbean, despite their sizable number and their important influence on the history of the region. Jews established trade routes between Europe and the

Caribbean as early as the sixteenth century and engaged in flourishing business ventures that were a mainstay of Europe's economy.

The Jewish presence in the Caribbean can be traced to the sixteenth century, with the emigration of Spanish Jews to the New World. During the Inquisition, King Ferdinand and Queen Isabella of Spain expelled the Jews from Spain the very year that Christopher Columbus set foot in the New World. There is speculation that perhaps Columbus himself might have been a *Marrano* (crypto-Jew).[15] The *Marrano* were Jews who converted to Christianity and were baptized in the church to escape persecution from the authorities but continued to practice Judaism clandestinely. During the Spanish Inquisition, it is estimated that as many as 100,000 Jews took refuge in neighboring Portugal (Arbell 2000:2). In 1496, the Spanish monarchs agreed to give their daughter's hand in marriage to King Manuel of Portugal with the proviso that he banish the Jews from his country. The Jews escaped once more and sought asylum in more hospitable places throughout Europe. A significant number joined an already thriving community in Amsterdam.

Through the middle of the sixteenth century, Spain and Portugal dominated the seas. Their precious cargoes of gold transported from the New World required protection against piracy by powerful naval forces, which eventually posed a threat to the security of their European neighbors. They vowed to annex as many territories and control as many Caribbean trade routes as they could. In this spirit, the Dutch sailed to Brazil's northeastern port of Recife and took control of that Portuguese colony in 1630. They sought to populate their new colony by relocating some 600 Jews to Brazil, and by 1645 that community reached 1,500. Under Dutch rule, Jews could practice their religion freely and openly, and they worked assiduously to create vibrant religious communities. They established new plantations on which slave workers grew sugar, coffee, and other crops for the local and foreign markets. By 1654, Portugal had reclaimed its Brazilian territory from the Dutch and signed a peace treaty by which the Dutch ceded the colony to the Portuguese. The Jewish community suffered from the effects of the Inquisition yet again. The colonial authorities imposed severe religious sanctions on the Jews and made it illegal for them to practice their religion freely. Like the Marranos before them, many declared their public allegiance to Roman Catholicism while practicing their religion under the cloak of secret societies throughout the colony. These societies were essential to the preservation of Judaism in the Caribbean. As the Portuguese widened the scope of the Inquisition, the colonial authorities sought out Jews for questioning. Those who did not renounce their religion were jailed, killed, or deported elsewhere. In an effort to rid Brazil of all its Jews, the Portuguese government made available sixteen ships to remove the Jews from the colony, and 150 Jewish families were forced to evacuate from Recife and emigrate to other places; some returned to Amsterdam, and others settled in New Amsterdam (New York today). But a significant number sought refuge on nearby islands in the Caribbean. This resettlement proved to be the beginning of the first Jewish settlements throughout the Antilles. Over time, they increased in number as new communities were started in Curaçao, Dutch Guyana (Suriname today), Jamaica, Barbados, and Martinique (Arbell 2000:3–5, 18).

The first synagogues in the Caribbean were built in the seventeenth century and were of the Spanish and Portuguese Sephardic tradition rather than the Ashkenazi, which was predominant in Central Europe. Both traditions followed the same teachings, but the Sephardic differed from the latter in the physical design of its synagogues, its customs, and its liturgy.[16] Among these differences were synagogue floors covered with sand, the ritualistic use of symbols, the congregants' singing of hymns, and the recitation of prayers in Spanish during the religious services.[17] A significant difference derived from the ritual use of the Torah (the law). The Torah was written on scrolls made of parchment and stored in a wooden cylinder to keep them upright and from which they were read during the Sephardic service. By contrast, among the Ashkenazi the scrolls lie flat on a table.

The Dutch were more tolerant of the Jews than the British, the Portuguese, or the Spanish. Toward the middle of the seventeenth century, twelve Jewish families settled in Willemstad in the Dutch colony of Curaçao, established the Mikveh Israel Emmanuel congregation in 1647, and built their first synagogue in 1694 (which still exists today). By 1750, the Dutch parliament had recognized the Jews as citizens, and the Dutch West India Company, which oversaw the Dutch colonies, encouraged them "to cultivate the lands under the penalty of their forfeiture" if they decided not to engage in agriculture. They were also accorded "the right to own slaves" and to work on their farms (Arbell 2002: 128).[18] What was perceived as the largesse of the Dutch caused the number of Jewish immigrants to soar to nearly 2,000 in just a relatively short time, so that by 1864, new settlers had arrived in Willemstad from England to establish the Liberal Jewish Congregation. The Jewish communities in Curaçao also engaged in trade and systemized trade routes and modes of exchange of goods to Europe and throughout the Antilles. By the end of the seventeenth century, Jewish communities in Curaçao had become wealthy enough to assist other congregations with the mortgage payments on their synagogues, not only in various parts of the Caribbean but in New York, Philadelphia, and Newport, Rhode Island (Arbell 2000:4, 37). It may be noted that the Jewish communities in the Caribbean were not isolated from their counterparts in other parts of the world and that some of their members maintained close connections with other congregations in Europe, throughout the Caribbean, and in the United States.

During the centuries that followed, new religious congregations were established in the British colonies in Port Royal, Jamaica, around 1704, and in Barbados in 1750. The history of the Jewish community in the British colonies was stained by moments of hardship and long periods of adversity on the part of the citizens and the colonial governments. The monopoly that Jews had over the trade routes was cause for so much resentment that in 1681 and again in 1695, powerful English settlers pressured the colonial parliaments of Jamaica and Barbados to levy surplus taxes on Jews under the pretext that these monies would be used for the "maintenance of highways" and for the "protection [of these colonies] against foreign invasions" (Arbell 2002:204; Andrade 1941:9). By the end of the eighteenth century, they had been prohibited from worshiping publicly, and the privileged absences from work accorded to them on the Sabbath by earlier decrees had been removed.

The cruelty of the Inquisition discouraged Jews from settling in Spanish Cuba, and the first wave of immigrants to arrive there occurred after the official end of the Inquisition in 1834. Most of them were Sephardic Jews whose ancestors had escaped persecution in Spain and who now were fleeing discrimination by the Turkish rulers of the Ottoman Empire. A smaller number, however, were of the Ashkenazi tradition from the United States. After Cuba's independence in 1902, the sugar industry there expanded, attracting a number of businessmen and financiers from the United States. They took up residence in Cuba to seek a fortune in the flourishing agro-industrial sector. A second wave occurred shortly after the end of the World War I as a result of the US National Origins Quota Act of 1924 that set limits on the number of immigrants from Eastern Europe and the countries bordering the Mediterranean.[19] Jews hoping to enter the United States went to Cuba with the prospect of entering the United States later, but many decided to settle there. They built local synagogues where they conducted religious education for their children and created thriving religious communities that, until 1959, the year of the socialist revolution, were some of the largest in the Caribbean.

France did not conduct an Inquisition as did the Spanish and the Portuguese, but the articles of the Code Noir of 1685, by which Catholicism increased its missionary zeal, discouraged Jews from settling in the French colonies. The code also called for the expulsion of the Jews from the French territories. Several communities managed to survive in the French colonies, but their members suffered from restrictions placed on them by the colonial authorities. In Martinique, which France captured from the Spanish in 1635, for instance, there were a number of wealthy Jews who had migrated there from other islands. By 1658, it is estimated that there were 300 Jews out of a population of 5,000 (Arbell 2002:37–39). They seemed to live in relative peace until the end of the seventeenth century. But, as in Jamaica, the Martiniquans resented their financial success and were instrumental in enacting several discriminatory decrees against their right to own land and conduct businesses in the colony. In 1683, Louis XIV ordered the Jews expelled from all the French colonies, but that order was not enforced strictly. Later, the French Revolution of 1789, which emphasized the ideas of liberty, fraternity, and equality, removed these restrictions and allowed Jewish communities to prosper and maintain their religious traditions.

Even the tiny Danish colonies of St. Thomas and St. Croix, which are part of the United States today, had a fairly substantial number of Jewish settlers. By the late 1700s, they had formed the congregation Berakah We-Shalom U-Gemilut

Hasadim in Charlotte Amalie in St. Thomas, which remained vibrant throughout the nineteenth century and into the beginning of the twentieth century.

During World War II, Venezuela and the Dominican Republic opened their doors to Jews from Europe. A wave of settlers established communities that could trace their ancestry to Spain and Portugal. Throughout the nineteenth and part of the twentieth centuries, Jews observed the high holidays and fasted on the required days of the year. Jewish youths studied the Hebrew language and learned the tenets of their religious traditions at rabbinical schools (*Yeshiva*) that were usually part of the local synagogues. These communities stayed in contact with congregations throughout the Caribbean and the United States, and even established links after 1948 with the newly created nation of Israel when emissaries from various synagogues there visited the Jewish congregations in the Caribbean to collect donations for their counterparts at home.

Despite the relative success of these communities in the Caribbean, the spirit of the Inquisition endures in the region even today. In the Catholic areas especially, the Jews are made to carry the weight of the blame for Jesus' death. During the Lenten period in Haiti, for instance, *raras* (festival bands) gather in various parts of the country to reenact Christ's passion in a festival called *bwile Jwif* (burn the Jew). Rara bands are large groups that can number tens of thousands of people; they are neither sanctioned nor assembled by the local clergy but are highly hierarchical in their organizational structures. During the week that precedes Easter Sunday, a community erects and publicly displays an effigy of a *Jwif* (Jew) which consists of a human figure stuffed with rags and old pillows and clad in trousers and a shirt. Onlookers are encouraged to "kick the Jwif," hit it with sticks, or scold it for killing Jesus. On the Saturday before Easter Sunday, the rara bands parade throughout various communities, carrying the effigy that they burn in a bonfire. Elizabeth McAlister notes that this festival is based on medieval European mystery plays in which the Jews were depicted as the villains who condemned Christ to death, but the roles of the Romans and that of Pontius Pilate were made inconsequential (McAlister 2002: 116). She also suggests that the observance of this festival is a part of a process of creolization wherein Christian "tropes" are captured in the imagination and are reformulated to express new social realities (McAlister 2002:122). *Bwile Jwif* can be analyzed in terms of the coincidence of opposites in which one can observe an exchange of the roles of the effigy and the members of the rara band. On the one hand, the effigy fulfills by turn the roles of the Jews who are guilty of Christ's death and that of Christ who is chastised by them. On the other, the rara band represents the Jews who have sinned and the Christian community that is redeemed by Christ's death. Moreover, McAlister notes that the effigy can be seen to symbolize the social dialectics in the class struggle between master and slave during the colonial period, and between the bourgeois elite and the oppressed poor in contemporary Haiti (McAlister 2002:122–123).

Such sullied depictions of the Jews have contributed to the clandestine practice of Jewish religious practice in the Caribbean. Many Friday night services are held in homes in which there are practically no visible symbols of a family's Jewish religious observances. The absence of the symbols of the faith, as well as the fear of derision among many Jews, has contributed to the gradual disintegration of the vitality of the Jewish communities in the Caribbean. Although most Jews would claim to identify with the world's "Jewish nation," many do not observe the Sabbath and hardly follow the conventional practices required by Jewish religious law. There are several reasons for the decline in these communities in the past fifty years. First, some families continue to send their children to study abroad, and many do not return home. Others who remain in the Caribbean find the Jewish Orthodox way of life (especially the dietary taboos) unsuited to a tropical environment and the conservative Sephardic tradition unattractive (Arbell 2000:342). Second, many Jews who convert to Christianity disrupt the integrity of their communities by leaving their neighborhoods and relocating elsewhere. Interfaith marriages with Gentiles also result in the gradual disappearance of Jewish customs and contribute to the erosion of the religious observances at home. Third, the introduction of the more liberal Reform tradition from the United States tends to abrade the vigor of Jewish religious orthodoxy and cause the gradual disintegration of many communities. Fourth, the importation of the Ashkenazi tradition by immigrants from Central Europe resulted in the predominance of this tradition over the Sephardic. This is true especially in St. Thomas and Venezuela, where the Sephardic congregations merged with the Ashkenazi and became virtually nonexistent. Young people in these areas today have scant knowledge of the Sephardic religious practices that once bound their forebears into strong communities. Moreover, in the Dutch areas where the Sephardic tradition is perhaps the strongest, the adoption of the Dutch prayers in the services as a substitute for the Spanish has lessened a sense of shared identity with the past. Fifth, in the case of Cuba, the 1959 revolution and its aftermath placed restrictions on religious practices. Many Cuban Jews fled the country and settled in other parts of the Caribbean, Latin America, and the United States.

More recently, there have been efforts to rediscover the Jewish heritage in the Caribbean. Organizations like the Caribbean Jewish Congress and Jamaica's United Congregation of Israelites have attempted to promote Jewish religious traditions and customs and recapture the history of various communities in the region. From these efforts, new forms of ritual practices may emerge in the future. They will undoubtedly bear the marks of the cultures to which they belong.

Islam

The first Muslims to arrive in the Caribbean came from Africa. They were black slaves from West Africa's Mandingo, Fulani, and other tribes, sold into slavery as early at the eighteenth century, but little is known about them, and scant historical records exist of their religious practices in the colonies. Historical records indicate that after emancipation in 1834, many slaves would not return to work on the sugar plantations. The absence of this lucrative labor force threatened the economy of the colonies, and the European colonists sought to recruit labor from North America, the Portuguese islands of the Azores and Madeira, and China. Great Britain turned to its colonies in the Middle East and South Asia for reliable sources of labor. British recruiters promised workers in India and in Indonesia that they would become prosperous in the New World— an expectation that brought great disillusionment to most, for the planters required of them the same back-breaking work as the slaves, and lodged them in shabby, unsanitary living quarters. But seeking to escape poverty in their own lands, more than 100,000 workers responded to the recruiters' call between 1845 and 1910, committing themselves to five years of labor. After that, they could stay and be given 10 acres of Crown land to farm (later reduced to 5 acres toward the latter half of the nineteenth century) or be offered remuneration for their services and allowed free passage back to their homelands. Most of them decided to settle in the New World. Although many migrated to other islands throughout the Caribbean, where they formed small close-knit groups, most settled in Trinidad, Guyana, and Suriname (formerly Dutch Guyana), where sugar production was prominent.

As the numbers of these immigrants increased since the mid-nineteenth century, so have the influences of their religious traditions. In addition to indentured servants, many immigrants to the Caribbean were refugees fleeing the ravages of wars in the Middle East; others came voluntarily in search of business opportunities in South America, stopped in the Caribbean, and decided to settle there. The Muslim community in the Caribbean was able to preserve its cultural traditions because, unlike Africans, many maintained Muslim traditions by returning home to visit family members. In the twentieth century, Muslim life in the Caribbean deepened with the founding of such organizations as the Anjuman Sunnat-ul-Jamaat Association in the 1930s and the Islamic Missionary Guild of South America and the Caribbean, in Guyana in 1960, both of which have sought not only to establish linkages between the various Muslim communities in the Caribbean but also to promote Muslim beliefs and practices throughout the region.

Islam has flourished in Trinidad, especially with the opening of the one million dollar Islamic Center in Kelly Village. This edifice includes classrooms used for worship, religious instruction, and various cultural activities. Islam has spread to other parts of the Caribbean as well. The largest concentration of Muslims is in Guyana, which boasts 133 mosques scattered throughout the country and a total of nearly 130,000 Muslims out of a population of 425,000 people; likewise, figures for Suriname and the Dutch-speaking islands show a total of more than 121,000 Muslims out of a population of 640,000. In the English-speaking

Caribbean, Jamaica has the largest population: there are more than 5,000 Muslims in that country out of a total of 3,000,000 people.[20]

A prominent Muslim sect that has flourished in Trinidad is the Ahmadiyya Muslim Jamaat, one of two Ahmadi sects in the world. It was introduced by East Indian immigrants from the city of Lahore in the 1930s. It was founded in the late nineteenth century by Mirza Ghulam Ahmad of Qadian, who claimed that he had come as a prophet and reformer (*Mujaddid*) who had been chosen to fulfill God's (Allah in Arabic) will. He taught that the advent of the coming of the end of days was predicted both by Jesus and Muhammad, as well as by other religious figures and sacred traditions of the world. Although the Ahmadi share with the larger Muslim community the value of prayer, charity, and fasting—three of the Five Pillars of Islam—they question the claim that Muhammad was the last of the prophets. Mirza Ahmad claimed to fulfill Muhammad's prophecy that another of Allah's messengers would come after him, and that he would be the sign of the Second Coming and the end of the world. Ahmad taught that the references to Jesus' second coming in the Bible were not literal and that he would fulfill these prophecies by being the one to return as the expected Messiah (*Mahdi*). The Messiah, or Imam Mahdi, are then one and the same person who will eventually defeat the anti-Christ (*Dajjal*) at the Second Coming and herald the triumph of Islam at the end of days, followed by an age of everlasting peace (Quran, Sura 22:48; 55:59). Moreover, the Ahmadi also teach that Jesus was crucified in Kashmir but survived the event. His disciples awakened him from a profound state of swoon, which made it possible for him to continue his ministry and prophesy the advent of the prophets Muhammad and Mirza Ahmad.

Many of the teachings of the Ahmadi sect are controversial, the most important of which is its teachings on the Second Coming and the Mirza Ahmad's status as a prophet. For that reason, this sect is regarded by the larger Muslim community in the Caribbean today as heretical. But its success in Trinidad is marked by the significant number of Ahmadi mosques and the passionate radio and television broadcasts throughout the country. The Ahmadi sect has had some degree of success among African Americans in the United States as well; imams and members of their mosques frequently visit those in Trinidad.

Since the 1960s, Louis Farrakhan's Nation of Islam (or black Muslim movement) has come to play an important role in the lives of Caribbean people. The Nation of Islam's recent success in the Caribbean can be attributed to several factors. First, the evangelistic efforts of African American missionaries (or Caribbean nationals who were converted to the Nation of Islam and returned to their homes from the United States) have converted many to Islam. Second, its emphasis on socioeconomic objectives has distinguished it from other theologies. More precisely, it couches its socioeconomic teachings in theological language by calling for social justice and an end to racism and poverty, affirming

The Jami Masjid (Jama Masjid), a historic mosque on
Picadilly and Queen Streets, old Port of Spain, Trinidad.

the need for equal opportunities for all persons of color. It teaches that people of color are in the majority and therefore represent a powerful force that can engender political and economic change in the world today. Moreover, the Nation of Islam upholds the banner of black nationalism in the Caribbean and takes its cue from the teachings of Marcus Garvey. As noted earlier, Garvey advocated racial pride and called for blacks to affirm their sense of transnational identity. All blacks in the New World possess a common spirit deriving from their shared historical experiences; they are the descendents of Africans who were severed from their kin groups and from their cultures and who were brought to the Americas as slaves by whites. According to the teachings of the Nation of Islam, slavery was supported by the Christian church, and therefore it would seem incongruous for the descendents of slaves to commit themselves to a religious faith that subjugated their ancestors and continues to oppress them even today.

The Nation of Islam, as well as the older traditions that preceded it in the Caribbean, has maintained the basic tenets of the faith as outlined in the Five Pillars of Islam. The first, *shahadah'*, is the belief in the oneness of Allah as the supreme and transcendent ruler of the universe. Muhammad is Allah's chosen prophet, to whom the Quran was revealed as the sacred scriptures via the intermediary of the angel Gabriel. The second is the *salat*, a command by which all Muslims must pray five times daily. Facing the Kaaba, the sacred site in

Mecca in Saudi Arabia, they communicate directly with Allah and express their gratitude to the Creator for the gift of life itself. The third is *zakat,* or giving alms. Muslims who are able are encouraged to practice charity and give a portion of their wealth to the poor. *Sawm* is the fourth pillar, mandating ritual fasting during the month of Ramadan, the ninth month in the Muslim calendar in which Allah revealed the Quran to Mohammad. And finally there is the hajj, which recommends that every Muslim make a pilgrimage to Mecca at least once in his or her life.

It is difficult to ascertain the exact number of Muslims in the Caribbean today. The local communities often have no membership rolls that indicate the exact number of adherents. There are still relatively few mosques throughout the region, but the numbers of Friday evening worship services are growing, although they consist mostly of informal ceremonies held in the devotees' homes and places of business.

The social and political state of affairs in the Caribbean is always changing, and the presence of Islam has never been felt so strongly in the region's history. Of late, new Muslim communities have emerged in Haiti, the Dominican Republic, and Puerto Rico. They have made their presence felt by emphasizing literacy and education of the young. They have also joined their Christian and Hindu brethren in calling attention to the increased problem of alcoholism and drug abuse in these countries and are attempting to recapture their societies' traditional values. Moreover, Islam fosters a spirit of transnationalism in the Caribbean. It awakens a spirit of racial solidarity with Africans and provides a sense of spiritual affinity with the peoples of the Middle East, South Asia, and Africa. In this way, it fosters the shared resolve to fight neocolonialism common to so many countries whose citizens seek to find their rightful places among other peoples of the world.

Hinduism

Hinduism also plays an important role in Caribbean cultures. There are small communities throughout the Caribbean, but the largest concentrations of Hindus live in Trinidad, Guyana, and Suriname. The presence of Hinduism in the Caribbean can be attributed to the same historical processes that brought large numbers of Muslims to the region. The importation of Hindu indentured laborers from India spanned the period between 1838 and 1910, with a brief interlude between 1848 and 1851 (Brereton 1974:26). During this span of seventy-two years, it is estimated that as many as 143,939 came to Trinidad (Brereton 1981: 103). Additional numbers were brought to Suriname, Guyana, Martinique, and Guadeloupe.

The East Indians who came to the Caribbean were bondsmen who worked long hours and, like the slaves before them, lived wretched lives. The working and living conditions were so appalling that many fled the plantations to live

Reconstructed Siewdass Sadhu mandir
("Temple in the Sea"), Waterloo, Central Trinidad.

with others who had completed their five-year term of service and who lived in squalid conditions in peasant settlements. When discovered by the police, those with unauthorized absences from the plantations were severely punished and jailed. As many as 70 percent of Indo-Trinidadians were agricultural workers, but those who were free bondsmen performed menial tasks for which they received barely adequate remuneration (Brereton 1974). Moreover, they were not considered truly free: they were restricted by criminal laws that curtailed their movements throughout the colonies, and the colonial governments issued immigrant certificates that East Indians had to show to the police upon request.

Their hopeless conditions generated unfavorable stereotypes about them in the larger society. Their manner of dress, languages, and customs contributed to the colonists' sense of their otherness. The colonists regarded the East Indians as inferior beings who were unable to improve their lot because of a lack of ability; they were also thought to be deceitful and immoral. Their religion reinforced these stereotypes about them and contributed to their low social status. The colonists were Westerners who regarded Christianity as a religion "superior" to all other creeds, and the Hindus' daily observances of such rituals as *puja* were condemned and considered idolatrous by the religious authorities. *Puja* is a rite of purification in which water is poured over an icon of a god. An oil lamp is lit and carried in a twirling motion around the room in which the ritual is performed, and the smoke emanating from the flame is believed to purify the room (and by extension the home) in which *puja* is observed. The

colonial government viewed the Hindus with contempt, claiming that such rituals were heathenistic, belonging to a barbaric religion. A 1911 article in the
Trinidad Review noted that "Indians were people of false religions" who had
"pagan minds" and were endowed with a low sense of morality that could be
transformed solely by the saving power of Christianity. This perception of
Hindus as immoral derived partly from their marriage rites, which were not
sanctioned by the colonial church and were considered illegal until 1945
(Khan 2004:37).

The suppression of a people often destroys what is benevolent and gentle,
but it also inspires in them the need to reclaim the very thing that is being eradicated from their culture. East Indians were persistent in maintaining their religious traditions and adapting to their new situation. Their ritual observances
in honor of the Hindu gods provided a sense of self-esteem and a refuge that
they believed protected them from derision. They looked to their religious
leaders (Brahmins) for guidance and trusted them as the custodians of their
way of life. They were successful in preserving their myths and many of the
rites of passage related to birth, initiation of their children, marriage, and death.
They retained many of the symbols of their religion and rekindled the need to
abide by the dietary restrictions associated with these rituals. Indo-Trinidadians
created a number of organizations to preserve Indian culture. As early as the
1890s, Hindu leaders formed the East Indian Association, the first Trinidadian
organization of its kind that sought to preserve Hindu traditions and to address
many of the social and economic issues related to the Indian community.
Later, in the 1950s, a new organization was formed, the Sanatan Dharma Maha
Sabha, whose primary goal was to strengthen East Indian national life in Trinidad and standardize Hindu worship. It eventually created a commission that supervised some sixty primary and secondary schools and promoted the teaching
of Hindu cultural and religious traditions among Indian youths (Khan 2004).

The prevailing Hindu tradition in the Caribbean teaches that there is one
Godhead (Brahman), the supreme creator and ruler of the universe whose transcendent nature is manifested in the personae of many minor deities. The
Hindu scriptures consist of a large compendium of sacred books that represent
complex philosophical systems persisting for than more 2,500 years. Among
these books are the *Vedas* and the *Upanishads*. But in the Caribbean the most
highly revered sacred writings are the epic stories of the god Krishna in the
Bhagavad Gita and Hanuman in the *Ramayana,* both of which are part of a
larger volume called the *Mahabharata*. The heroic exploits of both these gods
recounted in these texts mirror the situations of hardship that the early Hindu
settlers faced in the Caribbean. The *Bhagavad Gita* teaches the steadfastness in
and the value of one's work as a sacred duty. It also describes the need for one
to gain the knowledge of the transcendence of God as revealed by Lord Krishna,
who also affirms the sacredness of the human soul as deriving from the Godhead.
Likewise, there are many stories that are told in the *Ramayana* about Hanuman;

they picture him as a symbol of strength and perseverance, wisdom and astuteness. Perhaps one of the most popular accounts about the monkey god Hanuman is his maiden voyage to the island of Lanka (probably Sri Lanka today).[21] As he reached it, he was met by Sursa, a goddess whose duty was to test all newcomers to the island by having them pass through her mouth. When she tried to swallow Hanuman, he grew larger, which made Sursa also grow bigger. But suddenly he became smaller and escaped through the ears of the divine giant. Embattled by various demons and other demiurges in Lanka, Hanuman was wounded and sought to find a medicinal healing herb. He flew back to the Himalayas in India, but unable to find the exact location of the herb, he brought the entire mountain with him to Lanka.

In the study of religion, myths of any system of belief are its sources of power because these myths mirror the depths of the human character and reveal in most profound ways the forces that shape human destiny. The importance of myths to a religious community is that the stories authenticate life's crises, provide guidelines for human behavior, and serve as authoritative models for a community. Hence, myths belong to the realm of literature and the symbolic, and their importance lies not so much in the details of the stories they recount but in the philosophical truths that they impart. The story of Hanuman chronicles the hardships of Hindus in Trinidad, their cleverness in their struggle for survival before the colonial giant that sought to consume them, and the yearning to recapture the curative power of their culture as symbolized by Hanuman's return to the Himalayas. It also details the translocation of Hindu restorative traditions to the islands of the Caribbean as represented by the mythological land of Lanka.

Hindus demonstrate their belief in the holiness of the family and seek to ensure the sanctity of their homes by maintaining altars around which they perform many rituals such as *puja*. They pray to their gods at home, and those who are able meditate daily in the local temples. Many think that one gains knowledge of God through fasting one day weekly, for they believe that fasting helps turn one's attention from the physical cravings of the body and facilitates one's concentration on the knowledge of God's divine purity. At least once a year, Hindus perform a communal *puja* in which sages (*pandits*) read parts of the sacred text and perform *hawan*, the sacred fire ritual that recalls Hanuman's exploits in the *Ramayana*.

Among the most important annual religious observances is the Holi Phagwa, a festival held during the month of *Chaitra* in the Hindu calendar, which corresponds to the period of March or April in the Christian calendar.[22] This festival was first celebrated in Trinidad around 1845 with the arrival of East Indians from the Bihar region of India. Holi Phagwa is a liminal celebration that welcomes the spring planting season and extols the virtues of the Hindu religious and cultural traditions. It also rekindles the memory of the passage to the New World and the challenges that the East Indians' forebears had to face. The rhythmic music produced by the hand drums (*dholak*) and cymbals (*majeera*), accompanied by songs and dances, is said to rejuvenate the devotees in body and spirit. Water, colored by bright dyes and sprayed on the bodies of the participants, is believed to penetrate the skin to strengthen the body's subtle spiritual ions, which are thought to be the sources of health and beauty.

Despite the similarities that may exist between Hindu religious practices in the Caribbean and those in India, it cannot be said by any stretch of the imagination that Hinduism in the Caribbean is a South Asian religion that was transplanted in its unmodified form to the Americas. Through the years, the religion has evolved differently in the Caribbean than did its counterpart in South Asia. On their voyage to the Americas, East Indians found it difficult to maintain their religious laws. Hindus considered traveling to foreign lands on water to be taboo, but the hope for a better life abroad took precedence over religious considerations, and East Indian workers came to seek new opportunities in the Caribbean. Moreover, the journey overseas forced East Indians from different backgrounds, geographical regions, and social standing to share the same limited space on the ships that brought them to the Americas. Divisions between the castes became impossible. Historically, the caste system was understood as a means of indicating the degree of one's spiritual achievement. The higher the caste, the closer one was in one's journey toward spiritual enlightenment (*nirvana*). According to traditional Hindu beliefs, one's spiritual journey was not to be "polluted" by contact with a person of a lower caste. But while sharing a ship's limited space, Brahmins (the highest caste) had to eat meals with those of lower castes.

Once in the Americas, the preservation of the caste system became even more difficult because (1) the newcomers were regarded as having a lower status, even if they were Brahmins, and (2) the overcrowded conditions of the dwellings in which they lived near the sugarcane plantations made it impossible to recreate caste separation. East Indians bound for the Caribbean then were forced to begin anew and the rules on which castes were established had to be forsaken simply because of logistical difficulties.

Religion has played a considerable role in the preservation of East Indian culture in the Caribbean. It has enabled East Indians to maintain communal bonds through religious rituals and festivals. It sustained the inviolability of the family and emphasized the value of rearing youth in the Indian religious and cultural traditions. Finally, it allowed East Indians to assert the legacy of a sacred tradition that predates Christianity by more than 500 years.

■ Caribbean Religions as Global Religions

Since the 1950s, many Caribbean people have migrated to other places, notably to other parts of the Caribbean as well as Central America, the United States, Canada, and the United Kingdom (see Chapter 12 for Dennis Conway's description of the Caribbean disaspora). There they inhabit many of the world's largest cities, and despite the stresses of urban life and the lingering suspicions by outsiders of Caribbean religions as mere superstition and devil worship, Caribbean peoples have managed to maintain their religious beliefs and practices abroad.

For Cubans, what has been termed the *second diaspora* occurred shortly after their country's socialist revolution in 1959. Among some 1 million Cuban emigrants who settled in various parts of the world were priestesses and priests of Santería. They established thriving religious cells, or "houses," in Puerto Rico, Venezuela, and the United States and continue to wield a considerable authority over the people they serve. Although estimates of the numbers of practitioners and priests are difficult to determine, totals could run as high as the hundreds of thousands, with many more devotees of the *orichas* in the United States than in Cuba. The religion continues to play an important part in the lives of people in the diaspora and is often the primary agency for assisting poorer Cuban emigrants with health services and legal aid.

In the case of the Spiritual Baptists, the church has sent missionaries abroad in recent years. Several churches have opened in West Indian communities in London and Toronto. Among all the new churches in the diaspora, perhaps the greatest growth has occurred in Canada, Europe, and the United States. For example, St. Peter's Spiritual Baptist Church in Brooklyn claims to have more than 2,000 members, and two Spiritual Baptist churches in Toronto claim more than 1,000 members each. The New Jerusalem Spiritual Baptist Church outside London claims over 200 members.

Haitians also have recreated their religious traditions in the diaspora. They have established *ounfòs* (places of worship), as well as communities that approximate those of the African *lakou* (rural courtyard) that managed to survive throughout Haitian history. In Haiti, a *lakou* is an area shared by several families who live in separated dwellings, one of which may serve as the home of a person regarded as a spiritual leader. Haitians have recreated the *lakou* in the diaspora. The *house systems* in New York City are analogous to the *lakous;* they consist of an entire building in which several families live in individual apartments but share domestic and financial resources. The families gather around a priest or priestess, whose apartment often combines living quarters and a temple.

In the context of rituals, most of the paraphernalia used are readily available in most large cities in the diaspora. Even the pilgrimages are reproduced. For example, Halloween (October 31) in North America falls one day before All Souls' Day (November 1), the day consecrated to the souls of the dead in the Catholic, Santería, and Vodou calendars. Similarly, July 16, the day devoted to the Virgin Mary in the Catholic liturgical calendar, is reserved for Ezili in Vodou and Ochún in Santería. On that day, many Haitians in New York make pilgrimages to the Lady of Mount Carmel Church; those in Canada will go to St. Anne de Beaupré near Quebec.

Hindus are prominent in Canada, and temples can be seen in and near the major cities in the country. Several nonprofit organizations, such as the Hindu Conference of Canada, have attracted a significant numbers of devotees from the Caribbean, who have joined others from other parts of the world for religious rituals and pilgrimages. Through a system of reticulation Muslims in the Caribbean, especially devotees of the Nation of Islam, visit mosques in the United States and Canada, and the movement's leaders consult each other regularly concerning the community's commitment to teaching the religion. The same is true of Pentecostals who visit family members and with them attend religious services at the churches in the diaspora.

Perhaps one of the single most significant aspects of Caribbean religions in the diaspora is their multiethnic character. Ritual participation is open to members of cultural and ethnic groups from other parts of the world. This is especially true of the Rastafari, whose religious ideology and social message have had widespread international appeal, resulting in the creation of Rastafari communities in different parts of the world. In addition, the names of the spirits of Santería, the Spiritual Baptists, and Vodou have spread very quickly among nonnationals in the United States, notably among African Americans seeking to integrate black nationalism with an authentic African worldview. The emphasis on Africa and African cultures by the Rastafari has been particularly appealing to African Americans in the United States. In larger US cities, Santería is practiced by Americans of Dominican, Venezuelan, Colombian, and Mexican descent, as well as Anglo-Americans. The energy, creativity, and resources of these Caribbean religious communities in the diaspora have led to the formation of international organizations dedicated to fostering dialogue and cooperation in these emerging world religions. The participation of other cultural and ethnic groups will undoubtedly change these religions, for their members may incorporate their own cultural and religious traditions—a factor that may distinguish them from their counterparts in the Caribbean. It may well be that, for the second time in the history of these Caribbean religions, their traditions will become theologically diverse. And like the religions of the maroon republics in the period of slavery, the ethos of the theology of each religious center in the diaspora will depend upon its demographic composition and the theological inclination of its members as well as its leaders.

◼ Conclusion

Caribbean religions maintain some continuity with African religions traditions. However, because they developed in another cultural context, there are significant differences as well. Caribbean religions are multicultural to the core and derive their traditions from various regions, including Africa, Europe, and the Americas. Religious amalgamation occurred in different ways throughout the Caribbean and was facilitated through a system of reinterpretations whereby

African religious beliefs and practices were translated into Christian terms to hide them from unfriendly eyes. African beliefs and practices within Caribbean religions provide a commonly shared experience in a cultural context in which the combinations of African religious elements varied according to the preeminence of the religious traditions of a particular ethnic group or the theological inclinations of local religious specialists.

The multicultural character of Caribbean religions has made it possible for devotees to cultivate a transcultural identity and foster a sense of spiritual affinity with the larger world. Caribbean religions have spread to other areas as those emigrating from the region have maintained their traditions abroad in the diaspora. For the most part, Caribbean religions in the Caribbean and in the diaspora have neither set orthodoxies nor clearinghouses that provide official documentation of their beliefs and practices. They consist largely of independent, cell-like structures that are related to each other by a network rather than through a central bureaucratic hierarchy.

Caribbean religions have exhibited an extraordinary resilience that has enabled them to survive in the most adverse socioeconomic conditions throughout their history in the region and in the diaspora. Local autonomy has permitted ritual and theological innovations by leaders that have facilitated successful translocation into the most arduous socioeconomic and environmental conditions in the diaporas.

◼ Notes

1. The Pukumina is often referred to incorrectly as the *Pocomania,* named after the Spanish *poco maniacs* meaning *a little madness.* This term was applied to the movement to describe the behavior of its devotees during trance possession as bordering on madness.

2. We differentiate between folk and spiritual healing. Folk healing involves the extensive use of pharmacopoeia, whereas spiritual healing includes healing by the laying on of hands by a religious specialist.

3. Several days before de las Casas died in 1566, he recognized that slavery was wrong, that war was unjustifiable, and that the annexing of Indian land by Europeans was unscrupulous. He condemned all the European governments for transporting slaves from Africa.

4. A 1780 census revealed that 700 ships carried some 20,000 slaves into the colony annually. The black population outnumbered whites by 100 to 1 (Moreau de Saint-Méry [1797] 1958, vol. 1: 28–29).

5. Moreau de Saint-Méry, an eyewitness to Vodou during the eighteenth century, reported that makeshift altars and votive candles concealed the Africanness of their rituals (Moreau de Saint-Méry [1797] 1958, vol. 1: 55).

6. Note the change in orthography from *oricha* used in the context of Santería. Both terms have the same connotation in both religious traditions.

7. For a discussion of the proceedings, see Glazier 2001:318.

8. Trance possession and glossolalia by the Kumina is achieved by means of hyperventilation and what the devotees have termed *thumping,* that is, the grunting sound

produced by the exhaling of the breath passing through the vocal chords in synchronization with the rhythm of a song.

9. There are many biblical passages that depict the Cushites, but two are important to this chapter. Some passages describe the Cushites as noble, valiant warriors, whereas others allude to them as a poor, exiled people who were "led naked and barefoot, their buttocks shamefully exposed" (Isaiah 19:21) to the world. It may well be that the term *Ethiopia* as Liele used it would have a double meaning: it would have referred to the slaves' self-image as a poor and oppressed people living in an estranged land, and, as among the Rastafari today, it would have been used as a metaphor for social protest and resistance.

10. The emperor's coronation attracted so much of the world's attention that *Time Magazine* named him the 1930 "Man of the Year."

11. This term is a shortened but endearing version of Jaweh (or Yaweh), God's name in the Hebrew Bible.

12. The Rastafari interpret Selassie's death to be an ontological transformation from a bodily form to a spiritual essence. As Jah, the emperor is therefore active in the world and in their lives.

13. The Rastafari adopt the use of circumlocutions to suggest the uplifting of the human spirit. They use the word *over-standing* rather than *under-standing* and *livet-ary* rather than *die-tary*.

14. Cf. Leviticus chapters 11 and 18.

15. There may be a connection between the meaning implied in the terms *maroon* and *marranos,* both of which are derogatory words designating the flight of domesticated animals into a state of wildness or, as in the case of the Jews, into the diaspora in another land.

16. Sephardic synagogues are built around four poles that symbolize the "four matriarchs." The origin of this term derives from four prominent Jewish mothers in the Bible: Sarah, Rebecca, Leah, and Rachel. The number four is also symbolic of the four quarters of space. The synagogue can be said, then, to be a symbolic microcosmic representation of the world.

17. This is a tradition that derives from the need to muffle the sound of the feet of those who came to pray. Sephardic Jews in the Caribbean also believe that the sand-covered floors represent the children of Israel wandering through the desert (Arbell 2000:4). It also symbolized their own dispersion in the New World.

18. By and large, Jews owned very few slaves. Historical records indicate that their farms consisted of small plots that required merely one or two slaves.

19. Also known as the Johnson-Reed Act. It limited the number of immigrants admitted in the United States from any foreign country to 2 percent of the total number of people from that country residing in the United States. The object of this law was to limit the number of Eastern Europeans entering the United States.

20. Islam Awareness, "Muslim Situation in the Caribbean," http://www.islamawareness.net/Caribbean/carribean.html (accessed April 7, 2009).

21. Hinduism teaches that the world is sacred and that one should hold great reverence for all living things. Hanuman is the monkey god, the highest in the animal kingdom, who is thought to be the link between the human and animal worlds.

22. Pronounced "P'agwa" with an aspirated "h."

◼ Bibliography

Andrade, Jacob A. P. *A Record of the Jews in Jamaica from the English Conquest to the Present Time.* Kingston: Jamaica Times, 1941.

Arbell, Mordechai. *The Jewish Nation of the Caribbean: The Spanish-Portuguese Jewish Settlements in the Caribbean and in the Guianas.* Jerusalem: Gefen Publishing, 2002.

———. *The Portuguese Jews of Jamaica.* Kingston: Canoe Press, University of the West Indies, 2000.

Augier, Roy, M. G. Smith, and Rex Nettleford. *The Rastafari Movement in Kingston, Jamaica.* Mona, Kingston, Jamaica: University of the West Indies, 1960.

Barrett, Leonard. *The Rastafarians: Sounds of Cultural Dissonance.* Boston: Beacon Press, 1977.

Bascom, William. *Shango in the New World.* Austin, TX: African and Afro-American Research Institute, University of Texas, 1972.

Bastide, Roger. *African Civilizations in the New World.* New York: Harper and Row, 1971.

Birth, Kevin. *Any Time Is Trinidad Time.* Gainesville: University Press of Florida, 1999.

Brandon, George. *Santería from Africa to the New World: The Dead Sell Memories.* Bloomington: Indiana University Press, 1993.

Brereton, Bridget. "The Experience of Indentureship, 1845–1917." In *Calcutta to Caroni: The East Indians in Trinidad,* edited by John Gaffar La Guerre. London: Longman Group Limited, 1974.

Castor, Nicole. "Virtual Community: The Orisa Tradition in the New World and Cyberspace." Proceedings of the Sixth World Congress of Orisha Tradition and Culture. Port of Spain, Trinidad: Heritage, 1999.

Chevannes, Barry. *Rastafari: Roots and Ideology.* Syracuse: Syracuse University, 1994.

Desmangles, Leslie G. *The Faces of the Gods: Vodou and Roman Catholicism in Haiti.* Chapel Hill: University of North Carolina Press, 1992.

Encyclopedia of African and African American Religions. Edited by Stephen Glazier et al. New York: Routledge, 2001.

Garvey, Amy Jacques. *The Philosophy and Opinions of Marcus Garvey, of Africa for Africans.* Dover, MA: Majority Press, 1986.

Gerlach, Luther, and Virginia Hine. *People, Power, and Change: Movements of Social Transformation.* New York: Bobbs-Merrill, 1970.

Glazier, Stephen D. *Perspectives on Pentecostalism.* New York: University Press of America, 1980.

———. Marchin' the Pilgrims Home: A Study of the Spiritual Baptists of Trinidad. Salem, MA: Sheffield, 1991.

———. *Encyclopedia of African and African-American Religions.* London: Taylor and Francis, 2001.

———. "Demanding Deities and Reluctant Devotees: Belief and Unbelief in the Trinidadian Orisa Movement." *Social Analysis* 52 (2008): 19–38.

Homiak, John. "From Yard to Nation: Rastafari and the Politics of Eldership at Home and Abroad." In *Ay Bobo: Afro-Karische Religionen,* edited by Manfred Kremsner. Vienna: WUV-Universitatsverlag, 1995.

Hucks, Tracey. "I Smoothed the Way, I Opened Doors: Women in the Yoruba-Orisa Tradition of Trinidad." In *Women and Religion in the African Diaspora: Knowledge, Power, Performance,* edited by R. Marie Griffith and Dianne Savage, pp. 19–36. Baltimore: Johns Hopkins University Press, 2006.

Khan, Aisha. *Callaloo Nation: Metaphors of Race and Religious Identity Among the South Asians in Trinidad.* Durham: Duke University Press, 2004.

Lai, Walton Look. *Indentured Labor, Caribbean Sugar: Chinese and Indian Migrants to the British West Indies, 1838–1918.* Baltimore: Johns Hopkins University Press, 1993.

Lindsay, Arturo, ed. *Santería Aesthetics in Contemporary Latin American Art.* Washington, DC: Smithsonian Institution Press, 1996.

Lum, Kenneth. *Praising His Name in the Dance: Spirit Possession in Spiritual Baptist Faith and Orisha Work in Trinidad, West Indies.* Amsterdam: Harwood Academic Publishers, 2000.

McAlister, Elizabeth. *Rara! Vodou Power and Performance in Haiti and Its Diaspora.* Berkeley: University of California Press, 2002.

McCarthy-Brown, Karen. *Mama Lola: A Vodou Priestess in Brooklyn.* Berkeley: University of California Press, 1991.

Michel, Claudine, and Patrick Bellegarde-Smith. *Invisible Powers: Vodou in Haitian Life and Culture.* New York: Palgrave Macmillan, 2006.

Moreau de Saint-Méry, Médéric Louis-Elie. *Description topographique, physique, civile, politique, et historique de la partie française de l'isle de Saint-Domingue* (Topographical, physical, civil, political, and historical description of the French part of the island of Santo Domingo). 3 vols. New edition edited by Blanche Maurel and Étienne Taillemite. Paris: Société de l'Histoire des Colonies Françaises, 1958 [1797–1798].

Murphy, Joseph M. *Santería: An African Religion in America.* Boston: Beacon Press, 1988.

Rohlehr, Gordon. *Calypso and Society in Pre-Independence Trinidad.* Tunapuna, Trinidad: Gordon Rohlehr, 1990.

Simpson, George Eaton. "Baptismal, Mourning, and Building Ceremonies of the Shouters in Trinidad." *Journal of American Folklore* 79 (1966): 537–550.

———. *Black Religions in the New World.* New York: Columbia University Press, 1978.

Thomas, Eudora. *A History of the Shouter Baptists in Trinidad and Tobago.* Tacarigua, Trinidad: Calaloux, 1987.

Troeltsch, Ernst. *The Social Teaching of the Christian Churches.* New York: Harper and Row, 1960.

Weber, Max. *The Sociology of Religion.* Glencoe, IL: Free Press, 1960.

Zane, Wallace W. *Journeys to the Spiritual Lands: The Natural History of a West Indian Religion.* New York: Oxford, 1999.

11

Literature and Popular Culture

Kevin Meehan and Paul B. Miller

L iterature functions in the Caribbean, as elsewhere, as a documentary source that reveals the cultural patterns and social history that make up a civilization. Representative segments of every major cultural zone in the world—Amerindian, African, European, and Asian—have intermingled in the Caribbean, and this richness is reflected in the range and diversity of literature from the region. At the same time, because artists express their unique understanding of the world through literature and audiences come to share this understanding through reading, listening, and responding, literary texts also shape the history and culture of a given place as much as they reflect it.

Previous chapters have explored particular aspects of Caribbean reality, past and present. In this chapter, we look at traditions of verbal expression worked out over many centuries. In referring to specific writers and works, we introduce a series of creative tensions characteristic of Caribbean cultural identity. These tensions, which we view as sources of vibrant creativity in the Caribbean, include writing versus popular oral expression; the interplay of multiple languages; the dynamic of domination, resistance, and struggle for autonomy; the clash between individual island and collective regional identity; and the conflict between a desire to establish home and identity in the Caribbean, on the one hand, and the force of movement, displacement, and exile on the other. These tensions recur from the period of Amerindian settlement to the present day and allow us to examine diversity within the Caribbean as well as the common threads that suggest a unified regional culture.

Indigenous Cultural Patterns

Caribbean cultural history is often treated as if it began in 1492 with the arrival of Christopher Columbus off the shore of Guanahani, an island in the Bahamas that Columbus renamed San Salvador. As Stephen Randall reveals in Chapter 3, even scholars sympathetic to the idea of indigenous cultural influences in the region note pessimistically the near-total destruction of Taíno and other Arawak populations within one generation and the eventual military defeat of the Caribs in the 1790s, at which point British forces deported survivors from former Carib strongholds in the eastern Caribbean to Honduras and Belize.

Despite genocidal treatment at the hands of European colonists, however, native Caribbean peoples survive today on the islands of Dominica and St. Vincent and in greater numbers in mainland coastal settlements from Belize down to Guyana, Suriname, and French Guiana. Native culture is active in the fullest sense, and recent years have seen events such as the reunion of Carib communities in Honduras and St. Vincent; a renaissance in the formal study of indigenous songs, stories, dance, architecture, and foodways; growing partici- pation by Caribbean natives in indigenous peoples' movements worldwide; and publication of poetry in Caraib, Arawak, Trio, and Wayana (native languages spoken in Suriname). The currency of such poetry is suggested by a Trio song inspired by the sight of a low-flying airplane:

> *Jësinaewa ëhtëkëeirë / jekanawaimërë serë / jarëtono jarëtono mëëre jënë- tono mëëre / Jepananakirii jesautotao tïrïkë* (Weep and wail / for this is the giant canoe, / the cannibals are coming to get you; they're coming to eat you up. / Let's put some salt on him, the *pananakiri* [man-eater] says). (Jones 1998:511)

Here, the singer depicts airborne outsiders as man-eaters, thus reversing the usual association of Caribbean natives with cannibalism and savagery. Even when it is not articulated in indigenous languages, modern Caribbean expres- sive culture abounds with references to native civilization, ranging from the choice by rebel slaves in the former French colony of St. Domingue (the French form of Santo Domingo and the early name of Haiti) to reclaim the Taíno word *ayiti* (meaning "mountainous land") as the name of their independent country, to the recurring emphasis on Carib ancestry by the Antiguan writer Jamaica Kincaid, to the Cuban lutist Barbarito Torres's recent declaration in the song "Soy hijo del Siboney" (I'm a son of the Siboney/Ciboney). Such examples are not isolated, and they make it clear that the necessary starting point for any ex- ploration of Caribbean literature is the native Amerindian legacy.

Settlement
Even though native cultures in the archipelago did not reach the level of de- velopment seen in Maya, Inca, and Aztec societies, which boasted urbaniza- tion, monumental architecture, advanced technology, writing and sciences, and so on, it still is important to view the region as settled at the time of the Euro- pean incursion. Native arrivals began around 10,000 BC with the migration of

people from Florida and the Yucatán. They were nomadic hunter-gatherers who lived mostly in the larger islands (latter-day Jamaica, Cuba, Hispaniola, and Puerto Rico) and who became known as Ciboney. Much later, during the first four centuries AD, a second wave of natives moved into the archipelago from the Amazon Basin on the South American mainland. Agriculturally oriented, this second group was directly descended from the Galibi tribe in Guyana. As they blended with the Siboney and came to dominate the islands culturally and politically, members of this second wave were known collectively as Ahuruacos, or Arawaks, a word that means "flour-eaters" and identifies them with cassava, their main staple food. Subcultures developed at the local level, giving rise to other group names such as Lucayo, Kaketios, Ciguayo, Igneri, and— most numerous in the larger islands—Taíno.

Five centuries before the arrival of Europeans, a third wave of indigenous settlers known as the Caribs moved up from the south. Traditionally viewed as more warlike than the Arawaks, Caribs destroyed most of the male population in the smaller islands of the eastern and southern Caribbean and subjugated the surviving Arawak women. This history of conquest is the reason most often cited to explain the fact that Carib men spoke one language while the women spoke an entirely different language among themselves—one based on the preexisting speech of the Arawaks (Fouchard 1988:41–44). Over time, Carib settlements reached as far north and west as Cuba and Hispaniola, though in the larger islands the pattern was one of coexistence with Taíno inhabitants. Hispaniola (the island that today is divided between Haiti and the Dominican Republic) was, at the time of Columbus's arrival, divided into six *cacicats* (provinces), each one presided over by a *cacique* (chief). Two provinces were Taíno, two Carib, and two mixed Carib-Taíno.

A Template for Regional Culture

Hispaniola is a microcosm of the linguistic and cultural features of native Caribbean civilization. At least three languages were spoken: Carib was split into two branches along gender lines, whereas Taínos spoke their own unique language known as Marcorix. Together, these languages contributed vocabulary that describes important aspects of Caribbean flora (*cassava, guava, calabash*) and fauna (*lambi, coqui, agouti*), climate (*hurricane*), and material culture (*hammock*).

Although the three languages were distinct, Carib and Taíno people developed important shared features that allow us to speak of a unified or coherent culture of expressive arts. Stone carvings and paintings appear in caves, grottos, and hillsides, throughout Hispaniola and the entire archipelago from Jamaica to Trinidad. And though scholars still debate the precise meaning of these petroglyphs, there is general agreement that the inscriptions are sacred in nature and form part of a fully developed religious practice. The primary tenets of this religion, which was Taíno-Arawak in origin but found Carib adherents as well, revolved around veneration of spirits—referred to variously as *zemi, chemi, cimi,* or *semi*—that reside in the visible world (e.g., in stones, trees, and rivers). Some anthropologists and literary historians have argued that these petroglyphs are the work of an elite group of priest-historians, or *bovites,* and that we should consider such inscriptions the first example of Caribbean writing (Fouchard 1988:37–39, 79–81).

Popular verbal arts found expression in the songs of talented singers known as *sambas.* The cultural equivalent of medieval European troubadours or modern-day calypsonians, the *sambas* composed song-poems known as *areitos.* Examples of *areitos* include love songs, elegies, prayers, and war songs (Fouchard 1988:83–84).

Anthologies of Haitian and Dominican literature often begin with *areitos* such as "The Farewell to Racumon," "The War Song of Caonabo," and "The War Song of Cacique Enrique," none of which can be attributed to a specific composer. The sixteenth-century chronicler Gonzalo Fernández de Oviedo described in detail the music and dance of the Taínos in Hispaniola:

> These people had the good and gentle way of commemorating things past and ancient, which was in song and dance, and they called [*sic*] *areito.* . . . And as their joy and happiness would grow, they would at times join hands and at others go arm-in-arm, and, forming a circle, or ring, of them—man or woman—would take the initiative to lead, and would take certain steps forward and back. (Carpentier 1979:24)

Without question, though, one *samba* did emerge from the indigenous tradition to achieve almost mythological acclaim. That is Anacaona, the Taíno poet-queen. Named from the Taíno words for flower (*ana*) and gold (*caona*), she ruled over the *cacicat* of Xaragua, which had its capital at Yaguana, near the present-day Haitian city of Leogâne. Not only were Anacaona's songs known throughout the island, but also she was a multimedia performer and patron of the arts who included pantomime and large-scale choreographed pageants with her music and words. She also sponsored lavish feasts to mark seasonal changes and special affairs of state, and it was at one of these feasts marking a visit by the Spanish viceroy Nicolás de Ovando in 1503 that the Taíno hosts were massacred by their Spanish guests and Anacaona was hung from a post outside the smoking ruins of her city.

Sadly, such violence typified the dominant European response to native Caribbean civilization throughout the region. Despite the resulting disruption of indigenous cultural patterns, even this cursory examination reveals that native expressive arts contain many of the same characteristics—multilingualism, the coexistence of elite-based writing and popular-based oral performance genres, and lavish seasonal festivals—that also shape the scene of contemporary Caribbean literature.

▓ The Early Colonial Era:
Material Changes and Cultural Adaptation

Written literature in the region draws many of its distinctive images, themes, and political paradoxes from the diplomatic correspondence, travelogues, and histories produced during the first three centuries following 1492. Written for the most part (though not entirely) by Europeans, these texts are important documents in the ongoing project of creolization, or cultural adaptation. Although this adaptive process is comprehensive in scope, we are most concerned with literary aspects of creolization. Often what creolization boils down to from a literary perspective is the refashioning of languages—and, in some cases, the invention of entirely new languages—in order to make them capable of registering the unique social reality of the Caribbean.

Diplomatic Correspondence

The first three centuries of colonial writing in the region can be framed effectively by two texts, Christopher Columbus's "Letter of Columbus on the Discovery of America" (1493) and Toussaint L'Ouverture's "Letter to the French Directory" (1796). Written in April 1493 to the Spanish treasurer, Columbus's letter precedes the publication of his journals and is the first piece of commentary on the Caribbean to appear in Europe. It sets forth in uncanny detail many of the stock images that continue to characterize the region. The climate is Edenic, and Columbus is surprised to find trees that are "green and flourishing" despite having arrived at a time when a European would expect the onset of winter (Columbus 1892:3). Columbus offers a prospectus of the vast natural resources available as a return on the royal investment, including gold, spices, cotton, chewing gum, aloes wood, and "as many slaves for the navy, as their majesties will wish to demand" (Columbus 1892:11). This account establishes the logic of imperial control over Caribbean wealth and resources and shows already the presence of a strongly ingrained assumption that material and human wealth would inevitably flow out of the region. Writing about native inhabitants, Columbus alternates between celebrating the Taíno as noble savages who, for example, "go always naked, just as they came into the world," and depicting Caribbean society as tainted by underdevelopment, ignorance, and superstition (Columbus 1892:4). "They firmly believe," Columbus writes of the Taíno, "that all strength and power, and in fact all good things are in heaven, and that I had come down from thence with these ships and sailors" (Columbus 1892:6). In another passage, which might be seen as the first attempt to record native Caribbean speech, Columbus notes that the Taíno repeatedly proclaim his arrival with the phrase "Come, come, and you will see the celestial people" (Columbus 1892:7). In this initial rendering of Caribbean reality, allegations of native ingenuousness underwrite the magical aura ascribed to the region and help to secure the idea of Caribbean dependency on European military, political, economic, and cultural power.

Writing at the other end of the colonial era, and providing a sharp contrast to Columbus, is Toussaint L'Ouverture, a former slave who, during the 1790s, became the preeminent military and governmental leader of St. Domingue, the wealthiest French sugar colony and forerunner of the modern nation of Haiti. Toussaint's words reveal that official documents, even in the colonial era, could also voice the aspirations of African and mixed-race Caribbeans for dignity and freedom, thus challenging the assumption of dependence on European control. Penned in November 1796 during the height of the Haitian revolution (1791–1804), Toussaint's "Letter to the French Directory" denounces the scheme of white plantation owners to reinstate slavery, which the French government had abolished by decree in 1794. Adopting the rhetoric of patriotism and revolutionary ideals (liberty, equality, and brotherhood), Toussaint warns the French authorities that former slaves who fought to secure their freedom were willing to die in order to preserve it. While proclaiming loyalty to the "sublime morality" of republican France, Toussaint declares himself a "better father" to the people of the colony than the white planters (L'Ouverture 1989:197, 198). Toussaint's letter suggests that the model for effective leadership is a parent-child relationship, thus echoing the legacy of Columbus and setting the stage for critiques in twentieth-century Caribbean literature of patriarchal and patronizing leadership. At the same time, Toussaint's authoritative address and striking reference to the Caribbean colony as "my country" announce a note of radical Caribbean autonomy and bring colonial writing to the very brink of nationalism.

Travelogues and Histories

Between Columbus and Toussaint, regional expression gradually took shape in a steady stream of histories and travelogues. Initially, these documents were primarily in Spanish, including Columbus's *Diarios* (Diaries, 1493, 1498, 1503); *Brevíssima relación de la destruyción de las Indias* (Short account of the destruction of the Indies, 1542) and the multivolume *Historia de las Indias* (History of the West Indies, 1552) by Bartolomé de las Casas; *Historie del S. D. Fernando Colombo* (Fernando Colon's history of Santo Domingo, 1571) by Columbus's son; and later commentaries such as *Historia geográfica, civil, y política de la isla de San Juan Bautista de Puerto Rico* (Geographic, civic, and political history of the island of San Juan Bautista de Puerto Rico, 1788) by Iñigo Abbad y Lasierra and *Viaje a La Habana* (Trip to Havana, 1844), by Condesa de Merlín, among many others.

About a hundred years after Columbus, other Atlantic trading nations—the Netherlands, France, and England—began to challenge Spanish control of the islands, and we can see a corresponding rise in travel writing and histories in other European languages. Though the Dutch were the first to pose a serious threat to Spanish dominance over trade in metals, spices, agriculture, and captive Africans, their literature is comparatively slight in the early colonial period. Even so, two of the inaugural documents in the second wave of colonial historiography, Gaspar Ens's *Indiae Occidentalis historia* (West Indian history, 1612) and Jean de Laet's *Nieuwe Wereldt ofte Beschrijvigne van West Indien* (The New World, or the description of the West Indies [Old Dutch], 1625), are from Dutch writers.

Three monumental French travelogues—*Voyages aux isles de l'Amerique, 1693–1705* (Voyages to the islands of America, 1693–1705) by Jean Baptiste Labat, *Voyage a Saint-Domingue, pendant les annees 1788, 1789, et 1790* (Voyage to St. Domingue during the years 1788, 1789, and 1790) by François Alexandre Stanislaus de Wimpfen, and *Description topographique, physique, civile, politique, et historique de la partie Française de l'isle Saint-Domingue* (translated as "A civilization that perished: The last years of white colonial rule in Haiti," 1797) by Médéric Louis Élie Moreau de St. Méry—and two histories—*Histoire Général des Isles . . . dans l'Amerique* (translated as "Jean-Baptiste DuTertre on the French in St. Croix and the Virgin Islands," 1654) by Jean-Baptiste DuTertre, and *Histoire philosophique et politique des établissements et du commerce des européens dan les deux Indes* (Philosophical and political history of the settlements and trade of the Europeans in the East and West Indies, 1770) by Abbé Guillaume-Thomas-François Raynal—span the era from the mid-seventeenth through the late-eighteenth centuries and chronicle the rise of plantation society in Martinique, Guadeloupe, and St. Domingue. While English-language commentary on the Caribbean began in 1530 with Richard Eden's translation of *The Decades of Peter Martyr,* a Spanish text dealing with Columbus, the British travelogue tradition exploded in the eighteenth and nineteenth centuries with works like Edward Long's *History of Jamaica* (1774), Bryan Edwards's *The History Civil and Commercial of the British West Indies* (1793), and a cluster of volumes by British women travelers, most notably *Lady Nugent's Journal of Her Residence in Jamaica* (1801–1805).

Histories and travelogues provide details about the life of pirates, planters, and petty clerks while offering important, though often hostile, accounts of indigenous culture and, in later centuries, descriptions of the culture of enslaved Africans who, by the seventeenth century, formed the majority population throughout the islands. From a literary perspective, the history and travelogue tradition is significant in five ways. First, colonial texts chart the emerging plantation political economy. In their depictions of the changing regional landscape, historians and traveloguists establish images of gardens and houses that return in the belletristic fiction and poetry of later centuries as emblems of European domination.

Second, histories and travelogues serve as compendia of early literary efforts such as "The Sable Venus: An Ode," "The Repentant Sailor," and Francis Williams's "Ode," all of which appear in Long's *History of Jamaica.* Williams's verse, composed in Latin in 1759 to honor the Jamaican governor George Haldane and considered by many anthologists to be the first example of poetry by a native of the region, contains several lines that refer to the poet's own status as a black Jamaican, including "Minerva forbids an Aethiop to extol the deeds of generals," and "Nor let it be source of shame to you that you bear a white body in a black skin" (quoted in Boxill 1979:32).

Third, documentary writing by Europeans, even though it is typically hostile to enslaved storytellers, musicians, dancers, and religious leaders, nevertheless provides accounts of popular culture among Africans and Caribbean-born captives of African descent. Moreau's writing on St. Domingue and Long's on Jamaica, for example, contain the first important descriptions of Vodou and Myal, respectively. As Leslie Desmangles, Stephen Glazier, and Joseph Murphy discuss in Chapter 10, both Vodou and Myal are popular religions based on ancestor reverence, spirit possession, and group empowerment; their fully developed rituals focused resistance against the plantation regime and became foundations for national culture in the nineteenth and twentieth centuries.

Fourth, the extensive use of documentary genres anticipates important regional forms such as the slave narrative in the nineteenth century and the testimonial narrative in the twentieth century. Finally, Caribbean histories and travelogues have provided grist for literary artists who use these forms as templates for novelistic writing, beginning with Aphra Behn's *Oroonoko, or the Royal Slave* (1688) and Daniel Defoe's *Robinson Crusoe* (1719), stretching down to contemporary works by Wilson Harris, Edouard Glissant, Maryse Condé, Rosario Ferré, Edgardo Rodríguez Juliá, and numerous others.

◾ The Nineteenth Century: Toward Cultural Autonomy

The success of the Haitian revolution in 1804 inaugurated a new phase in the cultural history of the Caribbean. Whereas writing in the three previous centuries had been produced mostly by Europeans who identified very little with the region, from 1800 on Caribbean literature has been written more and more often by Caribbean people themselves seeking to fully define and celebrate Caribbean settings and identities.

And whereas writers in the early colonial era (pre-1800) were generally hostile to popular culture manifestations, Caribbean writers since then have increasingly sought to narrow the distance between written and popular culture. Indeed, the closer we get to the present moment, the more Caribbean writers see themselves in sympathetic dialogue with, and in many cases as products of, popular culture in all its complexity. The challenge of linking creative writing with popular songs, tales, dances, and so on is more characteristic of twentieth-century Caribbean literature and will be addressed in other sections of this chapter. Here, the focus is on Caribbean writing from the nineteenth century, in particular the contribution of romantic poetry, prose romances, novels, and documentary genres—all of which are linked to the central historical dynamics of abolishing slavery and solidifying independent national identities throughout the region.

Romantic Poetry and Prose

Weakened by the impact of the Napoleonic Wars in Europe, Spain began to lose control over its American empire in the 1810s. The wave of independence movements that swept across South America under the initiative of Simón Bolívar passed through the Caribbean as well. During a period of exile from the mainland, Bolívar penned the famous "Letter from Jamaica" (1814) advocating an integrated, independent Latin America. He subsequently sought refuge in independent Haiti and received money, arms, and a printing press from Haitian president Alexandre Pétion. In 1821 Spanish colonists in the eastern part of Hispaniola declared the formation of the Dominican Republic. Independence sentiments were brewing as well in Cuba and Puerto Rico, though in all three islands the struggle for national liberation would occupy the better part of the century and would be, in many respects, an unfulfilled quest.

Along with the political and economic aspects of nation formation, Caribbean people faced the cultural challenge of unifying groups divided by racial, class, and other antagonisms into a coherent national community. Writers struggled against isolation, censorship, and (particularly in the case of white Caribbean writers) their own racial chauvinism. Despite such obstacles, writers found numerous ways to play their part in initiating the process of unification. The Cuban poet Plácido penned "Despedida a mi madre" (Farewell to my mother) hours before being executed in 1844 for his part in an independence plot. Plácido was a mulatto who had been abandoned at birth by his white mother, and his final words reach out across the color line with a message that combines revolutionary conviction and antisentimental feelings: *"moro en la gloria, / Y mi plácida lira á tu memoria / Lanza en la tumba su postrer sonido"* (I calmly go to a death that is glory-filled, / My lyre before it is forever stilled / Breathes out to thee its last and dying note) (Plácido 1959:294).

Plácido's great successor at the end of the century is José Martí, who reanimated the themes of national reconciliation and Cuban autonomy. But whereas Plácido adopts the style of romanticism to convey his message, Martí's *Versos Libres* (Free verses, 1913) and *Versos Sencillos* (Simple verses, 1891) bring Spanish Caribbean poetry to the brink of modernism. Martí's lines are unrhymed, he employs a variety of meters other than the traditional ten-syllable foot, and his poetry focuses on symbols and objects in the world—for example, a *rosa blanca* (white rose) offered as a token of universal solidarity—in contrast to romantic writers' emphasis on exalted individual states of consciousness at odds with limiting social conditions.

Martí's contemporary in the Dominican Republic is Salomé Ureña de Henríquez. Recognized, like Martí, as the *musa de la patria* (national poet), and the author of an epic volume celebrating Anacaona, Ureña is most well known for lyric poems such as "A la patria" (To the homeland), "A Quisqueya" (To Quisqueya), and "La fe en el porvenir" (Faith in the future) that combined romantic nationalist fervor with an emphasis on positivism and ideals of rationality and progress. Ureña also evinces romantic style by exploring intimate emotions in poems such as "Melancolía" (Melancholy), "Angustias" (Anguish), "Tristezas" (Sadness), and "Amor y anhelo" (Love and desire).

Even more than poetry, the prose romance stands out as a key literary contribution to the development of nineteenth-century national culture, particularly in the Spanish-speaking countries. In addition to providing a birth-of-the-nation story, national romances usually feature ideal character types who represent the major divisions in a given society. When depicted as lovers whose desire reaches across such divisions, the characters' stories help consolidate national communities by imaginatively moving toward resolution of social conflict. Although typically associated with texts such as Anselmo Suárez-Romero's *Francisco* (1839) and Cirilo Villaverde's *Cecilia Valdés* (1839) from Cuba, and Manuel de Jesús de Gálvan's *Enriquillo* (1882) from the Dominican Republic, the national-romance genre also appears in Haiti, where the prose tradition begins with Emeric Bergeaud's *Stella* (1859). Interestingly, where Spanish Caribbean national romances present stories of romantic coupling, *Stella* uses the courtship theme to frame a story of fraternal strife in which two brothers, Romulus, a mulatto, and Remus, a black, vie for the affections of Stella, a white woman who symbolizes the spirit of the French Revolution transplanted in Haiti. In Bergeaud's text, resolution comes not from erotic coupling but rather from the brothers' reconciliation.

Interwoven with the national question—sometimes enhancing and sometimes impeding the push toward independence—was the fight to abolish slavery. Suárez-Romero's *Francisco,* for example, is a pro-abolition story whose ideal characters play out a love triangle that includes Dorotea, a tragic mulatto; Francisco, a noble black man too refined for the harsh regime of Cuban slavery; and Ricardo, a supremely bestial white planter. Against a real-life backdrop of constant slave revolts and fear that Cuba would become a second Haiti, Suárez-Romero depicts his enslaved lovers as docile martyrs, yet even that was too much for Spanish censors, who suppressed the novel for decades.

In the English-speaking islands, there is a parallel stream of novels that address the problem of slavery and its abolition. Typically, texts such as the anonymously authored *The Adventures of Jonathan Corncob* (1787), *Montgomery, or the West Indian Adventurer* (1812, 1813), *Hamel, the Obeah Man* (1827), and *Marley, or the Life of a Planter in Jamaica* (1828), as well as J. W. Orderson's *Creoloana* (1842), do not follow the prose romance pattern but instead adopt formulas such as the picaresque (bildungsroman). Nineteenth-century nationalist and abolitionist fiction is written almost exclusively by European sojourners or Caribbeans of European descent, and one thing these texts share is a tendency—inherited from the historians and travologuists—to represent plantation society from the point of view of white planters, even when depicting the brutality of the system and presenting calls to reform or dismantle it.

Documentary Genres

The voices of native Caribbean writers of color emerge primarily through documentary writing during the nineteenth century. Although their chosen genres and points of view on Caribbean society are very different from the European-authored texts, nonfiction writers such as Juan Francisco Manzano, Mary Prince, Jean-Baptiste Philippe, and J. J. Thomas are equally immersed in the social currents of abolition and nationalism. One of the most important texts in nineteenth-century Cuban literature is Manzano's *Autobiografía de un esclavo* (Autobiography of a slave, 1835). Born into slavery, Manzano, against the interdictions of his owners, teaches himself to read and write and escapes with the assistance of the del Monte group, an alliance of mostly white abolitionist thinkers and writers. With the proceeds from his own writings, Manzano purchases his own freedom, and at the behest of Domingo del Monte he writes a denunciation of slavery. His autobiography narrates a relatively pleasant childhood as a privileged, well-dressed slave belonging to a wealthy mistress. However, this carefree youth contrasts starkly with his adolescence and early adult life, when ownership is transferred to a new mistress, under whom he suffers continual torture and sadistic treatment. Manzano's *Autobiography* can be considered a founding text in Cuban writing, insofar as it laid the groundwork for combining a personal testimonial expression with a rhetorical denunciation of an inhumane institution that earned for both the genre and the author a lasting and universal appeal. Editions of Manzano's *Autobiography* in both the original Spanish and in translation are still printed today, and it seems clear that the text that marks the modern renaissance of the testimonial genre. Miguel Barnet's *Biografía de un Cimarrón* (Biography of a Maroon, 1968), was inspired by Manzano's title.

Building on the tradition of Olaudah Equiano, whose best-selling autobiography, *Equiano's Travels* (1789), included lengthy firsthand accounts of slavery in the Caribbean, Mary Prince's *The History of Mary Prince, a West Indian Slave, Related by Herself* (1831) exposed the slave experience from a black woman's point of view for the first time. Appearing in Britain precisely at the moment when the debate over abolition was reaching a climax, Prince's narrative went through three editions in one year. It caused an uproar in the press, the courts, and Parliament in the years immediately preceding the passage of an emancipation bill in 1833.

Apart from this historical and political significance, *The History of Mary Prince* is an important literary document for at least four reasons. First, it conveys a pan-Caribbean sentiment in the sense that Prince moves throughout the

islands, from her birthplace in Bermuda to Turks Island and, finally, Antigua before moving to England in 1828. Each place—even the hideous salt mine in Turks
Island—is described vividly and invested with great emotional attachment.

Second, the author's final destination is England, and in her expressions
of nostalgia for the family and places left behind, as well as the realization that
only outside the Caribbean is it possible to gain freedom and a public voice,
Prince anticipates the predicament and sentiments of émigré writers from later
generations. Third, her narrative casts typical Caribbean themes of displacement, hardship, resistance, and verbal wit within the framework of a woman's
story. Not only does this make clear how racial violence and the fight against
it are, for black women, waged over sexuality; it also lays the groundwork for
discussing a tradition of women's writing in the Caribbean.

Finally, even though Prince's story is filtered through the mediating figures of a British woman scribe and an abolitionist editor, and even though this
fact raises the problem of authentic voice, idiomatic Caribbean expressions
nevertheless break through. For example, Prince spent many days in the stocks
as punishment for her verbal rejoinders to white Antiguans, and when she
protests against excessive bondage with the complaint that the British in the
Caribbean "moor them up like cattle," Prince takes an important step toward
discovering a distinctive Caribbean voice in writing.

In a Trinidadian context, Jean-Baptiste Philippe's *Free Mulatto* (1824) defended the position of free persons of color by asserting that "the colored population of Trinidad have the same civil and political privileges with their white
fellow-subjects." Though Baptiste did not go so far as to call for the emancipation of enslaved blacks, his appeal challenged the regime of color prejudice
that, he claimed, had worsened when the island passed from French to British
rule in 1802. J. J. Thomas's *The Theory and Practice of Creole Grammar* (1869)
and *Froudacity, or West Indian Fables Explained* (1889) continue the development of Trinidadian cultural identity in the period after emancipation. Like
Philippe (and Prince, for that matter), Thomas begins both books as a protest
against a particular form of British imperialism, but each title ultimately im-
presses the reader less as a protest against colonial tyranny than as an affirmation of the Caribbean self. Particularly in the final section of *Creole Grammar,*
which contains a long list of Creole proverbs, we can see the author's love for
and appreciation of vernacular expressions like *même baton qui batte chein
noèr la pé batte chein blanc la* (the same stick that beats the black dog can beat
the white). Such expressions, Thomas claims, "prove that the Africans are not,
after all, the dolts and intellectual sucklings some would have the world believe them. . . . These applications are usually so truthful and ingenious that
they are worth volumes of comments and laboured definitions" (Thomas 1989:
121). Although the political drama of decolonization plays out more fully in
the twentieth century, it is clear from those nineteenth-century documents that
the cultural struggle toward independence was well under way and that the

voices of Caribbean majority populations were beginning to surface in literary texts.

▓ The Early Twentieth Century: Literary Movements, Vernacular Writing, and Cultural Unification

The first four decades of the twentieth century are characterized by an increasing confluence of popular and elite cultural activity.

Popular Culture and the Rise of Caribbean Literary Movements

In the wake of emancipation, which came in the 1830s for English-administered islands, the 1840s for French territories (Napoleon had reinstated slavery after the 1794 emancipation), the 1860s for Dutch, and the 1870s and 1880s for Spanish, changing economic structures resulted in the arrival of new populations from outside the region, including indentured labor from India, China, and Java, and free rather than slave labor from Africa. Britain also effected population transfers between various islands to manage labor crises and social unrest. Against the backdrop of such restructuring, Caribbean societies felt more than ever the shaping force of popular songs, dances, public speaking styles, and religious practices.

Sacred culture was pivotal in decisive moments of social upheaval, including the Haitian slave revolt, which started with a ceremony presided over by Boukman, a Vodou priest, and an unnamed woman priestess. Jamaica, too, had a history of militant uprisings being kicked off by religious leaders, including the so-called Sam Sharpe Rebellion in 1831 and the Morant Bay Rebellion in 1865, which were inspired by Baptist ministers Sam Sharpe and Paul Bogle, respectively.

Secular popular culture also grew in scope throughout the late nineteenth century. For example, carnival celebrations in Trinidad assumed much of their modern form during the period 1840–1900, combining the dances of pre-emancipation French Creole slave society (especially the calinda song form and dance style) with national dances brought by groups of liberated Africans after emancipation; the songs and dances of Anglophone migrants from Barbados and elsewhere; and the seasonal festivities of the old planter class that had traditionally celebrated with concerts, dancing, and picnics from Christmas until Ash Wednesday. Trinidadian carnival synthesized all these elements into an ensemble of marching bands, stick fighting, verbal boasting, and satiric songs (Rohlehr 1990:1–42). Even when carnival became a vehicle for expressing social strife, as in the famous Canboulay riot of 1881, it came closer than anything else to encompassing all strata of island life. Although the evolution

of Trinidadian carnival is unique, it does indicate the potential of popular culture throughout the region to integrate societies that had been fragmented and
divided under plantation slavery.

At the same time that popular practices were stamping their imprint on
Caribbean societies, elite groups were emerging everywhere in the region to
form salons and little reviews between 1900 and 1940. Thomas MacDermot,
editor of the *Jamaica Times,* created the All Jamaica Library publishing series
from 1905 to 1909; H. G. DeLisser edited Jamaica's principal newspaper, *The
Gleaner,* from 1904 until his death in 1944 and issued annual editions of
Planter's Punch beginning in 1920; Esther Chapman founded the *West Indian
Review* in 1934; O. T. Fairclough launched *Public Opinion* in 1937; and Edna
Manley directed *Focus,* a cultural spin-off of *Public Opinion,* beginning in
1943. All these journals appeared in Jamaica, which (with the possible exception of Haiti) witnessed the greatest quantity and quality of literary activity in
the region before 1940 (Cobham-Sander 1981:64–108). Alfred Mendes, C. L.
R. James, Albert Gomes, and others formed the Beacon Group in Trinidad,
where they produced two journals, *Trinidad* and *The Beacon.* Jacques Roumain
and others founded the indigenous movement as well as numerous journals
such as *La Revue Indigène* (The indigenous review), *La Relève* (Relief), and
La Trouée (Opening) in Haiti; in Cuba the *Revista de Avance* (Advance review), Gustavo E. Urutilla's column "Ideales de Una Raza" (Ideals of a race)
in the Havana daily *El Diaro de la Marina,* and the Club Atenas salon all helped
to organize literary culture and promote the efforts of poets Nicolás Guillén,
Regino Pedroso, and others.

Self-consciously literary in a way that had very little precedent (the Domingo
del Monte salon that produced Suárez-Romero and Villaverde in nineteenth-
century Cuba is perhaps the only earlier example), these elite groups sought to
codify and analyze popular culture and to develop distinctive literary expressions based on popular forms, including songs, proverbs in Creole, and animal
tales featuring Anancy the Spider, Compère Lapin (Br'er Rabbit), Frog and
Scorpion, and more. In the poem, "L'atlas a menti" (The atlas lied), which appeared in a 1927 issue of *La Revue Indigène,* Haitian writer Philippe Thoby-
Marcelin summons the folkloric character of Bouqui. Though typically depicted
as a dull-witted peasant who falls prey to the sly trickster Ti Malice, Thoby-
Marcelin's Bouqui speaks completely in Creole and becomes an icon of inas-
similable resistance, exclaiming to the other figure depicted in the poem, an
alienated, French-speaking Haitian schoolboy:

> *Dèhiè mônes gains mônes / HEIN? / Et lan cate-là / Blancs-yo fait Haiti piti /
> con-ça* (Behind the mountains are more mountains / EH? / And that's how /
> the foreigners make Haiti so small / with their maps).

Similar experiments with writing poetry based on popular speech can be
found in texts such as *Motivos de son* (Son motives, 1930), *Songoro Cosongo*

(1931), and *West Indies, Ltd.* (1934), by Guillén in Cuba; *Tuntun de pasa y grifería* (1937) by Luis Palés-Matos in Puerto Rico; and *Constab Ballads* (1912) and *Songs of Jamaica* (1912) by Claude McKay, who published these volumes of dialect poetry in Jamaica with encouragement and support from MacDermot and others before moving to the United States and eventually becoming associated with the Harlem Renaissance school. Within the same milieu of salons and little reviews, Caribbean prose writers were developing fictional equivalents of dialect poetry. Such efforts ranged from the work of Mendes, James, and DeLisser, all of whom embedded Creole-voiced characters within standard (i.e., British) English narration, to creative renderings of folk storytelling presented entirely in dialect. Examples of this latter type of writing appeared in the 1930s under the signature Wona in the Jamaican-based *West Indian Review.*

Viewed in a larger social and political perspective, the literature generated by the salons and little reviews points in three ways to intensifying anticolonial dynamics throughout the region. First, by deliberately promoting the incorporation of popular speech into written literary expression, these writers—even when they adhered to European or North American ideas of cultural excellence—enhanced literary creolization as a process of autonomous cultural development.

Second, salons, little reviews, and the movements associated with them addressed explicitly and implicitly the relationship of intellectuals and masses, as, for example, in the fiction produced by the Trinidadian writers of the Beacon Group. James and Mendes both project a hierarchical concept of this relationship by granting more authority to their frame narrators, who represent the observing Caribbean intellectual and whose standard English creates distance from working-class, dialect-speaking characters. Even here, though, such depictions produce a sort of freeze-frame image of divisions in society. Reproducing intellectual elitism this way in print did not in itself solve the problem of social stratification, but it could and in some cases did open up the possibility of critical awareness and the search for alliances among writers and mass groups.

Third, the by-product of thinking about such alliances was typically movement toward a more unified national culture and heightened resistance to outside domination. The tone of such resistance ranged from extreme anti-US sentiments in Haiti, where US Marine forces had occupied the country beginning in 1915, to the more conservative desire to achieve cultural autonomy (rather than outright independence) expressed by Jamaican writers associated with the Jamaica Poetry League, *Planter's Punch,* and *West Indian Review,* with other islands and movements falling somewhere in between these two poles. Particularly as a strong labor movement developed in the 1930s and as mass strikes broke out on island after island in the years preceding World War II, critical responses to literary experiments helped intellectuals to understand sympathetically and collaborate with popular movements, thus ameliorating some of the fragmentation and stratification in Caribbean society.

■ The Mid-Twentieth Century: The Dialectic of Exile and Nationalism

The two decades from the end of World War II to the mid-1960s mark a period of unprecedented breakthroughs in the writing, publishing, and worldwide reception of Caribbean literature. Ironically, it was the very experience of exile and migration out of the region that resulted in writers like Aimé Césaire, Mayotte Capécia, Edouard Glissant, Joseph Zobel, Alejo Carpentier, Una Marson, Louise Bennett, Samuel Selvon, V. S. Naipaul, George Lamming, Wilson Harris, and Derek Walcott gaining exposure to printing presses, theaters, radio stations, and other cultural resources located in metropolitan centers like London and Paris. National culture, then, seemed to reach its highest pitch precisely at the moment when Caribbean people, writers included, were leaving the islands in unprecedented numbers.

The dialectic of exile and nationalism was prompted in part by economics, particularly the lack of opportunities at home and the need to enlist Caribbean labor in the rebuilding of war-devastated European countries. In part, too, there was political fallout from a United Nations postwar mandate to dismantle colonial empires. This mandate created a feedback loop that quickened the progress toward regional autonomy that had been made by oil workers, miners, and farm labor during the strikes and agitation of the 1930s. In addition to political and economic developments, there were, as in the previous century, important cultural factors in the push toward nationalism. Even in cases such as Martinique and Guadeloupe, where the end of colonial status did not lead to national independence, cultural nationalism still supplied one of the major premises for moving beyond old-style colonialism.

Négritude

As a matter of cultural history, the literary outburst across the Caribbean that helped articulate nationalist consciousness featured new movements such as négritude in the Francophone societies, *negrismo* in Cuba and Puerto Rico, *Wie eége sanie* (Our own things) for Sranan-Togo writers in Suriname, and the Caribbean Artists Movement for Anglophone writers based in London. An important part of the literary infrastructure for such movements was the consolidation of journals and reviews. Négritude, for example, is often described as having sprung from the group of Caribbean and African writers who met as students in Paris and collaborated on the journal *Etudiant Noir* (Black student) (1934). Poetry volumes by two members of this group quickly followed. *Pigments* (1937), by Guyanese poet León Gontran Damas, and *Cahier d'un retour au pays natal* (Notebook of a return to my native land) (1939), by Martinican poet Aimé Césaire both denounce the French idea of colonialism as a civilizing mission. Damas and Césaire focus instead on the political violence of the slave trade: "How many of ME ME ME / have died / SINCE THEN / since they came that night," writes Damas in "Ils sont venus ce soir" (They came that night) (Kennedy 1989:45); the psychological violence of identity crises experienced by colonial subjects, as Césaire writes in *Cahier:* "*Dans cette ville inerte, cette foule désolée sous le soleil, ne participant à rien de ce qui s'exprime, s'affirme, se libère au grand jour de cette terre sienne*" (In this inert town, this desolate throng under the sun, not connected with anything that is expressed, asserted, released in broad earth daylight, its own) (1983:36–37); and positive reevaluations of African past and Caribbean present.

With the founding of *Présence Africaine* in 1948 as a quarterly journal and printing press located in Paris under the direction of the Senegalese editor Alioune Diop, négritude was able to consolidate itself as a transcontinental movement of black intellectuals. Composed of Caribbean figures such as Césaire, Damas, Frantz Fanon, Edouard Glissant, Jacques Stephen Alexis, René Depestre, and (somewhat later) Maryse Condé, and African figures such as Leopold Sedar Senghor, David Diop, Tchicaya U Tam'si, Jean-Joseph Rabérivelo, and Jacques Rabémananjara, *Présence Africaine* issued its review, published books by writers associated with the group, and sponsored important international meetings dedicated to promoting the goal of decolonization and recognition of African culture as a civilizing presence globally. Although négritude as an ideology has for the most part been supplanted by newer concepts such as Caribbeanness and creolization, its importance as a cultural and political catalyst in the Caribbean cannot be overstated.

The Caribbean Artists Movement

Among English-speaking Caribbean writers from the same generation, the infrastructure of journals and literary movements was somewhat more dispersed than in the case of négritude. Toward the end of the period we are considering here, however, a nucleus of writers and artists formed in London under the banner of the Caribbean Artists Movement. The foundations for a movement began in the 1940s with the establishment of the creative journals *Bim* (1942), edited in Barbados by Frank Collymore, and *Kyk-over-al* (1945), edited in Guyana by A. J. Seymour, along with the scholarly review *Caribbean Quarterly* (1948), published by the University of the West Indies, which regularly featured creative writing along with analytic pieces on regional history, politics, and culture.

Unlike earlier Caribbean-based journals that had short runs, these reviews appeared steadily throughout the 1950s and 1960s, as did *Caribbean Voices* (1946), a BBC radio series that began as "the brainchild of the Jamaican poet

Una Marson" (Cobham-Sander 1981:102). Broadcast out of London under the direction of Henry Swanzy, this show featured interviews and readings of creative works and is credited in accounts by George Lamming, V. S. Naipaul, and others as providing another important outlet for émigré writers.

In 1966, New Beacon Books, a store managed by Trinidadian poet and labor activist John La Rose, became the focal point for the Caribbean Artists Movement. The various projects born in the context of this movement included (1) theoretical discussions of Creole culture, "which is born in the West Indies and which contains non-European forms in large numbers" (Elsa Goveia, quoted in Walmsley 1992:97); (2) conventional literary responses—La Rose also operated a printing press, New Beacon Press, that published many new volumes of poetry and prose; (3) artistic forays into new media; (4) exploration of new venues for art exhibits, poetry readings, and conferences; (5) Marina Maxwell's Yard Theatre in Jamaica, and (6) numerous other developments designed to ensure that "Caribbean art, particularly its revolutionary new forms, would reach and activate a new range and generation of people" (Walmsley 1992:305).

The Caribbean Artists Movement typifies the dialectic of exile and nationalism because from its exiled grounding in London, it deliberately reached back to inspire and conspire with specific local projects in Trinidad, Guyana, Jamaica, the United States, and Canada. It thus summed up the cultural nationalist efforts that had been accumulating for a generation among displaced and itinerant Caribbean writers while also signaling a move beyond nationalism in the directions of pan-Caribbean regionalism and strengthening diasporic sensibilities.

A Boom in Caribbean Novels

The history of the first two postwar decades has been presented through the framing moments of négritude and the Caribbean Artists Movement, both of which were poetry-centered to a large extent. It is important to note before continuing, though, that this period of intense nationalist ferment is most remarkable in literary terms for the unprecedented number of excellent Caribbean novels published across the board in French, Spanish, and English. Cuba and the Cuban revolution were especially creative forces for the novel in the 1960s. Alejo Carpentier, who had led the way into the well-known boom in Latin American fiction with *El reino de este mundo* (The kingdom of this world, 1949), published *El siglo de las luces* (Explosion in a cathedral) in 1962. Carpentier was followed by other Spanish Caribbean writers. José Lezama Lima published his astounding and controversial epic *Paradiso* in 1968, and Reinaldo Arenas's *El mundo alucinante* (The hallucinatory world, translated as "The ill-fated peregrinations of Fray Servando," 1965) predated and anticipated many of the techniques of so-called magical realism. Another classic of the boom, *Tres tristes tigres* (Three trapped tigers, 1967), was written by a Cuban author-in-exile, Guillermo Cabrera Infante.

An important Puerto Rican writer from the period is Pedro Juan Soto, who, along with hosts of musicians from the island who went on to forge the salsa style, lived in New York and was one of the first Puerto Rican writers to incorporate this migratory and multilingual experience into his writing. His works include *Spiks* (1956) and *Usmaíl* (US Mail, 1959). Many Caribbean critics also claim the great novel *Cien años de soledad* (One hundred years of solitude, 1967) by Nobel laureate Gabriel García Márquez as a Caribbean novel because the mythical city of Macondo is located on the Caribbean coast.

In French, Haitian writer Jacques Roumain published *Gouverneurs de la rosée* (Masters of the dew, 1944), which is still the definitive attempt to depict Haitian culture in terms of the peasant majority. Haiti traditionally has been rich in literary production, and Roumain's novel was followed by numerous efforts to explore national culture and history, including Jacques-Stephen Alexis's *Compère Général Soleil* (Comrade General Sun, 1955), *Les arbres musiciens* (The musician trees, 1957), and *L'Espace d'un cillement* (The blink of an eye, 1957); and Marie Chauvet's *La Danse sur le volcan* (Dance on the volcano, 1957) and *Fonds des nègres* (Black valleys, 1960). In Martinique, the dilemmas of colonization, racial awakening, and historical consciousness inform Mayotte Capécia's *Je suis Martiniquaise* (I am a Martinican woman, 1948) and *La negresse blanche* (The white negress, 1948), Joseph Zobel's *Diab'-la* (The devil, 1946) and *La Rue Cases-Nègres* (Black shack alley, 1950), and Edouard Glissant's *La lézarde* (The ripening, 1959) and *Le quatrième siècle* (The fourth century, 1964).

Among Anglophone writers, H. G. DeLisser's *Jane's Career* (1914) and A. R. F. Webber's *Those That Be in Bondage* (1917) show some concern with defining local culture in Jamaica and Guyana, respectively. But the real run in cultural nationalist novels might be said to have begun in the 1930s with Claude McKay's *Banana Bottom* (1933), Alfred Mendes's *Pitch Lake* (1934) and *Black Fauns* (1935), and C. L. R. James's *Minty Alley* (1936). During the postwar period, the list of novels that imagine, define, and celebrate the contours of specific island settings is impressive and includes, in Trinidad, Ralph de Boissière's *Crown Jewel* (1952) and *Rum and Coca Cola* (1956), Samuel Selvon's *A Brighter Sun* (1952) and *Turn Again, Tiger* (1958), and V. S. Naipaul's *The Mystic Masseur* (1957), *The Suffrage of Elvira* (1958), *Miguel Street* (1959), and *A House for Mr. Biswas* (1961); in Jamaica, V. S. Reid's *New Day* (1949), Roger Mais's *The Hills Were Joyful Together* (1953), *Brother Man* (1954), and *Black Lightning* (1955), John Hearne's *Voices Under the Window* (1955), *Strangers at the Gate* (1956), and *The Land of the Living* (1961), Andrew Salkey's *A Quality of Violence* (1959), Sylvia Wynter's *The Hills of Hebron* (1962), and Orlando Patterson's *The Children of Sisyphus* (1964); in

Barbados, George Lamming's *In the Castle of My Skin* (1953), *Of Age and Innocence* (1958), and *Season of Adventure* (1960); and in Guyana, Edgar Mittelholzer's *Corentyne Thunder* (1941), *A Morning at the Office* (1950), *Children of Kaywana* (1952), *Kaywana Blood* (1958), and *Thunder Returning* (1960), Jan Carew's *Black Midas* (1958), *The Wild Coast* (1958), and *The Last Barbarian* (1961), and Wilson Harris's *Palace of the Peacock* (1960), *The Far Journey of Oudin* (1961), *The Whole Armour* (1962), and *The Secret Ladder* (1963). The foregoing list ranges widely in terms of narrative approach, emphasis on particular social groups (black, white, colored, East Indian, peasant, worker, planter, merchant, etc.), and projection of physical settings (Guyanese novels, for example, tend to convey a strong sense of the immense South American landscape that is absent in fiction set in the more limited physical space of islands). What they all share, however, is an affirmation of some aspect of local Caribbean reality.

■ The Late Twentieth Century and Beyond: The Dialectic of Return and Disillusionment

Inspired by political developments such as the birth of the West Indies Federation (1958) and the ousting of US-backed dictators in Cuba (1959) and the Dominican Republic (1961), many writers, artists, and intellectuals were returning to the region, literally as well as symbolically, even before the wave of national culture reached its peak in the mid-1960s. Perhaps inevitably, the idealism of homecoming clashed with the reality of enduring social divisions, political corruption, and economic dependence. Against a historical backdrop that included the breakup of the West Indies Federation in 1962 due to interisland rivalries, increasing restraints on free expression in Cuba after 1968, continuing problems of brutal dictatorship in Haiti and the Dominican Republic, and nagging dissatisfaction about the dependent status of Puerto Rico and French Caribbean territories, Caribbean literature from the past three decades has continued to express the desire for autonomy. At the same time, writers have posed radical questions about lingering barriers to full integration and liberation within single islands and the region as a whole. In Junot Díaz's Pulitzer Prize–winning mock-epic, *The Brief Wondrous Life of Oscar Wao,* for example, Dominican dictator-for-life Rafael Trujillo meets his end in a hail of bullets along a country road, but the system he embodied "was too powerful, too toxic a radiation to be dispelled so easily" (Diaz 2007:156). Lieutenants of the former regime continue to rule with corruption and violence, and eventually they destroy the life of Diaz's appealing antihero.

If the previous period was shaped by a dialectic of exile and nationalism, the most recent decades have been shaped by a new dialectic of return and disillusionment. The complexity of this dynamic is evident in "The Spoiler's

Return," a poem by the Nobel laureate Derek Walcott from his 1981 collection *The Fortunate Traveller.* Set in Port of Spain, Trinidad, "high on this bridge in Laventille" (Walcott 1992:432), the poem adopts the persona of Spoiler (Theophilus Phillips), a calypso king in 1953 and 1955, deceased in 1960, who was renowned for surreal, Kafkaesque lyrics featuring brain transplants, space travel, and irretrievable bank deposits (Rohlehr 1990:464–474).

Thematically, the poem follows in the calypso tradition of biting social critique, as Spoiler, upon his return from the grave, surveys the spectacle of postindependence decay. Objects singled out for commentary include unscrupulous business elites described as "sharks with shirt-jacs, sharks with well-pressed fins / ripping off we small-fry with razor grins"; murderous politicians "who promise free and just debate / then blow up radicals to save the state" (a reference to the 1981 assassination of historian and labor organizer Walter Rodney in Guyana); the once-popular Trinidadian prime minister, Eric Williams, whose disdain for the people is captured with the line "those with hearing aids turn off the truth"; and finally the general apathy that Spoiler attacks with the prediction that "all you go bawl out, 'Spoils, things ain't so bad.' / This ain't the Dark Ages, is just Trinidad" (Walcott 1992:433–434).

Against this scene of social decay, Spoiler's ghost becomes the perfect vehicle for protest, denunciation, and renewal with the claim, "I decompose, but I composin still" (Walcott 1992:432). Stylistically, Walcott embeds his social critique in the rhyming couplets utilized by calypsonians, signaling a primary identification with popular form. At the same time, he skillfully suggests a wider literary linkage by having Spoiler claim kinship with classical and neo-classical satirists Martial, Juvenal, and Pope, as well as his notoriously dyspeptic compatriot, V. S. Naipaul, whom Walcott-Spoiler dubs "V. S. Nightfall" (Walcott 1992:433).

The Influence of Popular Forms: Music, Film, and Drama

Walcott's immersion in calypso rhythms and rhetoric is indicative of a much broader process in the most recent decades of Caribbean literature, an intensification of links with popular cultural forms. Walcott's contemporary and peer, Kamau Brathwaite, has incorporated the faster rhythms of calypso as well as the slower Dread beats of reggae into his numerous volumes of poetry. In *History of the Voice* (1984), Brathwaite has theorized the practice of basing poetry on vernacular speech (including song), suggesting that the fundamental meter of Caribbean speech is dactylic in contrast to the iambic meter of British English (Brathwaite 1984:17). A younger generation of performance, or dub, poets has taken the linkage with music even farther. Artists such as Linton Kwesi Johnson, Michael Smith, Oku Onoru, Mutabaruka, and Binta Breeze have produced records and CDs on which they chant and sing their verse with backing from top-flight musicians. In prose writing, too, music has often been used in recent years to signal cultural resistance and recovery from cultural alienation. In Rosario Ferré's "Maldito amor" (literally, "cursed love," translated as "Sweet diamond dust," 1986), the title is taken directly from a nineteenth-century Puerto Rican composition and reflects the tortured interwoven histories of rich, poor, black, and white; the final vignette uses the clash between gangs favoring salsa and rock to symbolize rival political stances. Liliane Dévieux's heroine, in the short story "Piano-Bar" (1988), recovers a sense of her Haitianness and Caribbeanness by dancing to Dominican merengue and listening to "Haiti chérie," which evokes "the waves and undulations of the sea of the Antilles, the contours of our island, the bulging shapes of our mountains" (Dévieux 1991:74). In one of the most important recent follow-ups to Brathwaite's theorizing, poet and fiction writer Kwame Dawes has traced the influence of reggae on writing from Jamaica and the region as a whole. Referring to a "new reggae aesthetic," Dawes argues reggae music emerged as a working-class art form that "provided writers and other artists with an aesthetic model" and a "distinctively postcolonial aesthetic" from the 1960s down to the present (Dawes 1999:17–18).

Cinema, as well as music, has had a significant impact on popular and literary culture in the contemporary Caribbean. Cuban film throughout the post-revolution era has set consistently high standards both in quantity and quality. The work of Tomás Gutiérrez Alea, in particular, has been influential far beyond the local scene. His films range from *Memorias del subdesarrollo* (Memories of underdevelopment, 1968), *La muerte de un burócrata* (Death of a bureaucrat, 1966), and *Guantanamera* (1996), which offer biting critiques of intellectuals and bureaucratic absurdity; to *La última cena* (The last supper, 1976), a historical drama depicting a slave revolt on a colonial plantation; to *Fresa y chocolate* (Strawberry and chocolate, 1993), a comedy addressing the problem of homophobia and censorship. As elsewhere in the world, Caribbean cinema has included film versions of literary classics, including *El otro francisco* (1975, dir. Sergio Giral), a brilliant commentary on Suárez-Romero's 1839 novel *Francisco; Sugar Cane Alley* (1983, dir. Euzhan Palcy), a faithful rendering of Joseph Zobel's coming-of-age novel *La Rue Cases-Nègres;* and *The Orchid House* (1994, dir. Horace Ové), a six-hour miniseries for BBC based on Phyllis Shand Allfrey's novel. In one celebrated instance, the adaptation process worked in reverse, with Michael Thelwell's excellent novelization of the Jamaican cinema classic *The Harder They Come* (1972, dir. Perry Henzel).

Caribbean drama has also felt the impact of modern-day movements toward vernacular language and popular audiences. There has been a definite—though sporadic—art-house theater scene in the region from the time of colonial St. Domingue down to the contemporary period, with plays by Derek Walcott such as *The Sea at Dauphin* (1954) and *Ti Jean and His Brothers* (1958), as well as works by Aimé Césaire such as *La tragedie du Roi Christophe* (The tragedy of King Christophe, 1963) and *Une tempête* (A tempest, 1970). René Marqués (1929–1979) is Puerto Rico's most well-known playwright (as well as an important essayist); his *La carreta* (The oxcart, 1953) was another groundbreaking work that examined the conditions leading to the mass exodus of Puerto Ricans to New York. More recent decades, though, have seen the emergence of popular theater projects, beginning with Yard Theatre (mentioned above in the context of the Caribbean Artists Movement), Marina Maxwell's effort to produce theater by, for, and about the poor in Kingston, Jamaica. Also in Jamaica, drama has been used with great effectiveness as a tool of popular education and women's development by the Sistren Theater Collective. The success of Sistren extends not only to workshops on women's health, economic empowerment, and sex roles but also to video productions and a crucial volume of testimonial writing, *Lionheart Gal: Life Stories of Jamaican Women* (1986).

These significant developments in music, film, and drama, along with written literature produced in response to such popular forms, represented another attempt on the part of writers to work through the dialectic of return and disillusionment. Even as the experience of returning to the region has confronted artists and intellectuals with troubling examples of political and business leaders disconnected from the suffering majority, a large part of the creative response has been to push recent Caribbean writing ever closer to the majority voices by incorporating and responding to popular cultural forms.

The Achievement of Caribbean Women Writers

Unquestionably, the modern era is one in which women writers increasingly have come to define the field of Caribbean literature. The emergence of women (one is tempted to call it a *reemergence,* given the historical prominence of Anacaona, Prince, Ureña, Marson, Bennett, Jean Rhys, and others) is a phenomenon witnessed across the language groups. Recent anthologies of Caribbean women's writing like *Creation Fire, Green Cane and Juicy Flotsam, Her True-True Name,* and *The Whistling Bird* represent the transnational trend by including, in English-language publications, work from Francophone writers such as Mayotte Capécia, Marie-Thérèse Colimon-Hall, Marie Chauvet, Maryse Condé, Jacqueline Manicom, Simone Schwarz-Bart, Jan J. Dominique, and Edwidge Danticat (the latter two are Haitian writers who compose and publish primarily in English). Anglophone women writers include Erna Brodber, Michelle Cliff, Ramabai Espinet, Beryl Gilroy, Merle Hodge, Jamaica Kincaid, Velma Pollard, Olive Senior, and Jan Shinebourne. From the Spanish-speaking Caribbean, Julia Álvarez, Judith Ortíz Cofer, Rosario Ferré, Cristina García, Nancy Morejón, and Ana Lydia Vega have all published important, well-received works. Among Caribbean women writers from Suriname, the Netherlands Antilles, Aruba, and the Netherlands, key figures include Cándani, Thea Doelwijt, Chitra Gajadin, Trudi Guda, Nydia Ecury, Ellen Ombre, Astrid Roemer, Johanna Schouten-Elsenhout, and Bea Vianen.

Distilling any collective features out of such a diverse group of artists is practically impossible, but a few broad-brush comments may be useful for purposes of summing up the achievement of women writers in the Caribbean. Most important, perhaps, is that as a group women writers challenge many of the thematic concerns thought of as canonical in Caribbean writing. Women have not always enjoyed access to the material resources—such as academic scholarships—that allowed earlier generations of men to leave the region and experience what George Lamming called "the pleasures of exile." This is not to say that women have *not* traveled or that they have *not* contributed to the literature of exile and diasporic Caribbean living. There is, however, a marked emphasis on transforming immediate local reality, and this different focus is significant enough to challenge the exile-return dynamic that has defined so much male-authored Caribbean writing from the twentieth century.

Caribbean women also present serious challenges to the way male writers have thematized liberation and the quest for national autonomy. Women in classic Caribbean nationalist texts are often presented as marginal figures, passive objects, and helpmates, whereas men take the active roles in shaping history; not surprisingly, perhaps, women writers counter this tendency and place their women in more central and active roles. Also, whereas male-authored liberation narratives are often presented as externalized, filial rebellion modeled on the Caliban-Prospero conflict taken from Shakespeare's *The Tempest,* women writers often focus on internal states as the locus for freedom struggle, and they emphasize filial reconciliation with empowering ancestral traditions as much as rebellion against tradition.

▉ Conclusion

Caribbean literature in the early twenty-first century is vibrant and charged with the legacy of centuries—if not millennia—of intensive cultural adaptation to the material, political, and economic conditions of the region. Political domination and socioeconomic exploitation by first world powers and their local agents continue to structure cultural activity, as has been the case since 1492. Perhaps writers everywhere deal with social problems like poverty, unemployment, and violence that spawn alienation and disillusionment. Such problems, however, are particularly intense in the Caribbean. The resulting question of whether or not to commit one's art to social struggles is embraced by some— and rejected by others—but the pervasive urgency of the engagement question is a distinctive quality of Caribbean writing.

The tension between exile and return, or living a nomadic versus a locally rooted life, is one characteristic feature of the Caribbean experience that may have abated somewhat. The most recent generation of literary artists contains a significant number of writers, such as Julia Álvarez, Merle Collins, Edwidge Danticat, Junot Díaz, and others, whose work moves back and forth between pieces set in the Caribbean and others set in a diasporic milieu. These writers' responses to dislocation echo the work of earlier migrant voices stretching back to Mary Prince (at least), but the sense of binationalism and growing comfort with diasporic living evident in recent works arguably resolves some of the anxiety and polemics that have traditionally marked the issue of a Caribbean writer's physical location. Even the Cuban experience, which for decades was marked by a binary ultimatum characterized by exile or insularity, *gusanos* (traitors) or revolutionaries, Miami or Havana, has now become a much more flexible and dispersed arrangement, so that dozens of writers and artists come and go freely between the island and other destinations throughout the world. Cristina García's *Dreaming in Cuban* (1992), for example, narrates many passages back and forth between the island, South Florida, and New Jersey; each of the characters is in fact obsessed or preoccupied with his or her own private and diasporic idea of Cuba.

It is the capacity to reflect the region in all its kaleidoscopic diversity that defines Caribbean literature more than any other quality. Earlier periods have seen an emphasis on European, African, and East Indian cultural influences, and although those elements continue to be explored as aspects of Caribbean cultural identity, the present moment includes new developments such as the depiction of a Chinese Jamaican legacy (Patricia Powell's *The Pagoda,* 1998). As Surinamese literature becomes more widely disseminated through translation, English-language readers will be exposed to the growth in Javanese Caribbean writing, as well as literature in Sranantongo, the language of the maroon Bush Negroes, and writing in no less than four indigenous languages.

Fortunately for students and teachers interested in assimilating this vast field of literature, the contemporary period has also seen the Caribbean emerge as one of the most important arenas of literary and cultural criticism. The professionalization of literary studies through the University of the West Indies has produced a generation of first-rate critics and anthologists, including Carolyn Cooper, J. Michael Dash, Mervyn Morris, Kenneth Ramchand, Gordon Rohlehr, Elizabeth Wilson, and many others. There is also a pattern in the Caribbean of creative writers providing superb criticism. Literary figures including Antonio Benitez-Rojo, Kamau Brathwaite, Patrick Chamoiseau, Maryse Condé, Kwame Dawes, Edouard Glissant, Wilson Harris, George Lamming, and Sylvia Wynter have produced some of the most provocative and lucid critical commentaries available.

Again and again, in recent decades, critical discussions have returned to the idea of Caribbeanness as creolization. For Kamau Brathwaite, creolization refers to the "unplanned, unstructured, but osmotic relationship" that arises among various cultural traditions in a given island society (Brathwaite 1974: 6). Jean Bernabé, Patrick Chamoiseau, and Raphaël Confiant define *créolité* in similar terms as "the *interactional or transactional aggregate* of Caribbean, European, African, Asian, and Levantine cultural elements, united on the same soil by the yoke of history" (Bernabé, Chamoiseau, and Confiant 1990:889; emphasis in original). Creolization, critics emphasize, is a process of historical accretion, something one comes to understand through the work of historical recovery.

A useful concluding example explains both accretion and recovery as the keys that unlock Caribbeanness. This anecdote comes from Frank Martinus Arion, a multigenre writer from Curaçao, who explains how his efforts to track down the origins of the great curassow, a bird that symbolizes the island, opened up all the layers of colonial and precolonial history leading back to the Arawakan name for the bird, *pauwi*. After stopping the host of a radio show on animals in a Curaçaoan parking lot to show him an illustration of the bird, Arion writes, the two friends engage in the following conversation:

> "Are you in a hurry?" he asked at last.
> "No."
> "Let's go to my ranch then. I have a pair of them. Never knew this was the bird you were after. Had them all along. Got the hen from a doctor of Venezuelan descent. The cock from a lady when she heard I had a hen. Tremendously beautiful birds. They call them something like 'culo blanco.'"
> "Right. Pauwí culo blanco. Crax alector. Great Curassow. Black Curassow. Kòrsou Grandi. Pauwís. Powisi. Pauwili. Pauwiezen. Great Curaçao." I threw the groceries in his car and started for the Caribbean. (Arion 1998:452)

■ Bibliography

Abbad y Lasierra, Iñigo. *Historia geográfica, civil, y política de la isla de San Juan Bautista de Puerto Rico* (Geographic, civil, and political history of St. John the Baptist Island, Puerto Rico). Rio Piedras: Universidad de Puerto Rico, Editorial Universitaria, 1788.

Arion, Frank Martinus. "The Great Curassow or the Road to Caribbeanness." *Callaloo* 21, no. 3 (1998): 447–452.

Bernabé, Jean, Patrick Chamoiseau, and Raphaël Confiant. "In Praise of Creoleness." *Callaloo* 13, no. 2 (1990): 886–909.

Boxill, Anthony. "The Beginnings to 1929." In *West Indian Literature,* edited by Bruce King. London: Macmillan, 1979.

Brathwaite, Kamau. *Contradictory Omens: Cultural Diversity and Integration in the Caribbean.* Mona, Jamaica: Savacou, 1974.

———. *History of the Voice: The Development of Nation Language in Anglophone Caribbean Poetry.* London: New Beacon, 1984.

Bush, Barbara. *Slave Women in Caribbean Society, 1650–1838.* Kingston, Jamaica: Heinemann, 1990.

Campbell, Elaine, and Pierette Frickey, eds. *The Whistling Bird: Women Writers of the Caribbean.* Boulder, CO: Lynne Rienner, 1998.

Carpentier, Alejo. *Música en Cuba* (Music in Cuba). Havana: Editorial Letras Cubanas, 1979 [1946].

Césaire, Aimé. *The Collected Poems.* Translated with introduction and notes by Clayton Eshleman and Annette Smith. Berkeley: University of California Press, 1983.

Cobham-Sander, Rhonda. "The Creative Writer and West Indian Society: Jamaica, 1900–1950." Ph.D. diss., University of St. Andrews, Scotland, 1981.

Columbus, Christopher. "The Letter of Christopher Columbus on the Discovery of America." New York: Trustees of the Lennox Library, 1892.

Dawes, Kwame. *Natural Mysticism: Towards a New Reggae Aesthetic in Caribbean Writing.* Leeds, UK: Peepal Tree, 1999.

Dévieux, Liliane. "Piano-Bar." In *Green Cane and Juicy Flotsam: Short Stories by Caribbean Women,* edited by Carmen C. Esteves and Lizabeth Paravisini-Gebert. New Brunswick, NJ: Rutgers University Press, 1991.

Díaz, Junot. *The Brief Wondrous Life of Oscar Wao.* New York: Penguin/Riverhead Books, 2007.

Du Tertre, R. P. J. P. *Histoire Generale des Antilles Habiteés par les François* (General history of the Antillean French). Paris: T. Jolly, 1667, 1671.

Espinet, Ramabai, ed. *Creation Fire: A CAFRA Anthology of Caribbean Women's Poetry.* Toronto and Tunapuna, Trinidad: CAFRA and Sister Vision, 1990.

Esteves, Carmen C., and Lizabeth Paravisini-Gebert, eds. *Green Cane and Juicy Flotsam: Short Stories by Caribbean Women.* New Brunswick, NJ: Rutgers University Press, 1991.

Fouchard, Jean. *Langue et littérature des aborigènes d'Ayiti* (Language and literature of the natives of Haiti). Port-au-Prince, Haiti: Editions Henri Deschamps, 1988.

Goveia, Elsa. *A Study of the Historiography of the British West Indies to the End of the Nineteenth Century.* Washington, DC: Howard University Press, 1980.

Jones, Francis R., trans. "Kunawaraku's Song About Man-Eating Strangers." From a Dutch translation by Cees Koelewijn. *Callaloo* 21, no. 3 (1998): 511.

Kennedy, Ellen Conroy, ed. *The Negritude Poets: An Anthology of Translations from the French.* New York: Thunder's Mouth, 1989.

L'Ouverture, Toussaint. "Letter to the French Directory, 11/15/1796." In *The Black Jacobins: Toussaint L'Ouverture and the San Domingo Revolution,* by C. L. R. James. New York: Grove, 1989.

Mordecai, Pamela, and Betty Wilson, eds. *Her True-True Name: An Anthology of Women's Writing from the Caribbean.* Portsmouth, NH: Heinemann, 1989.

Philippe, Jean-Baptiste. *Free Mulatto.* Edited by Selwyn R. Cudjoe. Wellesley, MA: Calaloux, 1996.

Plácido [pseudonym of Gabriel de la Concepción Valdés]. "Despedida á mi madre" (Plácido's farewell to his mother). Translated by James Weldon Johnson. In *The Book of American Negro Poetry,* edited by James Weldon Johnson. New York: Harcourt Brace, 1959.

Prince, Mary. *The History of Mary Prince, a West Indian Slave, Related by Herself.* Edited by Moira Ferguson. Ann Arbor: University of Michigan Press, 1993.

Rohlehr, Gordon. *Calypso and Society in Pre-Independence Trinidad.* Tunapuna, Trinidad: Gordon Rohlehr, 1990.

Schomburg, Arthur A. "My Trip to Cuba in Quest of Negro Books." *Opportunity* (February 1933): 48–50.

Sistren, with Honor Ford Smith. *Lionheart Gal: Life Stories of Jamaican Women.* Toronto: Sister Vision Press, 1987.

Thomas, J[ohn]. J[acob]. *The Theory and Practice of Creole Grammar.* Introduction by Gertrude Buscher. London, Trinidad: New Beacon, 1989.

Walcott, Derek. *Dream on Monkey Mountain and Other Plays.* New York: Farrar, Straus, and Giroux, 1970.

———. *Collected Poems, 1948–1984.* London and Boston: Faber and Faber, 1992.

Walmsley, Anne. *The Caribbean Artists Movement, 1966–1972: A Literary and Cultural History.* London: New Beacon, 1992.

12

The Caribbean Diaspora

Dennis Conway

International migration is one of the Caribbean region's most fundamental demographic processes, contributing to the population diversity that characterizes the contemporary societies of this region. After the decimation of its indigenous peoples—some would characterize it as a genocide—following their encounter with early Spanish adventurers, the Caribbean was peopled largely by waves of immigrants from Europe and Africa with smaller proportions from Asia. Colonial conquests; mass movements from the Old World to the Americas; mass enslavement and forced migration; indentured recruitments; selective streams of influential or distinctive minorities; and significant return flows, counterstreams, and interregional transfers characterize the migration history of the region. The Caribbean was, therefore, settled by immigrants, and the subsequent Caribbean diaspora in part grew out of these early mobility patterns.

Old World movements beget New World movements. African and European diasporas were reformed to become Caribbean diasporas. There were substantial reversals in this transition as Caribbean diasporas crossed the Atlantic once again, with European colonial mother countries as their focus. Eventually, these ties to Europe, though persisting to this day in some Caribbean societies, would give way to ties to North America (both Canada and the United States). Other destinations in the Western Hemisphere would also host Caribbean immigrants and international circulators, both within the Caribbean and on the Central American isthmus. The Caribbean diasporas gradually became widespread and multilocal in their nature. As these systems evolved, the island home society remained the "homeland" hub, oftentimes functionally real but also imagined. In addition, the widening net of dispersed streams changed the circuits from bipolar linkages—as between island and mainland or between small island and large neighbor—to multiple island-to-island links and multiple

island-to-mainland enclave networks. Although early paths became well trod-
den and so traditional that they were entrenched in many a country's social
memory, new international paths were constantly being added as opportunities
arose elsewhere.

Changes also occurred in the character of the streams within the networks.
Notably, the last quarter-century has witnessed significant changes in the dynamics of Caribbean diasporas. Emigration (relatively permanent movement)
and return migration have increased in importance. International movements
within the region, as well as extraregional international moves, have contributed
to a more complex map of the diasporas than the commonly accepted models
of Caribbean–to United States movements would predict. International circulation (temporary, reciprocal, and cyclical movement) also has become a more
common voluntary transnational practice among the region's wealthier classes,
as well as an adaptation to the socioeconomic and biophysical crises the regions'
displaced and less fortunate people have experienced—rural poverty; crop
failures; and destruction caused by hurricanes, flooding, and volcanic activity.
As a distinct category of "forced" international moves, refugee flights—people fleeing persecution, economic hardship, or environmental destruction—
might be smaller in volume than other forms of international circulation, but
their size belies their significance in the political and economic affairs of affected Caribbean countries (Guyana and Haiti, for example), not to mention
their impact on host North American and European societies. Irregular migration, the more neutral term for the unauthorized, or illegal, "cross-border" movement of human trafficking and smuggling, for clandestine entry, or for those
overstaying their visiting visas, is also not a major outflow in comparison to
other Caribbean extraregional movements. Yet the widely accepted association
of irregular migration with illicit narcotics smuggling and with the threat of
terrorism has contributed to a rising tide of anti-immigrant xenophobia evident
within US political circles from the local to the federal level, making Caribbean irregular migration in North America an important contemporary policy
subject to be covered in this chapter.

Within the Caribbean diaspora communities of the twenty-first century,
transnational multilocal networks of migrants, families, and an ever-widening
circle of kin have become entrenched systems of interchange that link social
groups, diasporic families, and widely dispersed communities in the Caribbean, Europe, North America, and beyond. Oceania, East Asia, South Asia and
Southeast Asia, and even Russia are becoming emerging spaces of opportunity
for small numbers among the region's globally connected "skilled-workers
without borders." These networks facilitate the exchange of people, goods, information, ideas, cultural traditions, and material benefits among far-flung diasporas. For many, the Caribbean world has grown to incorporate Caribbean
communities in Toronto, Montreal, New York, Miami, Amsterdam, London, and
Paris into a wider pan-Caribbean network. Global corporate expansion, global

chains of resource extraction and production, and commercial and information exchange have exerted an increasing influence on patterns of international movement of the region's transnational elites, so that class and material wealth distinctions are adding further to the complexity of diasporic communities and their global reach. Through the first decade of the twenty-first century, they have become important extensions of the homeland society, in ways unimagined during the early postcolonial days of the mid-twentieth century.

A complete history of Caribbean diasporas would have to detail the interisland patterns of human movements of aboriginal people during the pre-encounter era, as well as the international mobility patterns of the next 500 years. However, a more modest agenda is proposed for this chapter. First, a brief historical account of the patterns of immigration and settlement of the region will demonstrate how mobility and its accompanying external influences gave each Caribbean territory its own cultural mosaic. Also demonstrated are the importance of immigration and emigration in the crosscurrents of interisland interdependence, as well as how the exchange of people within the region contributes to a common Caribbean experience. Eventually, in the first half of the twentieth century, and in large part as a response to the declining fortunes of national economies and ecologies, colonial neglect, and growing destitution of the masses, emigrations and wide-flung diasporas overtook immigration as the most significant demographic force. Profound socioeconomic and political changes across the region had a significant impact on patterns of emigration and on diasporic communities throughout the decades following World War II. In the aftermath of the events of September 11, 2001, heightened security concerns in the United States, and to a somewhat lesser extent in European destinations of Caribbean hopefuls, have prompted policy changes that may affect Caribbean peoples' cross-border options. Accordingly, the latter part of the chapter takes up these recent periods of transformation and illustrates the complexity of today's Caribbean diasporas as their accompanying transnational networks affect the migration options of many people differently and as the movers and stayers in turn affect their home societies, their mainland enclave communities, and the family networks that sustain these transnational mechanisms.

■ The Encounter with Europe: Domination of the Caribbean

The initial encounter between Europeans and Caribbeans in 1492 ushered in the first of a series of immigrant waves that would fundamentally influence the Caribbean's demographic trajectory. Claiming sovereignty over the newly discovered territory, the Spanish crown enlisted the services of adventurers such as Christopher Columbus to aid colonization. For political and religious reasons, only Spanish citizens qualified as immigrant colonists—*conquistadores* (conquerors), *encomenderos* (those to whom Indians were entrusted), or *hacendados* (landowners). However, the importance of these immigrants lay more with their power, authority, and influence than with their numerical size. Although their population continued to increase, albeit modestly, the numerically dominant Amerindian populations suffered calamitous declines. The causes were many: European-introduced diseases and epidemics, the destruction of indigenous systems, enslavement, and mass deportation to the New Spain mainland (Mexico). All too soon, the declining indigenous populations prompted the colonizers to seek new, replenishable sources of labor from across the oceans. They recruited yeoman farmers from Iberia, bought slaves shipped from Africa, and recruited indentured servants from other parts of their colonial empires.

For the Portuguese in Brazil, Dutch managers served their masters and developed sugarcane plantations, and later they were invited to British West Indian islands to improve technology and profits. Toward the end of the sixteenth century, an active slave trade was fostered. The Spanish operated their system directly from Africa to licensed ports in the Americas such as Santo Domingo, Veracruz, and Cartagena. The British, active in the slave trade and the intensive use of slave labor, trafficked slaves to their West Indian plantation colonies from West African ports. The French and Dutch colonists and planters also relied on the large-scale trading of slaves; as many as 12 million Africans were transported across the Middle Passage against their will—a forced transatlantic diaspora of lasting significance. Other parts of the respective colonial empires were continually being scoured for indentured labor or domestic servants, but this phase of forced importation of Africans brought about changes in regional population concentrations that would persist to the present day: the demographic dominance of Afro-Caribbean racial majorities. Just about all the Caribbean islands, regardless of European colonial ties, experienced a similar Afro-Caribbean racial transformation. Cuba was profoundly transformed, as was St. Domingue (the former French colony that became independent Haiti). Small islands like Barbados and Antigua soon had Afro-Caribbean majorities of 90 percent, and even among the larger West Indian islands, like Jamaica, an Afro-Caribbean majority emerged. Puerto Rico and the Dominican Republic, in contrast, did not experience such a dramatic racial transition.

Throughout the fifteenth and sixteenth centuries the slave trade and the plantation economies were so profitable that other European colonial powers successfully challenged Spanish hegemony. Buccaneers and privateers plundered the Caribbean's Spanish Main. As Stephen Randall shows in Chapter 3, French and British navies fought pivotal battles, armies built strategic fortifications and enlisted the services of indigenous militias, and politicians traded the dominions, haggling over terms that kept the colonial administrations in a constant state of insecurity. The island archipelago of the Lesser Antilles was one such battleground; the Caribbean coast of Central America was another region of British colonial expansion and mercantile control. Earlier recruitment

Former slave trading center, Curaçao.

of European yeomanry to settle and farm these possessions at first relied on land and property enticements and then arranged deportations and persecution of religious minorities. These efforts brought several ethnic minorities—Welsh Royalists, Dutch Jews, Syrians (Levantines), and Madeiran Portuguese—to the region. When plantations demonstrated their profitability, however, buying easily replaceable labor from Africa proved to be the Caribbean's answer.

Producing sugarcane with slave labor, the plantation economies of the French, British, and Dutch colonial possessions in the Caribbean became profitable. Enormous profits accrued to European colonialists, slavers, planters, crown governments and administrations, and the merchant classes. This agricultural industry flourished for the next 150 years, but most of the generated capital left the islands to promote commerce and industrialization in the imperial heartlands and to support political careers in Europe. Not surprisingly, the environmental consequences of this wholesale transformation of small-island landscapes to cultivable acreages were dramatic. As Duncan McGregor discusses in Chapter 7, eventually (and inevitably) many of the smaller islands' ecological systems became seriously degraded. There was, however, plentiful land for plantation expansion elsewhere in the Caribbean, and newer development in Trinidad, the British and Dutch Guianas, Santo Domingo, and Puerto Rico consolidated the need for more African slaves. Although Great Britain outlawed the slave trade in 1807 and called for the abolition of slavery in 1834, Caribbean plantations still needed labor. With many of the former slaves intent on moving off the plantation or off the island, if necessary, the newer plantations of the Guianas and Trinidad were able to recruit them, thereby initiating interregional migration streams from small islands to these larger territories (Richardson 1983). The plantations, however, needed more labor than could be provided by such interregional mechanisms.

Following the abolition of slavery and after a brief experimentation with apprenticeship arrangements, plantation owners and island administrations recruited indentured laborers to solve their labor shortages. The region therefore experienced another wave of mass immigration, this time from Asia. China was the largest source, followed by India. Chinese men and, later, women were brought into Cuba and several British territories (including Jamaica, British Guiana, and Trinidad) to work as plantation laborers. Although mainly recruited for field labor, many of the Chinese who took up their indenture option to remain rather than be repatriated gravitated to urban commerce, such as dry goods, laundries, and restaurants. Approximately 500,000 East Indians (as they were called) undertook indentured contracts to work on the plantations of Trinidad, Jamaica, and British Guiana. Remaining behind were approximately 150,000 East Indians in Trinidad, 21,500 in Jamaica, and 240,000 in British Guiana. Later, but under similar indenture contractual arrangements, 20,000 Hindustanis (also from India) and 30,000 Javanese (from the Dutch colony of Java) were brought to the new plantation estates in the coastal lowlands of Dutch Guiana. Unlike the Chinese, most East Indian laborers stayed in rural surroundings after their indentured contracts expired, some continuing to serve as plantation workers, while others formed a small-farmer sector.

However, indenturing wasn't the only labor recruitment strategy. There was continued recruitment of immigrant minorities from southern Europe and the European imperial homelands. In the Spanish colonies of Cuba, the Dominican Republic, and Puerto Rico, administrations and planters encouraged white immigration from Europe, in large part fearing the loss of cultural dominance and the demographic threat of the Afro-Caribbean racial majority.[1] Elsewhere among British possessions, there were attempts to attract former slaves from North America, and some colonization by free Africans was promoted and accomplished.

Seventeenth-century British colonization of the Atlantic Caribbean coast of the Central American isthmus also established enclave dominions in an area that would subsequently come under North American corporate control. The British encouraged their own settlers to exploit the forest and land resources in places such as British Honduras (Belize), Bluefields (in Nicaragua), and the Bay Islands off Honduras. Elsewhere along the Mosquito Coast of Nicaragua, the British allied with the native Indians in their conflicts with the weak Spanish administrators, trading firearms and even setting up British-educated puppet monarchs, who declared loyalty to the British crown. When the Central American republics gained political independence in the 1820s, Britain retained control of British Honduras, challenged the sovereignty of their republican claim over the Bay Islands and the Mosquito Coast, and generally supported British colonial enclave communities via commercial linkages. Later in the early nineteenth century, a more successful challenge to this British control would come from an independent United States (Sunshine 1985).

The eighteenth century witnessed the genesis of international connections between the Caribbean and the US–North American mainland, both in terms of capital investment circulating and people migrating. At the very beginning of the plantation era, the demise of white yeoman small farming in the West Indies had prompted the more adventurous to emigrate to the North American mainland colonies to start again. Later, some successful planters expanded their family properties to start mainland plantations. For example, Barbadian planters settled and prospered in South Carolina, and Barbadian merchant families established links with Baltimore. Louisiana–St. Domingue (Haiti) connections were entrenched from these earliest colonial beginnings, and migration and circulations between Cuba, St. Domingue, and Louisiana further enmeshed Caribbean and Gulf Coast societies in a common cultural heritage: part Creole, part Hispanic, part Acadian. The triangular trade of sugar, manufactured goods, foodstuffs, timber, cotton, and tobacco, which involved merchant houses with interests in Britain, its North American colonies, and the Caribbean, cemented imperial and transatlantic mercantilist linkages, served planter's interests, and furthered interconnections. In the process the trade deepened and entrenched the dependent relations of the Caribbean with external forces and influences. The wealth that was created in the region was always circulating out of it, and the region's people were to respond likewise as conditions worsened.[2]

■ Caribbean–North American Circulations, 1880–1970

Turmoil in the financial sector, including the failure of many banks in London, New York, and Boston during the financial depression of the 1880s, left many planters bankrupt and brought about wrenching structural changes in several small islands, among them St. Vincent and Tobago. Between 1880 and 1924, all the Caribbean's plantation economies became severely depressed; local populations suffered deepening impoverishment as a result. Several colonial administrations advocated or permitted safety-valve emigration, though few actually legislated this politically sensitive policy. Voluntary emigration and circulation was an option taken up by the more fortunate. Wealthier traders and businesspeople fled the hard times using the improved steamship services to New York, with Jamaicans, Barbadians, and Trinidadians emigrating to New York and Boston. Others moved with the help of their ethnic networks to havens in less-hard-hit Caribbean territories. Emigration to the colonial homeland was always an option for the more privileged elite classes, and sons and daughters were duly shipped off to be educated in European institutions, as befitting their social station in life.

International circulation via short-term labor contracts was the only available opportunity for the impoverished masses in the British West Indies. The Colonial Office and local administrations no longer viewed these possessions as good investments now that sugarcane was losing the competition with home-grown European beet sugar. The Asian economies of the British Empire promised much more, so the West Indies was basically neglected. Not surprisingly, British West Indian contract labor was recruited all over the Western Hemisphere, especially in Central and South America. US business interests were expanding in the hemisphere, and labor was much in demand. British West Indian men and women circulated, labored, and succumbed as they helped construct the Panama Canal. Between 1900 and 1914, some 60,000 Barbadians labored in Panama, and one estimate states that 20,000 died between 1906 and 1912. As many as 121,000 Jamaicans labored in Cuban sugar fields and factories between 1902 and 1932. Thousands of Leeward Islanders—Kittians, Antiguans, Nevisians, Montserratians—traveled as so-called deckers for temporary jobs in the US-owned sugar industry in the Dominican Republic. US Virgin Islanders and Bahamians circulated to Miami in the first decade of the twentieth century, helping to build a gateway metropolis in Florida. Middle-class Jamaicans, Barbadians, and Trinidadians and wealthier small-islanders circulated to West Indian communities in New York and Boston, with considerable emigration occurring as the return circuit was postponed indefinitely, the intended repatriation forgone in favor of staying in their adopted country. The diasporas were becoming embedded and the networks entrenched in the social fabric of the islands.

The 1924–1940 period was one of continued hard times and limited opportunities for the Caribbean masses. The Caribbean economy remained grim, and there was another crash in world sugar prices in 1933. Coincidentally, anti-immigrant (i.e., nativist) sentiments were heightened in the United States, in large part due to the massive influxes of new immigrants (from Italy, Greece, other southern and eastern European regions, and China) that the country had experienced during the preceding two decades. Accordingly, the Immigration Act of 1924 (the Johnson-Reed Act) promulgated a discriminatory national quota system for Asians and Caribbean peoples—limiting the number of immigrants from any country to an annual quota based on the number of nationals already in residence in the United States in 1920. Elsewhere in the Caribbean Basin, restrictive immigration legislation in Venezuela, Cuba, and the Dominican Republic also discriminated against previously welcomed black visitors. Repatriation was encouraged, and Haitians, Jamaicans, and small-islanders returned to swell the ranks of the unemployed masses back home. The only labor opportunities available in the region were in oil-related industries in the Netherlands Antilles (Aruba and Curaçao) and Trinidad. Small-islanders from places like Grenada, Barbados, Antigua, and St. Kitts took advantage of that employment opportunity. Other small-islanders continued patterns of circulation wherever they could find opportunities: in interisland trade and commerce or working passages and joining the merchant marine, often as not relying on networks provided by previous emigrants.

With US entry into World War II, labor needs increased as US men went off to war, and the agricultural sector and industries needed boosts in output; this started another international labor recruitment drive. *Braceros* (manual laborers) were recruited from Mexico as farm labor, and Caribbean cane cutters joined this program. For many of the unemployed in the Caribbean, circulation via short-term labor contracts to the United States was again possible under the US War Manpower Act, although the door quickly slammed shut again in 1952. In addition, World War II also saw many colonial regiments "doing their duty" in the European theater, and the mobilization of these war veterans would soon lead to a restructuring of colonial ties, to the growth of radical social movements, and to the onset of decolonization.

Predictably, the post–World War II period (1945–1965) was one of mass emigration from Caribbean colonies to a variety of European metropoles, particularly Britain, France, and the Netherlands. Emigrants left the British West Indies for British cities in response to massive recruitment schemes to staff service industries and administrations in the 1950s. Thousands of West Indians emigrated, exercising their right to take advantage of employment and educational opportunities in Great Britain. Some of the smaller Windward and Leeward Islands experienced depopulation and aging during this mass emigration; Montserrat lost almost 10 percent of its people, and Carriacou, a ward island of Grenada, lost 20 percent of its residents (Lowenthal 1972). Many intended to return, and some did return to their Caribbean homelands upon retirement, but significant numbers stayed. The influx of "New Commonwealth" immigrants from the West Indies, Pakistan, and India gradually aroused racist sentiments and fears, however. Eventually and abruptly, this alien immigration was terminated in 1962. The restrictive and discriminatory Commonwealth Immigration Act effectively stemmed the flow. Smaller numbers of Caribbean people of color also emigrated from French *départements d'outre mer* (overseas departments) like Guadeloupe, Martinique, and French Guiana to France and from the Netherlands Antilles (islands such as Aruba, Bonaire, Curaçao, and St. Maarten) and Dutch Guiana to the Netherlands. These streams were selective circulations, that is, emigrations of elites and youths from the small professional and middle classes among colonial societies. Most remained in Europe, and return flows were numerically small. Financial limitations (notably the high cost of transatlantic travel) prohibited most from considering this option, even if they had always intended to return (Rubenstein 1979).

In North America, a similar colony-to-metropole diaspora sprung to life as Puerto Ricans sought opportunities on the mainland. The rapid development plan for Puerto Rico (Operation Bootstrap) involved a massive restructuring of the island's agricultural sector. It embraced a modernization strategy of industrialization-by-invitation, and the ensuing rapid industrialization and urbanization in Puerto Rico were accompanied by mass circulation between the island and US metropolitan centers, particularly New York City and Spanish Harlem. Between 1955 and 1970, approximately one-third of the Puerto Rican population moved off the island, perhaps as many as 70 percent heading for New York City. By 1970 more than 1 million Puerto Ricans had moved to the mainland, with New York City, Miami, and Chicago hosting substantial enclave communities. Many moved back and forth between the island and their adopted city, attempting to achieve the best of both worlds—culture and identity in the former; money, material wealth, and skills in the latter (Ellis, Conway, and Bailey 1996; Lowenthal 1972).

Cuban links to the US mainland also strengthened during this period. A coup by Fulgencio Batista in 1952 prompted a stream of exiles to flee to Florida, where they set up an expatriate political base. Between 1951 and 1959, approximately 10,000 Cubans became permanent US residents, but this influx was swamped by the historic exodus following Fidel Castro's ascension to power in 1959. Between 1959 and 1962 the exodus of middle-class Cubans accompanied the consolidation of Castro's regime. Approximately 1 million Cubans fled, with two-thirds heading for the US mainland. A significant minority moved to Puerto Rico, where they soon formed a powerful immigrant business class. Miami and New York were the main destinations for these political refugees, and gradually, as their domestic power consolidated, the Cuban presence in Miami strengthened. Later, exiled Cubans moved to this Latino city, and Miami's Cuban community constituted more than 60 percent of the total Cuban American population (Boswell and Curtis 1984). For other Caribbean hopefuls in the region, the Immigration and Nationality Act of 1952 (the McCarran-Walter Act) reaffirmed the 1924 discriminatory quota system; it was not until 1965 that Caribbean people—other than Puerto Ricans and Cubans— were able to seek overseas opportunities in the United States.

A watershed moment for international mobility was the period from 1965 to 1970, dictated by fundamental changes in US immigration policy and practices. Additionally, a fundamental restructuring of Latin American and Caribbean economic fortunes ensued in the 1970s and persists to the present day. This chapter closes, therefore, with an examination and illumination of the latest phase in the development of complex Caribbean diaspora networks, where regional, hemispheric, and transnational mobility is bringing about significant demographic and cultural transformations of what were distinctive cultural milieus.

▪ Caribbean Diaspora Networks, 1970s to the Present

Prior to the 1970s, the Caribbean was a region first of significant immigration, then selective emigration streams, and then continued interregional immigration. Initially, European imperial powers received immigrants from their colonies, but eventually North American hegemony held sway. Emigration from the British West Indies in the decades following World War II was considerable.

In particular, during the 1955–1961 period perhaps as much as 6 percent of the islands' population left for the imperial homeland—150,000 Jamaicans, 19,000 Barbadians, and some 8,000 from the small islands of St. Kitts and Nevis, Dominica, Grenada, and St. Lucia. Those numbers were matched in succeeding decades by increased immigration and residence in the United States, in large part because of the longer duration of entry that country afforded to Caribbean petitioners. In particular, greater numbers of Trinidadians, Guyanese, and Antiguans moved to the United States in the 1970s than the United Kingdom during the peak entry period (1955–1961), many of them choosing New York City as their Caribbean "home away from home" (Conway and Cooke 1996).

The globalization of the world's economic order in accordance with market principles, which began in the late 1970s, continued through the 1980s and 1990s, and is still imposing neoliberal policies today, led to several changes in Caribbean migration patterns. Some migrations were continuations of past trends, whereas others evolved into new mobility forms and practices. Widespread indebtedness, recessions, increasing polarization of classes, and declines in living standards, among other things, have been structural realities throughout the region during this time, such that emigration continued as a survival strategy for the impoverished, the desperate, and the displaced. Although emigration has replaced immigration as the region's defining demographic process, interregional immigration was problematic for a few Caribbean islands (e.g., the Cayman Islands, the Bahamas, and Trinidad and Tobago) whose economic fortunes turned upward.

Throughout the 1990s, there was continued economic hardship for many at the bottom of the social order in the Caribbean. This was further exacerbated in some islands by outbreaks of civil unrest and violence, as well as by natural disasters and ecological calamities, which have initiated several streams of refugees—from Guyana, Haiti, and Montserrat, in particular. International circulation and temporary movements to neighboring or more distant places became a common strategy for many regardless of their skill levels, and well-entrenched networks facilitate such sojourning patterns. In addition, more opportunities arose for educated and highly skilled Caribbean people to leave for more education, better jobs, or skill enhancement, to the extent that policymakers bemoaned this extraregional "brain drain." Again, as a continuation of colonial and postcolonial practices, these Caribbean emigrants took advantage of these overseas opportunities in time-honored ways, drawing upon their flexibility, their resourcefulness, their initiative, and even their cultural capital (e.g., musical and athletic talents) to seek livelihoods in other parts of the Caribbean, in North America, in Europe, and farther afield in the globalizing marketplace for skilled professionals.

By the turn of the century, however, the pace of global economic expansion had diminished, yet the transnational networks and diasporic communities that had grown and deepened did not follow suit. Indeed, multilocal networks of social interaction and exchange across borders, within and between Caribbean island "stay-at-homes" and their family-linked, enclave extensions abroad continued to strengthen. These well-established transnational networks grew and diversified in terms of numbers involved, capital exchanged, and the stocks of human, social and commercial power and influence they generated for their participants. How Caribbean diasporas evolved into a hemispheric network incorporating North American and other metropolitan communities with their Caribbean counterparts is one of the final pieces of the story. The other "piece" is the growing political importance of Caribbean irregular migration into the United States, not so much because of any major increases, but more because of the growing anti-immigrant sentiments against "immigrants of color" fostered by the heightened tensions of the post September 11 era of a "geography of fear" and an accompanying hysterical obsession with border security (Miller 2006).

Three major immigration policy changes in the mid-1960s heralded this new era. First, restrictive legislation in Britain effectively "slammed the door" to that country's Commonwealth Caribbean immigrants in 1961. Then, in 1962, new Canadian immigration legislation removed racial discriminatory biases for entry requirements, opening another route to North America for Commonwealth Caribbean immigrants. In the United States, the 1965 Immigration and Nationality Act replaced the race-biased national origin–led entry system and established a set of seven preference categories, with family reunification as the underlying objective. Later, in 1976, the US Congress established a preference for countries in the Western Hemisphere, allocated ceilings for individual countries, and enacted conditions facilitating the entry of relatives and family of US residents. Then, the 1978 and 1980 amendments to the Immigration and Nationality Act extended the entry ceilings of this preference system. That opportunity was exploited by would-be Caribbean emigrants.

Well-established Caribbean communities in Miami, New York, Boston, Washington, D.C., New Jersey, and Hartford, Connecticut, provided family- and kin-based networks and links to support US-bound migration. Temporary trips (circulations) between island homes and mainland enclaves were open to many Jamaicans, Trinidadians, and Barbadians, among others; six-month sojourns using visitor visas became a common practice. Also beginning in the mid-1960s, there was a steady flow of professionals and youths from the Dominican Republic to New York City, which rapidly grew to mass circulation and emigration between island and city. By 1980, a net estimate of Dominicans residing on the US mainland was 400,000, most in the Washington Heights area of New York (Grasmuck and Grosfoguel 1997; Morrison and Sinkin 1982).

Prior to the 1970s, professional advancement, alienation with island society, and acclimatization to metropolitan ideals and standards of living (often inculcated while being educated abroad) had encouraged emigration of a self-selected group of highly educated individuals from the middle and elite classes, either to regional metropolitan countries or to Canada and the United States. The emigration of these groups of voluntary exiles (émigrés) was sometimes emulated by middle-class professionals—Trinidadian and Jamaican nurses,

Company providing services (transfer, telecommunications, travel)
to enable Latino immigrants to remain connected with
family members abroad, Washington Heights, New York.

for example, who were recruited by agencies or by others already established in New York City or Toronto's health sectors—who sought better opportunities in Canada and the United States, where they could practice their professions (Henry 1990).

In the 1970s this brain drain of émigré professionals translated into mass flights from the deteriorating conditions and political unrest brought about by mismanaged and often repressive regimes during the late 1960s and 1970s. During François "Papa Doc" Duvalier's regime in Haiti in the 1960s, almost three-quarters of the middle (i.e., professional) classes fled to French Canada. It was not until the 1970s that this exodus was followed by flights of small-business operators and peasants. These lower-class Haitians not only went to French Canada but also transited through the Bahamas to Miami or found their way to the Caribbean communities in Brooklyn (Conway and Cooke 1996). Later, political unrest continued to plague the country, even after Jean-Claude "Baby Doc" Duvalier fled into exile in 1986, and successive US administrations attempted (rather unsuccessfully) to establish a democratic regime in that troubled and impoverished country. The result was continued pressure to emigrate, and South Florida was the destination for an influx of Haitian boat people that was unfairly depicted by the media as an "invasion." The unfortunate refugees generally were not well treated by immigration authorities.

Cubans, by contrast, had to wait several years after the early-1960s mass exodus before the Castro regime relaxed its emigration restrictions and allowed more to leave. Immediately, Cuban Americans in Florida initiated a comprehensive airlift of Cuban refugees, and this private sector transport effort continued until 1973, with some 300,000 persons fleeing to Miami and elsewhere in the United States. During the remainder of the 1970s, the exodus became a trickle, with many fleeing the island via intermediate countries such as Mexico, Spain, Venezuela, and Jamaica. Then, in April 1980, aspiring émigré Cubans received another window of opportunity, and for five months a flotilla of small boats ferried more than 100,000 people between Mariél in Cuba and Miami in what has become known as the Mariél Boatlift-Bincops. However, these "Marielitos" were not treated as preferentially as their forerunners. Among them was a sizable group of Cuban prisoners, of whom some 5,000 had been released with significant criminal records (Boswell and Curtis 1984). This criminal stigma colored the US public's assessment of the Marielitos.

To the growing anti-immigration lobby in the United States, Cubans were no longer distinguishable from other invasions of colored foreigners from the Caribbean, Latin America, and Africa. Many of the hard-core criminals among the Mariél refugees received severe treatment and were incarcerated in high-security US federal penitentiaries. Despite the growing negative feelings directed at this latest wave of Cuban émigrés, Cuban refugees continued to receive preferential treatment from US immigration authorities because they were fleeing a communist regime. By contrast, many Haitians claiming political refugee status were not treated as well, and throughout the 1980s they were uncritically assessed as economic refugees and therefore didn't qualify for refugee admission. It wasn't until 1996 that US president Bill Clinton's administration mandated that all refugees (including Cubans) were to be treated similarly by the US Immigration and Naturalization Service (INS).

Illegal entry into and sojourns in neighboring Caribbean countries increased in importance and in volume from the mid-1970s onward. Many sought opportunities in other Caribbean countries experiencing relative prosperity due to tourism, the oil industry, or continued colonial support. In addition to attracting professionals from within the region, the tourism and oil industries provided opportunities for the less-skilled as they parlayed agricultural backgrounds into work in construction, repair, and maintenance. That continued a long-held tradition in many stagnant rural communities in the Caribbean, which use intraregional migration as a means to escape impoverishment in declining agricultural sectors at home while retaining home ties and the promise of return. Well-established paths emerged within and throughout the Caribbean, and current circulation and migration trajectories still follow such routes. Nevisians and Kittians transit to Antigua, St. Thomas in the US Virgin Islands, and elsewhere; St. Lucians transit to Barbados, to Trinidad, and elsewhere. The Grenadian-Trinidad circuit is well entrenched, and Vincentians who also go to Trinidad appear in appreciable numbers in New York City. Those from Dominica, by contrast, have chosen neighboring Martinique and Guadeloupe as their preferred transit, and some find their way to Paris and Europe via those islands.

Sometimes, routes include ports of call in San Juan, Puerto Rico, Miami, New York, or Toronto, metropolitan locales that may be terminals or transits. Retaining the widest set of options possible, Caribbean migrants anticipate or at least do not reject the possibility of returning to their Caribbean home. While in the United States, many prefer to retain their original citizenship. Others take US citizenship to sponsor further migrations of family members.

In the United States, passage of the 1986 Immigration Reform and Control Act granted amnesty to 2 million unauthorized alien residents and refugees, particularly Haitians, Dominicans, and Cubans. Eventually, through the early 1990s they would be granted green cards and permanent residency status. Not surprisingly, the "lost decade" of the 1980s witnessed the largest volumes of visiting and resident entries to the United States from the Caribbean of any decade in the twentieth century. In 1990 amendments to the Immigration and Nationality Act increased admission quotas for highly skilled young women and men in under-supplied occupations, such as nursing and medical technology, which opened the door to the recruitment of health services technicians and practitioners, scientists, and even athletes from the Caribbean. Still, unauthorized entries troubled US officials; the differential treatment of specific streams of refugees (such as the Haitians and Cubans) troubled civil rights groups; and the downturns of the Californian economy from the mid-1980s onward aided and abetted anti-immigrant rhetoric. The 1990s became a decade in which anti-immigrant sentiment and political positioning in California, and to a lesser extent in Florida, heightened tensions and fomented restrictive immigration policies. In 1996 there was a reversal of US immigration policies, with Congress passing the Illegal Immigration Reform and Immigrant Responsibility Act, which mandated the rapid deportation of "criminal" resident aliens; enacted higher penalties for overstayers; restricted legal immigrants' access to welfare programs and some of their benefits; and increased surveillance at the US-Mexican border. Yet the decade would end with less punitive provisions in place, as well as a mobilization of Latino voters in California that effectively reversed that state's anti-immigrant stance. Increases in recruitment of highly skilled immigrants were proposed and enacted, and security at the border with Mexico was couched more within the context of the war on drugs than as illegal, or irregular, immigration.

▣ The Deepening of Transnational Networks and Cross-Border Development

For the most part, the same migration mechanisms used in the 1980s and 1990s have remained in play, although multilocal transnational family networks beyond North America have widened further, and temporary visiting and circulating appears to be on the rise. Increases in migrant-donor activities across borders also have become substantial, with remittance flows now recognized as major transnational exchanges of capital (providing much needed "hard currency") flowing back to the migrants' home communities, particularly in times of crisis brought on by natural disasters such as hurricanes, volcanic eruptions, and flooding (see Table 12.1). Exchanges and transfers of knowledge, capital, commercial goods, and culture (in the form of art, literature, music, dance, and sports, for example) are now part of the contemporary "cross-border" activity that flows and circulates between Caribbean homelands and the overseas diasporic communities.

Caribbean peoples are transnationally mobile, exemplifying a resilience and adaptability that enables them to live between different worlds, as comfortable and familiar with their "away from home" place as their "home" place. Cosmopolitanism, transnationalism, and multiple identity formation are all commonly practiced experiences and hybrid existences in Caribbean peoples' extra- and intraregional lives and livelihoods (Foner 2001). Indeed, the increase in middle- and upper-class transnational mobility has altered the options for the latest generations of Caribbean "hopefuls" in those Caribbean islands that have turned the corner, through the maturing of either their tourist sector (e.g., the Bahamas, Barbados, St. Lucia), their offshore financial sector (e.g., the Cayman Islands), their diversified services (e.g., Puerto Rico), or their energy sector (e.g., Trinidad and Tobago). In what are now "emerging, middle-class societies," temporary migration is viewed as a viable alternative to permanent emigration, and "brain circulation" appears to be on the increase (though not in the emigration-stricken health sector). Transnational business activity has grown significantly, accompanying the expansion of the transnational upper- and middle-class elite, whose ranks have been swelled by returning nationals in several once-troubled Caribbean countries such as Jamaica, Trinidad and Tobago, Barbados, and Puerto Rico (Potter, Conway, and Phillips 2005). Remittances are helping too, though most are still first spent on immediate necessities, with only small proportions diverted to productive investments and community-level project development (Conway 2007a).

In addition to Cuban government restrictions on movement to the United States since the 1970s, Haitians were the other Caribbean people whose journeys to the United States were limited. Those from the Dominican Republic continued to visit New York, and the Washington Heights area became even more firmly identified with that Caribbean society. Similarly, many West Indians settled in Crown Heights, Brooklyn. After 1996 Cuban refugees no longer enjoyed the privileged status they had with previous administrations. However, hardships during the post-Soviet period continued to encourage Cuban defections and refugee flights, with *balseros* (those fleeing on rafts) choosing the most dangerous means of crossing.

Elsewhere, visiting patterns (i.e., nonimmigrant entries) to the United States from all over the region continued to be substantial. With the exception of the Dominicans and Haitians, the numbers of unauthorized illegal overstayers in the United States from the majority of Caribbean societies were not excessive

Table 12.1 Remittances into Caribbean Countries (US$ millions)

Country	Total 1996–2000	% Change 1996–2000	2001	2002	2003	2004	2005	Total 2001–2005	% Change 2001–2005
Barbados	412	64							
Belize	167	112			73	77	81	231	11
Dominican Republic			1,807	2,112	2,217	2,438	2,682	11,256	48
Guyana	211	15	90	119	137	143	270	759	200
Haiti			810	932	978	1,026	1,077	4,823	33
Jamaica	3,508	25	968	1,229	1,426	1,497	1,651	6,771	71
St. Kitts and Nevis	12.8	30							
St. Lucia	9.1	73							
Trinidad and Tobago	206	37	41	59	88	93	97	378	137
Total	4,526	30.8	3,716	4,451	4,919	5,274	5,858	24,218	60.4

Sources: Inter-American Development Bank, Multilateral Investment Fund, http://www.iadb.org/countries/index.cfm?language=English; Claremont D. Kirton, "Remittances: The Experience of the English-speaking Caribbean." In *Beyond Small Change: Making Migrant Remittances Count*, edited by Donald F. Terry and Steven R. Wilson (Washington, DC: Inter-American Development Bank, 2005), table 11.6, p. 273.

when compared to the irregular volumes of Mexicans, Salvadorans, Guatemalans, Colombians, and Chinese. Indeed, irregular influxes from Jamaica, Trinidad and Tobago, and the Bahamas had declined by the year 2000, according to INS estimates (Table 12.2). By that time, New York, New Jersey, Miami, Fort Lauderdale, Boston, Washington, D.C., and Los Angeles had vibrant, well-recognized Caribbean enclave communities where US-based families in the respective island-specific diasporas extended welcomes to their Caribbean-based kin, sponsored some, accommodated others, and both at "home" and "away from home," all generally viewed the United States and the Caribbean as their "global-worlds" (Conway 2007b). Many among the successful middle- and upper-middle-classes also continued to live transnational lives, returning to the Caribbean for celebratory festivals such as Trinidad's Carnival, Barbados' Crop-Over, and Jamaica's Reggae Sun Splash, family events, and any number of other reasons.

In Canada, Toronto's multicultural mosaic also had Caribbean enclaves, and Montreal and Quebec City both sustained a distinctive Haitian community. North American–Caribbean ties remained strong, and the multicultural presence of Caribbean communities in several North American cities certainly has enlivened them. New York City is home to the largest concentrations and most numerous mix of nationalities and remains the major destination for several groups. For example, more than 50 percent of Barbadians, Grenadians, Guyanese, and Vincentians have located there, along with nearly 50 percent of those from the Dominican Republic (Table 12.3).

The Caribbean's North American diaspora is not without its problems, however. One of the most troubling geopolitical features of contemporary US-Caribbean relationships is the "deportee problem." Since 1993, the United States has stepped up its enforcement of the deportation of immigrant criminals, with most of those deported being legal immigrants who had committed crimes and served their time in US jails before being shipped back to their Caribbean homelands. Smaller numbers of deportees were suspected or arraigned criminals who had overstayed their visitor's visas, immigrants who had entered illegally, or criminals whose parents were undocumented illegals. The Dominican Republic tops the list of countries with the highest number of deportees returned, but others significantly affected by this practice are Jamaica, Trinidad and Tobago, and Guyana (Table 12.4).

Within the Caribbean, criticism of the unannounced nature of the deportations was harsh. When domestic crime incidences increased in some affected countries, the association of these unwanted deportees with such increases further inflamed local opinion about the heavy-handed behavior of the US administrations of Presidents Clinton and George W. Bush in this regard. Regional concerns about this controversial enforced-return policy have continued to find their way into the local press and on Internet blogs throughout the region. And, at a recent congressional hearing in the summer of 2007, AnnMarie Barnes, the chief technical director of Jamaica's Ministry of National Security,

Table 12.2 Top Countries of Origin of Irregular Immigrant Populations in the United States, 1992, 1996, and 2000

Origin Country	1992 Population[a]	Origin Country	1996 Population[a]	Origin Country	2000 Population[a]
All countries	3,379,000	All countries	5,000,000	All countries	7,000,000
1. Mexico	1,321,000	1. Mexico	2,700,000	1. Mexico	4,808,000
2. El Salvador	327,000	2. El Salvador	335,000	2. El Salvador	189,000
3. Guatemala	129,000	3. Guatemala	165,000	3. Guatemala	144,000
4. Canada	97,000	4. Canada	120,000	4. Colombia	141,000
5. Poland	91,000	5. Haiti	105,000	5. Honduras	138,000
6. Philippines	90,000	6. Philippines	95,000	6. China	115,000
7. Haiti	88,000	7. Honduras	90,000	7. Ecuador	108,000
8. Bahamas	71,000	8. Poland	70,000	8. Dominican Republic	91,000
9. Nicaragua	68,000	9. Nicaragua	70,000	9. Philippines	85,000
10. Italy	67,000	10. Bahamas	70,000	10. Brazil	77,000
11. Honduras	61,000	11. Colombia	65,000	11. Haiti	76,000
12. Colombia	59,000	12. Ecuador	55,000	12. India	70,000
13. Ecuador	45,000	13. Dominican Republic	50,000	13. Peru	61,000
14. Jamaica	42,000	14. Trinidad and Tobago	50,000	14. Korea	55,000
15. Dominican Republic	40,000	15. Jamaica	50,000	15. Canada	47,000
16. Trinidad and Tobago	39,000	16. Pakistan	41,000		
17. Ireland	36,000	17. India	33,000		
18. Portugal	31,000	18. Dominica[b]	32,000		
19. Pakistan	30,000	19. Peru	30,000		
20. India	28,000	20. Korea	30,000		
All others	618,000	All others	744,000	All others	795,000

Sources: US Immigration and Naturalization Service (INS), *Statistical Yearbook of the Immigration and Naturalization Service* (Washington, DC: Department of Justice, 1992 and 1995); INS Office of Policy and Planning "Estimates of the Unauthorized Immigrant Population Residing in the United States: 1990 to 2000" (Washington, DC: Department of Justice, 2000).

Notes: a. INS estimates.

b. Problems persist with this relatively high estimate of entrants from Dominica because some are most likely entrants from the Dominican Republic.

argued that such a thoughtless policy and practice was actually a "counter-security" measure rather than a security solution. Her summation is compelling:

> Indeed, the mass relocation of criminal offenders from relatively high security environments to less secure societies that are by definition more criminogenic, has merely shifted the responsibility for managing such persons to their country

Table 12.3 New York City's Share of Legal Resident Admissions from Selected Caribbean Countries, 1990–1994

Origin	Population, 1990–1991	US Admissions, 1990–1994	New York City, 1990–1994	New York City/US (%)
Antigua	64,000	3,874	1,201	31.0
Bahamas	255,000	4,356	187	4.3
Barbados	257,000	5,480	3,101	56.6
Belize	187,000	9,071	1,159	12.8
Cuba	10,628,000	61,178	1,008	1.6
Dominica	86,000	3,944	748	19.0
Dominican Republic	7,110,000	222,178	110,140	49.6
Grenada	91,000	4,543	2,575	56.7
Guyana	795,000	48,138	30,764	63.9
Haiti	6,486,000	102,380	14,957	14.6
Jamaica	2,366,000	99,346	32,918	33.1
St. Kitts and Nevis	40,000	3,435	641	18.7
St. Lucia	133,000	3,336	895	26.8
St. Vincent and the Grenadines	114,000	3,649	2,057	56.4
Trinidad and Tobago	1,236,000	35,024	15,878	45.3
Other Caribbean	—	3,794	1,159	16.0

Sources: New York City, Department of City Planning, "The Newest New Yorkers, 1990–1994: An Analysis of Immigration to NYC in the Early 1990s" (New York: New York City Department of City Planning, 1996); US Immigration and Naturalization Service (INS), *Statistical Yearbook of the Immigration and Naturalization Service* (Washington, DC: Department of Justice, 1994).

Table 12.4 Annual Return Volumes of US Alien Criminals Deported, Fiscal Years 1993–2006

Country of Nationality	1993–1999	2000–2006	Total
Caribbean	20,787	36,611	55,398
Belize	635	820	1,455
Dominican Republic	10,700	15,775	26,475
Guyana	701	1,223	1,924
Haiti	1,518	2,678	4,196
Jamaica	7,459	10,143	17,602

Source: US Department of Homeland Security, *Yearbook of Immigration Statistics 2006* (Washington, DC: US Department of Homeland Security, Office of Immigration Statistics, 2007).

of birth. By expanding the locale for criminal enterprise, deportation poses serious challenges not only to national security interests in receiving countries, but also to the management and control of security globally. (US House Committee on Foreign Affairs 2007)

■ Conclusion

International circulation, temporary sojourning, and repetitive mobility have emerged as dominant and common patterns throughout the Caribbean. Extraregional diasporas have fostered overseas enclave communities in North America, and growing numbers of households and families have the transnational flexibility to live between two worlds. All this contributes to the cosmopolitan nature of the Caribbean. These diasporas also consolidate regional and metropolitan networks and links. Intraregional movements have long held sway as traditional paths for job searches, marriages, visiting, and short-term targeted earning. Some of these internal paths serve as transit stations for eventual journeys to Europe and North America, but some of these way stations retain Caribbean migrants (e.g., Puerto Rico's growing concentration of Dominicans, Antigua's retention of Kittians, and Guadeloupe's retention of Haitians and Dominicans from neighboring Dominica).

Far from being a simple safety valve or a demographic exodus caused by the lack of employment opportunities at home, the surplus of young people (and their unmet needs) and the complex patterns of short- and long-term international movements of emigration (displacement) and circulation (temporary, reciprocal movement) cement Caribbean societies with several North American metropolitan areas in a complex system of transnational interdependence. Short-term visiting appears to be one alternative to permanent residency. Repetitive visits maintain connections, and living a multilocal life has become a common survival strategy. Emigration continues to be a tradition for many islanders, too. Migration is more than ever a livelihood strategy in Caribbean societies, at home and abroad. Such a transnational life brings a multiplicity of identities to the fore, and there appears to be a growing pan-Caribbean consciousness in the cosmopolitan enclave communities of certain North American gateway metropoles—New York City, Miami, Toronto, and Montreal, in particular. Pan-Caribbeanism is being fostered by cross-cultural marriages, a widening and intertwining of Caribbean family networks, and the growing maturity of many Caribbean societies. Moreover, the further incorporation of these microstates into a globalizing new world order, where North American and European values and cultures themselves compete, change, or resist, has also contributed to the emergence of this consciousness.

Remittances—the flow of hard currency and in-kind transfers of material goods by migrants to families back home—have become an essential financial input for Caribbean families of all classes. Such funds are most commonly used to purchase needed goods—food, medicine, clothes, and the like—and consumption use is of considerable importance. In addition, remittances are important—and increasingly so—for both investment and savings. However, in many small states there are substantial constraints on the use of remittances. Contrary to earlier opinions, remittance flows appear to be sustainable over long periods with little indication of remittance decay over time. Though remittances are primarily used for consumption, there is also substantial investment in economic activities and in the well-being of others, some of which enables the perpetuation of the migration-remittances nexus (Connell and Conway 2000; Portes and Guarnizo 1991).

Return migration is a counter-flow of growing importance to Caribbean societies that have long witnessed emigration losses, experienced brain drains and separated families (Potter, Conway, and Phillips 2005). Notably, returning transnational middle-class and professional elites have recently been discovered (and their adaptation experiences examined) as a new cohort of youthful nationals, or "citizens by descent," who are returning to the islands of their birth, or the home-place of one of their parents, to "make a difference" or to "give something back" (Conway and Potter 2007). Furthermore, transnational Caribbean migrants provide their families at home and abroad with an extended range of options for various forms of familial, personal, and community development. Most importantly, remittances promote the development of human capital and growth of social and cultural capital stocks in local communities, with investments transferred at the appropriate scale (and scope) of effectiveness, that is, the people's—family or household—level (Connell and Conway 2000; Conway 2007a).

The Caribbean's many diasporas have matured and evolved to become embedded multilocal networks in which an adherence to one national identity is less adaptable than a transnational identity and having multiple identities is a more flexible response to today's uncertainties (Conway 2007b). Caribbean people continue to demonstrate their flexibility, their creativeness, and their fortitude despite the intractable social and economic problems they and their societies have faced since their incorporation into the colonial world in the fifteenth and sixteenth centuries.

▓ Notes

1. See Chapter 8 for further discussion of attitudes toward race, ethnicity, and class.
2. Chapter 5 contains an analysis of Caribbean economic patterns.

▓ Bibliography

Boswell, Thomas D., and James R. Curtis. *The Cuban-American Experience.* Totowa, NJ: Rowman and Allanhand, 1984.

Connell, John, and Dennis Conway. "Migration and Remittances in Island Microstates: A Comparative Perspective on the South Pacific and the Caribbean." *International Journal of Urban and Regional Research* 24, no. 1 (2000): 52–78.

Conway, Dennis. "Caribbean International Mobility Traditions." *Boletín Latino-Americano y del Caribe* 46, no. 2 (1989): 17–47.

———. "The Importance of Remittances for the Caribbean's Future Transcends Their Macroeconomic Influences." *Global Development Studies* (Winter 2006–Spring 2007), nos. 3–4 (2007a): 41–76.

———. "Caribbean Transnational Migration Behaviour: Reconceptualising Its 'Strategic Flexibility.'" *Population, Space, and Place* 13 (2007b): 415–431.

Conway, Dennis, and Tom Cooke. "Non-White Immigration, Residential Segregation, and Selective Integration into a Restructuring Metropolis, New York City." In *Social Polarization in Post-Industrial Metropolises,* edited by John O'Laughlin and Jurgen Frederichs. Berlin: De Gruyter and Aldine Presses, 1996.

Conway, Dennis, and Robert B. Potter. "Caribbean Transnational Return Migrants as Agents of Change." *Blackwell Geography Compass* (online) 1, no. 1 (2007): 25–45.

Ellis, Mark, Dennis Conway, and Adrian J. Bailey. "The Circular Migration of Puerto Rican Women: Towards a Gendered Explanation." *International Migration* 34, no. 1 (1996): 31–58.

Foner, Nancy, ed. *Islands in the City: West Indian Migration to New York.* Berkeley: University of California Press, 2001.

Grasmuck, Sheri, and Ramón Grosfoguel. "Geopolitics, Economic Niches, and Gendered Social Capital Among Recent Caribbean Immigrants to New York City." *Sociological Perspectives* 40, no. 3 (1997): 339–363.

Guengant, Jean-Pierre, and Dawn I. Marshall. *Caribbean Population Dynamics: Emigration and Fertility Challenges.* Barbados: Conference of Caribbean Parliamentarians on Population and Development, 1985.

Henry, Ralph. "A Reinterpretation of Labor Services of the Commonwealth Caribbean." Working Paper no. 61. Washington, DC: Commission for the Study of International Migration and Cooperative Economic Development, 1990.

———. "Cooperation in Human Resource Utilisation in the Commonwealth Caribbean." *Bulletin of Eastern Caribbean Affairs* 16, no. 1 (1990): 25–28.

Kirton, Claremont D. "Remittances: The Experience of the English-speaking Caribbean," In *Beyond Small Change: Making Migrant Remittances Count,* edited by Donald F. Terry and Steven R. Wilson. Washington, DC: Inter-American Development Bank, 2005.

Lowenthal, David. *West Indian Societies.* New York: Oxford University Press, 1972.

Miller, Byron. "The Geography of Fear: Fear as a Technology of Governance." In *Globalization's Contradictions: Geographies of Discipline, Destruction, and Transformation,* edited by Dennis Conway and Nic Heynen. London and New York: Routledge, 2006.

Morrison, Thomas K., and Richard Sinkin. "International Migration in the Dominican Republic: Implications for Development Planning." *International Migration Review* 16, no. 4 (1982): 819–836.

New York City, Department of City Planning. *The Newest New Yorkers, 1990–1994: An Analysis of Immigration to NYC in the Early 1990s.* New York: New York City Department of City Planning, 1996.

———. *The Newest New Yorkers, 2000: Immigrant New York in the New Millennium.* New York: New York City Department of City Planning, 2000.

Portes, Alejandro, and Luis E. Guarnizo. "Tropical Capitalists: US-Bound Immigration and Small-Enterprise Development in the Dominican Republic." In *Migration, Remittances, and Small Business Development: Mexico and Caribbean Basin Countries,* edited by Sergio Díaz-Briquets and Sidney A. Weintraub. Boulder, CO: Westview, 1991.

Potter, Robert B., Dennis Conway, and Joan Phillips. *The Experience of Return Migration: Caribbean Perspectives.* Aldershot, UK: Ashgate, 2005.

Proudfoot, John. *Population Movements in the Caribbean*. New York: Negro Universities Press, 1970.

Richardson, Bonham C. *Caribbean Migrants: Environmental and Human Survival on St. Kitts and Nevis*. Knoxville: University of Tennessee Press, 1983.

Rubenstein, Hymie. "The Return Ideology in West Indian Migration." In *The Anthropology of Return Migration*, edited by Richard E. Rhoades. University of Oklahoma, Department of Anthropology, 1979.

Sunshine, Catherine A. *The Caribbean: Survival, Struggle, and Sovereignty*. Washington, DC: Ecumenical Program on Central America and the Caribbean, 1985.

US House Committee on Foreign Affairs, Subcommittee on the Western Hemisphere. Testimony by AnnMarie Barnes, "Deportees in Latin America and the Caribbean." July 24, 2007, http://www.foreignaffairs.house.gov/110/bar072407.htm.

US Immigration and Naturalization Service (INS). *Annual Reports of the Immigration and Naturalization Service*. Washington, DC: Department of Justice, 1964–1968.

———. *1994 Statistical Yearbook of the Immigration and Naturalization Service*. Washington, DC: Department of Justice, 1994.

———. Office of Policy and Planning. "Estimates of the Unauthorized Immigrant Population Residing in the United States: 1990 to 2000." Washington, DC: Immigration and Naturalization Service, Office of Policy and Planning, 2000.

13

Trends and Prospects

Richard S. Hillman and Andrés Serbin

S ince the first edition of this book was published in 2003, there have been significant developments as well as continuities. Changes in Cuban leadership have brought new prospects for inter-American relations. Deteriorating security and social violence in Jamaica and the Dominican Republic, along with the increasing costs of travel, have affected their tourist industries. Instability in Haiti has continued, notwithstanding the continued presence since June 2005 of the United Nations Stabilization Mission in Haiti (MINUSTAH), constituted by mostly Latin American peacekeeping forces. Venezuela's attempts to build an alternative to US dominance in the region, signaled by the rhetorical and possibly material overtures of President Hugo Chávez and Nicaraguan president Daniel Ortega to the Colombian Revolutionary Armed Forces (FARC), have complicated Caribbean affairs. In addition, the Petrocaribe oil program has been expanding in the Caribbean and Central America, adding new beneficiaries and expanding the Bolivarian Alternative for the Americas to include Dominica and Honduras.

Such complications have occurred against a backdrop of continued US inattention and neglect and the persistence of failed policies. President George W. Bush's war in Iraq has certainly diverted attention from the Caribbean. Maintenance of the embargo against Cuba has done little to improve conditions on the island or to change the existing political system. Only the matter of immigration has entered into the American political discourse. However, the American public has weighed in by making a significant choice regarding the future direction of US policies, both domestic and international—including US-Caribbean relations. The election of Barack Obama has raised expectations both within the United States and the Caribbean. Yet Caribbean analysts recognize the enormity of the challenges facing the forty-fourth US president. Therefore, our cautious optimism must be tempered by issues that will at the very least require definitive new policies and serious attention over the long term, particularly when dealing with corporate interests and addressing structural issues.

The economic and fiscal crisis became of necessity the first and foremost priority of the Obama administration. The global impact of this crisis, however, means that its solution, or even reduction, will have salutary effects on Caribbean economies. Dennis Pantin and Marlene Attzs illustrate in Chapter 5 the ways in which the Caribbean economies are dependent upon the health as well as the fluctuations of the global economy. Similarly, US extrication from its overextended involvement in Iraq will allow US foreign policy to become more comprehensive—with possible correction of its neglect of the Caribbean.

As Thomas D'Agostino shows in Chapter 4, certain policies must be directed toward individual nations, yet a global approach to the region remains crucial. We therefore continue to assert the importance of understanding the Caribbean region as a whole. Despite linguistic, geographic, and other dissimilarities, common experiences and challenges compel an integrated approach to contemporary problem solving. Global trends, moreover, continue to require policymakers in the Caribbean to recognize the logic of regional integration as a means to achieve political and economic development.

This logic is compelling for insular microstates that individually are weak compared to the larger, more powerful states with which they must interact. Caribbean nations are similarly at a disadvantage with regard to market agents, such as transnational corporations, international financial organizations, and private banks. Also, as Jacqueline Braveboy-Wagner describes in Chapter 6, strategic importance of the region has been diluted since the end of the Cold War. Today the role of Caribbean countries as trading partners has supplanted the view that they are mere objects of the East-West rivalry. They can no longer play, either individually or as a block within the Organization of American States and other multilateral forums, one side against the other to their own benefit. At the same time, globalization processes and particularly the global financial crisis affect the entire region.

Although regional integration increasingly has been recognized as a serious option for the Caribbean, difficult obstacles inherent in intergovernmental dynamics and international relations have stultified its full realization. Since the 1990s, however, an interesting new trend has emerged as a potential catalyst for the promotion of modifications in intergovernmental and international initiatives that would support political, economic, and social development in the whole Caribbean region. There was hope that transnational civil society—formed by nongovernmental organizations (NGOs) and networks, old and new social movements, and professional and academic associations—would transcend the domestic sphere, extending its initiatives, agendas, and demands to regional and global levels.

Theoretically, transnational civil society—through the pressure, advocacy, and influence of regional and global nongovernmental networks—would act as a regulating (and potentially correcting) mechanism for the actions of nation-states and the international market. These networks would address social issues and promote increased participation of social actors in decisionmaking processes. In this regard, transnational civil society, still in its incipient and formative stages of organizing individual citizens and groups, has begun to assume an important role in the regional integration processes. Especially in the Caribbean, it was developing an unexpected regional leadership in promoting an intersocietal integration process while contributing to the advancement of the process of regionalism in which intergovernmental initiatives and social actors converged.

▓ The Intergovernmental Dynamic

The Association of Caribbean States (ACS), founded in Cartagena, Colombia, in 1994, crystallized the idea of a greater Caribbean by bringing together fourteen of the fifteen countries from the Caribbean Common Market (CARICOM), the Central American countries, the Group of Three (G3) countries (Colombia, Mexico, and Venezuela), Cuba, and the Dominican Republic. Associate members include Aruba, the Netherlands Antilles, and France (representing French Guiana, Guadeloupe, and Martinique). On the recommendation of the West Indian Commission as well as the G3 countries, particularly Venezuela and Cuba, the English-speaking members of CARICOM promoted this intergovernmental initiative within the framework of the Economic Commission on Latin America. Caribbean proposals for open regionalism and the technical support of the Latin American Economic System (Sistema Económico Latinoamericano, SELA) supported the initiative as well. (Venezuela withdrew from the G3 in 2006 to protest "creeping neo-liberalism" affecting the trade agreement.)

The ACS was founded due to the acceleration of subregional and regional integration processes in the Western Hemisphere in the 1980s and the 1990s. This rationale implied a desire for expanded economic relationships for the insular Caribbean states, a politically and socially stabilized region for the G3 countries, and the development of a common platform for negotiations with the United States and Canada (neither of which are members of the ACS) aimed at a speedier and smoother entry into the North American Free Trade Agreement (NAFTA). Although early on, the members of the ACS benefited from the Caribbean Basin Initiative (CBI) launched by the United States in the early 1980s, Cuba was a notable exception. Later, the members' long-term goal became entry into the Free Trade Area of the Americas (FTAA). Cuba sought to break its regional isolation and advocated increasing regional commerce and cooperation but was unsuccessful when the ACS allowed commerce to become a low priority on its agenda.

However, the inclusion of Cuba and the dependent territories, associated states, and overseas departments of European countries created difficulties for the ACS. Obstacles included US pressure on the Cuban government; complex negotiations regarding the distinctive status of the British-associated states and territories (the British Virgin Islands, the Cayman Islands, the Turks and Caicos, Montserrat, and Anguilla); the status of Aruba and the federation of the Netherlands Antilles as members of the Kingdom of the Netherlands; and the status of the overseas departments of Guadeloupe, Martinique, and French Guiana as French territories.[1] The inclusion of Puerto Rico posed similar difficulties. The US government was against its inclusion because it is a US Commonwealth, not an independent nation, despite the desire of several Puerto Rican governments to achieve full membership in the ACS.

These difficulties existed alongside others, including the internal negotiations leading to the establishment of a secretariat in Port of Spain, Trinidad; the appointment of a secretary-general (Ambassador Simón Molina Duarte of Venezuela); the definition of the budget and contributions from member countries; and the formulation of regulations, procedures, and internal rules. All have absorbed a great deal of the energy and available time in the ACS in the years since its creation, especially the negotiations during the technical and ministerial meetings and the creation of different commissions. But that is not the only reason for the lack of progress. The dynamic of hemispheric integration and the interrelationships among diverse actors of the greater Caribbean also have caused delays. One of the principal causes for the insufficient traction of the ACS was its members' lack of political will to establish and develop a solid institutional architecture for the ACS that would allow them to address more efficiently internal tensions and differences (such as the existing rift between the Caribbean and the Central American countries), external pressures, and a changing geopolitical and economic regional context.

Additionally, at the hemispheric level, the polarization between NAFTA and the Common Market of the South (Mercosur) has had an impact on the ACS. Mexico's membership in NAFTA, along with its active involvement in the political and institutional forging of the ACS, raised expectations among Caribbean countries. Some countries hoped to use their closer links with Mexico in the ACS as a bridge to NAFTA. Also, they wanted to counteract the negative impact of Mexican membership in NAFTA on the Caribbean Basin Initiative. Despite its influence in the formation of the ACS, Mexico chose to give more priority to NAFTA and to developing closer economic relations with its Central American partners.

Venezuela signed a free-trade agreement with CARICOM in 1991 as part of its active Caribbean policy and became an observer in this organization during the second presidency of Carlos Andrés Pérez. However, President Rafael Caldera and then Hugo Chávez at the beginning of his administration gave priority to relations with Brazil and Mercosur. Colombia also signed a similar agreement with CARICOM but then deepened its relations with the Andean Community of Nations and Mercosur. Later, Chávez gravitated toward the Caribbean. In the first decade of the twenty-first century, however, the region began a transition from the South American Community to the recently established Union of South America (UNASUR) under the leadership of Brazil. UNASUR includes the circum-Caribbean nations of Guyana and Suriname.

These trends resulted in the deceleration of the free trade agreements and integration processes initiated in the 1990s. By November 2004, there was a rift between the Mercosur member countries and Venezuela during the Mar del Plata Summit of the Americas. Then Venezuela's relations with the United States soured as that country gained the support of several Latin American and Caribbean countries aiming to establish the FTAA.

In the mid-1990s, the Dominican Republic, which (with Haiti and the CARICOM countries) was a member of CARIFORUM (an ad hoc organization that groups the Caribbean beneficiaries of the Lomé Convention with the European Union), offered to act as a "bridge" in building a "strategic alliance" between the countries of Central America and the Caribbean in the framework of the ACS in 1997 (Ceara Hatton 1997). Nonetheless, this strategic alliance had to contend with many obstacles on both sides.

The Central American countries advanced toward closer relations with Mexico and their traditional trading partner, the United States. The Central America–Dominican Republic–United States Free Trade Agreement (CAFTA-DR), which was signed on August 5, 2004, was designed to eliminate tariffs and trade barriers and expand regional opportunities for the various sectors of all the countries. CAFTA-DR would eliminate tariffs on more than 80 percent of US exports of consumer and industrial products, phasing out the rest over ten years. Eighty percent of imports from CAFTA-DR countries already enter the United States duty-free under the CBI, Generalized System of Preferences, and most-favored nation programs; the CAFTA-DR would provide reciprocal access for US products and services.

At the same time, steps were taken to deepen the integration of Central America through increased intraregional trade and political union. Banana production and the existence of export quotas for entry of that product into the European Union continued to be a point of friction between CARICOM and Central America, exacerbated by the dispute within the World Trade Organization between the United States and the European Union.

It became clear that there was a need for convergence toward a common position in response to the growing limitations of the Caribbean Basin Initiative, particularly in terms of competition from Mexican products. After a CARICOM–Central American meeting in Georgetown, Guyana, in 1998, however, the initiative for a strategic alliance received a cold reception. It was noted in the final declaration as being of "great interest," but no specific steps or commitments were taken to achieve it (Byron and Girvan 2000).

Also, full Cuban incorporation in the region remained problematic. The Cuba factor continues to reflect the inertial effects of the Cold War despite Cuba's membership in CARICOM and official observer status in CARIFORUM. However, there was a renewed dynamic of increasing relations among the insular Caribbean countries in 1999. This was closely associated with the CARICOM strategy to widen insular Caribbean interaction and consolidate the CARICOM integration process, and with Cuban aspirations to become an active member in the regional community, breaking the isolation imposed by OAS sanctions in the 1960s and the aggressive US policy associated with the economic embargo.

Representatives of Cuba and the Dominican Republic have been attending CARICOM meetings, Haiti has become a full member, negotiations regarding Cuba–Dominican Republic–CARICOM free trade agreements have advanced, and relations between Cuba and the Dominican Republic have deepened, with both countries actively engaged in the post-Lomé negotiations with the European Union (Ceara Hatton 2000). The transition of power from Fidel to Raúl Castro raised expectations in 2008 for the kind of political and economic transformation that would benefit Cuba's relations with Caribbean countries, already strengthened through the CARICOM-Cuba Commission. Moreover, Barack Obama's election as US president has increased hopes even further that normalized relations with the United States would enhance the ability of the entire region to integrate into a stronger hemispheric dynamic.

The regional geopolitical picture and the difficulties that have stood in the way of the development of the ACS were complicated, since its establishment, by disagreements over its agenda. Although the meetings of the ACS council of ministers and presidential summits focused on issues of tourism, transport, and trade, no significant advances were made. The Trinidad-Guyana proposal at the 1996 Havana summit for a regional free trade agreement met with indifference or reticence from other countries, especially Mexico. Similarly, the presidential summits have yielded paltry results. Neither Chávez nor Fidel Castro attended the Tenth ACS Presidential Summit. However, they both were at the 2001 Margarita Island meeting, where Venezuela actively promoted Petrocaribe.

There was, however, discussion within the ACS on the approval of preferential tariff agreements among member countries.[2] And progress has been made on important issues for the greater Caribbean, such as studies of sustainable tourism, coordination of transportation initiatives, and ACS special committees—especially the committee on natural disasters and catastrophes (Ceara Hatton 1997; Byron 1997).

After long delays, government representatives finally established a set of rules for the recognition and informal participation of social actors in the ACS in 1999. The Regional Coordination of Economic and Social Research (CRIES), a broad-based network of NGOs and research centers, was thereby admitted to the ACS. Unfortunately, although CARICOM approved a social charter on the initiative of the Caribbean Policy Development Centre (CPDC)—an umbrella organization for different island NGOs—social actors were not even granted formal consultative status in CARICOM.[3]

Finally, it is interesting to note that internal tensions evolved as a result of issues that would seem distant from the primary concerns of Caribbean integration. For example, while Mexico advocated the admission of the People's Republic of China for observer status, Central American countries argued for the admission of Taiwan. Both Mexico and Central America have had trade and cooperative relations with and have received economic support from these adversarial countries. There were similar tensions regarding the European Community, as well as the observer status granted to Russia and Egypt, which were admitted prior to many civil society groups.

Transnational Civil Society

Since the early 1990s, civil society has formed regional social networks by promoting intersocietal integration and by developing a dialogue with organizations involved in subregional integration (Serbin 1997). For example, the Civil Society Charter for the Caribbean Community was approved by CARICOM in 1999 (Jácome 1999; Byron and Girvan 2000; Yanes 2000). Another example is the Caribbean Policy Development Centre, which seeks

> to help NGOs in the Caribbean to understand where and how policies are made and how they affect our daily lives; to share information about these policies; to build the confidence and ability of Caribbean people to influence public policy; to work constructively with governments to design and support policies that benefit and improve the lives of Caribbean people; and to work together to change policies that do not benefit Caribbean people. (*CPDC Bulletin* 1996:8)

After the impact of Hurricane Mitch in 2006, Central American initiatives that had experienced problems nevertheless effected the restructuring of the Civil Society Consultative Committee of the Central American Integration System (SICA) (Yanes 2000). The present composition of this consultative committee includes a group of twenty Central American organizations from across the region,[4] and currently it has an office at SICA headquarters, as part of its official recognition as one of the mechanisms of the integration system.

CRIES, which was formed in 1982 and integrated into the ACS in 1999, both predated and paralleled some of these initiatives.[5] According to the organization, the CRIES strategy is based on two fundamental premises: First, "any solution for the major social and economic problems of the region's countries and territories necessarily has to pass through a regional project of Greater Caribbean integration." Second, "this project can only be built with the active participation of all the sectors of regional civil society" (CRIES 1997). Since 1997, CRIES has actively promoted a program for the participation of civil society in the integration process by organizing workshops, conducting studies, and using a specific strategy to intensify the dialogue between regional governments and actors from civil society. In this framework, CRIES, together with the Venezuelan Institute of Social and Political Studies (INVESP), actively promoted the Forum of Greater Caribbean Civil Society.

▇ The Forum of Greater Caribbean Civil Society

The forum began as a regional project on the sociopolitical agenda of integration, initiated by INVESP in 1995.[6] The project's original purpose was to identify the social actors involved in the regional integration process and their regional agendas, as well as to contribute to design mechanisms for participation by such actors in regional decisionmaking (INVESP 1996).

In the framework of this project, the first regional conference was held in Caracas in 1996, with the backing of SELA. A broad spectrum of representatives from NGOs, businesses and trade unions, and intergovernmental organizations from the greater Caribbean attended. During the conference, a proposal to organize the Forum of Greater Caribbean Civil Society was discussed, based on a 1996 study by the late Álvaro de la Ossa. The proposal gained support in successive workshops in 1996 and 1997 held in Guatemala, Caracas, and Barbados with political and academic actors and NGOs and was included in the extension of the INVESP project to the whole of Latin America and the Caribbean. Representatives of Mercosur and the Inter-American Development Bank attended one of those meetings.

In May 1997 the CRIES general assembly elected a new board (with a balanced representation from the insular Caribbean, Central America, and the G3 countries). A mandate was approved that outlined a strategic program. The regionalism and civil society program was designed to match the technical and academic capacities of CRIES to the needs and demands of the greater Caribbean civil society.

After the 1997 annual conference of the Caribbean Studies Association in Barranquilla, Colombia, the Colombian foreign minister and the ACS secretary-general invited regional academic networks and organizations to participate in the meeting of the ACS council of ministers to be held in Cartagena. The invitation explicitly mentioned the role played by CRIES in promoting a regional view of the greater Caribbean. Objections to the participation of civil society in the ACS, however, were based on the argument that no regulation had been approved as to the recognition and admission of social actors into the organization.

Nevertheless, the first Forum of Greater Caribbean Civil Society opened in Cartagena on November 23, 1997, with delegates representing more than

800 NGOs, social movements, and academic organizations. During the three days of the forum, a series of general documents were discussed and approved.[7] The decision to make the forum a permanent body was legally validated through a constitutive act. The executive committee was confirmed in its functions and given a two-year term. Its mandate was to proceed with the arrangements for future meetings, foster research, organize informational workshops, develop an education campaign, and support the work of committees. New committees were created to deal with issues of labor, education, science, and technology. A committee was also appointed to present the conclusions of the forum to the ACS council of ministers.

The presentation of the forum's conclusions to the ACS set a precedent not only for the greater Caribbean but also for the entire Western Hemisphere. The forum highlighted the dialogue between the civil society of the greater Caribbean and the ACS, the urgent need for the joint development of the region, and the importance of avoiding exclusion and insufficient democracy in regional decisionmaking. On the initiative of regional civil society and with the support of several governments, a significant step was taken on intergovernmental and intersocietal initiatives for integration in the greater Caribbean.

A series of workshops and the second forum (in Bridgetown, Barbados, 1998) and third forum (in Cancún, Mexico, 1999) resulted from intensive regional work by CRIES, INVESP, and other regional NGO networks. As a result of this process, the ACS council of ministers admitted CRIES as a regional social actor in 1999, which allowed CRIES to participate in council meetings and to work, on a consultative basis, with the different ACS committees in promoting a regional social agenda that would be based on the conclusions of the debates at the Civil Society Forum of the Greater Caribbean. The election of Norman Girvan as ACS secretary-general in 1999 opened the door to the increased participation of NGOs and academics in the regional integration intergovernmental scheme. His successor, Rubén Silié, a former director of the Latin American Faculty of Social Sciences in the Dominican Republic, also contributed to the growing participation by academics, introducing some new issues into the ACS agenda, such as conflict prevention and the achievement of the Millennium Goals. Although the forum gained official recognition by the ACS, the forum's ability to deliver results has been stymied by lack of resources and increasing regional fragmentation (Serbin 2007b).

Effectively, the forum has been replaced by the activities of other existing organizations. For example, CRIES amplified its mandate to include all of Latin America and the Caribbean in 2004, making possible a major relationship between organizations and networks of civil society. That led in July of 2005 to the participation of these groups in a UN conference on civil society designed to promote the prevention of conflicts and the building of peace. That same year, CRIES developed the constitution for the Plataforma Latinoamericana y Caribeña de Prevención de Conflictos y de Construcción de la Paz (PLACPAZ), which advances programs in the Caribbean and Central and

South America as part of the Global Partnership for the Prevention of Armed Conflict, which includes fifteen regional initiatives on the global level. PLAC-PAZ has produced a model that ties violent conflict prevention to the defense and promotion of human rights in Central America. Also, it has generated and supported initiatives regarding violence and youth in the English-speaking Caribbean and South America. Finally, CRIES and its member organizations recently initiated a program on civil society and climate change that focuses on the Caribbean and Central America, which provides continuity for some of the ACS initiatives regarding natural disasters. However, even with the cooperation of intergovernmental organizations like the OAS and subregional groups like SICA, in practice governments have been reticent to participate with the level of enthusiasm and support that could produce much-needed objective results.

■ The Future

These trends challenge the cautious optimism that characterized the first edition of this book. However, there are reasons to be hopeful that Caribbean problems will be addressed differently in the future. If the United States begins to implement policies that address regional issues in a mutually beneficial way, perhaps some of the intersocietal initiatives for integration in the greater Caribbean would gain sufficient impetus to provide far-reaching influences on the amelioration of endemic problems.

Clearly, the discussions contained in each chapter of this book lead to the conclusion that governments, economies, and societies in the region continue to experience debt, widespread domestic poverty, unemployment and crime, illegal migration, illicit narcotics trafficking, corruption, social violence, and societal malaise. Although transnational civil society has attempted to address these problems, its best hope is for coordinating initiatives with and lobbying existing political institutions, particularly regional and subregional organizations and integration schemes. Meetings, conferences, summits, and training workshops are only the beginning of a process of capacity building and political commitment that eventually could lead to greater cooperation for regional integration and a greater dedication to it by both citizens and governments.

If the past is prelude, the region's evolution as a crucible of many civilizations, its unique amalgamation of peoples and cultures, its beauty, and its potential will continue to produce important contributions to literature, music, art, technology, and racial and ethnic integration. The evolution to date, however, has been tortuous and the near future will probably present difficulties.

We have seen the impact of location, population trends, resource availability, and the environment on economic development and the people of the Caribbean. The multiple impacts of globalization processes, added to the legacies of colonialism, plantation society, and slavery that persist in influencing contemporary realities, have created challenges for socioeconomic and political development. Different political, social, and economic institutions have converged in similar patterns of patron-clientelism, elite dominance, and Creole fusion. Although many development strategies and economic programs have been tested, none appears to have mitigated the effects of dependency or general structural weakness. Regional integration offers hope. But the long history of external intervention has negatively influenced cooperative policies in the region, as has populist-inspired nationalism. Moreover, there are crucial issues regarding the ecology of the region, the natural assets and liabilities inherent in economies (many dependent on tourism) affected by hurricanes, depletion of coral reefs, and other forms of environmental degradation and pollution. Patterns of race, ethnicity, class, and gender are problematic as well as promising. Although these socially constructed concepts are often used to rationalize and legitimize disparities in status and wealth among different groups, the relative absence of ethnic and racial violence can be attributed in large part to the integrative Creole model inherent in the multicultural societies of the Caribbean. This dynamic is illustrated in the politicized nature of much of the region's literature and popular culture. Finally, the Caribbean diaspora will continue to affect the region's future.

Hopefully, civil society initiatives constitute a significant step toward the convergence of governmental and nongovernmental efforts to integrate the greater Caribbean. But this step must go well beyond the predominantly economic (and often purely commercial) dimension by including a broad spectrum of social, political, environmental, security, and cultural issues.

In essence, the Caribbean needs a legitimate interlocutor, especially for the social sectors that are excluded and marginalized from the benefits and the decisions related to the greater Caribbean integration process. In order to represent the interests of the greater Caribbean's civil society, it is necessary to articulate the needs and objectives of domestic social organizations and movements in each country (Duncan 1997; Jácome 1999). It will also be necessary to develop closer links with movements and organizations that are promoting regional and global agendas. For example, Venezuela's emergence as a regional leader, especially through policies that provide petroleum discounts to Caribbean states, offers an alternative direction toward integration. Inter-American relations, always affected by the machinations of external powers, have been complicated as a result. The Venezuelan option was viewed by the Bush administration as an unacceptable alternative to US dominance in the region. It remains to be seen whether the US-Venezuelan rivalry will transform into a Cold War–like adversarial relationship or whether future inter-American relations will be characterized by a theme of mutual respect and cooperation that the new administration in Washington seeks to foster.

Finally, global recognition of the need for alternative sources of energy and environmental protection could have a profound impact on a region in which wind and solar power are abundant. Diminished dependence on oil would have political consequences as well. Venezuela's aspirations for regional hegemony along anti-American lines would suffer from the lack of oil as a bargaining leverage. Whether or not a more empathetic US foreign policy would diminish the Chávez appeal, however, is widely debated. Some believe that an improved relationship could be achieved between Venezuela and the United States. Such improvement would benefit the Caribbean as a whole. Others see an increased US presence in the region as fodder for Chávez's inflammatory rhetoric. One way or the other, most analysts agree that the Caribbean must seek its own road to the future devoid of any form of dependency on the leadership of another country or community, whether the United States, Venezuela, the European Union, or Brazil.

In sum, progress depends on overcoming the political, organizational, and financial weaknesses plaguing regional organizations and networks, as well as overcoming the memory of integration attempts that have faltered in the past. It is crucial that there be continuous dialogue with regional governments and intergovernmental organizations to build equitable, participative, and sustainable development in the Caribbean. Although both civil society and political parties have the potential to play a vital role in the representation of popular interests, ultimately national governments must implement policies that address the region's endemic problems and fulfill the expectations of its people in order to ensure the future stability of the Caribbean region.

▓ Notes

1. This situation has been generating difficulties in the ACS. At present, France has associate status as the representative of its Caribbean overseas departments; in the Dutch Caribbean, the Netherlands is a member with observer status, the Netherlands Antilles has associated status, and Aruba has postponed its application for permanent membership. The United Kingdom joined the ACS as an observer, leaving to its associated states and territories the decision whether and how to join the ACS. Interestingly, Puerto Rico was willing to enter the ACS, but the United States would not allow it.

2. As noted by one scholar:

It could have considerable symbolic and practical importance. First it would provide tangible evidence of the existence of the ACS as a trade grouping and help to draw the attention of the business community to the opportunities for trade within the Caribbean Basin. Secondly, the CPT [Caribbean preferential tariff] provides for asymmetrical reductions based on differential levels of development among the member states. Acceptance of asymmetry by the larger ACS states could have a "spill-over" effect on the WTO [World Trade Organization] and the FTAA [Free Trade Area of the Americas] negotiations. It would establish a precedent that the small economies of CARICOM and Central America could use in pressing for special and differential treatment for countries that are less developed, or small and vulnerable. (Girvan 2000:6–7)

3. The twenty-one-member organizations of the Caribbean Policy Development Centre, based in Barbados, include Afrika Hall, Barbados; Association of Development Agencies and Association of National Development Agencies, Belize; Association of

Caribbean Economists, Jamaica; Caribbean Association for Feminist Research and Action, Trinidad; Caribbean Conservation Association, Barbados; Caribbean Conference of Churches, Trinidad; Caribbean Organisation of Indigenous Peoples, Guyana; Caribbean Human Rights Network, Barbados; Centre of Studies of America, Havana; Economic Research Center for the Caribbean, Santo Domingo; Caribbean Network for Integrated Rural Development, Trinidad; Eastern Caribbean Popular Theatre Organisation, St. Vincent; Women and Development Union, Barbados; and Windward Islands Farmers Association, St. Vincent.

4. See Rojas (1997:4) for a list of members.

5. CRIES maintained close links with the Caribbean Policy Development Center and the Iniciativa Civil para la Integración Centroamericana and is constituted by the following organizations: Association for the Advancement of Social Sciences, Guatemala; National Foundation for Development, Institute for Economic and Social Development of El Salvador; Salvadoran Programme for Development and Environment Research and TENDENCIES, El Salvador; Documentation Centre of Honduras, National Research and Studies Centre, and the Team for Reflection, Research, and Communication, Honduras; Centre of Research Studies and the Research Centre of the Atlantic Coast, Nicaragua; Training Centre for Development, Ecumenical Research Department, and the Central American Foundation for Integration, Costa Rica; Panamanian Center for Studies and Social Action, Training and Social Development Centre, Justo Arosemena Latin American Studies Centre and the Research and Teaching Centre of Panama, Panama; Centre Studies of America, Cuba; Centre for Research and Economic and Social Training for Development and Haitian Group of Research and Pedagogic Action in Haiti; Economic Research Center for the Caribbean, Research Center for Feminine Action and the Centre for Research and Social Promotion, Dominican Republic; Caribbean Policy Development Centre and the Women and Development Unit, Barbados; Society for the Promotion of Education and Research of Belize; Association of Caribbean Economists, Consortium Graduate School of Social Sciences, and the Institute of Social and Economic Research, Jamaica; Center for Studies of Puerto Rican Reality, Puerto Rico; Caribbean Network for Integrated Rural Development, Trinidad; Mutual Support Forum, Mexico; Institute for Political Studies and International Relations, Colombia; and the Venezuelan Institute for Social and Political Studies. For more information, see www.cries.org and www.invesp.org.

6. INVESP has been a member of CRIES since 1990. INVESP's president was elected to chair the board of CRIES in May 1997. The other elected representatives at this time were from the National Foundation for Development of El Salvador; Advancement of Social Sciences in Guatemala; the Mutual Support Forum of Mexico; and the Institute of Social and Economic Research, University of the West Indies (UWI), of Barbados and Jamaica. After CRIES broadened its regional scope in 2004, a new board was elected, including representatives from UWI, Jamaica; the Fundación Nuñez Jimenez, Cuba; Ecology Fund, a Colombian environmental organization; Instituto de Enseñanza para el Desarrollo Sostenido, Guatemala; Center for Caribbean Economic Research, Dominican Republic; and the State University of São Paulo, Brazil. The chair of the board was reelected.

7. The documents are available in a volume published by INVESP/CRIES in 1999.

▪ Bibliography

Acta Constitutiva de la Asociación de Estados del Caribe (Constitutive Act of the Association of Caribbean States). Cartagena de Indias, July 1994.

Byron, Jessica. "The Association of Caribbean States: New Regional Interlocutor for the Caribbean Basin?" Paper presented at the Fifth Conference of the Association of Caribbean Economists, Havana, November 30–December 2, 1997.

Byron, Jessica, and Norman Girvan. "CARICOM/CARIFORUM: Integración regional y los temas del comercio internacional" (CARICOM/CARIFORUM: Regional integration and the themes of international commerce). In *Anuario de la Integración del Gran Caribe, 2000* (Greater Caribbean integration annual report, 2000), pp. 59–82. Caracas: Nueva Sociedad/CIEI/CRIES/INVESP, 2000.

Caribbean and Central American Report—CCAR. London, July 15, 1997.

Caribbean Policy Development Centre (CPDC). "Intervention of the CPDC to the 18th Meeting of the CARICOM Heads of Government, Jamaica, 1 July 1997." *Pensamiento Propio* (Managua) no. 4 (May–August 1997): 140–148.

Ceara Hatton, Miguel. "El Caribe insular en la dinámica de la integración hemisférica" (The insular Caribbean in hemispheric integration dynamic). Paper presented at the Fifth Conference of the Association of Caribbean Economists, Havana, November 30–December 2, 1997.

———. "El Caribe: Cumbres, creación, de identidad e integración" (The Caribbean: Summits, creation of identity, and integration). Unpublished manuscript, March 2000.

CRIES (Regional Coordination of Economic and Social Research). Informational brochure, 1997.

de la Ossa, Álvaro. "Mecanismos políticos y económicos para la participación de los actores sociales en el proceso de regionalización" (Political and economic methods for the participation of social actors in the regionalization process). Paper, SELA/INVESP, Caracas, February 1996.

———. "Unificación centroamericana: La política primero, el desarrollo quién sabe" (Central American unification: First politics, development, who knows?). In *Anuario de la Integración del Gran Caribe 2000* (Greater Caribbean Integration annual report 2000). Caracas: Nueva Sociedad/CIEI/CRIES/INVESP, 2000, pp. 83–100.

———, compiler. *La integración social: Nuevas rutas hacia la discordia* (Social integration: New routes to disagreement). San José de Costa Rica: Fundación Fridrich Ebert/Fundación Centroamericana para la Integración, 1997.

Duncan, Neville. "Anglophone Caribbean Non-State Sectors in National Integration: A Vital Step in Caricom and Greater Caribbean Integration." Unpublished manuscript, 1997.

Girvan, Norman. "The ACS as a Caribbean Cooperative Zone." Paper presented to the Conference on Caribbean Survival in the Twenty-First Century, Port-of-Spain, Trinidad, March 2000.

Gonzalez, Anthony. "Globalización, regionalización y las relaciones entre el Caribe de habla inglesa y América del Sur en el contexto hemisférico" (Globalization, regionalization, and relations between the Anglophone Caribbean and South America in the hemispheric context). In *América Latina y el Caribe anglófono: ¿Hacia una nueva relación?* (Latin America and the Anglophone Caribbean: Toward a new relationship?), edited by Andrés Serbin. Buenos Aires: Instituto de Servicio Exterior de la Nación/Grupo Editor Latinoamericano, 1997, pp. 193–239.

Heron, Tony. *The New Political Economy of United States–Caribbean Relations: The Apparel Industry and the Politics of NAFTA Parity.* Aldershot, UK: Ashgate, 2004.

Hillman, Richard S., and Thomas J. D'Agostino. *Distant Neighbors in the Caribbean: The Dominican Republic and Jamaica in Comparative Perspective.* New York: Praeger, 1992.

Iniciativa Civil para la Integración Centroamericana (ICIC). "Posición y propuesta de las organizaciones aglutinadas en ICIC y CACI con respecto a la evaluación del sistema de integración centroamericana" (Position and proposal of the ICIC- and CACI-associated organizations with respect to the evaluation of the Central American integration system). *Pensamiento Propio* (Managua) no. 4 (May–August 1997): 159–167.

———. "Plan de trabajo encuentro de los pueblos" (Plan of job placement in towns). Unpublished manuscript, Guatemala, August 30 and 31, 1997.

INVESP (Venezuelan Institute of Social and Political Studies). *La agenda sociopolítica de la integración en el Gran Caribe, Programa Regionalismo y Sociedad Civil* (The sociopolitical agenda for greater Caribbean integration). Folleto explicativo, 1996.

INVESP/CRIES. *The Second Greater Caribbean Civil Society Forum: Documents and Proceedings.* Caracas: INVESP, 1999.

Jácome, Francine. "Las sociedades civiles frente al proceso de integración." In *La otra integración: procesos intersocietales y parlementos regionales en el Caribe* (The other integration: Intersocietal and regional parliamentarian processes in the Caribbean), edited by F. Jácome. Caracas: Cuadernos del INVESP, no. 4, 1999, pp. 73–105.

———. "El Foro Permanente de la Sociedad Civil del Gran Caribe: evaluación preliminar" (The Permanent Forum of Greater Caribbean Civil Society: Preliminary evaluation). In *Anuario de la Integración del Gran Caribe, 2000* (Greater Caribbean integration annual report, 2000). Caracas: Nueva Sociedad/CIEI/CRIES/INVESP, 2000, pp. 179–197.

Kaul, Inge, Isabelle Grunberg, and Marc Stern. *Bienes públicos mundiales: Cooperación internacional en el siglo XXI* (Global Public Welfare: International Cooperation in the Twentieth Century). New York: Oxford University Press, 1999.

Lewis, David. "Esquemas de integración regional y subregional en la Cuenca del Caribe" (Regional and subregional integration schemes in the Caribbean Basin). In *América Latina y el Caribe anglófono: ¿Hacia una nueva relación?* (Latin America and the Anglophone Caribbean: Toward a new relationship?), edited by Andrés Serbin. Buenos Aires: Instituto de Servicio Exterior de la Nación/Grupo Editor Latinoamericano, 1997, pp. 95–142.

Nogueira, Uziel. "The Integration Movement in the Caribbean at Crossroads: Towards a New Approach of Integration." Working Paper, INTAL Series. Washington, DC: Inter-American Development Bank, April 1997.

Ramsaran, Ramesh. "Economías pequeñas, preferencias comerciales y relaciones con América del Sur: Desafíos que enfrenta el Caribe de habla inglesa en una economía mundial cambiante" (Small economies, commercial preferences, and relations with South America: Challenges that confront the Anglophone Caribbean in a changing global economy). In *América Latina y el Caribe anglófono: ¿Hacia una nueva relación?* (Latin America and the Anglophone Caribbean: Toward a new relationship?), edited by Andrés Serbin. Buenos Aires: Instituto de Servicio Exterior de la Nación/Grupo Editor Latinoamericano, 1997.

Reinicke, Wolfgang, and Francis Deng. *Critical Choices: The United Nations, Networks, and the Future of Global Governance.* Executive summary. Washington, DC: Global Public Policy Project, January 2000.

Rojas, Zaida. "Organizaciones civiles buscan espacio en la integración" (Civil organizations seek a place in integration). In *Boletín PIECA* (Guatemala), no. 3 (October 1997): 2–6.

Serbin, Andrés. *El Caribe: ¿Zona de paz?* (The Caribbean: A peace zone?) Caracas: Comisión Sudamericana de Paz/Nueva Sociedad, 1989. Also published in English as *Caribbean Geopolitics: Toward Security Through Peace?* Boulder, CO: Lynne Rienner, 1991.

———. "Los desafíos del proceso de regionalización de la Cuenca del Caribe: Integración, soberanía, democracia, e identidad" (The challenges of the regionalization process in the Caribbean Basin: Integration, sovereignty, democracy, and identity). *Revista Venezolana de Economía y Ciencias Sociales* (Caracas) no. 4 (1995): 75–112.

———. "Globalización, déficit democrático, y sociedad civil en los procesos de integración" (Globalization, the democratic deficit, and civil society in the integration process). *Pensamiento Propio* (Managua) no. 3 (January–April 1997): 98–117.

———. *Sunset over the Islands: The Caribbean in an Age of Global and Regional Challenges.* London: Macmillan, 1998.

———. "Integración de la sociedad civil en el Gran Caribe: Balance de un año (1997–1998)" (Integration of civil society in the greater Caribbean: A one-year inventory, 1997–1998). In *La "otra" integración: Procesos intersocietales y parlamentos regionales en el Gran Caribe* (The "other" integration: Intersocietal and parliamentary regional processes in the Greater Caribbean), edited by F. Jácome. Caracas: Cuadernos del INVESP no. 4, 1999, pp. 5–24.

———. "Globalización, regionalismo e integración regional: Tendencias actuales en el Gran Caribe" (Globalization, regionalism, and regional integration: Current tendencies in the Greater Caribbean). In *Anuario de la Integración del Gran Caribe 2000* (Greater Caribbean integration annual report 2000). Caracas: Nueva Sociedad/ CIEI/CRIES/INVESP, 2000, pp. 11–35.

———."La Asociación de Estados del Caribe: Los límites políticos de las instituciones intergubernamentales." *Innovación y construcción institucional: Latinoamérica y el Este de Asia,* edited by R. Donner. Buenos Aires: CRIES/Icaria Editorial, 2007a, pp. 41–50.

———. "La integración regional: ¿Fragmentación y competencia de modelos?" In *2010 Una agenda para la región,* edited by Fabián Bosoer and Fabián Calle. Buenos Aires: TAEDA, 2007b, pp. 211–244.

Sutton, Paul. "El régimen bananero de la Unión Europea el Caribe y América Latina" (The banana regime in the European Union, the Caribbean, and Latin America). *Pensamiento Propio* (Managua) no. 4 (May–August 1997): 25–53.

Sutton, Paul, and Carlos Oliva, eds. *América Latina, el Caribe y Cuba en el contexto global.* Araquara: UNESP, 2002.

Yanes, Hernán. "Redes de ONGs e integración en el Gran Caribe" (NGO networks and integration in the greater Caribbean). In *Anuario de la Integración del Gran Caribe 2000* (Greater Caribbean integration annual report 2000). Caracas: Nueva Sociedad/ CIEI/CRIES/INVESP, 2000, pp. 161–177.

Acronyms

ACP	African, Caribbean, and Pacific group of states
ACS	Association of Caribbean States
ALBA	Bolivarian Alternative for the Americas
CACM	Central American Common Market
CAFTA-DR	Central American-Dominican Republic-United States Free Trade Agreement
CARIBCAN	Caribbean Canada Trade Agreement
CARICOM	Caribbean Common Market and Community (a Caribbean economic community)
CARIFORUM	Forum of the Caribbean Common Market and Community
CARIFTA	Caribbean Free Trade Association
CBI	Caribbean Basin Initiative
CIA	Central Intelligence Agency
CIM	Inter-American Commission of Women
CPDC	Caribbean Policy Development Centre
CRIES	Regional Coordination of Economic and Social Research
ECCB	Eastern Caribbean Central Bank
ECLAC	Economic Commission for Latin America and the Caribbean (United Nations)
EPZ	export-processing zone
EU	European Union
FARC	Colombian Revolutionary Armed Forces
F-CCA	Florida-Caribbean Cruise Association
FL	Fanmi Lavalas
FMLN	Farabundo Martí National Liberation Front
FSLN	Sandinista National Liberation Front

FTAA	Free Trade Area of the Americas
G-3	Group of Three Countries (Colombia, Mexico and Venezuela)
GDP	gross domestic product
GNP	gross national product
HDI	Human Development Index
IMF	International Monetary Fund
INVESP	Venezuelan Institute of Social and Political Studies
IPCC	Intergovernmental Panel on Climate Change
ISDHR	Institute for the Study of Democracy and Human Rights
ITCZ	Intertropical Convergence Zone
JLP	Jamaica Labour Party
JTA	Jamaica Teacher's Association
Mercosur	Common Market of the South
MINUSTAH	United Nations Stabilization Mission in Haiti
NAFTA	North American Free Trade Agreement
NGOs	nongovernmental organizations
NJM	New Jewel Movement
OECD	Organization for Economic Cooperation and Development
OECS	Organization of Eastern Caribbean States
PNC	People's National Congress
PNP	People's National Party
PLACPAZ	Global Partnership for the Prevention of Armed Conflict
PPP	People's Progressive Party
PRD	Dominican Revolutionary Party
PRG	People's Revolutionary Government
SELA	Latin American Economic System
SIDS	small island developing states
TWA	Trinidad Workingmen's Association
UFCO	United Fruit Company
UN	United Nations
UNASUR	Union of South America
UNDP	United Nations Development Programme
UNIA	Universal Negro Improvement Association
UNIFEM	United Nations Development Fund for Women
WIF	West Indies Federation
WTO	World Trade Organization

Basic Political Data

The United Nations Development Programme's Human Development Index (HDI) measures a country's achievements in terms of life expectancy, education (as reflected in adult literacy rates and combined primary, secondary, and tertiary school enrollments), and adjusted real income (through gross domestic product per capita in purchasing power parity in US dollars). HDI scores range from 0.0 (low) to 1.0 (high), with higher numbers indicating a greater level of development in the specified areas.

The Netherlands Antilles, consisting of Bonaire, Curaçao, Saba, St. Eustatius, and St. Maarten, is a former Dutch dependency that is now autonomous in internal affairs under the charter of the Kingdom of the Netherlands. Aruba, a former part of the Netherlands Antilles, assumed domestic autonomy as a member of the Kingdom of the Netherlands on January 1, 1986.

Antigua and Barbuda
Capital City Saint John's
Date of Independence from Great Britain November 1, 1981
Population 84,522
HDI Score and World Rank .830 (59 of 179)
Current Leader Prime Minister Winston Baldwin Spencer

Bahamas
Capital City Nassau
Date of Independence from Great Britain July 10, 1973
Population 307,451
HDI Score and World Rank .854 (49 of 179)
Current Leader Prime Minister Hubert A. Ingraham

Barbados
Capital City Bridgetown
Date of Independence from Great Britain November 30, 1966
Population 281,968

HDI Score and World Rank .889 (37 of 179)
Current Leader Prime Minister David Thompson

Belize
Capital City Belmopan
Date of Independence from Great Britain September 21, 1981
Population 301,270
HDI Score and World Rank .771 (88 of 179)
Current Leader Prime Minister Dean Barrow

Colombia
Capital City Bogotá
Date of Independence from Spain July 20, 1810
Population 46,000,000
HDI Score and World Rank .787 (80 of 179)
Current Leader President Álvaro Uribe

Costa Rica
Capital City San José
Date of Independence from Spain September 15, 1821
Population 4,000,000
HDI Score and World Rank .847 (50 of 179)
Current Leader President Oscar Arias Sánchez

Cuba
Capital City Havana
Date of Independence from the United States May 20, 1902 (occupation by the
    United States followed defeat of Spain in Spanish-American War of 1898)
Population 11,000,000
HDI Score and World Rank .855 (48 of 179)
Current Leader President Raúl Castro

Dominica
Capital City Roseau
Date of Independence from Great Britain November 3, 1978
Population 72,514
HDI Score and World Rank .797 (77 of 179)
Current Leader Prime Minister Roosevelt Skerrit

Dominican Republic
Capital City Santo Domingo
Date of Independence from Haiti February 27, 1844 (occupation by Haiti
    followed declaration of independence from Spain in 1821)
Population 9,500,000

HDI Score and World Rank .768 (91 of 179)
Current Leader President Leonel Fernández

Grenada
Capital City Saint George's
Date of Independence from Great Britain February 7, 1974
Population 90,343
HDI Score and World Rank .774 (86 of 179)
Current Leader Prime Minister Tillman Thomas

Guatemala
Capital City Guatemala City
Date of Independence from Spain September 15, 1821
Population 12,902,500
HDI Score and World Rank .696 (121 of 179)
Current Leader President Álvaro Colom

Guyana
Capital City Georgetown
Date of Independence from Great Britain May 26, 1966
Population 770,794
HDI Score and World Rank .725 (110 of 179)
Current Leader President Bharrat Jagdeo

Haiti
Capital City Port-au-Prince
Date of Independence from France January 1, 1804
Population 9,000,000
HDI Score and World Rank .521 (148 of 179)
Current Leader President René Préval

Honduras
Capital City Tegucigalpa
Date of Independence from Spain September 15, 1821
Population 7,000,000
HDI Score and World Rank .714 (117 of 179)
Current Leader President Manuel Zelaya

Jamaica
Capital City Kingston
Date of Independence from Great Britain August 6, 1962
Population 3,000,000
HDI Score and World Rank .771 (87 of 179)
Current Leader Prime Minister Bruce Golding

Nicaragua
Capital City Managua
Date of Independence from Spain September 15, 1821
Population 6,000,000
HDI Score and World Rank .699 (120 of 179)
Current Leader President Daniel Ortega

Panama
Capital City Panama City
Date of Independence from Spain November 28, 1821
Date of Independence from Colombia November 3, 1903
Population 3,000,000
HDI Score and World Rank .832 (58 of 179)
Current Leader President Martín Torrijos

St. Kitts and Nevis
Capital City Basseterre
Date of Independence from Great Britain September 19, 1983
Population 39,817
HDI Score and World Rank .830 (60 of 179)
Current Leader Prime Minister Denzil Douglas

St. Lucia
Capital City Castries
Date of Independence from Great Britain February 22, 1979
Population 159,585
HDI Score and World Rank .821 (66 of 179)
Current Leader Prime Minister Stephenson King

St. Vincent and the Grenadines
Capital City Kingstown
Date of Independence from Great Britain October 27, 1979
Population 118,432
HDI Score and World Rank .766 (92 of 179)
Current Leader Prime Minister Ralph Gonsalves

Suriname
Capital City Paramaribo
Date of Independence from the Netherlands November 25, 1975
Population 475,996
HDI Score and World Rank .770 (89 of 179)
Current Leader President Ronald Venetiaan

Trinidad and Tobago
Capital City Port of Spain
Date of Independence from Great Britain August 31, 1962
Population 1,000,000
HDI Score and World Rank .833 (57 of 179)
Current Leader Prime Minister Patrick Manning

Venezuela
Capital City Caracas
Date of Independence from Spain July 5, 1811
Population 26,000,000
HDI Score and World Rank .826 (61 of 179)
Current Leader President Hugo Chávez

■ Nonindependent Territories in the Caribbean

Anguilla Associated state within the British Commonwealth (1982)

Aruba Member of the Kingdom of the Netherlands (1986)

Bonaire Member of the Netherlands Antilles (1954)

British Virgin Islands British crown colony (1967)

Cayman Islands British crown colony (1972)

Curaçao Member of the Netherlands Antilles (1954)

French Guiana Overseas Department of France (1946)

Guadeloupe Overseas Department of France (1946)

Martinique Overseas Department of France (1946)

Montserrat British crown colony (1966)

Puerto Rico Commonwealth ("free associated state") associated with the
United States (1952)

Saba Member of the Netherlands Antilles (1954)

St. Barthélemy Administrative District of Guadeloupe (1946)

St. Eustatius Member of the Netherlands Antilles (1954)

St. Maarten Member of the Netherlands Antilles (1954)

St. Martin Administrative District of Guadeloupe (1946)

Turks and Caicos British crown colony (1976)

US Virgin Islands US territory with local self-government (1968)

Sources: United Nations Development Programme, *Human Development Report,* 2007–2008, http://hdr.undp.org (accessed March 2009); World Bank, *2008 World Development Indicators Database*, http://siteresources.worldbank .org/DATASTATISTICS/Resources/WDI08supplement1216.pdf; Central Intelligence Agency, *World Factbook 2008*, https://www.cia.gov/library/publications/ The-World-Factbook/ (accessed March 2009).

The Contributors

Marlene Attzs is lecturer in economics at the University of the West Indies, St. Augustine, Trinidad and Tobago.

David Baronov is associate professor of sociology at St. John Fisher College, Rochester, New York.

A. Lynn Bolles is professor of women's studies at the University of Maryland.

Thomas D. Boswell is professor of geography at the University of Miami, Florida.

Jacqueline Anne Braveboy-Wagner is professor of political science at City College and the Graduate School and University Center of the City University of New York.

Dennis Conway is professor of geography at Indiana University, Bloomington.

Thomas J. D'Agostino is executive director of the Hobart and William Smith Colleges and Union College Partnership for Global Education; director of the Center for Global Education; and visiting professor of political science at Hobart and William Smith Colleges, Geneva, New York.

Leslie G. Desmangles is professor of religion and international studies at Trinity College, Hartford, Connecticut.

Stephen D. Glazier is professor of anthropology and Graduate Faculty Fellow at the University of Nebraska–Lincoln.

Richard S. Hillman is professor emeritus of political science at St. John Fisher College, Rochester, New York.

Duncan McGregor is professor of geography at the University of London, England.

Kevin Meehan is associate professor of English and director of the UCF Haitian Studies Project at the University of Central Florida, Orlando.

Paul B. Miller is senior lecturer in the Department of Spanish and Comparative Literature, Vanderbilt University, Nashville, Tennessee.

Joseph M. Murphy is Tagliabue professor of interfaith studies and dialogue in the Department of Theology at Georgetown University, Washington, DC.

Dennis A. Pantin is senior lecturer and coordinator of the Sustainable Economic Development Unit for Small and Island Developing States at the University of the West Indies, St. Augustine, Trinidad and Tobago.

Stephen J. Randall is professor of history and director of the Institute for United States Policy Research, School of Policy Studies at the University of Calgary, Canada.

Andrés Serbin is professor of anthropology at the Central University of Venezuela, Caracas; director of the Venezuelan Institute of Social and Political Studies; and president of Regional Coordination of Economic and Social Research.

Kevin A. Yelvington is associate professor of anthropology at the University of South Florida, Tampa.

Index

417

About the Book

Carefully designed to enhance readers' comprehension of the diversity and complexities of the region, *Understanding the Contemporary Caribbean* ranges in coverage from history to politics and economics, from the environment to ethnicity, from religion to the Caribbean diaspora. Each topic is covered in an accessible style, but with reference to the latest scholarship. This new edition has been thoroughly updated to reflect recent events and trends.

Maps, photographs, and a table of basic political data enhance the text, which has made its place as the best available introduction to the region.

Richard S. Hillman is professor emeritus of political science at St. John Fisher College. His publications include *Democracy for the Privileged: Crisis and Transition in Venezuela* and *Understanding Contemporary Latin America.* **Thomas J. D'Agostino** is director of the Center for Global Education at Hobart and William Smith Colleges and executive director of the Hobart and William Smith Colleges and Union College Partnership for Global Education. He is coauthor, with Richard S. Hillman, of *Distant Neighbors in the Caribbean: The Dominican Republic and Jamaica in Comparative Perspective.*